THE LITERARY CULTURE OF NONCONFORMITY

The Literary Culture of
Nonconformity
in Later Seventeenth-Century England

N. H. KEEBLE

LEICESTER UNIVERSITY PRESS

1987

To Jen

First published in 1987 by Leicester University Press

Copyright © Leicester University Press 1987

Designed by Douglas Martin
Filmset in Linotron 202 Ehrhardt
Printed and bound in Great Britain by
The Bath Press, Avon

British Library Cataloguing in Publication Data

Keeble, N. H.
The literary culture of nonconformity
in later seventeenth-century England.
1. English literature – Early modern,
1500–1700 – History and criticism
2. Dissenters in literature
I. Title
820.9'382   PR439.D57

ISBN 0–7185–1207–3

Contents

Preface

Nonconformist writing of the later seventeenth century does not figure largely in our literary histories nor does it impinge at all forcefully upon our sense of the dominant character of Restoration literature. The received impression is that, as Puritanism petered out after its political defeat in 1660–2, its cultural and literary life became henceforth a backwater, increasingly narrow-minded, sectarian and dull, with nothing to offer as lively and interesting as the work produced for, and under the patronage of, the Restored court, church and *beau monde*. Since no such enfeebled tradition could have nourished the genius of Milton and Bunyan, they tend to be presented as the exceptions which prove the rule, men shaped by the revolutionary 1640s rather than the nonconformist 1660s and 1670s and liberated from their disabling religious constraints by their own individuality. The present study dissents from this view and seeks to claim for nonconformist writing as a whole a more significant place in our literary history than it has hitherto been accorded. Its earlier chapters consider the historical circumstances in which nonconformists wrote, particularly how imperative it was for them to communicate and to publish and how equally pressing were the penal obstacles put in their way, to conclude that literary creativity, composition and reading were vital not merely to the survival of nonconformity but to its very nature. In later chapters, discussion of the literary characteristics of this writing suggests that it was quite as interesting and innovative, and in some ways more persuasively *engagé*, more appealingly humane and more richly imaginative, than the witty posturings, satirical topicalities and urbane disinterestedness of Restoration plays, poems and prose.

My first and greatest debt is to Dr Isabel Rivers, now a fellow of St Hugh's College, Oxford, whose suggestion it was that I might write this book, and who supported its proposal to Leicester University Press. She subsequently advised me throughout its composition and undertook the onerous task of reading and commenting upon the entire typescript, much to its benefit. Her extensive knowledge of seventeenth- and eighteenth-century theological writing repeatedly alerted me to the unwary and the partial in my generalizations about the age. Half my text was read also by Dr Geoffrey F. Nuttall, whose comments have greatly improved the accuracy of my writing: no-one venturing into seventeenth-century ecclesiastical history could have a more learned, more generous, or more encouraging guide. Particular chapters are the better for having been read and commented upon by Mrs Felicity Riddy, Dr Ian McGowan and Dr David Bebbington. At various times I have pestered a number of other Stirling colleagues with queries: I should like especially to mention Dr John Drane, Dr Robert Rehder, now professor of English at the

University of Fribourg, Switzerland, Dr Robin Sowerby and Mr Martin Gray, to whose penetrating scepticism about my enterprise I owe more than he would suppose. And I must record the profit and pleasure I have had from many lunch-time conversations with Mr Norman Arthur in the churchyard of Greyfriars, Edinburgh. To all these friends and colleagues I am deeply grateful for saving me from many errors and infelicities; for those which remain I alone am responsible.

Preparation of this book has been greatly facilitated by the award of research grants by the British Academy, the Carnegie Trust for the Universities of Scotland and the Research Travel Fund of the University of Stirling. To each of these bodies I tender my thanks for their financial support. Most of my reading was done in the National Library of Scotland, and I should like to thank its staff for their speedy and helpful service.

Chapter 9 is based upon an article first published in *English*, XXXIII (1984), and some paragraphs in Chapters 6 and 7 are reworked from an article on *The Pilgrim's Progress* which appeared in *The Baptist Quarterly*, XXVIII (1980). To the editors of both these journals I am grateful for permission to revise and republish this material. Some passages in Chapters 3 and 8 derive from my *Richard Baxter: Puritan Man of Letters* (Oxford, 1982). On historical matters especially I am heavily indebted to secondary sources. I hope this is fully acknowledged in the footnotes, but I should like here to say that A. G. Matthews's *Calamy Revised* (Oxford, 1934) and Michael R. Watts's *The Dissenters: From the Reformation to the French Revolution* (Oxford, 1978) have been more or less constantly by me, and open, as I worked.

My handwriting would bring joy to no typist's heart: for the care with which they produced fair copy I am very grateful to Miss Mamie Prentice and Miss Yvonne McClymont, who dealt with most of my manuscript, and to Miss Elspeth McLellan. That copy is privileged to be published by Leicester University Press. I should like to acknowledge how much I owe to the expertise of the Press's staff and their patience with my corrections and second thoughts, and especially to the senior editor of the Press, Mrs Susan Martin, and to its Secretary, Mr Peter Boulton.

A sentence concluding this preface cannot attempt to repay my debt to my wife, and to our children, Oliver, Owen and Sophie, who have so patiently tolerated my many prolonged retreats from them to 'my nonconformists'. I may have written the book, but they made it possible.

University of Stirling
1 September 1986   N.H.K.

List of abbreviations

The following abbreviations are used in the notes; for publication details of a work referred to by author and short title see the earliest citation of it in the notes to that chapter. The place of publication is not given if it is London.

Arber, *TC*	Edward Arber (ed.), *The Term Catalogues, 1668–1709 A.D.*, 3 vols (*1903–6*; rpt New York, *1965*)
BJRL	*Bulletin of the John Rylands Library*
Bolam, *EP*	C. Gordon Bolam *et al.*, *The English Presbyterians* (1968)
BQ	*The Baptist Quarterly*
Braithwaite, *BQ*	William C. Braithwaite, *The Beginnings of Quakerism*, rev. Henry J. Cadbury, 2nd edn (1955; rpt York, 1981)
Braithwaite, *SPQ*	William C. Braithwaite, *The Second Period of Quakerism*, rev. Henry J. Cadbury, 2nd edn (1961; rpt York, 1979)
Browning, *EHD*	Andrew Browning (ed.), *English Historical Documents 1660–1714* (1966)
Bunyan, *CW*	*The Works of John Bunyan*, ed. George Offor, 3 vols (1860–2)
Bunyan, *GA*	John Bunyan, *Grace Abounding to the Chief of Sinners*, ed. Roger Sharrock (Oxford, 1962)
Bunyan, *HW*	John Bunyan, *The Holy War*, ed. Roger Sharrock and James Forrest (Oxford, 1980)
Bunyan, *MW*	*The Miscellaneous Works of John Bunyan*, gen. ed. Roger Sharrock, 12 vols in progress (Oxford, 1976–)
Bunyan, *PP*	John Bunyan, *The Pilgrim's Progress*, ed. James Blanton Wharey, rev. Roger Sharrock, 2nd edn (Oxford, 1960)
Burnet, *OT*	Gilbert Burnet, *Bishop Burnet's History of His Own Time*, 2 vols (1724–34)
CH	*Church History*
Cobbett, *ST*	William Cobbett (ed.), *A Complete Collection of State Trials and Proceedings for High Treason and Other Crimes and Misdemeanours*, cont. T. B. and T. J. Howell, 33 vols (1809–26)
CSPD	*Calendar of State Papers, Domestic*, 41 vols (1860–1947)
DNB	*Dictionary of National Biography*, ed. Sir Leslie Stephen and Sir Sidney Lee, 22 vols (1908–9)
EHR	*English Historical Review*
ELH	*English Literary History*
ELR	*English Literary Renaissance*

Fox, *JGF*	*The Journal of George Fox*, ed. John L. Nickalls, rev. edn (1975)
Harl. Misc.	*The Harleian Miscellany: or, a Collection of Scarce, Curious, and Entertaining Pamphlets and Tracts ... found in the late Earl of Oxford's Library*, 8 vols (1744–6)
Heywood, *AD*	Oliver Heywood, *His Autobiography, Diaries, Anecdote and Event Books*, ed. J. Horsfall Turner, 4 vols (Brighouse and Bingley, 1882–5)
Howe, *CW*	John Howe, *The Works*, ed. Henry Rogers, 6 vols (1862–3)
JEH	*Journal of Ecclesiastical History*
JFHS	*Journal of the Friends' Historical Society*
Jones, *CE*	R. Tudur Jones, *Congregationalism in England 1662– 1962* (1962)
JURCHS	*Journal of the United Reformed Church History Society*
Manton, *CW*	Thomas Manton, *The Complete Works*, 5 vols (1870–1)
Marvell, *P&L*	*The Poems and Letters of Andrew Marvell*, ed. H. M. Margoliouth, rev. Pierre Legouis and E. E. Duncan-Jones, 2 vols, 3rd edn (Oxford, 1971)
Marvell, *RT*	Andrew Marvell, *The Rehearsal Transpros'd and The Rehearsal Transpros'd. The Second Part*, ed. D. I. B. Smith (Oxford, 1971)
Matthews, *CR*	A. G. Matthews, *Calamy Revised: Being a Revision of Edmund Calamy's Account of the Ministers and Others Ejected and Silenced, 1660–2* (Oxford, 1934)
Milton, *CPW*	*Complete Prose Works of John Milton*, gen. ed. Don M. Wolfe, 8 vols (New Haven, Conn., 1953–82)
Milton, *PJM*	*The Poems of John Milton*, ed. John Carey and Alastair Fowler, 2nd corrected impression (1980)
Milton, *PL*	John Milton, *Paradise Lost*
Milton, *PR*	John Milton, *Paradise Regained*
Milton, *SA*	John Milton, *Samson Agonistes*
MP	*Modern Philology*
N&Q	*Notes and Queries*
OED	*The Compact Edition of the Oxford English Dictionary*, [ed. Sir James Murray *et al.*], 2 vols (1979)
Owen, *CW*	*The Works of John Owen*, ed. William H. Goold, 16 vols (1850–3; rpt Edinburgh, 1965–8)
Penney, *ESP*	Norman Penney (ed.), *Extracts from State Papers Relating to Friends 1654 to 1672* (1913)
Penney, *FPT*	Norman Penney (ed.), *'The First Publishers of Truth'* (1907)
PMLA	*Publications of the Modern Language Association of America*

PQ	*Philological Quarterly*
Rel. Bax.	Richard Baxter, *Reliquiae Baxterianae*, ed. Matthew Sylvester (1696): reference is to part, page and numbered section
RES	*Review of English Studies*
RHST	*Royal Historical Society Transactions*
Somers, *CT*	John Somers, *A Collection of Scarce and Valuable Tracts*, ed. Walter Scott, 12 vols, 2nd edn (1809–14)
SP	*Studies in Philology*
Steele, *BRP*	Robert Steele (ed.), *A Bibliography of Royal Proclamations of the Tudor and Stuart Sovereigns ... 1485–1714*, 2 vols (Oxford, 1910)
TLS	*Times Literary Supplement*
Turner, *OREN*	G. Lyon Turner (ed.), *Original Records of Early Nonconformity under Persecution and Indulgence*, 3 vols (1911–14)
Underwood, *EB*	A. C. Underwood, *A History of the English Baptists*, 2nd edn (1956)
Watts, *DRR*	Michael R. Watts, *The Dissenters: From the Reformation to the French Revolution* (Oxford, 1978)
Whitley, *BB*	W. T. Whitley, *A History of British Baptists*, 2nd edn (1932)
Wing, *STC*	Donald Wing, *Short-Title Catalogue of Books Printed in England, Scotland, Ireland, Wales and British America ... 1641–1700*, 3 vols (New York, 1945–51; vols I-II, 2nd edn, 1972–82)

Introduction

I REFORMATION SENTIMENTS

'Tis well known to such as have understood the state of Religion in this Kingdom, since the beginning of the Reformation, that there have been very different Sentiments about the Degrees of that Reformation itself.[1]

The English nonconformist tradition originates in the 'very different Sentiments' to which the Presbyterian John Howe, looking back from the late seventeenth century, here refers. Its antecedents, and something of its inspiration, lie, however, beyond the Reformation in the middle ages. Precedents are even older. Indeed, the first British churchman (and, incidentally, the first British writer) to achieve an international reputation, did so by defying the popes, councils and theologians of the Roman church. The monk Pelagius, having drawn from that prickly defender of orthodoxy, St Jerome, the unflattering observation that he was a corpulent Scottish dog weighed down with porridge, had his teachings condemned by two African councils in AD 416, and in the following year was himself excommunicated by Pope Innocent I. In Britain, however, his influence remained sufficiently great to bring St Germanus, Bishop of Auxerre, on a mission to the island in AD 429 specifically to combat Pelagianism. He worsted the heretics in debate at Verulanium (St Albans), but, despite a second mission in AD 447, an insistence on the part to be played by the human will in the scheme of salvation lingered in the teaching of churchmen from Britain and Gaul into the sixth century, when the first British nonconformist tradition finally died.[2]

Two centuries after Pelagius, it was church order and liturgy, rather than doctrine, which brought the British church into conflict with Rome. In the twelfth century the Benedictine Bishop of St Asaph, Geoffrey of Monmouth, recorded that when, in AD 603, St Augustine of Canterbury, leader of the mission dispatched by St Gregory the Great to evangelize the Saxons, 'asked the bishops of the Britons to submit to his orders', Dinoot (or Donatus), Abbot of Bangor, 'proved to him on a whole series of grounds that they owed him no allegiance at all'.[3] Though we may hesitate before trusting Geoffrey in matters of historical fact, this incident has a reliable source in the *Historia Ecclesiastica Gentis Anglorum* of St Bede the Venerable, for whom it exemplified the obstinacy and recalcitrance of the Britons in repudiating the jurisdiction of the 'universal church' and in refusing the 'universal practice' of that church in its calendar and liturgy, notably in its method of calculating the date of Easter and in its rite of baptism. The Synod of Whitby (AD 664) may have established *de jure* uniformity, but it is clearly with some irritation that Bede, having brought his narrative down to his own time in the early eighth century, has to admit the continuing nonconformity of the Britons. They still uphold 'their own bad customs against the true Easter of the Catholic Church' and

> continue even now, when the English nation believes rightly, and is fully instructed in the doctrines of the Catholic Faith, to be obdurate and crippled by their errors, going about with their heads improperly tonsured, and keeping Christ's solemnity without fellowship with the Christian Church.

Bede's *Historia* is, in fact, as much an account of the suppression of the indigenous Celtic church as it is of the evangelization of the Saxons. It was entirely in accord with the spirit of Bede that, in 1565, the Roman Catholic Thomas Stapleton dedicated to Elizabeth his translation of the *Historia*, the first since King Alfred's, explicitly to spur her to purge her realm of heretics, schismatics and nonconformists, and to return it to Roman allegiance. In Bede she might 'clearly see as well the misinformations of a few for displacing the ancient and right Christian faith, as also the ways and means of a speedy redress'.[4]

Pelagius' heresy was not of a kind to recommend him to later Puritans and nonconformists, who generally, from among the Church Fathers, had the highest regard for the predestinarian theology of his chief controverter, St Augustine of Hippo.[5] With the resistance of the British church, however, it was a different matter. Its rejection of Roman jurisdiction clearly had its counterpart both in the Reformation and in the later Puritan rejection of episcopal authority. Furthermore, its distrust of hierarchies and preference for a monastic or collegiate over a diocesan and parochial organization foreshadowed the Protestant and Puritan desire for a church order which restored to a minister an intimate relationship with, and full responsibility for, his people. Early Welsh monastic communities were independent families in the full sense that their abbacies were hereditary and their monks married and interrelated. The name 'Culdees', used of early Irish and Scottish monks and their followers, may derive from the old Irish for 'companion', and if, as the sixteenth-century Protestant Bishop of Ossory, John Bale, believed, their ministers were set apart not by episcopal ordination but by the vote of the congregation, then they anticipated the most radical Puritan church polity. In these various respects, the existence of such an independent native tradition not only encouraged reformers like John Foxe in their belief that Christianity in Britain was not of Roman but of Asiatic origin; it could also serve to highlight for them and their Puritan successors the spiritual inadequacies of Roman and episcopal jurisdiction.[6] Although defenders of the authenticity of the reformed episcopal Church of England might place it in the tradition of the Celtic church, as seems to have been part of Henry Vaughan's purpose in adopting the title 'Silurist', the widespread belief in the purity of a British church which flourished before Augustine's mission more readily inspired those seeking a more radical reformation and the abolition of episcopacy. Certainly Milton's sympathetic account of the Dinoot episode encourages us to interpret it as an encounter between humility and pride, pastoral care and officious lordliness, fraternity and hierarchy. And for Marvell, too, it was the introduction by Augustine 'of the Romish Ceremonies' which led the Britons to forsake 'the pure simplicity of the Primitive Church'. The 'Pontifical stiffness' of certain seventeenth-century Church of England divines towards non-episcopal 'Foreign Divines' and their greater sympathy for Rome than for Protestantism put him 'in mind of *Austin* the Monk, when he came into *Kent*, not deigning to rise up to the *British* or give them the hand, and could scarce afford their Churches either Communion or Charity, or common Civility ... [and] of *Austin's* Design, to unite them first (that is, under) the *Saxons*, and then deliver them both over bound to the Papal Government and Ceremonies'.[7]

The pastoral neglect and disregard for personal commitment, which in the Roman church scandalized the early Reformers as it did Puritans in the insufficiently reformed English church, and which both contrasted with the practice of the Celtic church, had become the common burden of literary depictions of Roman ecclesiastics long before the Reformation. The most famous English example is, of course, Chaucer. It is by the presentation of practical Christian commitment in the figure of his Parson that in *The Canterbury Tales* he brings into sharp focus the hypocrisy and moral turpitude of the regular clergy among his pilgrims. The coy Prioress is preoccupied with manners and fashion; the 'povre Persoun' 'waited after no pompe and reverence'. The carnal Monk spares no expense in pursuing the hunt; the Parson spares not in giving 'Unto his povre parisshens aboute/ Of his offrying and eek of his substaunce'. The venal Summoner readily perverts ecclesiastical discipline to line his own pocket; the Parson seeks 'To drawen folk to hevene by fairnesse'. For the avaricious Pardoner, homiletics is the art of fraudulent acquisitiveness; the Parson 'His parisshens devoutly wolde he teche'. What, above all, marks out this 'noble ensample', 'wonder diligent' is his unstinting pastoral service: 'He was a shepherde and noght a mercenarie.'[8] The mercenaries of the late medieval church were by none more directly challenged than by John Wycliffe, with whose teaching the Parson's tale has been thought to show affinities. Chaucer's Host does exclaim in dismay at the Parson 'O Jankin ... I smelle a Lollere in the wynd',[9] but this reaction is perhaps less evidence of the religious affiliation of the Parson (and Chaucer) than of the fact that 'Lollard', the term rather mysteriously applied to Wycliffe's followers, became, like the later 'Puritan', a disparaging sobriquet for any serious Christian witness.[10]

In the 1640s Milton found in Wycliffe an argument to spur the Long Parliament on its reforming course, for the career of the Oxford school-man showed that when 'God is decreeing to begin some new and great period in his Church, ev'n to the reforming of Reformation itself: what does he then but reveal Himself to his servants, as his manner is, first to his English-men':

the favour and the love of heav'n we have great argument to think in a peculiar manner propitious and propending towards us. Why else was this Nation chos'n before any other, that out of her as out of *Sion* should be proclam'd and sounded forth the first tidings and trumpet of Reformation to all *Europ*.

Had it not been for 'the obstinat perversnes of our Prelats', the work of Wycliffe, at which, so Milton alleged, 'all the succeeding *Reformers* more effectually lighted their *Tapers*', might have meant that neither 'the name of *Luther*, or of *Calvin* had bin ever known: the glory of reforming all our neighbours had bin compleatly ours'.[11]

This patriotic belief in the partiality of Providence was not peculiar to Milton. Wycliffe had become a common source of pride to English Protestants at an early date. Detecting in 'the valiant champion of the truth, John Wickliff, our countryman' a native precursor of Luther and Calvin and the 'Morning Star of the Reformation' (an echo of Ecclesiasticus l. 6 apparently first applied to him by Bale), they studied, edited and reworked Wycliffite texts throughout the sixteenth century.[12] It would be with Wycliffe that the early eighteenth-century Congregationalist Daniel Neal would begin his *History of the Puritans* (1732–8). Nor was this sense of indebtedness wishful thinking. It is now recognized that 'English nonconformity owes its origin ... to Master John Wycliffe', not only, or even primarily, because he anticipated the theological emphases of the Reformation and promoted biblical translation, but because his followers established a popular tradition of anti-clericalism and practical piety which endured until, and contributed to, the English Reformation, perhaps as significantly as either Henry VIII's marital problems or the religious genius of Martin Luther.[13]

This tradition of radical dissent is glimpsed in the ecclesiastical records of the early years of that Reformation. From these it is clear not only that the courageous integrity of Sir Thomas More had its counterpart among those whom he would have extirpated, but also that hardly were Luther's ideas known in England before ordinary men and women, encouraged by native Lollard traditions and by continental Anabaptism, were prepared to carry reform much further than was tolerable even to scholars and bishops sympathetic to it. The Roman Catholic Bishop of Winchester, Stephen Gardiner, was not more dismayed by the Protestantism of Thomas Cranmer, Archbishop of Canterbury, than was Cranmer by the spread and resilience of popular radicalism, epitomized, in the 1540s, by the determination of Joan Boucher, the 'Maid of Kent', to maintain her sacramental and incarnational heresies despite the entreaties of Cranmer himself.[14]

Joan of Kent was burned in 1550. Five years later Cranmer himself was the most eminent among the 300 or so Protestants burned by Mary Tudor in her attempt to reverse the religious developments of the previous two reigns and restore England to Roman jurisdiction. It was as the fire was being kindled at their feet that Hugh Latimer, Bishop of Worcester, encouraged Bishop

Nicholas Ridley with the words: '"Be of good comfort, master Ridley, and play the man. We shall this day light such a candle, by God's grace, in England, as I trust shall never be put out."' That they did light such a candle, and one which burned brightest in the prison cells of later Puritans suffering under episcopal persecution, was in large part due to John Foxe, who recorded Latimer's words. Throughout the seventeenth century his graphic record of the Marian persecution in his 'Book of Martyrs', *Acts and Monuments of Matters happening in the Church* (1563), would rouse the spectre of the 'Fires of Smithfield' whenever the Stuarts flirted with, or promoted, the restoration of Romanism, but his fiercely partisan and apocalyptic account of the heroism of English Protestants under trial spoke still more specifically to Puritans suffering for conscience' sake.[15] It was prized and recommended by Richard Baxter and was, with the Bible, John Bunyan's reading in prison, where it inspired the martyrdom of Faithful and supplied the only non-biblical historical figures in *The Pilgrim's Progress* (1678). It was from Foxe that Bunyan was able to quote Wycliffe at his trial in 1660, and in his writings it is to Foxe that he turns for examples of those who had courageously 'suffered for the word of God' and for evidence of the corrupt folly of popery.[16] When recording his trial in 1662 the Quaker John Crooke looked to Foxe for 'Presidents' for the persecution of conscientious saints. *The Book of Martyrs* could keep the Lancashire Presbyterian Roger Lowe, an apprentice mercer, engrossed for a whole morning, and, at his Lancaster trial in 1664, it supplied George Fox with examples justifying the Quakers' refusal of all oaths. [17]

Equally unintended by Mary Tudor was a second consequence of her policy: those who had fled to Calvin's Geneva and Bullinger's Zurich returned in 1558 with a renewed zeal and optimistic hopes of greater reformation under a Protestant queen, Elizabeth.[18] The Elizabethan settlement of the church in 1559 was an attempt to unite the nation by accommodating as many as possible of the divergent religious views now current in England. Such a compromise excluded the committed, of either Roman or Genevan persuasion, and created a national church which, as yet, wanted a religious identity. To the Protestants dissatisfied with it, it appeared but a pale copy of Rome, a hesitant, half-hearted flirting with Reformation. 'We in England', declared the anonymous *Admonition to the Parliament* of 1572, 'are so fare of from having a church rightly reformed, according to the prescript of Gods worde, that as yet we are not come to the outwarde face of the same.'[19] By that date the term 'Puritan' was already in use of adherents of this view.[20] What distressed them was the prescription in the *Book of Common Prayer* imposed by the Act of Uniformity of 1559 of unscriptural and popish ceremonies, and especially the wearing of the surplice.[21] The 1566 'Advertisements' of Archbishop Matthew Parker attempted to enforce uniform compliance, but their effect was to redirect the point of attack, if not to impel some Puritans towards outright separation from the established church.[22] What had begun as a quarrel over ceremonies and vestments became a quarrel over church government. It is episcopacy which the *Admonition* sees as responsible for the impurity of the English church. Following the lectures on Acts given by Thomas Cartwright, Lady Margaret Professor of Divinity, in Cambridge in 1570, Presbyterianism became the aim and hope of the Tudor Puritans. By the 1580s Archbishop John Whitgift was engaged in its active suppression; in 1589 his future successor at Canterbury, Richard Bancroft, found it necessary to defend episcopacy against Presbyterianism in a Paul's Cross sermon on I John iv.1, and in his *Daungerous Positions and Proceedings* (1593) he attacked the 'pretended reformation' of the 'Presbyteriall Discipline'. It was in controversy with the Presbyterian Walter Travers that Richard Hooker's *Treatise on the Laws of Ecclesiastical Polity* (1594–1662) originated, the most persuasive and enduring defence of episcopacy and of the *via media* of the established church.[23]

Presbyterianism involved no essential disagreement with episcopalians on the nature of the church. It thought still in terms of a national church, of a hierarchical government and of a parochial system. However, the *Book of Discipline* drawn up in 1586 by Walter Travers, with Cartwright's active involvement, and later published as *A Directory of Church-Government* (1644), vested authority not in any single individual but in a series of church courts, each having jurisdiction over inferior courts. Thus, a particular church was to be governed by its session or presbytery, consisting of the minister, teachers and elders; 12 or so presbyteries would elect representatives to the local classis (or sometimes, confusingly, presbytery); two dozen classes elected representatives to the half-yearly provincial synod; and the synods to the annual national assembly. Such a polity could be effected only by national legislation. Presbyterian hopes of passing this through parliament were defeated in the 1580s and there would be no second chance until the sitting of the Long Parliament in the 1640s. During the intervening fifty years Presbyterianism did not wane, but its energies were redirected and its nature changed. The intention of its projected church polity was to enable more direct and effective ministerial care over, and discipline of, parishioners than it was thought bishops overseeing large dioceses could exercise. This pastoral work might be, and was, promoted by conscientious ministers within the established church despite that church's continuing episcopal government. During the early seventeenth century the 'spiritual brotherhood' of Puritan ministers impressed upon their people in countless sermons the practical consequences of reformed theology and Puritan soteriology. This reformation of individual lives neither James I nor the bishops could prevent.[24]

A congregation organized according to what the episcopal historian Thomas Fuller later called 'presbytery in episcopacy'[25] would be characterized by one or more of the following practices: no wearing of the surplice; omission of the sign of the cross in baptism and of parts of the liturgy; reception of the sacrament sitting and the withholding of it from those who unrepentantly led demonstrably immoral lives; an emphasis on the sermon as the centre of worship. Herein lie the origins of modern nonconformity. The term, in its original sense, referred to beneficed members of the established church whose Puritan convictions led them to omit some parts of the liturgy and to refuse to conform to some of the ceremonies laid down in the *Book of Common Prayer* and the canons of the church. The *Oxford English Dictionary* records 'nonconformist' and 'nonconformity' in this sense from 1619 and 1618 respectively. Thus, the title of the Presbyterian John Geree's *Character of an Old English Puritane, or Non-Conformist* (1646) implies that these are synonymous terms, and in his text he firmly distinguishes the practice of such Puritan nonconformity from separatism. 'The corruptions that were in Churches' the nonconformist 'thought his duty to bewaile', but 'Perfection in Churches he thought a thing rather to be desired, then hoped for'. Hence, on the one hand he endeavoured 'amendment' and, though 'He reverenced Authority keeping within its sphaere', yet he 'durst not under pretence of subjection to the higher powers, worship God after the traditions of men'. On the other hand, 'he would not separate' from the Church of England as no true church in the hope of finding one of unspotted purity, for 'he expected not a Church state without al defects'. The Presbyterian reformation of church government which he did hope for 'he judged pertaining not to the being, but wel-being of a Church'. It is, as the historian Michael Watts remarks when quoting the passage at large, a characteristic 'combination of piety and realism, of humility and self-assertion, of deference and rebellion'. [26]

It was in this sense that Richard Baxter was a nonconformist from the earliest days of his ministry. When he was episcopally ordained in 1638 he 'had no Scruple at all against Subscription' and had been accustomed to join 'with the Common-Prayer with as hearty fervency as afterward I did with other Prayers! As long as I had no Prejudice against it, I had no stop in my Devotions from any of its imperfections.' At 'about 20 years of Age' (1635), however, his compliance had been disturbed by the example of

> very zealous godly Nonconformists in *Shrewsbury*, and the adjoyning parts, whose fervent Prayers and savoury Conference and holy Lives did profit me much. And when I understood that they were People prosecuted by the Bishops, I found much prejudice arise in my heart against those that persecuted them, and thought those that silenced and troubled such Men could not be the genuine Followers of the Lord of Love.

During the first year of his ministry he 'set upon a serious impartial Trial of the whole Cause'. His conclusions were: that kneeling to receive the sacrament was lawful; the surplice he 'more doubted of, but more inclined to think it lawful: And though I purposed, while I doubted, to forbear it till necessity lay upon me, yet could I not have justified the forsaking of my Ministry for it; (though I never wore it to this day)'; he made 'no Scruple' of the ring in marriage; the sign of the cross in baptism he concluded unlawful; a form of prayer he judged lawful, but the *Book of Common Prayer* he found 'to have much *disorder* and *defectiveness* in it, but nothing which should make the use of it, in the ordinary Publick Worship, to be unlawful to them that have not Liberty to do better'. His most significant conclusions were two: that the church wanted discipline (though at this stage he blamed this on 'the Bishops personal defects' rather than 'the very Frame of Diocesan Prelacy'); and that unqualified subscription 'was that, which if it had been to do again, I durst not do'. 'So that *Subscription*, and the *Cross in Baptism* and the *promiscuous giving of the Lord's Supper to all Drunkards, Swearers, Fornicators, Scorners at Godliness* &c. that are not Excommunicate by a Bishop or Chancellor that is out of their Acquaintance. These three were all I now became a *Nonconformist* to' (he seems to have forgotten the surplice). Baxter continued such a nonconformist all his life, but neither he, nor many of the very many who found themselves cited in the ecclesiastical courts for their behaviour, had any desire or expectation to separate from the established church. Indeed, Baxter 'daily disputed against the Nonconformists; for I found their Censoriousness and Inclinations towards Seperation [*sic*], (in the weaker sort of them) to be a Threatning Evil, and contrary to Christian Charity on one side, as Persecution is on the other'.[27]

To these fifty years of pastoral endeavour may be attributed the essentially practical genius of English Presbyterianism which, much to the consternation of the more rigorous Scots, was to prove far more concerned with Christian service than with ecclesiology. In the 1640s Presbyterianism at last had its political chance in England: the Long Parliament abolished episcopacy in 1642, summoned the Westminster Assembly to advise on a church settlement and, as a condition of the Scots alliance with parliament in the Civil War, passed Presbyterian legislation. Yet Presbyterianism was never established nationally. 'Presbyterians' had for so long operated without Presbyterianism that it is small wonder the term, in popular English usage and in the minds of many so addressed, came to denote not a man's ecclesiastical preference but his piety. In so far as they had a preference, the majority of those vulgarly called 'Presbyterian' were, so Baxter believed, to be distinguished from the 'rigid' or 'ancient' Presbyterians of the Tudor and Scottish type since, like Baxter himself, they favoured not the Presbyterianism of the *Book of Discipline* but the modified episcopacy which Archbishop James Ussher derived from Ignatius and Cyprian in his *Reduction of Episcopacie unto the Form of Synodical Government received in the Antient Church* (1656).[28] Many years later, in the course of controversies over the union of Scotland with England, James Webster, minister of the Tolbooth church, Edinburgh, feared for the security of Scottish Presbyterianism since 'We can't trust the *Presbyterian* Dissenters, who deserve better to be call'd *Episcopal* than Presbyterian'; 'were not their great toping men their Leaders, *Richard Baxter*, Mr. *How* and Mr. *Bates* for the lawfullness of Episcopacy?' These 'Reconcilers', as Baxter preferred to call them, were 'for Catholicism against *Parties*' and never, even at the Restoration, 'made one motion for Presbytery'. Nevertheless, it was as 'Presbyterians', that 'odious Name', that they were known to comtemporaries and are known to history.[29]

That Presbyterianism, which 'generally took in *Scotland*', continued 'but a stranger' in England was not due solely to the half-hearted support of these men, nor (as Alexander Gordon claimed) entirely to the influence of Baxter himself, nor wholly to the ill odour into which it was brought among English Puritans by the alliance between Charles I and the Scots in the Second Civil War.[30] There were, in the Westminster Assembly, eleven 'dissenting brethren', opposed to the Presbyterianism it was that body's business to implement. Early in 1644 their five leaders – Thomas Goodwin, William Bridge, Jeremiah Burroughes, Philip Nye and Sidrach Simpson – publicly explicated their preferred church polity in *An Apologeticall Narration*. 'Independency' is known to the *Oxford English Dictionary* from 1642, but in the previous year the term was used in controversy between the Presbyterian Thomas Edwards and Henry Burton, the rector of St Matthew's, Friday Street, whose opposition to the 'popery' of the episcopal church had led in 1637 to his being sentenced by the Court of High Commission to the pillory, a £5,000 fine, perpetual imprisonment and loss of his ears. The experience persuaded him the established church was no true church, and in 1642 he reorganized his London congregation as a gathered church. In 1641 the future Particular Baptist William Kiffin wrote of the 'Congregational way' but it was not until the end of the century that in England this term gained the currency it had enjoyed in New England since the 1640s and the publication of such works as John Cotton's *The Way of Congregational Churches Cleared* (1648). Baxter continued to use 'Independent' and 'Congregational' interchangeably until the end of his life. The generic noun 'Congregationalism' is not recorded in the *Oxford English Dictionary* before 1716.[31]

Unlike the challenge to the episcopalians of Presbyterianism, that of Congregationalism involved a radically different conception of the nature of the church. Where the Presbyterians sought reformation by re-forming the national church, the Congregationalists sought to recreate particular churches. Geree's nonconformist had supposed perfection in churches 'a thing rather to be desired then hoped for': they supposed the visible and invisible churches could and should be more closely approximated by 'gathering' churches composed only of members who testified publicly to their conversion and faith and who covenanted to join in fellowship together. John Gifford advised his Bedford church, which Bunyan joined in 1654, to admit a new member only 'after you are satisfyed in the worke of grace in the party you are to joyne with' and 'the saide party do solemnly declare (before some of the Church at least), that union with Christ is the foundation of all saintes' communion'. It was not the geographical accident of a parish boundary nor the deliberations of a church court but 'the *inward freeness, willingness* and *readiness* of the spirits of the *Confessors*', their voluntary commitment, which constituted such churches.[32]

In Congregational thought each such voluntary association of believers comprised an autonomous, self-governing society. In the early 1640s the writings of John Cotton had converted John Owen to Congregationalism, and it was Owen, hereafter to be the recognized leader of the Congregationalists as Baxter was of the moderate Presbyterians, who was largely responsible for the *Declaration of the Faith and Order Owned and practised in the Congregational Churches in England* (1658). The *Declaration* asserted that to each gathered church Christ 'hath given all that Power and Authority, which is in any way needfull' and that 'Besides these particular Churches, there is not intended by Christ any Church more extensive or Catholique entrusted with power for the administration of his Ordinances'. The *Declaration* allowed that it is 'according to the minde of Christ' for 'many Churches holding communion together' to 'meet in a Synod or Councel' for discussion and advice, but 'these Synods so assembled are not entrusted with any Church Power' and cannot impose their views on either churches or individuals. Congregational churches were hence subject to no external disciplinary or judicial authority: there are no 'Synods appointed by Christ in a way of Subordination to one another'. When to this is added the admission of members by the consent of the whole church, 'that so love (without dissimulation) may be preserved between the Members thereof', and the election of the minister of a particular church by its congregation, the democratic bias of the polity becomes clear.[33]

This insistence on congregational independence and the willing commitment of members carried a still more important implication:

> The *Spirit of Christ* is in himself too *free*, great and generous a Spirit, to suffer himself to be used by any humane arm, to whip men into belief: he drives not, but *gently leads unto all truth*, and *perswades* men to *dwell in the tents of like precious Faith*; which would lose of its preciousness and value, if that sparkle of freeness shone not in it.

In his *Reasons against the Independant Government of Particular Congregations: As also against the Toleration of such Churches* (1641) Thomas Edwards saw toleration of diverse opinions and practices as tending to religious and civil anarchy. His outrage that men were not whipped from their errors is still more pronounced in his heresiography *Gangraena, or a Catalogue and Discovery of many of the Errours, Heresies, Blasphemies and Pernicious Practices of the Sectaries of this Time* (1646). The watch-cry of the Independents, by contrast, was 'liberty of conscience': '*amongst all Christian States and Churches, there ought to be vouchsafed a forbearance and mutual indulgence unto Saints of all perswasions.*' However, though Independents might not wish, in Milton's words, 'to force consciences that Christ set free' and might perceive in the impositions of the Long Parliament that 'New *Presyter* is but old *Priest* write large', their own tolerance proved to have its limits when confronted by those seeking a reformation yet more radical than their own.[34]

There had, during the reign of Mary Tudor, existed in London Protestant congregations meeting in separation from the restored Roman church.[35] Their example was followed in the 1560s by a number of people, chiefly 'of the lowest order', who, convinced that the Protestant Elizabethan church was not merely inadequately reformed but no true church, absented themselves from their parish churches and met in small secret gatherings or conventicles. Concerted suppression and imprisonment fragmented the movement, but, ten years later, its conviction that the established episcopal church was invalidated by its popish tyranny and ceremonies and its flagrantly indiscriminate admission to the Lord's Supper was developed in the thought of the university men Robert Browne, Robert Harrison and Henry Barrow into a coherent ecclesiology justifying, in the words of one of Browne's titles, *Reformation without tarrying for anie* (1582). With the criticism Presbyterian Puritans agreed, but not with the conclusion or solution. While they wished for reformation within what was a flawed but true church, 'Brownists' and 'Barrowists' (terms recorded in the *Oxford English Dictionary* from 1583 and 1589 respectively), following II Corinthians vi. 17, came out from spiritual bondage and covenanted together in separatist churches.[36]

The Elizabethan response to the incipient separatist movement was to pass in 1593 *An Act for Retaining the Queen's Subjects in their Due Obedience*, which offered those not persuaded to conform by three months' imprisonment the choice of exile or death. Many preferred exile without the prompting of prosecution, most famously John Robinson, whose separatist church at Scrooby, Nottinghamshire, removed to the Netherlands in 1608 and thence, as the Pilgrim Fathers, to New England in 1620. It was probably while yet in England that the church had divided. John Smyth, pastor of the second group, resolved by simple yet drastic means an obvious illogicality in the separatist position: for those who repudiated and separated from the Church of England not to repudiate their baptism by its ministers invalidated their claim to gather a newly constituted and pure church. In 1609 Smyth baptized first himself (hence, the sobriquet 'Se-Baptist', 'Self-baptizer') and then the forty members of his Amsterdam congregation. This was a rejection not merely of the baptism of the Church of England but of infant baptism itself (paedobaptism). Believing true baptism to be not merely by water but by the Spirit, Smyth concluded that only adults mature enough to repent and make the commitment of faith could receive it. Believers' baptism was the mark of the separatist church founded by Smyth's erstwhile companion Thomas Helwys in Spitalfields in 1612. So, too, was Smyth's Arminian theology.[37] The Particular (that is, Calvinist) Baptists derive from the London congregation ministered to successively by Henry Jacob, John Lathrop and Henry Jessey, which, by the 1630s, had rejected infant baptism. This tradition also adopted what Bunyan would later represent in the Bath Sanctification. Smyth and Helwys baptized by affusion: the Particular Baptist *Confession of Faith* of 1644 prescribed baptism by immersion, in token 'that as certainly as the body is buried under water, so certainly shall the bodies of the saints be raised by the power of Christ, in the day of resurrection'.[38]

Contemporaries persisted until the end of the century in calling Baptists 'Anabaptists', that is, 'rebaptizers'. The term was not only wilfully inaccurate in that, by definition, a Baptist did not believe he had been previously baptized, but also deliberately tendentious in that it associated Baptists with the Munster enthusiasts who had so horrified the early Reformation. In his history of Broadmead church, Bristol, compiled after the Restoration, the Baptist elder Edward Terrill recorded that in 1640 the separatist and, later, Fifth Monarchist, John Canne had been denied a place to preach in the city because 'he was a baptized man, by them called an anabaptist, which was to some sufficient cause of prejudice'. Terrill was sceptical of the accuracy of accounts of what had happened at Munster, but it was not a scepticism generally shared. When he wished to convey his sense of the religious chaos of the Interregnum it was as 'Munsterian anarchy' that the Presbyterian Henry Newcome described it. For this 'anarchy' Baptists were not alone responsible. The social mobility and ferment, the revolutionary atmosphere and great expectations, the destruction of traditional authority in church and state, the promotion of religious toleration by Cromwell, all were conducive to the proliferation of an extraordinary number of radical sects, whose adherents came increasingly from the lower classes and whose extremism, both social and religious, attracted the opprobrium of more conservative contemporaries for tending all too literally to 'turn the world upside down' (Acts xvii. 16). In the eyes of Andrew Marvell they were a 'frantique Army' of 'Wand'rers, Adult'rers, Lyars, *Muns'er's* rest,/ Sorcerers, Atheists, Jesuites, Possest'.[39] Modern commentators are more sympathetic. It is in the sometimes quirky and bizarre, yet often incisively percipient and prophetic antinomian and millenarian ideas of this 'frantic army', rather than in the struggle between Cavaliers and Roundheads, that the true English revolution is now by many historians discerned. If so, it was a revolution in prospect, never in fact, for the amorphous groups of Levellers, Diggers, Seekers, Ranters and Fifth Monarchists were to disperse almost as quickly as they had come together in the 1640s.[40] All, that is, except the Quakers, a term first used in 1650 and found in official documents from 1654: but they were inspired by the greatest religious genius of the age, George Fox.[41]

This history bequeathed to the nonconformists of the Restoration period three distinctive convictions, present to varying degrees of intensity in different groups and individuals, but always present, and each in direct conflict with the premises and suppositions of the restored authorities. There was, first, the conviction that the work of the Spirit is active, dynamic and progressive. 'Truth', wrote Milton in 1644 in a gloss on Psalms lxxv.11 of which William Blake would have approved, 'is compar'd in Scripture to a streaming fountain; if her waters flow not in a perpetuall progression, they sick'n into a muddy pool of conformity and tradition.' The great enemy of spiritual enlightenment is custom 'rowling up her sudden book of implicit knowledge, for him that will, to take and swallow down at pleasure', whose adherents 'cry-down the industry of free reasoning, under the terms of humor, and innovation; as if the womb of teeming Truth were to be clos'd up, if shee presume to bring forth ought, that sorts not with their unchew'd notions and suppositions'. Since 'our faith and knowledge thrives by exercise, as well as our limbs and complexion', 'To be still searching what we know not, by what we know, still closing up truth to truth' is the mark of Christian commitment and fellowship, not 'the forc't and outward union of cold, and neutrall, and inwardly divided minds'. Just so, John Smyth defended his apparent changeableness. Though it 'may be thought most straung, that a man should oft tymes chandg his Religio*n*', this is a reprehensible inconstancy only 'if the Religion which a man chandgeth be the truth'. When further illumination reveals the inadequacies of anyone's professed faith, then 'not to chandge Religion is evil simply'. Therefore

> that we should fal from the profession of Puritanisme to Brownisme, & from Brownisme to true Christian baptism, is not simply evil or reprovable in it self, except it be proved that we have fallen from true Religion: If wee therefor, being formerly deceaved in the way of Pedobaptistry, now doe embrace the truth in the true Christian Apostolique baptisme: Then let no man impute this as a fault vnto vs.

In just this spirit, Terrill presented the early history of the Baptist Broadmead church as a progress, a 'going on to perfect separation' by stages as 'the Lord led them by degrees, and brought them out of popish darkness into his marvellous light of the gospel'.[42]

For George Fox, who in 1643 'left my relations and brake off all familiarity or fellowship with young or old' to go to 'many a priest to look for comfort', this quest for spiritual consolation or truth became an actual geographical journey. 'A man of sorrows' (Isa. liii.3), he 'travelled up and down as a stanger in the earth', 'seeking heavenly wisdom'. 'Through the countries' of England, through the Midlands and the Peak District, he sought out 'priests', 'dissenting people' and 'separate preachers', but found they 'were all miserable comforters': 'there was none among them that could speak to my condition.' And then, in 1647, 'when all my hopes in them and in all men were gone, so that I had nothing outwardly to help me, nor could tell what to do, then, Oh then, I heard a voice which said, "There is one, even Christ Jesus, that can speak to thy condition", and when I heard it my heart did leap for joy'. And so, keeping fellowship with no 'people, priests or professors, nor any sort of separated people, but with Christ', he grew in

> zeal in the pure knowledge of God and Christ alone, without the help of any man, book, or writing. For though I read the Scriptures that spoke of Christ and of God, yet I knew him not but by revelation, as he who hath the key did open, and as the Father of life drew me to his Son by his spirit. And then the Lord did gently lead me along ...

Richard Baxter had scant sympathy with the enthusiastic premises of Quakerism, yet he wrote that the true Christian 'sitteth not down contentedly in any low degree of grace': 'Heaven it self is perfection, and the work of a Christian is to press towards Heaven, and therefore 'tis to press towards perfection.' Bunyan was no more sympathetic, beginning his literary career in confutation of Quakerism, and yet his most famous work is, of course, entitled *The Pilgrim's Progress*. This commitment to spiritual progress would animate and distinguish nonconformist writing in an age committed to conformity, stability and uniformity in religious as well as in secular affairs.[43]

So to wait on the Spirit for guidance, to prefer conscience before tradition, is, as this bald survey has shown, to resist attempts to marshal opinion. To kill a king is to destroy the very root of traditional authority. The deed was emblematic of the import, if not the inclination, of Puritanism. Its ruthlessness and illegality shocked many Puritans. It would be a main theme of Presbyterian apologetic in the 1680s that it was none of their doing: 'it was a proud conquering Army, by the contrivance of *Ol. Cromwell*, and the applause of a *few fanaticks* that did it', wrote Baxter. But curtailment of regal (and episcopal) power had been the Presbyterians' own aim, enabling Milton in his defence of the regicide, *The Tenure of Kings and Magistrates* (1649), plausibly to claim they lacked the courage of their convictions. The degree of overt resistance might vary, but no Puritan could give unqualified assent to authority. Though they might disagree about its extent, toleration of and respect for the liberty of the subject, especially in matters of religious conviction, was preferred by all Puritans to dictatorial coercion. For some, this liberty extended very far indeed. In article 84 of the confession of faith he drew up Smyth made 'the first claim for full religious liberty ever penned in the English language': 'the magistrate is not by vertue of his office to meddle with religion, or matters of conscience, to force and compell men to this or that form of religion or doctrine: but to leaue Christian religion free, to euery mans conscience.' In *The Mistery of Iniquity* (1612), 'Whereas Smyth had appealed for liberty for all Christians Helwys pleaded for the toleration of all men', 'Let them be heretikes, Turcks, Jewes or whatsoever', since 'mens religion ... is betwixt God and themselves'.[44]

In the course of the Civil War, Cromwell came to similar convictions. After the victory at Naseby he wrote to William Lenthall, speaker of the House of Commons, that 'Honest men served you faithfully in this action ... He that ventures his life for the liberty of his country, I wish he trust God for the liberty of his conscience and you for the liberty he fights for.' Three months later, after the storming of Bristol, he concluded his report by remarking that

> Presbyterians, Independents, all had here the same spirit of faith and prayer ... they agree here, know no names of difference: pity it is it should be otherwise anywhere. All that believe, have the real unity, which is most glorious, because inward and spiritual ... As for being united in forms, commonly called Uniformity, every Christian will for peace sake study and do, as far as conscience will permit; and from brethren, in things of the mind we look for no compulsion, but that of light and reason.

This repudiation of the Stuart and Laudian concept of external uniformity, and its tyrannous enforcement, was above all what he looked for in the parliaments of the Interregnum. When, on 4 July 1653, he opened the Barebones Parliament, he exhorted its members to

> have a care of the whole flock! Love the sheep, love the lambs; love all, tender all, cherish and countenance all, in all things that are good. And if the poorest Christian, the most mistaken Christian shall desire to live peaceably and quietly under you, – I say, if any shall desire but to lead a life of godliness and honesty, let him be protected.

To his first Protectorate Parliament he protested 'Liberty of Conscience in religion [is] a fundamental ... a natural right' for all, not confined to any sect, nor in the whim of any magistrate, but 'very reciprocal'. Subsequent historians have borne out his claim in 1656 that, though he 'had boxes and rebukes on one hand and on the other, some envying me for Presbytery, others as an in-letter to all the sects and heresies in the nation', nevertheless he had 'through God's mercy, not been unhappy in preventing any one religion to impose on another'.[45]

Nonconformists were hence to prove far more sympathetic than the ecclesiastical and civil authorities of the Restoration to the proposition that people's consciences could not and should not be coerced. In 1660 the Quaker Edmund Burrough advised the restored regime that 'it is not given of God to any *Earthly King* or *Ruler* whatsoever, to exercise *Lordship* over the *Consciences of People* in the Matters of *Faith* and *Worship*, and the things pertaining to *God's* Kingdom'; 'if any man shall assume to *prescribe God a way* how he must be *Worshipped*, and shall *limit his Spirit* from this, or to the other *way of Religion*, and think *to be Lord in mens Consciences* in *religious Matters*, such are but *Usurpers*.' Burrough would soon be confirmed in what his words suggest he already feared and suspected, that the parliament and bishops of the Restoration saw things the other way about: religious prescription the duty of legitimate authority, its neglect the anarchic irresponsibility of such a usurper as Cromwell. Theirs was the last administration in England to attempt such enforcement, for the policy failed, completely and finally. If, as a consequence, Gilbert Sheldon, Archbishop of Canterbury (1663–77) and remorseless advocate of persecution, now appears to have been 'the product of a world which, if not dead, was fast dying', it is the nonconformists we have to thank for the anachronism.[46]

Dynamically inspired and more respectful of the individual conscience than of traditional authority, the religious tradition inherited by the nonconformists was also apocalyptic. The millenarianism most pronounced among Fifth Monarchists was not confined to them. Their advocacy of violent action and radical social change was distinctive, but chiliastic expectancy, a sense that God was intervening miraculously in history, informed the work of apparently far more conservative figures.[47] In New England in 1642 news of events in England led the serious and sensitive, but far from radical, Anne Bradstreet to apostrophize:

> Abraham's seed, lift up your heads on high,
> For sure the day of your redemption's nigh;
> The scales shall fall from your long blinded eyes,
> And Him you shall adore who now despise.
> Then fullness of the nations in shall flow,
> And Jew and Gentile to one worship go;
> Then follows days of happiness and rest;
> Whose lot doth fall to live therein is blest.[48]

Such a Restoration satire as Abraham Cowley's *Vision concerning his late Pretended Highness Cromwell, the Wicked* (1661) would attribute Cromwell's interest in the Jews to merely mercenary motives – to raise 'a present sum of Money'. However, that the conversion of the Jews, to which Anne Bradstreet refers, was a condition of the millennium was certainly a factor, and perhaps the decisive factor, in Cromwell's support for their readmission to England in 1655 (Rom. xi.25–6; Rev. vii.4–9, xiv.6, xx.1–7).[49] In his letters, dispatches and speeches, drawing inspiration from the God who routed Busiris' 'Memphian chivalry' and led Joshua, Gideon and Samson to victory, he made no doubt that 'the great hand of God' guided Parliament's armies in the Civil War and that it was the Lord who 'poured this nation from vessel to vessel' in the various constitutional arrangements of the Interregnum. In the victory at Bristol 'he that runs may read, that all this is none other than the work of God. He must be a very Atheist that doth not acknowledge it.' Scrutiny of the circumstances of Parliament's improbable victories proves it. That a 'poor and contemptible company of men, neither versed in military affairs, nor having much natural propensity to them' should prevail in three kingdoms can be attributed to nothing other than the 'strange windings and turnings of Providence', a 'miraculous appearance of God' which neither 'I nor no man living' could have foreseen, much less contrived. 'They that shall attribute to this or that person the contrivances and production of those mighty things God hath wrought in the midst of us' ascribe to cunning and policy more than it could ever achieve: 'My dear friend, let us look into providences; surely they mean somewhat. They hang so together ...'[50]

How persuasive an argument to this effect Cromwell's career could be is illustrated by the impression it made upon a mind so resistant to partisan cant and simplistic dogmatism as Andrew Marvell's. The 'Conversion of the *Jews*' had been for him an unimaginably distant prospect, and though by 1650 impressed, it was with studied ambiguity that in his 'Horation Ode upon Cromwell's Return from Ireland' he viewed the prospect of the 'restless *Cromwel*' who 'could not cease/In the inglorious Arts of Peace,/But through adventrous War/Urged his active Star'. By 1655 the irony had gone. Though scornful of the '*Chammish* issue' (Gen. ix.20–2) of Fifth Monarchists, Quakers and Ranters, and unwilling to commit himself to the view that these were the Last Days, he was yet moved by the prospect of the 'Angelique *Cromwel*' pursuing the Antichristian beast to its Romish lair famously to declare 'If these the Times, then this must be the Man.' Cromwell, it now seemed, made all things, if not certain, certainly possible: 'How might they under such a Captain raise/ The great Designes kept for the latter Dayes.' The possibility was irresistibly attractive:

> oft I think if in some happy Hour
> High Grace should meet in one with highest Pow'r,
> And then a seasonable People still
> Should bend to his, as he to Heavens will,
> What might we hope, what wonderful Effect
> From such a wish'd Conjuncture might reflect.
> Sure, the mysterious Work, where none withstand,
> Would forthwith finish under such a Hand;
> Fore-shortned Time its useless Course would stay,
> And soon precipitate the latest Day.[51]

2   RESTORATION SENTIMENTS

It was not the latest day but the Restoration which was precipitated. In the headily expectant revolutionary years of the 1640s Samson's victories had been in Milton's mind: 'Methinks I see in my mind', he had written in *Areopagitica* (1644), 'a noble and puissant Nation rousing herself like a strong man after sleep, and shaking her invincible locks.'[52] In the event, the Puritans proved no more invincible than Samson: it is his defeat Milton contemplates in *Samson Agonistes* (1671). They, no less than he, had believed themselves God's chosen, providentially led to 'mightiest deeds' and victory over 'cruel enemies', only to find that though, like Samson, unassailable by assault from without, their enemies had nevertheless triumphed as surely as his, 'in a trice', as Baxter wrote, when it was thought 'next impossible' and the Royalists, in Abraham Cowley's view, had not 'the least glympse of Hope' of it.[53] The Restoration so effectively, so painlessly and so quickly frustrated the whole range of Puritan aspiration that its beneficiaries could not but see it as a divine mercy: 'Never was there so miraculous a change as this, nor so great things done in so short a time', wrote the 72-year-old Bishop of Winchester, Brian Duppa, 'But *a Domino Factum est istud*: no humane widsom can claime a share in it.' As the Philistines once crowed over Samson, so now 'Clarendon's view that God had intervened miraculously to restore Charles II seemed more plausible than the view that the routed Parliamentarians had been the interpreters of God's will.' For Cowley, it was not merely more plausible but demonstrably true:

> Where are the men who bragged that God did bless,
> And with the marks of good success
> Sign his allowance of their wickedness?
> Vain men, who thought the divine power to find
> In the fierce thunder and the violent wind.

> God came not till the storm was past,
> In the still voice of peace he came at last.
> The cruel business of destruction
> May by the claws of the great fiend be done.
> Here, here we see th'Almighty's hand indeed,
> Both by the beauty of the work we see't and by the speed.

Poets such as Edmund Waller and John Dryden registered this miracle by swiftly transferring to Charles II their encomiums of Cromwell as the English Augustus. So excessive was the general jubilation at this Providence that it quite turned the head of John Wilmot, Earl of Rochester, in 1660 a 13 year old newly arrived at Wadham College, Oxford, and so, Gilbert Burnet conjectured, permanently debauched him.[54]

In the tracts and controversies of the next 30 years this was the stick most frequently used to beat the defeated Puritans: in a Tory pamphlet written during the Exclusion Crisis we read that

> from *Papist* sprung *Puritan*, from *Puritan Presbyterian*, from *Presbyterian Independent*, from thence *Anabaptists, Antinomians, Fifth-Monarchists, Sweet Singers in Israel, Quakers, Muggletonians*, and the Lord knows what, till by and through the Inconstancy of their Persons and Judgements, and the various Frekes of the several Humours, all was reduced to Chaos; so that neither a single Usurper, nor a Parliament without a King, nor Committee of Safety, nor Keepers of Liberties, or Councels of Officers, and Strength of Arms, could produce any Quiet, till God wonderfully restored Him, whose undoubted Right it was to sway the Sceptre of these Kingdoms.[55]

The imprint of John Lilburne's 1639 pamphlet *Come Out of Her My People*, issued when he was 'Close Prisoner in the Fleete for the Cause of Christ', had audaciously dated the tract 'in the yeare of hope, of ENGLANDS purgation, & the Prelates dissolution'. Restoration prison books would fly no such rousingly optimistic colours: England had been purged and prelacy dissolved, to no avail. The 'great persecution' of 1660–88 was endured not by those anticipating the dawn of that 'notable day', as the Ranter Abiezer Coppe had done in the imprint of *A Fiery Flying Roll* (1649), but by those for whom that day and its accompanying hopes had passed. '*It was the hopes of a Reformation that we fought and suffered for*' wrote Baxter of the Civil War:[56] deprivation, ostracism, prison and persecution were their reward. The penal religious legislation of the 1660s left no doubt that the Restoration settlement intended not the toleration and perpetuation of an alternative religious tradition but the extirpation, once and for all, of all sentiments about the Reformation not in accord with those of the re-established episcopalian church.

It failed of its aim and succeeded only in transforming Puritanism into dissent. To many, however, this survivor appears to have been but a pale shadow of his former self. Professor Kenyon's remark, in one of the standard histories of the century, is representative: the Restoration saw 'the collapse of Puritanism. This vital intellectual and spiritual force ... abruptly faded away in

1660, and with it the "Good Old Cause".' Deprived of significant parliamentary representation those, such as John Owen and John Howe, who had walked the corridors of power in Cromwell's time, were now the puppets rather than the masters of events. Their fortunes depended less upon their own arguments and endeavours than upon the intermittent attempts of the Stuart monarch to exercise his royal prerogative to suspend penal religious legislation. They thus found themselves caught helplessly in a cleft stick, bound either to submit to the persecution parliament willed upon them or to support the flexing of absolutist muscle on behalf of Roman Catholics. Christian's apprehensiveness at the lions before the House Beautiful reflects this vulnerability: no one could be sure whether the lions of persecution were chained, or when the senile Giant Pope might turn into the fearsome Giant Maul.[57]

Withdrawal and retreat we might expect to be the response of those so insecure and defenceless and so unequivocally worsted by events. After a life of energetic political and revolutionary activity the Cromwellian Independent Hugh Peter came to regret that he had for public affairs forsaken his pastoral service in New England, where he had ministered to Salem church (1636–41). In his petition to the House of Lords of July 1660 he undertook in future 'to be quiet in a corner (if I may) to let God alone with ruling the World ... yea to mind my own work, though never so small; to be passive under Authority, rather than impatient'. Execution as an abettor of the trial of Charles I, a fate which he met bravely, deprived him of such an old age, but the tenor of his words is echoed by those who survived. The Milton who had defended regicide and been England's voice throughout Europe issued, in the spring of 1660, 'the last words of our expiring libertie' to those 'now chusing them a captain back for *Egypt*' and sought no more to influence parliaments or to denounce kings. As his friends Marvell and the Quaker Thomas Ellwood both remarked, he lived henceforth 'a private and retired Life in *London*'. Baxter, denied even a curacy or unpaid lectureship at Kidderminster, the scene of his renowned Interregnum pastorate, retired with his wife to Acton in Middlesex 'that I might set my self to writing, and do what Service I could for Posterity, and live as much as possibly I could out of the World. Thither I came 1663 July 14.' Indeed, in 1661, growing 'wearied with this kind of Life, to be every day calumniated, and hear new Slanders raised of me', he had thought 'to go beyond Sea, that I might find some place in retired privacy to live and end my days in quietness, out of the noise of a Peace-hating Generation'. The charismatic witness of the Quakers became something perhaps finer and more determined, certainly something less histrionically demonstrative, after 1660. Under Fox's leadership their repudiation of 'carnal weapons' led to a quietist disengagement from politics and worldly affairs. And the great majority of the New Model Army seem to have returned quietly to civilian life. Though he perhaps (for good reason) overemphasized their contentedness, there is no reason to doubt the main thrust of the point made to Pepys in 1663 by his friend Robert Blackborne (or Blackburne), Secretary to the Admiralty under the Commonwealth:

of all the old army now, you cannot see a man begging about the street. But what? You shall have this Captain turned a shoemaker; the lieutenant, a Baker; this, a brewer ... and every man in his apron and frock &c., as if they never had done anything else ... the spirits of the old Parliament-soldier[s] are so quiet and contented with God's providences, that the King is safer from any evil meant him by them a thousand times then from his own discontented Cavalier[s].[58]

'Look for the great deliverer now' and you would find him, if not, like Samson, imprisoned, then in country retreat, on the continent, in New England, engaged in small trade, farming, teaching, everywhere harried and pursued.

Contemporary satirists exulted over this impotence, caricaturing the nonconformist heirs of the Puritans as embittered hypocrites gnashing their teeth in deserved frustration. Our own increasing admiration for the radical wing of the Puritan movement encourages us to take the same view, if less censoriously, for these were the men who most obviously failed and were most firmly silenced after 1660. If the real genius of Puritanism is to be found in its most enthusiastic sects, then their demise is its demise. And vanish they did, with startling suddenness and finality. A historian as sympathetic to the radicals' Interregnum heyday as Dr Christopher Hill inevitably sees here only loss, the end of a 'great period of freedom of movement and freedom of thought'. He is hence much less impressed by those more moderate Puritan groupings which contrived to continue in, and adapt to, a world where 'God was no longer served by the extravagant gesture' than by those which did not. He does not blame the restraint of the survivors, but neither does he admire it: 'The nonconformist minority became, through no fault of its own, provincial, "Sectarian" and "Puritan" in the pejorative sense of those words.' It was but a 'gloomy "Puritanism"' which in 1660 succeeded 'the defeat of the real Puritans'. After the enthusiasm of the Interregnum, another historian writes, 'only the wilderness of legalized Dissent lay ahead.'[59]

Little can be expected from such a gloomy and disillusioned minority. Their 'introverted characteristics', their 'separation from the mainstream of English intellectual and political life', their 'intellectually narrow' habits of mind and 'rabidly religious' *mores* 'unsuited to life in society' ensured that they would contribute 'little of permanent value' to our literature.[60] As it is the episcopal and royalist view of the defeated Puritans we echo in such comments, so it is the culture of the established church and court – the culture of the victors – which defines our sense of Restoration literature. Our reference and guide books assure us that 'Restoration literature is characterised by the wit and control of Dryden's poetry and the licentiousness of Rochester's satires.' Almost all of enduring value produced by the period was 'the work of the small upper class which wrote most of the poetry and drama ... or of educated middle-class writers who had access to it, accepted its standards, and succesfully imitated its mode of writing'.[61]

Two writers conspicuously did not accept its standards: John Milton, the greatest poet of the age, and John Bunyan, 'the greatest imaginative writer of the age', 'the most commanding, and in restrospect the most influential writer of the century'. Convinced as he is of the sudden collapse of Puritanism, Professor Kenyon is puzzled and finds it 'strange' that after the Restoration 'the main burden [in literature] was carried by Puritans or ex-Puritans',[62] and it is, indeed, a curious fact that these two 'obvious exceptions' to what is taken to be the prevailing literary temper of the age were both outstanding writers and nonconformists. Lest the received view of the sterility of the dissenting tradition be disturbed by this awkward anomaly, two arguments are commonly deployed, both of which minimize the relevance of the Restoration period to their literary achievement.

On the one hand, Milton and Bunyan are seen in the light of their Puritan predecessors rather than in the context of their nonconformist contemporaries: the experiences of the 1640s and 1650s are held to have been decisive for both the convictions and the literary achievement of each. Hence, although Milton's three great poems all postdate the Restoration, he will be found not in the later, where Dryden reigns supreme, but in the earlier (1600–60) seventeenth-century volume of the Oxford History of English Literature. He is similarly placed in 'The End of the Renascence (1625–1660)' section of the older *History of English Literature* by Emile Legouis and Louis Cazamian. Cazamian concedes that *Paradise Lost* is 'undoubtedly' the greatest work of the reign of Charles II, but goes on that the poem, 'as imposing as it is solitary, is foreign to the movement surrounding it. In the same way, the *Pilgrim's Progress* of Bunyan seems to belong to another world.' Milton is a 'belated writer' in an age whose 'best representative' is Dryden. For Cazamian, that Milton's personality 'should preserve the tone of its individual self after the world to which it belonged had disappeared ... is undoubtedly little else than what one might call a normal paradox', an 'inevitable exception' to the generalization of literary history. For Dr Hill the tone is less inexplicable, but anachronistic none the less: it is Milton's 'glory that in the time of utter defeat, when Diggers, Ranters and Levellers were silenced and Quakers had abandoned politics, he kept something of the radical intellectual achievement alive'.[63]

On the other hand, as a (not necessarily exclusive) alternative to this historical argument, recourse is had to the individuality of the two men. On this view, Milton was an idiosyncratic genius who 'can scarcely be called a true Puritan' and 'cannot be taken to represent anyone except himself'.[64] In a famous note, Coleridge similarly attributed Bunyan's achievement to his own genius:

in that admirable Allegory, the first Part of *Pilgrim's Progress*, which delights every one, the interest is so great that spite of all the writer's attempts to force the allegoric purpose on the Reader's mind by his strange names – Old Stupidity of the Town of Honesty, &c. &c. – his piety was baffled by his genius, and the Bunyan of Parnassus had the better of the Bunyan of the Conventicle – and with the same illusion as we read any tale known to be fictitious, as a novel – we go on with his characters as real persons.

Bunyan's imagination, that is to say, was so fired as to defeat his didactic purpose. *The Pilgrim's Progress* is lifted above the body of seventeenth-century Puritan writing precisely because its inspired author was liberated from the constraints of his theology and his nonconformist religious tradition. This train of thought leads to the view of the book as the work of a 'transcendent genius', 'as original as anything in literature can be', its innovative character unrelated to the circumstances of composition and inexplicable save by reference to its author's own daemon: 'No one has done so much with so little help from predecessors or contemporaries.'[65]

Whichever line we take, Milton and Bunyan are the exceptions which prove the rule and the impression remains that Puritanism peters out after the Restoration, its religious and cultural life henceforth a backwater. The difficulty of squaring this impression with the facts of literary history may be illustrated from Maurice Ashley's history of *England in the Seventeenth Century*. He takes the now familiar line that Milton and Bunyan stand 'apart' from the mainstream of Restoration literature as 'survivors from an earlier period'. If, however, we turn back to what he says of this earlier Interregnum period, it is to find the only 'consistently fine' writing of Puritan character located in the later Milton, in Bunyan, in Fox's *Journal* and *Reliquiae Baxterianae*, all pieces not only published but actually written after 1660.[66] We are thus asked to accept at one and the same time that the best work of these writers does not belong to the Restoration period in which it was produced, while the best work of the Interregnum period to which it does belong was produced by these very writers after the Restoration. The simple fact that, whatever in a political, religious, social, or military way it may have achieved in the 1640s and 1650s, Puritanism produced no enduring literary achievement until after 1660 offers a way out of the paradox. By accepting the cultural premises and contemporary evaluation of the victors, we have been misled into identifying the political defeat of Puritanism with its cultural demise. The contrary seems rather to be the case: political defeat was the condition of cultural achievement.

It is that proposition which this study advances: the literature of Puritanism, far from being left over from an earlier age, was generated by the Restoration experience of persecution and nonconformity. Milton and Bunyan appear as exceptions only so long as we accept the court's confident assertion of the universal hegemony of its taste and measure by the Caroline rule. They are indeed misplaced persons in a literary history which has room for a host of minor poets and dramatists, for the episcopalian prose of Robert South, Thomas Sprat, Isaac Barrow, Gilbert Burnet and John Tillotson, for the diaries of Samuel Pepys and John Evelyn, for the pamphlets and essays of George Savile, Marquis of Halifax, Sir William Temple and Sir Robert L'Estrange, but which can afford only a sentence to Lucy Hutchinson and to George Fox and William Penn (mentioned merely on the mistaken assumption that he was Fox's editor), and not even a clause to John Owen, William Bates, Thomas Ellwood,

Thomas Manton, John Howe, Robert Barclay, or Benjamin Keach. Such a history may, exceptionally, give a paragraph to Baxter, but only to characterize him as 'similar to the Anglican autobiographers', a comment which inadvertently reveals the criterion of selection at work.[67] If, however, we shift the rule, Milton and Bunyan appear as what they truly were, the surpassing representatives of a large and neglected body of writing which made a distinctive contribution to our literary history precisely because it was the product of a movement accommodating itself to the experience of defeat, repression and ridicule.

That accommodation is usually described as a compromise with the values of the new age, and it is quite true that after 1660 the rhapsodical inner voice no longer told women to expose themselves. In the 1670s the Scottish Quaker Robert Barclay would dismiss tales of Quaker women 'going naked for a sign' as 'calumnies' on a par with Romish libels about Luther's sorcery and Beza's sodomy.[68] And yet, after nearly thirty years' persecution, nonconformity was sufficiently independent, steadfast and resilient to resist the blandishments of James II in what Macaulay called 'the strangest auction in history' when monarch and episcopal church vied for nonconformist support for and against the royal policy of religious indulgence.[69] This is the crucial fact for an understanding of the literary achievement of later Puritanism. Those who resisted James clearly had in mind something other than political sway. The Interregnum had so nearly approached the ideal of the primitive church that even an opponent of Cromwell such as Baxter could write of that time 'where before there was one profitable Preacher, there was then six or ten; and ... I conjecture there is a proportionable increase of truly godly People.' This paradise had been lost, but nonconformists under James were clearly no more inclined to regain it by expedient political means than was Milton's Christ to adopt the 'politic maxims' urged by Satan as the effective means to win his kingdom. There remained, however, the 'paradise within', in the enjoyment of which, Michael promises the fallen Adam, he will be 'happier far' than in Eden. That its attainment is preferred to that of an earthly kingdom – even one ruled by King Jesus – is a characteristic bias of nonconformist writing which inclines to see the pursuit of power, from whatever motive, as evidence 'of human weakness rather than of strength'.[70] True strength consists in patient enduring. Baxter could write in 1663 to John Eliot, the 'apostle to the American Indians':

> As for the divine Government by the Saints ... I dare not expect such great Matters upon Earth, lest I encroach upon the Priviledge of Heaven, and tempt my own Affections downwards, and forget that our Kingdom is not of this World. Certainly if Christianity be the same thing now that it was at first, it is much unsuitable to a reigning State on Earth: Bearing the Cross, Persecution, Self-denial, &c. found something of another Nature ... He that surveyeth the present State of the Earth ... will be ready to think that Christ hath called almost all his Chosen, and is ready to forsake the Earth, rather than that he intendeth us such blessed Days below as we desire. We shall have what we would, but not in this World.[71]

Just so, Bunyan's Christian does not tarry to reform Vanity Fair but posts to the Celestial City.

This, though an expression of resignation, is not capitulation. It is rather a redefinition of the 'Good Old Cause'. The political ideal of the Interregnum, it has been said of the thought of Peter Sterry, one of the dissenters in the Westminister Assembly and a chaplain to Cromwell, was 'transformed into a spiritual realisation of Christ to the English saints ... the millenarianism of the 1650s into the realised eschatology of the 1660s'. 'It will never be well', wrote John Howe, 'till our own Souls be an Heaven to us ... 'Till we get a settled principle of holy quietude into our own breasts.' Such quietude is not quiescence: Michael points to continuing moral and spiritual effort as Adam's only way to regain paradise. Though the field of battle is no longer Edgehill or Naseby, there is yet a war to fight within each individual for, as Bunyan allegorized it in *The Holy War* (1682), possession of Mansoul. And, though not earthly, there is a kingdom to win:

> Yet he who reigns within himself, and rules
> Passions, desires and fears, is more a king.[72]

It is this emphasis on the 'reconstruction of individuals'[73] – this, if we will, forgoing of the chimera of the rule of the saints for pastoral ministration to a persecuted people – which, so far from betraying Puritanism, realized its true genius. The idealism remained: the challenge was not compromised: but it was issued now not to systems or organizations but to the individual conscience. The Milton who began by attacking episcopacy and haranguing the Long Parliament came finally to contemplate the solitary figure of Samson, 'a prisoner chained', yet drawing 'The breath of heaven'. The shared experience of disillusion and chastened optimism, though it took men off from social and political revolution, bred a new understanding of, and sympathy for, the complexities of human psychology, and a clear-sighted address to the actual conditions of fallen man. It was neither escapism nor defeatism but a sensitive awareness of human vulnerability in an inconstant world, of 'how variously the passions ... may be mov'd and stirr'd by ... variety of occasions' from 'a transport of high contentment' to 'a very Paroxysm of anguish and despair', which led John Howe to reassure his readers that 'this present state is only intended for trial to the spirits of men, in order to their attainment of a better state in a better world.'[74] Nonconformist literature bore an invaluably sympathetic witness to the apprehensions and aspirations of individuals in an age of increasingly complacent dismissal of any manifestation of individuality as a reprehensible aberration. It was not Civil War, nor regicide, nor Cromwell which released the Puritan imagination, but nonconformity.

To the circumstances which created the nonconformity of the Restoration, and transformed it into dissent, we must first turn, before going on to consider the literary consequence of those circumstances.

Chapter 1 'Fallen on evil days'
the historical circumstances of nonconformity

*And be ye not conformed to this world: but be ye transformed by
the renewing of your mind, that ye may prove what is that good,
and acceptable, and perfect will of God.*

*Rom. xii.*2

I   BLACK BARTHOLOMEW DAY

On 4 April 1660 Charles issued from Breda in Holland a conciliatory *Declaration*:

> because the passion and uncharitableness of the times have produced several
> opinions in religion, by which men are engaged in parties and animosities against
> each other ... we do declare a liberty to tender consciences, and that no man shall
> be disquieted or called in question for differences of opinion in matters of religion
> which do not disturb the peace of the kingdom, and that we shall be ready to
> consent to such an Act of Parliament as upon mature deliberation shall be offered
> to us for the full granting that indulgence.[1]

This augured well, but, as Baxter noted, though Charles seemed to have 'sent
over a Promise of Liberty of Conscience', he had in fact offered 'but a
Profession of his readiness to consent to any Act which the Parliament should
offer him to that end'.[2] Quite why Charles offered even this we cannot know:
policy, a naturally lenient and lax, if not morally cynical, disposition, and Roman
Catholic sympathies, probably all played a part; and possibly a genuine desire
for toleration.[3] Parliament, however, took no advantage of the offer, and drafted
no such Act. What is extraordinary about the Restoration is less the ease and
speed with which it was effected than that those who accomplished it took no
steps to safeguard themselves and their future. During its one month of
renewed life (February–March 1660), the Long Parliament never addressed
the question of the form of religious and civil government it envisaged. Indeed,
such was the desire for restoration among its Presbyterian majority, a desire
made urgent by John Lambert's attempted coup, that the question of terms
seemed quite secondary. Although the Presbyterians had lost their overall
majority in the Convention, which met on 25 April, they might yet have carried
legislation in alliance with the Independent members, but when Charles landed
at Dover on 25 May he was still bound by no more than the vague promise of
Breda. 'To the King's coming in without conditions may be well imputed all the

errours of his reign' the Scot Gilbert Burnet, afterwards Bishop of Salisbury, was to write in his *History of My Own Time.*[4]

This was no cause of dismay to Baptists, Quakers and some Independents, who suspected any Presbyterian inclination towards a treaty with the king as likely to impose on them a uniformity as intolerant as the episcopalian. 'God overthrew them, and turned them upside down, and brought the King over them' exulted George Fox, and, with that indifference to politics which was to characterize the Friends after 1660, dismissed the Restoration as irrelevant to Quakers since they 'did not concern themselves with the outward powers'.[5] Presbyterians, however, did concern themselves with such powers, and their hopes of an agreement were kept alive throughout the summer and autumn of 1660. 'Some plain and moderate Episcopal Men thought of Reconciliation and Union with the ... Presbyterians; yea, and a Reward to the Presbyterians for bringing in the King', and a number of 'Chief Presbyterians' were appointed chaplains to Charles.[6] In June the king 'took very well' Presbyterian proposals for 'a Conference for an Agreement', and, at a personal audience with Baxter, Edward Reynolds, Edmund Calamy, Simeon Ashe, John Wallis, Thomas Manton and William Spurstowe, he professed

> his gladness to hear our Inclinations to Agreement, and his Resolution to do his part to bring us together; and that it must not be by bringing one Party over to the other, but by abating somewhat on both sides, and meeting in the Midway; and that if it were not accomplished, it should be long of our selves, and not of him: Nay, that he was resolved to see it brought to pass, and that he would draw us together himself]: with some more to this purpose. Insomuch that old Mr *Ash* burst out into Tears with Joy.[7]

Later in the summer, the offer of the bishoprics of Hereford, Norwich and Coventry & Lichfield to Baxter, Reynolds and Calamy respectively (with deaneries to Manton and Bates) seemed to confirm the goodwill of the restored authorities.[8] In the Convention, the Presbyterians, in alliance with Independent members, passed on 4 September William Prynne's bill for *Establishing Ministers Settled in Ecclessiastical Livings*, which secured in their benefices all clergy appointed since 1642, unless the previous incumbent were alive or the present minister had sought the trial of Charles I, opposed the Restoration, or repudiated infant baptism.[9] On that same 4 September the Presbyterians received a draft of a proposed royal declaration concerning ecclesiastical affairs, and, after discussions on 22 October at Clarendon's residence, Worcester House, the amended *Declaration*, issued on 25 October, was couched in such moderate and conciliatory terms that, Baxter believed, 'any sober honest Minister might submit' to it. It provided for 'the advice and assistance of presbyters' in ordination and the exercise of episcopal jurisdiction; the appointment of suffragan bishops in large dioceses; the prohibition of 'arbitrary' episcopal power; the calling of a synod to revise the Prayer Book; and the toleration of 'the private consciences of those who are grieved with the use of some ceremonies'.

Baxter, receiving a copy on his way to an appointment with Clarendon, 'was so much pleased with it, that . . . I gave him hearty thanks' for its concessions to the Presbyterian point of view.[10]

If the Presbyterians thus seemed to have good cause to anticipate a church settlement sufficiently broad to accommodate them, three things that autumn boded less well. First, parliament was adjourned the day Charles signed Prynne's bill (13 September). Secondly, the beneficiaries of the Worcester House *Declaration* showed ominous divisions among themselves: some Presbyterians (including Zachary Crofton and Arthur Jackson) were against 'returning Thanks to the King . . . because their Thanks, would signifie an approbation of Bishops and Archbishops which they had covenanted against'. The published *Address of Thanks* (presented on 16 November) was signed only by those 'that were satisfied': 'some remained unsatisfied to the end'. Furthermore, some of the Presbyterians shared the Independents' chagrin that they had not been included in the negotiations, and that the Presbyterians were so forward on their own behalf when there was no word of toleration for those who could not accept the terms of the *Declaration*. At the Worcester House Conference Baxter had, despite Professor Wallis's importuning him to remain silent, actually spoken against toleration since 'it would secure the Liberty of the Papists'.[11] This would long rankle with the Independents. And, thirdly, on 28 October began the consecration of new bishops. John Sudbury's *Sermon* on the occasion, a celebration of 'the height and dignity' of the bishop's office, left no doubt that the restrictions of episcopal power proposed in the *Declaration* were far from the thoughts of those present.[12] 1660 may have seen the publication of such Presbyterian tracts as William Prynne's reissue of his 1636 *The Unbishoping of Timothy and Titus*, but no one was going to unbishop the bishops again. Parliament reconvened on 6 November. This combination of a revitalized episcopal bench and episcopalian members of the Convention, together with the disunity of the Puritans, meant that at the 'crucial moment' the division to pass the *Declaration* into law on 28 November was lost 183–157. 'So there', wrote Marvell in a letter, was 'an end of that bill and for those excellent things therein.' As a later satirist – perhaps Marvell again – put it:

> Then Bishops must reivive, and all unfix
> With discontent to content twenty six.[13]

The motives behind, and intentions of, the overtures to the Presbyterians during 1660 are as uncertain as those of the *Declaration* of Breda. Baxter's account, the earliest and most authoritative record of these events, interprets them as merely politic expedients to placate Presbyterian opinion and doubts that their implementation was ever seriously contemplated by court, bishops, or king. The chaplaincies were offered 'that the People might think that such Men as we were favoured and advanced, and consequently that all that were like us should be favoured, and so might think their Condition happy'. Those appointed 'made no doubt but that this was the use that was to be made of us', and the vote on 28 November seemed to justify his fear that the Worcester House *Declaration* 'was but for present use, and that shortly it would be revok'd or nullified'.[14] It is a view which has won the assent of many later historians, notably Robert Bosher, whose detailed survey of the Restoration negotiations interprets them as the pursuit of a Machiavellian policy designed to lull the Presbyterians into a false sense of security while the episcopalians consolidated their position. The 'real reason' for the recess of parliament was the growing preponderance of Presbyterians in the House as royalist and episcopalian members defected in increasing numbers; the consecration of bishops was intended, 'it may safely be assumed', to re-establish episcopacy before the House next sat; and the *Declaration* was 'a master-stroke of policy, well calcu-lated to relieve the dangerous state of tension'.[15] Charles, however, has had his supporters, who doubt the pursuit of a consistent policy to re-establish exclu-sively Laudian power and are prepared to credit his intention to implement the *Declaration*.[16] Charles was certainly cannier than Sir John Reresby's contem-porary assessment that he 'was not stirring nor ambitious' allows, but Reresby's additional comment that the king was 'easy, loved pleasures and seemed chiefly to desire quiet and security for his own time'[17] opens the way for a third view: that Charles did intend the implementation of the *Declaration* but not for religious reasons. He 'was no disinterested advocate of religious toleration, but a monarch bent on making much of monarchy', seeking 'monarchical emanci-pation' by 'enlarging the ranks of his potential supporters' and so escaping from dependence upon any one party.[18] But whatever the historical truth may have been, the experiential truth for Presbyterians was of deception and betrayal. Recalling these events in 1665, after the worst drought 'that ever Man alive knew, or our Forefathers mention of late Ages', during 'War with the *Hollanders*' and while the plague ravaged London, Baxter was a deeply dis-appointed and disillusioned man:

> O how is *London*, the place which God hath honoured with his Gospel above all Places of the Earth, laid low in Horrours, and wasted almost to Desolation, by the Wrath of God, whom *England* hath contemned; and a God-hating Generation are consumed in their Sins, and the Righteous are also taken away as from greater Evil yet to come.[19]

The vote of 28 November 1660 was the turning point. On 8 May 1661 the Cavalier Parliament met. Any lingering concessionary inclinations towards the Puritans had in the interim been dispelled by 'some discontented schismaticks' who, on 6 January, 'raised a small rebellion in London'.[20] Thomas Venner's Fifth Monarchist uprising was indeed a 'small rebellion', involving perhaps 50 people who were quickly overcome, but its suddenness and bloodiness (22 people were killed on each side) did much to convince apprehensive royalists and episcopalians that this was what could be expected from Puritans of any stamp.[21] In vain did Quakers and Baptists dissociate themselves from the uprising. Throughout 1660 the Secretary of State Sir Edward Nicholas had been receiving reports of 'wicked and disaffected persons ... termed Quakers', 'great store of anabaptists and quakers ... in every corner of the country' and of regular meetings of over 1,000 at Bristol 'to the great affrighting of this City'. Venner's rising merely confirmed what he and the government already supposed they had good cause to believe: that 'under the spetious *pre*tence of Religion & piety' enthusiasts hid 'their horrid designes'. A royal proclamation of 10 January forbade meetings of 'Anabaptists, Quakers, and Fifth Monarchy men, or some such like appellation' held 'under pretence of serving God', and upwards of 4,000 Quakers and Baptists were swiftly gaoled.[22] That any form of religious dissent was but a hypocritical cloak for rebellious sedition and political subversion was the firm conviction of the great majority of members returned to the Cavalier Parliament, men whose royalism had been further stirred by the coronation of Charles II, with full episcopal splendour, on St George's Day, 23 April.[23] Presbyterian representation was reduced to between 37 and 50 members. 'We have great hopes', wrote Secretary Nicholas, 'that this will prove a very happy Parliament, there being few Presbyterians in it.'[24]

This happy parliament quickly showed its temper: it voted to have the *Solemn League and Covenant* burned by the hangman and resolved that all its members should receive communion according to the rite of the *Book of Common Prayer*. The *Act for the Preservation of the King*, mindful that 'the late troubles and disorders did in a very great measure proceed from a multitude of seditious sermons, pamphlets and speeches daily preached, printed and published', made it treason to 'incite or stir up the people to hatred or dislike of the person of his Majesty or the established government', or to suggest they were popishly inclined, 'by writing, printing, preaching or other speaking'. The *Act against Tumultuous Petitioning* limited to 20 the number of signatories to a petition, and to 10 the number of its presenters. The Corporation Act (13 Car. II, st. II, cap. 1) required all civic officers and magistrates to take the oaths of allegiance and supremacy, to disclaim the lawfulness of taking arms against the king, to repudiate the *Solemn League and Covenant* and to receive the sacrament 'according to the rites of the Church of England' within the year preceding office.[25] On 3 July, even as the Savoy Conference, convened in fulfilment of the promise in the Worcester House *Declaration*, was debating the revision of the Prayer Book, a Bill for Religious Uniformity was introduced, drafted in part by the man before whom Bunyan had appeared, Sir John Kelynge, afterwards Chief Justice of the King's Bench. Clearly the House, which had restored bishops to their place in the Lords, had no intention of waiting upon amicable compromise, nor would anything like the *Declaration* ever pass an assembly which so identified compliance with its own religious ceremonies as the mark of loyalty and dissent from them as a disqualification from civic trust. The 'maxim was', so Halifax later recalled, 'it is impossible for a Dissenter not to be a rebel'.[26]

'We spoke to the Deaf', wrote Baxter of the Savoy Conference, and 'could prevail with these Prelates and Prelatical Men, (after so many Calamities by Divisions, and when they pretended Desires of Unity), to make no considerable Alterations at all' to the Prayer Book.[27] Baxter's own inexpert negotiating skills seem to have helped to close the episcopal ears. He took upon himself the main management of the Presbyterian case, but by the comprehensiveness and minuteness with which he presented it, caused only irritation and impatience. George Morley, Baxter's diocesan at Worcester and the man responsible for preventing his return to Kidderminister, wrote that the delegates were 'tending to an amicable and fair compliance, which was wholly frustrated by Mr Baxter's furious eagerness to engage in a disputation'. Izaak Walton recorded that even the 'patient' Robert Sanderson, Bishop of Licoln, was moved to expostulate 'with an unusual earnestness' at Baxter's *pertinacious confidence and less abilities*. And after the conference broke up without agreement in July, Baxter found Clarendon 'most offended at me. ... At our first entrance he merily [*sic*] told us [*That if I were but as fat as Dr Manton, we should all do well*]. I told him, if his Lordship could teach me the Art of growing fat, he should find me not unwilling to learn by any good means. He grew more serious, and said, That I was severe and strict, like a Melancholy Man, and made those things *Sin* which others did not.'[28] But even if 'The Puritan divines had not a statesman's head among them', the Savoy Conference was, by the time it met on 15 April, already doomed, hopelessly overtaken by events. What had, in 1660, been proposed as a conference between equals was, six months later, something very different: the Presbyterians were reduced by the 'admirable tactics' of the bishops to the position of suppliants to those in authority.[29] Even so, the revision of the Prayer Book, completed in Convocation by 20 December, showed some responsiveness to the Presbyterian exceptions raised at the Savoy. In its preface, Sanderson claimed that it deprived critics of '*occasion of cavil, or quarrel against the Liturgy of the Church*', and, less polemically and more positively, that it was a moderate document tending '*to the preservation of Peace and Unity in the Church*'. In Baxter's view, however, 'the Convocation had made the Common Prayer Book more grievous than before.'[30] If this is still a matter for debate, no two opinions are possible about the Act to which it was, without debate in the Commons, attached as a liturgical standard. The Act of Uniformity received the royal assent on 19 May 1662 and came into force on St Bartholomew's Day, 24 August.[31] It was expected, wrote Samuel Pepys, to 'make mad work among Presbyterian ministers'.[32]

The preamble to the Act (14 Car. II, cap. 4) looked back approvingly to the old 1559 Elizabethan Act of Uniformity and blamed upon 'the great and scandalous neglect of ministers' of its prescribed liturgy the 'great mischiefs and inconveniences during the time of the late unhappy troubles' and the 'factions and schisms' which were the 'scandal' of the Church of England and the 'hazard of many souls'. Believing that 'nothing conduceth more to the settling the peace of this nation ... than a universal agreement in the public worship of Almighty God', it enacted that the revised Prayer Book alone should henceforth be used in all places of worship and that every beneficed clergyman should, on one Sunday before St Bartholomew's Day, 'openly and publicly before the congregation ... declare his unfeigned assent and consent' to 'all and everything contained and prescribed' in it. Any clergyman who neglected to do so was *ipso facto* 'deprived of all his spiritual promotions'. Incumbents were further required to subscribe a declaration of non-resistance to the regal authorities of the state, of intended conformity to the liturgy and of the illegality and invalidity of the *Solemn League and Covenant*. And, finally, the Act broke decisively with England's history since the Reformation by recognizing the validity only of episcopal orders. Any incumbent not episcopally ordained by Bartholomew Day was deprived of his benefice. Taken together, these provisions were far more rigorous than the old Elizabethan Act, which had not mentioned orders and had required only a general undertaking to use the Prayer Book, not a public approval of every jot and tittle in it.[33] 'Present Conformity', wrote one unwilling nonconformist, 'is foreign and quite of another nature from conformity heretofore; Conscience being now much more forced and violated by them in the Chair.'[34]

Daniel Defoe was later to claim that 'above 3,000 ... quitted their Livings, because they could not comply' with this Act. At the time, William Hooke, a former chaplain to Cromwell, put it at '1,500 or 1,600 ministers of ability ejected, and ignorant, scandalous, and unworthy men in their places'. Baxter reckoned that 'When *Bartholomew-day* came, about One thousand eight hundred, or Two thousand Ministers were Silenced and Cast out', and his estimate is the one confirmed by subsequent research.[35] Not all of these were ejected in 1662. At least 695 had been put out in 1660 by the *Act for Establishing Ministers*, 290 as holders of sequestered livings whose original incumbents yet survived. Baxter himself was 'cast out (when many hundreds of others were ejected) upon the Restoration of all them that had been sequestred' and replaced as vicar of Kidderminster by his predecessor, George Dance.[36] The behaviour of Dance, whom Baxter had permitted to continue living in the vicarage throughout the Interrregum, contrasts with that of Thomas Fuller. On 18 October 1660 Fuller, who had in 1649 been succeeded in the living of Broadwindsor, Dorset, by John Pinney, signed a deed ceding to Pinney his legal right to the living.[37] Fifty-nine of those less fortunate than Pinney were yet more fortunate than Baxter, and succeeded in securing other benefices after being removed in 1660. But it was to no avail. In 1662 they, like Pinney, were among the Bartholomeans. The total number of clergy, lecturers, fellows and schoolmasters thus ejected in England by the summer of 1662 was computed by A. G. Matthews as 1,909, to which should be added 120 for Wales.[38] To this should also be added those such as John Owen, Peter Sterry and Increase Mather (unlike his brothers Nathaniel and Samuel) who were not put out merely because they held no benefice at the time. Indeed, large though the total is, it relates only to those beneficed in the Cromwellian church, and so is a measure chiefly of Presbyterian opinion (in its various shades). It includes only 194 known Independents and 19 known Baptists (most notably Henry Jessey), for many Independents, most Baptists and all Quakers had had nothing to do with the state church and so were never put out as they had never been in. To the 2,029 should therefore be added the sizeable body of more radical dissenters from the established church.[39]

As Bartholomew Day approached, there was some apprehension as to its possible consequences. In June 1662 it was reported to Sir William Compton, erstwhile member of the 'sealed knot' of royalist conspirators and now master of the Ordnance, that Fifth Monarchists and Republicans did but stay their hand until the more numerous Presbyterians, having 'tasted the scourge of the Act of Uniformity', joined them in a general uprising. In July, Secretary Nicholas received similar information that Commonwealth men were waiting only for Presbyterians to take the lead. Throughout the summer Samuel Pepys made anxious entries in his diary. On 22 June he was afraid that 'the Bishops will never be able to carry it as high as they do', and at the end of that month he recorded, 'All people discontented', the fanatics that 'the King do take away their liberty of conscience', and he feared 'the heighth of the Bishops, who ... will ruin all again'. Having heard a 'most eloquent' sermon by William Bates on 10 August, he gave it as his view that 'the Presbyters do all prepare to give over it all against Bartholomewtide.' Five days later his impression that 'the next Sunday will be the last of a great many Presbyterian ministers' was confirmed by what he heard while browsing among the bookstalls in Paul's churchyard: 'I pray God the issue may be good, for the discontent is great.' On 17 August (the last Sunday before 24 August), having heard William Bates's farewell sermon, he wrote: 'I hear most of the Presbyters took their leaves today. And the City is much dissatisfied with it. I pray God keep peace among us and make the Bishops careful of bringing in good men in their room, or else all will fly a-pieces.' On Bartholomew Day itself reports of disrupted services and the ripping apart of prayer books sounded 'very ominous'. On 31 August he prayed 'God preserve us!', since 'discontents ... by reason of the presbyters', rumours of plots and the imprisonment of nonconformists 'bode very ill'. On 3 September, the anniversary of Cromwell's victories at Dunbar and Worcester and of his death, a rising of 'Fanatiques and the Presbyters' was anticipated. It was with considerable relief that Pepys recorded on 30 September that the Bartholomeans had 'gone out very peaceably and the people not so much concerned therein as was expected'. That same month, Secretary Nicholas wrote with satisfaction to Lord Rutherford that all was quiet: many Presbyterians had conformed and London was generally appreciative of the quality and preaching of the conformist ministers.[40] That the nonconformists went 'peaceably' was a relief to the government, but for the reason they went at all we must look beyond the obstinacy, perversity, malice and hypocrisy attributed to them by royalists and episcopalians.[41]

2 'DIVERS SORTS' OF NONCONFORMISTS

'It is not to be thought', wrote John Howe, 'but among so many parties as come all under one common notion of dissenters from the public rule (and whom that rule did not find *one*, but made them so in the common notion,) there must be great diversity of opinions, and proportionably differing practices.'[42] And indeed there were.

In a monograph on Unitarian history Alexander Gordon wrote of the Bartholomeans that 'they did not go out on the grounds either of attachment or of antipathy to any theory of church government ... It was not episcopacy which they refused to sanction; it was the setting up of new, arbitrary and tyrannical terms of episcopalian conformity which excluded them.' He was thinking there of the Presbyterians, and particularly of Baxter's 'Reconcilers', the 'mere Christians', 'mere Catholics', 'of no Sect or party, but abhorring the very Name of Parties', who were 'perhaps a majority' of those ejected. Their withdrawal was prompted not by any one of the clauses in the Act of Uniformity – 420 of them were, like Baxter himself, in episcopal orders (including 45 ordained between the Restoration and 1662) and they had no objection to a set liturgy in principle. It was rather the Act's general implication that subscription to its provisions was an essential qualification for Christian fellowship which excluded them. This exclusivity was rejected by those who held that true Christianity was compatible with a wide range of theological opinions, liturgical practices and ecclesiastical structures and that to exalt any one of them into a condition of church member- ship was to mistake accidents for fundamentals. Though this view was held by some conformists, such as John Wilkins, Bishop of Chester, it was more commonly heard from such Presbyterian nonconformists as Thomas Manton: 'That which we detest is', wrote Manton, 'that the traditions of men should be made equal in dignity and authority with the express revelation of God.'[43]

That revelation set a value on something quite foreign to the Act of Uniformity. Explicating Matthew ix.13, and noting the echo of Hosea vi.6, Manton argued that 'if 'Sacrifices [which] were of God's institution' 'must give place to mercy, then externals of human institution ought much more to give place to mercy' and should never be insisted on if 'the urging of externals may cross mercy to the souls of men, by depriving them of the means of edification, and the gifts of a lively ministry, or crossing mercy to the bodies of men, by depriving them and their families of their necessary support and maintenance'. It is the argument Milton had deployed in favour of divorce: charity. To neglect this is to fall prey to a superstitious and partisan regard for shibboleths secondary to true religion. The New Testament teaches forbearance (Eph. iv.2,

3; I Pet. iv.8; I Cor. xiii.4, 7). It was just this case which Marvell, with the force not of biblical texts but of irony, urged against zealously partisan conformists. 'Truth for the most part lyes in the middle, but men ordinarily seek for it in the extremities', with the disastrous results which have been evident in Christian history since the Council of Nicaea. 'For one that is a Christian in good earnest, when a creed is imposed, will sooner eat fire than take it against his judgment.' Many things stand in need of correction 'which are far more ruinous in the Consequence, than the dispensing with a Surplice', and Marvell offered his own recommended impositions:

> before they admit men to subscribe the Thirty Nine Articles for a Benefice, they try whether they know the meaning. That they would much recommend to them the reading of the Bible. 'Tis a very good Book, and if a man read it carefully, will make him much wiser.[44]

To men of this mind, no scruple which did not touch the basic doctrines of Christianity was sufficient justification for excluding a man from communion. 'As long as we all agree in the Fundamentals', Baxter wrote, 'we are of one Religion for all our Differences': he who 'would unite the Church in Kings, in Councels, in any humane devices, will but divide it'. The Act of Uniformity was such a divisive device, needlessly fracturing the church. John Howe was, so Edmund Calamy recorded, for *'Union and Communion of all visible Christians; and for making nothing necessary to Christian Communion, but what Christ hath made necessary, or what is indeed necessary to one's being a Christian'*. When John Wilkins expressed surprise that men of Howe's *'Latitude ... continu'd* Non-conformists', Howe replied: 'That that *Latitude* of his, which he was pleased to take notice of, was so far from inducing him to Conformity, that it was the very thing that made and kept him a Non-conformist'. The nonconformity of these men was, ironically perhaps, but perfectly sensibly, a witness against the legislation which made nonconformity a possibility.[45]

For Presbyterians of less latitude particular clauses in the Act formed the chief obstacle to conformity, though these could weigh even with the Reconcilers. It was by Howe that the difficulty over reordination was famously put to Seth Ward, Bishop of Exeter:

> Why, pray, Sir, said the Bishop to him, what hurt is there in being twice Ordain'd? *Hurt*, my Lord, says *Mr Howe* to him; the Thought is shocking; it hurts my Understanding; it is an absurdity; For nothing can have two Beginnings.

Howe regarded his own ordination by Charles Herle, rector of Winwick, Lancashire, as 'truly primitive' by a 'Primitive Bishop', but for men of a stricter Presbyterian caste there could, quite apart from the hurt to their understandings, be no question either of receiving episcopal orders or of repudiating the *Solemn League and Covenant*. William Hooke, who claimed that 'most' Presbyterians had conformed, reckoned all of them would have done so 'had not the covenant pinched them'. Although this is the inaccurate and naughty reflection of an Independent upon the Presbyterians generally, it certainly reflects the scruple of some.[46]

Although Presbyterians rarely objected to a set liturgy *per se*, they had, as the Savoy Conference had shown, very considerable objections to that contained in the *Book of Common Prayer*. For them to make the comprehensive and unequivocal declaration of its acceptability required by the Act was consequently impossible. The anonymous author of *The Nonconformists Advocate* (1680) protested 'for peace sake I can submit, where I do not *like and chuse*' but 'assent and consent' is more than a simple undertaking to use what is disliked, such as the Elizabethan Act of Uniformity had imposed. Although he was prepared to perform what was required 'rather than break Communion with the Church', to declare his willingness to do so would, 'if a *Lye* be a transgression', be nothing less than wilful deceit: 'for in the bottom of my Soul, and in the truth of my Reins, I am utterly against it.' It was, furthermore, quite simply impossible for the majority of ministers living outside London to see the revised Prayer Book before 17 August, since it came from the press only shortly before. Burnet recorded that many 'well affected to the church' could not subscribe 'to a book that they had not seen' and so 'left their benefices on that very account', and Baxter pointedly asked 'how come *Bartholomew*-day 1662 to be so happy a day, as to bring at once 7,000 to sudden understanding and repentance, that never shewed that repentance till then?', and how came they to consent to a book 'which they had never seen', 'unless it was by changing with the times?' Forty years after Bartholomew Day the memory still rankled. 'Very few', the Presbyterian minister at Shrewsbury, James Owen, wrote in 1703, 'except those in or near London, cou'd possibly have a Sight' of the revised Prayer Book: '*Conformity* was usher'd in by an *Implicit Faith*, and the greatest Part of 2000 Ministers were turn'd out for not Assenting to a Book they had never seen.'[47]

The sense of injustice in such men was, however, most roused by the charge of schism, which they indignantly returned upon the heads of their accusers. 'Oftentimes the most Uncharitable Accusers of Schismaticks, and the most fierce and rigorous Punishers of it, are the greatest Causers thereof, and so most Guilty' wrote George Trosse, a Presbyterian minister at Exeter. 'When they are the *Imposers* of any disputable Doctrines, or Rites and Ceremonies, as *necessary Conditions of Communion*' they 'drive wilfully from themselves' those not satisfied of the indifference of the things imposed: '*These, These* are the great Dividers of the Church.' James Owen was of like mind: 'The Dissenters say the *Imposers* of *Unscriptural Terms* of Communion are the Schismaticks. The *Schism* lies at the door of the who contriv'd the *Act of Uniformity*.' Of Baxter, the inspiration of such men, Coleridge was to write that he 'is numbered among the Dissenters – with about as much right, as I might charge a man with desertion, whom I had thrown out of the window in the hope of breaking his neck!'[48]

So-called Presbyterians of the stamp of Baxter and Howe, who retained hopes of eventual comprehension within a more broadly based national church,

adopted a number of terms to distinguish themselves as unwilling nonconform-
ists and to point up what Defoe called their 'backwardness to separate'. Baxter
spoke of 'mere nonconformists' and sometimes 'episcopal nonconformists'.
The anonymous authors of *A Short Surveigh of the Grand Case of the Present
Ministry* (1663) described themselves on its title-page as 'conformable
Nonconformsits', and John Cheyney in 1680 published *The Conforming Nonconformist and the Non-conforming Conformist.* 'Partial conformists' and 'old
Puritans' were other terms used. These qualifying epithets and paradoxical
oxymorons were no mere play on words. They both capture the tension
inherent in the position of these men and accurately reflect their practice. '*The
Title of my Book*', wrote Cheyney, '*is the image of my Mind, and the Commentary of
my Practice.*' Unable to conform to a deliberately exclusive church, they would
yet not separate from it completely. Their habit of occasional communion with
parish churches fulfilled Cheyney's title. Occasional conformity was thus a
liberal and, originally, purely religious practice, defended as such by Baxter in
1671 and 1672, against the more rigorous separatism of Edward Bagshaw, who
thought 'it a sin to hear a Conformist'. It was an attempt at once to refuse the
partisan loyalty demanded by the Church of England without lapsing into
another, and equally damaging, partisanship. In 1702 Edmund Calamy told
Burnet it had been practised 'by some of the most eminent of our ministers
since 1662, with a design to show their charity towards the church'.[49]

It was a charity exercised in varying degrees. Zachary Crofton, ejected
Presbyterian curate of St Botolph's, Aldgate, approved of attendance at the
parish sermon, but not of hearing Common Prayer or receiving the sacrament.
The Flintshire Presbyterian Philip Henry participated in Common Prayer, but
would not receive. The seasoned campaigner William Prynne would receive the
sacrament sitting. Baxter, though, 'Had I my choice, I would receive the Lord's
supper sitting', was prepared, 'where I have not', to receive kneeling as
prescribed by the Prayer Book rubric. John Humfrey, 'though a Nonconformist
minister', was 'a Conformist parishioner', and would receive the sacrament only
in his parish church. And the antipaedobaptist John Tombes absented himself
only from infant baptism. It is pleasant to record that this charity was on
occasions reciprocated. On his deathbed Tombes was attended by Daniel
Whitby, rector of St Edmund's, Salisbury. Thomas Baldwin, Baxter's one-time
assistant at Kidderminster and afterwards nonconformist minister there, used
to attend the sermons of the vicar, Richard White. It was White who preached
his funeral sermon in 1693.[50]

To its critics, the practice of occasional communion by laymen seemed, and
sometimes inevitably was, a self-interested act to qualify for civic office under
the Corporation and, later, Test Acts. One of the most notorious cases was that
of the republican Slingsby Bethel, lampooned as Shimei by Dryden in *Absalom
and Achitophel*, who, elected a sheriff of London in 1680, duly attended the
Prayer Book service of Holy Communion as a qualification to serve. Defoe, in

his *Inquiry into the Occasional Conformity of Dissenters* (1701), implied that its practice by Sir Thomas Abney, a member of Howe's congregation chosen in 1700 to serve as Lord Mayor of London the following year, was an expedient of this kind. In his preface, Defoe challenged Howe either to vindicate or condemn the practice. Defoe's argument was vigorously straightforward: 'If a man Dissent from the Church, let him do so; and his Principles being well grounded for such Dissent, let him hold it; if not well-grounded, let him leave it'; 'Mediums are impossible'; 'Nothing can be lawful and unlawful at the same time'; and, scornfully,

> there is a sort of Truth which all men owe to the Principles they profess; and generally speaking, all men pay it: a *Turk* is a *Turk* zealously and entirely, an Idolater is an Idolater, and *will serve the Devil to a tittle*: None but Protestants halt between God and Baal, Christians of an Amphibious Nature, who have such Preposterous Consciences as can believe one Way of Worship to be right, and yet serve God another way themselves.[51]

Howe's reply, *Some Considerations of a Preface to an Inquiry concerning the Occasional Conformity of Dissenters* (1701), an unusually animated piece for him, maintains the distinction between occasional communion (signifying fellowship) and full conformity (signifying complete acquiescence) and rejects as an absurdly false distinction Defoe's application of I Kings xviii.21, as if 'the God of the dissenters and of the Established Church differ as the living God and Baal'. The debate would pursue its bitter and unedifyng course for another fifteen years, resentment at the practice finally reaching the statute-book in the Occasional Conformity (1711) and Schism (1714) Acts, which disqualified any official or schoolteacher who, having qualified for his post by taking the sacrament in the Church of England, subsequently attended a (now legal and tolerated) dissenters' meeting. In vain had such as the Presbyterian James Owen, in continuing controversy with Defoe and the indefatigable non-juring controversialist Charles Leslie, claimed that occasional conformity was the custom not of a 'mercenary' but a 'Catholick Spirit', which 'Confines not his Communion to any one Sect or Party of Christians, but has an Universal and Comprehensive Charity towards all'. The Church of England is, after all, but a church, not *the* church.[52]

For other nonconformists, it was only doubtfully, and sometimes certainly, not even that. Howe distinguished between those who, like himself, 'did not judge its Reformation so defective, that they might not communicate at all with it, nor so compleat, but that they ought to covet a Communion more strictly agreeable to the Holy Scriptures', and those who judged the established church 'so insufficiently Reform'd, as to want as yet the very being of a true Christian church'.[53] The majority of these were to be found among Independents, Baptists and Quakers. Their quarrel was neither with the exclusivity of the Act of Uniformity in general nor with its provisions in particular but with its premise that an ecclesiastical organization whose membership was coterminous with the population could in any sense be a church. Their argument was simply that faith, not nationality, was the qualification for church fellowship and hence that a church was recognizable by its distinction between the regenerate and the reprobate. I Corinithians v.11 was the oft-cited text, the epigraph, for example, to the anonymous *The Case of Mixt-Communion Friendly Discoursed* (1700), which contended that the process of excommunication in the established church was so prolonged, complex and inefficient that it in fact allowed membership to many excluded by this text. Though men 'must not *separate* from Christ, nor from his *Church – Catholick*, nor from *any particular Churches* in any thing, wherein they walk according to the Rule of Christ', they may and should separate from churches which admit the scandalous. Biblical precedents include Elijah's followers (I Kings xiv.18), 'an hundred *Nonconformist* Ministers . . . in a Cave' (I Kings xviii.13) and the Levites under Jeroboam (I Kings xii.26–33; II Chron. xiii).[54]

The temper of such separatists may be illustrated by the resolution of Mrs Hazzard. Her husband was a prewar nonconformist: beneficed at St Ewin's, Bristol, in 1639, he yet 'would not administer the sacrament to all the parish, and many other things in conscience he could not do'. His wife was, nevertheless, dismayed to find she could not bear to hear even him read the Common Prayer. In the ensuing 'very sore conflict in her spirit' between wifely duty and conscience, her eye lit on Revelation xiv.9–11: 'If any man worship the beast and his image, and receive his mark in his forehead, or in his hand, The same shall drink of the wine of the wrath of God . . . ' She and some friends forthwith 'separated from the worship of the world and times they lived in'.[55] Only apocalyptic imagery was adequate to express the detestation for the established church felt by those who, like Fox, regarded all traditional churches as 'cages of unclean Spirits', 'Synagogues of Satan'. The Quaker William Simpson's prophetic address is characteristic:

> Oh Church of *England*! This is unto thee, who livest in oppression and cruelty, pride and covetousness; a day of misery is coming upon thee . . . Oppression and cruelty hath been as a staff for thee, but the Lord is arisen to break thy Staff of Oppression, and thou shalt be left naked, though thou hast seemed to be the glory of the Nations with thy deceitful covers, but now thou shalt be left Naked, and Nations shall be ashamed of thee. Howl and weep ye Teachers, for the Lord is gathering his people from you, and ye shall devour his flock no more. The Day is coming upon you, that none shall buy your wares any more, ye Marchants of *Babylon*: All your Scarlet colour the Lord our God is coming to take off: Then your Nakedness shall appear.[56]

We should expect the separation of these nonconformists from the Church of England to be a good deal firmer than among Presbyterians, of whom by and large, they had no very high opinion. 'Being more than the rest against the Bishops, Liturgies, Ceremonies, and Parish-Communion', Independents and separatists, Baxter wrote, characterized 'those of us that were of another mind, and refused not Parish-Communion in some Places and Cases', as 'luke-warm

Temporizers, Men of too large principles, who supt the Anti-christian Pottage, though we could not eat the Flesh'. In *A Discourse Concerning Evangelical Love* (1672), John Owen argued against those prepared occasionally to attend the whole parish church service, a view supported by Stephen Lobb's *The True Dissenter* (1682). Early in 1684 there came into Baxter's hands 'a Manuscript of Dr Owen's (who was lately dead)' containing twelve 'Arguments against any conformity to Worship not of Divine Institution', which Baxter answered in *Catholick Communion Defended* (1684), not to everyone's satisfaction, for a 'swarm of revilers in the City poured out their keenest Censures' on him. By Quakers, occasional conformists were damned as 'hypocrites and dissemblers'.[57]

However, there was, even among Independents, a prewar tradition of attending at least the sermon at the parish church. Baxter recalled having heard in London in the early 1630s 'the Sectaries ... when they have on the Lord's Day stood at the Church Doors while the Common Prayer was reading, saying, *We must stay till he is out of his Pottage*'. The practice continued with some after the Restoration, much to the consternation of William Bridge, Congregational minister at Yarmouth, who threatened his people with excommunication if they persisted in it. Philip Nye, like Bridge a former dissenting member of the Westminster Assembly, was of another mind, and not only endorsed the practice but argued in *A Case: Whether we may Lawfully Hear the Now-Conforming Ministers* (1677) that it was not merely permissible but a duty to do so. *The Lawfullnes of Hearing the Publick Ministers of the Church of England Proved* (1683), which included Nye's pamphlet, went a stage further than allowing attendance at the sermon, and quoted Independents from John Robinson and Henry Jacob to Thomas Goodwin and Giles Firmin to authorize occasional full participation in Common Prayer.[58]

Howe was, then, entirely justified in remarking the 'great diversity of opinions, and proportionably differing practices' of nonconformists, but it was a heterogeneity scarcely regarded by the authorities. The Act of Uniformity was directed against nonconformsts within the established church. Subsequent legislation would make no distinction between these unwillingly ejected nonconformists and separatists who wanted no part of a national church. It treated all Howe's parties indiscriminately as a single group, defined by its relationship to the established church. And that relationship it radically altered. Writing an obituary character of Simeon Ashe, rector of St Austin's, London, Baxter described him as 'one of our oldest Non-conformists (of the old Strain; for now conforming is quite another thing than before the Wars)'.[59] And, by the same token, not conforming was quite another thing than before the wars.

There was continuity, of various kinds. Many of the Bartholomeans had fathers and grandfathers who had fallen foul of the ecclesiastical authorities. Edmund Calamy, grandson of the Smectymnuan and the third nonconformist divine of that name, proudly advertised his heritage on the title-page of his *Abridgment of Mr. Baxters History* (1702) where he described himself as

'Edmund Calamy *Edm. Fil. & Nepos*'. They themselves, leaders of nonconformity into the 1680s and 1690s, sometimes the eighteenth century, had often
begun their ministries before or during the Civil War. Seventy-two of them
were ejected from livings they had held since before 1640. Owen, who
embraced Congregationalism in the early 1640s, lived until 1683; Baxter,
ordained in 1638, survived until 1691; Howe, 15 years his junior, until 1705.
John Bunyan, who died in 1688, had been mustered in the Parliamentarian
army in 1644, and George Fox, who had undertaken his spiritual journey in the
1640s, lived until 1691. The doyen of the Bartholomeans was Thomas Nuttall,
who had held the rectory of Saxmundham, Suffolk, since 1616. Their last
survivor was Nathan Denton, vicar of Bolton upon Dearne, Yorkshire, from
February 1661 until 1662, who died in October 1720. Increase Mather,
Howe's Interregnum substitute at Great Torrington, Devon, who declined
English livings rather than conform, lived in New England until 1723. In the
congregations to which these men ministered were to be found the people they
had served in the Interregnum (most famously in the case of Owen), and they
continued to enjoy the same lay and political patronage they had received in the
past.[60] The Ashursts, Foleys and Hampdens continued to stand by Baxter, and
Philip, Lord Wharton, a lay member of the Westminster Assembly, was the
friend of Owen, Manton, Bates and, particularly, Howe. Denzil, Baron Holles,
who had held the Speaker in the chair in 1629 to secure the vote on the
Protestation against innovations in religion, was, after the Restoration, 'counted
the head of the Presbyterian party': *'Presbyter Holles'*, Marvell called him.[61]

And there were cases of the continuation of the 'old strain' of nonconformity.
Ralph Josselin, vicar at Earls Colne, Essex, since 1641, subscribed in 1662, but
maintained what Norman Sykes has called 'a half conformity' at best. For many
years he could bring himself to only intermittent and partial use of the Prayer
Book, and never wore a surplice. He was the subject of repeated complaints to
his diocesan from both parishioners and neighbouring clergy, and was
constantly apprehensive of archidiaconal and episcopal visitations. At last, on 16
May 1680, he put on the surplice, which, he wrote in his diary, 'I see no sin to
use, and shall endeavour to live as quietly as may bee to the end of my race.'[62]

Something nevertheless *had* changed. Howe wrote of Peter Vinke, ejected
vicar of St Catherine Cree, London, that 'not satisfied with some things in the
Act [of Uniformity], he calmly quitted his station, but not his ministry.'
Nonconformity 'of the old strain' had been practised by Puritans within the
established church, men whose desire for a reformed national church
distinguished them from those for whom the way of reformation lay in the
gathering of particular churches of visible saints out of, and apart from, the
national church. The unprecedented rigour of the Act of Uniformity made such
nonconformity henceforth all but impossible. Ralph Josselins were few, and
their behaviour hardly compatible with explicit undertakings to conform and to
use the Prayer Book. Those Presbyterians who, like Vinke, resolved, though

unwilling, to leave the national church but not to forgo their ministries had perforce to gather conventicles indistinguishable in practice from those of the separatists. Ecclesiological differences no longer counted for much. Following 1661, 'Presbyterians were forced to forbear all Exercise of their way: they durst not meet together (Synodically) unless in a Goal [*sic*]. They could not (ordinarily) be the Pastors of Parish-Churches. ... So that their Congregations were, through necessity, just of Independent and Separating Shape, and outward Practice, though not upon the same Principles.'[63] Willing and unwilling nonconformists found themselves in the same boat.

It was a boat parliament soon set about sinking. It was never the intention that the Act of Uniformity should purge the established church only to allow alternative religious traditions to flourish outside it. Having ejected nonconformity from the Church of England, ensuing penal legislation sought to eject it from England. In the event, it succeeded only in transforming nonconformity into dissent. The change in designation is significant, and the stages by which it came about instructive. It is partly legally explicable. Nonconformity is, from one point of view, a form of behaviour defined by law. Were the statutory definition of conformity altered (as Presbyterians hoped), or no longer universally enforced (as other nonconformists wished), nonconformity, though still practised, would no longer be nonconformity. This is what happened in 1689, but it is not the whole story. The term 'dissenter', which came into use in the second half of the seventeenth century, antedated the legislation of the 'Glorious Revolution', and it did not become the universal term for all the non-episcopal congregations of England until the early eighteenth century. During the intervening period, the continuing use of both terms reflected different perceptions of the status of nonconformity, different hopes for its future and different understandings of the relationship both between it and the established episcopal church and between its various constituent groups.

At the Restoration 'nonconformist' and the old Cromwellian 'tender consciences', whom Charles addressed from Breda, held the field, but after the *Act for Restraining Nonconformists from Inhabiting in Corporations* (1665), or 'Five Mile Act', 'dissenter' swiftly became the preferred term in official statements and in writings from the episcopalian side. Charles had already used it in his *Declaration in Favour of Toleration* (1662), and though the close of his later *Declaration of Indulgence* (1672) tactfully and prudently recalled Breda in its solicitation of 'truly tender consciences', its main address was to 'dissenting persons'. Sir Roger L'Estrange had set about 'dissenters' since the Restoration. When, in the 1680s, he did occasionally use 'nonconformist' in his paper *The Observator*, it was generally when animadverting upon a work which used that term in its title. Halifax addressed his famous *Letter* to a dissenter (1687) and the 1688 *Petition* of the Seven Bishops disclaimed 'any want of due tenderness to dissenters'. The comprehensiveness of the term by the end of the century is indicated by Charles Leslie's address in 1698 to 'the *Quakers*, and others of our

Dissenters from *Episcopacy'*. In 1702 Daniel Defoe, ironically adopting the point of view of just such a high churchman as Leslie, entitled his tract *The Shortest Way with the Dissenters*.[64]

We can understand why 'dissenter' made its way so readily on the episcopalian side if we look at usage amongst nonconformists themselves. Here, there is a distinction to be made. 'Dissenter' is very rarely used by Presbyterians, who, as in Baxter's many apologetic pieces, almost invariably prefer the old 'nonconformist'. This is the term used by Andrew Marvell in *Mr. Smirke* (1676) when defending Bishop Herbert Croft's recommendation in *The Naked Truth* (1675) of such conciliatory terms of comprehension as had been offered the Presbyterians in the Worcester House *Declaration*. In his biography of Baxter's admired friend and Chief Justice of the King's Bench, Sir Matthew Hale, Gilbert Burnet in 1676 reports Hale 'thought many of the *Nonconformists*, had merited highly in the Business of the *King's Restauration*, and at least deserved that the *terms of Conformity* should not have been made *stricter*, than they were before the war'. The thanks presented to William by John Howe on 2 January 1689 were published at *The Address of the Nonconformist Ministers* (1689), and in 1702, in his *Abridgment of Mr Baxters History of his Life and Times*, Edmund Calamy continued to use 'nonconformist'.[65]

However, when a Quaker like William Penn defended nonconformists he wrote *A Perswasive to Moderation to Church Dissenters* ([1686]). Independents, too, were happier with the term 'dissenter'. One such case, Stephen Lobb's *The True Dissenter* (1685), explains why. It is his argument that 'the true dissenter' is a *'thorough Nonconformist'*, one, that is to say, who has chosen complete separation from the established church. It is the idea of willing choice, with no desire for reunion, which informs 'dissenter'; of unwilling, and if possible temporary, necessity which informs 'nonconformist'. Despite their changed circumstances, Presbyterians continued to speak of themselves as 'nonconformists', thereby implicitly setting themselves in the tradition of the 'nonconformists of the old strain', men who, though they scrupled some ceremonies and impositions, were desirous of accommodation within a reformed national church. This is the tenor of Hale's remarks quoted from Burnet above – and Hale was himself engaged in drafting legislation to comprehend Presbyterians in the late 1660s. From the point of view of the episcopalian authorities, however, Presbyterians had chosen not to conform, and so were, like Independents, Baptists and Quakers, 'dissenters'. The individualistic and varied witness of the early Stuart period became, in the tidy and generalized fashion of the eighteenth century, a legally separate and corporate status. Presbyterians themselves came, if slowly and reluctantly, to accept that, after the Act of Toleration (1689), what they practised was not nonconformity but dissent. By 1702 Celia Fiennes, whose house was in 1730 registered as a Presbyterian meeting place, found it natural to describe the Presbyterians of Colchester, 'where formerly the famous Mr [Owen] Stockton was minister', as 'Dessenters'. Indeed, throughout the early eighteenth century journals of this granddaughter of 'Old Subtlety', the first Viscount Saye and Sele, and daughter of the Cromwellian Colonel Nathaniel Fiennes, it is invariably 'dissenters' who are numerous in Ipswich, Woodbridge, Bury St Edmunds, Norwich, Liverpool, Newcastle and Leeds. At Ashburton, in Devon, the 'great many Descenters' attended 'a Presbiterian an Anabaptist and Quakers meeting'.[66]

This terminological development can be confirmed from what at first appear to be anomalous cases. In 1700 Increase Mather published *A Letter to the Churches of the Non-Conformists.* Mather was no Presbyterian, and the date is late. However, Mather had, save for a visit to England in 1688–92, lived in New England since the Restoration: his is a fossilized example of the earlier usage. His up-to-date English animadverter, John King, though he picks up 'nonconformist' in direct reference to Mather, speaks himself of 'Dissenting Brethren', 'Dissenters' and the 'Dissenting Faction', as Mather never does. On the other hand, Edmund Calamy, who was, of course, both English and Presbyterian, still used 'nonconformist' in the three volumes of his epochal (the assessment is Roger Thomas's) *Defence of Moderate Nonconformity* (1703–5), when what he was actually defending, and defending so effectively that no less an authority than Locke thought his case unanswerable, was something Baxter would have regarded as separation and we recognize as dissent. Calamy prefers 'each worshipping Congregation in the Land, to manage itself in an entire Independency' to 'a National Church of one sort or another with *Penal Laws*'. Calamy pours this new wine into the old nonconformist bottle because, we may conjecture, to have adopted the term 'dissent' would have been to break too severely with the Baxterian tradition he regarded so highly. A few years later, Defoe's *Short View of the Present State of the Protestant Religion* (1707) was equally anachronistic, but in the contrary way. It is his contention that 'the State of things is somewhat altered' since the Restoration 'near 50 Years ago' and that 'the Dissenters in *England* are not of the same Mind now' and would not now conform even on the terms of the Worcester House *Declaration.* To describe the evolution of this altered state of things he has, at this date, only the term 'dissenter' available, and so uses it misleadingly of those at the beginning of the process as well as of those at its end.[67]

The two terms hence play off each other in various kinds of ways in the literature of the period. Although the episcopalian Burnet uses 'nonconformist' when indirectly reporting the view of Hale, 'dissenter' is the term which comes naturally to him when speaking in his own voice in the same work: 'moderate dissenters' is his phrase for Hale's 'nonconformists'. In controversy, 'dissenter' served episcopalians well since it tarred all nonconformists with the separatist brush. No distinction is made between 'Sectaries, or Dissenting Protestants' by such a fervent defender of the status quo as John Nalson, rector of Doddington in the Isle of Ely, and similarly Charles Leslie has no time for fine distinctions.

Attacking *Moderation a Virtue*, James Owen's defence of occasional conformity, the title-page of Leslie's *The Wolf Stript* (1704) promises to lay bare 'The Designs of the Dissenters', and the following year he impugned *The Principles of the Dissenters*. When distinctions are made, it is usually to score a controversial point. Leslie could single out the Presbyterians, but only to warn his readers against them since 'No other Protestant Dissenters grasp at our National Church', a phrase which inadvertently withdraws the distinction even while conceding it. Similarly, John Franklin distinguishes 'nonconformists' from 'separatists' throughout *A Resolution of this Case, Viz Whether it be Lawful to separate from the Public Worship of God in the Parochial Assemblies of England* (1683), but only to use their moderation as a stick with which to beat the more stringent separatists.[68]

Names, however, are more than polemical counters, and do not change without good reason. Presbyterians and Independents, Baptists and Quakers would never have come, all alike, to accept the common designation 'dissenter' merely because episcopalians and parliament willed it upon them. Rather, it answered to something in their experience. In 1702 the Whig pamphleteer John Tutchin, looking back at the history of the seventeenth century, wrote:

> Now, as this too much divided Nation has always been compos'd of two contending Parties, those Parties have been distinguish'd, *as in like Cases*, by Names of Contempt; and tho' they have often chang'd them on either side, as Cavalier and Roundhead, Royalists and Rebels, Malignants and Phanaticks, Tories and Whigs, yet the Division has always been barely *the Church and the Dissenters*, and there it continues to this Day.

The dichotomy which Tutchin detects in earlier seventeenth-century history had never been as stark as he suggests. His interpretation is, however, a revealing indication of the perspective created by the later seventeenth century. Though he is historically simplistic, he is experientially accurate of the Restoration period. The penal legislation which followed upon the Act of Uniformity visited persecution upon nonconformists of whatever persuasion. They faced a common foe and endured a common plight. What they thus shared together separated them as a group from the established church far more pressingly than anything which separated them from each other. It was this shared experience of persecution which created dissent out of the various nonconformities of 1660. When finally, and grudgingly, the legislators came to accept that their policy of extirpation had failed, the result was the division of which Tutchin writes. It was a division which appalled the eirenic temper of Howe. 'Let us take heed', he implored after the passing of the Act of Toleration, 'of having our Minds tinctur'd with a wrong Notion of this matter, as if the Indulgence divided *England* into two *Christendoms*, or distinguish'd rather between *Christians* and *Mahometans*, as some Mens *Cyclopick* Fancys have an unlucky art to represent things.' Have those, he asked, who identified godliness with one party or the other, or who took pride in 'being of this or that side of the severing Line', 'blotted *Rom.* 14 out of their Bibles?'[69] Yet Howe's very desire to bridge the gulf is evidence how it now yawned between churchman and dissenter. This was the legacy of the 'Clarendon Code'.

3   THE CLARENDON CODE

'And now came in the great Inundation of Calamities, which in many Streams overwhelmed Thousands of godly Christians' wrote Baxter of the aftermath of the Act of Uniformity.[70] The stream had, however, begun to flow two years earlier, when the Restoration put back into the hands of magistrates so minded a body of common and statute law already quite sufficient to harry nonconformists. The Elizabethan Act of Uniformity (1 Eliz., cap. 2) and the Jacobean Act against Popish Recusants (3 Jac. I, cap. 4) both provided for the fining of absentees from Sabbath worship in the parish church ('Sunday shillings'), but more serious, and more serviceable, was the Elizabethan Act against Conventicles (35 Eliz., cap. 1, *An Act for Retaining the Queen's Subjects in their Due Obedience*), whose penalties included banishment and death for those who refused to conform after three months' imprisonment, the latter sentence actually being passed after the Restoration, though not carried out, on 12 Aylesbury Baptists and a Bristol Quaker.[71] It was under this Act that Bunyan was imprisoned as early as November 1660, and although, as Bunyan argued, and as the Quaker Thomas Barker justly alleged when charged under it in 1683, 'that statute does not reach our Case, nor was made against us', it continued to be invoked since its penalties were more severe than those of Restoration legislation.[72]

Itinerant Quakers were liable to public whipping under the Elizabethan Vagrancy Act (39 Eliz., cap. 4), but their real vulnerability derived from their refusal of all oaths. By both Elizabethan and Jacobean statutes (5 Eliz., cap. 1, 3 Jac. I, cap. 4, 7 Jac. I, cap. 6) the oaths of allegiance and supremacy could be tendered to anyone over 18 years of age: persistent refusal incurred the penalty of *praemunire* (forfeiture of all goods and imprisonment during the king's pleasure). Though some Baptists refused oaths on principle,[73] it was against Quakers that this procedure was most persistently adopted. At Lancaster in 1664 a seemingly considerate justice, Sir Thomas Twisden, took this course with Margaret Fell, to avoid the severity of what nonconformists referred to tersely as '35 Eliz.', but more often prosecutions were openly brought under these acts because loss of goods and indefinite imprisonment were, like the penalties of '35 Eliz.', heavier than those of the Restoration Conventicle Acts. In the early 1670s Sir John Robinson wrote of the Quakers that 'there's no other way to proceed against them, but to indict them upon the Statute of Praemunire and seize their estates and imprison them during the King's pleasure. If this rule were more generally followed, it would break them without any noise or tumult.' Quaker outdoor meetings were further liable to be charged with the common law offences of unlawful assembly and riot. It was for perpetrating a riot and disturbing the peace that William Penn and William Mead were famously brought to trial at the Old Bailey in September 1670.[74]

To this body of law the Cavalier Parliament added the statutes known collectively as the 'Clarendon Code'.[75] The Corporation and Uniformity Acts were followed in 1664 by the First Conventicle Act (16 Car. II, cap. 4), passed on the pretext of the incompetent and poorly supported Derwentdale Plot.[76] This made generally applicable the provisions of the 1662 Quaker Act (13 & 14 Car. II, cap. 1). It forbade all religious meetings of five or more people not conducted according to the established church's liturgy. A first offence incurred a £5 fine or three months' imprisonment; a second, a £10 fine or six months in prison; a third, a £100 fine or transportation, whence it was commonly known as 'The Act of Banishment'. The Quaker Edward Billing pointedly recorded an occasion when this sentence was passed on some Quakers and the judge, uncertain where to send them, 'mentioned *Hispaniola,* (a place that never yet belonged to *England*) and one that stood by and heard him, said *Oliver did not get that for you*'. Even without judicial incompetence and grim farce, the ultimate penalty was not easily enforceable, ships' captains and crews on occasion refusing to carry those banished, 'it being contrary to ye Lawes of England to transport men *with*out their consent'.[77]

After, as it hoped, dispersing their adherents, parliament turned to the Bartholomeans themselves, denying them not only ministry but, in effect, any livelihood, by passing what John Pinney called the 'act of exile*ment*'.[78] The 1665 Five Mile Act (17 Car. II, cap. 2) was directed against those in holy orders who had not subscribed to the Act of Uniformity and who had 'taken upon them to preach in unlawful assemblies, conventicles or meetings under colour or pretence of exercise of religion ... [and] settled themselves in divers corporations ... thereby taking an opportunity to distil the poisonous principles of schism and rebellion into the hearts of his Majesty's subjects'. They could henceforth not come within five miles of any city, corporation, or parliamentary borough or any place where they had ministered ('unless only in passing upon the road') without having first taken the Oxford Oath (so called since the Act was passed by parliament meeting in Oxford during the Plague in London). This oath comprised a declaration of non-resistance repudiating the taking up of arms against the king, and an undertaking 'not at any time [to] endeavour any alteration of government either in Church or State'. The method of enforcement was as distasteful as the prohibition of any attempt (rather than any *unlawful* attempt) at political or ecclesiastical reform was tyrannical. Of the £40 fine incurred by an offender, one-third went to the crown, one-third to the poor of the parish where the offence was committed, and one-third to 'such person or persons as shall or will sue for the same', that is, to informers whose disclosures had led to conviction.

When the First Conventicle Act lapsed on 1 March 1669, informers were given a still more prominent place in its 1670 successor (22 Car. II, cap. 1). The Second Conventicle Act empowered not two (as in the previous Act) but any one justice of the peace, on the evidence of a confession, two witnesses, or merely 'by notorious evidence and circumstance of fact', to convict an accused of attendance at a conventicle. The simple satisfaction of the justice was to be taken as 'a full and perfect conviction', to secure which he had power to 'break open and enter into any house or other place' where a conventicle was suspected. Although its penalties were less severe than those of the First Conventicle Act (attenders were liable to fines of 5s. for a first and 10s. for subsequent offences, ministers to fines of £20 and £40, and the owner of the meeting place to a £20 fine), its imposition of fines of £5 on any who failed to inform and of £100 on justices who neglected to prosecute attracted to it widespread opprobrium as 'the Jnforming act'. To the many appalled at the compulsion to inform and the power given to individual justices, it appeared to be an erosion of fundamental liberties, 'the Quintessence of arbitrary Malice', as Marvell called it. This case was argued in such anonymous pamphlets as *The Englishman, or a Letter from a Universal Friend* (1670) and *Some Seasonable and Serious Queries upon the late Act against Conventicles* (1670), which was reported to Secretary Williamson as 'A most seditious Pamphlett', tending 'as much as is possible ... to ye stirring vp of Sedition and Rebellion'.[79] Outrage at the forcible entering of homes and the levying of fines 'by distress and sale of the offender's goods and chattels, or in the case of poverty of such offender upon the goods and chattels of any other person or persons who shall be then convicted', impassions *A True and Faithful Narrative of the Unjust and Illegal Oppression of Many Christians* (1671) and many subsequent pieces, including John Howe's *The Case of the Protestant Dissenters* (1689). Howe writes that by this 'horrid law', which is 'most principally grievous to us'

> our *Magna Carta* was torn in Pieces; the worst and most infamous of Mankind, at our own Expense, hired to accuse us; multitudes of Perjuries committed; Convictions made without a Jury, and without any Hearing of the Persons accused; Penalties inflicted; Goods rifled; Estates seiz'd and imbezel'd; Houses broken up; Families disturb'd, often at most unseasonable Hours of the Night, without any Cause, or Shadow of a Cause, if only a malicious Villain could pretend to suspect a Meeting there.[80]

Marvell's sardonic comment on this legislation was that such measures were to be expected from the episcopalians 'considering how empty of late the Church Magazines have been of that Spiritual Armour, which the Apostle found sufficient against all the assaults of whatever enemy, even of Satan'.[81] Be that as it may, its effect was to forge the corporate identity of dissent as all the parties in nonconformity shared together in the experience of exclusion and persecution they had hitherto in their history endured separately. Very few, no more than 210, joined the 7,000 or so conforming clergy.[82] The casuistry of

Bunyan's Mr By-ends is no very flattering reflection upon the motives of men who, in the damning phrase of the pamphleteer Ralph Wallis, 'stab'd their own consciences, and there's an end of the Persecution with them'. For moderate men the issue could be less clear-cut and the case of conscience the more agonizing. John Humfrey, Presbyterian vicar of Frome in Somerset, defended his decision to receive episcopal orders from William Piers (or Pierce), Bishop of Bath & Wells, by distinguishing between his ordination to the ministry (by his Presbyterian ordination in 1649) and the authorization of his exercise of that ministry in the Church of England (by his episcopal ordination in 1661). It was not an argument which long satisfied him, however, and within a year of the publication of his apologetic *The Question of Re-Ordination, whether, and how a Minister ordained by the Presbytery, may take Ordination also by a Bishop* (1661) he renounced his episcopal orders. John Pinney similarly came very close to conformity, but could not bring himself to take the final step of accepting a benefice. Finding his 'silence was very tedious and a great tempt.' he went so far as to receive episcopal orders. In his memorandum book he listed 'the tempt. to conforme' which prompted him as '1. Profit. putting a family from debt. 2. the tryumph of sectaryes on my outing. 3. the stifnes of the Bp. of Sar*um* [Humphrey Henchman] to out me. 4. Feare of future distrusting God' and 'Great feare that the *par*liam*ent* will doe more ag*ainst* nonconformists'.[83] It is a curt and telling enumeration of pressures material, ecclesiastic and spiritual.

The other sure way to avoid these pressures was by emigration, but this proved no more attractive than conformity. Although in 1662 there was 'great Talke of many Ministers with their congregations' removing to New England, only 15 ministers in fact crossed the Atlantic. A further 10 took up residence in Holland, and a few elsewhere. For a few of those who remained it proved possible to continue in their old parishes unmolested. The esteem of the local community enabled the Presbyterian John Angier, for example, to retain the curacy of Denton, Manchester, until his death in 1677, and the friendship of Sir Samuel Browne, justice of the Common Pleas and patron of Arlesey, Bedfordshire, allowed its ejected vicar, James Ashurst, to continue his ministry there as a nonconformist. But the vast majority of the great majority who neither conformed nor emigrated were left

> to the hostile sword
> Of heathen and profane, their carcases
> To dogs and fowls a prey, or else captived:
> Or to the unjust tribunals, under change of times,
> And condemnation of the ingrateful multitude.[84]

Considerable ingenuity, as well as heroism, was shown in the response to persecution. In September 1670 it was complained of Quakers in Bristol that 'Not *with* standinge all the endeavours of the Magistracy they cannot suppresse them by reason of theyre many trickes & evasions.' One such trick, adopted by the Congregational church at Norwich, was to avoid infringing the Conventicle

Act by meeting in 'small parcels'. To the same purpose, the Presbyterian Adam Martindale would preach over the same sermon several times to small groups. In Newcastle, the choice of a house 'where others are pretty rank on either side and opposite' enabled groups of auditors to hear the sermon from neighbouring windows. Members of the Broadmead Baptist church in Bristol 'broke a wall, up on high, for a window, and put the speaker in the next house to stand and preach, whereby we heard him as well as if in the room with us.'[85] If the Act was to be infringed, steps were taken to avoid detection: meetings were often held late at night, or in the early hours of the morning, and reached by people journeying separately along different routes, often apparently about legitimate business: the Presbyterian Richart Chantrye would go 'in the twilight to escape the informers, with a Bible in his pocket and a fork on his shoulder.' Should the meeting be detected, it was still possible to avoid charges by disguising its nature: Fox writes (disparagingly) of Presbyterian meetings having the appearance of feasts to deceive intruders. More often, the timely hiding or spiriting away of the minister removed the proof that the gathering was a conventicle, though this was rarely effected with the ingenuity of the Congregational minister Thomas Jollie. He would preach from the staircase to people gathered in the room below and separated from them by a door hinged in the middle which, when its top half was let down, constituted a pulpit, and a ready concealment when pulled up at the approach of informers or officers. This device depended on alert look-outs, and these were regularly posted at nonconformist meetings. Upon their signal, or the advance warning of a well-wisher, congregations were ready with a variety of expedients to delay the entry of intruders long enough for their ministers to escape (something, again, of which Fox disapproved). The definition in the First Conventicle Act of a conventicle as a meeting of five or more adults 'over and above the members of the household' afforded a convenient loophole: meetings not held in houses were apparently beyond its scope. It was with some consternation that in 1665 the authorities of Shadwell realized the Act could not be enforced against a Presbyterian conventicle held in a chapel. More often, meetings were held outdoors. Welsh Quakers met not only 'Sometimes by day, sometimes by night', 'not at certayne times', but also sometimes in 'a Barne' or 'by stealth ... in a Cave'. Quakers at Ashford, Derbyshire, 'intended to meete att the house of Hugh Marstin, but the Justices Warrant being brought to hinder them, they went into a Moore & kept their Conventicle'. The Second Conventicle Act more carefully specified 'any place ... house, field or place where there is no family inhabiting', but Quakers 'a boute looe' avoided at least the house-holder's or landowner's liability by meeting 'in the Rockes & vpon the sands to take off the fine thatt otherwise would lye upon the house & ffield'.[86]

This resourcefulness in countering persecution carries over into the spirit of adventure, the sense of omnipresent danger and the stress on alert watchfulness in nonconformist writing. Common experience taught the need for wariness, discernment, skill in detection and a ready responsiveness to unexpected eventualities. Daily life presented itself as a series of queries, quandaries and challenges: whether or not to conform, to attend a meeting, to take precautionary measures, to trust a stranger; how to respond to requests for information, to official interrogation, to legal proceedings; and, above all, how to endure material deprivation, destitution and impoverishment. Behind all these might lurk a larger, nagging question; was to consider them at all evidence of weakness, of compromise, of want of faith?

Many were convinced that it was. Bunyan was not to be put off from attending a meeting in November 1660 by the knowledge that a warrant had been issued for his arrest; from prison their pastor let the Broadmead congregation know of his disapproval when it began to 'meet more privately'; and Quakers were generally disdainful of all attempts to avoid detection and evade prosecution. Edward Billing admonished them that they were not to 'run shirking into holes, or skulk into corners by *threes* or *fours*'. An open and public witness alone was appropriate for those who have eaten 'of that Flesh, and drank of that Blood which admits not of hunger and thirst after the Inventions and Traditions of man'. Though the 'Furnace were or should be made seven times hotter than it already is' those who have received the everlasting Gospel 'cannot fly':

> Nay, nay; for our descent is legitimised by the Generator of the Just, and the Birth of our day is more Noble, our Principle and Spirit more public and true than so; and our mouths were not opened by, neither can they be shut in the will of man; insomuch, that what we receive in secret, that declare we openly and fully.

And declare it they did. When their meetings were disturbed and their members imprisoned, their meeting houses closed up or destroyed, the remaining Friends, often women and children, would meet as openly as before in the street, or in the ruins. Baxter, though in no doubt they were misguided and deluded, recognized the constancy of their witness. So, too, did Pepys: it both impressed and distressed him: 'They go like lambs, without any resistance. I would to God they would either conform, or be more wise, and not be ketched.'[87]

Once caught, however, they swiftly became very wise indeed in legal matters. It is at first disconcerting to find that those brought to court by their refusal to compromise made no scruple at all about securing an acquittal by pleading technical errors in the indictment, often of a trifling and inconsequential kind. This recourse to legalistic quibbling appears the more incongruous in view of the fact that not until the 1670s, and then largely as a result of the influence of the Quaker attorney Thomas Rudyard, could Friends be persuaded to use legal counsel. Yet the Fox who in *The Law of God ... and the corruption of English Laws and Lawyers Discovered* (1658) had no regard whatever for forensic skills and legal proceedings had no misgivings about recording his own courtroom successes achieved by picking holes in the indictments. Two facts afford an explanation. First of all, when the accused was entitled to know the charge preferred against him only when it was read in open court (and so had no chance to prepare a defence against it), when sworn testimony was unchallengeable and cross-examination hardly practised, and when the defendant could not appear as a witness in his own defence, to disprove the prosecution's evidence was all but impossible. Virtually the only way to gain acquittal was by invalidating the indictment.[88] And, secondly, the prevailing mood of the court was almost invariably hostile. There were sympathetic lawyers and judges, most notably Kelynge's successor in 1671 as Chief Justice of the King's Bench, the quite exceptional Sir Matthew Hale, 'the most learned lawyer of this or any period', 'a really beautiful character, comparable, among English judges, only to that of Sir Thomas More'. Burnet wrote of him that 'besides great charities to the *Nonconformists*, who were then, as he thought, too hardly used, he took great care to cover them all he could, from the severities some designed against them, and discouraged those who were inclined to stretch the laws too much against them', and in his *Additional Notes* (1682) on Burnet's *Life* Baxter wrote movingly of the admired friend he regarded as 'The pillar of Justice, the Refuge of the subject who feared oppression and one of the greatest Honours of his Majesties Government'.[89] However, the practice of appointing judges only during the king's pleasure (they were to be given tenure by clause iii of the Act of Settlement (1701)), led more commonly to judicial subservience and bias. The 'Wisdom and Probity of the Law', wrote Marvell in 1678, 'went off for the most part with good Sir *Matthew Hales*, and Justice is made a meer property.' The 'type of man that the crown found to be most amenable to its wishes was the political lawyer, without principles, with a fluent tongue, and with little knowledge of the law. Very perfect examples of this type were found in [Lord Chief Justice Sir William] Scroggs and [Lord Chief Justice George] Jeffreys.' Such men conceived it to be their business to secure verdicts in accord with the government's wishes. Judicial impartiality and the interest of the defendant had no more place in their proceedings than in those of Bunyan's Lord Hategood.[90]

Such judges further conceived it to be the jury's business to follow the direction of the bench, and woe betide any jury which showed an independent mind. The consequence is illustrated by the trial of Quakers held before Sir Richard Rainsford at Northampton Castle in 1665. Although the First Conventicle Act required prosecutions to be brought within three months of the alleged offence, and the defendants had been five months in prison, the trial nevertheless went ahead because 'they had a Jury upon whom they could set their own stamp as easily as upon a lump of Clay.' After the verdict of 'guilty' had been given in by the foreman, 'some of the *Jurymen* told the Prisoners' they had agreed on an acquittal, and when 'asked why they did not speak when they see such a gross miscarriage in the Court', their reply was 'they feared if they should have spoken, the *Judge* would have laid them by the heels'. When an Old Bailey jury acquitted about forty Quakers, they were exceedingly menaced, furiously interrogated, their Verdict by the Judge (so called) refused, and by him six of them bound over to answer it at the *Kings-Bench Bar*; and all this, because they could not without sufficient Witness, contrary to their Conscience, finde the Innocent *Guilty*. Are not the Jury Judges of matter of Fact (at least) and to give their Verdict according to their Conscience and Judgment? and is not the Judge obliged to receive the Juries Verdict.[91]

In 1670 legal history was made when the acquittal of Penn and Mead led to a case in which this fundamental principle of jurisprudence was at last confirmed. The jury which maintained its 'not guilty' verdict contrary to the advice of the judge and despite being kept two days and nights without food or water was imprisoned until payment of a fine of 40 marks by each juror for contumacy. The jury foreman, Edward Bushel, sued for a writ of Habeas Corpus, and Sir John Vaughan, Chief Justice of the Common Pleas, upheld his plea that he had properly fulfilled his duty as a juryman in returning what he had inferred from the evidence presented: 'the Jury, and not the Judge, resolve and find what the Fact is.' 'Never thing, since the King's Return', wrote Baxter, 'was received with greater Joy and Applause by the People' than this verdict in *Bushel's Case*. The bearing of Penn and Mead had secured far more than their own acquittal.[92]

Their bearing in court had been rather that of lions than of the lambs Pepys saw being led to slaughter. In the antipathetical theatre of the courtroom, defendants repeatedly seized the initiative from their judges and turned their trials into public vindications of themselves. Margaret Fell insisting that she address the jury, though the judge had ruled 'The Jury is to hear Nothing, but me to tender you the Oath', is a capital example of the use of the courtroom as a stage for defiant witness and vocal self-justification. Her 'everlasting Tongue', the exasperated judge was reduced to protesting, drew 'the whole Court' after her. At the same hearing, Fox showed his characteristic mastery of dramatic timing and gesture, manipulating the court's response in a fine moment of suspense. The judge directed:

> Lay your Hand on the Book: Give me the Book in my Hand. Which set them all a Gazing, as in Hope he would have sworn. Then, when he got the Book in his Hand, he held up the Book, and said: This Book commands me not to swear, if it be a Bible I will prove it; and he saw it was a Bible, and he held it up; and then they plucked it forth of his Hand again.

We can sense not only the judge's frustration at being upstaged but also his awe as he tried vainly to bolster his confidence and authority. 'I will not be afraid of thee, thou speaks so loud, thy Voice drowns mine and the Court's, I must call for three or four Cryers to drown thy Voice, thou has good Lungs.' This was no answer to Fox's pointed challenge that he should 'prison the Book' for proscribing oath-taking. Formally Fox may be convicted, but the affective movement of the swiftly printed account of these proceedings is quite otherwise: during a recess, Fox prays 'and I was so filled full of Glory, that my Head and Ears were full of it; and that when the Trumpets sounded, and the Judges came up again, they all appeared as dead Men under me.'[93]

The same mastery of the situation was demonstrated by Penn and Mead at their Old Bailey trial six years later. The bench was quite unable to direct the proceedings: it was challenged repeatedly from the bar not only on procedural and legal matters, but on larger issues. Mead pointed out to the jury the contradictory evidence of one witness and objected to the judge's asking him, the defendant, whether he was at the alleged riot. Penn engaged the judge in a heated exchange on the legality of the indictment and addressed judge, jury and the court in general on liberty and its infringement. Admonished to be silent, Penn replied: 'I am not to be silent in a Case wherein I am so much concerned; and not only myself, but many Ten thousand Families beside.' The Lord Mayor Samuel Starling was reduced by his impotence to melodramatic absurdity: 'Stop his mouth; Goaler bring Fetters, and stake him to the ground.'[94]

To their critics, such behaviour by Quakers might appear culpably histrionic. The Presbyterian Thomas Manton, comparing Matthew vi.6–8 with verse 16, wrote '*There*, Christ's scope is to commend and enjoin good works to be seen of men, *ad edificationem*, for their edification; *here*, his scope is to forbid us to do good works to be seen of men, *ad ostentationem*, for their ostentation.'[95] There was something irrepressible to the point of flamboyance about the defiance of these defendants. Court room scenes, with their clearly defined conflict, claustrophobic location and increasing suspense as they move through charge, counter-charge and disclosure to the climactic verdict, are intrinsically dramatic. The accused, casting themselves as the protagonists, conducted themselves very much as actors upon a stage. And, by putting these proceedings swiftly into print, they played before a far wider audience than the 12 men of the jury. Such reports, in which the participants are identified, the dialogue carefully attributed, and the exchanges reproduced *verbatim*, are dramatic texts as animated as, and far more searching and serious than, the staple fare of the Restoration stage. Though the matter is a trial, the business often pedantically legalistic, and the outcome a verdict, the issue transcends these circumstances. No opportunity to demonstrate the partiality, injustice, or brutality of legal procedures is missed, but, rather than the end of these pamphlets, revelation of the inadequacies of the judicial system is the means by which they exemplify their real concern: spiritual trial, combat and victory. What the court conducts as the interrogation of inferiors by the officers of a superior and unassailable law is rendered as a contest for mastery which, like the debates of *Paradise Regained* or *Samson Agonistes*, proceeding through linguistic fencing, the deployment of proof texts and a battle of wits, reveals the true stature and superiority of the (apparently) defenceless defendant and the (usually) condemned prisoner at the bar. His or her inadequacy proves as adequate to the challenge as the material helplessness of Milton's Christ; his or her hopeless plight as hopeful as that of

Milton's Samson. As the conflicting notions of law, duty and obedience engage, these reports become as deeply ironic as Bunyan's rendering of the trial of Faithful and Christian.

These qualities are all evident in Bunyan's own *Relation* of his imprisonment. That this is a contest, rather than a trial, is early made clear when William Lindall, vicar of Harlington, momentarily 'a little stopt' in his 'taunting' of Bunyan, is not 'willing to lose the day'. The self-assured superiority of Bunyan's interrogators prompts their repeated references to his low social status and to the fact that his hearers are 'none but a company of poor simple ignorant people'. We are, however, prepared for their true quality by Bunyan's association of the seemingly friendly lawyer William Foster with Judas. When they engage Bunyan on the field of doctrinal and biblical debate it is from their own mouths that we learn the real extent of their competence. One justice having protested that Bunyan 'will do harm; let him speak no further', Sir John Kelynge replies 'No, no, never fear him, we are better established than so; he can do no harm, we know the Common Prayer-book hath been ever since the Apostles time, and is lawful to be used in the church.' Upon this finely ironic and self-revealing disclosure of the incongruity between Kelynge's judicial assurance and spiritual ignorance, of the personal inadequacy behind the mask of authority, there follows swiftly, with fitting inevitability, Kelynge's discovery of just how insufficiently he is 'established', how much 'harm' Bunyan can do and how deeply he ought to 'fear' him. With foolhardy boldness Kelynge launches into a dispute on the right use of gifts and talents, only ignominiously to abandon his pretension: 'He said he was not so well versed in Scripture as to dispute ... And said, moreover, that they could not wait upon me any longer.' It is a dramatically telling and bathetic volte-face. Repeatedly Bunyan's adversaries are worsted, effecting an ironic role reversal: the judges become the judged, the convicted accused the innocent accuser. Bunyan may be all that his interrogators say he is in social, educational and legal terms, but it is not the Bench which has the mastery:

> LIND: Indeed I do remember that I have read of one Alexander a Coppersmith, who did much oppose, and disturb the Apostles. (Aiming 'tis like at me, because I was a Tinker.)
>
> BUN: To which I answered, that I also had read of very many priests and pharisees that had their hands in the blood of our Lord.[96]

It is hence not by direct address to the reader nor by tendentious commentary but by the ironic import of its dramatic presentation of events that the *Relation* comes to bear out Bunyan's contention that 'those that are most commonly counted foolish by the world, are the wisest before God. Also that God had rejected the wise, and mighty and noble, and chosen the foolish, and the base.' We have not the mere proposition but an evident demonstration that '*Christs* words [are] more than bare trifles, where he saith, he *will give a mouth and wisdom, even such as all the adversaries shall not resist, or gainsay*

[Luke xxi.15].' And, as the adversaries' case crumbles, so does their threatening power: 'verily at my return, I did meet my God sweetly in the prison.'[97]

4   SCHISM BY LAW

The provision in the Second Conventicle Act for the fining of negligent justices of the peace testifies to the fact that local magistrates could not be counted on vigorously to pursue persecution. Many of them were sympathetic towards, sensitive to the sufferings of, or even themselves committed to the nonconformists.[98] But if the degree of persecution hence varied from place to place, it also varied from time to time, since it took its cue from court and parliament, neither of whose attitudes towards nonconformists were consistently hostile. Even as penal legislation was being enacted and enforced, there were repeated moves to alleviate the predicament of nonconformists. These moves were not, however, disinterested. That Charles had been restored without conditions left open the very question over which a Civil War had been fought, namely, the extent of the royal prerogative. One of the stages by which that war had come about had been the trial in 1637 of John Hampden, the father of Baxter's friend, Richard Hampden. In the *Ship Money Case* it had been contended that the king was the sovereign power in the constitution, possessed of a prerogative no statute could limit or gainsay. Charles II probably never seriously contemplated any claim so sweeping: even under his more despotic brother, James II, in *Godden* v. *Hales* (1686), 'the highwater mark of prerogative pretention in the latter half of the seventeenth century', it was asserted only that the king had the prerogative to grant particular dispensations from the law. Nevertheless, Charles was concerned to defend as generous a conception of the prerogative as possible, while parliament was equally concerned to establish its predominance in the partnership of the constitution.[99] In this struggle, Roman Catholics and nonconformists assumed an importance far greater than might have been expected from their numbers and slight political power. As king and parliament vied with each other, their voice came to count for a great deal. They were at once the battleground, the ammunition and the prize of the fight.

The *Declarations* of Breda and Worcester House had suggested that, for whatever reason, Charles's inclination was less vindictive than that of the bishops and the Cavalier Parliament. On 11 May 1661 he issued a proclamation freeing Quakers imprisoned following Venner's uprising, and on 22 August 1662 another proclamation released Quakers imprisoned for holding unlawful conventicles. It was his intervention which pardoned those sentenced to death under 35 Eliz. Fox was persuaded that direct appeal to the king was the most effective means of redress for the persecuted, and on a number of occasions the king did show them clemency.[100] William Penn would similarly rely on James II. Even as the Uniformity Bill was passing through parliament, Charles,

Clarendon and the Lords, apprehensive of its potentially explosive and divisive effect, sought to modify its provisions, notably by the inclusion of clauses recognizing the royal dispensing power in ecclesiastical affairs.[101] Not for the first time, king and court were more kindly disposed to nonconformists than parliament, but not, as the nonconformist reaction to their next move recognized, from the purest of motives.

Following the Commons' rejection of the Lords' provisos and the royal assent to the unmodified Uniformity Bill on 19 May 1662, Charles and Clarendon sounded out the likely response of nonconformists to the exercise of the royal prerogative, in either dispensing with the Act in individual cases, or suspending it altogether. The response was not one of unqualified welcome: to avail themselves of royal clemency by bypassing parliament was contrary to the parliamentarian principles which, for all their differences, Puritans had espoused throughout their history. The petition Manton, Bates, Calamy and others drew up was consequently very guarded in its phrasing. In the *Declaration of Indulgence* he issued on 26 December 1662 Charles sought to overcome this difficulty by proposing to seek from parliament an Act which 'may enable us to exercise with a more universal satisfaction that power of dispensing which we conceive to be inherent in us' towards those ejected by the Act of Uniformity. Now a different objection came to the fore: while Congregationalists such as Philip Nye would have welcomed such toleration, Reconcilers such as Baxter abhorred the idea of a permanent schism in the religious life of the nation. Furthermore, there was a deep suspicion in both parties that the intended beneficiaries were the Roman Catholics, the 'greatest part of whom', so Charles averred in the *Declaration*, have 'deserved well from our royal father of blessed memory, and from us', and who were not excluded from it. Baxter recorded that 'Some of the Independents presumed to say ... they saw no reason why the Papists should not have liberty of Worship as well as others', but if the Presbyterians were expected 'to become Petitioners for Liberty of Popery, they should never do it, whatever be the issue'. Baxter and the Presbyterians therefore refused to offer the expected address of thanks, 'so that Mr *Nye* and his Brethren, thought it partly long of us that they mist of their intended Liberty'. Many nonconformists thus found themselves arguing the same case as Sheldon, whose forceful opposition to the *Declaration* was fuelled as much by antipathy to Romanism as by hostility towards nonconformists. This unlikely alliance against the king between nonconformists and their chief persecutor would be re-established, to far greater consequence, in 1688.[102]

On these twin grounds – of the exercise of the royal prerogative to overrule parliament and the toleration of popery – parliament in February 1663 refused to ratify the *Declaration*. Thus the nonconformists were initiated into their new role as pawns in the rivalry between court and parliament, and their reaction was the impolitic one it would remain throughout the period. Rather than capitalize on the opportunity that rivalry offered, they adhered to their principles against their own interests ('by breaking all these offers, we are our selves in our present afflicted state', Baxter wrote[103]) and the disunity which was both the genius and scourge of Puritanism appeared in their ranks. Though we should not be surprised: it is, on the level of national politics, but that same tenacious firmness, refusing to count the cost, which Bunyan had maintained before his judges.

Charles's second attempt of this kind was to have far more significant consequences. To free himself from financial dependence on parliament, and with signal disregard for either his own or the nation's integrity, on 22 May 1670 he entered into the secret Treaty of Dover with Louis XIV. In return for a subsidy from Louis, he reneged on the Triple Alliance with the Dutch and the Swedes by committing England to support France in a war against the United Provinces, and undertook publicly to declare himself a Roman Catholic. It is difficult to be confident about anything to do with this discreditable business: Charles may have been sincere in the religious clause, but at least one modern historian sees it as an attempt from his position of relative weakness to secure Louis' continuing support by identifying the alliance with the Roman cause.[104] To win nonconformist support, alleviate the plight of Roman Catholics, and to prepare the way for his public announcement (which never came), Charles on 15 May 1672 issued during the prorogation of parliament his second *Declaration of Indulgence.* On the incontrovertible grounds that 'by the sad experience of twelve years ... there is very litle fruit of all those forcible courses' of coercion, he professed himself 'obliged' to make use of his 'supreme power' in ecclesiastical affairs by declaring 'our will and pleasure to be that the execution of all and all manner of penal laws in matters ecclesiastical, against whatever sort of nonconformists or recusants, be immediately suspended'. Nonconformists were to be allowed public worship in 'allowed' places under 'approved' ministers; popish recusants 'the exercise of their private worship in their private houses only'.[105]

This was a good deal more comprehensive than the first *Declaration*, but the response to it was in some ways just what it had been ten years before. The episcopal church feared for its established status: in *The Rehearsal Transpros'd* (1672) it is, ironically, Marvell who appears as the champion of the king and the *Declaration* against Samuel Parker, afterwards Bishop of Oxford. Parliament was no more sympathetic: exchanges between Charles and the Commons finally forced the king to cancel his second *Declaration* on 7 March 1673.[106] The House went on to deliver 'the retort courteous to Charles' avowed purpose ... to give toleration to his co-religionists' in the First Test Act, which, *For preventing dangers which may happen from Popish recusants*, required all civil and military officers, and all members of the royal household to repudiate transubstantiation and to take the Lord's Supper according to the Prayer Book rite.[107] As in 1663, this constitutional and religious opposition by the Commons had nonconformist support. In the Test Act debates the Presbyterian member

William Love declared 'he had rather go without his own desired liberty, than have it in a way destructive to the liberties of his country, and of the Protestant interest'. This disinclination to promote the royal prerogative was coupled, as it had been in 1663, with a Presbyterian reluctance to accept toleration rather than comprehension: when 'the *London* Nonconformable Ministers were incited to return His Majesty their Thanks' for his *Declaration*, 'some were for avoiding Terms of Approbation, lest the Parliament should fall upon them; and some because they had far rather have had any tolerable state of Unity with the publick Ministry, than a Toleration.'[108]

Nevertheless, the counter-arguments had, after ten years of frustrated hopes and bitter persecution, less weight than formerly. Presbyterians had hitherto been in the main distinguishable from other nonconformists by their continuing hope that nonconformity would prove to be but a temporary phenomenon (a hope which, ironically, they shared with those episcopalians who wanted to cripple it). Their efforts towards comprehension (or 'accommodation') in a more broadly based national church had been pursued in 1667 in a bill, drafted by Sir Richard Atkyns, which waived reordination, omitted the word 'consent' and made optional disputed ceremonies; in discussions in 1667–8 with John Wilkins; and in a further bill, drafted by Hale. These efforts came to nothing, and the distinction between Presbyterians on the one hand and on the other Independents, Baptists and Quakers, who sought toleration (or 'indulgence') and contemplated permanent schism with equanimity, began to break down. In 1671 the future Secretary of State Sir Joseph Williamson observed 'all Presbyterians are growing to Independents.' This was so not only in ecclesiastical organization. While Baxter, Manton and Bates continued to press for comprehension, younger men were growing increasingly sympathetic to toleration, and so, implicitly, to the idea that nonconformity should become permanent dissent. Williamson christened the former group 'Dons' (in token of their seniority), the latter 'Ducklings' (in token of their youthful willingness to 'take to the water' of separatism).[109] These were led by the ejected vicar of St Giles, Cripplegate, Samuel Annesley, grandfather, through his daughter Susanna, of the Wesleys. It was in his congregation in what is now St Helen's Place that Defoe worshipped.[110] The approval of this group, which included William Whitaker, Thomas Watson, Thomas Vincent and James Janeway, was sought prior to the issue of the *Declaration* and they were ready to welcome it.[111]

Furthermore, pastoral concerns were now more pressing than ten years previously. The well-being of the people to whom they ministered was now in so much greater jeopardy that it persuaded the majority of Presbyterians to avail themselves of the opportunity for a more open ministry which the *Declaration* offered. Not to take this chance was to betray their charge: this was the burden of Baxter's *Sacrilegious Desertion of the Holy Ministry Rebuk'd* (1672). The constitutional argument was answered by John Humfrey: 'The Act of Parliament is against the command of God: the King permits what God bids.

Who should the subject obey, but God and the King?' It was not a comfortable position, but on 25 October 1672 even Baxter applied for a licence as an approved teacher.[112]

Thus, the *Declaration* became 'a watershed in the religious history' of the period. Fox mocked that those 'that had been stiff against toleration petitioned the King for meeting places and toleration, and gave great sums for licences, too', and all Quakers and many Congregationalists and Baptists refused to apply for licences on the grounds that the state could neither grant nor withold liberty to worship. As many as 1,610 licences were nevertheless issued in England and Wales. Of these, 939 were in the Presbyterian name, 458 Congregational or Independent, and 210 Baptist. Though an unreliable guide to denominational strength, partly because not every minister applied and partly because designation can be misleading (Bunyan was licensed as a Congregationalist, Tombes as a Presbyterian, and a few, notably Baxter, refused any denominational label), these figures are an impressive testimony to the resilience of nonconformity after ten years' persecution.[113] From this date Edward Stillingfleet, Dean of St Paul's and afterwards Bishop of Worcester, dated the 'Presbyterian separation', for not only had Presbyterians now a greater readiness to accept their nonconformist status, they also began to look to the organization and perpetuation of their churches as Independents and Quakers had done. The Presbyterian Oliver Heywood reordered his congregation in Northowram, Yorkshire, as a covenanted church and resolved to continue 'that publick way of preaching openly to all' when the licences were subsequently withdrawn; Presbyterian ordinations were held; meeting houses were built; and from November 1673 the Merchants' lectures at Pinners' Hall, London, offered a regular pulpit to both Congregationalists and Presbyterians.[114] The *Declaration* of 1672 thus confirmed that nonconformity had not been broken; but more, it impelled nonconformity towards its future in tolerated dissent. This final victory of toleration over comprehension was to be determined by the last Stuart attempt at absolutism.

After 18 years' duration the Cavalier Parliament was finally dissolved on 24 January 1679. If disillusion with the Restoration settlement at last had an opportunity to express itself it was, by the very circumstances which had forced the dissolution, exacerbated and refined. Resentment was given a grievance to seize upon. The revelations of the Popish Plot inflamed that anti-Roman feeling which was never far below the surface of English life, and which was annually reaffirmed in the burning of dummy popes on either 5 November or Elizabeth's accession day, 17 November. With hindsight popery might well appear 'a spent-force if ever there was one in the life of the nation', but to contemporaries nurtured on Foxe, the Fires of Smithfield, the Gunpowder Plot, the Irish massacre of 1641 and tales of Jesuitical duplicity, it appeared no such thing. They were, after all, confronted with the rising power of Louis XIV, were suspicious of Charles's religious commitment and aware, since James resigned his post as Lord High Admiral following the First Test Act, that the heir to the throne was a Papist. In January 1681 Heywood was able to list no fewer than 40 reasons for fearing 'that popery may again overspread England'. And popery meant tyranny and absolutism: witness the title of Marvell's *An Account of the Growth of Popery, and Arbitrary Government in England* (1677). Titus Oates's stories were believed precisely because they accorded with what everyone already half-believed. The Commons itself was, after all, persuaded that Papists were responsible for the Fire of London. 'It is not possible to imagin', wrote Sir John Reresby in his *Memoirs*, 'what a ferment the artifice of some, and the reall beliefe and fear of others concerning this plott, putt the two Houses of Parlament and the greatest part of the nation into.'[115]

This ferment was organized by the Achitophel of Dryden's *Absalom and Achitophel* (1681), Anthony Ashley Cooper, first Earl of Shaftesbury, into the first Whigs. The aim of the party was the exclusion of Charles's brother and heir James from the succession to the throne. This was presented as the only way to safeguard religious and civil liberty from popery and despotism, and the party therefore had a particular appeal for those who had suffered most. Both Presbyterians and old Interregnum radicals (who in their Indian summer enjoyed the patronage of Dryden's Zimri, George Villiers, second Duke of Buckingham) were found in the Whig ranks.[116] An intense lobbying and press campaign – in which the Baptist preacher and printer Francis Smith was conspicuous – was undertaken. Even Quakers joined in the effort to secure a sympathetic parliament. This activity bore fruit. At its close, the Cavalier Parliament had but 25 nonconformist members; the First Exclusion Parliament (1679) had 42; the Second (1680–1) 52. In part because of this improved representation, and in part because episcopalian hostility towards nonconformists decreased as their fear of popery increased, these parliaments were a good deal more sympathetic than the Cavalier had been. There were attempts to repeal 35 Eliz. and to pass both toleration and comprehension bills. The former Charles ordered not to be presented for signature; the latter were lost by prorogation.[117]

Charles fought exclusion and would 'not consent to disherison of the Crown' not so much from fraternal affection for James as from self-interest, for 'Without my leave a future King to choose,/Infers a Right the present to Depose.' More politic than James, Charles would yet have agreed with him that 'The Exclusion Bill destroys the very being of the monarchy, which, I thank God, yet has had no dependency on parliaments nor on nothing but God alone, nor never can, and be a monarchy.'[118] So their father had thought. Sir Robert Filmer's exposition of the divine right of hereditary monarchy, *Patriarcha*, originally composed and circulated in defence of Charles I's cause, was forty years later published in 1680 on behalf of his sons. It was a view which, through Charles's timely use of the prerogative right of prorogation and dissolution and a 'sheer political genius' which has won the respect of modern historians, survived the Exclusion Crisis. Armed with a new subsidy from Louis XIV, Charles was able, on 28 March 1681, to dissolve the Third Exclusion Parliament after it had sat for only a week, and to rule thenceforth without a parliament. With exclusion lost, the Whigs crumbled, and the nonconformists, as the most readily identifiable of their supporters, bore the brunt of the 'Tory revenge' of 1681–6 in the most severe and sustained period of persecution they were called on to endure. It was, wrote Heywood in February 1684, their darkest day.[119]

It is small wonder that, pitched suddenly into persecution from a position of political influence, some took to revolution. Though it never even reached the stage of detailed planning, let alone execution, the Rye House Plot of June 1683 seemed to justify all the Tory charges and further inflamed persecution.[120] Nor is it any wonder that, poorly represented in James II's first parliament of May 1685 and confronted with a determined Roman Catholic monarch, many nonconformists, including Defoe, supported the rebellion of Charles's illegitimate son, James Scott, Duke of Monmouth. After all, in his declaration of war of 11 June (of which the ejected Presbyterian and Rye House plotter Robert Ferguson was probable author) Monmouth undertook to defend both 'the Protestant Religion' and a 'limited Monarchy' against James's 'Conspiracy against the Reformed Religion and the Rights of the Nation'. He pledged himself never to 'lay down our Arms' until 'all the Penal Laws against Protestant Dissenters be repealed, and Legal Provision made against them being disturbed by Reason of their Conscience'. Nonconformists formed a substantial part of Monmouth's support. Erstwhile Cromwellian officers such as the Baptist Henry Danvers led them to Sedgemoor. And they figured prominently amongst those executed and transported by the Bloody Assizes Jeffreys held during August and September 1685. Those who suffered included the Baptist Elizabeth Gaunt, a woman, in Burnet's view, of 'exemplary charity', who was burned alive for harbouring a man she did not know to be a rebel, the last woman executed in England for treason and one of the last persons to die by fire.[121]

In his Romanizing policies James at first looked for support to the Church of England, and apparently with good reason. As long ago as 1661 Seth Ward, afterwards Bishop successively of Exeter and Salisbury, had, in his 5 November sermon preached before Charles, *Against Resistance of Lawful Powers*, claimed that the obedience of the subject was 'deeply, and firmly rooted in the Foundation of our *Religion*'. In 1683 the Convocation of Oxford issued a decree directing the university's tutors to instruct students 'in that most necessary doctrine, which, in a manner, is the badge and character of the Church of England', namely, absolute passive obedience to the monarch 'without exception'. Episcopal divines admonished Monmouth on the scaffold 'If you be of the church of England, you must acknowledge the doctrine of non-resistance to be true.'[122] And it was to the prevalence of this conviction that James himself owed the defeat of exclusion and his own peaceful accession. However, despite these precedents, episcopalians proved less subservient to the royal will than James expected. In the spring of 1686 he consequently looked elsewhere for allies, and began to foster nonconformist support for his planned repeal of the Test Acts on behalf of his co-religionists. On 10 March 1686 he issued a General Pardon to all imprisoned for conscience' sake and soundings were taken as to the likely nonconformist response to an indulgence.[123]

'All on a sudden the Churchmen were disgraced, and the Dissenters were in high favour.' This was a more dramatically abrupt change of fortune for nonconformists than even the experience of 1681; it was to prove also of more consequence, and, at the time, more searching. James's overtures presented a starker choice than had those of his brother. No one could believe of this monarch, as was just possible of Charles, that a genuine sympathy was at work. James's first *Declaration of Indulgence* of 4 April 1687 openly declared 'We cannot but heartily wish that all the people of our dominions were members of the Catholic Church' and, while it suspended all ecclesiastical penal laws, it also relieved civil and military officers of the oaths of supremacy and allegiance and of the sacramental test, and granted freedom of worship 'in private houses or places purposely hired or built for that use' to nonconformists and Roman Catholics alike. This was to go far beyond Charles's 1672 *Declaration* and left no doubt of the intended beneficiaries. 'Whatever reasons were alleged, the true reason appeared to most men to be a design thereby to weaken the Church of England ... to devide the Protestant churches, that the popish might find less opposition (Devide et impera).' Would the nonconformists pay the price?[124]

Some 80 addresses of thanks were received. Nevertheless, as Defoe later wrote, 'The Generality of the Dissenters saw the hook thro' this Bait, and tho they accepted their Liberty ... yet they professed their Dissatisfaction at having it given in an unparliamentary manner.' Many of the addresses carefully insisted on the need for subsequent parliamentary ratification, many were not spontaneous but elicited by court pressure, and many of the Presbyterian 'Dons', notably Baxter, Bates and Howe, refused all expressions of gratitude. Not all, however, were so reluctant. Henry Nye published his father, Philip's, *The King's authority in Dispensing with Ecclesiastical Laws, Asserted and Vindicated* (1687) 'to express my Gratitude' for the *Declaration* and 'to promote the Designs of Your Princely Clemency'. The Bartholomean Vincent Alsop, licensed as a Congregationalist in 1672 and from 1677 pastor of the Presbyterian meeting in Tothill Street, London, where he was succeeded in 1703 by Edmund Calamy, was one of the most conspicuous examples of a man who unreservedly welcomed the indulgence. His action brought down on him the ire of Ferguson, who heatedly berated all those who co-operated with the Romish tyrant: 'this new practice of *Addressing*', Ferguson wrote, was 'never in fashion, unless either under a *Weak* and *precarious Government*, or under one that took *illegal courses'*, for 'he who *Ruleth* according to the standing *Laws* of a *Country* ... needs not seek for an Approbation of his Actions from a part of his *Subjects.'* The Quakers, and particularly William Penn, were of another mind. They had benefited most from the Pardon of 1686, which had released perhaps 1,200 of them from prison, and support for the king's prerogative and the extending of toleration to Roman Catholics is the burden of Penn's *Perswasive to Moderation to Church-Dissenters* (1686), *Good Advice to the Church of England* (1687) and *Some Free Reflections upon Occasion of the Public Discourse about Liberty of Conscience* (1687).[125]

James's radically altered policy towards nonconformists necessarily involved the Church of England. The predicament in which it found itself is nicely exemplified by the attempt of the recent Roman Catholic convert John Dryden to further his royal master's policy as he had done that of Charles in *Absalom and Achitophel. The Hind and the Panther*, composed during the winter and spring of 1686/7, adopts the perspective of the earlier phase of James's strategy. In the beast fable the Independent Bear, Quaking Hare, Baptist Boar, Presbyterian Wolf and Socinian Fox are presented as monsters which such Roman Catholic realms as Italy and Spain are fortunate to have been spared; other nonconformist sects are 'A slimy-born and sun-begotten Tribe', 'gross, half-animated lumps'. By contrast, the Church of England Panther is 'fairest ... of the spotted kind', 'least deform'd, because reform'd the least', next only to the 'milk white *Hind*, immortal and unchang'd' of Roman Catholicism. The doctrinal and ecclesiastical debate between the Hind and the Panther, which forms the second and third parts of the poem, is intended to vindicate Roman Catholicism and the royal lion's protection of its adherents, to dissuade the Panther from any alliance with her 'ancient foes' the sectarian beasts and to persuade her to support the royal policy of repealing the Test Acts. The poem, however, was overtaken by events. Completed two weeks after the publication of James's *Declaration* it carried, when published, an incongruous preface which sought to square the text with James's new ecclesiastical bias. The preface praises those nonconformists who, supporting the royal policy of indulgence, '*have withdrawn themselves from the Communion of the* Panther', and, remarking that '*This Indulgence being granted to all the Sects, it ought in reason to be expected that they should both receive it, and receive it thankfully'*, it reminds them that the king '*expects a Return in* Specie *from them; that the Kindness which He has Graciously shown them, may be retaliated on those of his own perswasion'*. The villains of the poem have become the heroes of the preface, where the sectarian beasts replace the Panther as the ally favoured by the Hind and royal Lion. Hence, where the poem itself argues only for repeal of the test, the preface claims repeal of both test and penal laws is the aim.[126]

Dryden's Panther was accustomed to thinking of itself as the exclusive ecclesiastical partner of the monarch. It now found the monarch, whom 'I cannot disobey', in alliance with its opponents and showing every sign of abolishing its established status with their help. Archbishop William Sancroft realized its 'perilous predicament' and so, in its turn, the episcopal church began to make overtures to the nonconformists. This was what Macaulay called 'the strangest auction in history'. Meetings and negotiations in 1686/7 sought to persuade nonconformist leaders that James's intentions were not in their best interests, and the suggestion began to be made that they should cast in their lot with the growing number of William of Orange's episcopalian supporters, since he could be relied upon to carry the repeal of the penal laws through parliament with episcopalian support without tolerating Catholicism.[127]

It was as part of this campaign to wean nonconformists from James that Halifax wrote his famous *Letter to a Dissenter* (1687). Its burden was Ferguson's, but where Ferguson exclaims, berates and ejaculates in impassioned fervour, Halifax is urbane, ironic and judicious. Ferguson's tract is an urgent missive from the front line; Halifax's a cool assessment from HQ. In his *Apology for the Church of England* (1688), Burnet was about the same business. Like Ferguson, he is distressed by the addresses of thanks, and especially Alsop's 'Imprudent strains'. And, like Ferguson, he is alive to the timely persuasiveness lent to his argument by Louis XIV. In his *History of My Own Time* he commented that the revocation of the Edict of Nantes in October 1685 and the persecution of the Huguenots 'came very seasonably to awaken the Nation' to the true nature of Roman Catholic monarchy. As Ferguson had put it, Louis XIV's action showed 'how far the *Promise* and *Royal Word* of a *Catholic Monarch* is to be trusted unto'; 'His Majesty of Great *Britain*, hath a pattern lately set him, and that by the Illustrious *Monarch*, whom he so much admires, and whom he makes it his ambition and glory to imitate.' Penn stood almost alone in his willingness to credit James II. Where Halifax cautioned nonconformists against trusting their monarch, Penn, in his reply *The Great and Popular Objection against the Repeal of the Penal Laws and Tests* (1687), cautioned them against trusting their new found friends, the episcopalians. It was a reasonable point: even if James was not to be trusted, was the Church of England?[128]

James's *Order in Council* of 4 May 1688, commanding that his second *Declaration of Indulgence* of 27 April should be read from all parish pulpits, unwittingly resolved the doubt and cemented this alliance. It seemed a neat move: an episcopal refusal to distribute the *Declaration* to their clergy might be expected to antagonize nonconformists; episcopal compliance to win nonconformist gratitude to the king who had stayed persecution. Either way, nonconformists would be drawn into the royalist camp. The tactic, however, backfired: instead of alienating the established church, it allied that church with nonconformists in opposition to the king. Extensive nonconformist support for the stand of Sancroft and the six bishops against the *Declaration* was confirmed by the careful disclaimer, in their *Petition* of 18 May begging to be excused the *Order*, of 'any want of due tenderness to dissenters' and its expression of a willingness 'to come to such a temper' with them 'as shall be thought fit when that matter shall be considered and settled in Parliament and Convocation'. These considered phrases were the result of negotiations with the nonconformists following publication of the *Order*, at which it was agreed nonconformist support for episcopalian refusal to comply would be matched by an episcopalian commitment to a new religious settlement. Obedience, even for Tories and episcopalians, after all had its limits.[129]

No addresses of thanks for the second *Declaration* were forthcoming from nonconformists; nonconformist ministers visited the bishops in the Tower; and nonconformists joined in the general jubilation at their acquittal of the charge of publishing a seditious libel, namely, the *Petition* 'which they presented to the King conteaning the reasons why they could not order his Majesty's declaration … to be read in churches'. Halifax later told William of Orange that he regarded the trial of the Seven Bishops 'as that which hath brought all the Protestants together and bound them into a knot that cannot easily be untied'. The knot was sealed by Sancroft's *Articles* to his bishops of 16 July requiring them to have 'a very tender regard to our brethren, the protestant dissenters' and 'to visit them at their houses and receive them kindly at their own'. Things had indeed changed since Sancroft's predecessor, Sheldon, had in 1668 led the opposition to Hale's comprehension bill.[130]

What pulled the knot tight was the prospect of a Catholic dynasty raised by the birth of James's son, the future Old Pretender, on 10 June 1688. In the letter dispatched to William of Orange on 30 June, the day of the Seven Bishops' acquittal, he was urged to intervene to safeguard the religious and civil liberties of the nation on the grounds that the birth of this child, 'which not one in a thousand here believes to be the queen's', jeopardized the succession to the throne of his wife and James's daughter, Mary. Early in 1688 John Hampden, grandson of his famous namesake and son of Baxter's friend Richard Hampden, who had been convicted of treason by Jeffreys after the Rye House Plot, was one of the first nonconformists to commit himself to William. Nonconformist support had grown as the year wore on, and to the certainty of it was in large part due the 'astonishing providence' (the phrase is the Presbyterian Henry Newcome's) of William's landing at Torbay on 5 November and the final flight of James on 23 December. When 'a bloody cloud hanged over us, of popery', wrote Heywood, 'all on a sudden a bright sun appeared out of the East'. Over fifty nonconformist divines, with John Howe as their spokesman, on 2 January 1689 presented an address of thanks to William. Of all the monuments in Westminster Abbey, Celia Fiennes would later choose to remark that:

> in Harry the Sevenths Chapple layes our great and good as well as ever glorious King William, and Queen Mary his Royal Consort whome noe tyme can ever obliterate the memory of, their being Englands deliverers in Gods hands from popery and slavery which King James by the King of Frances power was involving us in.[131]

For the second time in 30 years a king came from over the sea, but William, though welcome, did not come as Charles had done, unconditionally and with an undisputed right to the crown. That right and those conditions were to be determined by parliament. The Convention of 1689, putting its authority beyond question by its first enactment legalizing its proceedings, undertook a comprehensive constitutional and religious settlement. In both the Lords, where they were led by Philip, Lord Wharton, and the Commons, where their leader was Richard Hampden, nonconformist members were active in the debates and committees which led to the resolution that James had abdicated by his flight and to the offer of the crown jointly to William and Mary on the terms of the *Declaration of Rights* presented by Halifax on 12 February, terms which, subordinating the king to parliament and, denying his prerogative right to suspend laws, became statutory in 'our greatest constitutional document since Magna Carta', the Bill of Rights (16 December 1689). Despite their best efforts, however, the religious settlement proved to be but grudging. The negotiations towards an agreement with the nonconformists lost a prime mover on the establishment side when Sancroft's conscientious refusal to break his oath of allegiance to James by recognizing William and Mary led to his suspension (1689) and deprivation (1690). The retreat of the Roman Catholic threat, the possibility that many Presbyterians might enter the Church of England should comprehension be carried and the fact that William himself 'seem'd to countenance Presbutery more then ... the Church of England' and 'to favour Calvanisme' all combined to persuade episcopalians to look to their authority and so weakened their resolve to honour the understandings of 1688. The comprehension bill Sancroft favoured was lost, as were attempts to repeal the Corporation and First Test Acts.[132]

What did reach the statute-book was *An Act for Exempting their Majesties' Protestant Subjects Dissenting from the Church of England from the Penalties of Certain Laws*, which, with its 'chilling title', was the least that could be done to redeem the promises of the previous two years. It repealed nothing, and had no effect upon the civic status of nonconformists. For those nonconformists who took the oaths of allegiance and supremacy as rephrased in the Act Legalizing the Convention, who subscribed the 1678 Test Act's declaration against transubstantiation and who were trinitarians, it suspended penal ecclesiastical legislation and granted freedom of worship, provided that this was conducted only at registered meeting houses with unlocked doors by ministers who subscribed the doctrinal articles of the Church of England. Baptists were excused article 27 and Quakers were permitted to affirm.[133]

It was not much, but even the little that it was is a remarkable testimony to the courageous integrity of the last Puritans. Through all the vicissitudes of these 30 years their constancy had testified 'that conscience towards God may have a greater hand ... in guiding men the different ways they take than is commonly thought'. Milton had long ago posed the rhetorical question: 'What more binding then conscience?' This might serve as a sub-title to Marvell's *Rehearsal Transpros'd*, and, indeed, as the motto of the body of nonconformist writing. It was a principle nonconformist witness had brought the law to recognize. When Howe, who accompanied Wharton to the United Provinces in the late 1680s, met Burnet at Utrecht, the future Bishop of Salisbury observed that nonconformity 'could not subsist long ... when Mr *Baxter* and Dr. *Bates*, and he, and a few more were once laid in their Graves, it would sink, and die'. To this, Howe replied: it did not 'depend upon *Persons*, but upon *Principles*, which when taken up upon grounds approv'd upon search, could not be laid aside by Men of Conscience'.[134]

Chapter 2 'Hand in hand'

the literary response of nonconformity to persecution

> *Let us hold fast the profession of our faith without wavering; (for he is faithful that promised;)*
>   *And let us consider one another to provoke unto love and good works.*
>   *Not forsaking the assembling of ourselves together, as the manner of some is; but exhorting one another*
>
> Heb. x.23–5

I   REBELS AND SCHISMATICS

Conscience was the one thing Gilbert Sheldon, Archbishop of Canterbury, would not allow to nonconformists. It is his name, rather than Clarendon's, which should be attached to the penal legislation, for, whereas Clarendon had worked to mitigate the severity of the Act of Uniformity and had promoted Charles's policy of toleration, Sheldon was an inveterate opponent of both toleration and comprehension and an implacable pursuer of nonconformists.[1] In 1665, 1669 and 1676 he initiated censuses throughout the English and Welsh dioceses, the chief intention of which was to determine the numbers and distribution of 'yᵉ crafty ... turbulent ... factious Inconformist ministers' and their adherents. There seems little doubt that these enquiries were intimately linked with Sheldon's promotion of the Clarendon Code. 1665 was the earliest convenient moment after Sheldon's elevation to the see of Canterbury on the death of William Juxon in 1663 to secure an authoritative list of the Bartholomeans and assess the effect of the Act of Uniformity. Furthermore, since the First Conventicle Act had been passed the previous year, the returns would make it possible to identify and watch likely offenders. In 1669 that Act expired, and the figures obtained in that year's census would enable him to show nonconformity had not been crushed and so to argue for the Second Conventicle Act. And the 1676 census could assess the effect of the issuing of licences in 1672.[2]

If we ask why Sheldon was so anxious to secure statistics and to measure the effect of repression, we may find an answer in the phrases he used in the letter to Humphrey Henchman, Bishop of London, which accompanied the 'Orders and Instructions' for the 1665 census. Sheldon writes of the 'great disorders and disturbances caused by ye crafty insinuations and turbulent practices of factious Inconformist ministers'. He was convinced, that is to say, that the nonconformists were, at best, intent on disturbing the peace and, at worst, seditious rebels merely pretending to religion. This was certainly the view taken by the legislators. The Five Mile Act spoke of ejected ministers holding unlawful assemblies 'under colour or pretence of exercise of religion', and the Second Conventicle Act was directed against 'the growing and dangerous practices of seditious sectaries and other disloyal persons, who under pretence of tender consciences have or may at their meetings contrive insurrections', phrases which Fox tried (unsuccessfully) to argue put peaceable Quaker meetings beyond the scope of the Act. 'Under a pretence of religion' is the phrase Sheldon himself used of conventicles in his letter with the instructions for the 1669 census, and the returns were drafted in just this spirit. From Canterbury diocese, for example, it was noted that the Canterbury congregation of 'John Durant, excom*municated* Independ*ent* Preach*er*' included 'Tho: Scott Esq: a Ringlead*er* of the Petic*ion* for the K*ings* tryall' and that the Sandwich nonconformist Bartholomew Coombes was 'very active in the late Rebellion'. In 1676 Samuel Parker, then Archdeacon of Canterbury and afterwards Bishop of Oxford, still felt obliged to note that 'The Heads and Preachers of the severall Factions [of nonconformists] are such as had a great share in the late Rebellion'. To recall their separatist and prewar origins he even now calls the Independents 'Brownists'.[3]

It was hence possible for a pamphlet seeking nonconformist support for James's policy of indulgence to argue, without intended irony, that no one had 'suffered for their Consciences' since 'none are punish'd for Matters of meer Religion'. The 'Principle, that Conscience ought not to be compell'd' could be said to have been 'yielded', since compulsion was used only for the civil and political, not religious, offences of holding illegal meetings and refusing the non-resistance and Oxford oaths. It was a line of thinking totally unimpressed by such a plea as William Penn's for *Moderation to Church Dissenters* ([1686]), whose premise was 'there is such a thing as *Conscience* and the *Liberty* of it, in reference to *Faith* and *Worship* towards God'. On the contrary, by the authorities 'Liberty of Conscience is counted a *Pretence for Rebellion*, and Religious Assemblies, *Routs* and *Riots*'.[4] Neither church nor state would concede that conventicles were, not merely (and incidentally) illegal gatherings, but churches. Indeed, they could not concede it, for the Act of Uniformity had recognized the established church as the only true church and only those in episcopal orders as true ministers. Whatever went on at conventicles, it could not, therefore, be religion. Dark suspicion lurks in the parenthesis of the Bishop of Bristol's admission to Sheldon in 1665 that in his diocese, in Dorset, 'There are many non Conformist Ministers who neither hath nor will take the oath enjoyned them by the late act of parliament, but have gotten them private habitations 5 miles from any Corporate towne, where they often meet together (about what, noe man knowes)'. For the truth of the matter, the Bishop had no need of access to such unpublished church records as those of Bunyan's Bedford congregation: he could, the next year, have learned from *Grace Abounding* what was in the minds of such ministers. Its intense sense of vocation was, however, disallowed: certainly, the pretence of it conferred no pastoral or ministerial authority. The ministers of nonconformist congregations appear in the episcopal returns as merely 'heads', 'teachers', sometimes 'preachers', even 'Seducers', and their followers are 'abettors'.[5]

What they abetted was the marvellously unflagging and tirelessly repeated cry of countless pamphleteers and polemicists: rebellion. No one was to forget that beneath the quietest lamb's clothing there lurked a ravening wolf. In his *Shortest Way with the Dissenters* (1702), Defoe, ironically adopting the persona of a high churchman, summed up the charges preferred through-out the Restoration period: 'You have *Butcher'd* one *King*, *Depos'd* another King, and made a *mock* King of a Third'. His fellow Whig pamphleteer, John Tutchin, rightly described the great theme of establishment writing during the 40 years following the Restoration as being the loyalty of the Church of England and the inevitable disloyalty of nonconformists. With equal justification he singled out as the burden of Sir Roger L'Estrange's many publications the contention that 'the very Nature and Tendency of their Profession is destructive of Kingly Power, and the Government of the Nation'.[6] It was for just such destructive tendencies that Baxter was, as he believed at L'Estrange's instigation, brought to trial for sedition and convicted by Jeffreys in 1685.[7] In 1702 the publication, among the 'many *Lewd* and *Poisonous Pamphlets* of Late spread Abroad to *Debauch* the *Nation*', of Edmund Calamy's *Abridgment* of the *Reliquiae* of 'that *Arch-Rebel*' Baxter incensed the non-juror Charles Leslie. Leslie's hostility is unusually venomous but not otherwise exceptional. It is one of his more temperate allegations that 'that *Hypocritical* and *Bloody Faction*', having murdered the 'unparallel'd *Goodness* and *Condescentions* of so *Pious* and *Meek* a King' as Charles I, 'still glory in it, Repeat it every Year in their *Calves-Head-Feasts*, where they *Sacrifice* to the *Legion* that possesses them. And not satisfied with the *Royal Blood* they have *Drank* [sic], still Thirst for more'. The Quakers are no better. In the first decade of the eighteenth century Leslie is still convinced they '*Disturb the Peace in all Civil Societies, and Preach up the Lawfulness of Disobedience to Human Authority*', that they '*Propagate* their Abhorr'd Principles of *Schisms* and *Rebellion*' and that they intend to put the nation 'in a flame'.[8]

For much of the later Stuart period rhetoric had the better of reality with the government too. It believed the image its propagandists fostered. Certainly, there were disaffected Cromwellians and republicans, especially during the years immediately following the Restoration and, to a degree, until the accession of William and Mary. Certainly those who had exercised power during the Interregnum were often to be found in nonconformist congregations, in none more conspicuously than in John Owen's. Owen, who had been closely involved, if not instrumental, in the fall of Richard Cromwell and the subsequent attempts to secure a republican state settlement, had, early in 1659, gathered a church which to many appeared as much a political caucus as a congregation. It may have met at Wallingford House, Major-General Charles Fleetwood's London residence, and its members included many former army grandees. Following the Restoration, Owen continued to minister to Fleetwood and to such Cromwellian major-generals as James Berry and John Desborough. And, certainly, there were plots. But by how much the government was a victim of its own prejudice and exaggerated nervousness is well illustrated by the illusory career attributed in the state papers to Colonel Edmund Ludlow, as fine a fiction as the age produced.[9]

On 20 June 1660 the regicide and convinced republican Edmund Ludlow surrendered himself to the authorities, but in August he escaped to Dieppe. On 1 September a proclamation for his apprehension was issued; in October he was rumoured to be in Gloucester; in December an immediate and extensive search was ordered, but no trace of him was found. Ludlow, however, refused to go away. In August 1661 he was said to have landed in Essex with his fellow regicide, Major-General Edmund Whalley, who had reportedly returned from his refuge in New England. In October he was set to be the greatest man in England, with 40,000 old soldiers at his call. Later that month he was thought to be lurking about Cripplegate. Eight months later he was again seen there, this time disguised; then he was spotted in Westminster. The following month, July 1662, he was reported to be the general of a planned uprising, with Desborough as his lieutenant-general, Archibald Campbell, earl of Argyll, commanding in Scotland, and Henry Cromwell and Sir Henry Vane's son having commands in England. In August, Lord Fairfax was to be the general, and Ludlow the commander in the West. In October an informant predicted a rising before the 28th of the month involving Ludlow, Major-General John Lambert (imprisoned on Guernsey) and William, Lord Steele. In November another informant promised the rising before Christmas.[10]

One might have supposed him by now played out, but the 'grand old rebel' had hardly begun his career. His was the name on every informer's lips. In February 1663 a warrant was issued to search a house in West Charleton, Devon, for him. He was said to be planning a West country uprising and his supposed correspondents were imprisoned. In March he was near Whitechapel with 100 men of the New Model Army, then with 500 men in St Giles. In May he was still in London, with Whalley and the regicide Major-General William Goffe poised in Brussels, and the regicides William Cowley and John Lisle in Normandy. He was, inevitably, implicated in the Derwentdale plot. In October he was in Somersetshire to lead 10,000 men from Wales. And so it went on into

1664. He was bringing 5,000 men from the West and planning insurrection in Holland. In 1665 he was plotting with Desborough in Leiden and suspected conspirators were interrogated about their links with him. In 1666 an invasion from Holland was promised. Not until 1667 does his name fade from the state papers and the fevered imaginations of the government and its spies.[11]

What he had actually done was to travel quietly through France and settle in Geneva. Rather than plot against England, he refused complicity in such schemes and was himself the victim of assassination plots: his companion John Lisle was murdered at Lausanne on 11 August 1664. He was, as were the majority of those suspected by the government, engaged not in the seditious promotion of the Good Old Cause but in its literary commemoration and vindication: he was writing his *Memoirs*.[12]

2   'THESE SO MUCH CENSURED MEETINGS'

The conclaves of plotters of which the government and its pamphleteers believed conventicles consisted were as chimerical as Ludlow's numerous uprisings. Of the real business of conventicles Howe gives a very different account in controversy with Edward Stillingfleet, then Dean of St. Paul's and afterwards Bishop of Worcester:

> I do particularly believe, – as I doubt not but God is graciously present with those that in the sincerity of their hearts have chosen to serve him in the way which the law prescribes, – so that if Dr Stillingfleet had known what proofs there are of that same gracious presence in these so much censured meetings, his thoughts would have been very different of them from what they are. I do not speak of proselyting men to a party, which I heartily despise as a mean and inconsiderable thing: but have known some and heard of many instances of very ignorant and profane persons, that have been led, perhaps by their own curiosity or it may be by the persuasion of some neighbour or friend, to hear and see what was done in such meetings, that have (through God's blessing upon so despised means) become very much reformed men, and, for ought that could be judged, serious and sober Christians. And whereas some, that have very prejudicial thoughts of all that frequent such meetings, may be apt to suspect all effects of that kind to be nothing else but illusions of fancy, or a disposition at least to enthusiasm, or an artificial and industrious hypocrisy; I am very confident that if the Doctor had had the opportunity frequently to observe and converse with such, – as we have had, – and heard the sobriety and consistency of their discourse, and seen the unaffected simplicity, humility and heavenliness of their conversation, he could not have allowed himself the liberty of such hard censures.[13]

The impression Howe gives not merely of a godly but also of a thriving community capable of attracting converts can be confirmed by such official reports as, barring its inevitable gloss, this entry in the 1669 episcopal returns:

> In the Towne of Hartford, there are publick conventicles held every Sunday at ye time of Divine service. There is one meeteing of Anabaptists to ye number of 400 & upward, to whom one Capt. [John] Spencer is the preacher; another there is of

Quakers (of as great number) to whom Capt. [John] Crooke is preacher. He was a Justice of peace under Cromwill; is of dangerous principles, a subtle fellowe, & one who hath too much influence upon the people of that Towne & the country about: each of these have their publick places fitted for their meeteings as if they were allowed by authority.[14]

London Presbyterians did not wait until the indulgence of 1672 before putting up buildings specifically for meetings. It was, again in 1669, reported that houses had been 'new built on purpose' for the congregations of Thomas Doolittle in Mugwell (now Monkwell) Street, Thomas Vincent in Hand Alley, Bishopgate Street ('spacious ... with galleries') and his brother Nathaniel in Farthing Abbey, Southwark, and Samuel Annesley in Spittlefields ('*with* Pulpit and Seates').[15] It was, perhaps, more usual for ministers to preach 'as the apostle Paul did', in their own homes,[16] but clearly one could hardly move around London and remain unaware that these domestic and meeting houses were the focus of worshipping communities.

In the country, and in other denominations, it might be very different – in 1669 Quakers at Radclive, Buckinghamshire, met 'at ye house of Mary Armalt, a poore simple wench' – but not necessarily so. The frequency with which the established church's own buildings were used points to a remarkable confidence. At Penistone, Yorkshire, where Henry Swift retained the living despite not subscribing, Congregationalists met 'At the *pa*rish Church there being noe lawfull Incumbent'. Even without such explanation, conventicles might be held in the church, as at Pudsey, Yorkshire, and we hear even of Quakers meeting in the 'Chappelry' at Rippon, Yorkshire.[17] At Banbury the Quaker meeting house built in 1657 was in 1665 moved to a new site in the town. At Henley-on-Thames, Friends purchased a meeting house and burial ground in 1672 and in Somersetshire 'great Meeting Houses' were built at Gregory Stoke and Ilminster 'about ye year 1670'. They 'saw needfull to build a meeting house' near Crossfield, Cumberland in 1667, and at Broughton, also in Cumberland, 'aboutt the year 1687, ffriends Increased soe in Number thatt mostt of the dwelling houses was to litle to Contain the Meeting, so thatt the ffriends belonging to thatt Meeting, agreed to build a Meeting House att litle Broughton'. At Colchester, they were the most resilient and determined of all:

Jn ye time of ye Great Persecution in 1663 and 1664, and while ye Cruel Troopers were in Town and friends Sorely Persecuted, they built a Large Meeting House, which was an amazement to ye Whole Town.

Jn ye year 1670, Wm. Moore was Mayor again, and Caused ye Meeting House to be Twice planked and Bricked up, which was Twice broken up, but at last Friends were forced to Meet in ye Street in ye Winter in Rain and Snow, though pretty free from Disturbance. Two Friends were imprisoned for breaking open ye Meeting house doors, but were quickly Released. Thus Truth through Great Sufferings got ye Victory.

Jn ye Year 1673, Friends Pulled down part of ye Meeting House to build it more Convenient, when one John Vickers, an old Adversary to Truth, petitioned the Quarter Sessions that while our Meeting House was Pulling down it might be utterly laid Wast and Razed to ye Ground, but they took No Notice of it.[18]

This account of the experiences of the Colchester Quakers makes it clear how much the fortunes of nonconformists depended upon the attitude of the local magistracy, constabulary and corporation officers. Persecution was chronologically intermittent because of the fluctuating policies of court and parliament, but geographically variable because of the differing persuasions of justices. On the one hand, local inhabitants might find themselves suddenly at the mercy of such a fit of loyalty as that of Sir Giles Strangways in 1675. Having been 'lately made Privy Counsellor', he went 'into the Country, swoln with his new Honour, and with Venom against the Fanatics' and 'set his Informers to work'. In this case, the fit was short-lived: Marvell recorded with ironic satisfaction that he 'dyed suddenly, notwithstanding his Church's Letany, *From sudden Death, good Lord*, &c.'. On the other hand, they might enjoy the circumstances reported in 1670 to Joseph Williamson, then Arlington's secretary, but afterwards knighted and Secretary of State. He was told 'that Whitby and the country adjacent are too much planted with all sorts of Dissenters and Quakers, who herd together, and that most of the neighbouring justices wink at it, if not favour their proceedings'. The ejected Presbyterian minister Simon Barret was known to preach 'at Lambourne, Berkshire, at ye house of Mr Philip Garrard high Constable', his auditors including 'Charles Fettiplace Esq. Just. of Peace'. In 1681 it was in consternation reported that the mayor of Canterbury had married the daughter of the Congregationalist John Durant, ejected rector of St George's, Canterbury, and 'the most seditious conventicle preacher in this country and the principal agent in getting hands to that damnable petition for bringing his late Majesty to his trial and death'.[19]

The Colchester experiences also show how the execution of the Clarendon Code centred on meetings and meeting houses. The term 'meeting house', common to all the nonconformist denominations, accurately describes not only the domestic architecture of their buildings but also their conception of the bond between those meeting within. They were all, whether by ecclesiastical tradition or force of circumstances, effectively, if not always strictly, covenanted members of gathered churches, coming together not by custom but by choice. For the Congregationalist Stephen Lobb, the essential distinction between Congregational and episcopal churches was that, whereas the procedures of the former are '*personal* by all the Body of the Church', those of the latter are 'not *personal* ... but only by the Intervention of Delegates, Messengers, Officers or synods'. Under a diocesan polity, 'We have no converse with one another ... for we never know one of five hundred in the Diocess', but members of a Congregational church help 'each other towards heaven, by provoking each other to Love and to Good works' and by comforting each other. Members of a particular congregation, that is to say, constituted a family, or, as the Quakers would later call themselves, a society of friends, bound to each other and separated from the world and established church. It was 'Love (without dissimulation)' which the 1658 Savoy *Declaration* had sought to preserve between the members of particular churches and, as its architecture suggested a home, so it is the image of a loving and welcoming family which characterizes church fellowship in nonconformist writing.[20]

The readiest example lies in *The Pilgrim's Progress*. As Christian is about to leave the house of the Interpreter his host prays 'The Comforter be always with thee good *Christian*, to guide thee in the way that leads to the City'. This divine guidance leads Christian directly to the Palace Beautiful. That the palace stands 'just by the High-way side' may be taken as a realistic detail (no building could plausibly stand in the road) with the stress on the house's proximity ('just by' rather than 'back from'). The suggestion that its wayside position implies church membership is not essential to a successful pilgrimage sorts ill with Bunyan's depiction of Christian's reception and experience at the palace.[21] The palace is not easy to reach – the lions of persecution have seen off Timorous and Mistrust – but its doors stand open to receive the persevering, for it was built 'for the relief and security of Pilgrims'. This is the key to Bunyan's handling of the episode. Christian is at his most helpless when he comes to the palace after a series of physically and emotionally draining experiences: the strenuous assent of Hill Difficulty; the disturbing encounter with Timorous and Mistrust; the far more disturbing discovery of his negligent loss of his roll, with its consequent 'great distress'; and finally, the ordeal of daring the lions. Never before on his pilgrimage have Christian's isolation and vulnerability been so evident, either to himself or to the reader. Nor has the sheer effort of keeping on, the demand on the will, been so much insisted on: up Hill Difficulty 'he fell from running to going, and from going to clambering upon his hands and his knees, because of the steepness of the place'; Timorous and Mistrust, with their tale of the lions, reduce him to a fearful quandary; night comes on as he retraces his steps to search for his roll, all the way sighing, weeping and chiding himself; it is fully dark as he resumes his way, 'bewayling his unhappy miscarriage' and haunted by the thought that the lions, who 'range in the night for their prey', might at any moment tear him in pieces; and it is 'trembling with fear' that he at last reaches the palace. He arrives, that is to say, lonely, 'weary and benighted', desperately in need of a refuge from the hostile world and of comfort against his own inadequacies. These the Palace Beautiful supplies. And the solace it offers the exhausted and hunted individual is that of companionship. Discretion, questioning Christian in the way of a Congregational church admitting a new member, calls 'two or three more of the Family' who welcome him 'in to the Family'. The entertainment is not only edificatory discourse, biblical reading and instruction; it is also supper, 'with fat things, and with Wine that was well refined' and rest in the Chamber called Peace whose 'windows opened towards the Sun rising'. By such administrations these 'good Companions' enable Christian to descry Immanuel's Land and send him on his way no longer so vulnerable but now armed 'lest perhaps he should meet with assaults'.[22]

Though misconstrued as the complicity of factious cliques and seditious cabals, this was the fellowship the Clarendon Code was designed to break. It did so in the most direct way possible: by destroying the families, homes and meeting houses of nonconformists. Fines were not only heavy but often ruinous. After paying fines totalling £100 the Devonshire minister Robert Collins had to sell his house and flee to Holland to maintain his family. When levied by distraint and sale of goods, such fines deprived families not only of comforts but often of essentials, even of the tools of the trade upon which their survival depended. Frequently, goods in excess of the fines were taken, but the surplus was rarely returned, for it was, of course, all profit to the informer: many

> have had their Houses broken open by the Informers, Constables, and other Officers, who, like so many *Dragoons*, have for a long time kept the Possession, plundring and stealing, as well as distreining their Goods: And what was taken under colour of Law, though of greater value than the Fine amounted to, yet no return has been made of the Overplus.

One Yorkshire informer contrived to amass £2,000 in 14 months by this trade.[23] Imprisonment of the head of the family for any length of time was alone sufficient to ruin poorer households. Grim though these penalties were, the shock and horror of the experience of raid and arrest could be as devastating. Meetings were frequently broken up with violence, the doors of private houses broken down, their occupants seized without warning at any time of the day or night, even from their beds, and driven, the old, sick, women, without preparation and no matter how far, to prison, their children left to fend for themselves. What might be coolly contemplated as a legal procedure to be undergone by an individual frequently proved in practice to be a frighteningly unpredictable and vicious physical and psychological assault on family and friends.[24]

If this forcible dismemberment of the nonconformist body was not to prove mortal it was crucial that a sense of fellowship, of belonging to a community, be maintained among individuals however long they might be separated or widely scattered. To endure the hardship of arrest and sentence was trial enough, and carried with it sufficient risk of apostasy; to suffer besides from a sense of abandonment, desolation and isolation would be an all but insupportable experience of betrayal. The Clarendon Code would have done its work and the fellowship would die. People in adversity have need of friends, but, when membership of a church has directly caused that adversity, for the church then to fail the sufferer would make a mockery of the sacrifice. Both to avoid, if possible, arrest and trial, and to mitigate its consequences, it was essential to maintain communication between the members of nonconformist churches, between particular churches and between the nonconformist body and the world which sought its extirpation.

At the most elementary and immediate level the security of meetings depended upon the vigilance and timely signal of look-outs. Often, though, the action of the authorities was anticipated before the arrival of officers. In 1665 it was reported to Joseph Williamson that it was extremely difficult to surprise any London conventicle since they were all so linked together that news of any warrant issued was sure to be known. Should members of a meeting nevertheless be arrested and committed, other resources were available. In prison, members of a particular church or of a communion seem not to have been separated, and might thus continue to enjoy mutual support and the fellowship of worship. In his autobiography Thomas Ellwood, for example, records many cases of Quakers supporting each other in prison not only spiritually but materially, those wealthier and with the benefit of relatives visiting them sharing their food and bedding with those less fortunate. Quakers especially seem often to have enjoyed the trust of their gaolers. Fox records a number of cases of Friends being granted temporary liberty, even to attend worship. When imprisoned in Bridewell, Ellwood, on his own undertaking to return, was allowed out to visit Friends imprisoned in Newgate. And from Ellwood we also learn that Quakers in London took the practical step of allocating each city prison to a few Friends so that, no matter where held, Quaker prisoners could be sure of provision, visitors and a means to convey messages to the world outside.[25]

Meanwhile, it was essential that the church, however depleted, should continue to meet. The simple act of meeting at all, in spite of persecution, was itself a declaration of the continuing identity of the church and of its resolve. It was a declaration consciously directed both to outsiders and to the church's own members. To the former it might act as a provocative declaration of war: Marvell in 1670 wrote of the harassment by 'the Train Bands in the City, and Soldiery in *Southwark* and Suburbs' of conventiclers who 'met in numerous open Assemblys, without any Dread of Government', that 'they wounded many, and killed some Quakers, *especially* while they took all patiently'. But this patience could speak more movingly, as we have heard Pepys testify. It was not only Quakers who were aware of the effectiveness of such witness: persecuted Christians, wrote Bunyan, should persevere 'in ways of godliness, both with respect to morals and also instituted worship ... [and] keep close to gospel worship, public and private'. The Bristol Baptist church at Broadmead was encouraged to continue public meetings specifically to win sympathy and converts.[26]

That 'the world' had to be denied occasion to deride and exult over nonconformists was a factor in Bunyan's determination on 12 November 1660 to attend a meeting at Samsell, a village about 13 miles from Bedford, in the full knowledge that to do so was to court arrest. His account of the event shows, however, that something else was uppermost in his mind. He might have avoided being taken since 'there was whispering that that day I should be taken, for there was a warrant out to take me'. When a friend, 'being somewhat timorous', counselled the prudence of absenting himself, Bunyan replied: 'By no means, I will not stir, neither will I have the meeting dismissed for this.

Come, be of good chear, let us not be daunted, our cause is good, we need not be ashamed of it'. His reflections after this exchange, when he 'walked into the close ... somewhat seriously considering the matter', though sensitive to the likely use which would be made of his absence by the world at large, centred rather upon the effect his withdrawal would have upon his own people:

> I had shewed myself hearty and couragious in my preaching, and had, blessed be Grace, made it my business to encourage others; therefore thought I, if I should now run, and make an escape, it will be of a very ill savour in the country. For what will my weak and newly converted brethren think of it? But that I was not so strong in deed, as I was in word. Also I feared that if I should run now there was a warrant out for me, I might by so doing make them afraid to stand, when great words only should be spoken to them ... if I should fly, it might be a discouragement to the whole body that might follow after. And further, I thought the world thereby would take occasion at my cowardliness, to have blasphemed the Gospel, and to have had some ground to suspect worse of me and my profession, than I deserved. ... I came in again to the house with a full resolution to keep the meeting.

'Great words only should be spoken to them': to attend the meeting and so allow himself to be silenced was Bunyan's most eloquent testimony to the world, but primarily his most moving sermon to his people.[27]

3   'DEARE FRIND MY DEARE LOUE SALUTS THEE'

It was, however, a sermon which could be preached only once: thereafter, other means had to be used. It was to writing that the nonconformists turned, as Paul had done in the earliest days of imprisonment and adversity. To the written word, above all else, was due the preservation of nonconformity. By this means, the letter of the law could be observed. Ministers might not only preach over a sermon several times to ensure their people could meet safely in small groups, but might also, like Obadiah Grew, have it transcribed 'to be read to four or more writers in short-hand, every Saturday night or Lord's day morning; and every one of these read it to four new men who transcribed it also: and so it was afterwards read at twenty several meetings'. But much more frequently, and much more significantly, it was by writing that nonconformists frustrated the dissevering intention of the Clarendon Code. By their letters they maintained a sense of community and fellowship despite being forcibly separated. The encouragement to the Broadmead church to continue public meetings mentioned above came in a letter written from prison in 1670 by Thomas Hardcastle, later its pastor. Two years afterwards, the church issued a circular letter encouraging steadfastness in its meetings. What was in 1765 published as Bunyan's *Relation of his Imprisonment* consisted of five reports or letters originally written by him from prison to encourage the Bedford congregation. During imprisonments in Aylesbury during the 1660s the Quaker Isaac Penington wrote regularly not only to his wife ('it was pretty hard to me to miss of a letter from thee on the Third-day' he confides when worried about her health), but to magistrates ('Why do ye persecute and afflict a man who desireth to live in the love and peace of God towards you? ... think what ye are doing ... Read *Is.* xxiv and *Rom.* ii 2, 9'), to neighbouring meetings, to relatives, to friends and to Friends ('Dear George [Fox], thou mayest knowest my wants and desires more fully than my own heart. Be helpful to me in tender love').[28]

Penington's correspondents included Ellwood, the man whom his own and his wife's example had drawn to Quakerism. Ellwood's *History* gives a fine indication of the value of such letters, especially to a young convert such as in 1661 he was. 'It was quickly known' in Oxford that an arrested Quaker was confined in the house of the city marshal: 'whereupon (the Men *Friends* being generally Prisoners already in the Castle) some of the Women-*Friends* came to enquire after me, and to visit me'. By them, 'an Account was soon given to the *Friends*, who were Prisoners in the Castle, of my being taken up', and one of these, Thomas Low (or Loe), the man who had unwittingly caused Ellwood's arraignment, wrote to him 'a very tender and affectionate Letter' of encouragement. 'Greatly was my Spirit refreshed, and my Heart gladded, at the Reading of this Consolatory Letter from my Friend', but when Penington also wrote from Aylesbury gaol, 'I had Cause ... to double, and redouble my thankful Acknowledgment to the Lord my God.' Such 'Epistolary Visits' were being made constantly to nonconformists, no matter where in the kingdom they might be imprisoned.[29]

The authorities were quick to realize what indefatigable correspondents nonconformist ministers and their people were. The rather ill-defined responsibilities of the Restoration Secretaries of State included, as those of Cromwell's Secretary John Thurloe had done, the gathering of intelligence at home and abroad and the dissemination of news for domestic consumption. To these ends they had a monopoly of newspaper publication, they operated an extensive spy network and they controlled the post, with authority to open mail. It was from intercepted letters that much of Whitehall's knowledge of non-conformist activities was culled:

> They watched at the Post-House for my Letters, to know with whom I corresponded in *England*, where they found several Letters of mine, when they opened them ... and if they did find any thing they could wrest to their turn, they did keep my Letters, and if they found nothing that could touch me, they caused to seal up my Letters again, to be delivered to me.

This was written by William Dundas, a Scottish Quaker, but his experience was not peculiar to Scotland. The confinement of Ellwood in 1661 came about after he found himself before the deputy-lieutenants of Oxfordshire because a letter he had written inviting the Oxford Quaker Thomas Low to attend a meeting in Ellwood's home town of Crowell, 'instead of being delivered according to its Direction, was seized, and carried (as I was told) to the Lord *Faulkland*, who was then called *Lord-Lieutenant* of that County'. Unbeknown to Ellwood, Low had already been committed to Oxford Castle in the campaign prompted by Venner's uprising, and in the period immediately following this 'mad Prank, of those infatuated *Fifth-Monarchy-Men*' the authorities were especially nervous and vigilant: 'hereupon Letters were intercepted, and broken open; for the Discovery of suspected *Plots*, and *Designs* against the Government.' But much later Vincent Alsop still thought it prudent on occasion to take the precaution of sending his letters unsigned.[30]

Marvell's regular letters to his Hull constituency illustrate just how wary one had need to be. He is habitually reticent, confining himself to mere rehearsal of parliamentary affairs without comment, and even then never saying all that he could. A cautious and cautionary note is repeatedly struck in the correspondence. Having, in a letter of 1670, written in some detail of parliamentary debates on taxation to George Acklam, mayor of Hull, he concludes:

> These things I have been thus carefull to giue you a plain account of, not thinking a perfunctory relation worthy your prudence but must in exchange desire you will not admit many inspectors into my letters. For I reckon your bench to be all as one person: whereas others might chance either not to understand or to put an ill construction upon this openesse of my writing & simplicity of my expression.

There is, indeed, an almost conspiratorial understanding between sender and recipient, not always merely implicit. To mayor William Shires Marvell wrote on 21 October 1672 that

> neither do I write deliberately any thing which I feare to haue divulged yet seeing it is possible that in writing to assured friends a man may giue his pen some liberty and the times are something criticall beside that I am naturally and now more by my Age inclined to keep my thoughts private, I desire that what I write down to you may not easily or unnecessarily returne to a third hand at London.

Finding, two weeks later, that what he had written was known in London, he warned 'there is some sentinell set both upon you and me. And to know it therefore is a sufficient caution.'[31]

To set beside Marvell's constituency correspondence his letters to his nephew William Popple is to realize just how bland and non-committal the former is. Popple elicits from Marvell far more pointed and more personal reflections upon the times. This we might expect. Not only did uncle and nephew enjoy an affectionate relationship, but Popple's political bias was Marvell's. He was the friend of Penn, and the man who wrote in his preface to what was probably his own English translation of Locke's *Letter concerning Toleration* (1689) 'Absolute liberty, just and true liberty, equal and impartial liberty, is the thing we stand in need of.' Whereas the full account of the provisions of the Second Conventicle Act Marvell sent to mayor John Tripp contains no word of comment, to Popple it is described as 'the terrible Bill ... the Quintessence of arbitrary Malice'. To Tripp Marvell merely reports as 'extraordinary' Charles's attendance at the Lords' debates in April 1670, for which the upper house tendered 'thanks for the honour he did them'; to

Popple, this is presented as an action which, though it had precedent, 'it is now so old, that it is new, and so disused that at any other, but so bewitched a Time, as this, it would have been looked on as a high Usurpation, a Breach of Privilege.' And yet even to Popple it is 'for some Reasons not fit to write' that Marvell in June 1672 expects an early peace with the Dutch:

> There was the other Day ... a severe Proclamation issued out against all who shall vent false News, or discourse ill concerning Affairs of State. So that in writing to you I run the Risque of making a Breach in the Commandment.[32]

In February 1662 Williamson received a copy of an intercepted Quaker letter 'containeing such suspicious expressiones' that the justices of Cockermouth, Cumberland, had felt bound to proceed to 'take the Examinacions of the Parties' and forward the result to London. What so aroused their suspicion was a letter from John Dixon, yeoman of Lowsewater, to Hugh Tickell, yeoman of Portinscale:

> deare frind my deare loue saluts thee & thy wife with the rest of thy famaly this is to sertifie thee of our *pro*seedings att ye month meettinge you are desired to seend your Collecttion y^t was for London with speed for it steayes for youres & mosdals [Mosedale's] and you must seend yt which is for our owen county seruis & it is ordered yt there be a Collectione this month for ye seruis of the truth & to be brought in to the next month meetinge att quartell [Quarry?] hill at Tho: Porters.

What, the justices wished to know, were these collections for? For the relief of the poor, for necessitous Friends overseas and for prisoners in Carlisle and elsewhere was the reply. And what was this monthly meeting's business? To discover who stands in need of relief. As the justices wrote to Williamson: 'Admitt their explanacion thereof bee truth & they as harmlesse & innocent people as they *pre*tend to bee.' 'Yett', they went on, their collections, meetings and journeys 'may give to[o] great an opp*or*tunity to malicious disatisfied spiritts through such like pr*e*tences to effect their daingerous designes to ye pr*e*iudice of the pr*e*sent Gou*er*nment'.[33]

This incident is telling evidence of the ability of the Quakers to maintain a corporate sense of identity through regular nationwide contacts, letters and the keeping of records. It was an organizational genius recognized at the time: a letter of 21 January 1661 from Hull to Sir Francis Cobb at Whitehall reported that

> in searching for Armes there was found at Risum [Rise?] in Holdernesse in a Quakers house diverse papers wherein it doth appeare that they have constant meetings & intelligence all over the Kingdome, & contributions for to carry on their horrid designes, though masked under the spetious pr*e*tence of Religion and piety ... they also keep Registers of all ye affronts & injuryes y^t is done to any of them, when, where & by whome. Therefore it doth appeare they are an actiue subtill people.

The inspiration behind this organization was Fox, who was directly responsible for founding the Meeting for Sufferings whose business it was to monitor the effect of persecution throughout the country, to identify Friends in need and to arrange their relief. Fox also, from an early date and repeatedly, stressed the importance of written records. What William Braithwaite called his 'historical instinct' ensured the preservation of a mass of letters, journals, minutes, records of sufferings and other papers of early Friends, material which was used by Fox himself in the composition of his *Journal*. The London Yearly Meeting in 1676 reminded county Monthly Meetings 'to keep an exact account among themselves of those that first brought the message of glad tydeings among them'. This was reiterated in 1680, and the Yearly Meeting for Sufferings in 1682 seconded the request to send reports to London. It was a process which culminated, early in the eighteenth century, in the published broadside *Directions to Collect Matters for a General History of the Entrance and Progress of Truth in this Age By Way of Annals*.[34]

Though most conspicuous and impressive in the case of the Quakers, this desire to identify, to maintain correspondence with and, eventually, to preserve the memory of the members of their fellowship is to be found also in other denominations. Baxter's voluminous correspondence evidences the same impulse, and it was precisely because he did not lose contact with the Bartholomeans that he was able to cast the later sections of his autobiography as an account of their shared experiences. The character sketches he wrote of many of those who 'suffered for not swearing, subscribing, declaring, conforming, and for refusing Re-ordination' as a 'duty which I owe to the honour of God's graces in them' were based not on 'hearsay, but personal acquaintance'.[35] In the successive editions of Calamy's *Abridgment* of Baxter's autobiography, this was the part of the *Reliquiae* which received the most generous treatment. In the first edition of 1702 the *Account of many ... of those Worthy Ministers who were ejected* (to quote the title-page) already occupied over half the volume. In the enlarged two-volume edition of 1713 the 'account' was given a volume to itself, and it was yet further augmented by the publication in 1727 of the two-volume *A Continuation of the Account* ... Nor was this impulse confined to biographical and autobiographical writings. Readers have supposed that in Mercy and Christiana Bunyan commemorated his first and second wives, that Great-heart was based upon a Parliamentarian officer or Puritan minister (perhaps Gifford) and that the allegorical figures of *The Holy War* (1682) included characterizations of contemporary nonconformists.[36]

4   'THE PRESS HATH A LOUDER VOICE THEN MINE'

As these examples indicate, to go into print was a natural and inevitable extension of this ubiquitous use of the pen in correspondence and records. If communication and writing were essential to the continuance of nonconformity, it was upon publication that its ultimate survival depended. Among the resources to which nonconformists turned to counter persecution the press was seized upon by all parties as the most potent and effective means by which to contradict the premises of persecution and to bring in a true verdict upon the behaviour of the oppressed. This is, in one way, as we should expect. It is a commonplace that the Reformation enjoyed one inestimable advantage denied medieval reform movements: the press. Within three years of voicing his initial misgivings in the manner of a medieval schoolman, Luther became a modern publicist. In 1517, when he nailed his hand-written, 95 Latin theses to the door of the church in Wittenberg Luther was, in the traditional way, inviting scholastic, private and oral debate upon his contentions. The publication of his three treatises of 1520, two of them in German, represented an epochal departure from this form of argument and of communication: it was an appeal to the public at large by the means of print. There would be no turning back: the subsequent course of the Reformation was to be charted by books. In England, it was in print, not in the schools or the cloister, that More and Tyndale argued it out; and it was in English, not in Latin. Thereafter, it was in print that each church declared, defended and promoted its distinctive doctrine and ecclesiology. Gentlemen poets might still disdain to publish ('the fault that I acknowledge in myself is to have descended to print anything in verse ... I wonder how I declined to it, and do not pardon myself' wrote Donne in 1612);[37] professional writers might continue to seek noble patronage; and scholars might yet prefer Latin: but by the seventeenth century no religious cause could make its way without the public as its patron, the vernacular its medium of expression and print its means of communication. For evidence of this we need only mention the extraordinary collection of over 22,000 tracts assembled by the bookseller George Thomason during the Civil War and Interregnum. Nor was this impulse merely polemical and controversial. The preponderance of works of homiletic, practical, devotional and casuistical divinity in earlier seventeenth-century booksellers' catalogues continued unchallenged in the later Term Catalogues.[38]

The nonconformists were, then, heirs to a literate, literary and bookish religious tradition. Their circumstances, however, gave them a particular incentive to publish. 'The Press', wrote Baxter explaining his own publications, 'hath a louder voice then mine',[39] and nonconformists had need of a voice which would carry far if they were to be heard from the exile – in prison, the provinces, or abroad – to which the Clarendon Code banished them. In their various kinds of seclusion, they could in writing come to terms with the events which had, apparently so finally, overthrown them; and through publication they could declare their continuing, and renewed, commitment despite those events, their willing submission to God's Providence. This commitment could use the printed book to refute the government's presentation of them as seditious rebels and episcopalian caricatures of them as hypocritical dissemblers. And, above all, by the printed word nonconformists could overcome the isolation and separation caused by the Clarendon Code and prevent the disintegration it intended.

The case of Ludlow, mentioned earlier, exemplifies the first of these motives, but in this Ludlow was entirely characteristic. It was precisely 'to set my self to writing, and do what Service I could for Posterity' that Baxter lived 'as much as I possibly could out of the world'. One of the first works he embarked upon was the autobiographical *Reliquiae Baxterianae* (1696), a comprehensive account of his own past in relation to the nation's past, the body of which is given to an exhaustive analysis of the events of 1660–2 and their aftermath. This account, written 'lest the fable pass for truth', is intended to vindicate the Presbyterians and evidence the injustice of their treatment, but it is also one man's reaffirmation of his commitment to the cause which had brought himself and his companions only disappointment and suffering, and of his confidence in it despite this experience.[40] This is no less the implicit burden of Bunyan's very different autobiography, *Grace Abounding to the Chief of Sinners* (1666). The very brevity of his treatment of his trial and imprisonment, which appear as a kind of coda to the book's main concern, Bunyan's conversion, cannot but imply their inconsequentiality, their total inability to jeopardize or call in question the saving experience of grace. Bunyan, as his readers well knew, wrote in prison: what of that? The structure of the book dismisses this mere circumstance as surely as its title. Certainly, imprisonment tests Bunyan's resolution, but this testing is constructive and creative, the final confirmation of the sincerity of his profession. He has in prison received so 'much conviction, instruction and understanding' that his readers may 'take encouragement, should the case be their own, *Not to fear what men can do unto them*'.[41]

Just so in his retirement Milton completed *Paradise Lost* and composed *Paradise Regained*, certainly, and *Samson Agonistes* almost certainly,[42] each of them centred on a hero under trial, two of them meditations upon apparent failure and defeat, and one a study of a man in prison oppressed by the apparent injustice of the ways of God. This was, indeed, Dryden's criticism of *Paradise Lost* ('his subject is not that of an heroic poem, properly so called. His design is the losing of our happiness, his event is not prosperous, like that of all other epic works'), as it was Ellwood's, whose objection, by his own account, that Milton had said a good deal about the loss of paradise but nothing of its regaining prompted the composition of the sequel.[43] Neither of them had taken the measure of the epic which, though not triumphant in traditional epic terms, wrests victory from defeat as surely as does Milton's Samson, finds, indeed, failure to be the condition of victory. The 'paradise within thee, happier far' is attainable only by fallen man, and, more specifically, by fallen man living in the time which Michael foresees when 'heavy persecution shall arise/ On all who in the worship persevere/ Of spirit and truth'.[44] And even in *Paradise Regained*, where the question of failure never arises, Milton's marvellously innovative and percipient psychological treatment stresses the positive benefits of trial by having the Messiah discover his true nature and mission through the course of the temptations in the wilderness. Although the final dismissal of Satan is a foregone conclusion, the full impact of that dismissal is not. The Christ, who, Milton insists, is, though 'exalted', a man, with the limitations that implies, is initially unsure of his vocation and course of action. He has no recollection of his earlier encounter with Satan upon the fields of Heaven, depends upon Mary for his knowledge of the events surrounding his birth and cannot foresee 'to what intent' he is led into the wilderness. Before encountering Satan, uncertain what it means to be the Son of God, he has turned over in his mind the course of his earlier life and has meditated upon the significance of Messiahship, 'Musing and much revolving in his breast/ How best the mighty work he might begin'. What ensues in the course of his trial – a trial in which his isolation and defencelessness are stressed, notably in the storm – is a process of revelation ('For what concerns my knowledge God reveals').[45] So it is too for Satan, who engages this man precisely to discover his true nature and identity ('Who this is we must learn ...'). The resolution of the final temptation of the Temple (Milton's purpose requires the Lucan rather than the Matthaean order) thus becomes not only a rejection of Satan and a refusal to test God, but also an affirmative declaration of self-discovery, of divine identity. It is, for protagonist, antagonist and reader alike, a moment of epiphany compressed into a line of stunning finality:

Tempt not the Lord thy God, he said and stood

That final monosyllable comprises the thrust not merely of this poem but of every nonconformist meditation upon the course of individual lives, the challenge of trial and the meaning of vocation held by the defenceless. Neither in abandoning, nor in defying, still less in challenging, but in trusting God the persecuted might withstand Satan's assaults as surely as this 'perfect man' stood where it was impossible to stand. And then there is the consequence:

But Satan smitten with amazement fell.[46]

Men who found their future so contrary to what they had worked and prayed for might well scrutinize their past, but Bunyan clearly has his eye also on the present. He writes, as we heard him say, to encourage those who might be, or who might be fearful of being, in a like case. Introspection in nonconformist writing is never merely backward or inward looking, never merely a private business; it is a means to restore the confidence of others. Self-renewal, the affirmation that, in Milton's words, 'I sing ... unchanged', was more than an individual's boast, a personal cry of defiance at the government; it was a service to the nonconformist body which tended, as Baxter said of the purpose of his Kidderminster farewell sermon, to its 'strength & stedfastness'.[47] Nor was it merely a defensive reaction. Often such personal testimony was vigorously offensive. This was particularly so in accounts of trials and imprisonments which were frequently not only immediately written but immediately printed. Publication of the undaunted bearing of defendants and prisoners was certainly intended to inspire, but such pamphlets essayed also the larger task of influencing public opinion by setting against the official record an experiential account of the persecutors' proceedings. Of this, Penn and Mead's account of their Old Bailey trial in 1670 is a capital example.

Their report of this trial justifies its publication in the following terms: 'well knowing, how industrious some will be, to misrepresent this Tryal to the disadvantage of the Cause and the Prisoners, it was thought requisite, in defence of both, and for the satisfaction of the People, to make it more publick.' 'The People' here would include Quakers facing the possibility of similar treatment, but were primarly the public at large. The preface is addressed not to Penn's co-religionists but 'To the English Reader' and appeals not to particular religious convictions but to the patriotism and fundamental rights of his fellow citizens. Penn appears not as a Quaker but as a wronged Englishman. The denial of *his* right to 'Religious Liberty [and] civil Freedom (as if to be a Christian and an English-man were inconsistent)' is an attack upon the rights of all, and therefore concerns the reader, whatever his religious persuasion:

> *How much thou art concern'd in this ensuing* Tryal *(where not only the Prisoners, but the Fundamental Laws of England, have been most Arbitrarily Arraigned)* read, and thou may'st plainly judg ... O! *What monstrous and illegal Proceedings are these? who reasonably can call his Coat his own,* when Property is made subservient to the Will and Interest of his Judges? *Or, who can truly esteem himself a Free-man,* when all Pleas for Liberty are esteem'd Sedition, *and the Laws that give, and maintain them so many unsignificant pieces of Formality?*[48]

It is this general appeal which inspirits the account. Penn takes his stand not on Quakerism (which would have denied him a hearing with many) but upon the ancient rights of Englishmen. Charged under common law with perpetrating a riot (that is, with holding a meeting for some 300 people in Grace-church Street, London), Penn pressed the judge to explain the legal justification for the indictment. The answer 'Upon the Common Law' did not satisfy him: 'Where is that Common Law?' To this the recorder, Thomas Howell, (understandably) replied that he could not 'run up so many years, and over so many adjudged Cases, which we call Common Law, to answer your curiosity', but Penn, in one of what Marvell called his 'very pertinent' replies, retorted 'if it be Common, it should not be so hard to produce' and he refused to plead until convinced the charge was legal. He capped the exchange with fine wit:

> *Rec.* You are an impertinent Fellow; will you teach the Court what Law is? It's *Lex non scripta*, that which many have studied thirty or forty years to know, and would you have me to tell you in a moment?
>
> *Penn.* Certainly; If the Common Law be so hard to be understood, it's far from being very common.

This hint of arbitrary proceedings Penn then enlarged into an outright attack on the liberty of the subject. 'Is this Justice or true Judgment? Must I therefore be taken away, because I plead for the Fundamental Laws of *England*?' He conjured up for the jury the prospect of anarchic tyranny:

> Certainly our Liberties are openly to be invaded, our Wives to be ravished, our Children slaved, our Families ruined, and our Estates led away in Triumph, by every sturdy Beggar and malicious Informer, as their Trophes, but our (pretended) Forfeits for Conscience sake.

The rhetoric may seem extreme, but the judge came in right on cue:

> Till now I never understood the reason of the Policy and Prudence of the *Spaniards*, in suffering the Inquisition among them: And certainly it will never be well with us, till something like unto the *Spanish* Inquisition be in *England*

These words from the pamphlet especially outraged Marvell, and would be recalled by him in *The Rehearsal Transpros'd*. An extraordinarily foolish utterance from the point of view of the prosecution, they could, for the rhetorical strategy of the report, hardly be bettered: as Penn has presented himself as a free-born Englishman, so the judge adopts the persona of tyrannical Inquisitor. Penn's parting shot reinforces the point: 'I can never plead the fundamental Laws of *England*, but you cry, Take him away, take him away. But it is no wonder, since the *Spanish* Inquisition hath so great a place in the Recorder's Heart.'[49]

Though acquitted on the main charge, Penn and Mead were imprisoned until fines for contempt were paid. Penn justified his refusal to submit on the grounds that he could not be silent in 'a Case wherein I am so much concerned, and not only my self, but many Ten thousand Families beside'. Publication of the trial ensured those many thousands could hear how Penn had spoken not merely in his own but in their defence. It is acquittal at the bar of public opinion which is sought. When arrested and imprisoned at Lancaster in 1660, Fox issued *The Summ of Such Particulars as are Charged against George Fox in the Mittimus by which he stands Committed: Together with George Fox his answers to the said Particulars*, a public vindication of himself and an appeal beyond the courts of law. This motive to publication is still more explicit in the account of the 1665 trial of Quakers at Northampton, which concludes: 'And now all moderate People may judge, whether here is any matter of Fact proved, or found to be done (by the aforesaid Innocent harmless People) against the King, or that might make for the disturbance of the peace of the Kingdom.'[50] The titles of this and similar tracts make clear this appeal to the common English sense of justice: *The Voice of the Innocent uttered forth; Or, The Call of the Harmless and Oppressed for Iustice and Equity* (1665); *The Peoples Antient and Just Liberties Asserted* (1670); *Another Out-cry of the Innocent & Oppressed. Being a true Account of the unjust and illegal proceedings of Richard Rainsford and Roger Norwich, and others* (1665): E[dward] B[illing], *A Faithful Testimony for God & my Country: Or, Retro-spective Glass for the Legislators And the rest of the Sons of the Church of England, (so called) Who are Persecuting the Innocent* (1664).

As this last example shows, pamphlets might to the same end be more particularly addressed to episcopalian divines and to members of parliament. From Reading gaol the Quaker Benjamin Coale issued a pointed plea for toleration in his challenge *To the Bishops and their Ministers* (1671). Imprisonment might confine Coale himself, but in print he could nevertheless make 'a Visitation unto unto [*sic*] you all, that you may consider what you are doing' Such pamphlets were often of a controversial, rather than a journalistic, nature, but might, like Baxter's series *The Nonconformists Plea for Peace* (1679), its *Second Part* (1680) and *Defence* (1680), draw evidence from actual cases of suffering. 'Knowing how many are apt to take things upon trust' and that the Quakers 'are People so generally Reproached' was the justification Robert Barclay offered for a public defence in one of his controversial pieces, but Quaker writings, especially in the earlier years of the Restoration period, more commonly took the form of jeremiads, lamentations, denunciations and prophetic warnings, reminding parliament, bishops and lawyers of their subordinate, fallible status, chastening them with Old Testament examples of vengeance on the cruel and the corrupt, and predicting the time when these persecuting justicers should appear at 'the Barr of [God's] Divine Judgement ... to give a True, Just and Clear answer to the True and Infallible Bill of Indictment preferred against you by the Infallible witness of the Eternal Light of the Everlasting God in your Consciences, which Bill will be found against you by the Grand Jury of Gods holy Martyrs'.[51]

To influence opinion such pamphlets might have a still more specific reference and be directed to particular officers, to members of parliament, or to the king himself. In 1664 the Quaker William Stout published *The Innocency and Conscientiousness of the Quakers Asserted and Cleared from the Evil Surmises ... of Judge Keeling.* John Owen sought to prevent the passage through the Lords of the Second Conventicle Act by *The State of the Kingdom with Respect to the present Bill against Conventicles,* and John Humfrey, like his friend Baxter an advocate of comprehension and 'though a Nonconformist minister, a Conformist parishioner', endeavoured to influence the Revolution settlement by having copies of his single quarto sheet *Advice Before It Be too Late* ([1689]) handed to members of the Convention Parliament.[52] From the Tower the Quaker Charles Bayley was in 1665 prompted by the Plague to make public an earlier appeal to Charles II in *The Causes of Gods Wrath Against England: And a Faithful Warning from the Lord to Speedy Repentence; Fore-told by, and delivered in, a Letter to the King, Dated the 4th of the 7th month 1663.*

Often though, the address was more intimate. Fox was throughout his life an indefatigable correspondent and pamphleteer, addressing himself, in the manner of the examples just cited, to the king, to judges, magistrates, priests, as occasion demanded: but he also, and most frequently, wrote to and for Quakers suffering under persecution. He was intimately familiar with Friends at home and abroad, not only (and most obviously) because of his ceaseless itinerant ministry but also (and perhaps more extensively) because of a lifelong exchange of letters. In 1698 the Second Day's Morning Meeting was able to issue a collection of over 400 of them, a mere fraction of those available. Fox's last service was to ensure that this channel of communication should not be closed by his death. In a posthumously opened letter he directed 'All Friends in all the world, that used to write to me of all manner of things and passages, and I did answer them – let them all write to the Second-day's Meeting in London ... and the Second-day's Meeting in London for them to answer them in the wisdom of God'.[53]

Fox did not, however, restrict himself to private letters: he also issued frequent general, often printed, pastoral epistles and pamphlets to encourage and advise congregations deprived of their leaders. 'It was upon me to write a few lines to Friends to strengthen and encourage them to stand fast in their testimony, and bear, with Christian patience and content, the suffering that was coming upon them.' This was in 1670, but it might have been almost any year in his life since 1650, when he first 'writ a few lines for the comfort and encouragement of the faithful'. His many imprisonments served only to free him to make this service his most immediate concern, 'For Paul wrote epistles to the saints, though he was in prison.' Fox's account of his detention in 1674 illustrates this connection between confinement and composition: 'During the time of my imprisonment in Worcester ... I writ several books for the press ... Besides these I writ many papers and epistles to Friends to encourage and strengthen them in their service for God.'[54]

This pastoral motive and Pauline precedent might inspire far more substantial works. Though hardly a letter, Bunyan's *Grace Abounding* echoes in its title a Pauline prison epistle of encouragement to the persecuted (I. Tim. i.14–15) and is similarly addressed 'to those whom God hath counted him worthy to beget to Faith, by his Ministry in the Word'. Publishing, that is to say, offers Bunyan a way to continue the ministry Kelynge's application of 35 Eliz. would prevent:

> *Children, Grace be with you,* Amen. *I being taken from you in presence, and so tied up, that I cannot perform that duty that from God doth lie upon me, to you-ward, for your further edifying and building up in Faith and Holiness,* &c., *yet that you may see my Soul hath fatherly care and desire after your spiritual and everlasting welfare; I now once again, as before from the top of* Shenir *and* Hermon, *so now from* the Lions Dens, *and from* the Mountains of the Leopards (*Song* 4.8), *do look yet after you all, greatly longing to see your safe arrival into* THE *desired haven.*

Bunyan had learned at his trial that '*The Philistians understand me not.*' No matter: though '*I stick between the Teeth of the Lions in the Wilderness*', the bond between himself and his people is not broken; and they will understand him. The relationship, indeed, continued so close through over ten years' imprisonment that even before his release in 1672 Bunyan was elected pastor of the Bedford church. If writing *Grace Abounding* was a consolation to Bunyan himself, its publication was a relief to the frustration of his silencing. He might take comfort not only from recording his spiritual experience, and so bringing *'fresh into my mind the rememberance of my great help, my great support from Heaven, and the great grace that* God *extended to such a Wretch as I'*, but also from the opportunity this provided to serve, express his concern for and talk to those he loved.[55]

Such an address, and such a text, maintained the sense of community the Clarendon Code would fragment. Just so, from York Castle William Dewsbury issued prophetic, admonitory and hortatory letters to fellow Quakers to be 'sent abroad to be read, in the fear of the Lord, in the holy Assemblies of the Church of the first born, where she is scattered to the ends of the Earth'. *The Word of the Lord, To his beloved Citty New-Ierusalem* ([1663]) restores to those so scattered, frightened and in danger of apostasizing their sense of purpose and identity as God's chosen: 'Oh come away, come away, out of all your thoughts, desires, doubts, and unbeleife, which would turn you aside from the enjoyment of the dear love of God in Christ Jesus.' Dewsbury's main theme is 'the unspeakable love of God in *Christ Jesus* the Husband of the Bride, the Lambs Wife' which will *'deliver his Captives, and establish them in his glorious freedom'*, and his main purpose is to ensure the survival of particular meetings: *'All feel the love of God enlarging your hearts one to another, that the strong may bear the burthen of the weak.'* The same concern informs the writings of church members as well as those of their pastors. The *True and Faithful Relation from the People of God (called) Quakers, in Colchester* (1664), having detailed their sufferings, affirms

> yet our keeper is the Lord of Hosts, and we cannot but testify to all our brethren every where, to whom this Relation shall come, that he hath been abundantly good unto us, and hath sweetned our cup of bitter tribulation unto us aboundantly, and our strength and courage have not failed.

This does not merely keep the brethren informed: it encourages them to remain brethren with its assurance that though persecution may seem fearful it is not insupportable. John Samm would have all Quakers enjoy a still more fervent rapture of love despite all adverse circumstances. 'Oh! drink a full draught with me', he implores, 'for I am as if I were sick with love: Oh! the weight of the glorious love of my God with me feel ... that your tongue may be touched and your lips may be opened that living songs and Hallelujahs may arise.' 'Oh! be not daunted or dismayed although the Sea may swell, the Lion like nature roar, and the Devil may rage', for, he insists, 'they shall never prevail against the least Babes, as they abide in the faith,' The real force of these exhortations is, though, reserved for the close of the tract, where we are told, what was never hinted at in the text, that it was *'Given forth in the pure love and fear of God, in the County Gaole of* Northampton, *being twelve steps under ground.'*[56]

The printed word might restore a relationship even more intimate than that of church fellowship. Bunyan addressed *Grace Abounding* to his 'children', like Paul in his epistles establishing a familial and parental relationship to his congregation, but actual, as well as spiritual, fathers, husbands and mothers addressed their relations in print. In the Tower in 1660 Hugh Peter wrote to his daughter Elizabeth *A Dying Father's Last Legacy to an Only Child*, recommending her to pursue a retired life, uninvolved in the vain world. Lucy Hutchinson wrote (though she did not publish) her *Memoir* of her regicide husband John Hutchinson for her children, to restore to them the father imprisonment, obloquy and death had taken from them. Nor were such pieces always the product of the reflective aftermath of persecution. At the close of a vituperative and humorous attack on episcopacy in the prefatory epistle to *More News from Rome* (1664), dedicated, somewhat oddly it had seemed, to his wife, Ralph Wallis's tone suddenly softens in a moving attempt to span the distance persecution has put between them:

> *I am the more large in my Epistle, not having seen your face nor my Childrens a long time, whilst head and heart hath stood almost an hundred miles asunder; not knowing when I may, I take leave; and the good-will of Him that dwelt in the Bush be with you and yours: which is the desire of your truly affectional Husband.*[57]

It is an entirely personal moment, so that the reader becomes suddenly an intrusive outsider. And we may conjecture that Wallis cast the pamphlet itself in the form of a dialogue between a man and his wife for personal reasons as well as for satirical and polemical effect. Though prevented from joining his wife and risking detection should he write to her, he may yet express himself as if to her. Furthermore, he does so in just that situation of trust and calm he has been driven from. That the two talk over topical affairs together alone in their house, in bed at night, creates an impression of mutual support, of companionship, of an island of sanity in a world of rabid bishops, fanatical persecutors and grotesque Romish superstitions. It recreates and re-establishes in writing that relationship broken by persecution.

Out of the circumstances of persecution there thus comes a tract which, though scurrilously and abusively in that tradition which goes back to Martin Marprelate, is affirmative as well as derisive: while it defames, berates and ridicules the Restoration authorities, it contains within itself the experiential justification for its outrage. What it affirms is entirely characteristic of the nonconformist response to persecution. The Clarendon Code bribed friends to betray friends, forcibly dispersed meetings, broke open houses, split families, ruined households, in short, despoiled the fruits and perverted the bonds of creaturely affection. Nonconformists replied with a firm confidence in the capacity of those bonds to withstand the strain. Though in a very different key to Wallis, Milton, at the close of *Paradise Lost*, restores to each other another husband and wife whom greed, deception and malevolent scheming had separated. It is together, hand in hand, that Adam and Eve go to encounter the world beyond Eden. To walk holding hands it is necessary to walk side by side. Milton's epic culminates not in Adam leading Eve from paradise but in an image of equal companionship, of a relationship restored and enduring, through grace, despite the machinations of Satan. The greatest poem of the age shares with the least nonconformist tract a belief in the sanctity of human affection, a belief for which we will look in vain in the brittle world of marital discord in Restoration drama. And, furthermore, both the blind poet, 'fallen on evil days', and the hunted pamphleteer, separated from wife and family, shared with imprisoned ministers and persecuted nonconformists the conviction that it was by the written and printed word they could best safeguard not only the 'link of nature' but also the fellowship of the just.

Chapter 3 'Truth shall retire'
nonconformity and the press

Write the things which thou hast seen, and the things which are,
and the things which shall be hereafter.

Rev. i. 19

I LICENCES, LIBELS AND BONFIRES

'*Preachers* may be silenced or banished, when *Books* may be at hand.'[1] That the press might be the preservation of nonconformity under persecution the authorities realized quite as well as Baxter. They had not, however, denied to Presbyterians and Independents the pulpits of the established church, nor to all nonconformists the right to gather, merely in order to allow them to propagate their views in print. If literary composition and publication were the lifeline of nonconformity, it was a lifeline the authorities were determined to cut. Throughout our period, nonconformist writers, printers and publishers were in conflict with a government resolved to frustrate and prevent their endeavours.

There was nothing novel about the introduction of censorship. On the contrary, this, as Milton observed, had been the immediate response to the challenge of Wycliffe and Lollardy: in 1408 all unapproved biblical translation was banned and all manuscripts intended for copying were required first to be submitted to ecclesiastical censors for scrutiny. The renewed challenge posed by the appearance of Lutheran books in England in the 1520s ensured that, from its earliest days, printing too would be subject to ecclesiastically controlled censorship. Despite the political and religious revolutions of the next 170 years the policy towards the press of those in power under Tudors and Stuarts was remarkably consistent: to suppress what they regarded as heretical and seditious. No matter the prevailing temper of sovereign , parliament or established church: Roman Catholics, English episcopalians and Puritans alike successively took up and refined the censorship machinery of their predecessors. On the assumption that the right to control the press fell within the royal prerogative, this consisted initially, under Henry VIII, simply of royal proclamations, a steady stream of which were issued in the 1530s and 1540s. These were at first directed exclusively against heretical books, but by 1538 no book in England was to be printed without both the pre-publication authorization of the king, a member of the Privy Council, or a bishop, and its printer's name on the imprint.[2]

This *ad hoc* arrangement was in 1557 regularized and considerably better organized by the charter incorporating the Stationers' Company.[3] By this charter the government turned to its purpose the self-interest of those most concerned with, and knowledgeable about, printing and publication. It granted the Company a monopoly of printing and the right both to search for unregistered presses and books and to proceed against offenders. Though strictly the Company pursued printers operating outside its control, in practice it was 'a detective agency intended to assist in the uprooting of heresy and sedition'. In order to safeguard printing for its members, no book could be printed until it had been 'licensed', 'allowed', or 'tolerated' by one of the two Wardens of the Company and (for a fee) 'entered' in the Company's Register.[4] This entry constituted a record of copyright, which was then vested not in the author but in the owner of the copy (however he might have come by it). Not until 1710 would there be a Copyright Act in the modern sense. The Wardens, however, would so license and enter only manuscripts which had already been (rather confusingly) 'licensed' by authority. Although the Wardens themselves sometimes exercised this authority, the external censors were, by the Injunctions of 1559, specified as: the queen; six members of the Privy Council; or any two of the Archbishops of Canterbury and York, the Bishop of London, the Chancellors of Oxford and Cambridge, and the Bishop and Archdeacon of the place of printing. This generally meant that the Bishop of London and one other acted, and their imprimatur was required to be printed at the end of every published work 'for a testimonye of the allowance thereof', though in fact very few books actually carried it.[5]

Since, then, an unentered book would also be an unlicensed book, in seeking out the former to protect its own interest the Stationers' Company's searchers at the same time sought out the latter in the government's interest. The government, which had realized it 'could no longer control the press without the aid of a specialized and interested organisation', thus found in the incorporation of the Company 'a means of obtaining further control over the all-powerful and obnoxious printing press'. When, on 10 November 1559, Elizabeth confirmed the charter granted by her predecessor, Mary, she subscribed to Mary's avowed intention which was, by granting the charter, to 'provide a suitable remedy' to deal with the 'seditious and heretical books rhymes and treatises ... daily published and printed by divers scandalous malicious schismatical and heretical persons, not only moving our subjects and lieges to sedition and disobedience against us ... but also to renew and move very great and detestable heresies against the faith and sound catholic doctrine of Holy Mother Church'.[6] The Company was still more openly identified as an executive agent of the government by the Decree of 1566 issued by the prerogative court of Star Chamber, the judicial arm of the Privy Council. This empowered it to search for, seize and destroy any books offensive to the government and printed contrary to the law of the land. In 1576 the Company appointed 12 pairs of searchers who were between them to inspect every London printing house once a week. This right to search was reaffirmed by a further Decree 20 years later, which simplified the licensing process by designating as censors of any book 'before the ymprintinge' the Archbishop of Canterbury and the Bishop of London. These two between them could not pretend to read every manuscript intended for the press; the task was informally delegated to their chaplains and, by Archbishop Whitgift in 1588, to a panel of 12 clerics. The 1586 Decree also prohibited the setting up of any new press anywhere save in London, and only there with episcopal permission.[7]

This machinery was given its fine tuning by the Star Chamber Decree of 1637. Like that of 1586 its provisions dealt with both the printing and the licensing of books, but its 33 clauses were far more exact and comprehensive, taking in also the retailing of books. As regards the first, it limited to 20 the number of permitted master printers in Oxford, Cambridge and London, and to two the number of presses worked by each. No vacancy (deemed to have occurred only on a printer's death) could be filled without episcopal approval, and every printer had to undertake not to deal in unlicensed texts. As far as licensing was concerned, the pre-publication licensing and entering of books continued to be obligatory, but the Decree now required the submission of two copies of every manuscript (one to be retained to ensure no alterations were made to the copy between licensing and printing), the relicensing of any subsequent reprint and the printing in published copies of both the licence and the names of author, printer and publisher (or 'bookseller' as he was generally called in contemporary terminology). The Company's right to search for both unlicensed and unentered books was reaffirmed, and the censors were now more carefully designated: books on law fell to the Chief Justice or Chief Baron; on history or affairs of state to a principal Secretary of State; on heraldry to the Earl Marshal; books printed at Oxford and Cambridge to the respective Chancellors of the universities; and all other books to the Archbishop of Canterbury or the Bishop of London, or their appointees. And, finally, the right to sell books was withdrawn from shopkeepers in general and confined to members of the Stationers' Company; foreigners were prohibited from retailing books and no English books were to be printed abroad; all imported books were to be landed at London and opened only by an official of the Company and a cleric.[8]

In July 1641 the court of Star Chamber was abolished, and with it went the censorship founded on its prerogative authority. The respite was, however, but brief, and slowly but surely the elaborate 1637 apparatus was set back in place. The sudden upsurge in printing not only, to the Company's alarm, often infringed copyright and broke its monopoly, but also, to the alarm of the Long Parliament, disseminated ideas too heterodox, radical, or subversive for its liking. In June 1643, partly under pressure from the Company, the Parliament passed *An Ordinance for the Regulating of Printing*, which restored the substance of the 1637 Decree (though without specifying licensers or restricting the number of presses). This was the occasion of Milton's *Areopagitica*, one of many pleas for liberty of the press to be heard in the early 1640s from such Leveller and radical pamphleteers as William Walwyn, Richard Overton and John Lilburne. Despite this campaign, a further *Ordinance against Unlicensed or Scandalous Pamphlets*, passed in 1647, specified penalties for offenders. This was followed by *An Act against Unlicensed and Scandalous Books and Pamphlets and for better regulating Printing* (1649, revised in 1653) which, at least, did not resort to the hideous physical punishments meted out by the Star Chamber.[9]

Where the Long Parliament and Commonwealth had feared to tread the Cavalier Parliament was not likely to venture. The Restoration authorities quickly showed they had no intention to be more liberal than earlier regimes. Books by Milton and by his fellow republican and Arminian John Goodwin were burned by proclamation in August 1660, and thereafter Charles and his successors continued to the end of the century and beyond to issue regulatory press proclamations, directed usually against specific titles.[10] These, however, were inconsequential compared to the *Act for Preventing the Frequent Abuses in Printing Seditious, Treasonable and Unlicensed Books and Pamphlets, and for Regulating of Printing and Printing Presses*, which received the royal assent on the same day as the Act of Uniformity, 19 May 1662. On 10 June, when it came into force, 'The clock was put firmly back to 1637.' Since it was enacted by the king in parliament the Act could lay claim to greater authority than earlier pronouncements based on the royal prerogative alone or on the sole authority of the House of Commons, but little else distinguished it. Its drafters, thinking still in Tudor terms, readopted the provisions of the 1637 Decree, itself based on the Decree of 1586. The Act prohibited the printing of unlicensed and unentered books and reappointed the 1637 censors; it required the licence to be printed at the beginning of every book (whence 'Licensing Act'); it reimposed the limit of 20 on the number of master printers (with a maximum of two presses and two apprentices each) and of four on the number of type founders, all to be appointed by the Archbishop of Canterbury or the Bishop of London; and it reaffirmed the company's right to search, now additionally empowering the Secretaries of State to issue general search warrants.[11]

This Act (14 Car. II, cap. 33) lapsed on 13 March 1679, and for a few years there was a period comparable to the freedom of the early 1640s. There was an immediate drop in the number of entries in the Stationers' Company's Register and an immediate increase in the number of works printed. This, as Christopher Hill has pointed out, was the period of Bunyan's major works, but the predominant temper of most of the material published during these years was controversial and polemical. Nonconformists who had hitherto been unable legally to argue their case in print ('while men have call'd to us [*What is it that you would have?*] ... they would not give us leave to tell them' wrote Baxter) now engaged vigorously in its defence. Baxter's *Nonconformists Plea for Peace* (1679) was not only the first of his many apologetic pieces but was also one of the earliest books in a sustained and ramifying literary controversy which came to involve men of every party and which was hardly silenced until 1688.[12] The lapse in 1679 occurred because of the more pressing preoccupations of the First Exclusionist Parliament, and that the 'explosion of polemical pamphleteering', as one historian has called it, coincided with the Exclusion Crisis only increased its intensity. Nonconformist authors, printers and booksellers were active in the political campaigning and controversies surrounding the elections to, and policies of, the Exclusion Parliaments, and such newspapers as the Baptist Francis Smith's *Protestant Intelligence, Domestick and Foreign* were begun in rivalry to the official *London Gazette*. The government's response was judicial suppression; a series of proclamations; the counter-attack of Sir Roger L'Estrange's newspaper *The Observator*, which began publication in 1681; and, eventually, the renewal of the Licensing Act in 1685.[13]

After a futher renewal in 1693 the Act finally expired on 3 May 1695. That it was then allowed to do so seems, however, to have been due less to any parliamentary desire for press freedom than to recognition of the Act's ineffectiveness, to the needs of commercial enterprise and to the Whig campaign to discredit the Tory Secretary of State, Daniel Finch, Earl of Nottingham.[14] There were liberal ideas abroad. The Whig and deist Charles Blount had, in his *Just Vindication of Learning* (1679), condemned censorship as 'an old Relique of Popery' and rehearsed against it the arguments of Milton, who was never more the prophet he claimed to be in the headnote to 'Lycidas' than in *Areopagitica*. Blount wrote with all of Milton's anti-clericalism, and with something of his pointed scorn: censorship

> reflects upon our Church and Clergy, of whose Labours we should hope better, and of the Proficiency which their Flock reaps by them; than after all this Light of the Gospel, all this continual Preaching, they should be still frequented with such an unprincipled, unedifyed and laick Rabble, as that the Whiff of every new Pamphlet should stagger them out of their Catechism and Christian Walking. This may have much Reason to stagger and discourage the Ministers, when such a low Conceit is had of all their Exhortations, and Benefiting of their Hearers, as that they are not thought fit to be turned loose to three Sheets of Paper, witout a License; that all the Sermons, all the Lectures, preached, printed, and vented in such Numbers and such Volumes, should not be Armour sufficient against one single *Enchiridion* unlicensed.

At the time of the 1693 debates on the Act's renewal Blount returned to the Miltonic argument that 'Licensing and Persecution of Conscience are two Sisters that ever go Hand in Hand together' in *Reasons Humbly Offered for the Liberty of Unlicensed Printing* (1693), which was seconded by an anonymous *Supplement* (1693). And Locke, who had supported the Act's expiration in 1693, in 1694 drew up a 'Memorandum' of arguments against its further renewal which resented the allowance of only such books as chimed with the 'humours' of the government of the day, the exercise of ecclesiastical control over men's minds and the authority to search private premises upon mere suspicion (Locke's own papers had in 1681 been confiscated during the Exclusion Crisis). But even Locke laid a pragmatic emphasis on the commercial disincentives of the Act and certainly did not envisage a completely free press: 'I know not why a man should not have liberty to print whatever he would speak; and to be answerable for the one, just as he is for the other, if he transgresses the law in either.'[15]

Locke here touches on one of the strongest arguments against the renewal of the Licensing Act: there was without it a body of statute and common law quite sufficient to control the press. Of this the judiciary has been well aware ever since the Restoration. When the stationer Thomas Brewster, the printer Simon Dover and the bookbinder Nathan Brooks were tried in 1664 for seditious publication, they were indicted at common law, not charged under the Act. In his summing up, Chief Justice Sir Robert Hyde declared: 'by the course of the common law before this new act was made, for a printer or any other ... to publish that which is a reproach to the king, to the state, to the church, nay to a particular person, it is a misdemeanour.'[16] Common throughout our period, this course was the only one to take during the period of the Act's lapse. Between 1679 and 1685 the Tory campaign to break the opposition involved, amongst others, the 1680 trials for libel of the Baptist stationers Benjamin Harris and Francis Smith (both publishers of Bunyan) and of Jane Curtis; the trial of Henry Carr (or Care) for his newspaper *The Weekly Pacquet of Advice from Rome*, also in 1680; and the 1685 trial of Baxter for seditious libel.[17]

On defamation, slander, libel and sedition the law was at once remarkably vague and remarkably comprehensive. This was what made it so serviceable: it cast a far wider net than the Licensing Act, which enabled the prosecution only of the printers of unlicensed books. Restoration courts continued to act on the Star Chamber principle that any adverse reflection upon the sovereign, government, or established church was malicious and culpable since it fostered discontent, if not subversion and sedition.[18] Furthermore, to assist in the dissemination of such comment by any means was as criminal as to originate it. In the case against Harris, Scroggs ruled that 'all persons that do write, or print, or sell' scandalous or malicious material were equally guilty. In the case against Brewster, Hyde would not admit the defence that publication was the defendant's trade and that no bookseller could be familiar with every page of his stock.[19]

Few other lines of defence were available. The accuracy or truthfulness of the offensive text was immaterial. At Carr's trial Jeffreys declared that 'no persons whatsoever may expose to the public knowledge any manner of intelligence' without authorization. Nor need criticism be explicit. Baxter's defence counsel, Richard Wallop, argued that, as there was in Baxter's *Paraphrase* no explicit reference to the Church of England or its clergy in the glosses on priestly hypocrisy, formalism and persecution, 'they who drew the information, were the libellers, in applying to the prelates of the Church of England those severe things.' Jeffreys was not impressed by this deft substitution of the indictment for Baxter's text as the libellous document ('Mr. Wallop I observe you are in all these dirty causes') nor by the suggestion that the libel was in the mind not of Baxter but of the prosecution. Though Wallop claimed 'there was no colour' for the alleged 'innuendos' since the glosses were 'natural deductions from the text', Jeffreys preferred to deduce from the character of the defendent his seditious and libellous intent.[20] Nor was it necessary even to publish critical material, in the sense of making it available to a third person, to risk prosecution. Sir Samuel Barnardiston was in 1684 convicted for political opinions expressed in a private letter; the main evidence against Algernon Sidney in 1683 was taken from private papers discovered in his desk; and the 'publication' for which the Seven Bishops were tried in 1688 was the single copy of their *Petition* to the king.[21]

Whether or not the Licensing Act was in force had no bearing on this *post factum* censorship. Ten years after its final expiry Chief Justice Sir John Holt advised the jury in the trial of John Tutchin for seditious libel that to 'possess the people that the government is male-administered' is libellous since 'If people should not be called to account for possessing the people with an ill opinion of the government, no government can subsist. For it is very necessary for all governments that the people should have a good opinion of it.'[22] Nor had the Act any bearing on treason. This was a charge less likely to be incurred by writing and publication than that of seditious libel, but it was a real possibility: Brewster was told by Hyde he was lucky not to be tried capitally; it was contemplated as a charge in the case of Baxter; and it was, of course, for treason that Sidney was executed.[23] Under the old treason statute of Edward III it was sufficient for a conviction to prove merely that the defendant had 'imagined' the king's death, without any overt act to that end. The evidence of Sidney's republican papers that he had contemplated a non-monarchical constitution was thus sufficient to convict him, whether or not he ever intended its implementation. *The Act for the Safety and Preservation of His Majesty's Person* (1661), however, noting the contribution to the 'late troubles' of 'a multitude of seditious sermons, pamphlets and speeches daily preached, printed and published with a transcendent boldness', explicitly added to its definition of treasonable behaviour 'any printing, writing, preaching or malicious and advised speaking' which compassed, imagined, invented, devised, or intended the king's harm or death.[24] This was sufficient to condemn the Presbyterian Thomas Rosewell to death in 1684 for likening the popish Charles II to Jeroboam, claiming faith could work greater miracles than monarchy and asserting the people who flocked to the king to be cured of the King's Evil would do better to attend such a conventicle as the one at which he was preaching.[25] Rosewell was pardoned by Charles, but, in 1664, there had, despite his pleas, been no intercessor for the printer John Twyn. Unbeknown to him, his house was under surveillance, and in October 1663 he was surprised at 4 a.m. printing an incitement to rebellion entitled *A Treatise of The Execution of Justice* for Elizabeth Calvert. He also admitted having printed *Mene Tekel: or the Downfall of Monarchy*, a tract in favour of elective rather than hereditary monarchy. He was hanged, drawn and quartered.[26]

The imaginings and imagined intentions of the defendant bore on cases of seditious libel as well as of treason. These trials make strange and depressing reading now not only because the judges acted as prosecutors but also because it was they, and not the jury, who decided whether any publication was scandalous, malicious, or seditious. It was the jury's business to determine solely the fact of publication. 'If', Scroggs directed the jury in Carr's case,

> you find him guilty, and say what he is guilty of, we will judge whether the thing imports malice or no ... If this thing doth not imply it, then the judges will go according to sentence; if it doth, so that it concerns not you one farthing, whether malicious or not malicious, that is plain. Now, there remains only this one thing, that is, Whether or no he was the publisher of this book?[27]

Defence counsel in the case of the Seven Bishops hence took the sensible course of challenging not the alleged nature of the *Petition* but the fact of its publication. At his trial in 1664 the Baptist Benjamin Keach could not hope successfully to take this line: there were 1,500 copies of his catechetical *The Childs Instructor* for sale. Equally, however, it was futile for him to attempt to deny the charge that, in its antipaedobaptism and millenarianism, the book was malicious and seditious. When he attempted to address the court on his doctrine and the particulars of his indictment (which he had had only an hour to read), Hyde quickly cut him short: 'You shall not speak here, except to the matter of fact: that is to say, whether you writ this book or not.' Hyde's own instruction to the jury that the *Instructor* was contrary to the established church order and Prayer Book was not to be challenged. The jury's misgivings that the quotations in the indictment did not correspond with the printed text were overruled, and a guilty verdict was duly returned: Keach was pilloried, fined £20 and imprisoned until payment of sureties for good behaviour.[28]

The fact that sentence depended upon the judges' interpretation of a defendant's meaning and intention in a published text explains the scorn, derision, unsubstantiated allegations and browbeatings that issued from the bench. These tirades were not purposeless or merely splenetic: to attribute to defendants the worst possible character and record established malicious or seditious intent. For Hyde to assert, before any verdict had been brought in on Keach, 'you are a Fifth Monarchy Man; and you can preach, as well as write books; and you will preach here, if I would let you: but I shall take such order as you shall do no more mischief' was to prepare for an appropriate sentence when the inevitable verdict of guilty of the fact of publication was eventually delivered. Jeffreys' harangue may have had nothing to do with what Baxter actually wrote, but it had all to do with the fact that he was Baxter, and therefore naturally, whatever his precise words may have been, intended to incite sedition. 'There was not an honest man in England, but what took him for a great knave.' This was not the verdict of the trial but its premise. Baxter was imprisoned until payment of a fine of 500 marks was made and bound over for seven years.[29]

The exemplary nature of these sentences is evidenced by the continuation of the practice of exacting punishment upon the books themselves. Ever since the subsequently canonized martyr John Fisher had, in 1521, preached at Paul's cross at a royally authorized burning of Luther's books,[30] every authority had continued to light bibliographical bonfires. By Elizabethan proclamation the works of the Familist Hendrik Niclaes were burned in 1583; in 1590 the Stationers' Company burned in its hall immoral books, including Marlowe's translation of Ovid; in 1633 Star Chamber ordered, besides the mutilation of Prynne, the burning of his *Histrio-Mastix*; the Long Parliament burned Charles I's *Book of Sports* in 1642; and during the Civil War and Interregnum both conservative royalist and radical Ranter pieces were burned. The Restoration regime, traditional in this as in so much else, in 1661 burned the *Solemn League and Covenant* and the legislation which had brought Charles I to trial, and subsequently incinerated Milton's defences of regicide, Keach's *Child's Instructor* and Thomas Delaune's *Plea for the Nonconformists* (1684). Delaune, his wife and two children all died in Newgate after his conviction and imprisonment for publishing a seditious libel. Defoe's claim, in his preface to the 1706 edition of the *Plea*, that Delaune was 'One of near 8000 Protestant Dissenters that perish't in Prison, in the Days of that Merciful Prince King *Charles* the Second' was something of an overstatement, but not his assertion that 'The Treatment the Reverend and Learned Author ... met with, will for ever stand as a Monument of the Cruelty of those Times.'[31]

The greatest of these bonfires came during the reaction following the Exclusion Crisis. On 21 July 1683, the day of William Russell's execution, the Convocation of Oxford University issued its *Judgment and Decree ... against certain pernicious Books and damnable Doctrines destructive to the sacred Persons of Princes, their State and Government, and of all human Society*. Directed against any and all views which contemplated any restraint on the royal prerogative, the Decree is couched in terms which might have come from some Elizabethan denunciation of rebellion and schism a hundred years before. Determined to root out all 'the attempts of open and bloody enemies and machinations of treacherous heretics and schismatics', it lists, under 27 heads, those doctrines 'fitted to deprave good manners, corrupt the minds of unwary men, stir up seditions and tumults, overthrow states and kingdoms, and lead to rebellion, murder of princes, and atheism itself'; it declares every one 'of these propositions to be false, seditious and impious, and most of them to be also heretical and blasphemous'; it prohibits the books which contain them to members of the university; and it decrees that such books should be 'publickly burnt, by the hand of our marshal in the court of our schools'.[32]

Those so condemned, whose names L'Estrange gleefully reported in *The Observator* of 1 August, comprised a company ranging in time and opinion from Julian the Apostate to Hobbes, Cardinal Robert Bellarmine to John Knox. The nonconformists named included John Goodwin and John Milton (for their defences of regicide); Owen (for *Righteous Zeal Encouraged* (1649), his 'Sermon before the regicide'); and Baxter (cited five times, for allegedly allowing in *The Holy Commonwealth* (1659) the legitimacy of *de facto* authority and of oaths of allegiance to it, the deposition of tyrants, that the king may be overruled by Lords and Commons in England's mixed constitution, and that Charles I was properly resisted by subjects upon whom he made unlawful war). Quakers and Fifth Monarchists were repudiated *en masse*, the former for holding oaths to be contrary to the word of God and for expecting revelations, the latter for wishing to set up Christ in the place of 'the powers of this world'. They must have made quite a blaze: but in 1710 the Decree was itself burned by order of Oxford Convocation.[33]

2   MR FILTH

Though these measures and proceedings were pretty much what authors and printers had had to contend with throughout the sixteenth and earlier seventeenth centuries, the government's identification of nonconformists as the likeliest fomenters of sedition made them the commonest suspects, pursued with all Jeffreys' certainty of their guilt, if not always with his unbalanced fanaticism. This unenviable vulnerability was rendered the more acute by the appearance on the scene of the one agent of press control who had no precedent in earlier English press history, an agent who shared to the full the conviction that anything written by a nonconformist was *ipso facto* false, certainly malicious, probably seditious and very possibly treasonable. In Bunyan's *Holy War*, one of the steps which Diabolus, having won Mansoul, takes to secure the town is to cause

> by the hand of one Mr. Filth, an odious, nasty, lascivious piece of beastliness to be drawn up in writing, and to be set upon the Castle Gates: whereby he granted, and gave his license to all his true and trusty sons in *Mansoul*, to do whatsoever their lustful appetites prompted them to do, and that no man was to lett, hinder, or controul them, upon pain of incurring the displeasure of their Prince.

Bunyan's marginal note on this passage is: 'Odious Atheistical Pamphlets and filthy Ballads & Romances full of baldry'. Among Bunyan's contemporaries, the only man possessed of the power here attributed to Mr Filth to allow such publications and to prohibit criticism of them was Roger L'Estrange.[34]

L'Estrange had had a somewhat chequered career. He narrowly escaped execution in 1644 for endeavouring to secure Lynn for the royalists, an experience which may have a bearing on his later vendetta. After imprisonment and an inglorious part in the Second Civil War he went into exile in 1653. 1659 found him engaged in the pamphlet warfare which preceded the Restoration and, rather ironically, assuming the role of seditious libeller which would soon, when played by others, be such anathema to him. Following the Restoration, he showed none of the politic restraint towards the Presbyterians displayed by his masters. In a series of heated pamphlets he set about denying them the esteem they currently enjoyed as agents of the Restoration. His attitude is tersely summed up in the sub-title to his reply to the Presbyterian John Corbet's *Interest of England in the Matter of Religion* (1660): *The Holy Cheat* (1662; actually, 1661). The unauthorized and anonymous publication of the Presbyterians' Savoy Conference papers in *A Petition for Peace* (1661) drew from him *The Relapsed Apostate* (1661) and its supplement *State Divinity* (1661). In the former he accused Baxter not only of writing the papers, which was true, but also of arranging their publication, which was false. Thus began his 25-year campaign to discredit Baxter, a campaign which the next year engaged him in vituperative exchanges with Edward Bagshaw, the ejected vicar of Ambrosden, Oxfordshire. This series of anti-Presbyterian tracts culminated in *Toleration Discuss'd* (1663), which hammered away at the points L'Estrange would reiterate until 1688: that the Restoration was not due to Presbyterian assistance; that the nonconformists were factious and schismatic; that 1641–2 showed what was really in their minds; and that nothing less than their complete suppression would secure the realm.[35]

There was one other insistent theme running through L'Estrange's pamphlets: that since nonconformists were hypocritical subversives, to allow them the freedom of the press was the greatest folly. It is there in *Toleration Discuss'd*, in *A Modest Plea* (1661), *Apology to Clarendon* (1661), *A Memento* (1662) and *Truth and Loyalty Vindicated* (1662). In *A Memento* L'Estrange claimed that 'Libels were not only the *Fore-runners*, but in a high Degree, the *Causes* of our late *Troubles*', and now, in 1662, 'If we look well about us',

> we may find this Kingdom, at this Instant labouring under the same Distempers; the Press as *busie* and as *bold*; Sermons as *factious*; Pamphlets as *seditious*; the Government *defam'd*. The Lectures of the *Faction* are throng'd with pretended *Converts*; and scandalous *Reports* against the *King* and *State*, are as currant now as they were twenty years ago.

This was reprinted in 1682. L'Estrange's conviction that the 'first step' on the road to civil disobedience is 'to *Dispute*', for the 'very *Doubt* of *obeying*, subjects the *Authority* to a *Question*, and gives a dangerous Hint to the People, that *Kings* are accountable to their subjects', led him to detect rebellion lurking behind every critical or dissenting remark: 1682 might go the way of 1642 no less than might 1662 have done. In *A Seasonable Memorial in some Historial Notes upon the Liberties of the Presse and Pulpit* (1680) he warned that 'the Presses and the Pulpits all this while giving life and credit' to the seditious aspirations of the 1640s is likely to have the same consequences. And in *An Account of the Growth of Knavery* (1678), his reply to Marvell's *An Account of the Growth of Popery*

(1677), he asserts 'The Libels in fine of 77. are so exact a Counterpart of the others of 41. that two Tallies do not strike truer: And undoubtedly such a Correspondence in Method, cannot be without some Conformity also of Design.' This fear both fed on and nourished the belief that there were vast amounts of such material in circulation. In *A Word Concerning Libels* (1681) it is said to be 'the opinion of Men well vers'd in the Trade of Book-Selling, that there has not been so little as 30000 Reams of Paper spent upon this Seditious Subject, in the Late Liberty of the Press' (that is, since 1679). It had, apparently, been as bad following the Restoration. In *Truth and Loyalty Vindicated* L'Estrange drew the attention of the Privy Council to the fact that 'upon a *Modest Calculation* ... not so few as *Two-Hundred-Thousand* Seditious Copies have been Printed, since the blessed Return of his Sacred Majesty ... To These may be added divers *Millions* of the *Old Stock*.'[36]

L'Estrange's one-man campaign at the Restoration did not go unnoticed or unappreciated. By Secretary Sir Edward Nicholas, L'Estrange was on 24 February 1662 made Surveyor of the Press with warrant to search for and seize seditious, scandalous, or unlicensed publications and to apprehend offenders. L'Estrange's expression of impecunity in *A Memento* suggests, however, that the position carried no emolument, and in *Considerations and Proposals in order to the Regulation of the Press*, which appeared on 3 June 1663, L'Estrange argued for the establishment of a formal office of Surveyorship of the Press. He first clears the need for some greater degree of control with his familiar claim that 'There have been *Printed*, and *Reprinted*' since the Restoration 'not so few as a *Hundred Schismatical Pamphlets*' of which 'The *Instruments*' are '*Ejected Ministers, Booksellers* and *Printers*'; no less than 'near *Thirty Thousand Copies of Farewel-Sermons*' have appeared 'in Defiance of the Law'; '*Scarce any one* Regicide or Traytor *has been brought to* Publique Justice ... *whom either the* Pulpit *hath not* Canonized *for a* Saint, *or the* Press Recommended *for a* Patriot, *and* Martyr.' L'Estrange believed, in fact, in the existence of a well-organized publishing underground: stationers, he alleged,

> hold Intelligence *Abroad* by the means of *Posts, Carryers, Hackney-Coachmen, Boatmen*, and *Marriners*: and for fear of *Interceptions* they Correspond by *False Names*, and *Private Tokens*; so that if a *Letter*, or *Pacquet* miscarry, people may not know what to make on't. As for the Purpose; so many *Dozen of Gloves* stands for so many *Dozen of Books*. Such a *Marque* for such a *Price* &c.[37]

Granted, then, 'the Necessity' of better '*Regulating* the Press' the question is 'in what *manner*, and by what *means* This may be Effected'. L'Estrange's reply is a cogent one. It cannot be left to the Stationers' Company acting under the Licensing Act since, while it is in the Company's interest to protect its monopoly and seek out unentered printing which infringed copyright, it is not in its interest to pursue seditious printing which, often, not only had its members' sympathy but was actually produced by them. 'Diverse of the very *Instruments*, who are *Entrusted* with the *Care* of the Press' are in fact 'both *Privy*, and *Tacitly Consenting* to the *Corruptions* of it'. In the 'Prodigious *License*, and *Security* of *Libelling*' which results, however, 'let but any Paper be Printed that Touches upon the *Private Benefit* of the *Concerned Officer*: The *Author* of *That Paper* is sure to be *Retriev'd*, and *Handled* with sufficient *Severity*.' Stationers, being 'both *Parties* and *Judges*', are

> Entrusted (effectually) to *search* for their *own Copies*; to *Destroy* their *own Interests*; to *Prosecute* their *own Agents*, and to *Punish Themselves*: for they are the Principal *Authors* of the Mischiefs which they pretend now to *Redress*.

The Company, which L'Estrange believed warned its members of impending searches, could not be expected to declare war on itself in this way: an independent authority could. On 15 August 1663 a warrant was issued 'for erecting the office of Surveyor of printing and printing presses, appointing Roger L'Estrange surveyor ... With power to search for and seize all treasonable and schismatical books and papers'.[38]

The pamphlets L'Estrange had already published made it abundantly clear whom he would suspect to be the authors of such books and papers and that he would construe his appointment as a licence to harry mercilessly nonconformist authors and printers. And so he did. It was his animus and zeal which made censorship and press control during the Restoration period so much more vindictive and so much more partisan than anything experienced before, for it was not the Stationers' Company, nor the courts, nor the Licensing Act, but L'Estrange who saw to it that no offender was left unpursued and that, though detection and trial might not necessarily attend unlawful writing and printing, these would always be undertaken in circumstances of apprehension and fearful risk. Just how menacing L'Estrange could be is illustrated by an episode in 1672 recorded by Baxter:

> There came out a Posthumous Book of A[rch] Bishop [John] *Bromhall's* [i.e. Bramhall's *Vindication of Himself and the Episcopal Clegy from the Presbyterian Charge of Popery* (1672)], against my Book, called, *The Grotian Religion* [(1658)] ... And before the Book was a long Preface of Mr. [Samuel] *Parker's*, most vehement against Dr. *Owen*, and some-what against my self: To which Mr. *Andrew Marvel* ... did Publish an Answer [*The Rehearsal Transpros'd* (1672)] so exceeding Jocular, as thereby procured abundance of Readers, and Pardon to the Author, Because I perceived that the Design of A. Bishop *Bromhal's* Book was for the Uniting of *Christendom* under the old Patriarchs of the *Roman* Imperial Church, and so under the Pope ... I had thought the design and this Publication look'd dangerously, and therefore began to write an Answer to it. But Mr. [Nevill] *Simmons*, my Bookseller, came to me, and told me, That *Roger Lestrange*, the Over-seer of the Printers, sent for him, and told him, That he heard I was Answering Bishop *Bromhall*, and Swore to him most vehemently, that if I did it, he would ruin him and me, and perhaps my Life should be brought in question: And I perceived the Bookseller durst not Print it, and so I was fain to cast it by.[39]

Threats were not, however, always so effective: Ralph Wallis turned his encounter with L'Estrange to positive polemical advantage, and, for once, the Surveyor was worsted.

In January 1664 Wallis was reported to be hiding in London, and intercepted letters between him and his wife revealed not only that he had books to dispose of and manuscripts nearly ready for the press which he hoped soon to complete, but also that money was being collected for them to be printed by the ejected Scottish rector of St Mary de Crypt, Gloucester, James Forbes, a leader of nonconformity in the West of England and a learned man, though now said to be a shoemaker in Clapham. On 12 May a warrant was issued for Wallis's arrest in order for him to be examined by Secretary Sir Henry Bennet (afterwards Earl of Arlington), but in June Wallis was still free and freely dispensing his books. A letter intercepted on the 15th of that month boasted that he would frustrate all the designs of William Nicholson, Bishop of Gloucester, Thomas Warmestry, Prebendary of Gloucester and Dean of Worcester, and 'the devil's bloodhound' L'Estrange. This was as good as a direct challenge. On 20 June a second warrant was issued to L'Estrange to apprehend him and keep him in safe custody.[40]

It was not easily done. He not only continued at liberty but publicly taunted his pursuers in print. In *More News from Rome* (1664) the cat-and-mouse game being played out in real life becomes part of the rhetorical strategy of the pamphlet. Wallis adopts the persona of an ordinary man, a cobbler, of straightforward mind and down-to-earth integrity, unjustly victimized by episcopal malice. Audacious humour plays through his denunciations of the pluralism and episcopal trappings of Nicholson and Warmestry as he mercilessly taunts his pursuers with their inability to catch him. Against the impotent vindictiveness of the 'blood hound' L'Estrange is set the honest poor man's innate strength:

> *What's the matter these Mastive fellows quarrell about it* [i.e. his publications] *and be ready to come out with a* Bowgh wough *at me. I have seen a country man walking by a country house, which hath stood somewhat solitary, out comes a great Dog with a* Bowgh, wough, wough, *at him, the country man spreads his arms, runs to meet him, as if he would catch him in his arms, the dog seeing it, claps his tail between his legs, away he runs, the Countrey-man cryes out,* Begone ye cowardly Cur, begone, *what afraid of a naked man! ... So I say to these Mastive Fellows,* Begone ye cowardly fellows, begone, *what afraid of a naked-man?*[41]

Within the pamphlet, Wallis's parade of gross and bestial caricatures are powerless to quell, let alone catch, his 'naked man'. L'Estrange, 'Old Crack-fart', may threaten '*with* Gate-house *and* Gallows, *and Warrants granted forth for my apprehension*' but such weapons from '*the Antichristian Armory*' merely prove that the persecutors' true allegiance is to '*the Angel of the Bottomless Pit*': '*Have ye no weapons in* David's *Armory to fight withal? sure he is not your King.*' Their true concern is not the well-being of the church, nor their true motive pastoral: time-serving self-interest directs them the surest way to worldly advancement. Why did the Warmestry who preached against sedition and fanaticism at Gloucester (as he did to Baxter's old parishioners at Kidderminster) keep his peace throughout the Interregnum and 'stand so long before be brought the

Message'?: because he would deliver it only at no risk to himself and when it 'would bring meat in the mouth of it, his Prebends place at *Gloucester* . . . What's become of all those souls which died in the fifteen years' before the Restoration? The reductive wit of Wallis's 'naked man' strips his pursuers of all dignity. More pointedly, it deprives them of all power to quell him, armed though they may be with the force of the law: a group of drunk clergymen 'joyned with L'Estrange to apprehend me lately, who very uncharitably suspects me for a Witch, thinking that I can transform my self into several Shapes, and therefore hunts me in the day with his *Beagles* for a *Hare*, and himself at night for a *Badger*'.[42]

This would have made galling reading for L'Estrange during the summer of 1664. When, by the autumn, Wallis had still not been apprehended, a renewed and concerted effort was made to trace him. On 13 September Bennet issued a warrant to L'Estrange to arrest Forbes and to seize any books or papers in his possession. To aldermen of Gloucester he issued warrants to search the houses in Gloucester of Toby Jordan, bookseller, William Jordan, apothecary, Edward Eckly and Wallis's wife, Elizabeth. Any seditious papers found were to be forwarded to Bennet and their possessors detained. Perhaps as a result of information secured during the searches, L'Estrange was able to report to Bennet on 28 September that he had at last secured Wallis (now alias Gardiner). Wallis, however, would not reveal the address of his lodging, with (as L'Estrange suspected) its incriminating evidence, and L'Estrange turned his attention to Forbes, who had so far eluded him, and to his Gloucestershire contacts, in an effort to discover the address.[43]

The suspects were finally all gathered in. Under examination by the Privy Council on 1 October Thomas Rawson, journeyman shoemaker, of Little Britain, admitted Wallis was his lodger and that he had brought many books there. Wallis himself admitted authorship of *Magna Charta, Good News from Rome* ([1662?]), *More News from Rome* and *The Honour of a Hangman*. James Forbes claimed not to have read, nor even to know how he came to possess, the books L'Estrange had found in his study. Wallis, however, was not to be detained for long. He was released on 27 October after submitting petitions to Bennet from Newgate, the one pleading that a poor family should not starve for his scribbling a little drollery which satirized priests only to prompt their reformation and claiming he would as readily write of fanatics in the same vein when the mood took him; the other advising that his bail would be put up by Sir Richard Browne, a Presbyterian and former parliamentarian major-general who had supported the Restoration and won considerable acclaim for his swift action, when Lord Mayor of London, in suppressing Venner's rising.[44]

Wallis might have meant to reform priests but he had himself no intention of reforming. In April 1665 Nicholson complained to Sheldon that Wallis was again selling his books openly in Gloucester, boasting of his scurrility, denying the royal supremacy, defaming the liturgy and winning loud popular applause for so doing. He was so little daunted that in 1666 he reissued *More News from Rome*. So he went on for three years. In April 1668 L'Estrange wrote to Secretary Williamson enclosing *Room for the Cobbler of Gloucester* (1668), 'the damnedest thing has come out yet'. Wallis had vanished once more, but L'Estrange knew at least he was in disguise and was confident of tracking him down, provided neither Williamson, Arlington nor Sheldon, if shown the tract, let it be known L'Estrange was on Wallis's trail. Controlling the press, wrote L'Estrange in a revealing aside, is no easy matter and it is better to work by surprise, making no move or sign until the capture of suspects was sure. In this case, however, it was death, not the Surveyor, which found Wallis in February 1669.[45]

Wallis's reference to a 'great Dog' alludes to L'Estrange's nickname 'Towzer the dog'. It was not only as a monstrous and popish, but also a grossly lecherous, dog that L'Estrange was represented in the pope-burning processions of 1680 and 1681. It was commonly alleged that, though a printer could expect no sympathy from the Surveyor, a printer's wife might. The stationer John Dunton was in no doubt L'Estrange would 'wink' at unlicensed printing for a feminine smile, and one of Wallis's jibes is that his wife is a *'hansome woman'* but *'too honest'* for the *'corporal uncleanness'* in which L'Estrange and his 'Tribe love to deal'.[46] A more substantial restraint on L'Estrange's activities was the resentment of the Stationers' Company, which, understandably, did not readily accept that it could not itself adequately control the press and did not take kindly to the Surveyor's interference in its affairs.Their 'uneasy partnership' was marked by indignation on L'Estrange's side at the Company's uncoopera- tive attitude; and on the Company's side by an unwillingness to proceed against members whose illicit activities did not infringe copyright or involve psalters, primers and almanacks, the Company's exclusive privilege.[47]

Otherwise, L'Estrange had a free hand, and employed every handy method. In his *Considerations* he had recognized it was 'hard' to discover an anonymous author or illegal press unless someone informed, and he was quite prepared to offer 'Rewards' to encourage such would-be informers, including even the promise of a recommendation to the first vacancy to appear in the statutory quota of printers. The moral turpitude is deepened by the fact that L'Estrange knew he was tempting *'Necessitous Persons'*. In the first number (13 August 1663) of his paper *The Intelligencer* (his Surveyorship carried with it a monopoly of licensed news), with its extraordinary editorial announcing 'a Publique mercury should never have my vote, because I think it makes the multitude too familiar with the actions and counsels of their superiors', L'Estrange offered rewards of 40s. to any informer of a secret press, £5 for information about libels in the process of printing, 10s. for unlicensed books being printed and 5s. for the discovery of hawkers or sellers of seditious books. These were offers which might on occasions be much improved: the *London Gazette* in March 1678 offered rewards of £50 for the discovery of the printer and £100 for the author of the anonymous *Account of the Growth of Popery* (1677).[48] Like his masters the Secretaries of State, L'Estrange seems, in fact, to have operated a spy network, a network which was itself, not surprisingly, susceptible to bribery.[49]

Once a culprit was located, L'Estrange acted with alacrity, often raiding printing houses in person. It was L'Estrange who had had Twyn's house watched and who surprised him at four in the morning, and it was L'Estrange who attempted to force the door of Nathan Brooks' neighbour 'with a smith's sledge'. When apprehended, a suspect would be imprisoned, perhaps even without examination, let alone trial. Usually, however, he was interrogated by L'Estrange or one of the Secretaries of State. Trial might follow, but, more often, months of imprisonment. In this latter case, freedom was generally eventually offered on condition the detainee either undertook to inform on illicit printing activities in future or entered into a bond for good behaviour. The Licensing Act specified a bond of £300, but this (and more) was exacted from many who had never been tried, let alone convicted, under the Act.[50]

A glance at some of the inmates of the Gatehouse prison, Westminster, during 1663 will illustrate these procedures. On 10 January 1663 Thomas Leach, printer of Shoe Lane, was examined for printing reports of the trials of the regicides acquired by his wife. He refused to name the publisher and was committed to the Gatehouse. Later that month he was released on security of £500 for good behaviour. On 23 June the printer Peter Lillicrap was arrested, and a warrant issued for his wife the next day. In July he petitioned Bennet for release from his seven weeks' confinement for printing farewell sermons, undertaking himself to seek out seditious material. Suspected accomplices were examined on 4 August and, after another petition in September, Lillicrap was released from the Gatehouse on 7 September. As Lillicrap was petitioning for his release the booksellers Henry Marsh, Robert Cutler and John Brudenell were committed to the Gatehouse by Bennet's warrant, dated 21 July. Marsh was released in September after entering into a bond of £300, but in November he was again a petitioner to Bennet having been once more committed to the Gatehouse, this time by the staunch royalist John Egerton, Earl of Bridgewater (as a boy the performer of the Elder Brother in Milton's *Comus*). After examination by Bennet in February 1664 he was discharged in March. Brudenell was a co-signatory of the November petition to Bennet for his release on bail from his confinement for the unlicensed printing of David Lloyd's anonymous *The Kingdome Saved* (1663). In September he entered into a £300 bond. Cutler had secured his release by the same means, but more expeditiously: petition, bond and warrant for release were accomplished by 1 August.[51]

Six days after Lillicrap's committal, Elizabeth Calvert joined him in the Gatehouse. She petitioned Bennet for her release, arguing that she had, to supply her wants, merely and inadvisedly delivered a few illegal books for her husband (the radical publisher Giles Calvert). On 24 July she entered into a bond of £600 for good behaviour and an undertaking to appear before a Secretary if required. In October, however, it was found necessary to issue to L'Estrange a warrant to apprehend her for examination by Bennet. She seems to have eluded him, and a second warrant was issued on 22 October. In the State Papers there is an undated petition to Bennet from Richard Stevenson for the release of his son, Matthias, from the Gatehouse, to which he had been committed because his mistress, the widow Elizabeth Calvert, was being sought for libellous publication. The father alleged his son had no knowledge of her whereabouts. L'Estrange, however, found her, and in February 1664 she was arrested, put in close confinement in the Gatehouse and examined concerning the printer and author of *Mene Tekel*. In March she petitioned Bennet for her release, enclosing a doctor's testimony that her son, Nathaniel, who had himself in November entered into a £300 bond to refrain from seditious printing or retailing, was now terminally ill. Neither she, nor any other of the detainees, had been brought to trial.[52]

3   WITH AUTHORITY, OR WITHOUT

To see a manuscript safely through this barrage into print demanded resourceful tactical manoeuvres as well as heroism. Sometimes the attempt was not even made. Milton's *De Doctrina Christiana* is the most celebrated, but by no means the only, example of a substantial work written up in a fair copy but never submitted for licensing or delivered to the press.[53] Confinement of copy to manuscript did not, however, necessarily mean that it was not 'published'. On the contrary, here was one way to escape the provisions of (at least) the Licensing Act. Ever since the invention of the press the older practice of manuscript-copying and circulation had remained a common, if limited, form of publishing not only poetry which disdained the vulgarity of print but also proscribed material. Charles Morton, who ran the principal Congregational academy in London at Newington Green, is known to have written a republican utopia entitled *Eutaxia* which circulated in manuscript but was never printed and has not survived. Most of Marvell's political and religious satires were available only in anonymous manuscript copies until they began to appear in the 1689 *Collection of the Newest and Most Ingenious Poems . . . Against Popery* and its successive volumes of *Poems on Affairs of State*. Marvell himself passed to Sir Edward Harley handwritten instalments of *The Growth of Popery* before its publication.[54]

The government was well aware of this circulation of illicit material. As the case of Algernon Sidney and the experience of Locke made clear, even privately kept papers had to be safely guarded. It was not only Pepys who wrote 'in characters'; so did the ejected Presbyterian Roger Morrice. The Presbyterian Philip Henry made erasures in his diary and resolved henceforth to be 'more cautious' when his friend Richard Steele's diary was seized. A government so inquisitive was fully alive to the greater threat posed by clandestine copying. It was on the grounds that they were places where not only printed but transcribed libels were read and copied that proclamations were issued to close and control coffee-houses.[55]

Men thus schooled to wariness must, as Christopher Hill has remarked, have exercised a good deal of self-censorship, both in what they withheld from the press and in the composition of what they did send to it. We do not know why Baxter's *Reliquiae*, begun in 1665, was not offered to a publisher in his lifetime, but the improbability of obtaining a licence for such a work must surely have been a factor. To Milton's awareness of the sensitivities of the censor Christopher Hill would attribute the moderation of *Of True Religion*, which was licensed; scholars also often point to this to explain the comparative absence in *Paradise Lost* (which was submitted for a licence) of the heresies of *De Doctrina*. We may similarly note the small part played in *The Pilgrim's Progress*, licensed under the Act, by persecution, politicking and intrigue; in *The Holy War*, published after the Act had lapsed, they are the driving force of the plot.[56]

A rather different form of self-censorship was exercised by the Quakers, the majority of whose publications were unlicensed and so not tailored to satisfy the censor. In the 1650s Quakers had been accustomed to consult Fox before having a work printed. With the increasingly frequent imprisonment of Fox and other Quaker leaders in the 1660s this had become less easy and less common, and in 1672 the Yearly Meeting appointed ten Friends to oversee and authorize all Quaker books. The following year, the weekly Second-day's Morning Meeting was instituted to supervise Quaker publications and to ensure copies were kept of every Quaker and every anti-Quaker text. No Quaker printing was to go ahead without the Meeting's prior approval, and the titles of all authorized books were to be entered in the Meeting's records. This control was, however, exercised not in deference to the Licensing Act but to safeguard the integrity of Quaker literature: it was, in Fox's words, 'to see that young Friends' books that was sent to be printed might be stood by'. If they might, then let them be published, law or no law.[57]

The practice of unlicensed printing was commonest among Quakers, partly because they did not recognize the state's right to silence the printed any more than the spoken word ('our mouths were not opened by, nor can they be shut in the will of man' wrote Billing), and partly because it would have been futile to seek licences for the kind of material they produced. It was not, however, confined to them. Writers and publishers of every persuasion on occasion bypassed the Licensing Act in this way, as they had evaded all such regulations ever since Henry VIII first required authorization. Of this we may be sure, but just how much unlicensed material was published we cannot confidently determine. The requirement in clause iv of the 1637 Decree that licences should be printed in authorized books had never been observed by more than a third of legal publications. The similar provision in the Licensing Act was as rarely followed, even in books which had, in fact, been licensed. We cannot, therefore, apply the simple rule of thumb that a book which had passed the censor would declare itself: were we to do so, we should have to conclude that the vast majority of books printed were unlicensed. Nor can we turn to the Stationers' Register for reliable guidance. Although a book there entered would have been previously licensed (unless fraud was involved), by no means all licensed books were entered. Indeed, as the Stationers' hold on the press steadily weakened during our period, the number of entries came to bear no relation to the amount published. We can, then, determine which books certainly were licensed (from the presence in the printed text of the *imprimatur*, entry in the register, or advertisement in the Term Catalogues, which, themselves licensed by L'Estrange, dealt only in authorized material); and we can determine which books certainly were not (from their precautionary use of a false or defective imprint to conceal the place of printing); but there remains a mass of books which might appear either legal but want substantiating evidence of authorization, or suspect (because, for example, of their authors' anonymity) though they may have been licensed.[58]

What we can say is that unlicensed printing, with its additional safeguards of authorial anonymity and imprints restricted to 'Printed in the Year — ', was rarely practised by Presbyterians. Their more conservative outlook and greater regard for law and authority disinclined them to undertake it, and, in any case, their writing on devotional and doctrinal, if not historical, matters was sufficiently orthodox to pass the censor. Baxter is representative of their position. Following the Savoy Conference he told Peter Gunning, afterwards Bishop of Ely, that he supposed none of the Presbyterian delegates 'intended to be so presumptuous as to publish [their papers] without Authority', and Baxter himself advised Secretary Sir William Morice of the printing of the *Petition for Peace* 'that he might send a Messenger to surprize' it in the press. Baxter was accustomed 'to put my Name to my Writing', was 'not used to publish any thing unlicensed' and did not think it 'fit to break the Law of Printing without necessity'. For him, such necessity arose but rarely. His *Fair-warning: or XXV Reasons against Toleration and Indulgence of Popery*, published in 1663 following Charles's first *Declaration of Indulgence*, was anonymous; so was his piece on the occasion of the second *Declaration* which encouraged nonconformists to an active pastorate (*Sacrilegious Desertion of the Holy Ministry Rebuked* (1672)). A glance down the entries of Donald Wing's *Short-Title Catalogue* under Bates, Manton, or Howe reveals a similar disinclination. From this, though, we should infer not so much that authorized publication was readily available to Presbyterians as that, when it was not, they generally preferred to keep silent. When Oliver Heywood sent a manuscript for publication, 'if it may passe the presse' he implied that he would proceed no further should it be refused. When some of Baxter's practical writings were refused a licence, he withheld not only those, but also some controversial pieces, which would have been authorized, rather than have the censor determine the bias of his publications.[59]

It is nevertheless true that Presbyterians had readier access to licences than their fellow nonconformists. As we move through Independents, Baptists and Quakers the incidence of anonymity, false and defective imprints greatly increases. Owen was far oftener anonymous than Baxter – fifteen times after 1660 – though his publisher (generally Nathaniel Ponder) disclosed himself. Bunyan's pieces of the early 1660s occasionally had blank imprints, but thereafter publishers' names regularly appear (usualy Francis Smith or Ponder, to whom Owen may have introduced him). Only *The Pilgrim's Progress*, however, seems to have been properly licensed. Bunyan was anonymous only once. Benjamin Keach frequently was, as were his printers and publishers. On occasions, Keach seems to have acted as his own publisher ('For the author ...', 'Printed, and sold by the author, and William Marshall', 'sold by John Harris, and at the author's house, Southwark'). Fox was habitually anonymous following the Restoration, and it is only in the 1680s that the name of Andrew Sowle, a committed Quaker printer since the 1650s, or that of his daughter, Tace, or his former apprentice, John Bringhurst, begin to appear on his title pages. Penn affords a nice example of the Quakers' blithe insouciance: committed to the Tower for the unlicensed *Sandy Foundation Shaken* (1668) he there promptly wrote the classic *No Cross, No Crown*, and not only turned to the advantage of his cause the punishment inflicted on him but did so by repeating the offence: the book appeared in 1669, unlicensed and with a blank imprint.[60]

And, equally, the more topical, political, or satirical a work the greater the likelihood of its being unlicensed. Save for cases of flat heresy, the censors seem to have been generally unconcerned about the finer points of theology. About early church history they were less happy, since it could so easily reflect adversely upon episcopacy. English history was still more sensitive, unless, as in the work of the sub-dean of Westminster Peter Heylyn, it was handled from an explicitly royalist and episcopalian point of view. From Milton's *History of Britain* (1670) the censor cut anti-episcopal passages, and a licence was refused his letters of state. Brabazon Aylmer, who had been preparing to publish them, had instead to issue Milton's familiar letters and Cambridge prolusions, which were authorized. Baxter's *Church-history of the Government of Bishops* (1680), with its apologetic preface, attack on such royalist historians as Heylyn, and general thesis that prelacy was 'the diseasing tumour of the Church', appeared only during the lapse of the Act. So, too, did its sequel, *The True History of Councils Enlarged* (1682) and Baxter's defence of non-episcopal orders in *A Treatise of Episcopacy* (1681).[61]

Current affairs and political theory were the most sensitive material of all, unless, again, the treatment defended the status quo. Any adverse reflection upon contemporary authorities or suggestion that the constitution was imperfect was disallowed. Such reflection could be inferred from doctrinal, homiletic, or exegetical works. This Baxter learned at his trial, though hardly to his surprise, for he had had to omit from *The Divine Life* (1664) 'the quantity of one Sermon ... wherein I shewed what a mercy it is to one that hath walked with God, to be taken to him from this World; because it is a dark, a wicked, a malicious, and implacable, a treacherous deceitful World, &c. All which the Bishop's Chaplains must have expunged, because men would think it was all spoken of them.' When such general meditations upon the fallen world were deemed unacceptable directly topical and satirical accounts of it were inevitably proscribed. L'Estrange, meeting with Marvell's anonymous and unauthorized *The Rehearsal Transpros'd* when it was already for sale, promptly seized the second impression at the shop of its publisher, Nathaniel Ponder. In this case, he was overruled. Charles himself so appreciated Marvell's wit and drift that, through the Earl of Anglesey, he directed L'Estrange to license it, which, under protest and with some passages excised, he did. When the excisions were restored in copies for sale L'Estrange promptly withdrew his imprimatur until a 'Second Impression with Additions and Amendments' was printed incorporating his alterations. This rather humiliating experience perhaps explains the vehemence with which L'Estrange prevented Baxter from seconding Marvell's reply to Parker. Robert Ferguson's address to any who may 'be deluded into a good opinion of his Majesty' James II was, predictably, unlicensed, as was Vincent Alsop's *Anti-sozzo* (1675), a rather too protracted attempt to subject to Marvellian irony the rationalism and moralism of *The Knowledge of Jesus Christ* (1674) by William Sherlock, afterwards Dean of St Paul's. In 1680 no licence was needed for Alsop's defence of nonconformity against Stillingfleet's *The Mischief of Separation*, but *The Mischief of Impositions* was still anonymous.[62]

To take a public line critical of the government was, even for a conformist, to be forced into unlicensed printing. An eminent case was that of Herbert Croft, Bishop of Hereford, whose *The Naked Truth* (1675), an argument for comprehension and against persecution, was anonymous, and unlicensed. For this he apologized in his preface, but with no explanation, which he could hardly offer without giving offence. It was not a chance which could be let pass by his animadverters, Peter Gunning and Francis Turner, each of them a Master of St John's College, Cambridge and each of whom ended his career as Bishop of Ely. Their replies boasted full imprints, with the imprimatur of G[ulielmus] Jane, chaplain to the Bishop of London, and afterwards Regius Professor of Divinity at Oxford. Croft's whole thrust was, alleged Gunning, 'as contrary to the known Laws as his Printing without License confestly was'; Turner scorned Croft's apology since he 'sins on ... all this while he goes on with his Printing and Publishing it without a License'. In *Mr. Smirke* (1676) Marvell rallied to the defence of the bishop against the 'Licensed Clergy', pointing to the partisan operation of censorship:

> It is something strange, that to publish a good Book is a sin, and an ill one a vertue; and that while one comes out with Authority; the other may not have a

Dispensation. So that we seem to have got an Expurgatory Press, though not an Index; and the most Religious Truth must be expung'd and suppressed in order to the false and secular interest of some of the Clergy.

And Marvell turned against the animadverters their apparently needless anonymity: this 'Trick' is

> ordinary with many others of them, who while we write at our own peril, and perhaps set our names to it, ... they that rail for the Church of *England*, and under the Publick License and Protection, yet leave men, as it were at Hot Cockles, to guess blind fold who it is that hit them ... sure theirs is not *so Vile a Cause* too that they dare not abide by it. Or are they the Writers conscious [*sic*] to themselves that they are such Things as *ought not once to be Named among Christians*? Or is it their own sorry performance that makes them ashamed to own their own Books? Or is there some secret force upon them that obliges them to say things against their Conscience?

This last suggestion that they were but government hacks was perhaps the unkindest cut of all.[63]

In the Second Part of *The Rehearsal Transpros'd* (1673) Marvell had similarly chided Samuel Parker, afterwards Bishop of Oxford, on the 'sculking method' of publishing anonymously his *Reproof to the Rehearsal Transpros'd* (1673). Parker should have known better, for the anonymity of his *Ecclesiastical Politie* (1670), its *Defence* (1671) and Parker's preface to Archbishop John Bramhall's *Vindication of Himself* (1672) had already given Marvell an opportunity which, in the First Part of *The Rehearsal Transpros'd* (1672), he had improved to derisory polemical advantage. It was because Parker 'hath no Name or at least will not own it, though he himself writes under the greatest security' that Marvell bestowed on him the mocking appellation 'Mr. Bayes', immediately thereby reducing all Parker's efforts to the farcical inconsequentiality of Buckingham's play *The Rehearsal* (1671), of which Bayes, a composite caricature of Davenant and Dryden, is the hero. Parker is as absurd a divine as is Bayes an heroic dramatist: 'our Divine, the Author, manages his contest with the same prudence and civility, which the Players and Poets have practised of late.'[64]

Marvell is here almost gleeful as he puts down Parker's fanatical pomposity and he does seem to have relished the cat-and-mouse game of anonymous and unlicensed printing. He writes in a letter that the anonymous *Mr. Smirke* 'said to be Marvels makes what shift it can in the world but that Author walks negligently up & down as unconcerned'. Of the recent anonymous publication of *The Growth of Popery* he writes with ironic satisfaction to Popple:

> There have been great Rewards offered in private, and considerable in the Gazette, to any who would inform of the Author or Printer, but not yet discovered. Three or four printed Books since have described, as near as it was proper to go, the Man being a Member of Parliament, Mr. *Marvell* to have been the Author; but if he had, surely he should not have escaped being questioned in Parliament, or some other Place.

And we can glimpse him deliberately planning to outwit his opponents. Having in May 1673 read in manuscript Parker's forthcoming reply to *The Rehearsal*

Transpros'd Marvell, while yet unsure whether publicly to answer it, will 'for mine own private satisfaction forthwith draw up an answer that shall haue as much spirit and solidity in it as my ability will afford & the age we liue in will endure'. He would not, however, lose the element of surprise should he decide to proceed to the press, and in a letter desires 'that all the discourse of my friends may run as if no answer ought to be expected to so scurrilous a book'.[65]

Unlicensed work had perforce to be surreptitiously printed, either on secret presses or secretly on registered presses. Such clandestine operations were almost as old as printing itself. Tyndale had issued works from the continent with false imprints in the 1520s, as did John Bale, both under Henry VIII and during exile under Mary. Martin Marprelate's anti-episcopal tracts had been printed on an illegal mobile press in the 1580s, and during the late sixteenth and early seventeenth centuries there was a steady stream of Puritan publications from presses in Holland – John Lilburne's prison tracts were printed in Amsterdam in the 1630s by the separatist pastor John Canne.[66] Illicit printing on this scale did not survive into the Restoration. The Licensing Act's restriction of printing to Oxford, Cambridge and London seems not to have been evaded, though there were secret presses in the capital. L'Estrange discovered one in October 1662. In 1668 Elizabeth Poole was committed to the Gatehouse for keeping a private press for unlicensed printing, and that same year L'Estrange was enquiring after a secret press run by John Darby, his wife Joan and Brewster's widow, Ann. A spy was confident it was in 'one of five houses in Blue Anchor Alley; but by reason of so many back doors, bye-holes, and passages, and the sectarians so swarming thereabouts, I have been afraid of being discovered in scouting'.[67]

The imprints of works illegally produced would generally, and understandably, admit to no more than the year of publication, if that. Sometimes they were deliberately misleading. 'Printed at *Amsterdam*' doubtfully claim the imprints of the 1677 and 1678 editions of Marvell's *Growth of Popery*, and Robert Ferguson, the alleged author of its unlicensed and anonymous second part, disguised its London printing in 1682 with the imprint 'at Cologne'. The 1698 edition of Ludlow's *Memoirs*, 'Printed at *Vivay* in the Canton of *Bern*', was almost certainly printed in London, probably by Darby. Sometimes imprints were tauntingly witty in the manner of Martin Marprelate's tracts and Leveller pamphlets: Marvell's *Rehearsal Transpros'd* was initially printed 'for the assigns of John Calvin and Theodore Beza' and Ralph Wallis's *More News from Rome* carried the saucy imprint 'Imprinted at *London* for the Author, for the only benefit of his Wife and Children'.[68] It seems that in this case Wallis, like Keach, acted as his own publisher. Such clandestine operations might, however, involve not fewer but more people than the usual publisher, printer and author. The ejected vicar of Monmouth Nicholas Cary, who practised as a physician in London, arranged for his patient Denzil Holles the printing of Holles's anonymous and unlicensed *Some Considerations upon the Question Whether the*

Parliament is Dissolved (1676). Under examination by Secretary Williamson, Cary professed not to know whether his patient, whom he refused to identify, were its author. Cary was committed to the Tower, his house was searched and he himself subsequently fined £1,000.[69]

Work which was submitted to the censor in accordance with the law seems in one way to have been very rigorously treated and yet in another to have been quite cavalierly allowed. The likelihood of finding a sympathetic licenser among the chaplains (with whom nonconformists had chiefly to deal) was slim. He would not hold his chaplaincy were he not a good party man. It is hence no surprise to find Baxter's eirenical *Cure of Church-Divisions* refused a licence by the Samuel Parker who, while Sheldon's chaplain and a censor, appeared in print as an uncompromising defender of the monarch's absolute supremacy over private consciences and as a remorseless advocate of persecution to enforce conformity. One of Marvell's targets in *The Rehearsal Transpros'd* was the partisan licensing policy of Parker and his fellow chaplain Thomas Tomkins, like Parker a polemicist against nonconformity in general and Baxter in particular. Of these 'two Say-masters of Orthodoxy ... all Theology must ask License'. The result is not the authorization of sound doctrine but 'a more authoriz'd way of libelling' while those libelled must keep silent.[70]

Furthermore, it was in the licenser's own interest to err on the side of caution since he was himself at risk and subject to higher authority. An imprudent licence could be revoked and the licenser punished, as happened with increasing frequency in the 1680s and 1690s during the last attempt to reimpose the Licensing Act. The Scot James Fraser, whom Anthony à Wood called 'the Presbyterian Licenser', was in 1692 put out of his post for having incautiously licensed Anthony Walker's *True ... Account of the Author of a Book entitled* Εἰκὼν Βασιλική (1692). He was replaced by Edmund Bohun, who acted as licensing deputy for the Secretary of State Daniel Finch, Archbishop Tillotson and the Bishop of London, Henry Compton. Bohun himself was, however, imprisoned for allowing Charles Blount's anonymous *King William and Queen Mary Conquerors* (1693). In his autobiography he complained of the difficulty of exercising judgement acceptably. One safe course was, as Baxter testifies, to look to the author: were he suspect, the manuscript was safest refused. On this ground, Thomas Grigg, chaplain to the Bishop of London Humphrey Henchman, told Baxter that his manuscripts would be turned down even if from an unexceptionable author the same material would have been licensed.[71]

On the other hand, precisely because censorship was left to individual judgement, there was flexibility and inconsistency in the system. The book Grigg refused, *Directions for Weak Distempered Christians*, subsequently appeared in 1669, duly licensed. The *Cure* which Parker rejected was authorized two years later by Henchman's chaplain Robert Grove and published in 1670. To this man, Baxter made grateful acknowledgement in the *Reliquiae* as:

the only Man that Licenseth my Writings for the Press, (supposing them not to be against Law, which else I could not expect;) And besides him alone, I could get no Licenser to do it. And because being Silenced, Writing is the far greatest part of my remaining Service to God for his Church, and without the Press my Writings would be in vain, I acknowledge that I owe much to this Man, and one Mr. *Cook*, the Arch-bishop's Chaplain heretofore, that I live not more in vain.

Furthermore, licensers were, like everyone else, subject to pressure from above. Owen in 1668 acknowledged that it was 'through the countenance of [the] Favour' of Secretary Morice that his works 'received Warrant to pass freely in the world'. Secretary Sir John Trevor, Morice's successor, may similarly have acted on Owen's behalf. It was also commonly believed that a guinea would do the trick, even with L'Estrange. Marvell ironically hoped that Parker had dealt in private with the Surveyor and 'payd his Fees' for his *imprimatur*.[72]

Nonconformists unable, like Owen, to call on influential patronage, or, like Baxter, to find a sympathetic censor, or unwilling to resort to bribery, might still benefit from the fact that licensers were underpaid and overworked. At his trial in 1680 the Baptist printer Francis Smith complained that the delay in waiting for authorization deprived topical works of their market. Milton had long ago pleaded the impossibility of giving every submitted manuscript thorough scrutiny as an argument against censorship, and the position did not improve after 1662. In 1676 Henry Oldenburg, first Secretary to the Royal Society, resigned his position as licenser of books on affairs of state after only three months 'because of the tenderness of the employment and the vast expense of time it requires'. Bohun made the same point, 'reading to the hazard of my health and eyes' to dispatch the business, and Blount wrote of the inadequacy of 'the hasty view of an unleisured Licenser'. It would have required uncommon dedication to an unenviable and ill-regarded task to have read carefully through the entirety of every submission even were the pressure of work not so great. Consequently, remarkable things got through, such as the biting topicality of Faithful's trial at Vanity Fair, or Milton's extraordinary opening to *Paradise Lost*. At that date the word 'restore' could bring to mind only one Restoration, yet here is Milton implicitly dismissing it as an irrelevance and directing attention instead to a real restoration. *Paradise Lost* seems, indeed, to have received only token objection (to I.594–9) from Thomas Tomkins, its licenser, perhaps because he read no further, or read inattentively. Had he done so, he would surely have baulked at the 'lewd hirelings' who climb into God's church; the 'tedious pomp that waits/On princes'; the application of the terms 'dissent' and 'sect' not to Satan but to Abdiel; the 'evil days' on which the poet has fallen in Restoration England; and the 'carnal power' which Michael predicts 'shall force/On every conscience.[73]

One final expedient remained to the authors of licensed books: through the ambiguity of multiple reference (or 'plurisignation' as it is sometimes inelegantly called) to smuggle into an allowed text illicit meanings and applications beyond, and more topically inflammatory than, the expressly stated sense. To liken Satan to the misty early morning or eclipsed sun is, overtly, no more than to image his impaired brightness; but since the sun was a traditional symbol of divine royalty it may implicitly, as the licenser realized, associate evil with kings and Satan with Charles I. Christopher Hill, believing censorship to have been the most important conditioning pressure on seventeenth-century literature and the circumstance most neglected by literary critics, has argued that such use of implication, ambiguity, suggestive allusiveness and obliquity was resorted to far more often than is recognized, that the period's texts should be approached as 'cryptograms to be decoded' and that the 'fit audience' for Milton, 'the great equivocator', would have been comprised of initiates into the secrets of his sub-text, characterized by their sensitivity to the verbal nuances of his poetry.[74]

As the case from *Paradise Lost* just cited illustrates, it was (and is) a matter of interpretation. It was upon this point that Baxter's conversation with Grigg turned. When Grigg 'askt me, whether I did not think my self that Nonconformists would interpret ... as against the Times' what Baxter had written 'of the Prosperity of the Wicked, and the Adversity of the Godly', Baxter replied: 'Yes, I thought they would; and so they do all those Passages of Scripture which speak of Persecution and the Suffering of the Godly; but I hoped Bibles should be licensed for all that'. When Bates advises that as part of our self-examination we should 'consider the Quality of the Times we live in, to discover what Sin is predominant in us ... there is ... no Contagion more catching than of National Sins', he does not himself enlarge on what those sins might be. He is, however, encouraging his reader to discern and identify them in the contemporary world. When Manton explicates Pharisaical hypocrisy as consisting in greater concern for ritual than for commitment it is difficult to resist the surmise that he has the Act of Uniformity in mind. Though he makes no such specific application of his theme and concludes 'But I will prosecute this no further', a nonconformist reader almost certainly would prosecute it further, might, indeed, be thought to be encouraged to do so by the very explicitness of Manton's refusal to pursue it himself. Such biblical exegesis could, though, work against the author as well as for him: only a direct denial of a contemporary application (and no divine would deny the Bible contemporary relevance) could prevent the authorities, as well as sympathetic readers, from drawing their own conclusions. At his trial, Baxter claimed that his glosses on the hypocrisy of Pharisees were not aimed at the Church of England, but Jeffreys would have none of it. The barrister William Atwood cited precedents to the effect 'that words ought to be taken in the milder sense, and not in the strained, by *Innundos*', but Jeffreys exclaimed 'Baxter for bishops' ... that is a merry conceit indeed!' and directed the jury that 'he could mean no men else' than the conforming clergy.[75]

Fictional worlds were perhaps safer. The tyranny of Milton's Satan might, to those so minded, recall Charles I, but it is Satan, not Charles, who is described.

That Bunyan's Mr Worldly-Wiseman 'looked like a Gentleman' and directs Christian to Civility as well as to Morality might make a point about Bunyan's social superiors, but it is only a fictional character that is delineated. It is Lord Hategood, not Jeffreys or Kelynge, who berates Faithful. That the 'chief strength' of Diabolus' third army lies in his '*Bloodmen*, who 'would fasten upon any; upon father, mother, brother, sister', may all too pointedly have recalled for nonconformists their persecutors, but Bunyan's assurance that they are 'though mischieveous and cruel ... chicken-hearted men, when they once come to see themselves matched and equal'd' is, in the design of the allegory, a perfectly proper encouragement to resist the forces of Antichrist, not those of law and order. The 'Red-coats, and Black-coats' who corrupt Mansoul during the second Diabolonian occupation are certainly soldiers and priests but, on one allegorical level at least, they are medieval papists rather than Restoration royalists and episcopalians. It is Mansoul which becomes 'vile and filthy', not Caroline England. Baxter did not , and almost certainly could not, publish his autobiography, in which the Great Plague is interpreted as a visitation on London for its sins; Bunyan could and did publish *The Holy War*, in which the apostasy of Mansoul brings plague in its train.[76]

4   CONFEDERATES AND CONGERS

None of these expedients would, however, have been of any avail were there not individuals prepared to print nonconformist texts. An author without a printer was as good as silenced whether or not he continued to compose in the privacy of his own room. To gain access to a press was his most immediate need, as to deny it him was the government's chief aim. The printer thus became the key figure in the struggle between the government's press officers and nonconformist writers. This was the person at the centre of everyone's attention, and the one who ran the greatest risks. Not only did the nature of the occupation necessarily confine the printer to one conspicuous place surrounded by incriminating evidence, but it was against the printer as the producer of dissident literature that the Licensing Act and L'Estrange's efforts were first and foremost directed. The printer might also act as publisher (or 'bookseller') and as retailer as well, but when the manuscript was procured, and capital invested by, another, and distribution undertaken by a third party, these fell next to the authorities' attention. Only finally did they turn to the more elusive, and in himself less influential, creator of the literature, the author. Prosecutions of printers far exceed in number those of authors. The printer was, indeed, not merely the author's agent but his ally and first line of defence: upon his or her silence depended the strength of the shield of anonymity. The very existence of nonconformist literature was thus itself a witness to a shared commitment; its production a testimony of fellowship.[77]

It is consequently no surprise to find that the stationers prepared to risk handling nonconformist material were themselves often nonconformists whose business commitment was of a piece with their other activities. The London publishers Brabazon Aylmer, Dorman Newman, Thomas Cockerill and Ponder, for example, in 1672 acted as agents to procure licences under Charles's *Declaration*. Cockerill was later a manager of the Presbyterian fund. Benjamin Alsop served in Monmouth's army. Francis Smith was a General Baptist, licensed as a preacher in 1672, whose publications included a devotional work of his own authorship, *Symptomes of Growth and Decay in Godliness* (1660). The Baptists' *Humble Apology* (1661), disowning Venner's uprising, was sold by Smith and printed by a Particular Baptist, Henry Hills. Giles Calvert, the most prominent early Quaker publisher, though not himself a Quaker, attended Quaker meetings, and his son, also Giles, may have been a Friend. His sister, Martha Simmonds, wife of the Quaker printer Thomas Simmonds (or Simmons), was the chief of James Nayler's 1656 Bristol followers.[78]

We may distinguish several groups of such stationers. The first to come to the authorities' attention was the radical Cromwellian printers and publishers dubbed by L'Estrange 'the Confederate Stationers': Giles Calvert, Thomas Brewster and Livewell Chapman. Chapman, who had served his apprenticeship under the Puritan publisher Benjamin Allen, whose widow he married, became in the 1650s 'the publishing bastion of the Fifth Monarchy' and the owner of a press that, in the opinion of Secretary Thurloe, did 'much mischief'. He was imprisoned briefly in 1654, and in 1660 he eluded the warrant for his arrest issued for his publication of Milton's *Considerations ... to remove Hirelings out of the Church* (1659). With Brewster and Calvert he issued farewell sermons and the regicides' *Speeches and Prayers* (1660). To this commemoration of the restored regime's most prominent enemies as victims and martyrs the trio added a riposte to the public burning of the Covenant, *A Phenix: or the Solemn League and Covenant* (1661), which publicized Charles II's acutely embarrassing acceptance of the Covenant at his Scottish coronation in 1650, and a book of portents intended to refute royalist interpretations of recent providences, *Annus Mirabilis: or the Year of Prodigies* (1661). This was reputedly the work of the Baptist Henry Jessey. Under examination he denied its authorship, but it seems he did at least contribute material to it.[79]

The detection of this group was L'Estrange's earliest success and probably the chief reason for his promotion to the Surveyorship. In *Truth and Loyalty Vindicated* he tells how, in October 1661, he procured a warrant and seized 'about 120 copies' of the *Phenix* 'together with the Printer [Thomas Creake]' and 'One Stationer (of the three that were Partners in the Impression)', namely Giles Calvert.[80] Creake turned king's evidence. Elizabeth Calvert was committed to the Gatehouse and released on £500 security in December. Her husband Giles, with Henry Hills and Brewster a former official printer to the Council of State (1653), a publisher of Penington since 1648, of Fox since 1653 and of over 200 Quaker titles, entered into a bond of £500 in November 1662. He died nine months later.[81] Chapman, who had fled abroad, returned to England, was arrested in March 1663 and examined by Secretary Bennet in April. In March 1664 L'Estrange visited him in the Gatehouse, after which he was released on £300 security that neither he nor his wife, Ann, would deal in illicit publications.[82] And Brewster, the third confederate, was discovered in Bristol in February 1663, and, after some months' enquiries, arrested in October. He was (rather unusually) brought to trial in February 1664 for having maliciously and seditiously published the *Speeches and Prayers* and the *Phenix*. With him in the dock were Simon Dover, charged with seditious printing, and Nathan Brooks, charged with selling the works. Creake testified that Calvert, Brewster and Chapman had had him print an impression of 3,000 copies of the *Speeches* 'with as much privacy and expedition as I could', and 2,000 copies of the *Phenix*, and that Dover continued the printing. L'Estrange testified he had, after forcing entry, discovered at Dover's and Brooks's houses incriminating evidence (despite a desperate attempt to destroy this by fire). All three were fined, pilloried and imprisoned during the king's pleasure. Brewster died soon after this verdict.[83]

The radical press was not, however, so easily silenced. The confederates had had an associate in their enterprise: Francis Smith. He went to the Gatehouse for it, but, unlike his companions, survived to pursue for another twenty years a vigorous career of radical publishing through a bewildering succession of arrests, examinations, imprisonments and pursuits by L'Estrange and his spies (he was on one occasion the object of Lillicrap's attentions).[84] Nor did the work of the other confederates die with them. Elizabeth Calvert, who was to die a Baptist in 1674, took over her husband's business, his sign of the Black Spread Eagle and his publishing policy. Her encounter with L'Estrange in 1663–4 did not at all daunt her. In 1665 there was again a warrant issued for her arrest. In 1667 a consignment of her books was seized at Bristol, and the printer James Astwood was examined concerning Calvert stock. In January 1668 she and the printer John Darby were examined by Secretary Morice; in April she was committed for keeping a private press; and in May she was joined in the Gatehouse by Darby and Brewster's widow, Ann. Ann Brewster's name rarely appears in the *Short Title Catalogue*, presumably because she used blank imprints. At the time, she was certainly thought to carry on, like Elizabeth Calvert, where her husband left off. L'Estrange believed she had a hand in Marvell's *Growth of Popery*, she was probably the 'A.B.' who printed the first impression and pirated 'second edition' of *The Rehearsal Transpros'd*, and she was reputed to run the illegal Blue Anchor Alley press with Darby. Darby printed for Ponder the corrected, censored, second impression of *The Rehearsal Transpros'd*, and may also have printed for him Part I of *The Pilgrim's Progress*. His wife, Joan, was as active in disseminating nonconformist literature as was he, 'the *Religious Printer* ... [who] goes to Heaven with the Anabaptists', dedicated to printing it. Indeed, she and Ann Brewster were, in L'Estrange's view, 'a couple of the craftiest and most obstinate in the trade'.[85]

This involvement of wives, widows and, remembering Nathaniel Calvert's bond, of families, is further evidence of the shared commitment involved in the publication of nonconformist literature. The Widow Inman of Addlehill, Thames Street, who was known as a printer of seditious books, had succeeded to the business of her husband, Matthew. The widow of the Simon Dover tried with Brewster and Brooks was 'a common prenter for all Scandalous pamfletts'.[86] Jane and Langly Curtis were, in the 1670s and 80s, equally committed publishers of dissident material, and equally familiar with L'Estrange, prisons and courts.[87] Andrew Sowle, the pre-eminent Quaker publisher, in the early 1670s founded a firm which continued in business, and in the family, until 1829. He was actively supported by his wife Jane and daughter Tace, who succeeded to the business in the early 1690s. Quakers seem, indeed, to have organized themselves into a kind of religious counterpart to the Stationers' Company. Calvert's successors in the 1670s and 1680s, men such as Benjamin Clark and John Bringhurst, worked closely with the Morning Meeting, which not only authorized publication but discussed details of format and setting, safeguarded copyright and might itself even mark up copy for the press.[88] This shared involvement was not, though, peculiar to radicals and Quakers. The Benjamin Simmons who in the early 1680s published from the Three Golden Cocks near the West End of St Paul's was a relative of Baxter's publisher, Nevill Simmons, to whose London business he had succeeded. Benjamin was himself succeeded by Nevill's son, Thomas. A younger Nevill Simmons, bookseller in Sheffield, may also have been a relative. All the London men published Baxter and Presbyterian works.[89]

The Simmons family takes us to a rather different group of stationers which operated from shops chiefly in the Poultry, a street running the short distance from the east end of Cheapside to the stock market, where the Mansion House was afterwards built. It took its name from the medieval poultry market on this site, but it had, since the early sixteenth century, been a publishing centre. This group included such men as Benjamin Alsop, Brabazon Aylmer, Thomas Cockerill, John Dunton, John Lawrence (or Laurence), Dorman Newman, Nathaniel Ranew, Jonathan Robinson, William Rogers and the man Dunton called 'the most eminent Presbyterian Bookseller', Thomas Parkhurst, in 1703 elected Master of the Stationers' Company. These men had a publishing policy as marked, though different from, that of the 'Confederates' or the Quaker stationers of George Yard, Lombard Street. Brabazon Aylmer, for example, in Dunton's estimation 'a very just and religious man', though he came to own the copyright of *Paradise Lost* and issued Milton's *Epistolarum Familiarium Liber* (1674) and *Brief History of Muscovia* (1682), published chiefly works in the latitudinarian and Baxterian traditions. From *The Duty and Reward of Bounty* in 1671 until the end of the century he was the regular publisher of Isaac Barrow, including three editions of his *Works*, and of John Tillotson (Archbishop of Canterbury 1691–4), often in partnership with William Rogers, with whom he published Tillotson's *Works* in 1696. His list also included Richard Kidder, ejected vicar of Stanground, Huntingdonshire, who conformed in 1664, and Edward Fowler, later Bishop of Gloucester. This apologist for the latitudinarians (in *The Principles and Practices of Certain Moderate Divines* (1670)) was thought by Baxter to be 'a very ingenious sober Conformist'. When his *The Design of Christianity* (1671) was impugned as too moralistic (by, among others, Bunyan in *A Defence of the Doctrine of Justification* (1672)), Baxter came to its defence in *How Far Holinesse is the Design of Christianity* (1671).[90]

As well as such latitudinarians and low churchmen, who had a common background with and considerable sympathy for Presbyterian nonconformists (Tillotson had a high regard for Baxter and joined with him in a scheme for comprehension), Aylmer was the main publisher of William Bates, the ejected Presbyterian and friend who preached Baxter's funeral sermon. With Jonathan Robinson Aylmer published Edward Pearse, ejected lecturer at St Margaret's, Westminster, and in partnership with either Robinson alone or with Nathaniel Ranew and Robinson (who named his son Ranew) Aylmer issued some Bates titles, but of the majority of Bates's works he was the sole 'undertaker' or publisher. His printer for many of these was John Darby. Aylmer published also several pieces by Howe, though Howe more frequently published with Thomas Parkhurst, with whom, fittingly, Aylmer joined to issue Howe's funeral sermon on Bates. In 1678 Aylmer published Manton's *Sermons*. Manton's works went more often to Robinson, with whom Aylmer joined to issue *XVIII Sermons* (1679). The five-volume *One hundred and Ninety Sermons* (1681–1701) was initially undertaken jointly by Aylmer, Parkhurst, Robinson and Benjamin Alsop. And there was, finally, one other regular author in Aylmer's list: following the 'apostasy' of the 'Christian Quaker' George Keith, Aylmer became the most usual publisher of his pieces against the Quakers.[91]

The close personal, religious and professional ties between these men, hinted at by this mere listing of Aylmer's publications, may be further illustrated by a glance at the career of John Dunton. The man Pope was to describe in *The Dunciad* as 'a broken Bookseller and abusive scribbler' had been, though an unpredictable eccentric in the best seventeenth-century tradition, a vigorous and prominent stationer in the 1680s and 1690s. He was apprenticed to Parkhurst, and took his first shop near Parkhurst in the Poultry, before succeeding in 1685 to Alsop's shop, also in the Poultry, when Alsop took his commission in Monmouth's army. It was with Parkhurst that he published his first title, *The Lords Last Suffering* (1682), by Thomas Doolittle, the ejected Presbyterian rector of St Alphage, London, whom Baxter had supported at Cambridge in the early 1650s. By exchanging this title for the publications of other stationers Dunton was able to stock his shop and establish himself as a bookseller. He attended Doolittle's meeting, and was recommended by a friend to propose to his daughter so that he could 'have her Father's Copies for nothing', but in 1682 he married Samuel Annesley's daughter, Elizabeth, after Parkhurst had given Annesley a testimonial to his character. Annelsey's son-in-law Samuel Wesley (or Westley), afterwards the rector of Epworth, Lincolnshire, and father of the Wesleys, presented them with an epithalamium. Through Annesley, Dunton also met Defoe. His list subsequently included titles by Annesley and Wesley, and Wesley and Defoe collaborated with Dunton in the production of the twice-weekly *Athenian Mercury* (1691–7).[92]

In 1685 Dunton sailed for New England, where he met Increase Mather, some of whose works, as well as those of Increase's son, Cotton, he was later to publish, with Astwood as his printer. This trip may have been necessitated by complicity in Monmouth's rebellion: Dunton's apprentice, Samuel Palmer, was involved, and was to remain in New England. Dunton himself was in hiding in 1686–7 and then visited Holland, where he met Alsop, settling in England again only after the accession of William and Mary. His biographer, however, believes it more likely that it was his creditors he fled. Certainly, his wife Elizabeth (the 'Iris' of the autobiographical *Life and Errors* (1705)) took a far more diligent and professional interest in the business than her husband, as Dunton himself generously acknowledged. On her death in 1697, though still in his thirties, he retired from publishing.[93]

Here is a remarkable density of Presbyterian and nonconformist connections whose professional, personal, familial, literary, religious and political strands it is impossible to disentangle. Despite Dunton's waywardness, and a willingness to include in his list whatever was saleable, Dunton's publications were often of the Poultry type, and issued with Poultry partners. They included Baxter, and the man who took up Baxter's part in the antinomian controversy of the 1690s, Daniel Williams. Dunton's was one of the names on the imprint of the *Heads of Agreement assented to by the United Ministers* (1691) which resulted from the negotiations for union between Presbyterians and Congregationalists and which Baxter, only months before his death, supported in *Church Concord* (1691), produced by Parkhurst. Dunton published both Keith and Benjamin Keach's two allegorical fictions, *The Travels of True Godliness* (1683) and *The Progress of Sin* (1684). He was to have published Cotton Mather's *Magnalia Christi Americana*, but this appeared in 1702 with Parkhurst's imprint. Dunton, though, had joined with Parkhurst, Robinson and the 'upright and honest' John Lawrence to issue Baxter's *Reliquiae* (1696). One reason Leslie was incensed by the publication in 1702 of Calamy's *Abridgment of Mr. Baxter's History* was the audacity of the appearance on its title-page of not one stationer but three, namely the three remaining from the *Reliquiae* partnership, Parkhurst, Robinson and Lawrence.[94]

Dunton had previously joined with each of his *Reliquiae* partners separately to share the cost of publication, as well as with Alsop and Thomas Cockerill. And they, in their turn, had each associated with other members of the group.

Newman and Alsop were in 1682 partners in the production of Bunyan's *Holy War*, and that same year were joined by Cockerill in undertaking the publication of Stephen Charnock's *Several Discourses upon the Existence and Attributes of God*. The following year, the Alsop, Aylmer, Parkhurst, Robinson collaboration which had produced Manton's sermons was joined by Cockerill and Newman to publish the *Annotations upon the Holy Bible* of the ejected Presbyterian Matthew Poole. After Alsop's flight and Newman's bankruptcy, the remaining four were joined by Lawrence and Thomas Cockerill junior in issuing subsequent editions of Poole.[95]

What these various professional associations represent is a deliberate policy to ensure the publication of substantial works and collections of nonconformist divinity. These same men were associated in other business ventures, but what gave coherence to their publishing group was their commitment to nonconformity. Dunton first used the term 'conger' of the joint undertaking of publication (and sharing of copyright) which grew out of the wholesaling agreements of the late 1670s and early 1680s, but if the conger was a business arrangement designed to safeguard its members financially by spreading the cost and sharing the risk of publication, its incentive was rather religious than commercial. The desire to publish such material preceded the need to make arrangements to do so. And the material certainly was overwhelmingly nonconformist. To the determination of these men to see it in print the modern publishing industry owes its origin.[96]

Chapter 4 'Fit Audience Though Few'?

nonconformist writers and their readers

> Let no corrupt communication proceed out of your mouth, but
> that which is good to the use of edifying, that it may minister
> grace unto the hearers.
>
> Eph. iv. 29

I   CADMUS' DRAGON'S TEETH

L'Estrange had his successes: printers were harassed and imprisoned; authors
and booksellers were prosecuted. The final conclusion on his press campaign
must, however, be that it was a failure. The Surveyor never came anywhere
remotely near controlling the press. So far were he and the licensers from
silencing dissenting voices that they were hardly able even to mute them. *The
Rehearsal Transpros'd* opens with a passage ironically decrying 'The Press (that
villanous Engine) invented much about the same time as the Reformation' for
having 'done more mischief to the Discipline of our Church, than all the
Doctrine can make amends for'. Marvell picks up Parker's avowal that he is
'*none of the most zealour Patrons of the Press*' in order to taunt him with the
inefficiency of the licensing system and L'Estrange with his inability to exercise
his Surveyorship effectively:

'Twas an happy time when all Learning was in Manuscript, and some little Officer,
like our Author [Parker], did keep the Keys of the Library. When the Clergy
needed no more knowledge then to read the Liturgy, and the Laity no more
Clerkship than to save them from Hanging. But now, since Printing came into the
World, such is the mischief, that a Man cannot write a Book but presently he is
answered. Could the Press but once be conjured to obey only an *Imprimatur*, our
Author might not disdain *perhaps* to be one of its most zealous Patrons. There have
been wayes found out to banish Ministers, to fine not only the People, but even
the Ground and Fields where they assembled in Conventicles: But no Art yet
could prevent these seditious meetings of Letters. Two or three brawny Fellows
in a Corner, with meer Ink and Elbow-grease, do more harm than an *hundred
Systematical Divines* with their *sweaty Preaching* ... Their ugly Printing-Letters, that
look but like so many rotten-Teeth, How oft have they been pull'd out by [Sir John]
B. [irkenhead] and L. ['Estrange] the Publick-Tooth-drawers! and yet the rascally
Operators of the Press have got a trick to fasten them again in a few minutes, that
they grow as firm a Set, and as biting and talkative as ever. *O Printing*! how hast
thou disturb'd the Peace of Mankind! that Lead, when moulded into Bullets, is not
so mortal as when founded into Letters![1]

Marvell's irony mocks the conservatism of Parker and L'Estrange, but it hardly travesties their point of view, nor is his ridicule of their inability to control printing simply satirical exaggeration. He goes on to liken the fertility of the press to Cadmus' dragon's teeth, and with good cause. The Licensing Act had, like the Star Chamber Decree of 1637, restricted to 20 the number of master printers and allowed no more than two apprentices to each.[2] There were fewer printers and presses in London than in comparable European capitals in the seventeenth century, but in his *Considerations and Proposals* (1663) L'Estrange estimated that about 60 master printers with 'above 100 Apprentices' were at work and, though the Plague and Fire of London may have temporarily reduced this number, the entries in Henry Plomer's *Dictionary* of stationers active between 1668 and 1725 makes it clear that it could never have been restricted to the statutory limit. During the 1670s at least 52 printers were at work in England for all or part of the decade, and 13 stationers who were both booksellers (or publishers) and printers; during the 1680s, 76 and 23; during the 1690s, 77 and 31; and in the single year 1700, 50 and 25. Nor was the limitation of each to two presses observed: in 1668 James Fletcher was reported to have five presses in operation.[3] A contemporary catalogue lists 3,550 titles for the period 1666–80, or an average of 254 per year. A print run was probably in the region of 1,000–1,500 copies,[4] so we may conjecture that, of authorized publications alone, somewhere in the region of 10,000 titles were printed between 1660 and 1700, with the number of copies running into millions.

What precise percentage of this output may be classified as 'nonconformist' only a sustained statistical analysis of Donald Wing's *Short-Title Catalogue* could determine. We may, however, be confident that the number of titles published and of copies printed was, in absolute terms, very considerable, and comparatively far higher than the nonconformist proportion of the population would warrant. We have heard L'Estrange exclaim at the millions of illegal copies abroad. This sounds like polemical exaggeration, but he seems not to have exaggerated the number of printers (rather the contrary) and a wildly improbable figure would have carried no weight. Similarly, Thomas Creake's testimony that 3,000 copies of the regicides' *Speeches and Prayers* and 2,000 copies of *A Phenix* were printed may not have been the fancy of an informer anxious to please, nor the fancy of vanity Dunton's claim to have printed 10,000 copies each of the third edition of *The Practice of Godliness* (1690) by the Congregationalist Henry Lukin and of Keach's *Travels of True Godliness* (1683).[5] We may, after all, trust Baxter when he writes that some 20,000 copies of *A Call to the Unconverted* were printed in the year of its publication (1658), and this had by 1685 reached a twenty-third edition, or another 25,000 or so copies. His *Saints Everlasting Rest* (1650), a very substantial work of over 700 quarto pages, had reached a thirteenth edition by 1688. The 22 seventeenth-century editions of *The Pilgrim's Progress* probably represent over 30,000 copies.[6] Nothing on the conformist side can match these figures. And, though these were exceptional best sellers, anything up to six reprintings seems not to have been unusual for practical and devotional nonconformist divinity, particularly of a Presbyterian or Congregational persuasion. Apart from the frequent cases in Baxter and Bunyan (including *Grace Abounding, Mr. Badman* and *The Holy War*), examples are to hand in the bibliographies of Bates, Corbet, Keach, Heywood, Howe, and Owen, to look no further.[7]

Although Robert Barclay's *Catechism* (1673) and *Apology* (1678) ran to five and four editions respectively, and the enlarged 1682 version of Penn's *No Cross, No Crown* to six, Quaker pieces were more commonly brief and frequent than substantial and reprinted, but they were astonishingly frequent. Only three of Penington's tracts were reprinted (and then only once each), but, from 1648 until his death in 1679, he failed to publish only in the six years 1652, 1655, 1657, 1669, 1673 and 1676, and he often produced several pamphlets in one year (11 in 1660).[8] The total number of pieces published by early Quakers has been variously computed. From Donald Wing's *Catalogue* and Joseph Smith's two-volume *Descriptive Catalogue of Friends' Books* (1867), the most recent such calculation finds that, by 1700, 3,103 new Quaker titles had been published, 469 reprints and 187 memorials (often prefaced to other works). Of these, 2,939 were published between 1660 and 1699 inclusive.[9]

To produce such quantities of books was one thing; to bring them to readers, another. This remarkable productivity would have been to no avail – would, indeed, have been financially impossible – were not nonconformists able to distribute and retail what the government would much rather remained unobtainable. In London there was little difficulty. Potential purchasers might easily browse in the stalls in Paul's Churchyard or Little Britain, and there read the title-pages of licensed material posted up as advertisements (hence their descriptive fullness and large, sometimes strident, claims), or turn the pages of the author's prefaces, directed often to engaging the attention and interest of just such casual browsers.[10] Penn's preface to the greatly enlarged second edition of his *No Cross, No Crown* (1682), to take a random example, is at once disarmingly courteous and direct: 'Come, Reader, hearken to me awhile; I seek thy salvation; that is my plot; thou wilt forgive me.' With fine poise, Penn at once entices and challenges. He entices by the personal disclosures which engage sympathy, confer authority and offer promise: 'the following Discourse, first written during my confinement in the Tower of London, in the year 1668' traces a 'path' in which

> God, in his everlasting kindness, guided my feet in the flower of my youth, when about twenty-two years of age: then he took me by the hand, and led me out of the pleasures, vanities, and hopes of the world. I have tasted of Christ's judgments and mercies, and of the world's frowns and reproaches: I rejoice in my experience, and dedicate it to thy service in Christ.

He challenges by the unassailable assertiveness of his opening premise ('The great business of man's life is to answer the end for which he lives, and that is to glorify God and save his own soul: this is the decree of Heaven, as old as the world'); by his concern for the reader ('O! Reader, as one knowing the terrors of the Lord, I persuade thee to be serious, diligent, and fervent about thy own salvation'); and by his assurance (Christ is 'as infallible as free; without money, and with certainty'). His comprehensive purpose ('that thou, Reader, mayest be won to Christ; and if won already, brought nearer to Him') allows no reader to discard the book as irrelevant to his case. Thus is the reader drawn gently into a relationship of such seriousness, yet such open and equable friendliness, that by the end of the preface he will not wish to part company with Penn.[11]

In the last three decades of the seventeenth century London stationers began to engage their customers more actively by auctioning books. Dunton disposed of books in this way, and Milton's friend Edward Millington, who may have sold Milton's library in 1669/70 and whose wit and dramatic sense of timing won Dunton's praise, became the most famous auctioneer of the time.[12] More significantly, the development of subscription publishing as a means both to raise capital for printing and also to guarantee a market was almost entirely the innovation of nonconformist stationers. It was the existence of a committed nonconformist readership which made possible this appeal to the patronage of the public. To subscribe to the second edition of Baxter's *Paraphrase on the New Testament* (1695) was after all, in view of its history, to declare oneself pretty emphatically. The method was frequently used in the 1680s and 1690s, particularly by the Poultry stationers, to secure the publication of substantial nonconformist texts. A single bookseller might, understandably, be unwilling to take upon himself the entire risk of such a venture. Nevill Simmons, for example, declined Baxter's *Methodus Theologiae Christianae* (1681). Baxter himself undertook to pay for its printing, but at considerable loss to himself: 'some friends contributed about Eighty pounds towards it; It cost me one way or other about Five hundred pounds: About Two hundred and fifty pounds I received from those Non-conformists that bought them.'[13] Subscription might not be more successful: in 1683 Samuel Simmons still had unsold copies of the two-volume complete edition of the Congregationalist Joseph Caryl's *Exposition upon Job* for which he had, ten years before, invited subscriptions of 50s. and offered for sale to the public at £4. They were still available, from William Marshall, Newgate Street, in 1690, at 30s. (40s. bound). The shifting partnerships of the Poultry stationers, however, managed the business more successfully and 'from the early sixteen-eighties onwards displayed a continuity of subscription enterprise in prompting nonconformist divinity'.[14] In the Term Catalogue for February 1680 they advertised Manton's sermons on Psalm cxix to subscribers undertaking to pay £1 4s., '10s. in hand towards the carrying on of the said work; and the remaining 14s. upon the delivery of the said Book to the Subscriber'. In the *Athenian Mercury* of 29 October 1695 Dunton printed proposals for the publication of the *Reliquiae Baxterianae* at 17s. 6d. to subscribers and 20s. to other purchasers. By this method Jacob Tonson more famously published the fourth edition of *Paradise Lost* in 1688. The printed list of subscribers included the name of Sir Roger L'Estrange.[15]

Clause x of the 1637 Decree and the Licensing Act had both restricted the retailing of books to members of the Stationers' Company, but outside London there was an extensive distribution network by means of which nonconformist texts, both licit and illicit, were made available throughout the kingdom. Stationers themselves might distribute their publications, by post, carrier, coach, or ship, to provincial booksellers, to county fairs and to a variety of other outlets. When the Bristol bookseller Richard Moon was raided in 1663 he was found to have received books from Brewster and Calvert. It was during the Fair at Bristol that Brewster himself was discovered in lodgings in the town with two boxes of largely unlicensed books. Legally, Oliver Heywood received regular large consignments of books from Thomas Parkhurst.[16]

The trade of such men as Parkhurst was open and above board, and even surreptitious stationers constituted a fairly small group, who could be harassed, if not always caught. There was, though, a far larger and far less manageable body of men involved in the trade. When L'Estrange analysed the book trade, his list of the 'usual *Agents* for *Publishing*' included, besides stationers and printers, '*Hawkers, Mercury-women, Pedlers, Ballad-singers, Posts, Carryers, Hackney-Coach-men, Boat-men,* and *Mariners*'. It had been from a 'poor Pedlar' that in Shropshire Baxter's father had been able to buy Richard Sibbes's *Bruised Reed*, and they seem to have continued to carry books, both licit and illicit, as a matter of course, despite L'Estrange's irritation and government attempts to prevent them. The grant of a patent in 1665 to Edward Gray and Thomas Killigrew to license pedlars and chapmen quite failed to control their trade, as it hardly could, since there seem to have been about 10,000 of them in the 1680s. From London, and from market towns, these men carried books into the remotest areas.[17] While Parkhurst and his fellow stationers supplied London with large folios, these pedlars made available to a dispersed county market the substantial number of godly chapbooks and nonconformist tracts in the price range 2d. to 9d., easily carried and within the means of poorer readers.

A main intention of the 1665 patent had been to prevent the distribution of Quaker books, but this was something for which Quakers had no need to rely upon pedlars. Itinerant Quakers carried books as a matter of course on their missions. The Scottish Quaker William Dundas was in Dieppe in the early 1660s when two women Quakers arrived from England 'to bear a Testimony to the Truth against the *Protestants* of that Nation, and brought with them several Books of Friends translated into *French*, and distributed in the Town, and gave me also to distribute'. The same practice was adopted in England, sometimes with substantial works. An advertisement for George Keith's reply to Barclay's *Apology, The Standard of the Quakers Examined* (1702), describes Barclay's work as 'a Book they very much boast of; having been at the Charge of printing it in Latine, Low Dutch, French; and several editions in English; which, at a publick

Expence, they have given away; looking upon it as the Foundation of their Opinion'. Quaker stationers themselves undertook the warehousing, dispatching and retailing of books throughout England and in the New World, not always finding it easy to have their accounts settled. So, too, did individuals not in the trade. There is in the State Papers a list, dating perhaps from 1664, of 44 'Dispersers' of Quaker books. Its geographical spread is remarkable: York, Lincoln, Nottingham, Warwick, Huntingdon, Northampton, Hertford, Colchester, Gloucester, Bristol, Weymouth and Ryegate are all represented. No wonder Ellis Hookes, Clerk to the Morning Meeting and the Meeting for Sufferings and the man chiefly responsible for collecting, collating and preserving early Quaker records, could write without remark or explanation that the 'many faithfull Testimonyes to the Truth' left by Richard Hubberthorn 'in bookes and Epistles' had since his death been not only printed but also 'dispersed among friends'.[18]

To these various endeavours should be added those of the authors themselves. In one of his diaries Oliver Heywood wrote that 'My book of heart-treasure [*Heart Treasure* (1667)] being printed, I had and paid for 10£'s worth of them, and they are all dispersed and disposed of and I hear they doe some good, blessed be god.' Whether they had been purchased or received as payment from his publisher (usually Thomas Parkhurst), he made a habit of thus giving away his own books. In 1687 he 'distributed gratis to my hearers about home, my relations and friends abroad in Lanc – at York – &c' 162 copies of his *Baptismal Bonds Renewed* (1687). He records the names of those to whom, in 1679, he gave 138 copies of *Life in God's Favour* (1679). In the four years 1667–71 he disposed of over 200 copies of *Heart Treasure* and nearly 300 copies of *Closet-Prayer a Christian Duty* (1671) in this way. When his brother Nathaniel's *Christ Displayed* was published in 1679, Heywood's widowed sister-in-law received from Parkhurst 'by John Stot carryer' 100 copies 'for the copy' and Heywood and his friends undertook to buy 300 copies. Some of these Heywood gave away, some he sold and some went to local stationers to sell. Indeed, besides his own benefactions, Heywood seems to have operated the equivalent of a modern mail-order service, receiving from neighbours money for books ordered from Parkhurst.[19]

Baxter took a similar course throughout his life. During the Interregnum, while at Kidderminster, he 'gave to every family in Town and Parish (being beside a great Borough about twenty Villages) a Catechism, and some of my lesser Books, and of every Book I wrote usually as many as my Purse could well afford. And to every Family a Bible, which either for want of money, or of willingness to buy, had none, where any one in the house could read.' After the Restoration, though he 'never came near' his Kidderminster people again, he 'sent them all the Books which I wrote'. When, in 1674, his *Poor Man's Family Book* was published, he 'found it a useful work of Charity to give many of them (with the *Call to the Unconverted* [(1658)]) abroad in many Countries, where neither I, nor such others had leave to Preach (and many Hundreds since, with good success)'. He had always encouraged his readers to give books as one of their acts of charity, especially to poorer families; but, as these words suggest, the Bartholomew ejections and Clarendon Code made this a still more urgent duty. He appealed particularly to the rich: 'if Rich Men will give their Tenants and Neighbours such Books as are suitable to the instruction of Families, and the People will diligently use them, it may do much to keep up saving Knowledge and Practice, where the publick Ministry faileth most.'[20]

After the publication of *The Saints Everlasting Rest* (1650), for which he received £10, Baxter came to an arrangement with his publishers Thomas Underhill and Francis Tyton, and subsequently with Nevil Simmons, his main publisher between 1655 and 1681, in order to facilitate the giving of books and to ensure that his own works were sold as cheaply as possible. He described this arrangement in an appendix to his *Five Disputations of Church Government and Worship* (1659) intended to scotch the rumour that he made £300–£400 annually from his books:

> I agreed with them [his publishers] for the fifteenth Book, to give to some few of my friends, hearing that some others agreed for the tenth. Sometime my fifteenth Book coming not to an hundred, and sometime but to a few more, when of Practical Books I needed sometime 800. to give away. Because I was scarce rich enough to buy so many, I agreed with the Bookseller, (my Neighbour, [Simmons]) to allow 18d. a Ream (which is not a penny a quire,) out of his own gain towards the buying of Bibles, and some of the practical Books which he printed, for the poor: Covenanting with him, that he should sell my Controversial Writings as cheap, and my Practical Writings somewhat cheaper then books are ordinarily sold. To this hour I never received for my self one penny of money from them for any of my Writings, to the best of my remembrance: but if it fell out that my part came to more than I gave my friends, I exchanged them for other Books.

In a letter which Matthew Sylvester appended to *Reliquiae Baxterianae* Baxter reiterates that 'I never received more of any Bookseller than the fifteenth Book, and this Eighteen pence a Rheam', adding that any profit which remained after the purchase of books was put into a trust for charitable use.[21]

These arrangements demonstrate a particular concern that books should be within the means of the poor, available to husbandmen, craftsmen, artisans, servants, cottagers and day-labourers. To reach them, books had to be not merely printed and distributed but cheaply priced. The book trade in general catered for this market with single sheet ballads selling for 1d. (or two a penny), chapbooks and three- or four-sheet small books of 24–36 pages for 2d. to 6d. Longer romantic and historical fictions sold for up to 9d., or 1s., but these prices were already beyond the poorer members of society. In the earlier seventeenth century an agricultural labourer's average daily wage was 12d., when work was in season. In the 1690s the herald and genealogist Gregory King estimated (and probably somewhat underestimated) that this amounted to an annual family income of £15, or £4 10s. per labourer. He put a cottager's family income at no more than £6 10s. per year. For yeomen or freeholders, shopkeepers, tradesmen, small merchants and professional people, whose incomes King estimated at £45 for tradesmen and shopkeepers, £72 for clergy, £91 for wealthier freeholders and £198 for merchants, stitched plays sold generally for 1s., duodecimos and small octavos for 2s. to 3s. 6d., and octavos for up to 6s. For the bibliophiles amongst them, for merchants in a rising way of business and for the gentry, there were quartos and folios for 7s. to 20s. (or more, especially if ornately bound).[22]

In the main, nonconformists offered nothing to rival the very cheapest items available, though Quaker tracts sold for very little, and the anonymous *Lamentation over the House of Israel* ([1664?]) carried on the title-page the rhyme 'This is not to be sold/For Silver, nor for Gold/For unto Thee/This Book is free,/ Without Monie.' They were, however, rivals for the chapbook market. Indeed, the 'godly books' which formed over 30 per cent of the chapbook publishers' trade were often versions, or alleged versions, of nonconformist texts: Baxter's name was attached to chapbook sermons; extracts and selections from his works were published piratically in cheap format; there was in 1684 a 22-page version of *The Pilgrim's Progress*; and nonconformist sermons appeared as chapbooks.[23] A good many homiletic, practical and devotional nonconformist texts were available for 6d.: Baxter's *God's Goodness Vindicated* (1671), for example, and his *Duty of Heavenly Meditation* (1671); Bunyan's *Strait Gate* (1676) and *A Book for Boys and Girls* (1686); John Corbet's *Self-Imployment in Secret* (1681); Nathaniel Vincent's *Little Childes Catechisme* (1679); and Keach's *A Summons to the Grave* (1676). This last was a sermon, and 6d. was the usual price for a book made up of a single sermon. Brief pieces, such as Thomas Doolittle's *The Swearer Silenced* (1689), sold for as little as 4d.[24]

The great majority of nonconformist texts fell, however, at the lower end of the next price range. For 1s. or 1s. 6d. a reader might select from a wide variety of works by Baxter, Bunyan, John Cheyney, John Corbet, Thomas Doolittle, Giles Firmin, Theophilus Gale, Thomas Gouge, John Humfrey, James Janeway, Benjamin Keach, Owen, Penn, Matthew Poole, John Tombes and Thomas Vincent, to name but a few.[25] These included *Grace Abounding* and each part of *The Pilgrim's Progress*, Keach's *Travels of True Godliness* (1683) and Baxter's *Call to the Unconverted*.[26] For 2s. there was Oliver Heywood's *Heart-Treasure* and Owen's *Nature ... of Indwelling Sin* (1668); for 2s. 6d., Joseph Alleine's *Alarme to Unconverted Sinners* (1671); for 3s., Howe's *Blessedness of the Righteous* (1673) and Baxter's *Cure of Church-Divisions* (1670).[27] Between 4s. and 7s. there were substantial works such as Baxter's enlarged *Life of Faith* (1670), the *Morning Exercises* edited by Samuel Annesley and Owen's *Doctrine of Justification by Faith* (1677).[28] The price of the *Samson Agonistes* and *Paradise Regained* volume was 4s.; 6s. the price of Milton's *History of Britain*.[29] There seems then to have been rather a gap until we come to the large folio collections of works, biblical annotations and doctrinal and scholarly treatises selling for over 15s. a volume. These were of a Presbyterian or Congregational stamp, and included the works published by subscription. Thomas Goodwin's *Works*, Caryl on Job and Owen on Hebrews fall into this class.[30]

2   THE IMPLIED READER

Nonconformist writing presupposed a reader. Its composition was not a private pursuit for personal ends (however personal its immediate occasion and inspiration may have been), but a public service, and, furthermore, a service whose full performance demanded not only diligence in writing but an equal diligence in transmitting the text to potential readers and in persuading them to acquire it, read it and act upon it. Nonconformist texts were very rarely thought of as having intrinsic merit; their virtue resided in their potential to transform lives. Milton may have had his eye on posterity and have intended to 'leave something so written to aftertimes, as they should not willingly let it die', but in this he was exceptional. Baxter's disclaimer is far more representative: 'I write not to win thy praise of an artificial comely Structure; but to help souls to Holiness and Heaven.' Such an explicit declaration of a design upon the reader is to be found wherever we turn in nonconformist writing. We heard Penn deliver another in the preface to *No Cross, No Crown*, but the bias hardly requires exemplification. It was common to all, including Milton. He may, exceptionally, have intended an enduring contribution to Western culture, but the moralistic, educative and didactive purpose of nonconformist writing – its functional and utilitarian nature – is as clearly expressed in the opening paragraph of *Paradise Lost* as in Baxter or Penn. Its concluding line is ambiguous, but this ambiguity serves only to throw into prominence the significance of the reader to Milton's enterprise. Milton's syntax at once poses and answers the question: 'justify to whom?' Unless an adjudicator is persuaded, justification fails to justify. The poem's grandly announced intention to justify God's dealings with men can be directed only to a reader, and fulfilled only in a reader's response. To 'justify the ways of God to men' Milton must justify to men God's ways. Someone must hear him.[31]

This much the determination to sow Marvell's dragon's teeth throughout the kingdom tells us, but where did the teeth take root and multiply? For whom in particular did Milton write of the general predicament of 'man'? Later in the poem, he appears to anticipate but 'few' readers. In context, however, this is less an expression of resignation at their paucity than an encouragement and compliment to his readers and a reiteration of the seriousness of purpose declared at the poem's opening. The passage encourages the reader by establishing with him a special relationship as one of the chosen for whom Milton writes. It compliments him by contrasting him with Bacchus' (Cavalier) revellers, with their hedonistic, and ultimately fatal, excapism. And it reaffirms Milton's purpose by distinguishing the illuminating heavenly inspiration of his muse from the 'empty dream' inspired by Orpheus' mother, Calliope.[32]

We may, then, suppose Milton hoped for more than a 'few' readers, but how many readers may we conjecture for nonconformist texts generally, and who were they? To form some opinion on this, we need first some impression of who *could* have read them. Gregory King estimated a total English population of 5,500,520: modern demographers estimate a population declining from 5.2 million in the 1650s to 4.8 million in the 1680s, thereafter rising again to 5 million in 1700.[33] What proportion of this population was fully literate is irrecoverable with certainty. Historical sociologists have established that barely a third were able to sign their names in this period, and that this ability declined with social satus. While all clergymen could sign and generally 90 per cent of the gentry, only 60–65 per cent of yeomen were able to do so, 50–55 per cent of tradesmen, 15–20 per cent of husbandmen and 10–15 per cent of labourers. This kind of evidence leads Peter Laslett to the view that this was a society still mainly 'oral in its comunications', where 'the ability to read with understanding and to write much more than a personal letter was confined for the most part to the ruling minority.'[34] Strictly, however, such statistical evidence tells us only of the ability (or willingness) to sign, and not of the ability to write or the (commoner?) ability to read, still less of the fluency or competence with which these skills, if possessed, were practised.[35] Margaret Spufford's detailed attention to, and inferences from, particular cases leads her to the view that historians are 'probably being far too conservative in their estimates of the spread of reading ability' at least. She concludes that 'illiteracy was everywhere face to face with literacy', that by 1700 even popular culture was literate rather than oral and that, though 'we shall never be able to assess' the 'true size' of the late seventeenth-century reading public, it was almost certainly greater than statistics alone suggest.[36]

A number of Margaret Spufford's examples are drawn from nonconformists: the famous case of Bunyan, the son of a poor husbandman and 'mechanic' or artisan; the case of Oliver Heywood's first wife Elizabeth, daughter of the ejected minister John Angier, who could 'read the hardest chapter in the bible when she was but foure years of age' and was able, at six years old, 'to write down passages of the sermon in the chappel' (Heywood himself was far less forward); and the evidence of Quaker publication and spiritual autobiographies. Other examples are plentiful: when an apprentice mercer in the Lancashire village of Ashton-in-Makerfield, the Presbyterian Roger Lowe acted as a (sometimes paid) secretary for illiterate neighbours and friends; Joseph Lister, a Bradford Presbyterian orphaned at the age of six who worked as a servant in London after his apprenticeship was terminated by the outbreak of the Civil War, 'learned to write both long and short hand, and characters very well, that I might be of use in the family', apparently when he was 10 to 12 years old.[37]

As these examples suggest, literacy rates were higher amongst nonconformists than in other sections of society. Not only did they write copiously, confident of nonconformist readers, but they were heirs to the educational drive of Puritanism and, as we shall see in the next chapter, continued to be enthusiastic advocates of the benefits of literacy, encouraging all classes of society, and especially children, to learn to read and to write and to be diligent practitioners of these skills. This was one aim of Bunyan's *Book for Boys and Girls*, as it was of the *Primmer and Catechism for Children* (1670) put out by Fox and Ellis Hookes. They were also, as William Braithwaite noted a little wryly in view of Fox's own orthographical idiosyncracies, responsible for *An Instruction for Right Spelling.*[38]

But how many nonconformists were there? There are four sources of evidence which afford an answer to this question: individual contemporary estimates; the episcopal returns prepared for Sheldon; an episcopal return prepared for William III in 1693; and, fullest and most reliable, the dissenters' own survey conducted in the early eighteenth century. The first of these tend to be impressionistic. They vary widely and are usually computed to further a controversial point. Algernon Sidney remarked sardonically of a bill for the relief of nonconformists that 'intending to oblige above a million of men' it would have been better first 'to consult with one of that number, concerning the way of doing it'. By contrast Francis Turner, in his reply to Bishop Croft, played down the number of committed nonconformists. 'Dissenters properly so call'd', he wrote,

> are not in some Dioceses above one in twenty. Many absent themselves from our Churches out of pure Indevotion and Laziness. Many frequent the Meeting-houses out of Curiosity, and many for want of room in their Churches and Tabernacles at *London*, or because of their distance from their own Parish Churches in the County. The stiff and irreconcilable Dissenters appear to be a handful of men in comparison.

Samuel Parker proposed the same proportion, drawing from Marvell the retort that 'the Nonconformists value themselves … upon their Conscience and not their Numbers'. In 1692 Defoe put the figure at two million; and an anonymous pamphlet of 1732 at 700,000.[39]

The episcopal returns at first appear more authoritative, but their editor, G. Lyon Turner, points out that they should be treated with caution: not all the returns are extant; they were made with varying degrees of thoroughness and accuracy; they almost certainly minimize the figures, partly because the necessary secrecy of nonconformist meetings made accurate figures difficult to come by, and partly to confirm the impression that this contemptible minority could be finally extirpated by further penal legislation; and estimates are often vaguely phrased ('The number uncertaine', the number 'cannot be learnt', 'great numbers', 'many not yet discovered doubtlesse').[40] Turner's conclusion is, from the 1669 returns, between 120,000 and 123,000 nonconformists. The 1676 census computed the proportion of nonconformists to conformists as 1 to

22 of the adult population, but, since this calculation treated everyone who did not actively dissent as a committed conformist, it inflated the conformist figure and correspondingly reduced the nonconformist. Even so, working with a conformist total of 2,123,362, this admits nearly 100,000 as the smallest nonconformist estimate which could be offered.[41] The conclusions of the 1693 census were very similar: 2,447,254 conformists to 108,676 nonconformists, which again gives the proportion of 1 to 22.[42]

In the second decade of the eighteenth century a committee of the Three Denominations (Presbyterian, Congregationalist and Baptist) undertook a survey of dissenting congregations, probably as part of a campaign for the repeal of the Schism Act. Its results were written up by the Congregationalist and historian of Puritanism Daniel Neal, and by the Presbyterian John Evans. These lists have been analysed by Evelyn Bebb and, more recently and in fascinating detail, by Michael Watts. The former concluded that nonconformists (excluding Quakers) numbered 150,000–250,000 in the period 1660–1700, and 250,000–300,000 in the period 1700–40. Michael Watts put the figure for all dissenters in England (including Quakers) at 338,120 in the early eighteenth century, with another 17,770 in Wales, or some 6 per cent of the population. Of these, Presbyterians were by far the most numerous (185,430), nearly three times the number of Congregationalists (67,580). Dr Watts calculates 63,370 Baptists and 39,510 Quakers (excluding Wales). These could constitute as much as 8 per cent of the population in areas of highest density (such as the Presbyterians in Lancashire and the West Country), but through large areas of the kingdom their representation was less than 5 per cent. Only the Presbyterians had a significant presence everywhere. Baptists made no impression in the North, and Congregationalists were thinly dispersed there and in the West Midlands. The greatest strength of both lay in South Wales and the Home Counties, where they amounted to 5 per cent of the population. Quakers were widely, though more thinly, dispersed, but most prominent in the north-western area of their origin, Cumberland, Westmorland and Lancashire, in Bristol, and in London and the northern Home Counties. Only in Bristol, however, did they exceed 2 per cent of the population.[43]

This, then, was the primary and immediate market for nonconformist texts. The figures may seem comparatively slight, but this impression is for two reasons misleading. First, a higher proportion of the nonconformist body than of the population generally was literate. 330,000 nonconformists in a nation of 3.5 million adults, a third of whom were literate, may have accounted for 13–15 per cent of the literate population. And secondly, unlike national population statistics, the nonconformist figures are, for all their shortcomings, a measure of positive commitment, a significant part of which consisted, especially when persecution prevented meetings or removed the minister, in literary study. Nonconformists were not only able but diligent readers. If, then, the nonconformist figures represent a potential readership greater than one might expect, and greater than that of a group of comparable size from the population at large, equally, when viewed absolutely, they are far from inconsiderable. No other body of seventeenth-century literature could address itself to so readily definable and so large a readership. Although episcopal works apparently had a larger public, their sales suggest an actual readership which, with a few exceptions, was smaller than that enjoyed by nonconformist works. Polite letters addressed an audience fractional by comparison. Drama may have been, from one point of view, 'the dominant literary form' of the period, but plays were only rarely reprinted, and so seldom reached more than 1,000 or so readers.[44]

The composition of this readership was diverse. Nonconformist authors generally make it clear, on their title-pages and in their prefaces, to whom their books are primarily addressed. They characterized their intended readers in one of two ways: by their religious state or their secular calling. The former descriptions classify readers as unregenerate; as believers who have reached a particular stage of spiritual maturity; as members of particular congregations; and as adherents of a denomination. The first of these were not commonly intended as the sole readers. Although Baxter's *Call* was enlarged and constantly reprinted, Alleine published his *Alarme to Unconverted Sinners* (1671) and Bunyan his *Come & Welcome, to Jesus Christ* (1678), evangelism to the public at large was usually not the main purpose but a subsidiary aim in books primarily directed to the consolation and encouragement of believers, and particularly nonconformists. Penn's *No Cross, No Crown* was directed to both groups of readers, and so was *The Pilgrim's Progress*. By chalking '*out before thine eyes,/The man that seeks the everlasting Prize*', showing '*whence he comes, whither he goes*' and '*how he runs, and runs,/Till he unto the Gate of Glory comes*', it encourages both its unconverted reader to begin the journey and its converted reader to continue in the way.[45] Milton's purpose in *Paradise Lost* would seem to be equally comprehensive: a persuasive to those who doubted the justness of God's ways, and a confirmation to those who accepted it.

Baxter's was the most sustained attempt to address the second group of readers. He undertook to compose an entire body of practical divinity dealing with every stage of Bunyan's journey, its several volumes addressed to the 'several ranks' of the spiritual life. After his *Call* to 'impenitent unconverted sinners', he addressed 'those that have some purposes to Turn', and so successively 'the babes in Christ', 'lapsed and backsliding Christians' and 'the strong'.[46] No one else was so comprehensive, but many other nonconformists addressed themselves to particular religious states and, since religious and physical maturity have some relationship, also to different age groups: children, students, young men and women and the old are specified in titles and prefaces by Keach, Bunyan, Gale and Baxter, for example. Baxter's plan also took in 'some special errors of the times, and ... some common killing sins', and these too were commonly taken up. In *The Pilgrim's Progress* Atheist, Formalist and Hypocrisy have neither entered by the gate nor stayed in the Palace Beautiful, and texts on such themes might be addressed to the general public. Counsels to avoid despair, self-ignorance and apostasy were more specifically directed to nonconformists, as were encouragements to the joys of faith. To say so directly would, of course, be to invite the censor's veto, but it is pretty clear for whom Howe intends his discourse on Psalm xxxvii. 4 in *A Treatise of Delighting in God* (1674): 'This Psalm, by the contents of it, seems to suppose an afflicted state of good men, by the oppression of such as were in that and other respects very wicked ... Hence, the composure of it is such as might be most ... serviceable to the fortifying of the righteous against the sin and trouble which such a state of things might prove the occasion of unto them.'[47]

John Owen's literary career had begun with *The Duty of Pastors and People Distinguished* (1643), a book addressed to his congregation at Fordham, Essex, and many later nonconformist texts derived from manuscripts and sermons originally prepared by their authors for the people in their ministerial care. Although printed for a larger public, these were often published as a token of continuing pastoral concern for the particular congregation from which the author was now separated. Howe's *Blessedness of the Righteous* (1668) contained the substance of Interregnum sermons preached at Great Torrington, Devon, and *Delighting in God*, dedicated 'To my much valued Friends, the Magistrates and Other Inhabitants of Great Torrington', consisted of a revision of 'sundry sermons ... preached twenty years ago among you' and now published as 'both a testimony of my affection and an advantage to you'. Baxter continued to address his Kidderminster people in the same way. Such texts need not always have lain twenty years in a desk drawer. It was sometimes possible to publish sermons preached at conventicles, as did Bunyan, for example.[48]

The fourth group of religiously directed titles includes the considerable mass of controversial material produced. This was often, and often acrimonious, professional and scholarly debate between theologians and ecclesiastics of different parties from which the 'general reader' is all but excluded. It was by no means always conducted between nonconformists on the one side and episcopalians (or Romanists) on the other. Doctrine could divide Presbyterian from Congregationalist, as it did to the ruin of the Happy Union between them in the early 1690s, and so could ecclesiastical policy and polity, especially as they bore on comprehension, toleration and occasional conformity. On these things Baxter and Owen could never see eye to eye.[49] Bunyan began his literary career in controversy with Edward Burrough, and each gave as good as he got. Even here, however, and particularly in controversy with conformists, a pastoral motive can often be discerned in a concern for the predicament of ordinary lay nonconformists and in anxiety about the disabling effects of the errors under which members of other denominations laboured.

Except when they specify him as, to take random examples, an MP, a justice, or an apprentice, descriptions of the reader in social or secular terms tend to be vague. Very often the 'poor' and the 'vulgar' are addressed, and it was frequently urged that, in Manton's words, 'Usually God's true people are the meanest and most contemptible, not being so noted for outward excellency as others.' But when, in the same book that he explains '*Discourse*' means '*ratiocination*' in order not to be mistaken 'by the vulgar Reader', Howe freely deploys Hebrew, Greek and Latin, it appears his notion of 'the Vulgar' is somewhat elastic. In *The Living Temple* he endeavours to 'make the case as plain as possible to the most ordinary capacity', and yet his readers are expected to know their Hobbes, Descartes and Locke, and not to be stumbled by Platonism, Pythagoreanism or Epicureanism. The 'meanest and most contemptible' would, literally, be unable to read Howe, and the literate vulgar person of 'ordinary capacity' would find him very hard going indeed.[50]

This we might put down as the exceptional case of a man naturally of a scholarly and philosophical frame of mind,[51] and yet the image of well-ordered domesticity and of a competent, if not lavish, financial context created in Baxter's *Poor Man's Family Book* (1674) and its sequel, *The Catechizing of Families* (1683), suggests that here, too, the 'poor' reader is expected to be in sound circumstances. The one thousand authors and works of Baxter's recommended '*Poor mans Library*', which ... cometh short of a Rich and Sumptuous Library' have clearly lost touch with any real impoverishment. In *The Pilgrim's Progress* it is noticeable that, unlike the pilgrims, Mr Worldly-Wiseman 'looked like a Gentleman', By-ends marries a lady's daughter and Mr Brisk is 'of some breeding'.[52] Nevertheless, poverty is not a source of temptation to Christiana and her companions, nor are financial constraints a trial. The dominant impression in Part II is of a settled prosperity, and this, we may suppose, was an image to which Bunyan expected his readers to respond as a reflection of their (and his) experience of communal life and the fellowship of a gathered church. This corresponds to the implication of nonconformist book prices surveyed earlier. Those prices extended from the poorest to the richest pocket, but were concentrated in the range 1s. to 4s., within the means of freeholders, tradesmen, shopkeepers and the mercantile classes. Nonconformist writers appear to have anticipated a readership which was predominantly urban and drawn from what might be called, cautiously, the lower middle and middle classes.

In this, they were doing no more than address themselves to those social groups which constituted the strength of nonconformity. From an analysis of the social composition of nonconformity Michael Watts concludes that it corresponded by and large to that of the population generally, save that nonconformists were more likely to live in towns, labourers were poorly represented and a higher proportion of nonconformists were engaged in commerce and manufacture.[53] Quakers might be much poorer. A petition from 56 Quakers in Reading gaol in July 1664 asked that their plight be taken note of, 'beinge manie poore men, & women, & saruants', and this 'the principall tyme of the yeare for Laborers and husbandmen, of which our Companie doth much consist'. The destitution of their poor families with 'little else to maintain them but their daily labour' was the recurrent plea of imprisoned Quaker men.[54] The episcopal returns invariably spoke slightingly of the social status of Quakers – 'meane in quality', 'not considerable for estate', 'Meanest Mechanicks', 'All of very poore condition, scarce a yeoman amongst them', 'none of note', 'of ye inferior Gang'.[55] But though a higher proportion of Quakers than of other denominations came from very humble backgrounds, even amongst them yeomen and traders were half as common as artisans and far outnumbered labourers. A petition to the king from Norwich gaol in 1683 spoke of the impending ruin of the prisoners' families 'having all of us Dependency on our Industry and Trades for a Livelihood, yet by reason of our strait Confinement we are necessitated both to shut up our Shops and lay down our Trades'. And Quaker converts did of course include aldermen, justices, teachers, clergy and gentry.[56]

The episcopal returns were no more complimentary about Baptists, or Anabaptists, as they of course called them: 'Chiefly women', 'inferior people', 'meane for ye most part', 'Inconsiderable persons', 'Poore people', 'Most Women and Girles', 'Very meane, ye best scarce worth ye title of Yeoman'. Bunyan's own church was described as of the 'Meanest sort'. That this superlative was Bunyan's own description of his family's social status in *Grace Abounding* suggests, however, that 'mean' and 'inferior' denote not the very poorest but mechanics like Bunyan, artisans, and husbandmen. Labourers – still less vagrants – seem hardly to have registered as part of society at all. If they are mentioned, even by nonconformists, it is likely to be disparagingly, as when Howe, illustrating the absurdity of heavenly expectations without preparative moral effort, writes that it 'were a like thing as if an unbred peasant should go thrust himself, with an expectation of high honours and preferments, into the prince's court'.[57]

Of Presbyterian and Congregational conventicles, the adjective tended to be 'middle' or 'ordinary' rather than 'mean', and it was often conceded that they were attended by 'Tradesmen or Yeome*n*', 'the better sort', 'persons of good estates & Quality', 'of pretty good Qualitie', 'men of co*m*petent *pa*rts and breeding ... some of 500^{lb} a yeare, some 200, some 100, some 60 some 30, besides people of meaner sort'. This impression may have been partly due to their greater numbers, and hence to the inevitably higher representation of the gentry, rather than solely to what was, comparatively, a significantly more elevated social composition. Certainly, husbandmen and artisans figure prominently in Dr Watt's analysis.[58]

It does appear, however, that the commercial and industrial enterprise of nonconformists met with marked success. It may be that exclusion from political, civic and academic life directed their energies along these channels. An anonymous pamphlet of 1687 in support of James's policy of indulgence observed that the 'Fanaticks', who at the Restoration had been thought by their persecutors to be 'but few, and these very illiterate, inconsiderable and obstinate', had, after 20 years, proved in fact to be 'Men of some Sense, Moderation, and Candour, and, in good earnest, the Trading part of the Nation'. Of the Quakers Leslie wrote in the 1690s that 'G. Fox *was ... Inconsiderable ... and got none, at the beginning, to follow him, but from among the* Poor *and most* Ignorant *of the* Herd; *who have since swell'd to a* Rich, *a* Numerous, *and a* Potent *People, over-spreading these* Three Nations; *and stocking whole* Plantations *Abroad'*. If, in the late seventeenth and early eighteenth century, 'Congregationalism was very much the religion of the economically indepen- dent', the same was increasingly true of nonconformity generally.[59]

And yet the matter cannot quite be left there. This may have been the prevailing bias of nonconformist writing, but it was not exclusive. Burnet said of Marvell that 'from the King down to the tradesman, his books were read with great pleasure', and in the preface to Part II of the *The Pilgrim's Progress* Bunyan wrote of the Pilgrim of Part I that all ranks of society in *'City, and Countrey will him entertain'*.[60] The folk tale conventions and romance motifs of Part I, besides telling us something of Bunyan's own youthful reading, imply an originally intended readership rather below the level of yeomen, the people who bought chapbooks and popular romances.[61] The milieu of Part II is more realistically social and sociable, that of a country town. *Mr. Badman* is addressed to city merchants. And the complex allegory of *The Holy War* implicitly appeals to the cultivated taste of a more sophisticated élite. In short, Bunyan catered for everybody. If the great dividing line in seventeenth-century society was between the gentry and nobility on the one hand, and everyone else on the other, then the only comprehensive term available to describe the non-gentle populace was 'vulgar'. It would, in a hierarchical society, be no recommendation of a book to associate the gentry with the vulgar as its intended readers, but the very copiousness of the term 'vulgar' excludes no one save the very small percentage of the population who could claim to be gentle or noble.[62] We should interpret it not as designating a particular class of people, not even a vague 'middle class', but as appealing to the largest possible number of people. 'The vulgar' was the seventeenth-century equivalent of the medieval 'everyman' or the modern 'common man'. To write for the 'vulgar' was not to write for Dryden's audience or Tillotson's, but it was to write for everyone else. Nonconformist writing was in the vanguard in recognizing them, rather than their influential but numerically insignificant superiors, as the patrons of literature.

3   THE AUTHORIAL PERSONA

There is no stereotype of the nonconformist author. Nonconformity was, in its very nature, an individualist witness, and that individualism is abundantly in evidence in the characters, backgrounds, opinions and styles of its writers. We can, however, say that, if nonconformists were more likely to read than the general populace, they were also more likely to write. They took to authorship with remarkable readiness. Of those listed in *Calamy Revised*, at least 131 are noted as having produced one publication and 315 as having produced more than one. Fourteen of these cases are posthumous, but that still leaves 432 publishing authors in a total of 1,909, or just over 22 per cent. One estimate is that by 1700 nearly 650 Quakers (including at least 82 women) had appeared in print. So common was nonconformist authorship, and so prodigal, that Leslie could write: 'It wou'd be the work of a *Society of Writers*, such as they have, to Answer every one of that *Multitude of Pamphlets*, which, now more than ever, come out Thick and Threefold upon us every Day, to Propagate their Abhorr'd *Principles*.' Although, in his reply, Defoe was right to deny the formal existence of any such 'society' and to claim that nonconformist books were less the 'Design of a Party' than the work of committed individuals, nonconformists were, nevertheless, emphatically a society of writers.[63]

The great majority of the authors were ministers. Presbyterians and Congregationalists were generally university educated men, and the eminent among them were, if not Londoners by birth, residents and ministers in or near the capital. Many had had considerable political influence during the Civil War and Interregnum, and continued to enjoy the friendship and patronage of peers sympathetic to nonconformity, who supported their meetings, offered sanctuary in their houses and granted financial aid. Anna (Lindsay), Countess of Balcarres, was a particular admirer of Baxter; Anne (Russell), Countess of Bedford, was apprehended at a conventicle where Manton was preacher, and Elizabeth, Countess of Anglesey at one conducted by Owen.[64] Edward Bagshaw served as chaplain to her husband, Arthur Annesley, who intervened on behalf of James Forbes when he was imprisoned under the Five Mile Act. Henry Hurst also acted as the earl's chaplain, and as chaplain to Margaret (Montagu), Countess of Manchester. Thomas Adams was chaplain to Elizabeth (Holles), Countess Dowager of Clare, and Roger Morrice to Denzil, Lord Holles. The Countesses of Bedford, Manchester and Clare joined with Philip, Lord Wharton, to pay fines levied on James Bedford. Wharton was, indeed, conspicuous in his patronage. He granted Cornelius Todd £8 a year and was the patron and benefactor of Thomas Gilbert, George Griffiths, Matthew Hill, John Howe and John Witlock. Thomas Benlowes, Theophilus Gale, Abraham Clifford, Thomas Elford and John Nott all served him as tutors to his sons or chaplains to his family.[65]

Despite the readiness with which examples such as these can be adduced, the social standing of these men was not high in an age when even clergy of the Church of England were only doubtfully gentlemen. The unpaid Baptist and Quaker preachers,[66] who often continued to practise their trades or crafts, certainly were not. The tinker Bunyan was no exception. The 'heads & teachers' of his own Bedford church were reported in the episcopal returns as 'John Fenne, Hatter, Thomas Honylove, Cobbler, Samuel Fenne, Hatter, &

Thomas Cooper, Heele maker'. Amongst Baptists who published, Keach was a tailor, Thomas Grantham a tailor and farmer, and John Spilsbury a cobbler. By contrast, however, we can cite Hanserd Knollys, the son of a Lincolnshire rector, who had received episcopal orders, as had Francis Bampfield, an alumnus of Wadham College, Oxford, and the physician William Russell, who was Chemist-in-Ordinary to Charles II.[67]

The same is true of the Quakers. Fox himself was a weaver's son, who, brought up in the Leicestershire village of Fenny Drayton, worked as a shoemaker; Dewsbury was a shepherd in the East Riding; John Audland a linen draper. The many Quakers moved to publish an autobiographical book of testimony were often very humble people. But George Keith was a graduate of Aberdeen; Robert Barclay, the son of a Colonel and MP, was educated in Paris; Penington, whose father had been Lord Mayor of London, was an educated and cultured man. And in William Penn, the son of Admiral Sir William Penn, who was the 'quasi-ward' of James and, at the age of 37, received from Charles the grant of Pennsylvania in settlement of royal debts to his father, Quakerism had a courtier as intimate with royalty as any in the land.[68]

Save for Penn, none of these men was wealthy, and many were severely strained financially by the Clarendon Code. The review undertaken by the Common Fund set up by Presbyterians and Congregationalists in 1690 records stipends from £100 per annum to as little as 20s., with the majority below the £28 reported as the 'ye least a minister can Subsist on in this County' of Derbyshire.[69] It was not, however, impecuniosity which prompted them into print. For one thing, when profits went to the owner of the copy (namely, the publisher), a significant income from authorship was rare, and a living by that means alone impossible. Payment for copy was often in kind (as in the case of Nathaniel Heywood, cited above), and, when in cash, rarely exceeded the £5 Milton received for *Paradise Lost*. Nor had the author any redress against piratical printing. It was Ponder as the man concerned, not Bunyan, who pursued Thomas Braddyll for his piratical editions of *The Pilgrim's Progress* and who repudiated the spurious Part III put out in 1693 by Josiah Blare.[70] Even were considerable financial rewards possible, however, this would not have moved nonconformists to publish, as the case of Baxter demonstrates. We saw in Chapter 2 that their chief motive was pastoral. They wrote as ministers to a suffering people who were determined to fulfil their vocation despite the proscription of the Clarendon Code.

This intimate relationship between persecution and publication is caught in the opening sentence of *The Pilgrim's Progress*: 'As I walk'd through the wilderness of this world, I lighted on a certain place, where was a Denn; And I laid me down in that place to sleep: And as I slept I dreamed a Dream.' The wilderness of trial leads to the den of imprisonment which inspires the dream of imagination and the act of literary composition. However, although a dream of escape, Bunyan's is not an escapist dream. Nonconformist writing did not attempt to free nonconformists from their dens in the way of the seventeenth-century Baroque tradition, a tradition which delighted in wonder and admiration and sought to liberate the human spirit by (and into) aesthetic and sensory enjoyment. Baroque artists to this end sought out extreme situations and forms of behaviour and adopted the extravagant and extraordinary means to deal with them best known in English from the poetry of the Roman Catholic convert Richard Crashaw. The kind of wonder they sought to induce hardly saw moral instruction, or, indeed, any kind of instruction, as a literary aim. Nonconformists emphatically did. They were counsellors. A taste responsive to the Baroque will find them guilty of 'confusing the function of the literary artist ... with the function of the preacher'. The Milton in whom critics discern some, at least, of the Baroque's delight in fanatasticality and ripe exuberance, would feel himself ill served by a reader who merely gasped in wonder at *Paradise Lost*.[71]

This gives to the nonconformist writer, for all the biographical variety surrounding him, a distinctive literary persona. He is above all else concerned about the bearing of his theme upon the daily lives of his readers, and will expend his greatest energies on drawing out its implications for their behaviour. Whatever he writes about, he applies, practically, morally and spiritually. It has been well said of *Paradise Lost* that it is 'about how men should live in the real world'. Milton's epic is not, as Wordsworth misleadingly described it in order to distinguish his own poetry from Milton's, 'A history only of departed things,/Or a mere fiction of what never was'. On the contrary, it recounts the Fall that its readers may better understand not the past but their own present fallen state, and may learn, as Wordsworth hoped his readers would learn, that paradise is not an old fable but 'A simple produce of the common day'. It is Milton's reader, as well as Adam, who receives just this assurance from Michael.[72]

Although within his allegories Bunyan has (largely) forgone direct address, they are governed by the same determination to instruct. He cannot be content to rely on implication and indirect narration. He is, like all nonconformist writers (including even Milton in *Paradise Lost*), intrusive, constantly watching and guiding his reader's responses. That is why he is so persistently and conscientiously present in the margins of his texts. The self-reflexive nature of Bunyan's fictions insists that they be read as a means, not an end. This was essential to his literary purposes. His marginalia were not incidental additions but an integral part of the design of his allegories. Through its several editions he continued to make substantial additions to the marginalia of *The Pilgrim's Progress*,[73] and it is with a statement of their significance to *The Holy War* that he concluded its preface:

> *Nor do thou go to work without my Key*
> *(In mysteries men soon do lose their way)*
> *And also turn it right if thou wouldst know*
> *My riddles, and wouldst with my heifer plow.*

> *It lies there in the* window, *fare thee well,*
> *My next may be* to ring thy Passing-Bell.

The obligation this passage, whose penultimate line is marginally glossed 'The margent', imposes upon the reader had been laid on him with equal directness in the prefatory 'Apology' to Part I of *The Pilgrim's Progress*: "*My dark and cloudy words they do but hold/The Truth, as Cabinets inclose the Gold.*' It is the reader's business to unlock that cabinet. The existence of a long emblematical tradition in Puritan writing led Rosemary Freeman to allege that Bunyan never doubted 'his audience's capacity or inclination to penetrate to the truths that lay beneath the surface'. Nevertheless, he took the precaution of reiterating in the book's conclusion his warning against undue delight in the fiction for its own sake:

> *Take heed also that thou be not extream,*
> *In playing with the* out-side *of my Dream:*
> *Nor let my figure, or similitude,*
> *Put thee into a laughter or a feud:*
> *Leave this for* Boys *and* Fools; *but as for thee,*
> *Do thou the substance of my matter see.*
> *   Put by the Curtains, look within my Vail;*
> *Turn up my Metaphors, and do not fail:*
> *There, if thou seekest them, such things to find,*
> *As will be helpful to an honest mind.*[74]

This notion of a mystery to be unlocked by a key characterized Bunyan's literary thinking. Bunyan described both his own works and their inspiration and authority, the Bible, in just such terms. Of Part II of *The Pilgrim's Progress* he wrote:

> *Besides, what my first* Pilgrim *left conceal'd,*
> *Thou my brave* Second Pilgrim *hast reveal'd;*
> *What* Christian *left lock't up and went his way,*
> *Sweet* Christiana *opens with her Key.*

And in *The Holy War*, after the first reunion of Emanuel with Mansoul, a feast is given, following which '*Emanuel* was for entertaining the Town of *Mansoul* with some curious riddles of secrets drawn up by his Fathers Secretary, by the skill and wisdom of *Shaddai*'. When Emanuel expounds these riddles, which are glossed in the margin 'The holy Scriptures', 'Oh how they were lightned! they saw what they never saw, they could not have thought that such rarities could have been couched in so few and such ordinary words.'[75] That is precisely what Bunyan hoped might be the experience of a reader of his allegories.

To this way of thinking, literary form is not organic but a structure separate from, and subservient to, theme. The first poem in Bunyan's first book of poems, *Profitable Meditations* (1661), makes explicit his 'sugared pill' theory of poetry:

> *When Doctors give their Physick to the Sick,*
> *They make it pleasing with some other thing:*
> *Truth also by this means is very quick,*
> *When men by Faith it in their hearts do sing.*

Here matter and manner are kept as far apart as in the preface and conclusion to *The Pilgrim's Progress*, and there is the same firm expression of priority:

> 'Tis not the Method, but the Truth alone
> Should please a Saint, and mollifie his heart:
> Truth in or out of Meeter is but one;
> And this thou knowst, if thou a Christian art.

In Bunyan's poetry generally image and import are separated out, but in the *Book for Boys and Girls* the very appearance on the page keeps mystery and key discrete. The poems are usually in two parts, the first describing the subject and the second, often headed 'Comparison', drawing the moral. We might feel that on occasions 'the first part is complete in itself without the comparison which follows' but Bunyan's defence of his strategy in the book's preface points to the second part as his justification:

> What tho my Text seems mean, my Morals be
> Grave, as if fetcht from a Sublimer Tree

It is the gravity of the moral which counts and is the *raison d'être* of each poem.[76]

And so, in the margins of his allegories, Bunyan is there, pointing up the moral and taking us off from a preoccupation with the outside of his dream. Even as the imaginative power of his text invites the suspension of our critical faculties in involvement and identification with the tale and its characters we are inhibited from making this response by being alienated from the text. Through our affections, aroused by the fiction, Bunyan works on our will and understanding, but to achieve this our understanding must be kept alert: '*lay my Book, thy Head and Heart together.*' Most obviously and frequently he supplies biblical texts as an interpretative key to (and justification of) his allegory, but he can often more explicitly 'turn up' his metaphors. He may move only partially outside the world of his fiction, in his comment mingling tenor and vehicle, or he may do no more than gloss a particular symbol or character: in *The Holy War* we are several times reminded that 'castle', 'wall' and 'gates' stand for 'heart', 'flesh' and 'senses' respectively; the dog at the Gate in *The Pilgrim's Progress* is glossed '*the Devil*', the light of the Interpreter's candle '*Illumination*', '*Madam Bubble*' as '*this vain World*'. Often, though, Bunyan will draw out the thematic drift of incidents. Even when the text itself calls our attention to the significance Bunyan is happier if the margin also alerts us: when Gaius advises that the prospect of a well laid table should 'beget *in* thee a greater desire to sit at the Supper of the great King in his Kingdom' the margin adds '*What to be gathered from the laying of the Board with the Cloath and Trenshers*'. Such comments may sharpen the satirical bite: when Great-heart and his party find the spring at the foot of Hill Difficulty muddied since Christian's time, the margin observes "*'Tis difficult getting of good Doctrine in erroneous Times.*"[77]

Moments of tension in the plot are never allowed to pass without our absorption in the detail of the allegory being disturbed in this way. Civil War and biblical sieges mingle when Diabolus' followers enter Mansoul and make 'great havock of what ever they laid their hands on; yea, they fired the Town in several places; many young children also were by them dashed in pieces; yea, those that were yet unborn they destroyed in their mothers wombs.' What is truly awful here is not, however, the sufferings of those in the sacked town but the moral collapse of a saint: 'Guilt. Good and tender thoughts'. The raped women of Mansoul are similarly glossed: 'Holy conceptions of good'. The cries of Christiana and the children when Giant Maul fells Great-heart are so realistically apt that, were it not for the check of the margin, we should almost certainly read on with relief at the human level that the cries rouse Great-heart and so miss the encouragement to petitionary prayer which the episode is offering to the least member of a church: *'Weak folks prayers do sometimes help strong folks cries.'*[78]

Such interpretative glosses may be explicitly addressed to the reader. The frequent hand in the rubric column is to attract the reader's attention. Often, 'Mark this' is spelled out, sometimes as an admonition directed to a specific reader: Christiana's feelings for Christian are glossed *'Mark this, you that are Churles to your godly Relations.'* In *Mr. Badman*, Bunyan frequently turns to people in this or that situation, under this or that temptation, in the way of the Puritan sermon and practical treatise: 'young thieves take notice', 'A story for unclean persons to take notice of', 'Good counsel to those godly maids that are to marry', 'Servants observe these words.' In *Mr. Badman* again Bunyan turns to the reader to substantiate his preface's claim that he has 'as little as may be gone out of the road of mine own observation of things': 'The desperate words of one H.S. who was once my companion'; 'This was done at Bedford.' These comments bear on the integrity of his work: very occasionally it is the writer, not the preacher, who addresses us. A lyric is glossed *'The Dreamers note'* to ensure we do not mistake it for Hopeful's and a charge of literary pretentiousness is offset by the gloss on *'ex Carne et Sanguine Christi'*, *'The Lattine I borrow'*. When it is the preacher who speaks it is not always in the imperative mood: we are admonished (*'We lose for want of asking for'*), encouraged (*'Tis good to cry out when we are assaulted'*), exhorted (*'Pray, and you will get at that which yet lies unrevealed'*) and challenged ('See now what's the work of a backsliding Saint awakened').[79]

As they near the end of their pilgrimage Christian and Hopeful are proof against Atheist, but a subtler snare awaits Hopeful. In that 'Countrey, whose Air naturally tended to make one drowsie' he quickly becomes 'very dull'. Were it not for Christian's insistence that he remain awake, watchful and actively engaged in rehearsing and assessing his experiences, he would have succumbed to the lure to forget himself. It is just such an office Bunyan in his marginalia performs for the reader. As we read, some one is there with us, looking over our shoulder. It is this awareness which ensures that we remain conscious as we read that we *are* reading, alive to our obligation to seek out the *'Truth'* within this *'Fable'*. We are prevented from yielding ourselves completely to the enchanted worlds of the allegories as surely as Hopeful was prevented from yielding to the '*inchanted ground*'.[80]

4   GOOD BOOKS AND BAD

Bunyan thus remains our guide as surely as does Great-heart the pilgrims'. He is leading us. Neither he, nor any nonconformist writer, will allow mere literary pleasure or aesthetic satisfaction to deflect or detain us from pursuing the way they would have us go. They are determined, as Howe wrote of one of his publications, 'that such as into whose hands this little treatise shall fall, may be induced to consider the true end of their beings' and act accordingly.[81] And yet, there is another side to all this. Bunyan does, after all, write poetry and allegory, despite his avowedly homiletic purpose, and he does so on precisely the grounds advanced in Sidney's *Defence of Poetry*: the imaginative recreation of spiritual states has a more compelling and enduring effect than discursive analyses of them. '*My fancies*', he claimed in 1678, '*will stick like Burs.*' When he repeated this image in 1684 he made more explicit the appeal of his method to the whole person, to intellectual and imaginative faculties alike:

> *I also know, a dark Similitude*
> *Will on the Fancie more it self intrude,*
> *And will stick faster in the Heart and Head,*
> *Then things from Similies not borrowed.*

Bunyan clearly recognized and welcomed the affective potential of imaginative literature. His 'fancies' will 'stick' because they move and intrigue. He made no attempt to disguise the pleasure his method afforded. On the contrary, this was its recommendation. Bunyan evidently enjoyed riddles, and expected his readers to do so too. They are to anticipate '*something rare*' in Part I of *The Pilgrim's Progress*; '*nimble Fancies*' are invited to solve the '*Riddles*' that '*lie couch't within*' the '*Misterious lines*' of Part II. The book entices with the prospect of something '*pleasant*': '*Wouldst thou divert thy self from Melancholly?*'[82]

This pleasure Bunyan did not regard as antipathetical to godliness. It is to entertain, as well as to instruct, the town of Mansoul that Emanuel starts riddling. The recreation after supper at Gaius's house, when the pilgrims are 'very Merry', is, again, riddling. Christian's smile in the House of the Interpreter is a smile not merely of admiration but of satisfaction and pleasure at fathoming the emblem of the valiant man. When Mercy and the boys blush for failing to solve the 'Riddle' of the spider it is not merely the application which affects them: it is also their want of percipience, of wit. Christiana, by contrast, is a 'Woman of quick apprehension'. Her companions have been caught out, and that ill becomes a saint, for the godly are an alert and curious people:

> *Things that seem to be hid in words obscure,*
> *Do but the Godly mind the more alure;*
> *To study what those Sayings should contain,*
> *That speak to us in such a Cloudy strain.*[83]

And so, in his marginalia, Bunyan is not merely an expositor of his text. His advice had been not to ignore but to '*be not extream,/In playing with the* out-side *of my Dream*', and he readily alerts the reader to that 'out-side'. He may do so simply by summarizing or signposting the plot ('Mr. Badman plays a new prank'). Often, though, such summaries have a colloquial sharpness missing in the text itself: when, coming to Doubting Castle, Great-heart and his party 'consulted what was best to be done', in the margin 'They ... have a mind to have a pluck with Gyant Dispair'; in the text Mr Fearing is 'ashamed to make himself much for Company' in the House Beautiful, but in the margin he is '*Dumpish at the house* Beautiful'; Christian's reproof to Hopeful is glossed 'Christian *snibbeth his fellow*'; in the margins Christian '*roundeth up* Demas' and Talkative '*flings away from* Faithful'.[84] In such comments, a responsiveness to the text as story, rather than as allegory, is beginning to supplant plot summary.

This tendency can be still more pronounced. Bunyan will often comment as a reader, caught up in the action of his fiction and apparently oblivious of his own reader, though actually, of course, heightening the degree of response to the drama of the plot. 'Poor *Mansoul*' comments the margin when Diabolus exhorts his army '*that yet more and more ye distress this Town*'. In the course of the preparations for Diabolus' second attempt on Mansoul Bunyan reiterates in the margin 'Take heed *Mansoul*', 'Look to it *Mansoul*'. Diabolus' account of the intentions of Emanuel's army earns the retort 'That's false Satan'; Diabolus' claim that Emanuel's mercy is mere policy provokes the disclaimer 'Very deceivable language', 'Lying language'. 'No, no, no, not upon pain of eternal damnation' Bunyan exclaims at Diabolus' suggestion that he and Mansoul should '*renew our old acquaintance and friendship again*'. He has other moods: he applauds Christiana's reply to Mrs Timorous as '*A pertinent reply to fleshly reasonings*' and Great-heart's bearing to Mr Feeble-mind as '*A Christian Spirit*'. He can be ironic, too: '*O brave* Talkative'.[85]

Bunyan's marginalia are, then, quite as concerned to bring to his reader's attention the pleasure as the profit of reading his texts. Certainly he meant his books to be useful: but equally certainly, he meant reading them to be fun.[86] He was bolder than most in the degree of play he admitted, but Bunyan is not otherwise exceptional. We have stayed so long with his marginalia because the dual interest and purpose they so clearly reveal characterize nonconformist taste in general and nonconformist literary attitudes in particular. It is easy to typify the former in terms of austere sobriety. Ellwood records that the visit he and his father paid the Peningtons in 1658, when they had converted to Quakerism, was not as anticipated: 'So great a Change from a Free, Debonair and Courtly sort of Behaviour (which we formerly had found them in) to so strict a Gravity as they now received us with, did not a little amuse us, and disappoint our Expectation of such a pleasant Visit, as we used to have.' Dinner was 'very handsome; and lacked nothing to recommend it to me, but the want of Mirth and pleasant discourse'. We can multiply nonconformist strictures on the fashionable Caroline times. Howe takes issue with Cavalier gallants as rakes and debauchees, Epicurean atheists who 'reckon they have arrived to a very heroical perfection, when they can pass a scoff upon anything that carries the least signification with it of the fear of God; and can be able to laugh at the weak and squeamish folly of the softer and effeminate minds, that will trouble themselves with any thoughts or cares how to please and propitiate Deity'. Such a demeanour took its cue from the licentious Charles, the *'Royal Refugee'* who, Defoe later wrote, 'our Breed restores,/With *Foreign Countries*, and with *Foreign Whores*;/And carefully repeopled us again/Throughout his Lazy, Long, Lascivious Reign'. 'All places are full of vomit and filthiness, so that there is no place clean' wrote Bunyan. 'As the world is older, it is worse', wrote Penn, 'and the example of former lewd ages, and their miserable conclusions, have not deterred, but excited ours; so that the people of this seem improvers of the old stock of impiety.' The 'invention' the age bestows upon self-gratification, and the 'excess' to which it pursues it, have turned Caroline England into the 'spiritual' Sodom and Egypt of Revelation xi. 8.[87]

We can equally readily represent nonconformists as deeply suspicious if not fearful, of sensuousness and imaginative pleasure. The aphoristic 'Notes for My Self' of the Presbyterian John Corbet include 'Entertain not a sensual Imagination for a moment'; 'In every delight of Sense, watch against all Brutishness.' Bates rebukes 'The sensual Wretch [who] surveys his Carnal Paradise, and personates the Pleasures of Sin by impure Imaginations. His Fancy runs riotously over tempting Beauties.' Howe repudiates the 'satisfying of lusts' as 'the commensurate end of man': 'a debauched sensualist that lives as if he were created only to indulge his appetite', 'vilifies the notion of man, as if he were made but to eat and drink and sport, to please only his sense and fancy'. Meeting houses were 'plain, void of pomp or ceremony' as befits Christian simplicity, rather than 'gaudy and worldly ... accommodated to the most carnal part'. James Owen describes organs and instrumental music in public worship as fit only for 'superstitious *Fops*, and empty *Noddies*', a distracting 'Theatrical Pomp, and noisie Ostentation': it is 'a sad lame Devotion, that stands in need of a few tweedling Organ-pipes to make it more brisk and lively'. And we need not look far to find nonconformists speaking as slightingly of drama and romance as their Puritan forebears had done. 'A Gazette or a Play-book' is expected to be the reading of the unregenerate. A reader of *The Blessedness of the Righteous* 'looking on these pages, with a wanton rolling eye, hunting for novelties, or what may gratifie a prurient wit, a coy and squeamish fancy', had better go 'read a Romance, or some piece of Drollery'. Marvell's analogy for the spurious and deceitful is 'some vain *French* Romance'.[88]

To leave matters there (as is often enough done) would, however, be to misrepresent the nonconformists. Theirs was not a kill-joy, sombre and ascetic taste. Thomas Manton noted that Christ did not lead 'a strict austere course of life' but 'came eating and drinking' to persuade people not to place religion in outward austerities and observances. Men superstitiously appoint to themselves unnecessary tasks, and forbid themselves many lawful things, and this they call by the name of holiness. When Satan, who is usually a libertine, pretendeth to be a saint, he will be stricter than Christ himself. Christ foresaw this spirit would be working in the world [Col. ii.21, 23] ... That men were apt to place religion in simple abstinence from the common comforts of life, under a pretence of more than ordinary mortification: neither eat, nor taste, nor touch.

Manton goes on to echo Baxter ('Over-doing in externals is undoing in religion'), but the point had received what was to become a more famous formulation from Milton: 'who bids abstain/But our destroyer, foe to God and man?' A proper mortification 'consists not ... in a monkish discontent with the world, but a holy contempt of it when we most freely use it'. Howe was of like mind: God 'never intended to forbid the gratification of the faculties, nor hath given us any reason to doubt but that the lower delights that are suitable to them might be innocently entertained'. Gaius the hospitable innkeeper (cf. Rom. xvi.23, III John 1–6) plays a prominent part in Part II of *The Pilgrim's Progress*, and in Part I Christian at the Palace Beautiful sits down to a table 'furnished with fat things, and with Wine that was well refined'.[89]

Nor was theirs an exclusively utilitarian aesthetic which tolerated only the didactic and homiletic. It did tolerate only the edificatory, but the sources of edification were many, various and delightful. It was not immediately apparent to all nonconformists that imaginative literature was one of them, for the predominant end of Restoration drama, fiction and poetry was certainly not godliness. This understandably bred prejudice against them occupying the time of nonconformist writers or readers. It was, however, a prejudice nonconformist authors themselves sought to counter. Rather than reject any literary genre *per se* they distinguished between the prevailing literary temper of Restoration society and the use which might be made, and had in the Bible itself been made, of metaphor, parable, story and poetry. As Bunyan remarked: 'for what are these things Ordained, but that we might by the godly use of them, attain to more of the knowledge of God, and be strengthened by his Grace to serve him better. But there is a vast difference between using of these things, and a using of them for these ends.'[90] In their apologetic prefaces and by their practice, nonconformist authors sought to persuade their readers imaginative literature might indeed serve these ends.

So, when Milton essayed drama, it was with explicit Pauline authority and neither intended for the stage nor in the manner of the contemporary theatre. For this, that theatre was as much responsible as Milton's Classicism. Thomas Gouge wrote of 'Stage-plays' that 'many ... are stuffed with filthy and obscene speeches, and set forth with many lascivious gestures, by which they are very prone to infect the mind with effeminate lust, and dispose your heart for unclean and filthy actions. The stage is a decoy for the stews.' The language is severe, but the point is easily substantiated, both from the texts themselves and from such play-goers as Pepys. And that severity should not be allowed to obscure the fact that, since Gouge's is a moral, not a literary outrage, the criticism is directed not at drama but at the contemporary use of drama ('many' plays). Implicitly, drama need not be stuffed with such speeches nor set forth such gestures. Similarly, when Marvell slights Parker by associating him with drama and romance he does so by appealing not to the intrinsically reprehensible nature of these genres but to their inappropriateness in this context: Parker is being accused of indecorum. And, though the Congregationalist Theophilus Gale had no time for '*Romances*, which so much please the wanton wits and humours of this corrupt Age', it was yet entirely possible to invent to better purpose, as the Bible shows.[91]

This is the line of argument developed in Bunyan's 'Apology' for Part I of *The Pilgrim's Progress*. Biblical precedent not only authorizes fiction but exemplifies its capacity to grasp pointedly and movingly the facts of experience. To be sure, it is mere idle time-wasting to lose oneself in the escapist other-worlds of popular romance. Bunyan would have been in full sympathy with the implication of Samuel Butler's rhetorical question, 'what else/Is in them all, but Love and *Battels*?' As reworked by Bunyan, however, there is a good deal else. He does observe the '*Romantique* Method' of alternating adventurous and recuperative episodes, and we do have a journey, a hero, combats, giants, monsters, castles and dungeons, challenging terrain, darkly mysterious places, narrow escapes from death and enticing women, the very things, that is to say, Penn castigated as constituting the absurd unreality of the illusory romance world: but circuitous errantry has become a purposeful quest, pursued not through magical forests but along recognizable seventeenth-century roads, undertaken not by a chivalric exemplar but by a common man who is hampered by ordinary, petty, selfish people and whose battles are fought within himself. Hence, to read Bunyan is '*far from folly*', a '*profitable*' means to greater self-knowledge. To '*loose thy self*' in his fictional world will be to '*find thy self*'. Though he fabled, Bunyan could hence claim in a poem to write '*no Fables*'. This contrast between the 'feigning' of romance and the realistic accuracy, the truth to experience, of his fictions, was made more explicitly by Bunyan in the preface to *The Holy War*:

> *Some will again of that which never was,*
> *Nor will be, feign, (and that without a cause)*
> *Such matter, raise such mountains, tell such things*
> *Of Men, of Laws, of Countries, and of Kings:*
> *And in their Story seem to be so sage,*
> *And with such gravity cloath ev'ry Page,*
> *That though their Frontice-piece says all is vain,*
> *Yet to their way Disciples they obtain.*
> *But, Readers, I have somewhat else to do*
> *Than with vain stories thus to trouble you;*
> *What here I say, some men do know so well,*
> *They can with tears and joy the story tell.*[92]

Experiential authenticity legitimized imaginative literature.

This claim was Milton's too. His repudiation of the 'tedious havoc' of medieval and Renaissance romances was a repudiation not of romance but of falsity ('fabled knights/ In battles feigned') and indulgent luxuriance. Coming to doubt the historicity of Arthur he could not write the Arthuriad he originally planned: truth was his subject. Yet this admirer and heir of Spenser remained a romancer. For one last example we may turn to Lucy Hutchinson, the widow of the regicide Colonel John Hutchinson. She distinguishes her *Memoirs* of her husband from romance, and passes by 'all the little amorous relations, which if I would take the paynes to relate, would make a true history of a more handsome management of love than the best romances describe'. These are things 'to be forgotten, as the vanities of youth'. And yet romance conventions organize her account of their courtship, John Hutchinson falling in love with her reputation and fainting at the (false) news she is married before ever he has met her; and her description of him would grace the hero of any Renaissance romance.[93]

These are examples not of the repudiation but of the redirection and reapplication of received conventions. There are others, notably in the adoption of poetry as part of communal worship, a development to which Keach contributed so signally. Congregational hymn-singing owes its origins in large part to the nonconformists and was to be become established through the hymns of the eighteenth-century dissenters Philip Doddridge and Isaac Watts.[94] These hymnodists were following Corbet's advice: 'Never terminate in the sensitive Pleasure, but make use of it to raise thy Heart to God.' Their determination to make use of 'sensitive pleasure' in worship is a particular example of the general determination of nonconformist writers to profit their readers by, as Bunyan put it, 'aluring' them. They recognized that the edificatory and the enjoyable were not inimical; the one might serve the other. It was clearly with approval that Howe wrote of Bates:

> Nor was he wont to banish out of his conversation the pleasantness that fitly belonged to it; for which his large acquaintance with a most delightful variety of story, both ancient and modern, gave him advantage beyond most; his judicious memory being a copious promptuary of what was profitable and facetious, and disdaining to be the receptacle of useless trash. To place religion in a morose sourness was remote from his practice, his judgment and his temper.[95]

Chapter 5 'Knowledge within bounds'
learning and creativity in nonconformity

> *Knowledge puffeth up, but charity edifieth.*
> *And if any man think that he knoweth any thing, he knoweth*
> *nothing yet as he ought to know.*
> *But if any man love God, the same is known of him.*
>
> *I Cor. viii.*1–3

I   EDUCATION AND THE SPIRIT

'*Preachers* may be silenced or banished, when *Books* may be at hand.' Essential to survival in these terms books may have been, and they may have offered 'pleasing diversions' from melancholy, but were they intrinsically essential to the Christian life? In *The Pilgrim's Progress*, after all, Christian reads only one book: the Bible. His progress is guided not by a course of reading but by Scripture, by Evangelist, by the illumination of the Holy Spirit and by experience. In this respect (as in so many others) his history corresponds to that of Bunyan himself, whose progress to faith and assurance is depicted in *Grace Abounding* as a series of intense private experiences, revelatory moments and fervent (and fervid) meditations upon biblical texts. Bunyan was advised by his own Evangelist, John Gifford, first pastor of the Independent (and subsequently open-communion Baptist) church as Bedford, not to pay much attention to what others said or wrote: 'he pressed us to take special heed, that we took not up any truth upon trust, as from this or that or another man or men, but to cry mightily to God that he would convince us of the reality thereof, and set us down therein, by his own Spirit in the holy Word.' Bunyan had received some schooling, but in *Grace Abounding* this is mentioned to the credit of his parents, not as a testimony to his own attainments, which he disparages:

> But yet not withstanding the meanness and inconsiderableness of my Parents, it pleased God to put it into their heart, to put me to School, to learn both to Read and Write; the which I also attained, according to the rate of other poor mens children, though to my shame I confess, I did soon loose [*sic*] that little I learned, even almost utterly, and that long before the Lord did work his gracious work of conversion upon my Soul.

Coming in the third paragraph of his spiritual autobiography this clearly establishes that the ensuing 'gracious work of conversion' owed nothing to, and certainly was not dependent upon, books and reading.[1]

This is a recurrent emphasis throughout Bunyan's publications. Playing down the actual extent of his reading (which included not only, by his own admission, Dent, Bayly, Foxe and Luther, but also a good swathe of contemporary practical and controversial divinity[2]), he turns his ignorance to defiant homiletic advantage. What he writes allegedly gains authority precisely because it derives from no authority other than Scripture and experience: 'I have not writ at a venture, nor borrowed my Doctrine from Libraries. I depend upon the sayings of no man: I found it in the Scriptures of Truth, among the true sayings of God.' Just so Gifford's successor John Burton recommended Bunyan's first publication, *Some Gospel-Truths Opened* (1656), on the grounds that he well knew Bunyan's 'ability to preach the gospel not by humane art, but by the spirit of Christ', and two years later I.G. (probably John Gibbs, later ejected Baptist vicar of Newport Pagnell) similarly wrote of Bunyan in the preface to *A Few Signs from Hell* that though 'his humane learning [is] small, yet he is one that hath acquaintance with God, and taught by his Spirit.' Bunyan's claim that he does not know 'the Mode nor Figure of a Sylogism' is the more provocative when prefaced to a substantial theological treatise, *The Doctrine of the Law and Grace Unfolded* (1659). He barely concedes that this flaws his method; certainly he does not concede that it disables him from tackling the vexed questions of the covenant of grace, predestination, the significance of works, assurance and perseverance:

> Reader, if thou do finde this book empty of Fantastical expressions, and without light, vain, whimsical Scholar-like terms, thou must understand, it is because I never went to School to *Aristotle* or *Plato*, but was brought up at my fathers house, in a very mean condition, among a company of poor Countrey-men. But if thou do finde a parcel of plain, yet sound, true, and home sayings, attribute that to the Lord Jesus, his gifts and abilities, which he hath bestowed upon such a poor Creature, as I am, and have been.

Even in the fictional world of *The Pilgrim's Progress* Bunyan takes the precaution of glossing a Latin tag with the marginal comment *'The Lattine I borrow'*. He writes not as a man who knows what we do not know but as a man who has experienced what we have not experienced (but may): 'I preached what I felt, what I smartingly did feel, even that under which my poor Soul did groan and tremble to astonishment.'[3]

With all this we may contrast the case of Richard Baxter, whose conversion, by his own account, was brought about almost entirely by reading. Where Bunyan presents his soul 'led from truth to truth by God', Baxter traces the stages of his early spiritual development through a succession of secondary texts. His schooling was irregular and inadequate. In the Shropshire villages of Eaton Constantine and High Ercall the 'School-masters of my Youth' were a series of barely literate, often drunk clergymen, 'most of them of Scandalous Lives'. After his tenth year, when he moved from his maternal grandparents to the parental home, his father, now a reformed man though formerly 'addicted to Gaming in his Youth', became 'the Instrument of my first Convictions'. He set Baxter 'to read the Historical part of the Scripture, which suiting with my Nature greatly delighted me'. Subsequently, 'a poor Day-Labourer in the Town ... had an old torn Book which he lent my Father.' This was the Jesuit Robert Parson's *Firste Booke of the Christian Exercise appertayning to Resolution* ([Rouen], 1582), 'corrected' by the Protestant Edmund Bunny, which had enjoyed successive reprintings since its first publication in 1584: 'in the reading of this Book (when I was about Fifteen years of Age) it pleased God to awaken my Soul, and shew me the folly of Sinning, and the misery of the Wicked, and the unexpressible weight of things Eternal, and the necessity of resolving on a Holy Life, more than I was ever acquainted with before.' 'And about that time it pleased God that a poor Pedlar came to the Door that had Ballads and some good Books: And my Father bought of him Dr. [Richard] *Sibb's bruised Reed* [(1630)]. This also I read.' 'After this we had a Servant that had a little Piece of Mr [William] *Perkins's* Works ... And the reading of that did further inform me, and confirm me. And thus (without any means but Books) was God pleased to resolve me for himself.' In the early 1630s Baxter continued to be an avid reader of Puritan theology – he mentions Robert Bolton, John Preston, Edward Elton, Thomas Taylor, William Whately, Robert Harris – and, during a period of 'Doubts of my own Sincerity in Grace'

> the reading of Mr *Ezek. Culverwell's* Treatise of Faith [(1623)] did me much good, and many other excellent Books were made my Teachers and Comforters: And the use that God made of Books, above Ministers, to the benefit of my Soul, made me somewhat excessively in love with good Books; so that I thought I had never enow, but scrap'd up as great a Treasure of them as I could.[4]

It hence comes as no surprise to learn that he accumulated a remarkable library,[5] and that, from an early age, study, reading and scholarship were his delight and his goal. He engagingly tells against himself the tale of how, as a schoolboy at the free school at Wroxeter, when Richard Allestree, afterwards Regius Professor of Divinity at Oxford and Provost of Eton, was moved 'up into the lower end of the highest Form, where I had long been Chief, I took it so ill, that I talkt of leaving the School: whereupon my Master gravely, but very tenderly, rebuked my pride, and gave me as my Theme, *Ne sutor ultra crepidam*'. His youthful ambition was nevertheless for '*Literate Fame* ... the highest Academical Degrees and Reputation of Learning'. As a young man 'my inclination was most to *Logick* and *Metaphysicks* ... Which occasioned me (perhaps too soon) to plunge my self very early into the study of *Controversies*; and to read all the School-men I could get ... because I thought they narrowly searched after Truth.' In his early thirties he exclaimed:

> What delight have I found in my private studies, especially when they have prospered to the increase of my knowledge! me thinks I could bid the world farewel, and immure my self among my books, and look forth no more (were it a lawful course) but as [Daniel] *Heinsius* in his Library at *Leyden*) shut the doors upon

me and as in the lap of Eternity, among those divine souls, imploy my self in sweet
content, and pitty the rich and great ones know not this happiness.[6]

In the autobiographical 'Love Breathing Thanks and Praise', written after the
Restoration and published in 1681 in *Poetical Fragments*, the memory of his first
discovery of that 'sweet content' is still fresh:

> The many precious Books of holy men,
> Thy Spirit used on me as his Pen:
> *Perkins, Sibbs, Bolton, Whateley,* holy *Dod,*
> *Hildersham, Preston,* other men of God,
> How pertinently spake they to my case?
> They open'd Heaven and Hell before my face ...
> They search'd my heart; help'd me to try my state;
> My earthy Mind they help'd to elevate:
> What strong & quickening motives did they bring,
> To raise my heart, and winde the slackned spring?
> These happy Counsellors were still at hand;
> The Maps, and Landskips of the Holy Land.
> This food was not lockt from me; but I could
> Go read a holy Sermon when I would.
> How cheaply kept I many Rare Divines?
> And for a little purchas'd Golden Mines?

Though advanced on characteristically commonsensical grounds, it is clearly
this personal experience which informs Baxter's general advice in *A Christian
Directory* (1673) to seize upon books as a chief means of grace:

> The Writings of Divines are nothing else but a preaching the Gospel to the eye, as
> the *voice* preacheth it to the ear. Vocal preaching hath the preheminence in moving
> the affections, and being diversified according to the state of the Congregations
> which attend it: This way the Milk cometh warmest from the breast: But Books
> have the advantage in many other respects: you may read an able Preacher when
> you have but a mean one to hear. Every *Congregation* cannot hear the most judicious
> or powerful Preachers: but every *single person* may *read* the Books of the most
> powerful and judicious; Good *Books* may be kept at a smaller charge than
> Preachers: We may choose Books which treat of that very subject which we desire
> to hear of; but we cannot choose what subject the Preacher shall treat of. Books we
> may have at hand every day and hour: when we can have Sermons but seldom, and
> at set times. If Sermons be forgotten, they are gone. But a Book we may read over
> and over till we remember it: and if we forget it, may again peruse it at our pleasure,
> or at our leisure. So that good Books are a very great mercy to the world.[7]

These remarks make it clear that the differing estimates of the significance of
books in the thought of Bunyan and Baxter are, in part, a reflection of
contrasting experience and temperaments. Bunyan's youthful instability, the
intensity of his anguish and despair, fed by visions and dreams, could be
answered by nothing less than immediate and overpowering raptures. The man
who came to exclaim 'How lovely now was everyone in my eyes, that I thought
to be converted men and women! they shone, they walked like a people that
carried the broad Seal of Heaven about them', 'Christ was a precious Christ to
my Soul that night; I could scarce lie in my Bed for joy, and peace, and triumph,

thorow Christ', this man had not been able to 'express with what longings and breakings in my Soul, I cryed to Christ'; he had been 'ready to sink where I went with faintness in my mind', going 'up and down bemoaning my sad condition', in 'great straights', prone 'to dispond', fallen 'as a Bird that is shot from the top of a Tree, into great guilt and fearful despair'. Thus 'driven to my wits end', 'bereft of my wits', only something other than wit could answer his case. His own attempts at rational argument proved hopelessly futile: they would merely 'return again upon me'.[8]

There is hence no intellectual – and certainly no literary – intermediary between Bunyan and the Bible, or Satan, or Christ. All act with an immediacy whose forcefulness only images of physical irresistibility can convey. Animated scriptural texts assail him: 'that saying came in upon me'; 'that Scripture fastned on my heart'; 'that piece of a sentence darted in upon me'; Luke xxii.31 'sometimes ... would sound so loud within me, yea, and as it were call so strongly after me, that once above all the rest, I turned my head over my shoulder, thinking verily that some man had behind me called to me, being at a great distance, methought he called so loud'. Satan is actually and tauntingly present, engaging in dialogue as directly as to Milton's Christ: 'Now also did the Tempter begin to mock me in my misery'; 'Which when the Tempter perceived, he strongly suggested to me'; 'sometimes I have thought I should see the Devil, nay, thought I have felt him behind me pull my cloaths.' And when consolation comes, it is simply, and personally, 'the Lord' who 'did more fully and graciously discover himself to me', who 'did also lead me into the mystery of Union with this Son of God'. In this world of unpredictable encounters, understanding, if it come at all, comes unbidden, suddenly and finally: 'thus at that very instant it was expounded to me.'[9]

Baxter's doubts as to his election were prompted not immediately by Satan but mediately (and characteristically) by his reading. The first of the 'chiefest Causes' he lists is 'Because I could not distinctly trace the Workings of the Spirit upon my heart in that Method which Mr [Robert] *Bolton*, Mr [Thomas] *Hooker*, Mr [John] *Rogers*, and other Divines describe'. His lack of assurance derived from his inability to point to an indisputable and traumatic conversion experience, and 'because my *Grief* and *Humiliation* was no greater, and because I could weep no more for this'. He sought the Slough of Despond Bunyan knew: 'all my Groans were for more *Contrition*, and a *broken Heart*, and I prayed most for *Tears and Tenderness*.' It was to no avail: 'whether sincere conversion began *now*, or *before*, or *after*, I was never able to this day to know.' Reflection upon his experience led him to reject as definitive and prescriptive the model he had found in his reading – but it did not lead him to reject reading: quite the contrary. His misgivings that, because he knew not 'the Time of my Conversion, being wrought on by ... Degrees', '*Education* and *Fear* had done all that ever was done upon my Soul, and *Regeneration* and *Love* were yet to seek', yielded to the perception that '*Education* is God's ordinary way for the

Conveyance of his Grace, and ought no more to be set in opposition to the Spirit, than the preaching of the Word ... the Soul of a Believer groweth up by degrees.' And his failure to experience the emotional anguish of a broken heart led to the realization that 'God breaketh not all Mens hearts alike, and that the gradual proceedings of his Grace might be one cause, and my Nature not apt to weep for *other* Things another'.[10]

This recognition that temperaments differ, his own gradual growth in grace and the part played therein by books, all combine in Baxter's recurrent insistence that spiritual enlightenment comes not (ordinarily) in such intense revelatory moments as Bunyan experienced but through a slow educative process which works by means, of which the chief is reading. 'Man being a *Rational wight*, is not taught by *meer Instinct* and *Inspiration*'; 'It is true, that the saving knowledge of Divinity must be taught by the Spirit of God: But it is false that *labour* and *humane* teaching are not the means which must be used by them, who will have the teaching of the spirit.' All knowledge is the gift of God, but 'he giveth it by means', namely, instruction by teachers and diligence by learners. Consequently, learning is not merely the business of children: 'We must go on to learn as long as we live.' All Christians should be 'much in *Reading*', engaged upon thorough and systematic study,[11] for

> Grace presupposeth Nature; We are *men* in order of Nature at least before we are Saints, and Reason is before Supernatural Revelation. Common knowledge therefore is subservient unto faith: We must know the Creator and his works ... Humane learning in the sense in question is also Divine: God is the Author of the light of nature, as well as of grace.

Those who rely solely upon the Spirit are hence as far astray as those who rely solely upon Scripture, since both distinguish and oppose what is indistinguishable and complementary. The former expect miracles which, though not impossible, are self-evidently not the common experience of Christians since the time of the Apostles. The latter, who 'say, no other *Books of Divinity* but *Scripture* are useful', who would set it up 'instead of the *whole Law*, and *Light of Nature*' and who 'feign it to be instead of all Grammars, Logick, Philosophy, and all other Arts and Sciences' equally affront plain common sense: the Bible is, after all, written in Hebrew and Greek! Baxter's distaste for the irrationality of enthusiasm picked upon the very habit which meant so much to Bunyan: the application to one's condition of isolated biblical texts. '*Think not that because some strong imagination bringeth some promise to your minds, that therefore it belongeth unto you.*' Experience had shown him that 'upon true enquiry' it was almost invariably found that such a practice misappropriated the text. Bunyan might prefer what he 'smartingly did feel' to syllogistic reasoning, but Baxter, for whom faith was the 'rational Act of a rational Creature', 'must say no more than [he] can prove'.[12]

Baxter was hence far readier to recognize – and to allow – uncertainty than Bunyan. Where Baxter could admit doubt and scepticism without feeling his faith threatened, and could hold many and seemingly contrary positions in catholic and eclectic harmony, Bunyan must have a single and sure answer. In the famous 'self-review' in *Reliquiae Baxterianae* Baxter wrote:

> Among Truths certain in themselves, all are not equally certain unto me; and even of the Mysteries of the Gospel, I must needs say with Mr *Richard Hooker, Eccl. Polit.* that whatever men may pretend, the subjective Certainty cannot go beyond the objective Evidence: for it is caused thereby as the print on the Wax is caused by that on the Seal ... I am not so foolish as to pretend my certainty to be greater than it is, meerly because it is a dishonour to be less certain ...

Bunyan could not so admit degrees of certainty: doubts about some of the very things Baxter admits to having misgivings of appear in Diabolus' army in *The Holy War*. *Grace Abounding* is a passionate quest for assurance: Baxter, characteristically, did not regard assurance as a necessary consequence of saving faith, an infallible mark of the true Christian. In Bunyan questions – and *The Pilgrim's Progress* begins with *the* question, *'What shall I do to be saved?'* – demand and admit answers. There is but one way, 'as straight as a Rule can make it'.[13] For Baxter, the way was less direct and less easy confidently to discern. Bunyan's certitude is well attested by his deft, near riddling, exchanges with his inquisitors in the *Relation of the Imprisonment*. The aphoristic skill with which he there puts down his opponents derives from the absolute sureness of his convictions. Baxter would have needed far longer and far more words to do justice to his discerning awareness of the subtle and complex ways in which his own views both corresponded to and differed from those of his questioners. The brevity and single-mindedness of *Grace Abounding* compared to the length, confusion and comprehensiveness of the *Reliquiae* is a measure how much more firmly Bunyan drew the lines.

2 HUMANE LEARNING

The points of view of Bunyan and Baxter are not, however, merely matters of personal inclination and temperament: their positions correspond to two apparently contrary thrusts in the Puritan tradition. Bunyan's exaltation of the work of the Spirit and corresponding denigration of reason and study may be paralleled in the writings of many Interregnum radicals, from whom, indeed, we hear far more strident and comprehensive rejections of intellectual endeavour than from Bunyan. One of the earliest and most influential formulations of this anti-intellectualism was *The Sufficiencie of the Spirits Teaching without Humane Learning*, published in 1640 by the cobbler and London separatist pastor Samuel How, and commended, in the 1655 edition, by the Baptist William Kiffin. How allows all must know their native language, else the saving condition of Romans x.14 cannot be fulfilled, 'But the human learning which I oppose ... is the knowledge of arts and sciences, diverse tongues, much reading, and persisting in these things, so as thereby to be made able to understand the mind of God in his word: this is it that I condemn' on the grounds of I Corinthians ii.13. Carnal men, though learned, 'cannot perceive the things of God', and those who 'have had this kind of learning, when they came to know Christ, they forsook it all'. If, as I Corinthians ii.10 alleges, the Spirit 'searcheth the deep things of God', 'what need we more?' How is in no doubt that of two men in a state of grace, the one learned, the other not, the latter is to be preferred for the ministry for 'the wisdom of the world is foolishness with God' (I Cor. iii.19).[14]

How's contention – that carnal reason and human learning are of no help in understanding the will of God – became a main plank in the radical case against a state-supported, university-educated clergy, and a distinctive feature of both the anti-clericalism and the revolutionary confidence of Civil War enthusiasts and lower-class Interregnum sects. The antinomian New Model Army chaplain William Dell rejected the need for a university-trained clergy since 'if Christ call him and pour forth his spirit on him, that and that only makes him a true minister.' The corollary of this in radical thought was not that education is no alternative to, or substitute for, spiritual vocation, but that it is antipathetical to it. Christ's own Apostles were, observed Dell, 'poor, illiterate, mechanic men', and yet, wrote Penn, Christ so endued these 'poor mechanics' with 'his spirit and power' that 'in a few years many thousands' were by them converted.[15] The Seeker William Erbery was of like mind, so was Isaac Penington. Penington, from moving in Seeker and Ranter circles in the late 1640s and early 1650s became a Quaker, and from Quakers such as James Nayler were heard repeated attacks on the anti-christian 'men of learning' to be found in parish pulpits who searched 'into the hidden things of God by your own wisdom, which is carnal' instead of following 'the pure light of God dwelling in you'.[16]

Penington believed, and with justice, that many of the earliest Quaker preachers were 'for the most part mean, as to the outward, young country lads, of no deep understanding or ready expression, but very fit to be despised every where by the wisdom of man', and yet

> O how did the Lord prosper them in gathering his scattered wandering sheep into his fold of Rest! How did their words drop down like dew, and refresh the hungry thirsty souls! ... How did they batter the wisdom and reasonings of man, making the loftiness thereof stoop and bow to the weak and foolish babe of the begettings of Life!

But the classic Quaker statement is, of course, from Fox. In 1646, when Fox was 'walking in a field on a First-day morning, the Lord opened unto me that being bred at Oxford or Cambridge was not enough to fit and qualify men to be ministers of Christ; and I stranged at it because it was the common belief of people'. No Evangelist guided Fox, still less books: he came to the saving knowledge of God 'experimentally':

> My desires after the Lord grew stronger, and zeal in the pure knowledge of God and of Christ alone, without the help of any man, book or writing. For though I

read the Scriptures that spoke of Christ and of God, yet I knew him not but by revelation, as he who hath the key did open, and as the Father of life drew me to his Son by his spirit. And then the Lord did gently lead me along, and did let me see his love, which was endless and eternal, and surpasseth all the knowledge that men have in the natural state, or can get by history or books.

As Dryden later, and unsympathetically, wrote of these times:

> The Spirit gave the *Doctoral Degree*:
> And every member of a *Company*
> Was of *his Trade*, and of the *Bible free*.[17]

The Baxterian point of view, on the other hand, was commonly that of Presbyterians and Congregationalists. In his satirical burlesque *Hudibras*, Samuel Butler observed a distinction between, on the one hand, his Presbyterian hero, who is educated in Aristotelian logic, Classical rhetoric, Greek and Roman literature and scholastic and metaphysical divinity, and, on the other hand, Hudibras's Baptist squire, Ralph, who, though 'not far behind' the knight, is possessed of knowledge

> of another kind
> And he another way came by't:
> Some call it *Gifts*, and some *New Light*;
> A Liberal Art, that costs no pains
> Of Study, Industry, or Brains.

In a general way, this distinction is sound. Amongst Presbyterians and Congregationalists, the great majority of whom had university degrees, the former certainly and the latter usually supported a stipendiary and educated ministry. In the 1653 debates in the Barebones Parliament John Owen, an Oxford MA and afterwards DD, argued against the abolition of tithes advocated by the great majority of Baptists, Levellers and Fifth Monarchists, and by some radical Independents: and Owen was Dean of Christ Church and Cromwell's Vice-Chancellor of Oxford (1652–7). The most renowned of Christ Church's students during Owen's headship was John Locke, tutored by Thomas Cole, a Congregationalist ejected in 1660 who was to open an academy at Nettlebed, Oxfordshire, for training ministers; but the students also included at least 25 men who were to become nonconformist ministers.[18] Owen, who provocatively used Latin to refute Quakerism in his *Exercitationes adversus Fanaticos* (1658), fully supported the defence of the traditional role of the universities in the training of ministers against such attacks and calls for reform as that of the former army chaplain, and Erbery's editor, John Webster in *Academiarum Examen* (1654). To be the Congregational head both of a former cathedral house and a formerly Laudian university was no easy task. It may be, as his biographer believes, that Owen never managed to resolve the 'basic tension between a conservative academic and social outlook and a fairly radical religious viewpoint', but, for our purposes, it is that continuing commitment to academic and bookish values which is significant. It was a commitment which, in the experience of students, was not at all at odds with Owen's equal commitment to the promotion of Oxford as a centre of godliness. George Trosse thanked 'God from the bottom of my heart that I went to Oxford when there were so many sermons preached, and so many excellent and practical divines to preach them. ... Then, Religion was in its glory in the University.' And the Flintshire Presbyterian Philip Henry recalled his days at Christ Church with equal gratitude: 'he would often mention it with thankfulness to God, what great helps and advantages he had then in the University, not only for learning, but for religion and piety.'[19]

Owen may have gathered a church at Christ Church. Thomas Goodwin, a former dissenting member of the Westminister Assembly and part author of the Congregational *Declaration of Faith and Order*, certainly did at Magdalen, of which he was president. John Howe, who on the title-page of *The Blessedness of the Righteous* (1673) identified himself as 'sometime Fellow of *Magdalen* College, *Oxon*', was a member of this church, though, characteristically, upon '*Catholick Terms*'. Howe had all the Presbyterian's usual distrust of revelatory inspiration. Calamy records that he lost Cromwell's favour for preaching against the 'ill tendency' of 'the Notion of a *particular Faith* in Prayer', the view that those 'as were in a special manner favour'd of God' could confidently predict the response to their supplications and have 'pointed out to them future Events beforehand, which in reality is the same with Inspiration'.[20] For Howe, as for Baxter, reason was the defining attribute of man which distinguished him from the material creation. No form or state of matter, 'however modified and moved to the utmost subtilty or tenuity', could attain 'the powers of ratiocination or volition'. 'If to understand, to define, to distinguish, to syllogize, be nothing else but the agitation and collision of the minute parts of rarified matter among one another, methinks some happy chemist or other, when he hath missed his designed mark, should have hit upon some more noble product, and by one or other prosperous sublimation have caused some temporary resemblance, at least, of these operations.' Spared a time when this no longer seems 'quite out of the reach and road of artificial achievement', Howe was consequently convinced 'there must be somewhat else in man ... that is distinct from his corruptible part, and that is therefore capable, by the advantage of its own nature, of subsisting hereafter.'[21]

'The subjective Certainty cannot go beyond the objective Evidence': Baxter's inference from man's rationality was also Howe's, though by him put less tersely and pointedly: the knowledge of God is not 'by way of enthusiastical impulsion, without any reference to the external revelation that is rationally and aptly suitable to the working of the effect'. It is a mistake to suppose only 'rapturous, transporting apprehensions' constitute an authentic experience of grace. An '*enthusiastical assurance*' which 'excludes any reference to ... external revelation, and exercise of our own enlightened reason and judgment thereupon' is no safe evidence of regeneration. Howe concedes that God may 'if he please, imprint

on the mind the whole system of necessary truth, and on the heart the entire
frame of holiness, without the help of external revelation', but he sees little
point in pursuing the question whether God, in fact, ever does. It is not a
'matter of such moment that we need to be either curious in inquiring or
positive in determining about it' since subjective confidence will, if justly
grounded, always be verifiable from Scripture and objective observation no
matter what an individual may claim to be its source. Such a Lockean frame of
mind was very little interested in the particularities and peculiarities of religious
experience. In this, Howe, 15 years junior, was more of the age than Baxter,
who remained inveterately curious about the great variety of possible human
conditions, physical, psychological, emotional and spiritual. Howe works on an
altogether more abstract and rarefied level. His writings are remarkable
amongst those of nonconformists for their lack of specificity, of detail, about
both his own experience and the observable world. Appearances did not much
move him.[22]

What he did respond to, and respond to with a fine sensitivity, was something
else:

> To the altogether unlearned it will hardly be conceivable; and to the learned it need
> not be told, how high a gratification this employment of his Reason naturally yeilds
> [sic] to the mind of a man: When the harmonious contexture of truths with truths;
> the apt co-incidence, the secret links and junctures of coherent notions, are clearly
> discerned: When *effects* are traced up to their causes; *Properties* lodged in their
> native *subjects*; *Things* sifted to their Principles. What a pleasure is it, when a man
> shall apprehend himself regularly led on (though by a slender thread of discourse)
> through the Labyrinths of Nature; when still new discoveries are successfully
> made, every further enquiry ending in a further prospect, and every new Scene of
> things entertaining the mind with a fresh delight! How many have suffered a
> voluntary banishment from the world, as if they were wholly strangers, and
> unrelated to it; rejected the blandishments of sense; macerated themselves with
> unwearied studies, for this pleasure: making the ease and health of their bodies, to
> give place, to the content and satisfaction of their minds.[23]

To 'employ reason' for Howe meant to rise above particularities to the
perception of the 'harmonious contexture of truths', to 'trace effects to causes'
and to 'sift things to their principles'. This was his joy, and he delighted in the
company of any who were upon the same aspiring quest. As a student at
Christ's, Cambridge, in the late 1640s, he met the Cambridge Platonists Ralph
Cudworth ('the incomparable Dr. Cudworth' Howe called him) and John
Smith, and formed a lasting friendship with Henry More. To this Calamy
attributes 'that *Platonick* Tincture, which so remarkably runs thro [his]
Writings'. This is most evident in his responsiveness to 'this famous sect, the
Platonists', the 'school' of Pythagoras, which might better be called a 'church',
and the 'ethnic philosophers' whom he can often discuss more interestingly and
at greater length than biblical texts. Maximus Tyrius ('that most ingenious
pagan author'), Hermes Trismegistus, Pythagoras, Plotinus, Empedocles,
Heraclitus, Philo, Porphyry, Philostratus, Dionysius Halicarnassus, Epictetus

and Diogenes Laertius are just some of those whom he quotes in Greek and whose guidance he welcomes.[24]

The 'Platonick Tincture' is not, however, merely a matter of naming names. Howe makes his own the thought of 'the great Pagan Theologue', Plato. The idealism of the *Phaedo*, its aspiration to free the soul from its mortal confines and its imagery of the soul as a bird, wingless or encaged in the body, drew from him a heartfelt response. The 'instability and fluidity' of man's 'corporeal being' which 'hath nothing steady or consistent in it' is the main theme of *The Vanity of this Mortal Life* (1672), but to it Howe constantly returns throughout his writings. The predicament of the nonconformist as a victim in the Restoration world, more usually rendered by the direct recording of cases of suffering or injustice, or by the irony of satire, is in Howe presented not with historical particularity or satirical topicality but by general and Platonic meditation upon the human condition: life is but 'a dark umbrage or shadow' of 'actual essence', 'nothing but 'εἴδωλον,ψεῦδος – α *mere semblance*, or a *lie*'. Howe, who here refers to Plotinus, habitually finds a mutually consistent and confirmatory witness in pre-Socratic and Platonic philosophers on the one hand and in the Bible on the other. Heraclitus' aphorism, 'All things flow, nothing stays, after the manner of a river', is paralleled by I Corinthians vii.31, which 'more elegantly expresses' 'the scheme, the show, the pageantry' of 'the whole scene of things in this material world'. Paul 'speaks of it but as an appearance, as if he knew not whether to call it something or nothing'. And so, as Paul consequently requires that 'the affections ... be as if they were not', Howe himself concludes from the insubstantiality and unreliability of the world that we should '*endeavour for a calm indifferency and dispassionate temper of mind towards the various objects and affairs that belong to this present life*'. Psalms lxxiii.20, xxxix.5–6, Job xx.8 and Ecclesiastes similarly teach 'the exility, and almost nothingness, of man's being'.[25]

Not every Congregationalist or Presbyterian was of Howe's mind, however, – nor even every erstwhile fellow of Magdalen. Theophilus Gale was Howe's contemporary at Oxford, and, like him, a member of Goodwin's church. Ejected in 1660, he was for two years tutor to Philip, Lord Wharton's sons, and subsequently served as John Rowe's assistant and successor, ministering to a London Congregational church. While Howe delighted in his 'ethnic philosophers', Gale's life's work, the massive five-volume, 1,800 quarto-page *Court of the Gentiles* (1669–78), was devoted to showing that, as ancient pagan learning and literature was derived from, and at best, a misunderstanding, at worst a diabolical perversion of the Hebrew traditions preserved in the Old Testament, it is not in itself an adequate or proper area of study. It may be used incidentally as a gloss on Scripture, or to supply historical information, but to prefer it to Christian theology, or to adopt its methods to expound that theology, leads only to error, heresy and atheism. Gale has the Cambridge Platonists and latitudinarians in his sights. Intending to confirm '*the* Authoritie of the

Scriptures, *and so by consequence* the Christian Religion' he sets out *'to beat down that* fond persuasion, *which has of late crept in among, and been openly avowed by many, too great* Admirers *of* Pagan Philosophie, *(especially that of* Plato) *as if it were all but the* Product *of* Natures Light'. On the contrary, so far from being the triumph of unaided reason, *'the choicest* Contemplations *of* Gentile Philosophie, *were but some corrupt* Derivations, *or at best some broken* Traditions, *originally traduced from the* Sacred Scriptures, *and* Jewish Church.'[26]

Gale's marvellously erudite, endlessly fascinating and largely misguided demonstration of this thesis is his own, but the thesis itself is not. He can cite in support an impressive list of Church Fathers, Jewish historians and the Greeks themselves. His favourite text, reiterated throughout the first two volumes, is Plato's assertion in *Cratylus* that the Greeks received their learning 'from certain Barbarians, more ancient than ourselves': these barbarians, on the authority of Clement of Alexandria and Augustine, Gale identifies as Hebrews.[27] To do so, he reconstructs the lines of transmission. Phoenicians and Egyptians were the intermediaries. The Phoenicians were, he claims, Canaanites who, after Joshua's conquests, migrated in large numbers around the Mediterranean world but who nevertheless retained sufficient contact with Canaan to carry with them a knowledge of Hebrew customs and learning gained both during the residence of the Patriarchs in Canaan and since the Israelite occupation. For their part, the Egyptians were 'no way famous for *Wisdom*, or *Philosophie*, before the abode of the Patriarchs', but 'received the best part of their Laws from the *Mosaick Constitutions*, besides what they had immediately from *Joseph* their great *Legislator*'. Their gods, 'all younger than the Patriarchs', were but degenerate recollections of them; Osiris, for example, was 'an *Hieroglyphick* of *Joseph*'. Later, during the Babylonish Captivity, many Jews fled to Egypt, and were instrumental in establishing at Alexandria 'the most flourishing' school in the ancient world by 'seasoning that Fountain of Learning with Scripture Light'. What the Egyptians thus learned from the Hebrews became the inspiration of Greek philosophy through the travels to Egypt of such as Thales, Pythagoras and Plato.[28]

All this was very far from being nonsense. Old Testament usage implies no firm ethnic or cultural distinction between Canaanites and Phoenicians. Modern scholars, noting the common reference of Akkadian 'Canaan' and Greek 'Phoenicia' to trade in purple dye and textiles, do not distinguish categorically between them.[29] Certainly, they had what Gale calls 'familiar *commerce*' with the Israelites, notably in the tenth century, when David and Solomon had commercial and diplomatic dealings with Hiram, king of Tyre (II Sam. v.11; I Kings ix.11–14), and in the ninth, when Ahab famously (and infamously) married the Phoenician princess of Sidon, Jezebel (I Kings xvi.31–2). Equally certainly, Jews were resident in Egypt since before the Exodus, where they so increased that by the first century AD there may have been a million Greek-speaking Jews resident in Egypt and Alexandria had become 'a centre of world

Jewry'. And certainly, too, from the Egyptians the Greeks took their mathematics and astronomy, and from the Phoenicians their alphabet.[30]

But so, too, did the Hebrews. What weakens Gale's case is not his account of interaction between ancient peoples but his claim that the interaction was almost exclusively one way: his comprehensive and single-minded determination to establish the primacy of the Jewish revelation by deriving from it all ancient learning, tirelessly sustained through hundreds of pages, finally undermines his seriousness. He traces not only all ancient culture to the Jews – all languages derive from Hebrew, all letters from Moses, all 'Pagan *Theologie* or *Idolatrie*', philosophy, poetry, historiography, law, rhetoric and myth from 'sacred Oracles'[31] – but also every detail of it. Tales of Bacchus are 'corrupt and broken ... Traditions' of Noah, Moses and Nimrod; Typhon derives from Moses, Hercules from Joshua, Saturn from Noah. Homer's style shows he had 'many of his *Fictions* from some *real Scripture Tradition*, which he gathered up whilest he was in Egypt'. Plato's androgynous man in the *Symposium* is a muddled echo of the creation of Eve from Adam's rib; the Classical Golden Age recalls Eden; Deucalion's flood in the *Timaeus* is a memory of Noah; the Pythagorean academy was modelled on Jewish temple rites and the practice of the Essenes.[32] But where modern anthropologists and folklorists would see in his parallels evidence of the basic types of primitive story and of the common function of poetry and myth in primitive cultures, Gale detects not parallels but imitation, misunderstandings and diabolical perversions of a sacred original. Denying the possibility of rival or comparable insights in different cultures, he detects only degeneration from that original. Modern theologians would be likely to draw from Gale's premise that God 'is the *original Idea* of all truth, the *eternal wisdom* and fountain of all light' the possibility of various revelations of that truth; Gale will admit only one. He hence allows nothing to the insight of Greek philosphers themselves, and has no sense of the difference between the Hebraic and Hellenic mentality. Where Howe saw enlightenment, Gale finds only darkening gloom. Plato '*discolored*, and *disfigured* the *habit* of his *Jewish traditions*'. In his chapter 'How Jewish Traditions came to be mistaken by Pagans' Gale instances their mythologizing tendency, linguistic ignorance, misapplication of Hebrew stories to new heroes, misunderstanding, contempt for the Jews, but above all their unregenerate pride and wilful perverseness:

> notwithstanding those rich, and resplendent *Derivations* of *Divine Revelation*, how much did the *Gentile* world solace it self in its own native darknesse? what mixture of *vain Imaginations* with *Judaick Traditions*? what muddie, dirtie *phantasmes* did they mingle with those *broken Traditions*, they received from the *waters* of the *Sanctuarie*?[33]

An irony of course attends the whole of Gale's *magnum opus*: his refutation is only possible because of his possession of just such Classical knowledge, familiarity with arcane learning and facility in ancient tongues as he argues against. A similar irony attends a more famous and, apparently, even more uncompromising repudiation. The man who 'had so keen an appetite' for 'the study of literature' that he came better than any other to satisfy Ben Jonson's demand of a poet ('that which we especially require in him is an exactness of study, and multiplicity of reading, which maketh a full man') and of whom the Quaker Thomas Ellwood wrote 'In tongues he so much skill had got,/He might be called *The Polyglott*',[34] this man had Christ in *Paradise Regained* adopt what seems to be Samuel How's position: 'he who receives/Light from above, from the fountain of light,/No other doctrine needs.' Milton's Christ rejects Plato in particular as one who 'to fabling fell and smooth conceits' and the body of Classical philosophy in general as 'false, or little else but dreams,/Conjectures, fancies, built on nothing firm'. To his mind, as to Gale's, the self-evident superiority of Hebrew literature to Classical declares that 'Greece from us these arts derived.'[35]

3   'TRUST NOT ONLY TO YOUR UNDERSTANDINGS'

And yet Gale and Milton are not the idiosyncratically anomalous cases they at first appear, nor are either they or the Baptists and Quakers to be categorically distinguished from Presbyterian and Congregational defenders of humane learning. We are dealing, in fact, not with differences of kind but of degree, not with opposing contentions but with a shared position based upon a premise common to all nonconformists; that though man may be rational, he is not merely rational. Neither the repudiation of learning by anti-intellectualists, nor its defence by academic apologists was absolute and unqualified. Though the extent to which they admitted humane assistance differed (and even this was a difference which narrowed through our period), all admitted that assistance; and though all admitted it, none trusted finally to it. But did Milton's Christ then not mean what he said?

In *Paradise Lost* ignorance is clearly not a virtue. Prior to the Fall, the Father sends Raphael to Eden explicitly to teach Adam that he may fully understand his hazardous situation. Furthermore, though the burden of Raphael's information is admonitory, the Father envisages a conversation between friends withdrawn from the business of the world which recalls not only Exodus xxxiii.11 but also the setting of Plato's dialogues: 'Go therefore, half this day as friend with friend/Converse with Adam, in what bower or shade/Thou find'st him from the heat of noon retired,/To respite his day-labour.' To learn is enjoyable. Just how enjoyable, and how natural and proper, the relationship between preceptor and pupil evinces. By letting slip a reference to the Satanic rebellion Raphael, like a good teacher, arouses Adam's curiosity. And when Adam, who has listened 'attentive' and with 'delighted ear', implores his 'Divine instructor' to give a 'full relation', the archangel willingly obliges. His narration of the war in heaven so impresses Adam that he is 'Led on, yet sinless, with desire to know/What nearer might concern him', and this 'thirst ... of knowledge', too, Raphael satisfies with an account of the creation. He does so, however, with a caution:

> commission from above
> I have received, to answer thy desire
> Of knowledge within bounds; beyond abstain
> To ask, nor let thy own inventions hope
> Things not revealed ...
>   knowledge is as food, and needs no less
> Her temperance over appetite, to know
> In measure what the mind may well contain,
> Oppresses else with surfeit, and soon turns
> Wisdom to folly, as nourishment to wind.[36]

The implications of this caution to be temperate in the pursuit of 'invention', which may include scientific experiments as well as metaphysical speculation,[37] are drawn out in Book VIII. The book falls into two halves: in the first, Raphael answers Adam's astronomical queries; in the second, Adam relates his experiences since his creation. A common theme, however, unites the two. Adam concludes his account with a moving confession of the emotionally disturbing effect Eve's beauty has upon him. So strong is the 'passion' aroused by 'the charm of beauty's powerful glance' that 'All higher knowledge in her presence falls/Degraded, wisdom in discourse with her/Looses discountenanced, and like folly shows.' This draws from Raphael, 'with contracted brow', the stern line: 'In loving thou dost well, in passion not.' True love, he argues in Neoplatonic vein, 'hath his seat/In reason' and 'is the scale/By which to heavenly love thou mayst ascend'.[38] And just as true love can, if immoderately pursued, degenerate into 'carnal pleasure' and lust, so too can intellectual curiosity become a debasing passion. In reply to Adam's 'doubt' that the whole universe could have been created 'merely to officiate light/Round this opacous earth', Raphael, while not rebuking Adam's desire for knowledge ('To ask or search I blame thee not ...'), diverts it to practical and moral concerns. The validity of Copernican and Ptolemaic cosmologies 'imports not': Raphael himself disconcertingly offers both geocentric and heliocentric accounts of the universe. What does matter is that Adam should occupy his mind not 'with matters hid' but with 'what concerns thee and thy being', namely, to 'serve and fear' God, for this, as Raphael had said earlier, is what 'best may serve/To glorify the maker, and infer/Thee also, happier'.[39]

As we approach the Fall in Book IX the force of Raphael's lesson thus becomes clear. As Adam's desire for a companion in Eden is according to the divine will, so too is the play of man's mind upon the creation. Neither human love nor intellectual curiosity is intrinsically evil: both are a means to 'infer men happier'. Neither, however, can in itself confer happiness. Since their proper function is to encourage not self-reliance but creaturely devotion to the Creator, to pursue them for their own intrinsic pleasure is to pursue them for Satanic ends. Humane study which fosters either a merely rational scepticism or a merely intellectual speculativeness is as much a culpable self-indulgence as sensuality. There can be an intellectual intemperance and disobedience no less than an emotional. Adam takes the point:

> apt the mind or fancy is to rove
> Unchecked, and of her roving is no end:
> Till warned, or by experience taught, she learn,
> That not to know at large of things remote
> From use, obscure and subtle, but to know
> That which before us lies in daily life,
> Is the prime wisdom.[40]

But, as he will be guilty of emotional excess ('How can I live without thee ...'), so Eve will be of intellectual. It is as 'Mother of science', the earthly *scientia* which, in Augustinian thought, was far inferior to *sapientia*, heavenly wisdom, that Satan addresses the Tree. And it is for *scientia*, to escape what she is persuaded is her ignorance in 'speculations high and deep', that Eve eats. To remain 'lowly wise' rather than intellectually assertive is an act of faith she cannot, at that moment, perform.[41]

The passage in *Paradise Regained* is not a hardening of this Miltonic position, a withdrawal of the willing admission of intellectual curiosity and rational investigation, but a reiteration of its subordinate status. In the poem Milton handles the three wilderness temptations in the Lucan order, but the first is tersely introductory and the third climactically brief. The body of the poem is given to an expanded treatment of the mountain temptation which, in all its guises, is prompting Christ to answer one, crucial, question: 'all thy heart is set on high designs,/High actions; but wherewith to be achieved?/Great acts require great means of enterprise.' Satan proposes a succession of means by which Christ might establish his kingdom, many of them uncomfortably reminiscent of the policies and methods of Puritans during the Civil War and Interregnum. To the bearing on nonconformity of Christ's rejection of them all we shall return later. Here, we need to notice that given the choice between a Satanically inspired design to 'Be famous then/By wisdom' and faith in God there is only one choice possible, or go the way of Eve. In the dramatic context of the encounter only an unqualified negative will serve. Milton had himself drawn attention to the significance of context in assessing the general applicability of a character's remarks when he pointed to its Pharisaical audience to claim an admonitory rather than a prescriptive force for Christ's prohibition of divorce.[42] Just so here: the implication is not that learning or its pursuit are intrinsically evil, but that they are not essential and that to trust to them is fatal. When, to complete the lines quoted earlier, Christ says that 'he who receives/Light from above ... No other doctrine needs, though granted true', he denies only the necessity of learning, and allows it need not be erroneous. Were the repudiation absolute rather than relative, it is difficult to believe a poet as consistent and decorous as Milton would have allowed Christ's earlier praise of Socrates to stand, or that he would have had Christ so often express himself in Classical terms, or that he would have published the poem with, as its companion piece, *Samson Agonistes*, a poem explicitly modelled on Greek tragedies. Nor, to conclude anecdotally, would he in 1662 have taken on Thomas Ellwood, the man who claimed to have prompted the composition of *Paradise Regained*, to improve the Quaker's Latin![43]

'Knowledge within bounds': this Miltonic position was not peculiarly his but was shared by all nonconformists. Even among radicals, the prevailing bias of Puritan educational theory had been for the reform and promotion, not the abolition, of education. It was not learning itself but 'humane learning', the arid scholasticism and traditional Classicism of Oxford and Cambridge, which was repudiated.[44] This was damned as an escapist folly on a par with monasticism, with which, of course, it shared a popish origin. So William Dell, despite his diatribes against universities, continued master of Gonville and Caius College, Cambridge, until the Restoration, and proposed far-reaching and forward-looking reforms which included the founding of universities in all major provincial towns and the adoption of a more comprehensive and practical syllabus. This bias would be reflected in the curricula of the dissenting academies, which have won the admiration of historians and which even some conformist contemporaries recognized as an innovative improvement on university tuition.[45] Similarly, Gale's five volumes berating 'ethnic philosophers' did not not prevent him from tutoring Wharton's sons, or in his will leaving his books to Harvard and funds for the support of poor scholars. And though the Baptist ministry continued generally unlearned until the end of the century, in 1679 Edward Terrill made provision for the education of Baptist ministers. The Bunyan whose schooling was irrelevant had, after all, confessed 'to his shame' that he forgot it. In *The Holy War* we find precisely the Miltonic balance. Learning is certainly a trifle, subject to prevailing fashions, not to be trusted. Mr Tradition, Mr Human-wisdom and Mr Mans Invention quickly make their peace with Diabolus, declaring 'that they did not so much live by *Religion*, as by the fates of *Fortune*. And ... since his Lordship was willing to entertain them they should be willing to serve him.' But they had previously just as readily served Emanuel. In a loyal Mansoul, learning subserves faith; it is Mansoul's capitulation which perverts it to diabolical ends. And so, in his *Book for Boys and Girls* (1686), Bunyan took care to instruct his young readers in the elements of literacy and numeracy, encouraged them that '*Some Boys with difficulty do begin,/Who in the end, the Bays, and Lawrel win*', and insisted '*Nor let my pretty Children them despise;/All needs must there begin, that wou'd be wise.*'[46]

Even in a Quaker family we find the Ellwood who sought out Milton because his Latin was rusty, and who had never quite lost his youthful 'natural Propensity to Learning', engaged early in 1663 as a tutor to Isaac Penington's children. Indeed, Ellwood protested that he was not 'rightly sensible of my Loss' in having neglected his studies 'until I came amongst the *Quakers*. But then I both saw my Loss, and lamented it; and applyed my self with utmost Diligence, at all leisure Times to recover it: so false I found that Charge to be, which in those Times was cast, as a Reproach upon the *Quakers*, That *they despised and decried all Humane Learning*; because they denied it to be essentially necessary to a *Gospel-Ministry.*' This is at first startling. Had not Fox trenchantly observed that 'the beginning of ... many languages was *Babel*; and *Pilate* he could not open the Scriptures with Hebrew, Greek and Latine, but crucified Christ, who is the substance of the Scriptures, and when he had done, he set many languages on the top of him'? We rather expect from a Quaker such a bias as we find in the account of his conversion written by George Keith, an Aberdeen graduate. He turned to Quakerism when he discovered that it was not the educated clergy but Friends 'who were taught of God who pointed me to true principles; and, though some of them could not read a letter, yet I found them wiser than all the teachers I ever formerly had been under.' Keith was, during his Quaker period, a vigorous defender of the ministry of the ignorant. In his sprightly *The Woman-Preacher of Samaria; A Better Preacher, and more Sufficiently Qualified to Preach, than any of the Men-Preachers of the Man-made-Ministry in These Three Nations* (1674) it is that 'she was taught by Christ, by Christ himself; she was taught immediately' which is for him the crucial point of John iv: 'Her Preaching was not any Humane design, either of her, or any Man, or men else, but it was wholly Divine.' It is hence no surprise to find that Keith's definition of the two '*cheife and principall veins, and arteries, which convey the very Blood, life and Spirit of the Christian Religion, into the true members of that body*' appears to leave no scope at all for humane learning: '*that ther is no saving knowledge of God ... but by the* Immediate Revelation *of Jesus Christ*' (the subject of Keith's *Immediate Revelation* (1668)), and that the 'Image, Word and Light, *which is* Jesus Christ ... *doth shine forth* in some measure universally, *and enlighten every man that comes into the World, and thereby giveth unto him, a day of visitation, wherein it is possible for him to be saved*' (the subject of *The Universall Free Grace of the Gospell Asserted* (1671)).[47]

 And yet Keith also argued that to hold these '*two maine and principall things*' in Quaker belief was not to repudiate other sources of enlightenment and instruction. In the first place, though the Spirit has primacy, the Bible is to be valued as 'a clear and perfect copy as to *essentials* and necessaries of Christian religion'. In *Quakerism Confirmed* (1676), a work he wrote together with Robert Barclay, Keith charged those who accused Quakers of neglecting the Bible with confounding 'the *materiall* and *formall objects of faith*, as if we did hold that inward revelation without Scripture did propound unto us the material objects of faith, which is false'. That we should believe is a spiritual revelation; what and how we should believe we learn from Holy Writ. Quakers 'pretend to no ... *doctrines*, which are not conform [*sic*] to the Scriptures of Truth'. To the charge that this is specious since Quakers allow authority to the Bible only so far as it is confirmed by inner conviction, and hence treat it not as an objective rule but a subjective whim, Keith replied, somewhat casuistically, and perhaps, as we shall in a moment hear Locke argue, fallaciously:

> we know the Scriptures testimony by the spirit *tanquam a priori*, as we know the effect by the cause, and we know the Spirits testimony by the Scriptures, *tanquam a posteriori*, as we know the cause by the effect, and so both are objective, and yet in divers kind, because the objective evidence of the spirit is a self-evidence and primary, the objective evidence of the Scripture is but derived and secondary.[48]

If it is false that Quakers undervalue the Bible, equally, in Keith's view, it is false that they reject the 'usefulness of all means, and instruments whatsomever [*sic*], whether books or men':

> And as concerning *the sufficiency of this light unto salvation*, wee doe not understand it in opposition, to either the *necessity* or *usefulness* of the *outward coming of Christ*, and his sufferings and death for our sins, nor in opposition unto the *service and use* of any teachings *in the outward*, that come from the Spirit of God, or any outward things to be done or practised, which his spirit leadeth unto all.

Keith, writing in the late 1660s and early 1670s, thus bears out what Ellwood was later to recollect of that time in his *History*: it was not the usefulness but the indispensability of secondary means which Quakers rejected. To neglect 'the service of any means', Keith writes, is reprehensible but, he adds, 'we may not overvalue them, so as to set them up in God's room, as if we could not live without them'. We are back, in fact, to 'knowledge within bounds'. In Keith's view, no less than in Milton's, the pursuit of learning for its own sake is Satanic: 'the enemy makes a prey of their souls, and fetters their feet in this snare, of gathering knowledge from books, or any other way, to keep them from the true knowledge.' But Keith, no less than Milton, can cite Greek philosophers and historians. Similarly, Francis Howgill, one of Fox's earliest converts and perhaps a university man, though he argues against the necessity, even the desirability, of ministerial learning, still brings to *The Great Case of Tythes* (1665) extensive Hebraic and Patristic learning and shows himself conversant with early church history and with conciliar and canonical pronouncements and law.[49]

And, equally, 'knowledge within bounds' was the burden of the defenders of learning. Baxter welcomed 'subservient sciences', but only so long as they were subservient. He is as anxious as Raphael to dissuade from *'presumptious curiosity'* in prying 'into Gods Secrets' and, again like Raphael and despite his youthful passion for the medieval schoolmen whom Gale stigmatized as the worst sophisters, came unequivocally to prefer practical to metaphysical divinity:

> In my youth I was quickly past my Fundamentals, and was running up into a multitude of Controversies, and greatly delighted with metaphysical and scholas- tick Writings ... But the elder I grew the smaller stress I layd upon these Controversies and Curiosities ... as finding far greater Uncertainties in them, than I at first discerned, and finding less *Usefulness* comparatively ... And now it is the fundamental Doctrines of the Catechism, which I highliest value, and daily think of, and find most useful to my self and others: The Creed, the Lord's Prayer, and

> the Ten Commandments ... are to me as my daily *Bread* and *Drink* ... I had rather read or hear of them, than of any of the School Niceties, which once so pleased me.

Whereas he once had a high opinion 'of Learned Persons and Books', experience taught him 'we are all yet in the dark. And the more I am acquainted with holy Men, that are all for Heaven, and pretend not much to Subtilties, the more I value and honour them'. He was hence, like Milton, in no doubt that an uneducated man who had 'never heard of most of the Questions in *Scotus*, or *Ockham* or *Aquinas*' but who had 'a double measure of the knowledge of God in Christ' was 'far richer in knowledge, and a much wiser man, than he that hath these Controversies at his fingers ends'. No amount of reading would in itself serve: *'Trust not only to your understandings, and think not that study is all which is necessary to faith. But remember that faith is the gift of God, and therefore pray as well as study.'*[50]

Just so, Howe argued that 'rational certainty', '*intellectual certainty*' does not constitute faith and is, therefore, inadequate: 'as the inward revelation uses not to do its work without the outward ... so nor is the outward revelation able, alone, to beget that which, in the more eminent sense, goes in Scripture under the name of faith.' Like Raphael, he allows Ptolemaic and Copernican cosmologies indifferently ('as this or that hypothesis best pleases us') since we should never so far trust our own minds as to allow them to dictate to us either certainties or doubts: 'The notion of the goodness and righteousness of God, methinks, should stick so close to our minds and create such a sense in our souls, as should be infinitely dearer to us than all our senses and powers.' He quotes John xiv.16–21 to the effect that 'a communicable privilege and favour to holy souls' is the gift of the Spirit, 'an inward manifestation of divine love'.[51]

Hence, Howe was not, any more than Baxter, who had something of Howe's regard for the Cambridge Platonists, tempted to suppose Christianity was not mysterious.[52] The first part of *The Living Temple* (1676) is an early and sustained refutation of deism which insists that any profession of belief in a deity who is not immanently present is mere atheism since it denies the true nature of God. For Howe, God has not only a 'capacity and propension' to communicate with humans, but also a 'gracious inclination of will thereunto', 'an aptitude thereto': 'that *Being* is not *God*, that cannot converse with men.' For all his urbane poise and rational idealism, an intimate and affectionate relationship between God and individuals hence remains for Howe the essence of faith. He pointedly observes that the claim that the existence of the deists' God can be proved not from experience or revelation but 'from nature' would be weightier if 'some of them had told us or could tell us what they meant by *nature*'. In fact, its very remoteness from human experience proves this God a mere intellectual fabrication: in a passage unusually patterned for Howe, he writes

> they who have imagined such a Being and been pleased to call it God, have at once said and unsaid the same thing. That Deity was but a creature, and that only of their own fancy; and they have, by the same breath, blown up and blasted their own

bubble; made it seem something and signify nothing; have courted it into being, and rioted it again quite out of it; in their conceit, created it a God, in their practice a mere nullity.

That it does not impinge upon practice and carries no obligation of service or devotion in Howe's view explains why this fabrication is so invidiously attractive. It is an attraction which incites Howe to ironic derision. To 'admit of this fictitious Deity' can 'do no prejudice to their affairs' since

> They are not his creatures, but he is theirs; a precarious Deity, that shall be as long, and what, and where they please to have him ... There shall be a God, provided he be not meddlesome nor concern himself in their affairs to the crossing of any inclinations or humours which they are pleased shall command and govern their lives.

This is no more than a disguised atheism, a licence for the immorality and licentiousness of the Caroline *beau monde*. Howe hence designates the deist position 'Epicureanism': 'the *Epicurean* Deity ... is a Being of either so dull and phlegmatic a temper that he *cannot* be concerned in the actions and affairs of men; or so soft and easy, that he will not.' This is no God since we 'owe him no more homage than we have to the great Mogul or Cham of Tartary ... In one word, all converse between him and man, on his part by providence and on ours by religion, is quite cut off.'[53]

4 'STILL AS I PULL'D, IT CAME'

'All converse between him and man ... is quite cut off': Howe's objection to deism points to what it was all nonconformists shared, what it was which, despite their particular differences of emphasis on the significance of learning and the role of reason, marked them off as a group from the increasingly confident rationalism of their age. In the terminology of the theologians, they continued to prefer *fiducia* (trusting and affectionate commitment) to *fides* (intellectual assent to propositions) or *fides historica* (compliance with tradition), what Milton, among others, called an 'implicit faith'. It was because, in his view, it was possible for Roman Catholics to believe only 'as the Church believes' that, in *Of True Religion*, published in 1673 following the dispensation to worship privately granted papists by Charles's 1672 *Declaration of Indulgence*, Milton excluded popery as 'the only or the greatest Heresie' in Christendom from the toleration he advocated for all holders of explicit faith, that is, Protestants of any persuasion. The saving commitment of self involves more than submission to authority and deference to precedent. It also involves more than doctrinal rectitude. While *fides* may indeed accept what is actually true, and may itself be a necessary part of faith ('Can you love and serve a God that you *Know* not?' Baxter asks rhetorically), it is not in itself a sufficient or saving faith. That consists in an emotional cleaving to God which is, wherever we turn in nonconformist writing, the gift not of understanding but of grace, the fruit not of study alone but of experience. This (entirely typical) passage is from Thomas Manton:

> There is in faith an assent, which is sufficient when the object requireth no more. As there are some speculative principles which are merely to be believed ... there an intellectual assent sufficeth. But there are other things which are propounded, not only as true, but good. There, not only an intellectual assent is required, but a practical assent ... a consent to choose it for my portion and happiness ... Trust is not a bare opinion of Christ's fidelity, but a dependence upon his word.[54]

Intellectual positions hence in themselves count for relatively little. In *Of True Religion* Milton argues that though members of different Protestant sects may in their various ways be doctrinally mistaken, they are yet 'no Hereticks. Heresie is in the Will and choice profestly against Scripture; error is against the Will, in misunderstanding the Scripture. ... It is humane frailty to err, and no man is infallible here on earth.' In his depiction of the Fall in *Paradise Lost* Milton had carefully maintained this distinction between error (which is intellectual) and sin (which is wilful). Although 'credulous' and deceived by the snake, Eve remains 'sinless' until persuaded by her intellectual error to trust the snake rather than God. Though prompted by logic and argument, the sin resides not in the mind but in the heart, which is why Adam, who is not deceived, can yet commit it. This is also why Abdiel can sound so like Satan: what distinguishes them is their loyalty. As this leads us to expect, on these matters Milton's *De Doctrina Christiana* is entirely orthodox. Milton adduces James ii.19 ('The devils also believe and tremble') to show the inadequacy of *fides*. It is 'necessary for salvation' but cannot in itself attain it (I Tim. iv.1). It is valuable but as a means to saving faith, 'a receiving of God and an approach to God' (John i.12), or, as Milton quite properly calls it, 'love', which may know about theology but knows God directly, experientially. This was the position Baxter developed in the second part of his *Treatise of Knowledge and Love Compared* (1688). The doctrines he there draws from I Corinthians viii.3 are:

Doct. 1   *Knowledge is a means to a higher end, according to which it is to be estimated.*
Doct. 2   *The End of Knowledge is to make us Lovers of God, and so to be known with Love by him.*
Doct. 3   *Therefore knowledge is to be valued, sought and used, as it tendeth to this holy blessed end.*
Doct. 4   *And therefore those are to be accounted the wisest and best-knowing men, that love God most: and not those that are stored with unholy knowledge.*

So it was that, despite his theological dissent from what he took to be the errors of Bunyan's antinomianism, Baxter could recognize in him a man possessed of this love. And Bunyan, we recall, preached 'what I smartingly did feel'.[55]

As presented in *Grace Abounding* what Bunyan felt was, as we noted earlier, hardly under his own control. The clear implication of his narrative is that no man can think himself into *fiducia*, reason himself into love. This may, indeed did, denigrate man's intellectual faculties, but Bunyan's dismissal of his learning was no more mere anti-intellectual irresponsibility than was Baxter's more restrained qualification of its usefulness merely a tactical concession to legitimize scholarly pursuits. Both were defending as vital an aspect of human nature increasingly disdained by the temper of their age. 'Knowledge within bounds' was not a restrictive tenet but a liberating one, for, whatever the degree to which it subordinated 'subservient sciences', it did so precisely in order to admit the intuitive, the emotional, the imaginative and the spiritual. Its ubiquitousness is evidence neither of a stultifying imperviousness to innovative thinking nor of a sectarian biblicism but of a dynamically held conception of man more comprehensive and more generous than that fostered by Lockean rationalism, Newtonian mechanism and deistic moralism. The 'converse between God and man' which Howe would safeguard was conducted on a level beyond the rational and engaged far more than a man's mind. From the historical point of view, 'knowledge with bounds' was a rearguard defence of modes of perception and apprehension which would hardly again be championed until the work of Wesley and, in his engravings of 1788, William Blake dismissed deism with the words 'Man's perceptions are not bounded by organs of perception; he percieves [sic] more than sense (tho' ever so acute) can discover.'[56]

This, of course, was what the age condemned as enthusiasm. Although, at the end of the seventeenth century, Charles Leslie properly noted that 'The Word *Enthusiasm* signifies *Inspiration*; and may mean a *Good* as well as an *Evil* Inspiration', he went on, 'from the frequent False Pretences to it, it is generally us'd in the worst sense.' It had, indeed, been used almost exclusively of what its user regarded as false claims to enlightenment and revelation since becoming current early in the century. Milton's nephew, Edward Phillips, confined his definition of '*Enthysiasts*' in *The New World of English Words* (1658) to 'a certain Sect of people which pretended to the Spirit and Revelations' (his definition of 'Quakers' as 'a modern Sect of Enthusiasts' was hence damning). In *The Anatomy of Melancholy* (1621) Robert Burton had set the tone of later discussions when, in his discourse on 'Religious Melancholy' he attributed enthusiasm to Satanic apparitions, and associated it with the 'infatuated' Munster Anabaptists, 'pseudo-prophets' and 'pseudo-Christians' subject to visions, 'a company of giddy heads', 'the ruder sort ... carried headlong with blind zeal' who 'turn prophets, have secret revelations, will be of privy council with God Himself, and know all His secrets'. Burton's view that enthusiasm was certainly the product of a diseased imagination and often of a diseased body was developed by Henry More in *Enthusiasmus Triumphatus* (1656), and More's fellow Cambridge Platonist, Benjamin Whichcote, stated categorically that 'Enthusiasm is the Confounder, both of Reason and Religion: therefore nothing is more necessary to the Interest of Religion than the prevention of *Enthusiasm*.' In *Leviathan* (1651) Thomas Hobbes, dismissive equally of the possibility of Satanic or divine inspiration, equated enthusiasm with madness, but it was left to the less outrageous Locke to deliver the *coup de grace* in the chapter 'Of Enthusiasm' which he added to the fourth edition (1700) of *An Essay Concerning Human Understanding* (1689/90).[57]

In this culmination of the rationalistic trend of the century the line of thought illustrated by Baxter's correlation between subjective certainity and objective evidence and by Howe's insistence on the 'external revelation' becomes a refutation of the epistemological fallacy of enthusiasm. Locke begins with the premise that a lover of truth is defined by his 'not entertaining any Proposition with greater assurance than the Proofs it is built upon will warrant' (where 'proofs' means 'rational verification'); the convictions of enthusiasts certainly do surpass the evidence of such 'proofs'; *ergo* their confidence is proof not of the validity of their claim to immediate divine enlightenment but only of how smartingly they felt what they smartingly did feel. Since reason alone (or 'natural *Revelation*') is his touchstone, a truth for Locke is verifiable only 'by its own self-evidence to natural Reason; or by the rational Proofs that make it out to be so'. Should an enthusiast's assurance pass this test, it will be vindicated, but, of course, as a truth naturally known 'without the help of Revelation'. If not, no amount of enthusing about the irresistible experiential force of the divinely inspired 'Light within' will establish it, for this is mere unsubstantiated assertion 'that leads them continually round in this circle; *It is a Revelation, because they firmly believe it*; and *they believe it, because it is a Revelation.*' To 'examine a little soberly this internal Light, and this feeling on which they build so much' is to discover that, when 'strip'd of the Metaphor of seeing and feeling' it amounts to no more than that 'they are sure, because they are sure'. Thus what for the enthusiast vindicated the authenticity of his converse with God was for Locke an abnegation of rational responsibility, the easy way out, 'Immediate *Revelation* being a much easier way for Men to establish their Opinions and regulate their Conduct, than the tedious and not always successful Labour of strict Reasoning'. 'Reason', he exclaimed despairingly, 'is lost upon them, they are above it ... they feel the Hand of GOD moving them within, and the impulses of the Spirit, and cannot be mistaken in what they feel.' Butler had made the same point: 'What e'er men speak by this *new Light/* Still they are sure to be i'th' right.'[58]

The phrase 'the light within', which Locke picks up, became the virtually exclusive refrain of Quaker writing, and it was the Quakers who attracted the most withering denunciations for their enthusiasm. Quakerism, wrote Leslie, '*is but one branch of* Enthusiasm; *tho the most* spread *and* Infectious *of any now known, in this Part of the World*'. But though most pronounced and pernicious in this case, enthusiasm was not confined to Quakers: 'Enthusiasm *has been the Root of the greatest Evils that have befallen the* Church ... *And from hence our several sorts of* Dissenters *took their* Rise.' Leslie himself recognized (and from him it is quite a concession) that by the later seventeenth century it would not do simply to describe all nonconformists as 'enthusiasts' without qualification ('*once* Settl'd *and* Established ... [they] *wore off from it by Degrees*'), but, as the survey in this chapter has shown, he was not far astray in detecting *something* in nonconformity which distinguished it from Lockean rationalism even in the thought of its most rational adherents.[59] Leslie would call it 'enthusiasm'; they would call it 'experimental faith'. It is this which, in the world of Locke, informs nonconformist writing and gives it its distinctive authenticity. Affection and feeling count for as much as, usually more than, reason. Looking back after the Restoration to 'the beginning of the late troubles of the Nation' Penington attributed them to the growing hold of reason over men's minds. They were drawn by Satan

> from the living feeling, and from the inward power of Religion, into Disputations and Contentions about Forms of Worship and Church-government, which drew out the reasoning part, and withdrew the spirit of the mind from feeding on its proper nourishment; and so Life decayed in the Spirit, while Wisdom and Knowledge and Subtlety encreased in the Understanding.

Though many of his fellow nonconformists would have put the opposition less starkly, and would have allowed ratiocination and dialectic to come to their aid, for all of them, as for Penington, truth was, as Keats would later say, the product not of 'consequitive reasoning' but of 'Sensations rather than Thoughts', what is 'felt upon the pulses'.[60]

In the letter of 1817 from which these phrases are taken Keats was making the commonplace Romantic distinction between the inferior perceptual capability of reason and the superior percipience of intuition, or, in their terminology, imagination working under inspiration. In the same year as Keats's letter Coleridge, in chapter xiii of *Biographia Literaria*, held that the imagination is 'the living power and prime agent of all human perception, and as a repetition in the finite mind of the eternal act of creation in the infinite I AM'; and three years later Shelley opened his *Defence of Poetry* with the categoric assertion that 'Reason is to the imagination as the instrument to the agent, as the body to the spirit, as the shadow to the substance.' For such men, the insights of imagination were the gift of visionary moments beyond their recipients' control or prediction. Wordsworth's 'spots of time' are, in such a poem as 'Resolution and Independence', unsolicited and startling moments of 'renovating virtue', granted as if 'by peculiar grace,/A leading from above, a something given'. Literary composition, the 'expression of the imagination' in Shelley's phrase, was hence the fruit of inspiration: in another letter Keats wrote, in a famous sentence, 'if Poetry comes not as naturally as the Leaves to a tree it had better not come at all.' This the seventeenth century would have called an enthusiastic theory of literary creativity and would have given it short shrift. Augustan aesthetics thought no more highly of literary inspiration than did Augustan philosophy of religious enthusiasm. Both, in Leslie's words, 'possessed the Imagination' and 'clouded' and disabled reason. When discussing the desirable attributes of a poet in the preface to his 'heroic poem' *Gondibert* (1651), William Davenant cautioned that 'inspiration' is 'a dangerous word'. Its ill-effects are evident in Spenser, whose allegory resembles 'a continuance of extraordinary Dreames' akin to the hallucinations of a 'Feaver'. In his answer to this preface, Hobbes agreed: 'Fancy' is the least faculty of a poet; it is 'Judgement [which] begets the strength and structure' of a poem. In his criticism, Dryden insists repeatedly that judgement should control wit, fancy, or imagination. For him, as for Hobbes before him, 'Fancy, without the help of Judgement, is not commended as a Vertue ... without Steddinesse, and Direction to some End, a great Fancy is one kind of Madnesse.' In its Augustan phase the English Classical tradition remained as firmly convinced as Ben Jonson had been that 'there goes more to the making' of a poet than mere trust in inspiration, to 'think he can leap forth suddenly a poet by dreaming he hath been in Parnassus, or having washed his lips in Helicon'.[61]

When nonconformists speak of the process of composition, however, they sound, as we are beginning to expect, far more like the later Romantics than these contemporary Augustans. The *locus classicus* for inspiration in English literature is, after all, Bunyan's account of the genesis of Part I of *The Pilgrim's Progress*: it was an unexpected, unpremeditated and irresistible urge to write what he never intended which produced the book. In writing it, he was not planning the work ('*I did not understand/That I at all should make a little Book/In such a mode*'): indeed, he put aside the intended tract he was engaged upon ('*Nay, I had undertook/To make another*'). He was surrendering himself, just as he surrendered himself that night when he could scarce lie in his bed for joy: falling '*suddenly into an Allegory*', fancies multiplied '*Like sparks that from the coals of Fire do flie*'. Nor was he thinking in any deliberative way. The book came effortlessly, unbidden, not only like Keats's leaves but also like those texts of Scripture which darted into Bunyan's mind in *Grace Abounding*: when he '*set Pen to Paper with delight*' he '*quickly had my thoughts in black and white./For having now my Method by the end;/Still as I pull'd, it came.*' This may remind us of Milton's 'celestial patroness', Urania, who similarly deigns 'Her nightly visitation unimplored,/And dictates to me slumbering, or inspires/Easy my unpremeditated verse'. Milton's early eighteenth-century editor Jonathan Richardson was told that when composition had proceeded 'with a certain *Impetus* and *Æstro*' Milton would rise in the morning eager to dictate what the night had vouchsafed him. And Quakers habitually justified their writings (as all their actions) as directly experienced divine 'movings'. We may take as an example Ellwood's account of the composition of his first publication, *An Alarm to the Priests* (1660). When Ellwood felt himself 'commanded' to 'proclaim the Lord's controversy' with hireling priests:

> Fain would I have been excused from this Service, which I judged too heavy for me: Wherefore I besought the Lord to take this Weight from off me (who was, in every respect, but young;) and lay it upon some other of his Servants (of whom he had many) who were much more able and fit for it. But the Lord would not be entreated: but continued the Burden upon me, with great weight; requiring

Obedience from me, and promising to assist me therein. Whereupon I arose from my Bed, and in the Fear and Dread of the Lord, committed to Writing what He, in the Motion of his *Divine Spirit*, dictated to me to write.

And what was dictated was not what Ellwood himself would have chosen to write: 'When I had done it, though the Sharpness of the Message therein delivered, was hard to my Nature to be the Publisher: yet I found Acceptance with the Lord, in my obedience to his Will, and his Peace filled my Heart.' Ellwood's powerlessness is not an exhilarating experience like Bunyan's, nor a blessed reverie like Milton's, but it shares with Bunyan and Milton that sense of vocational inevitability Baxter caught in the phrase 'I was but a Pen in God's Hand.'[62]

During the Interregnum the Quaker habit of presenting their writings as the irresistible and extemporaneous product of revelatory moments had often invoked the precedent of inspired biblical figures. The first verse of the book of Ezekiel is, for example, recalled in the opening of Luke Howard's *A Few Plain Words of Instruction* (1658): 'On the eleventh day of the third Moneth, 1658. as I stood at my labour in my outward calling, with my mind staid on the Lord I was moved of [the] Lord in the clear spirit of truth.' In the early years of the Restoration, Quakers continued to adopt such prophetic personae. Richard Crane's title page to *A Lamentation over Thee, O london* (1665) recalls not only Jeremiah but, with its epigraphs from Luke xix.41 and Matthew xxiii.37, Christ's denunciation of Jerusalem. John Philly's *The Arrainment of Christendom* (1664) has, as its title suggests, a wider compass: Philly warns not only Charles II but also the pope, the Holy Roman Emperor and all kings and princes that the last days are come. On his title-page he presents himself as:

JOHN, the Servant of the *most Hy God* Being a Prisoner, (*with my companion in travel* at a plas called *Great Gomorra*, on a Certain Yland in *Hungaria*, the *East of Christendom*) For the Word of God which liveth, and abideth for eyer, & for a Testimony of JESUS, which I held – on the 19 *Day* of the *first Month* in the Year according to Christendoms account 1662. The *Living, Eternal,* & *pur Power* of God moved in me, & revealed unto me that I should wryt.

Here is the same combination of temporal and geographical accuracy, personal experience and revelation as in the example from Howard. For us it may recall not only the oracles of Ezekiel and other Old Testament prophets but also just this same combination of realism, subjectivity and visionary experience in Wordsworth's 'Tintern Abbey', with the precise location of its sub-title, the insistent personal pronouns of its opening lines and its subsequent testimony to 'visions of God'.[63]

The Wordsworth who believed in 'Powers/Which of themselves our minds impress' and who could consequently write quite as disparagingly as Bunyan of books and study –

Enough of Science and of Art;
Close up those barren leaves;

> Come forth, and bring with you a heart
> That watches and receives.

– this Wordsworth was, in those 'blessed' moments of enlightenment, 'laid asleep/In body, and become a living soul' which could 'see into the life of things'. This, of course, is precisely what happens to Bunyan at the beginning of *The Pilgrim's Progress*. The device of the dream is not merely a narrative and structural technique to ease us into the world of the allegory: it is a state analogous to Wordsworth's visionary trance. Bunyan's sleep is what makes insight and literary creation possible, not merely in the biographical sense that the dream stands for the inspired day-dream of the book's composition but also in the thematic sense that we can see into the life of things only when our meddling and murderous intellects (in Wordworth's phrases) are quietened. In *Paradise Lost* Milton refers to his blindness to similar effect. Far from being, as his royalist opponents alleged, divine punishment for his Puritanism, it was a divine gift which, by denying him physical sight, enabled him to see more than the organs of sense perceive. It set him in the company of the blind prophet-poets and king, Thamyris, Homer, Tiresias and Phineus as one who enjoyed the 'celestial Light' which 'Shine[s] inward' to reveal 'things invisible to mortal sight'.[64]

It thus emerges that, far from denigrating literary composition and the exercise of the imagination, nonconformity welcomed them as the natural and inevitable expression of the graciously inspired and heart-felt experience of faith, and, furthermore, that it encouraged in its writing just those qualities which contemporary critical canons would warily restrain. Though its politics were no longer revolutionary, perhaps because its politics were no longer revolutionary, nonconformity realized the revolutionary literary implications of Puritanism. It was, after all, to gain the 'liberty' which the 'bondage' of fashionable heroic couplets would deny him that Milton wrote *Paradise Lost* in blank verse. But this liberty was conceptual as well as formal. In his chapter 'Of Pagan Poesie, and its Traduction from Sacred Oracles' Gale gives us as fine a statement of Romantic aesthetics as we could hope for. Although predictably arguing that '*Ethnick Poesie*', that is, classical Greek poetry, descends from the divine poetry of the Hebrews, he unusually discourses on their '*parallel Ends and Designes*', which leads him to discern a single character and purpose in the poetry of all cultures. The '*original ground* and first *occasion* of all *Poesie* [was] stupendous *Miracles*, and *affecting Providences*, which God vouchsafed the infant state of his *Church*'. Such a deliverance as the Red Sea crossing could not but 'make a deep *impresse*, on the tender and soft *Affections*' of the Hebrews, so that the Jewish church

> being struck with the sense of these prodigious *Appearances* of *Divine power* in her behalf, was not able to contain her self within bounds, (for Affections melted are very diffuse) without venting her self in *Poetick Hymnes* and *Raptures*. For *Affections* are the greatest Wits that may be, and delight to vent themselves in *Poesie*; which is

a *Witty Art*, or rather *passion*; and therefore the most *expressive* of extraordinarie and choicer Affections. Alas! who so dull or *flegmatick*, but can, upon some more than ordinary experiments of *Divine Providence*, find some *poetick* strains to vent his more *warme* and *melted* Affections in and by? Thus much *Experience* learnes us, that where any *extraordinary occasion* happens for the moving the Affections, especially *Admiration, Love, Joy* or *Sorrow*; there this *Poetick vein* is most *pregnant* and *ripe*. For as *speech* was given to man for the communicating his *conceptions* or mind unto others; so *Poesie* (which is the most witty and affectionate speech) seems for the more *lively representation* of our choicer *Apprehensions* and *Affections*, stirred up by some extraordinary *events* or *experiments* of *Providence*. This seems to be the genuine and original *ground* or occasion of all *Poesie*, especially *sacred*.[65]

This association of poetry with the pressure of subjective experience and the power of emotion, so contrary to the generalizing and urbane poise often assumed by Augustan verse, is not peculiar to Gale. It recurs, for example, in Ellwood's 'easing his spirit' in Bridewell by allowing his 'mournful Muse' to 'vent' herself in 'a close *Exprobation*' and in his tendency at other times to break into expostulatory poems. The Quaker John Crooke, in April 1664 a prisoner in Ipswich gaol, there wrote for his friend John Samm, who had died the previous month in Northampton gaol, an elegy in heroic couplets, 'The free flowings of my pure soul to J.S. whose Decease I do condole'. The loss of his brother Nathaniel in 1677 and of his nephew James Crompton in 1680 moved Oliver Heywood to poetry, and in 1677 he subscribed a poem 'these verses I compile/ in the *heat* of my devotion,/not caring for the stile/nor yet intending notion/ *rouzing my heart* the while/to some diviner motion'. 'Passion' was equally what moved Baxter to poetry, and it was the pressure of his grief at the death of his wife which prompted the publication of his *Poetical Fragments* (1681).[66]

Since the most extraordinary and affecting experience possible was regeneration, poetry was for Gale a natural concomitant of religious devotion: 'in the World's *Infancie* (when *Atheisme* had so little rooting) the *senses* and *minds* of men were more struck with the *Admirable* Experiments of *Divine power*, whence flowed deep *Admiration*, and *commotion* of Affections, which are very *witty* and *natural Poets*.' 'Ethnick Poesie' continued to fulfil not only the '*secondarie* lower ends' of 'Divine' poetry (to 'give *lively colors* and *representations* unto things' and to express 'our choicest *concernings*, and most raised *Affections*') but also this '*supreme end*, though in relation to a different *Object*', namely: '*to celebrate the great name of God, appearing in the stupendous operations of his hands; and therefore to maintain his Adoration and Worship in the world*'. This service the Orpheus who haunted Milton's imagination performed for the Greeks, just as Moses had performed it for the Hebrews.[67]

Gale's theory of poetry, conceiving of it as a matter of heart and emotion, rather than mind and judgement, is predominantly expressive and subjective, not rhetorical and mimetic. It is also enthusiastic, not only in its stress on poetry's affective moving power, the power of the poet's enthusings to enthuse others, but also on its admission of the inspired nature of these enthusings in both Hebrew and Classical poetry. As God granted his people '*Poetick Raptures* and *Hymnes*', so Satan communicated to his '*Devoti* a *Diabolick* gift of *Enthusiastick Poesie* ... Thus, as God was wont to deliver his sacred *Oracles* in *Ecstatick Poesie*, so also the Devil in his *Diabolick Enthusiasme*'. Both were hence in 'Forme or Mode' enthusiastic. Gale adduces Plato's *Ion* on the Classical side, and in the Bible points to 'the Songs of *Moses*, and *Miriam*, Exod. 15.1 [which] were by *Divine Afflation*, or Extemporarie Enthusiasme'. Old Testament prophets were similarly 'transported' under a '*Divine* Ecstasie' (I Sam. x.5–6), and the songs of Simeon and Anna and I Corinthians xiv.26 suggest that this habit of extempore composition continued in the early Christian church. The prefatory apology to Benjamin Keach's poetic dialogue *War with the Devil* (1673) takes just this line. It associates poetic with religious inspiration not to invalidate but to vindicate it. Keach's defence stands the views of Davenant, Hobbes, Dryden and Locke on their head: poetry

> 'tis no human Knowledge gain'd by Art,
> But rather, 'tis inspir'd into the Heart
> By Means Divine, for true Divinity
> Hath with this Science great Affinity.[68]

It is for the blessing of this inspiration that, in the opening invocation of *Paradise Lost*, Milton prays the 'heavenly Muse, that on the secret top/Of Oreb, or of Sinai, didst inspire/That shepherd, who first taught the chosen seed'. Gale's remarks may help us to see that to implore such divine aid was not the 'saucy familiarity' with God William Davenant took it to be but an appeal to the only true source of, and justification for, poetry. Nor was the undertaking of a poetic theodicy quite as paradoxical as it might seem. To justify the ways of God to men was not primarily (though it was partly) to win his readers' intellectual assent to theological propositions; it was rather to move their hearts and so win their commitment as full human beings. This required more than logical demonstration of verities: it required poetry. Donne may have been content to reduce his readers to the role of 'Understanders', intellectually adroit and uncommitted admirers of his ingenious misapplication of ideas, and Dryden might have thought *Paradise Lost* better rhymed, but poetry was, for Milton, neither the witty 'toys' of metaphysical 'fantastics' nor the judiciously restrained and predictable formalism of Augustanism. It was a divinely inspired affective medium, the 'simple, sensuous and passionate' mode of address which enabled Spenser to excel Aquinas as a teacher. Only this could not merely inform the understanding but also move the heart to trust.[69]

Chapter 6 'A paradise within'

internalization, introspection and individualism in nonconformist writing

> *My kingdom is not of this world: if my kingdom were of this world, then would my servants fight, that I should not be delivered to the Jews: but now is my kingdom not from hence.*
>
> *John xviii.*36

I   NO CROSS, NO CROWN

To ask that nonconformists trust in the justness of God's ways was, apparently, to demand that they should not trust the plain evidence of what went on around them. The Rule of the Saints had not only failed, but failed dismally and ignominiously. No great battle, no last stand, no heroic encounter with overwhelming odds marked the end of the Good Old Cause in 1658–60: it collapsed into petty bickering, partisan quarrelling and spiteful vindictiveness, and expired in self-mutilation, the setting-up and pulling-down of governments, almost week by week, nearer to grim farce than to tragedy. The proffers of toleration in 1660 and 1661 may not have been trusted, but the incompetence of Puritan politicians and the ineptness of Puritan negotiators were so far from winning concessions that they barely delayed the re-establishment of Cavalier and episcopal hegemony.[1] And, after bad, there was worse: exclusion, ejection, persecution, prison and, for too many, death. Of Quakers alone it has been estimated some 450 died in prison during the Restoration period.[2]

And. again of Quakers alone, more than 15,000 experienced imprisonment. Small wonder that prison, or the threat of confinement, are so constantly present in nonconformist writing, nor that the image of life it depicts is, in one way, a grim one. Fox is in and out of prison throughout his *Journal*, mocked, ridiculed and execrated; Lucy Hutchinson's husband has died disgraced and in miserable circumstances; Milton's Samson is blind, captured and in despair; Mr. Badman's wife is humiliated and abused; Mansoul can hope for no victory in the Holy War, merely continuing struggle. At the very beginning of *The Pilgrim's Progress* Bunyan lights upon a 'Denn', marginally glossed 'The Gaol', and his representative heroes Christian and Faithful are warned by Evangelist that 'in every City, bonds and afflictions abide in you; and therefore you cannot expect that you should go long on your Pilgrimage without them, in some sort or other'. In the town of Vanity Fair, 'you will be hardly beset with enemies, who will strain hard but they will kill you.' And there is, of course, no way round Vanity Fair (Eccles. i.2, 14, iii.19), where freedom might be no better than imprisonment. In a letter of 1685 Howe wrote:

> Nor have I found any thing more destructive to my Health, than Confinement to a Room for a few Days in the City Air, which was much better and more healthful to me formerly, than since the Anger and Jealousys of such as I never had a disposition to offend, have of late times occasioned Persons of my Circumstances very seldom to walk the Streets.

'Men', he wrote in *Of Thoughtfulness for the Morrow* (1681), 'have nothing here but gloom and cloudy darkness before them ... What new scene shall first open upon them, they cannot tell. And, as is natural to them that converse in dubious darkness, their thoughts turn all to fear.' Indeed, life itself is, metaphorically, 'a Dungeon'. 'Be always expecting some Trouble or other, to interrupt thy outward Pace [*sic*] and Rest' Corbet cautioned himself.[3]

The bewilderment such experiences might cause, and the temptation to distrust they posed, is at the heart of *Samson Agonistes*:

> God of our fathers, what is man!
> That thou towards him with hand so various,
> Or might I say contrarious,
> Temper'st thy providence through his short course.

The apparent perversity of God's dealings with his chosen ones wrings this exclamation from the Chorus as it views the humiliation and degradation of that 'glorious champion' Samson. He, God's 'nurseling once', 'His destined from the womb', had been led on 'to mightiest deeds', only to find himself 'cast ... off as never known' and left 'helpless' in the power of the Philistines, those 'cruel enemies' whom, by God's 'appointment', he had 'provoked'. The publication of *Samson Agonistes* in 1671 could not but encourage its readers to discern in Samson's plight that of the Puritans after 1660. Too many of them were, or might at any moment be, 'prisoners chained', scarcely able to 'draw/ The air imprisoned also, close and damp,/Unwholesome draught'. Their consciousness was as bitter as the Chorus's that this was meted out to 'such as thou [God] hast solemnly elected ... To some great work, thy glory,/And people's safety, which in part they effect'. Samson had been such a one, but the Chorus is speaking generally, not specifically. To a contemporary reader that subordinate clause would all too pointedly recall those who had, in part, effected the people's safety in the great work of the Good Old Cause. And the examples the Chorus adduces of God's contrary dealings are precisely the experiences during the 1660s of those who had been so dedicated to God's glory: abandoned to the 'heathen and profane' and 'captived' they were brought before 'the unjust tribunals, under change of times', or 'perhaps in poverty/ With sickness and disease thou bow'st them down'. Samson's despair and the

Chorus's disillusioned conclusion were to nonconformists too real a threat, and for the same reason:

> Just or unjust, alike seem miserable,
> For oft alike, both come to evil end.[4]

That Samson suffered 'Eyeless in Gaza at the mill with slaves', and not in a Restoration prison, may have enabled Milton to treat *the* case of conscience facing nonconformists without the censor's intervention, and so freed him to handle those issues with which nonconformists had perforce to engage in their attempts to perceive and to accept God's purpose in and after the Restoration. This choice of subject, however, also enabled him implicitly to make the one point upon which nonconformist writers insisted more than any other in their attempts to counter disillusion and despair: this had happened before. So far is it from being an inexplicable, undeserved and unique experience that persecution has been the common lot of the faithful through all ages: '*Many and great in all Ages unto this day have been the* Afflictions, Tryals, *and* Oppressions *of the* Righteous, *as have been foretold by the holy Prophets, Christ and his Apostles since the world began.*'[5]

The pattern was set in only the second generation of mankind: Cain fell '*upon righteous* Abel, *for no other cause than the* worshipping of God *according to his* Conscience, *in the* Faith *and* Power of God, *which was not consistent with* Cain's hypocrisie *and* formality'. Old testament examples thereafter are numerous: the Israelites enslaved in Egypt and Daniel were frequently adduced. Indeed, in Fox and Hookes's *Primmer* Daniel receives a more extensive account than any other biblical figure or episode (including Jesus) in the list of '*Proper Names in Scripture*'. If persecution thus marked the beginning, and characterized the course of, the history of both mankind and the Israelites as a nation, so did it too the history of the Christian era. It was endured by Paul and the Apostles. In the early Church, wrote Penn, 'the spirituality of the Christian worship' was soon perverted, 'making it rather to resemble the shadowy religion of the Jews, and the gaudy worship of the Egyptians, than the great plainness and simplicity of the Christian institution', with the result that, as Christian ministers 'grew ambitious, covetous and luxurious', they

> with ... pride and cruelty, blood and butchery and ... with unusual and exquisite tortures, ... persecuted the holy members of Christ out of the world; and that upon such anathemas, as far as they could, they ... disappointed them of the blessing of heaven too. These true Christians call martyrs; but the clergy, like the persecuting Jews, have styled them blasphemers and heretics.

In Bunyan's *Seasonable Counsel: or, Advice to Sufferers* (1684), written because 'many at this day are exposed to sufferings', repeated reference is made to Daniel, to Paul, to the experience of the early church and to cases from Foxe.[6] The 'Great Persecution' of 1660–88 thus takes its place in Christian history as only what is to be expected by the Christian.

This is to make it not commonplace but immensely significant. In this perspective, persecution becomes an evidence not of God's abandonment of his elect but of the fidelity of the faithful: suffering is the badge of the saint. 'We be called to soffre. For with oute sofferinge no man can be the sonne of god' William Tyndale had long ago glossed Hebrews xii. 'That which purifies us is triall' Milton later wrote. This was his theme in *Comus* ('Eye me blest Providence, and square my trial/To my proportioned strength'),[7] but in the circumstances of the 1660s it was a contention to be vindicated with both a new urgency and a new compassion, not only in Milton's own poems but in nonconformist writing of every persuasion. The immediate occasion of the Congregationalist Thomas Goodwin's *Patience and its Perfect Work* (1666) was the Fire of London, but since its text (James i.1–5) is interpreted as referring to the persecution of Acts viii.1, the book's treatment of 'sore tryals' bears on the general experience of nonconformists. Noting that in I Peter i.7 trial is associated with the refining and purifying power of fire, and that there 'The Apostle saith, *the tryal of your Faith is more precious then Gold*', Goodwin is in no doubt

> That your graces are so highly valued by God, is the reason, why he tryes them; he would not be at the pains and cost of it, else. And *they being tryed*, and holding to be right, and true gold indeed, they have thereupon his approbation upon that tryal; and he sets his *Royal Tower Stamp*, and mark upon them.

William Penn's observation that 'Apostacy and superstition are ever proud and impatient of dissent: all must conform or perish' similarly implies that those who suffer are neither apostate nor superstitious, that they suffer precisely because they do not conform to the world. 'The people of God are a suffering people', wrote Bunyan, because 'the Lord has put such darkness betwixt Egypt and Israel, as will not suffer them to come together.' So for the early Christians, wrote Howe, 'any common state of suffering to them was the visible prejudice of [their] cause and interest'. And in *Paradise Lost*, the persecution which Michael foresees is not random or haphazard: it is visited by those who 'seek to avail themselves of names,/Places and titles, and with these to join/Secular power, though feigning still to act/By spiritual' upon those who 'in the worship persevere/Of spirit and truth'.[8]

'The Faithfull Followers of Christ', must, then, 'Expect Troubles in this World' (Luke ix.57–62), of need be 'all the days of our lives', must not only expect them, but welcome them as divine gifts:

> The vile world knows nothing but carnally, after a fleshly manner and interpretation; and too many that would be thought enlightened are apt to call providences by wrong names, for instance, afflictions they style judgments, and trials, more precious than the beloved gold, they call miseries.

If this should seem an outrageous suggestion and an impossible demand, we are to remember that God made it of his own son. Saints 'who are in their passage to heaven to be exposed to great difficulties and trials' may have comfort and hope in their Redeemer' for 'he himself submitted to be tempted'. We should 'remember our general' not only because he too suffered, but more especially because, above all other biblical precedents, his life exemplifies the necessity of temptation and suffering to salvation and his victory offers the assurance that trial is not in vain. In the words from Luke xix.23 which Penn tok as his curt title, *No Cross, No Crown*: 'To reign, it is necessary first to suffer (II Tim. ii.12; Rom. viii.17)'. Manton adduced Hebrews xii.2 (Christ himself 'for the joy that was set before him endured the cross'), and James i.12 ('Blessed is the man that endureth temptation: for when he is tried, he shall receive the crown of life') to conclude, paraphrasing Mark x.30, 'That is enough to content a Christian, the eternal reward is sure. In this world he shall receive with persecution an hundredfold, but in the world to come eternal life.' On this, Presbyterian, Quaker and Baptist were as one: Manton's 'this is great comfort to the church and people of God, when the powers and principalities on earth are employed against them, to consider what powers and principalities attend on Christ' is but a less rapturous formulation of Crooke's '*blessed are they for ever who are found* faithful unto Death, *for they shall have* the Crown of Life; *for* sincerity *shall prevail over* hypocrisie, *and the* Power *against all* Idolatry *and* Formality; for the Lord hath spoken it.' The faithfulness, patience and bravery of those who endure will, wrote Bunyan, 'in the day of God, abound to their comfort, and tend to their perfection in glory'. Each of these comments might serve as a gloss on *Paradise Regained*.[9]

2   THE LAMB'S WAR

Victory was promised: but not victory in the old way. There would not be, could not be, any successors to Cromwell's Ironsides: Sedgemoor was not another Naseby. Militant millenarianism died with Venner. And the 'Glorious Revolution', though it significantly modified the constitution, fell far short of the aspiration of the Interregnum. Baxter had never sympathized fully with these endeavours, but his reflections in 1664 do not merely draw from history confirmation of his misgivings: they touch a chord common to all nonconformity:

> I am farther than ever I was from expecting great matters of Unity, Spendor or Prosperity to the Church on Earth, or that Saints should dream of a Kingdom of this World, or flatter themselves with the Hopes of a Golden Age, or reigning over the Ungodly, (till there be a *new Heaven and a new Earth wherein dwelleth Righteousness*). And on the contrary I am more apprehensive that Sufferings must be the Churches most ordinary Lot, and Christians indeed must be *self-denying Cross-bearers*, even where there are none but formal nominal Christians to be the *Cross-makers*: And though ordnarily [*sic*] God would have Vicissitudes of Summer and Winter, Day and Night, that the Church may grow *extensively* in the Summer of Prosperity, and intensively and radicatedly in the Winter of Adversity; yet usually their *Night* is longer than their *Day*, and that *Day* its [*sic*] self hath its Storms and Tempests.

The ten reasons adduced for this resignation include: 'The Tenour of the *Gospel* Predictions, Precepts, Promises and Threatnings, are fitted to a People in a suffering State. And the Graces of God in a Believer are mostly suited to a State of Suffering. Christians must imitate Christ, and suffer with him before they reign with him; and his Kingdom was not of this World.' Above all, 'The Observation of God's dealing hitherto with the Church in every Age confirmeth me: and his befooling them that have dreamed of glorious Times.'[10]

The text from John which Baxter there quotes, and which serves as an epigraph to this chapter, was cited time and time again; the golden age will be not here but hereafter. It recurs like a refrain through the later pages of Fox's *Journal*. In a letter written to Charles from Lancaster gaol in 1660 Fox cites it as proof he is no enemy to a king of England; in the potent and mystical year 1666

> I was moved to give forth a paper to them who looked for Christ's personal coming <in an outward form and manner> ... and some of them did prepare themselves when it thundered and rained and thought Christ was coming to set up his kingdom; and then they thought they were to kill the whore without them. But I told them the whore was alive in them and was not burnt with God's fire ... And they looked for Christ's coming outwardly, to set up his kingdom, and their looking was like unto the Pharisees 'Lo here' and 'lo there'; but Christ was come and had set up his kingdom above sixteen hundred years since ... And when Christ was come he said his kingdom was not of this world.[11]

In the *Journal*, the Restoration merits hardly a mention, for 'the Lord's power was over all ... and all would be well whether the King came in or no, to them that loved God and were faithful to him.' Disengagement from political hopes and fears was rarely so complete among nonconformists of other persuasions, but all were as convinced as Fox that Venner was wildly misguided. Such chiliastic texts as I Peter iv.7 and I Corinthians x.11, Manton explained, were expression not of temporal but of experiential facts: 'it is as certain to faith as if he were already come.' I Corinthians ix.24–5, II Timothy iv.8 and Revelation ii.10, iii.11, were the commonly cited proof texts that the 'incorruptible' crown that is promised is not of an earthly rule, even by the saints, but a crown in the kingdom of heaven won only at death by those who hold fast through 'many tribulations': so, Evangelist exhorts Christian and Faithful, 'run that you may obtain it'.[12]

With the world no longer the scene of victory, worldly means to its attainment became inadequate. All they could win was the world, a mortal crown, and with that the nonconformists now had little to do: 'this present state is only intended for trial to the spirits of men, in order to their attainment of a better state in a better world.' Circumstances may have conspired to make nonconformists spectators only of public affairs, but this quietism was neither the precaution of expedient self-interest nor the lethargy of impotence. It was a role now actively sought and recommended. If disappointment and disillusion prompted reappraisal of the Good Old Cause, the lesson learned was a positive one: that those who trust to the world and its ways will be deceived. Christians, wrote

Howe, should 'with a proportionble unconcernedness ... look on, and behold the various alternations of political affairs; no further minding either the constitution or administration of government, than as the interest of the universal Ruler, the weal and safety of their prince or country, are concerned in them'. The old zeal for the reformation of institutions had gone. Where, in the past, political and military means had recommended themselves as a legitimate response to monarchy, episcopacy and social injustice, recourse to them now was viewed with deep sceptism. Howe continues: 'But how many, under the specious pretence of a public spirit, make it their whole business to inspect and pry into these affairs ... with no other design than to catch at an opportunity of serving their own turns!' A 'public spirit' is not one of Christian's qualities: with Vanity Fair he has no more to do than he must, and he certainly does not tarry to endeavour its reformation. Nor do he and Faithful plot the downfall of the authorities of the town, and, though he does not suffer Faithful's fate, Christian no more attempts to contrive his own escape than does his companion. 'A Christian', wrote Bunyan, in *Seasonable Counsel*, 'must be a harmless man'; we should not strive 'to deliver ourselves from ... affliction' but should 'with quietness submit ourselves', suffering with the active 'consent of the will', deliberately choosing 'suffering rather than sin'. We should prepare to meet our trial, 'not with carnal weapons, but with the graces of the Spirit of God', studying 'to be quiet ... to be at peace with all men'.[13]

This trend was most marked amongst Quakers. This is Fox answering the charge that he plotted insurrections:

> This is false, to these things I am as a Child, and knows [*sic*] nothing of them, and never learned the *postures of War*, and my Weapons are *Spiritual, and not Carnal*, and with Carnal Weapons I do not fight; and my *Kingdom is not of this* World saith Christ, and those that follows [*sic*] Christ in the Spirit, the Captain of their Salvation, denies the Carnal Weapons, who denies drawing any Carnal Weapons against the *King* or the *Parliament*, or any man upon the Earth ... and I witnesse against all *Murtherous plots*, and all such as would *imbrew the Nation in Blood*, which be not in Peace, and I am innocent of all these things and knows [*sic*] them not, and it is not *in my Heart* to have any mans life destroyed upon the Earth.

In 1659 he warned 'All Friends, everywhere, keep out of plots and bustling and the arm of the flesh' for 'Friends did not concern themselves with the outward powers', and in 1661 he was the first of twelve signatories to *A Declaration from the Harmless and Innocent People of God, called Quakers, against All Plotters and Fighters in the World*, which asserted 'All bloody principles and practices, we, as to our own particulars, do utterly deny, with all outward wars and strife and fightings with outward weapons, for any end or under any pretence whatsoever.' This political quietism and, especially, this pacificism, Fox was to preach repeatedly and uncompromisingly, for, were Christ's kingdom of this world, 'his servants should fight, but it was not and therefore his servants did not fight'. The Quaker way was, averred a pamphlet addressed to king and parliament, 'when any thing hath been imposed upon us, which for Conscience-sake we could not actually conform unto, we have patiently conformed to suffer the penalty thereof, without any resistance, or secret seeking revenge'. This was to act, as the authors of this pamphlet wrote, 'in the patient long-suffering Spirit of the Lamb'.[14] It was the way, in the phrase so often heard from Quakers, of the Lamb's War (Isa. liii.7).[15]

'*Who fights for God must not Man's Weapons use*': this moral Ellwood drew from the defencelessness of David before Goliath, and just this renunciation is the theme of *Paradise Regained*. Its interpretation of the temptations in the wilderness is addressed directly to this contemporary issue for nonconformists, for the poem presents the encounter as a struggle between Christ and Satan over the means by which he should win his kingdom. It is not a narrative of the regaining of paradise, as *Paradise Lost* had narrated the history of the Fall; it is an argument about how paradise should be regained, and, more particularly, an argument about how a person lacking every advantage of status, accomplishment and power might regain it. Structurally, the debate on this issue occupies the body of the poem: its resolution precipitates final victory. And in the course of the prolonged second temptation Satan systematically and comprehensively advocates every means by which power might be achieved. Under this trial, Christ refuses to resort to the 'politic maxims, or that cumbersome/Luggage of war' recommended by his adversary. Challenged by Satan's question 'thy heart is set on high designs,/High actions; but wherewith to be achieved?', the Son rejects as appropriate 'means of enterprise' social and financial aggrandisement, political wiles, military force, rhetorical arts and intellectual expertise. Contrary to Satan's supposition that 'prediction still/In all things, and all men, supposes means,/Without means used, what it predicts revokes', the 'ostentation vain of fleshly arm', though 'Plausible to the World', is to the Son 'worth naught', merely 'argument/Of human weakness rather than of strength'. 'Who best/Can suffer best can do; best reign, who first/Well hath obeyed.'[16]

But what, then, of *Samson Agonistes*? The Samson who 'hath quit himself/Like Samson, and heroically hath finished/A life heroic, on his enemies/Fully revenged', who lies victorious 'Soaked in his enemies' blood' and covered with 'clotted gore', this hardly seems an unworldly hero as meek as a lamb.[17] And yet that is what he is. The so-called 'Hebraic' spirit of this Classical tragedy on a Christian theme has troubled many commentators, who find it distressingly vengeful, a celebration of Jehovah's triumph over Dagon through the wanton destruction wrought by his barbarous champion Samson. The catastrophe is, in John Carey's words, 'morally disgusting'.[18] More particularly, and more positively, Andrew Milner has seen in this aspect of the poem a significant change of emphasis from the solution *Paradise Regained* proposed to the problem posed to nonconformists by the Restoration and ensuing persecution.

Milner argues that the pacific theme of the subdued 'anti-epic', with its plot confined to 'personal redemption' and 'devoid of almost any action at all', had been 'an indication of the general fatigue in the revolutionary movement', to which, having lost the 'capacity for resistance', 'quietism appeared the only remaining viable option'. In *Samson Agonistes*, however, Milton is 'apprehensible of the weaknesses of such ... fatalism' and reasserts 'the possibility of political activism and, indeed, of political victory'. Within a few years of 1660 'the endemic instability of the restored monarchy became increasingly discernible'. *Samson Agonistes* reflects the reviving optimism amongst radicals and opposition groups, the 'movement from quietism to activism' which was to lead to the Exclusion Crisis. Samson himself forsakes the 'stoic heroism' of *Paradise Regained* for action, regaining his 'martial vigour', particularly in the episode with Harapha. Indeed, though *Paradise Regained* had 'perfectly captured the tone of patient stoicism which informed the Quaker-quietist response to the Restoration', even there the rejection of 'the kingdoms of the world' had been conditional, not absolute, a tactic, rather than, as with Fox, a strategy. Milton 'is concerned with the appropriateness, rather than the morality, of political action', which he no more rejects out of hand than he does the pursuit of learning.[19]

There is one difficulty with this cogent and suggestive argument: it is impossible at one and the same time to look towards political or military action and to be in a state which makes such action morally and spiritually acceptable. Even if, somewhere, some day, they might be appropriate, to desire or to choose such means is, as the body of *Paradise Regained* makes abundantly clear, to be Satanically motivated. The person who prefers them, no less than the person who prefers learning to spiritual enlightment, will pursue them not as means but as ends. If ever they are appropriate, it will be in God's good time, at his disposal, not man's, and granted only to those who have repudiated them. But the possibility hardly arises: despite its conclusion, *Samson Agonistes* offers no encouragement to anticipate, still less to trust to, God's blessing on such means.

Samson initially rejects out of hand the Messenger's command to attend the festival of Dagon, and when he does agree to go it is not in submission to Philistine authority ('Commands are no contraints') but because

> I begin to feel
> Some rousing motions in me which dispose
> To something extraordinary my thoughts.
> I with this messenger will go along,
> Nothing to do, be sure, that may dishonour
> Our Law, or stain my vow of Nazarite.
> If there be aught of presage in the mind,
> This day will be remarkable in my life
> By some great act, or of my days the last.

Samson does not know what is going to happen. He is inwardly moved to attend, just as Quakers, certainly never constrained by commands, invariably presented themselves to be spectacles at court trials when charged to do so. Like them, he is resolved not to compromise his conscience; but no more than could they can he foresee that this witness will not result in further ignominy and degradation. He does have a premonition of something momentous, but its nature is unclear to him. It may be glorious or disastrous ('some great act, *or* of my days the last'). The ironic knowledge that it will be both is the reader's privilege. Samson himself has no assurance he is not a lamb being led to the slaughter, as Pepys thought the unresisting Quakers were. And yet he goes. This is to go not in a state of political or military preparedness, nor with premeditated plans of action: it is to go in faith.[20]

The Samson first presented to us has no such faith, no such readiness to trust despite circumstances, no such sensitivity to inner promptings. It is less his confinement by the Philistines which the opening soliloquy insists on than his confinement in the dungeon of despair, 'Myself, my sepulchre, a moving grave', where he languishes 'As one past hope, abandoned'. His resistance to those who would stir him is not, at this stage, a positive disinterest but the lethargy of disillusioned uninterest, and the indifference of one convinced by events that 'the strife/With me hath end':

> My hopes all flat, nature within me seems
> In all her functions weary of herself;
> My race of glory run, and race of shame,
> And I shall shortly be with them that rest.[21]

This man would make nothing of the opportunity which is later offered.

It is now generally agreed that it is Samson's progress from this despair which supplies the answer to Dr Johnson's objection that in the drama 'the intermediate parts have neither cause nor consequence, neither hasten nor retard the catastrophe'. The middle of the play traces Samson's regeneration, a renewal of faith and hope which alone makes possible the catastrophe. We must, however, be wary of any such contention as Andrew Milner's that 'Samson's own individual redemption, is indissolubly linked to the political solution.' It is quite true that the latter is predicated on the former: but the former does not necessitate the latter. They are indissolubly, but not inevitably linked. Samson's renewed faith makes the catastrophe possible but does not guarantee it. Christopher Hill's formulation is similar: the two themes of *Samson Agonistes* are 'Samson's recovery and the liberation of his people. The latter depends on the former.' True: but the former would have been complete and perfect without the latter, is, indeed, complete and perfect before the latter. That is why Samson goes with the Messenger.[22]

We must consequently be equally cautious of overstating or misrepresenting the optimism of the drama. To entitle a chapter on *Samson Agonistes* 'Hope Regained', or to write of it as 'profoundly optimistic', is to reduce Christ's withstanding of Satan in *Paradise Regained* to an inconsequentiality, or at least a matter of no very great encouragement to the reader. It implies that Samson's victory is altogether more invigorating. What is meant, of course, is that revolutionary hope is regained. Samson acts, and acts successfully, 'exclusively in this-worldly terms'. Unlike *Paradise Regained*, *Samson Agonistes* is hence persuaded of the possibility of 'political regeneration'. This is its optimism.[23]

Three points mitigate the persuasiveness of this interpretation. First of all, despite Samson's personal triumph, victory is by no means assured to Israel ('let but them/Find courage to lay hold on this occasion'). Secondly, the catastrophe is not, in any accurate sense, a political victory. It is Manoa, who hopes 'to work [Samson's] liberty' by negotiation and financial arrangements with the Philistine lords, who is the politician. He is the one who makes proposals to the worldly powers. And, though he does so successfully, his endeavours come to nothing. They are frustrated by unforeseen Providential intervention, an intervention which brushes political means aside as lamentably inadequate and misguided. The Manoa who, thinking exclusively in this-worldly terms, had looked forward to nursing his son back to health and vigour, comes to accept that the divine resolution surpasses his own schemes: 'Nothing is here for tears.'[24]

And, thirdly, that intervention, destructive and bloody though it is, is not military. The catastrophic meeting of man and circumstance in the 'spacious theatre,/ Half round on two main pillars vaulted high' is uniquely Samson's and could offer no reader hope of a like opportunity.[25] Nor could any reader, however optimistic, anticipate anything like Samson's success with Samson's complete lack of preparation, forethought and allies. Whatever import the catastrophe carries, it cannot be literal. If, then, it is not a model of political or military action, it must bear a dramatic significance. And, if our text has any pretension to unity, that significance must derive from what has gone before. The context and occasion of the preceding scenes may have been, loosely, political, but their content was not. How Samson might yet smite the Philistines is never a point at issue. His feelings about his present circumstances are the concern of each of his visitors (and, in the ironic way of Classical tragedy, never what they expect or what they hope to arouse). For the catastrophe now to announce a political triumph – even one contingent upon the hero's regeneration – would be to rupture the play. Rather, it declares in the historical terms of the play's action the thematic fact that the hero has found himself: Samson has quit himself like Samson. Were the point of the catastrophe the decimation of the Philistines, the drama would indeed have no middle – and no beginning either. Were its moral the assurance of bloody victory over enemies, it would indeed be disgusting. But neither is the case. What is remarkable about *Samson Agonistes* is not Milton's fidelity to the facts of his biblical story but his subordination of them to his theme of personal regeneration.[26] And that is the great theme of nonconformist writing generally.

3 'CHRIST HIS SCHOOLS'

In the years immediately following the Restoration it was still possible to hear the old millenarian expectancy. This is the Quaker William Bayly, writing in 1662:

> Therefore *TREMBLE* ye *CARELESSE DAUGHTERS*, and let all *flesh* be silent
> before *him*, who is come to *reign* in Mount *Sion*, and in *Jerusalem*, and before his
> *Antients Gloriously*; *Awake*, therefore, ye that make mention of his *Name*, *Retire*,
> *retire*, into the Habitation of his *Holiness*, and let the *Tongue* cleave to the roof of its
> Mouth that makes mention of his *Name*, and not in *Righteousness*; in this the mighty
> day of his power and *Wonders*, for thy God hath remembered thee oh *Sion*, and will
> yet again build thee up O *Jerusalem*.

Two years later another Quaker, John Philly, warned all worldly powers that
'The dread-ful, and most terribel *Battel Ax*, of the most *just*, *Ryteos*, *Powerful
Lord God of vengeans* is now laid to thy *Root*, and that Power, and spirit by which
thou art now acted and in which thou now standest, will the Lord God now *hew
down, root up and utterly destroy*.' The Lord is 'drawing neer to plead the caus of
his crucified Son, his cruelly tortured, and murdered saints, his greatly spoyled,
and oppressed Peepel in thee. Wo, Wo, Wo ... ' 'The *day* is com which shal
shak open al thy prison doors, for the *first* born of the Egyptians is neer hand
slayn, & the *great sea* divyding ... '[27]

This kind of thing did not, however, long survive. Two years after Philly,
Goodwin's title, *Patience and its Perfect Work, under Sudden & Sore Tryals*,
captured both the circumstances commonly addressed and the response usually
recommended by nonconformist writers. No hope is held out in this work that
the trials of nonconformists might abate, or that the saints will enjoy a sudden
and glorious victory, or that the Last Days are at hand. And yet the work is
deeply compassionate, optimistic and encouraging. Goodwin concedes that the
injunction to the persecuted of James i.2 ('count it all joy') is 'the *strangest
Paradox* ... that ever was': 'when their miseries are so great, that they *cannot be
endured*, that yet their joy must be so great, as more *cannot be expressed*. This is
the hardest duty, that ever was required of the distressed hearts of men.' Yet it
would not be enjoined were it impossible. We are to strive not for an active
response to active persecution but for a '*constant persisting* ... with *submission*,
and *quietness*, and *cheerfulness*, to the *end of a man's days*'. This was the burden of
Manton's 1662 farewell sermon on Hebrews xii.1 ('let us run with patience the
race that is set before us') in which he draws encouragement from the examples
of those who 'have borne the cross of Christ with an invincible patience'.
Elsewhere he wrote 'Many times we must be content, not only to be active
instruments, but passive objects of God's glory. And therefore if God will
Glorify himself by our poverty, or our disgrace, our pain and sickness, we must
be content.'[28]

To aspire to be a passive object was not, as it may at first appear, to abnegate
humanity, a cowardly retreat from the challenge of human responsibility or the
potential of human thought and feeling. Christian patience was not presented as
an abject capitulation to circumstances, and never described as the 'lethargy'
Andrew Milner detects in Restoration radicalism. On the contrary, it was
carefully distinguished from the stagnant quiescence of hopelessness, the
indifference of helplessness and the resigned stoicism of pessimism. Like

Goodwin, Manton argued that the paradoxical proposition in the opening of James's epistle that 'affliction or trial, which is the cause of all murmuring or impatience, should work patience', does not mean that familiarity with suffering breeds dull insensitivity: 'this is a stupidity, not a patience.' Patience is the attribute not of a paralysed or hardened but of an alert and sensitive soul, a dynamic virtue which endures adversity positively and cheerfully, confident Providence and not fortune rules the sublunary world. It is the bearing of the heavenly-minded, of those convinced that mortal suffering is inconsequential beside eternity. It is also a demanding and challenging virtue. We must, wrote Howe, 'endure to the end': 'In reference to an afflicted, suffering condition, how ungrateful so ever it be to our Flesh, a filial subjection to the Father of our spirits is required.' That subjection must be maintained whatever persuasions to renege flesh may experience. The Pauline and apocalyptic exhortation to 'stand fast' (I. Cor. xvi.13; Rev. ii.25, iii.11), Manton pointed out, is a military metaphor opposed not only to revolt but also to cowardice. Such heroic patience , such obedient submission, is the theme of *Paradise Lost* ('the better fortitude/ Of patience and heroic martyrdom') and is everywhere in Milton the key to his understanding of how to regain paradise. The 'deeds/ Above heroic' recounted in *Paradise Regained* consist in refusing to be heroically active, in preferring 'deeds of peace ... wisdom ... patience ... temperance' to 'ambition, war or violence', for, in the words of the Chorus in *Samson Agonistes*:

> patience is more oft the exercise
> Of saints, the trial of their fortitude,
> Making them each his own deliverer,
> And victor over all
> That tyranny or fortune can inflict.[29]

Although this was to persuade to submission not to submissiveness, nonconformist writers were sensitive to the charge that it might nevertheless be construed as a falling off from the old zeal. Repeatedly they insisted that though the form of witness had changed this represented no weakening of vocation, no decline from the militant and charismatic Christianity of the Interregnum. They preached not a betrayal of (to speak anachronistically) the revolution but a rediscovery of the true sphere of faith, of the true obedience of a Christian, a quietism in which the Spirit was as actively present as in any rapturous ecstasy or militant campaign. The Quaker Patrick Livingstone wrote as follows to those tempted to forsake the Friends because of their subdued quietism:

Now those that were with us, and are gone from us, they pretend to own the first coming forth, and they cry, *Where is the Power that was at first?* but this Power thousands witness, and are established in it: But here we see the subtilty of the Enemy, because the mighty motions of the bodies of *Friends* are ceased, and *Friends* are still and cool, and quiet; therefore these persons are made to think that the same Power is not in Meetings. But O ye foolish ones, and beguiled by the Enemy! can ye not discern the times, that time and this time? When Physick is given to the Body, and when all is purged out, the Physick leaves working, and the Body is still?

> Were not all the breakings and meltings, and terrible shakings and quakings of
> Friends bodies, to purge out sin, and to bring to coolness and calmness of mind?

This, Livingstone continues, is not merely a consequence of, and in no way a
reprehensible compromise with, changed times; it is a preferable spiritual state:
the

> terrible shakings, breakings and meltings were … but for a little time, and so were
> quickly gone again, and the Voice of the Lord was not distinctly discerned there …
> the stillness being come, that's a durable thing, a solid condition; and here the
> mind is brought into a capacity to discern the Voice of the Lord.[30]

The Presbyterian Howe wrote in a very similar vein. We are to conceive of
patience 'not under the notion of dull and sluggish impotency, but of power, an
ability to endure'; 'it gives a man a mastery and conquest over all undue and
disorderly passions. It fixes the soul in a composed serenity, creates it a region
of sedate and peaceful rest'; 'The temper of spirit it introduces, in opposition to
angry and querulous repinings, is a dutiful silence.' To attain to patience, the
virtue of *singular perfection*, as Goodwin called it, was perfect discipleship,
since its practice marked the end of Christ's own life (Heb. ii.10). In Romans
xv.5, 'God is pleased to style himself in his Word "the God of patience"':
patience is 'his very image in the soul.'[31]

It was a perfection attainable only by those who practised self-denial. The
unmortified Christian and the heathen, are, writes Penn, of the same religion,
'For though they worship not the same idols, they worship Christ with the same
heart': 'the deity they truly worship is the god of the world.' Worshipping him,
they are wholly at the mercy of changes of state and circumstance. The true
Christian, however, dies to the world. Penn explores the contrast through the
familiar image of a journey:

> The true self-denying man is a pilgrim; but the selfish man is an inhabitant of the
> world: the one uses it, as men do ships, to transport themselves or tackle in a
> journey, that is, to get home; the other looks no further, whatever he prates, than to
> be fixed in fulness and ease here, and likes it so well, that if he could, he would not
> exchange.

This is the meaning of the 'figurative speech', the Cross of Christ. The
metonymy expresses a contempt for, and indifference to, both worldly comfort
and worldly pain: 'It is a holy resignation to God, and confidence in Him
testified by a religious obedience to his holy requirings, which gives more
evidence to the soul of the things not seen … ' This is the force of the images of
purgation so often applied to trial: 'A golden potshed may shine bright till it
cometh to a scouring. In trying times God heateth the furnace so hot, that dross
is quite wasted.' For Howe, the name 'christian' 'betokens obedience', 'for what
is Christianity but the tendency of souls towards God … Therefore is the initial
precept of it, and the condition of our entrance into that blessed state, self-
denial.'[32]

And the person who does attain to this state is free. Patience is rarely mentioned without bringing liberation in its train. It is this which offsets the grim picture with which this chapter began and which characterizes noncon-formists writing from, and about, prison. The great work of persecution is to teach self-denial; its great reward, the gift of spiritual freedom. Gaols become, in Bunyan's words, 'Christ his schools', teaching 'filial subjection'. More familiar than Howe's phrase is Milton's description of the unfallen Adam 'in true filial freedom placed'. The truth of the oxymoron is what Adam is taught by the trauma of the Fall and by Michael: freedom is won not by the Satanic pursuit of power and self-gratification but through self-denial and submission ('Henceforth I learn, that to obey is best ... ').[33]

It is a truth we meet on every side. This is Gale:

> actual Conformitie unto God implies *subjection and submission to his providential Wil, both Afflictive and Directive.* And herein also much moral Libertie doth consiste. Is not that mind most noble, great, and free, which can bear great crosses with equanimitie and patience? Doth not this give more libertie and enlargement than any temporal affliction can deprive us of? O! what a sweet thing is it to have a free generous mind under a straitned confined condition! How facile are burdens made hereby! A virtuose Spirit, that follows God in afflictive providences, becomes a King over his crosses: his losses prove his gain; his reproche his glorie; his confinement his libertie.

It is, writes Howe, 'a delightful thing to the spirit of a man, when he is sensibly disentangled and at liberty from the care, desires, griefs, and fears that were wont to inwrap his heart'. Images of soaring flight are inadequate to express this liberation: a 'bird escaped from a Cage ... with what joy doth it clap its wings, and take its flight' is but a 'faint Emblem' of the liberty of the mortified Christian. To his freedom there are no limits:

> It is reckoned a brave and manly thing, to be in the temper of one's mind a citizen of the world, meaning it of this lower one; but why not rather of the universe? And it is accounted mean and base that one should be so confined by his fear or sloth to that spot of ground where he was born, as not upon just inducement to look abroad, and go, for warrantable and worthy purposes, – yea, if it were only honest self-advantage, – as far as the utmost ends of the earth. But dare we not venture a little further? These are too narrow bounds for a truly great spirit. Anything that is tinctured with earth or savours of mortality, we should reckon too mean for us ...

For an autobiographical example of the demeanour of such a 'truly great spirit' we may turn to Fox. In Scarborough Castle in 1665 he was mocked by drunken prisoners and soldiers, and by one of them challenged to a fight. 'And the next morning when they were more sober I told him that challenged me I was come to answer him, with my hands in my pockets, and <reaching my head towards him, said> there was my hair and my back ... <But he skipped away ... a-laughing ... and one of the officers said, "You are a happy man that can bear such things".'[34]

What emerges from Restoration prisons is hence a literature positive and optimistic beyond all reasonable expectation, a literature affirmative and celebratory of the human spirit's capacity to transcend adversity. It offers no political programme: but it is a triumphant literature. It affirms, in Bunyan's phrase, man's 'liberty of soul'. George Hughes, ejected vicar of St Andrews, Plymouth, writes: 'Free communion with God in prison is worth a thousand liberties, gained with loss of liberty of spirit. The Lord keep us his free men.' An unidentified imprisoned nonconformist minister gave to James Woods, an ejected Lancashire Presbyterian, a copy of verses beginning 'Though I am shutt from Thy house and my one,/I both enjoy in Thee, my God alone.' And to Pinney, the Presbyterian Isaac Clifford wrote as follows, probably in 1666 while serving a term in Dorchester gaol whose effects, Calamy believed, 'brought him immaturely to his grave':

> The fear of a prison is more than the harm. We have great cause to praise God, who hath made a prison very comfortable. I was never better in health or more cheerful in spirit than since my imprisonment, glory be to God. The best liberty which none can take away we have here, and enjoy much peace and quietness and precious opportunities, which many who are abroad much want. We have this advantage by a prison, we are free from the fears and snares, y^t much disturb and endanger others.[35]

Although this is not a political, nor even, from one point of view, a reasonable optimism, it impresses the reader as an authentic experience. We share no escapist fancy but a realistic address to the facts of the case. We can get some sense of this if, for a moment, we cast our minds back to 1642. In that year Richard Lovelace found himself in the Gatehouse prison for supporting the 'Kentish Petition' to parliament. He was there able famously to declare, 'Stone Walls doe not a Prison make,/Nor Iron bars a Cage' by transporting himself from confinement in recollections of amorous play with the Althea to whom his poem is addressed and of boisterous loyalist carousing 'When thirsty griefe in Wine we steepe,/When Healths and draughts go free' in the company of those with whom

> (like committed Linnets) I
> With shriller throat shall sing
> The sweetnes, Mercy, Majesty
> And glories of my KING.[36]

This is freedom won by imaginative escape from the present plight into recognized royalist roles – lover, tippler, loyalist. Lovelace is too cavalierly confident to pay his immediate situation any heed. The matter of his poem ignores the circumstances of his imprisonment and its tone implies his confinement is at worst a mere interruption, undeserving of attention. He happily continues on his way, oblivious to the events which brought it about and not in the least concerned to assess his involvement in them. The world, we may say, passes him by.

From the Bedford county gaol in 1665 Bunyan issued his verse *Prison Meditations*, which contains the following stanza:

> For though men keep my outward man
> Within these Locks and Bars
> Yet by the faith of Christ I can
> Mount higher than the Stars.

The editor of Bunyan's *Poems* comments on these lines that 'The sentiment and imagery are strongly reminiscent of Lovelace.' Bunyan's relationship to his prison and the means by which he wins his spiritual freedom, are however, quite different. He does not present himself as one who happens to have fallen on hard times: in stanzas surveying his earlier ministry, he recognizes his own responsibility for his internment and reaffirms the decision which brought it about. The circumstances of place are admitted as well as the process of time. Bunyan shares his experience with the community of the persecuted – the *Meditations* are addressed to 'Suffering Saints' – and, enduring it, he is at the mercy of a legal system which brands him 'Heretick, Deceiver ... the Churches foe', of public opinion which dismisses nonconformists as 'Fools', of deceitful 'Politicians' who 'now appear to us at best/But Machiavilian Friends', and of common criminals and 'Rogues'. Bunyan, that is to say, is paying attention: his poem has a context, personal, temporal and circumstantial, and its theme is how he, as an individual, responds to and masters that context. Where Lovelace took refuge in the past, Bunyan engages with the present. It is this squaring up to the facts which transforms 'Gaols' (*sic*) into 'Christ his schools' where 'my Mind/ Is free to study Christ' and enables him to enjoy just such empire as Milton's Christ exemplifies and the Chorus in *Samson Agonistes* describes. The truly valorous, Bunyan writes, are not such as those who, like Lovelace in 'To Lucasta Going to the Warres', can manage to prefer 'Honour' to a mistress, but those who

> do conquer their own Hearts
> All worldly fears, and then
> Also the Devils firy darts,
> And persecuting Men.[37]

What Bunyan describes is a process of spiritual reappraisal and growth through meditation upon the occasion and circumstances of his imprisonment, a process which culminates in a renewed commitment and a public declaration of constancy. Trial, as Bunyan's image of Christ's schools suggests, was not only challenging, purging and liberating: it was also enlightening. It was, indeed, the deeper awareness of self fostered by adversity which liberated. 'God's tempting is not to inform himself', wrote Manton, 'but to discover his creature to themselves and others ... that what is known to him, and yet unknown to ourselves, that that which lodgeth and lieth hid in our heart may be discovered to us.' 'In trials we discern the sincerity of grace, and the weakness and liveliness of it; and so we are less strangers to our own hearts.' It was this redirection of the punitive intention of persecution to the positive end of 'self-searching and self-ingaging', as Heywood's imprisonment in York Castle in

1685 moved him to renew his covenant with God, which made possible such public witness as the Quaker John Swintoun urged:

> the sum, the main of all to be minded is, What spirit thou art born off [sic], led by, possessed with, joyned to: for who are born of the Spirit, are led by the Spirit, and who are joyned to the Lord are one Spirit. So all know what spirit you are of; for this is the tryal of this day, to try what spirit you are of: and this shall abundantly be manifested before this day be over ... it is he or they, who endure to the end, receive the Crown.[38]

It is such a process of enlightenment that both Milton's Christ and his Samson experience. To Milton's conviction that trial purifies we may attribute the fact that the temptation in the wilderness was 'the one event in the life of Jesus which appealed to him'. He could write of this, rather than the Atonement, under the title *Paradise Regained* because it exemplified man's capacity to emerge from trial victorious over Satan with a new trust and a new self-awareness. All the tempter's endeavours serve only to clarify and to intensify the Son's understanding of himself and his mission. A similar irony attends the efforts of Manoa and Dalila to persuade Samson to accept a comfortable old age. Each poem ends with an affirmative declaration of the protagonist's true identity as one not parted from God, a public witness born of the revelatory experience of self-discovery under trial.[39]

4   HEART RELIGION

This liberation into self-hood was necessarily experiential. The freedom won through adversity is, in nonconformist writing, no more an abstract theory than it is a political possibility: it is a felt fact, a state of being. The millenarianism of the Interregnum was transmuted into what a modern theologian would call 'realized eschatology', the doctrine that the kingdom of God belongs not to the future nor to the world but is founded within each believer who possesses, in Milton's phrase, 'a paradise within'. This, wrote Howe, is 'our *principal business*', '*to adorn and cultivate our inward man*': 'It can never be well, till our own Souls be an Heaven to us ... 'Till we get a settled principle of holy quietude into our own breasts; and become the sons of peace, with whom the peace of God may find entrance and *abode.*' It was in these terms that Keith and Barclay turned back the charge of enthusiasm: what had become 'a term of reproach' 'properly signifies ... *God within*'. Picking up the Pauline usage in I Corinthians vi.19 to which Milton alludes in the proem of *Paradise Lost*, Penn (though it might be any Quaker) wrote that God dwells not in buildings but within each believer: 'This is the evangelical temple, the Christian church, whose ornaments are not the embroideries and furnitures of worldly art and wealth, but the graces of the Spirit: meekness, love, faith, patience, self-denial, and charity.' The church, declared Fox, is the people 'and not the steeplehouse'. Nor is Christ's coming a future prospect: millenarian Baptists and Fifth Monarchists mistake his 'reign to be outward, when as he was come inwardly in the hearts of his people to reign and rule there ... Christ is come and doth dwell in the hearts of his people.'[40]

This is the essence of the insistent Quaker distinction between 'inward' and 'outward'. Theirs was the most radical attempt to carry the Reformation to its logical conclusion by repudiating all 'outward' mediatorial help. In his *Journal* Fox thus described his mission as it was revealed to him in the late 1640s:

> when the Lord God and his son, Jesus Christ, did send me forth into the world, to preach his everlasting gospel and kingdom, I was glad that I was commanded to turn people to that inward light, spirit, and grace, by which all might know their salvation, and their way to God ... I was to bring people off from all their own ways to Christ, the new and living way, and from their churches, which men had made and gathered, to the Church in God ... and off from the world's teachers made by men, to learn of Christ ... and off from all the world's worships, to know the spirit of Truth in the inward parts ... And I was to bring people off from all the world's religions, which are vain, that they might know the pure religion ... And I was to bring them off from all the world's fellowships, and prayings, and singings, which stood in forms without power, that their fellowships might be in the Holy Ghost ...

We are, wrote Penn, 'negative to forms: for we leave off, we do not set up forms'.[41] 'Our *Masters* letter', wrote Barclay, alluding to the common proof text II Corinthians iii.1–3,

> is writt *in our hearts*, and ther wee ar to find it, neither is our *Master* separated from us, as those *Masters* are, who use to write *letters* to servants to set them on work, while they are absent, and cannot help them by their presence, for our Master is alwayes with us, and he requires us to doe all our works by his *immediate* counsell, direction and assistence [*sic*], as present with us, and *in us*.[42]

Though most pronounced amongst Quakers, to preach 'Christ within' and so bring men off from 'forms of power' to the immediacy of the 'living way' had been the Reformed mission ever since Luther took his stand on justification by faith. Romans ii.28–9 was cited not only by Quakers but by all parties within Puritanism. The consequent experiential basis of the Puritan doctrine of the Holy Spirit was the subject of a seminal study by Geoffrey F. Nuttall, first published in 1946, and the introspective bias of Puritanism has since become familiar to students of English language and literature. To it the English language owes many compounds and adjectives with 'self' as the first element (including 'selfish')[43] and to it English literature in large part owes the emergence of autobiography as a distinct genre.[44] With their hopes of powerful worldly forms now finally eclipsed, nonconformist writers came to concentrate still more markedly than their Puritan forebears upon the 'paradise within' as the sole felicity and aspiration of Christians. Experience became still more pressingly the court of appeal for those who refused the judgements of Restoration courts. During the proceedings against Bunyan, his examiners and judges were much put out that he should presume to know better than his betters. The knowledge in which he excelled was the fruit of an individualistic method so rigorously and fiercely inductive and 'experimental' (as the word was) that it would have affronted any Baconian or Lockean philosopher.[45] Bunyan's full defence of his right to meddle in spiritual things came in 1666 in *Grace Abounding*. It proved that, in the words from I Peter iv.10 which Bunyan had quoted at his trial, he had 'received the gift'. It did so experientially. Truth in *Grace Abounding* is an experiential fact as undeniable as physical pleasure or pain. On this authority, Bunyan speaks as incontrovertibly as a Hebrew prophet.

This inward (but not introverted), man-centred (but not anti-social) emphasis is evident in the structure and strategies, as well as the content, of nonconformist works. Milton defers to precedent in *Paradise Lost* by beginning *in media res*, but, being Milton, is no slavish imitator. His structural design makes a thematic point. The chronologically prior war in heaven is subordinated to man's story. It is recounted by Raphael solely for the benefit of Adam and Eve, having significance only in so far as it bears on, and prompts a reaction in, them. From (potentially) an epic tale in its own right it is reduced to a parenthetical episode in the history of humankind. What goes on in the hearts of Adam and Eve is what counts. Similarly, in *The Holy War*, the paraphernalia of social and political dealings and all the 'luggage' of war are transmuted into a metaphor for the individual's attainment of resolute patience: its military campaigns are an individual's spiritual struggle with doubt. Furthermore, the chief Doubters in Diabolus' army are not intellectual queries about doctrine but self-doubts, misgivings about the authenticity of personal experience (Election-doubters, Vocation-doubters, Grace-doubters, Faith-doubters, Perseverance-doubters). The resolution of self-denial, the fortitude of patience and the joy of liberation are possible only to those whose faith is beyond doubt. The struggle now was to have trust sufficient to set against the passive obedience so assiduously fostered by the established church the passive disobedience of conscience, to be able to say, as did an early Quaker protestation of loyalty to Charles, that if the king

> shall require ought of vs, which for conscience sake we cannot doe, wee shall rather choose, patiently to suffer, then sin against ye God of our life. Nor can wee, or shall wee, rise vp with carnal weapons to worke our owne deliverance, but in patience & well doeing Commit ourselves vnto ye Lord.[46]

With the field of battle become the heart of man the real enemy is not the persecuting authorities but the Satan who alone, by persuading to doubt, compromise and apostasy, can bring the individual to yield. 'Experience teaches every son and daughter of Adam' that 'the heart of man is the seat of sin': 'the enemy's temptations' are 'within: if they take not, the soul sins not'. Only the vigilance of introspection and meditation can guard against such revolt. To 'decline to audit accounts in thy own conscience' (the words are Penn's, but the image was ubiquitous) is to lay oneself open to doubt (by missing the encouragement of evidences of grace) and to risk desertion (by founding one's religion on a self-regard which neglects evidences of sin). Such conscientiousness in Quakers was by episcopalians dismissed as the tiresome scrupulosity of fanaticism. Penn neatly turned the point. Those who 'say we strain at small things, which becomes not people of so fair pretensions to liberty, and freedom of spirit' are the very ones provoked by these 'small things' into a persecuting rage: 'So that if we had wanted a proof of the truth of our inward belief and judgment, the very practice of them that opposed it would have abundantly confirmed us.'[47]

The appeal to conscience, the insistence on the need for sincerity and the urging of the corresponding duty of introspection were, however, not peculiar to Quakers. They were common to nonconformity, even in its most rational and least enthusiastic forms. Howe, for example, was adamant that 'The general aversion of mens spirits to this so necessary work of *self-reflection*, is one of the most deplorable Symptoms of lapsed degenerate humanity.' The capacity to turn the mind, 'a *rational sun*', inward was for him a distinguishing attribute of man: 'what *power* is there in man, more excellent, more appropriate to reasonable nature, than that of *reflecting*, of turning his thoughts upon himself'. Conscience, the 'name of this reflecting power', 'discovers, at the same time, the ugly deformities of a mans Soul and the means of attaining a true spiritual comliness'. Since 'a constant self-inspection' is the best means by which to attain the design of Christianity, for a person to 'name himself a Christian, and yet be under gross ignorance touching the temper and bent of his own soul' is to be but 'a vain trifler'.[48]

Baxter was of like mind. In 1662 he published a series of sermons on II Corinthians xiii.5 under the title *The Mischiefs of Self-Ignorance*.[49] These mischiefs were by Bunyan conceived to be of such consequence that in *The Pilgrim's Progress* they merit particular treatment. The ignorance of Bunyan's Ignorance is a self-ignorance, a misconception about his spiritual state. He has not struggled in the Slough of Dispond nor entered the way by the Gate, and yet, unregenerate and ignorant of 'the workings of faith', he walks confidently in the way 'wise in his own conceit'. He is, in fact, Howe's 'vain trifler'. When Christian urges on him the doctrine of justification by faith, Ignorance is brusquely dismissive, and to Hopeful's query 'if ever he had Christ revealed to him from Heaven' he retorts '*What! you are a man for revelation! I believe that what both you, and all the rest of you say about that matter, is but the fruit of distracted braines.*' It is when urged to 'Be awakened then, see thine own wickedness, and flie to the Lord Jesus', when, that is, his attention is directed from outward behaviour to inward disposition, that he parts company with Christian and Hopeful. But we have not heard the last of Ignorance. Unlike the other false pilgrims, he is not confined to a single episode in the book. He is with or in the vicinity of Christian and Hopeful, and their topic of conversation, for over 30 pages, and the tenacity of his misconception carries him through even to the gates of the Celestial City. No other false pilgrim stays the course or is so constant a presence. He seems the most like a true pilgrim of them all: the temptation he represents is ever-present. And yet he is the least like. Bunyan is so acutely aware of the dire threat posed by such a confident, self-righteous (Ignorance echoes the Pharisee in Luke xviii.9–14) but parodic religion of works devoid of self-awareness that he is led to give his last word not to the glorification of Christian and Hopeful but to the damnation of Ignorance. The narrator leaves the reader with the awful warning 'Then I saw that there was a way to Hell, even from the Gates of Heaven.'[50]

Ignorance, then, failed to audit his spiritual accounts: had he done so, he would have found the balance wanting. Those who would avoid his error were advised not only to engage in self-examination regularly and diligently but also to keep a record of the findings of such introspective analysis in what Baxter called a 'Book of *Heart accounts*'. The advice to this affect of the afterwards ejected Presbyterian vicar of Garstang, Lancashire, Isaac Ambrose, in his very popular *Media* (1650), seems to have been specially fruitful: John Angier, Henry Newcome, Adam Martindale and Oliver Heywood, ejected ministers whose lives and ministries traversed Cheshire, Lancashire and Yorkshire, all left autobiographical papers, diaries and written meditative reflections, as did the Lancashire Presbyterian layman Roger Lowe.[51] At the beginning of the record known as his *Autobiography* Heywood thus described the incentive to its composition:

> tis my desire to search & see what obedience & grounds of hope I haue to beleeue & be persuaded that my soul is built upon the rock of ages, that I am within the bond of the covenant, and sealed up to the day of redemption, wch I doe to this end that I may giue diligence to make my calling, and election sure, not in itselfe, but to my selfe.

He undertakes 'A Relation of the most considerable passages of my life' in order 'to compare my past and present state and obserue my proficiency in christianity, to see whether I be better this year then the last'. The passage of the Five Mile Act prompted him to begin a diary which he overlooked in January 1681: 'The review of by-past providences may in after times be of singular use to mine owne soule in humbling my heart, making me trust in god for the future, in greater straits, not to despair whatever may befal me.'[52]

For Heywood, and for many, many other nonconformists, to secure assurance of a title to the 'paradise within' was thus a literary endeavour. He was, in no facetious sense, the author of his own life, its historian and interpreter. As its reader, he drew from it confirmation that he was within the covenant, consolation in trial and resolution under persecution. For just these purposes the former Hampshire rector and London nonconformist John Corbet kept, at irregular intervals between 1663 and 1680, written assessments of his spiritual life:

> In order to peace of Conscience and assurance of my good Estate towards *God*, it must in reason be supposed, that I may rightly understand the Marks of Sincerity set down in *God's* Word, as also the predominant Inclinations and Motions of my

own Soul; and that I may be so far assured of my right understanding of the things aforesaid, as to have no reasonable ground of doubting thereof. For I have no other ordinary way to know my sincerity in order to the said Peace and Assurance, but to examine it according to my best Understanding, by the Marks thereof set down in *God's* Word. [Psalm cxxxix.3][53]

Corbet's papers were published. Though originally a private duty, this literary self-analysis frequently found its way into print, and by no means always posthumously. *Grace Abounding* is but one of a large number of introspective and autobigraphical nonconformist works intended by their authors for publication – a number which perhaps includes *Samson Agonistes*.[54] As the Restoration receded, however, this continuing bias became increasingly unfashionable. Episcopalians did not write spiritual autobiographies; their divines were chary of the inner life and offered no encouragement to be intimate or self-revealing in print. Edmund Calamy and Thomas Ellwood would endeavour to set forth Baxter's *Reliquiae* and Fox's *Journal* in a suitably polite and impersonal style by refining their authors' plain dealing and moderating their individualistic idiosyncrasies, but in the 1690s and the first decade of the eighteenth century both texts were, from one point of view, anachronistic.[55] The world had moved on. Its proper study was no longer individual people (still less the individual self) but the genus Man.[56] Contempories nurtured on latitudinarian theology, on the philosophy of Locke and on episcopalian historiography saw themselves as emerging from the chaos of misrule into order, and from the fallacious fanaticism of subjectivity into the '*clear, unchang'd*, and *Universal* light' of an impartial and impersonal rational epistemology. 'God said, *Let Newton be*! and all was *Light*' tells us as much about what had happened to God and divine illumination as about Pope's esteem for science. He no longer revealed himself directly to individuals ('the Universal Cause/Acts not by partial, but by gen'ral laws') but through the predictable order of the intellectually fathomable creation. In this world, the ungovernability of the 'paradise within', its repudiation of properly constituted worldly authority, was, at best, embarrassing, and, at worst, downright dangerous. 'They will be Ty'd to no *Rules* or *Government*', wrote Leslie of nonconformists, 'but of their own Framing, and Alterable at their Pleasure. They have said, *We are Gods*, and who are *Lords over Us*!' To such enthusiasm Leslie ascribes more '*Mischief*' than has been wrought 'by the open *Assaults* of *Atheists*'; it is responsible for 'Most of the *Heresies* and *Schimsms* which have *Disturb'd* and *Divided* the *Church*'.[57]

This refusal of loyalty to the developing intellectual and cultural hegemony of the age was not, however, merely the sullen insubordination of a frustrated faction pilloried by Leslie; nor was it the stultifyng imperviousness to new ideas of an increasingly narrow-minded and stagnant tradition which to many modern intellectual and literary historians it appears. There was a positive, even prescient, side to this recalcitrance. As the subjectivity of nonconformist writing preferred the personal to the abstract, so the strategies it deployed to delineate and articulate the 'paradise within' offer a compelling alternative to the generalizing and universalizing techniques of the dominant literary tradition. It is always as an individual that a nonconformist writer commands his reader's attention. Whereas the type depicted by Lovelace through the deployment of literary conventions owes none of its features to the particularities of its author's life and character, Bunyan in his *Prison Meditations* writes as a specific person encumbered with all the circumstances of an exact biography. *Mr. Badman* is the fruit of one man's reflections on what he himself has witnessed: despite the literary artifice of the dialogue form he has

> as little as may be gone out of the road of mine own observation of things. Yea, I think I may truly say that to the best of my remembrance, all the things that here I discourse of, I mean as to matter of fact, have been acted upon the stage of this world, even many times before mine eyes.

Seeking, in *Ebal and Gerizzim* ([1665?]), to persuade sinners of 'that amazing love/Of God, we read of', Bunyan turns not to books but to himself for convincing arguments:

> If you would know, how this can operate
> Thus on the soul; I shall to you relate
> A little farther, what my soul hath seen,
> Since I have with the Lord acquainted been.

What he has himself seen and experienced supplies not only matter and argument but also the inspiration and authenticating commitment of what he writes:

> I never endeavoured to, nor durst make use of other men's lines, *Rom.* 15.18, (though I condemn not all that do) for I verily thought, and found by experience, that what was taught me by the Word and Spirit of Christ, could be spoken, maintained, and stood to, by the soundest and best established Conscience: and though I will not now speak all I know in this matter; yet my experience hath more interest in that text of Scripture, *Gal.* 1.11, 12 than many amongst men are aware.[58]

The frequency of personal pronouns in these quotations is characteristic. Even in *Paradise Lost*, where Milton has his 'richest robes' about him, the narrator is still an individual in a specific context ('fall'n on evil days'), not merely a bardic voice. Baxter's works are replete with autobiographical anecdotes and illustrations. The appeal to experience is a chief argument in homiletic, apologetic and controversial works. It also personalizes the author.[59] If we would find a precedent for the intrusive narrators of eighteenth-century novels who are themselves as much the subject and source of interest in their books as their plots, we can do so here. And as in those novels this narrative technique makes for an intimate relationship between writer and reader, so too here. The autobiographical emphasis and habit of direct address which carries over from the pulpit and pastoral instruction into the printed word is in the mode of familiar converse rather than of formal literary composition. It is the manner of a man willing freely to disclose himself. He could hardly do otherwise, for sincerity alone could lay claim to the 'paradise within'. And sincerity embraced a person's relationships and dealings with others, as well as with himself and with God.

Nonconformist writing was consequently private in an age which was going public. In personal conversation with an individual, rather than public display before an audience, it prefers intuitive insight to general commonsense. The observation in the preface to the 1662 *Book of Common Prayer* that only '*private fancies*' had sought liturgical change implicitly dismisses the case for reform a idiosyncratic and therefore out of court. That is to be the spirit of the new age. In Dryden, 'private' is a pejorative epithet: 'What weight of antient witness can prevail/If private reason hold the publick scale?'[60] Literature henceforth was to be characterized by public address to topical public issues, by general *dicta* rather than personal particularities, by Nature rather than individual natures. By contrast, there is curiously little generalization or topicality in nonconformist writing. Christian doctrine is turned to specific cases and public affairs are dealt with from the point of view of one who experiences (and usually endures) their consequences, as Adam comes to know the consequences of the war in heaven. Certainly, there were political pamphlets, and satire, but (save for Marvell) these did not engage the literary energies of nonconformity. What did was something else: the significance of personal experience. This certainly has a temporal and geographical context (of which political affairs are a part), but the emphasis falls upon the response to that context. And that response is conditioned not by the context but by the individual. Destiny is not contingent. So, in *Paradise Lost*, Hell is a place, but the real horror is the experiential hell which knows no boundaries: 'myself am hell'. This Satan inhabits no matter where in the cosmos he flies. Truly, 'The mind is its own place, and in itself/ Can make a heaven of hell, a hell of heaven.' That is why the self-created dungeons of Giant Despair's castle threaten a far worse confinement than the merely physical walls of Restoration prisons. These, to a mind rightly disposed, may offer visionary dreams and the freedom of paradise. During Monmouth's rebellion in 1685 Philip Henry was confined in Chester Castle. He was there 'in nothing uneasy all the while ... it is guilt that makes a prison.'[61]

Although Milton did not, like Donne, prefer interiors as the settings for his poems, this bias gives to his poetry, for all that it ranges through time and space and exemplifies momentous issues in exceptional heroes, a far more persuasively intimate and secluded privacy than Donne's. Where the earlier poet, with a hectoring assertiveness which belies insecurity and doubt, insists (or hopes by insisting) that this bedroom excels the public world beyond its windows, Milton's poetic structures assume, without the ambiguous tone of strained logic and audaciously inappropriate analogies, that the private is the only world that matters. His strikingly domestic Eden is a case in point. This far distant spot, which preoccupies Hell and Heaven, upon which all history depends, and towards which, with Satan, we undertake a prolonged and laborious journey through Hell Gates, across Chaos, past the *primum mobile*, though the Universe, by the Sun and over the boundary of Eden itself, proves, when we finally arrive, to be not an idyll of exotic other-worldliness nor a paradise of preternatural perfection but a place where a man and a woman live, eat, drink, sleep and do a little gardening. Its ordinariness and self-contained privacy – its inconsequentiality, we might say – are Milton's most daring stroke: this is the centre of creation. Samson may be Israel's (and God's) champion, but the reader knows a man bothered by relatives, friends and acquaintances, who has out of his own incapacity to discover exceptional ability. And there is the close of *Paradise Regained*: the reader has witnessed an action played out 'in secret', whose victor 'unobserved/Home to his mother'd house private returned'.[62] It is as if nothing has happened, and, of course, from the point of view of public affairs, the commonsensical world of which, in the poem, Satan is the spokesman, nothing has. That is the point.

Howe's 'proportionable unconcernedness' thus creates not a literature of introverted withdrawal but a personal and intimate literature in which people count for more than politics, a literature fascinated by people's lives (the conversations in *The Pilgrim's Progress* nearly always turn on the pilgrims', or someone else's, experience) and convinced of the value of the individual self. It had one other significant characteristic. The *'experimental confession'* Faithful advances as the way to disclose one's faith to others was no more in the Augustan line than it was in Talkative's. In *The Spectator* Addison would find such detailed attention to the minutiae of individual lives and spiritual experience downright hilarious. The introspective and autobiographical bias of nonconformist writing was, however, defending something badly in need of defence. Taking their cue from Charles II, Restoration wits found, of all feelings, religious sentiment and commitment the least becoming. In *The Pilgrim's Progress* Shame, anxious to be in the socal swim, knows it to be his part to object to religion as a 'pitiful, low, sneaking business' beneath the notice of 'the brave spirits of the times'. It is the social stigma, the sheer vulgarity of carrying religion to such indecorous and immoderate lengths which affronts those who, in Bunyan's *Prison Meditations*, object that 'we do disgrace/Our selves by lying here' and which is the commonest objection made to the exhortations of Keach's True Godliness. What he recommends is simply 'ill-bred'.[63]

In resisting this trend towards propriety and polite disdain nonconformist literature was championing the claims of emotion and sentiment. Introspection was necessary to establish sincerity precisely because it could only be confidently affirmed on the basis not of outward actions but of inward disposition and feelings. Were external actions reliable, hypocrisy would be no danger. But it was: the Master's letter Barclay described 'is writ *in our hearts*', not in Ignorance's dutiful observances.[64] The *'familiar knowledg'* of God which in the previous chapter we heard Howe prefer to '*notional* and *speculative*' knowledge is best described 'by the name of *acquaintance*'. Philip Henry similarly stressed the intimate and loving nature of the relationship when he replied to those hesitant about engaging in extemporary prayer

> God regards not elegancy in prayer. He cares not how little there is of the head in the duty , so there be a great deal of the *heart* ... We must approach God in prayer as children to a father ... Is not a tender-hearted father far more delighted with the lispings and stammerings of his little child, when it first begins to speak, than with the neatest, finest, speech that he can hear from another? And what is the reason? Why, it is his *child*.

To 'be as inward with [God] as we can, to familiarize our selves to him' is to have, in Penington's phrase, 'a living feeling' of and for him, or, in Howe's words, 'a spiritual sensation'. Spiritual commitment and devotion are conceived in terms, and expressed through images, of physical sensation, human affection and transporting emotion. This is Penington again:

> Eye hath not seen, ear hath not heard, nor hath it entered into the heart of man to conceive, what the power of Life hath wrought through them [ie Quaker preachers] in the hearts or consciences of those, who have longed after and waited for the Lord. O the breathings and meltings of the soul, the sence of the living presence of God, the subjecting of the heart unto the Lord, the awakening of and giving strength unto his Witness, the falling down and weakening of the powers of darkness, the clear shining of the Light of Life in the heart, and the sweet running of the pure streams thereof into enlivened souls ... [65]

It was hence a heartfelt longing and devotion which introspection sought to establish and generate. Psalm xlii.1 prompts Manton to advise, 'Search then for such a restless and strong desire; try if there be such an ardency and earnestness upon your affections that nothing can satisfy but Christ.' We may know whether we indeed have such a desire by analogy with human love: 'When we strongly desire a thing, the heart fainteth under the want of it. Amnon was sick for Tamar, 2 Sam.xiii.1–4. And the spouse was sick of love for Christ, Cant.v.8.' Howe recommends reading the Psalms 'to have your hearts alike affected and transported': 'there is no such thing as real, solid delight in God anywhere existing, or ever will be, separately and apart from a supreme love and addictedness of heart to him.'[66] Across its range, this religious tradition is aspiring to rapture.

And across its range, the literature of this tradition is far from being restrained or staid. It welcomes the transporting power of feeling; it delights in the amorous and sensory; and, in contrast to the sober moralizings of Richard Allestree's *Whole Duty of Man* (1657) or Tillotson's sermons, it offers a model of the religious life which demands the full responsiveness of emotional and sentient beings. We should weep, literally, for our sin, writes Gouge; be 'fervent' in our devotion; and 'allured' by the amiableness of God. Sentiment without moral action would be mere sentimentality; but deeds drew their validity from the sentiment. And so when, in his diaries and notebooks,

Heywood set himself, as he frequently did, 'to deale truely and faithfully with my own soul in self-examination', 'to review my state and especially my course of life', his spiritual exercise contemplated his moral failings as a means to create an emotional conviction of need which would compel devotion and make his 'hart suitable' for 'converse with god'. And sometimes his heart was 'warmed',

> wonderfully wrought upon, and exercised in deep expression of godly sorrow for my sin, in strong breathings and pantings after god for suitable supplys, in raised ravishing admiration of his goodness, and free grace to such a vile wretch and the lord comes in sometimes with the gales of his grace, refreshing my hart, sealing his loue to my soul ... [67]

The emotional sterility so often attributed to Puritanism and the nonconformists developed not here but in the work of court dramatists and poets and of episcopalian divines. It was there people grew ashamed of their humanity. The province of nonconformist writing was, as Wordsworth's was to be, 'the heart of man' , a country too rarely visited by the writers of a 'hard bitten age which showed little interest in natural human feeling'.[68]

Chapter 7 'The better fortitude'
realism and the nonconformist hero

> *And he saith unto me, My grace is*
> *sufficient for thee: for my strength is*
> *made perfect in weakness.*
>
> *II Cor. xii.9*

I À LA MODE

A variety of literary heroes and heroines were available to Restoration writers. Renaissance romance survived in the popular chapbook form known to Bunyan, and the genre enjoyed an Indian summer in the *roman de longue haleine* of Madame de Scudéry, so much admired by Dorothy Osborne. Madeleine de Scudéry and her English imitators pursued comely princes and princesses through complex and exotic histories, and still more complex and prolonged love affairs.[1] Their theatrical counterpart was the rhymed heroic drama in which, ruled Dryden in the preface to his *The Conquest of Granada* (1672), 'Love and Valour ought to be the subject' – love and valour, we should add, as practised and experienced by the socially privileged in far-away places. Indeed, these virtues were implicitly only attainable by such people in such places. In their very remoteness from common experience lay the appeal of such plays. They 'ought not to imitate conversation too nearly': 'an heroic poet', wrote Dryden, 'is not tied to a bare representation of what is real.' Buckingham was being no more than accurate when, in his burlesque *The Rehearsal* (1671), he had a character describe the authors of such plays as 'fellows that scorns to imitate Nature; but are given altogether to elevate and surprise'.[2] Nothing is conceded to probability or reality as the brave, handsome and devoted lover is followed through alternating ecstasies and despairs. Only an audience's willingness to surrender itself in uncritical indulgence can save his rhetoric from bombast, his plot from farcical bathos. The easy gasp of wonder and astonishment is demanded, not the intensity of sympathetic involvement.

The vogue for such extravagance did not long survive the 1660s, but it was succeeded by forms equally, though differently, extravagant. In fiction, amorous intrigue became the province of the shorter *nouvelle galante* and 'secret history' which, in the preface to his *Incognita* (1692), Congreve distinguished from romance as of 'a more familiar nature'. They were also likely, as in Congreve's novel, to undermine their own seriousness through the ironic use of an intrusive narrator, but this they could do only because the affected posturings of love in rare, high places remained their subject. Although Congreve dismisses romance as 'all a lye' the difference between the genres is less one of kind than of degree, for Restoration novels still, as Congreve concedes, 'represent to us intrigues in practice, delight us with accidents and odd events'. To claim these are 'not such as are wholly unusual or unpresidented' is to lay great stress on the adverb.[3] The incongruity between the belittling common sense of Congreve's narrator and the impassioned fervour of what he narrates in fact results from the novel's continuing dependence upon romance for its subject. In a similar way, the tradition of anti-romance, stemming from *Don Quixote*, depended for its effect upon recognition of the romance conventions implicitly invoked. The burlesque of *Hudibras* would fail with a reader not familiar with its chivalric model, as would that of Buckingham's *Rehearsal* with an audience ignorant of heroic drama. The tendency of such works towards greater realism is rhetorical rather than conceptual in origin. So, too, is the apparently still greater realism of picaresque rogue-fiction, exemplified in *The English Rogue* compiled by Richard Head and Francis Kirkman (1665–71). It intends not to elevate the commonplace to literary seriousness but to startle, amaze and outrage by its hero's audacious rejection of received values. The rogue is as ingeniously and improbably dexterous in his manipulation of low-life dealings as is the fashionable Restoration *roué* in his mastery of polite society.[4]

Here was another model. In the witty comedy of manners the *beau monde* admired what it took to be its own sophistication, its liberation from disabling sentiment, its epigrammatic retort to serious thought: 'You should have just so much disgust for your husband as may be sufficient to make you relish your lover.' The names Freeman and Courtall from Etherege's *She Would if She Could* (1668) strike the note. The description of these two in the list of *dramatis personae* as 'two honest gentlemen' refers not to any such integrity as Bunyan represented in his Mr Honest but to social position and, more particularly, to a social adroitness which is never wrong-footed. It is Courtall who, discovered in a deceit, extricates himself with the expostulation 'fie, fie, the keeping of one's word is a thing below the honour of a gentleman'. A hedonistic disdain for intellectual or moral aspiration and a distrust of any professed motive which does not admit immediate self-gratification characterize a libertine such as Dorimant in Etherege's *The Man of Mode* (1676). Out-manoeuvering and conquering the woman counts for more than loving her; the idea of serving her is preposterous. Hence, Wycherley can build *The Country Wife* (1673) on a hero (none too subtly called Horner) who has his way by affecting impotence. In this world, those not young, fashionable and sceptical can expect only ridicule and indignity. To be from the country, middle-aged, mentally unexceptional or sincere is to be marked down for a fool. Indeed, merely to be decent is to be disqualified from interest: Pinchwife's ascription to his wife of 'no beauty but her youth; no attraction, but her modesty, wholesome, homely, and huswifely' is meant not only to send Horner packing but also to be intrinsically risible.[5] It is its want of sympathy for human nature which confines Restoration drama to a mere appendix of Renaisssance drama.

What none of these heroes or heroines would dare venture is simple, honest plain-speaking. To do so, when human relationships are conceived almost entirely as struggles for mastery, would serve no purpose and would run a grave risk. It would be to sacrifice the chance of victory and almost certainly to subject oneself to domination by another. It is this fear which prevents Millamant from an open admission of love for Mirabell in Congreve's *The Way of the World* (1698). If not engaged in deliberate deception, these heroes and heroines are embellishing what they believe they feel in as elaborate a fashion as they can manage. To encounter another human being is, for each of them, to be put on his or her mettle: upon the quality of the ensuing performance, all depends. The tireless attention to details of dress and appearance, the sensitivity to forms of courtesy and address, the shame of a social gaffe or indiscretion, the vulnerability of the dressing room before one's body has been attired for the social encounter, these are not the accidentals but the essence of human relationships. The whole energy of Restoration protagonists is devoted to the effort to persuade, impress, outwit, cajole, coerce, overcome, in short, to have their way, by the unanswerable wit, the impenetrable falsity or the overpowering fulsomeness of their protestations. Whether by deliberate deceit or elaborate self-preservation, the way of this world, and the common way of the Restoration hero, was to manipulate others.

This was the common way, too, of Restoration society. Such a literary vogue could thrive only with the support of its audience and readers. These plays and fictions were aimed at, patronized and read by London society, which evidently found in them something to its taste. Their reduction of human character to caricature and grotesque, of human relationships to elaborate rituals, of conversation to wit-combats and of thought to generalization and epigram must have answered to something in the *mores* of society itself. To John Lilburne and the Levellers, army commanders under Cromwell had seemed grandees little different in their desire for power from hereditary peers and magnates. It would be rash to claim ambition was abolished with the monarchy, but that public life then had a quality subsequently lost may be appreciated after only a few hours at Charles II's court. Here, self-seeking, disguised under politic (or hypocritical) cloaks of many hues, was the order of the day. The desperation with which courtiers ignominiously scrambled for office through the frauds of impeachment and attainder was encouraged by the cynical dubiety of Charles himself, the king, in Rochester's words, 'Whose promise none relyes on'.[6] The uncertainty which Charles's own dissimulation generated about his true inclinations and preferences inevitably led to a wary disinclination to commit themselves among both his courtiers and those members of society who took their cue from the monarch.[7] Self-disclosure and avowed commitment were dangerous and, before long, socially vulgar. Poses were struck instead, as they are, for example, in the poetry of Rochester, a calculated attempt to impress by being unimpressed with any circumstance or conviction: 'Our selves, with noyse of Reason wee doe please/In vaine: Humanity is our worst Disease.' His cynical and libertine disdain safeguards him from the demands, and from the vulnerability, of commitment to others. In a different key, the disinterestedness of the 'trimmer' Halifax is a similar attempt to remove the individual from too close involvement with others. Portraiture may make the point: to set beside the portraits of Cromwell by Samuel Cooper, of Bunyan by Thomas Sadler and of Baxter by John Riley (?) those of Charles II, Dryden and Congreve by John Michael Wright's studio and Sir Godfrey Kneller, is to exchange for the variety of individual features openly disclosed the uniformity of a type rendered by the externals of dress and, most obviously, by those ubiquitous wigs. In *Paradise Lost* Adam and Eve's virtue consists in a state of being; by the time of *The Rape of the Lock*, virtue has become a socially acceptable and prudently self-interested form of behaviour. In Clarissa's speech, it is the way to a comfortable old age.[8]

It was a way with which nonconformists would have nothing to do. To be a nonconformist was to put a premium on, and to strive for, if not always to attain, sincerity. If, as the previous two chapters have suggested, nonconformists were individualists wary of implicit faith, possessed of 'private reason', reliant upon personal experience and persuaded by the inner testimony of feeling and conviction, then they could be no compliant followers of contemporary fashions, nor could they assume roles as circumstances or personal advantage might dictate. This independent integrity was most notoriously demonstrated by the Quaker refusal of 'hat honour': 'when the Lord sent me forth in the world', Fox writes

> he forbade me to put off my hat to any, high or low; and I was required to 'thee' and 'thou' all men and women, without any respect to rich or poor, great or small. And as I travelled up and down, I was not to bid people 'good morrow' or 'good evening' neither might I bow or scrape with my leg to any one.[9]

In less overt forms, this defiance of prevailing social fashions was common to nonconformity: artificial manners and elaborate dress are rebuked by writers of every persuasion. Even though we can towards the century's end detect a willingness to admit that a Christian might be polite and a gentleman we shall find no suggestion that he should compromise to be polite, or that the conventions of social decorum should dictate his behaviour. Matthew Henry approvingly quoted his father's saying 'Religion doth not destroy good manners; it destroys not civility but sanctifies it' with the comment 'Sanctified civility is a great ornament to Christianity'; Howe wrote 'how lovely is the conjunction of the well-accomplished gentleman and the serious Christian'; and Gouge that 'religion requires courtesy, as well as piety, good manners, together with good consciences.' Each of them, however would have been as appalled as Bunyan by Worldly-Wiseman's advice to Christian to be eased of his burden by civility alone. In the 1720s Defoe's Roxana was still surprised to find 'that QUAKERS may ... understand Good-Manners, as well as any-other People'.[10]

This is not merely a contrast between fashionable and unfashionable forms of behaviour. Nonconformists would readily have admitted that incivility might be as much an affectation as civility, that plainness in dress and manners might be as much a matter of convention as ornamentation and elaboration. The distinction is between not the forms of, but the significance accorded, behaviour and dress. The nonconformists' stress on inwardness meant that for them, as for the Puritans, hypocrisy and formalism were above all the vices to guard against. Since salvation depended upon the sincerity of one's Christian profession, neither the frequency nor the quality of the performance of external works, no matter how assiduous, diligent, or elaborate, counted for much in itself. 'A renewed heart, that is unfeignedly set to please God in all things is more than all the pomp of external duties.'[11] Such a 'renewed heart' would declare itself in outward actions, but it could not be reliably asserted on their evidence alone. After all, with a little effort, anyone could manage them; Bunyan's Ignorance did. For the Restoration hero, however, the 'outward' was all: he was defined not by his inner life but by the quality of the performance he put up in meeting whatever situation the plot confronted him with. His heroism rested on his ingenuity and adeptness at assuming roles.

Clearly, such a hero could be of no service to nonconformist writers. Indeed, Manton's (entirely typical) description of a hypocrite might be a characterization of him. His attention is concentrated on 'outward observances', on 'the flesh' rather than the 'heart and spirit'; he fusses inordinately about details of ritual and etiquette; and he has a high esteem of his own virtuosity, and a corresponding scorn for the abilities of others. 'But now true religion maketh men humble and lowly in their own eyes ... and maketh men pitiful and compassionate towards others, more ready to help than to censure them'.[12] The Restoration hero is present in nonconformist writing: but he has become the villain.

This is explicitly the case in Penn's *No Cross, No Crown*. Its five chapters 'Of Luxury' draw their wealth of sharply observed examples 'of excessive indulgence of self' from the social customs and recreations of a world given over to 'Plays, parks, balls, treats, romances, music, love-sonnets, and the like'. Penn fully realized that a society and its art sustain each other and that the latter inspires, as well as mirrors, the former. Of all the 'wretched inventions' of self-indulgent luxury 'the playhouses, like so many hellish seminaries, do most perniciously conduce to [its] sad and miserable ends; where little besides frothy, wanton, if not directly obscene and profane humours are represented, which are of notoriously ill consequence upon the minds of most.' The ways of society and of its art have both to be rejected:

> They that will have Christ to be theirs must be sure to be his; to be like-minded, to live in temperance and moderation, as knowing the Lord is at hand. Sumptuous apparel, rich unguents, delicate washes, stately furniture, costly cookery, and such diversions as balls, masques, music-meetings, plays, romances, &c., which are the delights and entertainment of the times, belong not to the holy path that Jesus and his true disciples and followers trod to glory.

In literature, as in society, 'men become acceptable by their trims and the à-la-modeness of their dress and apparel; from whence respect to persons doth so naturally arise (James ii.1–9), that to deny it is to affirm the sun shines not at noonday'. Penn does deny it. Arguing that Matthew vi. 31–3 'comprehends all external things whatsoever' he dismisses the whole charade. The following is a description of society's preoccupations, but it would serve equally well as a description of its literary preoccupations:

> What buying and selling, what dealing and chaffering, what writing and posting, what toil and labour, what noise, hurry, bustle, and confusion, what study, what little contrivances and overreachings, what eating, drinking, vanity of apparel, most ridiculous recreations; in short, what rising early, going to bed late, expense of precious time is there about things that perish![13]

2   IN THE WORLD

The Restoration hero not only applied the wrong values in the pursuit of the wrong ends; he was also in the wrong place. The self-denial advocated in nonconformist writing is carefully distinguished from an enclosed religious life. In a famous sentence in *Areopagitica* Milton had derided monasticism: 'I cannot praise a fugitive and cloister'd vertue, unexercis'd & unbreath'd, that never sallies out and sees her adversary, but slinks out of the race, where that immortall garland is to be run for, not without dust and heat.' This Puritan disdain for what was regarded as a cowardly retreat remained characteristic of nonconformist writing. 'A recluse life, the boasted righteousness of some', is not, averred Penn, 'much more commendable, or one whit nearer to the nature of the true cross' than formalism or self-indulgence. It is both 'unnatural', in seeking to deny the sociable and emotional nature of people, and futile, since 'The Christian convent and monastery are within, where the soul is encloistered from sin.' Since 'Evil comes from within, and not from without: how ... can an external application remove an internal cause; or a restraint upon the body, work a confinement of the mind?'[14]

'True godliness', then, 'does not turn men out of the world, but enables them to live better in it.' For all its repudiation of political and military means, its stress on the inward rather than the outward, the nonconformist conception of the Christian life was of an active engagement with, not a passive withdrawal from, the world. That, indeed, was the consequence of inwardness. A disposition to converse with God will at one and the same time dispose to converse with men. Love for the one is inseparable from love for the other and love, as we heard Manton say, is not love if it fails to generate a desire actively to serve. (The parable of the Good Samaritan (Luke x.25–37) and Matthew xxv.31–46 were the commonly cited texts.) It is sometimes said that the Puritan tradition promoted observance of the First Table of the law (duties to God) above the Second (duties to man, Exod. xx.1–17, xxxii.15–16, xxxiv.1–4).[15]

Certainly, in Manton's words, 'Simple duties of the first table are greater than duties of the second' (Job xxxiii.12; Matt. xxii.38), but such a contention positively encourages the performance of the duties of the Second Table: 'because I love, or fear, or would honour God, therefore I perform my duty to man for the Lord's sake.' Nor does it subordinate the whole of the Second to the whole of the First: the comparison must be 'rightly made; the chief of the first table with the chief of the second, the middle with the middle, the least with the least ... Thus the circumstantial and ceremonial duties of the first table must give place to the necessary and moral duties of the second.' A monastic life devoted to the Divine Office consequently appeared negligent, selfish and slothful: it is, wrote Penn, 'a lazy, rusty, unprofitable self-denial, burdensome to others to feel their idleness'. To avoid the world was not self-denial but denial of the opportunity to serve: we should not, wrote Baxter,

> causelessly withdraw from humane society into *Solitude*. A weariness of converse with men, is oft conjunct with a weariness of our duty: And a retiring voluntarily into solitude, when God doth not call or drive us thither, is oft but a retiring from the place and work which God hath appointed us: And consequently a retiring rather from God, than to God.[16]

The comprehensive term 'godliness', preferred by nonconformists as by Puritans, hence encompasses both private and public duties and allows no distinction between service to God and service to others. The business of the world is a saint's business.

Moralism and materialism were ever-present dangers, to be sure, but dangers to be encountered, not shunned. 'Every son of Abraham ought to mind some particular calling' wrote Gouge, citing Genesis iii.19, for 'idleness is the root both of beggary, and of all manner of wickedness', but, he adds, 'Follow your worldly business with a heavenly mind, as a citizen of heaven, and a pilgrim on earth.' Works alone do not justify, but, wrote Bunyan, those who discount them and lapse into antinomianism ''tis evident have not known what 'tis to receive the spirit of adoption'. In *A Holy Life* (1684), which was written to enjoin to 'good Works', Bunyan was sensitive to the difficulty of maintaining a correct balance: 'If faith be preached as that which is absolutely necessary to *Justification*; then faith-fantastical, and looseness and remisness of life (with some) are joyned therewith. If holiness of life be preached, as necessary to *salvation*, then faith is undervalued, and set below its place.' His own answer, and the general nonconformist answer, is implied by the compound 'faith-fantastical': faith, if saving and not illusory, has '*effects*', as Christian retorts to Ignorance's claim that the doctrine of justification by faith would 'loosen the reins of our lust'. Bunyan put the point thus:

> *A Professor is a Professor though he hath no good Works; but that, as such, he is truly godly; he is foolish that so concludeth. Not that Works make a Man good; for the Fruit maketh not a good Tree, it is the Principle, to wit, Faith, that makes a Man good, and his works that shew him to be so.*

> *What then? why, all Professors that have not good Works flowing from their Faith, are naught; are Bramble bushes; are nigh unto Cursing, whose end is to be burned. For Professors by their fruitlessness declare that they are not of the planting of God* ...
>
> *Verily good works are necessary, though God need them not, nor is that Faith, as to Justification with God, worth a rush, that abideth alone, or without them.*[17]

The margin refers us to Matthew vii.16–18, Luke vi.44 and James ii.14–26, all passages commonly cited to this effect.

If, then, it was to conduce to godliness, nonconformist writing had to address itself to public service in the world, and, more particularly, to the world of its readers' experience. The prevailing bias of its divinity was consequently neither ascetic nor devotional in any narrow sense, but practical and casuistical. It confronted not the demands placed upon those of high birth nor the dilemmas posed by exceptional circumstances but the problems and situations commonly encountered in ordinary lives. From the religious bias and pastoral concern of nonconformity there thus emerges a fairly clearly defined literary world, the scene of the Christian's labours. Baxter's *A Christian Directory* (1673), for example, undertook 'the resolving of *practical Cases of Conscience*, and the reducing of Theoretical knowledge into serious *Christian practice*'. The titles of its four books indicate its scope and province: 'Christian Ethicks (or private Duties)'; 'Christian Oeconomicks (or Family Duties)'; 'Christian Ecclesiasticks (or Church Duties)'; 'Christian Politicks (or Duties to our Rulers and Neighbours)'. It is a guide for a person employed and with a family, an individual, but an individual who is a member of a household, a church, a local community and a national society. Every possible relationship in each of these contexts is treated, sympathetically, but also with a clear-sighted directness which does not blanch at the vulgar, shun the unseemly, or gloss over the indelicate. And these are handled with a minute particularity which eschews both the abstract prescription of absolute norms and the misleading finality of the epigrammatic generalization. Either course would simplistically reduce to order and coherence – to uniformity – what is, in fact, and in experience, disorderly and incoherent. People, times and places are too varied and various, too elusive and subtly individualistic, to allow such responses to serve as practical advice. 'The differences of Natures as well as of actual Cases' demand realistic accuracy.[18]

This is a domain foreign to Restoration literature, which rarely leaves the drawing room or ventures beyond the park gates. The Town, its almost invariable setting, affects a fine scorn for everywhere, and everyone, outside London. The Town offers Etherege's Lady Cockwood 'freedom' after the melancholy of the country, where, complains Sir Oliver, a man grows 'a sot for want of gentleman-like recreations' (namely, swearing, drinking and whoring). For Dorimant 'all beyond High [Hyde] Park's a desert'; the extremity of his protestation of sincere love when his 'passion knows no bounds' extends to undertaking to live in Hampshire. The desire of Wycherley's country wife to go out walking provokes appalled amusement in Alithea: 'A walking, hah, ha;

Lord, a Country Gentlewomans leisure is the drudgery of a foot-post; and she requires as much airing as her Husbands Horses.' 'I nauseate walking, 'tis a country diversion. I loathe the country and everything that relates to it', declares Millamant. The proper use of the country, as of a mistress, is , rules Dorilant, 'not to dwell in constantly, but only for a night and away; to taste the Town the better when a man returns'. Such disdain marks a literature of very limited social (and thematic) range, a literature directed exclusively to an enclosed élite. 'I loathe the Rabble', asserts Rochester, who is content should his peers – Wycherley, Godolphin, Buckingham – 'Approve my Sense'. The absurdity of the claim of Buckingham's laureate hero Bayes that he loves 'to write familiarly', and the bathos of the Brentford setting, are part of the joke of *The Rehearsal*. From the point of view of its patrons, of course, what this literature depicted *was* the world. Scant regard is paid to those not sufficiently affluent or well-bred to be excused from earning their living since they are socially inconsequential. The only 'business' worth giving time to is conducted at Whitehall or in the playhouse, not in a shop, and certainly not in a field.[19]

The nonconformist bias is directly contrary: it inclines to regard the 'world' of Restoration literature as a kind of secular and literary monasticism, self-preoccupied, withdrawn indulgent. In nonconformist writing the 'world' is an altogether larger and more varied place, and it is located beyond the Restoration pale. William Bates warns people against pride in their social status and in 'the Nobility of their extraction', and even a courtier like Penn shares Milton's scorn for 'the tedious pomp that waits/On princes'. He tilts vigorously at the 'folly' of, and 'pother' about, 'noble blood'. He does so for a reason we can by now anticipate: the mere external circumstance of heredity has no bearing on a person's own individual state. 'An ancestor's character is no excuse to a man's ill actions ... and since virtue comes not by generation, I neither am the better nor the worse for my forefather.' 'To be descended of wealth and titles fills no man's head with brains or heart with truth: those qualities come from a higher cause.' Besides, even the most ancient family had its rise in some such 'upstart gentleman' as now outrage 'persons of blood'. If we go far enough back, it is to discover we are all of one family, 'all descended from one father and mother'. Penn is no proto-communist revolutionary: 'I would not be thought to set the churl on the present gentleman's shoulder; by no means; his rudeness will not mend the matter.' Penn's thinking remains hierarchical, but social position in itself counts for very little: true honour consists not in external circumstances *per se* but in what a person of either high or low degree makes of those circumstances.[20]

Nonconformist literature consequently rarely visited the court or the salon and it had a particular regard for those beneath the notice of polite literature. Its 'familiar' manner could mention Brentford without incongruity. It set its hero down firmly in the world of domestic, commercial and social dealings, and directed him there to exercise himself: 'the best recreation is to do good', for

> men and women ... to follow their respective callings; frequent the assemblies of
> religious people; visit sober neighbours to be edified, and wicked ones to reform
> them; be careful in the tuition of their children, exemplary to their servants; relieve
> the necessitous, see the sick, visit the imprisoned; administer to their infirmities
> and indisposition, endeavour peace amongst neighbours: also, study moderately
> such commendable and profitable arts, as navigation, arithmetic, geometry,
> husbandry, gardening, handicraft, medecine, &c.; and that women spin, sew, knit,
> weave, garden, preserve, and the like housewife and honest employments, the
> practice of the greatest and noblest matrons, and youth, among the very heathen:
> helping others, who for want are unable to keep servants, to ease them in their
> necessary affairs ... [21]

Set in the world and directed to its betterment, such moral endeavours demand
attention to the world. A saint may appear to the world a fool for rejecting its
ways, but he cannot afford to be a fool in the world. Christian service is possible
only to those who notice occasions to minister, needs to be met. The attention
to self in nonconformist writing was matched by an equal attention to the
external world in which the self had to act.

This watchfulness, which was so frequently enjoined, involved not only a
sensitivity to opportunities for service but also a reflective wariness. The world
could deceive no less than the human heart. It was the adversary, as well as the
field of combat. To be a Christian was to be alert, curious and reflective,
vigilant against external temptation as well as inner doubt. It was also to
'improve' what was observed by assessing, interpreting and applying it to one's
own condition. 'Let us', says Christian to Faithful after they have identified the
monument of Lot's wife, 'take notice of what we see here, for our help in time
to come.' Christian's progress in fact takes place not during the incidents of his
pilgrimage but during those analytical discussions of these events, their
interpretation in the light of Scripture, which, to readers who approach *The
Pilgrim's Progress* merely as a novel, appear irritating interruptions to the action.
They are the action: at least, the only action that matters. Faith does not put our
mental faculties into retirement: it is by reflective attentiveness that we grow in
grace. An individual who does not meditate on what has happened to him has,
in fact, had no experiences. He has no history. And as it is only the human
mind, alert and waiting on the guidance of the Spirit, which can, by
recollecting, comparing and assessing experience, give purpose and order to a
life, so it is in the response of Christian's mind that the true story lies.
Ignorance, after all, sees the same things as Christian, and does complete the
fictional journey. He remains, however, impervious to what goes on around
him. Progress is possible only to the Christian pilgrim. And so Christian's own
progress is measured, in large part, by the growing confidence with which he
accurately discerns the true nature of those whom he meets. At the beginning
he falls an easy prey to Mr Worldly-Wiseman, but he is later able to see through
Talkative and to dismiss the casuistry of Mr Money-love. He attains, finally, to
the generous wisdom of his comments on Little-faith. The Discretion who had

questioned him at the Palace Beautiful and perceived he was a true pilgrim would, in modern English, be named 'Discernment'.[22]

The particularity of nonconformist divinity, the habit of observant attentiveness it fostered and the curiosity it expected in the alert saint give to nonconformist writing the kind of texture which Defoe was to use to such advantage. The distinctive mark of his fictions (and journalism) is a precise grasp of facts. By circumstantial detail he persuades us of the reality of plague-stricken London or Crusoe's island. The itemization of Moll's acquisitions and the precisely delineated scenes in which she operates are so factually compelling they obscure the otherwise glaring improbabilities of her life, the confused narrative points of view and the inconsistencies in her character. If not always clearly understood or organized, Defoe's fictional worlds are sharply observed. This argues in him not only a practical but an inveterately curious nature, one which collected and hoarded the minutiae of the external world. His *Tour through the whole Island of Great Britain* (1724–6) took him far afield in search of them, as did what her editor calls Celia Fiennes's 'unappeasable craving for new facts'. These are often of a businesslike and domestic sort, especially culinary: she remarks the way 'oat Clap bread' is baked and eaten in the Lake District and borders of Scotland, the preparation of 'Codlings' in Scarborough or of rennet in Colehill, near Coventry. West Country apple pies, with clotted cream, are 'the most acceptable entertainment that could be made'.[23] She is interested in market prices, especially as the provinces compare with London, and in industrial methods. The working of Huguenot paper mills in Cambridge, coal mines at Chesterfield and tin mines in Cornwall all engage her.[24] And, as she details the luxurious appointments of noble seats, so she observes the dress and manners of poor people, though with some impatience at the taciturn (and dialectal) unhelpfulness of Yorkshiremen who 'say its good levell gate all along, when it may be there are severall great hills to pass'. Towards the Scots she is even less sympathetic: their sloth results in very 'nasty' domestic and social habits.[25]

This no-nonsense attitude is evident in her comments on the sights which, like a good tourist, she took in. In St Winifred's Well

> there is some small stones of a reddish coullour ... said to be some of St Winifreds blood ... which the poore people take out and bring to the strangers for curiosity and relicts, and also moss about the bancks full of great virtue for every thing – its a certaine gaine to the poore people, every one gives them something for bringing them moss and stones, but least they should in length of tyme be quite gather'd up they take care to replenish it dayly from some mossy hill and so stick it along the sides of the Well.

Similarly, St Mungo's Well, at Copgrove in Yorkshire, 'Setting aside the Papists fancyes of it I cannot but think it is a very good Spring, being remarkably cold', which she knew from bathing in it. This preference for ascertainable facts over tales is characteristic. Though 'the story is' of the 'confused' stones of Stonehenge that 'none can count them twice alike', 'I have told them often and bring their number to 91.' Similarly she (quite rightly and from her own experience) points out that the Wrekin in Shropshire, though 'noted for the highest piece of ground in England', can be supposed to be so only 'by those that live in the heart of the kingdom and about London', for it is slight in comparison to the fells of Cumberland and Westmorland, or even the Malverns 'not 40 mile distant'.[26]

In the first decades of the eighteenth century, a dissenter like Celia Fiennes enjoyed the freedom to travel, observe and write at leisure. Though her sharply drawn and practical observations set her journals in the nonconformist tradition, they lack the urgent attentiveness and pressing literary purpose of earlier non-conformist writing. There, literary realism is a means by which to win freedom. Circumstantial accuracy is, for example, turned to apologetic purpose in Quaker reportage. *A True and Faithful Relation From the People of God (called) Quakers, in Colchester* (1664) seeks to win sympathy not by arguing the Quaker case but by a detailed presentation of what they endured. The pamphlet does note that not even their persecutors believed they were disturbers of the peace, and hence that the treatment meted out to Quakers is monstrously unjustified, but it is in the factual reporting of the steady escalation of this treatment that the force of the tract lies. On the '*25th* of the *8th* month [October]' the mayor and his officers merely broke up a meeting. On the '*1st* day of the *9th* month' this was repeated, but, 'being not satisfied with this', on the '*10th* of the same month' there came a 'Party of the County Troops' who beat the Friends and vandalized their meeting place. Denied admission thereafter, the Friends met in the street. On the '*6th* day of the *10th* month', 'a Troop of the Kings horsemen', in armour, with drawn swords, carbines and pistols, 'crying *what a Devil do ye here*', broke up the meeting, wounded many and chased others through the streets. The following day 'they got them great Clubs' (Bunyan's Clubmen were, it seems, all too real), 'and one Trooper beat a Friend with his drawn sword till the blade fell out of the Hilt, which when the friend saw, he said, *I will give it thee again*, and so giving it to the souldier, said, *I desire the Lord may not lay this daies work to thy charge*'. As the pace quickens, so the detail intensifies:

And on the *27th* of the *10th* month they used another stratagem to terrifie us withal, *viz.*, they set Centinels on horseback and some on foot, to guard the waies where friends should be driven away, and then came 38 armed men on horseback riding upon friends in such a desperate sort, as would have amazed any that had had nought but an arm of flesh to trust to, and being come did with their Clubs and Carbines, lay on in such a manner, as moved the standers by to great compassion.
    And as if all these cruelties were not enough for these men to inflict upon our bodies, against the 6 day of this month being the 4 day of the week, the souldiers prepared themselves with a new kind of weapon to torment the women friends withal, which made some of them say, *if they might choose, they might rather have been beaten with their grevious Clubs* ... The weapons by which they now thought to satiate their cruel minds upon us, was to take iron spikes, and drive them into the ends of their clubs, and sharpen them with a File, and so they might easily enter through womens clothes.[27]

For such a report to succeed it must appear to be impartially accurate and trustworthy. Hence, each incident is carefully dated, details are precise (one Quaker's wound was 'above four inches by rule') and plausible ('sharpen them with a File'). The narrator is not above comment ('cruel minds'), but he prefers to allow events to speak for themselves, leaving explicit reaction to the 'standers by'. When an inference is drawn, it emerges naturally from the facts of the case: when two troopers beat a constable who endeavours to restrain them 'all men' may indeed see 'how much these men regard peace, or the Kings name'. The alleged upholders of the law have declared themselves to be its violators. It is the steady eye and unimpassioned voice of the narrator which gives the *Relation* its stark horror.[28]

It is characteristic of such steadiness to recognize the true nature of things, but not to be overawed by them, nor to be persuaded by them to adopt conveniently simplistic responses. In 1660 Burrough handled a number of royalist doubts, misgivings and questions about the Quakers. If his intention was to allay their fears he can hardly have succeeded, for to each query he replies with a common sense and a reliance on the facts of the case which must have incensed any royalist worth his salt. Did Quakers, with their claim to inspiration, foresee the Restoration? 'God respecteth neither *persons* nor *names*, but doth give the *Kingdoms of the World* to whomsoever he will', which seems to put Charles II and Cromwell pretty much on a par, an inference consistent with Burrough's view of the Restoration as a judgement on the Interregnum authorities. Is it not just that Charles should enter into his hereditary right? It is clearly the divine will at the present, but as to its justness, let us wait until we have experience of his rule. Will his reign be blessed? Who knows? It will be 'according as he walketh in the fear of the Lord'. Should he persecute the conscientious, 'the reward will be *Sad* and *Heavy* upon *him*', as it was upon the Interregnum. Burrough is too clear-sighted and too clear-headed to give politic (and polite) answers.[29]

The nonconformist hero could, then, be an awkward guest. If he rarely entered the drawing room, equally, when he walked, it was not to stroll in the park but to journey, and to journey both far and with purpose. Though Celia Fiennes is a tourist rather than a pilgrim, the perceptive acuity, the circumstantial ordinariness, the mundane inconsequentiality we find in her journals, the fresh air we breathe, the anticipation with which we await what is round the next bend in the road, all these are characteristic of earlier nonconformist writing. They are qualities unknown in fiction before *The Pilgrim's Progress*. That 'way', it has been often noticed, is a muddy, poorly signposted seventeenth-century road. Those who travel it have to tackle difficult terrain, endure bad weather and watch out lest they are benighted or miss their way; dogs will bark at them, footpads molest them, travellers misinform them; they will pass stately homes, busy market towns and bleak moors; they may meet, or make, a friend, but often they will fall out with their acquaintances; they will gossip about neighbours, but often be lonely, hungry, sometimes afraid and, above all, weary. In Fox's autobiographical *Journal* we are again much of the time on the road and with him travel the length and breadth of Britain (and beyond). Visionary perceptions jostle mundanities with no sense of incongruity or bathos to the confusion of our categorical distinctions between the natural and the supernatural. The way of faith may be miraculous, but it pursues a very ordinary course through this world.

The Restoration hero might, of course, travel, but not this way. His journeys would lie through the far distant realms of romance. There, the nonconformist hero could not venture. One of Penn's denunciations of idle pastimes develops into a sustained critique of romance, a critique which, incidentally, reveals he had, before his conversion, considerable familiarity with the genre. If we bid members of society reflect on the recreations in which they indulge,

> the best return that is usual is reproachful jests (Eph. v.3,4), profane repartees, if not direct blows. Their thoughts are otherwise employed: their mornings are too short for them to wash, to smooth, to paint, to patch, to braid, to curl, to gum, to powder, and otherwise to attire and adorn themselves (Psalm xii.2; Isa. v.12; lix.3, 4); whilst their afternoons are as commonly bespoke for visits and for plays; where their usual entertainment is some stories fetched from the more approved romances; some strange adventures, some passionate amours, unkind refusals, grand impediments, importunate addresses, miserable disappointments, wonderful surprises, unexpected encounters, castles surprised, imprisoned lovers rescued, and meetings of supposed dead ones; bloody duels, languishing voices echoing from solitary groves, overheard mournful complaints, deep-fetched sighs sent from wild deserts, intrigues managed with unheard-of subtlety; and whilst all things seem at the greatest distance, then are dead people alive, enemies friends, despair turned to enjoyment, and all their impossibilities reconciled: things that never were, nor are, nor ever shall or can be, they all come to pass. And as if men and women were too slow to answer the loose suggestions of corrupt nature; or were intent on more divine speculations and heavenly affairs, they have all that is possible for the most extravagant wits to invent; not only express lies, but utter impossibilities to very nature, on purpose to excite their minds to those idle passions, and intoxicate their giddy fancies with swelling nothings but airy fictions which not only consume their time, effeminate their natures, debase their reason, and set them on work to reduce these things to practice, and make each adventure theirs by imitation: but if disappointed, – as who can otherwise expect from such mere phantasms? – the present remedy is latitude in the greatest vice.[30]

What is striking in this passage is that Penn is put out quite as much by the unreality as by what he takes to be the immoral effects of romance. Indeed, the latter stems from the former. Romance arouses expectations which life cannot satisfy: its fruit is frustration, bitterness and the opiate of self-gratification. Penn's accumulated epithets, stressing the improbabilities of plot and the extravagances of incident characteristic of the genre, lead to a clear enunciation of his own literary, as well as moral, touchstone: 'things that never were, nor are, nor ever shall or can be' avail nothing. 'Truth to nature' is the literary counterpart of moral truthfulness. The phrase is one which was to be heard often during the coming century, but for the nonconformist it was conceived not in terms of those 'general properties and large appearances' Dr Johnson's Imlac would later recommend as the concern of the poet, but as consisting in precisely that delineation of the 'individual' rather than the 'species' Imlac warns against. The nonconformist did 'number the streaks of the tulip [and] describe the different shades in the verdure of the forest', declining to enter the cloister of abstraction or to take refuge in generalization.[31]

3 'ABOVE HEROIC'

'The friendship of the world is emnity with God' (James iv.4). The Restoration ideal is a person of the world who enjoys its friendships and masters its ways. In defending and depicting its contrary ideal, a person in the world but not of it, nonconformist literature incidentally created a new kind of literary hero. This is most famously the case in Milton's rewriting – or unwriting – of epic.[32] In *Paradise Lost*, the martial heroism of Classical epic, of medieval romance and of Renaissance romantic epic is the attribute of Satan. He first appears as every inch the epic hero: resolute, defiant in defeat, accoutred with Achilles' shield and spear, and saluted by a feudal host which, bearing triumphal trophies, 'in perfect phalanx' 'Breathing united force with fixed thought/Moved on in silence to soft pipes' such as 'raised/To highth of noblest temper heroes old/Arming to battle, and instead of rage/Deliberate valour breathed'.[33] This association of old heroes with the fallen angels, and of Satan with epic exempla, is disconcerting, especially since Milton repeatedly insists that those we meet in the first two books of the poem are deservedly in Hell, perverse, corrupt, with but the 'Semblance of worth, not substance'. This implication that martial heroism is insubstantial and evil recurs throughout the poem. The old ideal is consistently associated with the adverse party. It is Satan who trusts to the power of force ('to be weak is miserable') and who sees in the exercise of domination the only promise of fulfilment. His conviction that it is 'Better to reign in hell, than serve in heaven' later becomes Eve's: 'inferior who is free?'. Throughout the poem, such a conviction brings chaos and havoc in its train. Destruction is what Satan, 'our destroyer', sets against divine Creation ('only in destroying I find ease') and whenever a hero is mentioned we can expect carnage to attend him. Michael predicts that in future times:

> might only shall be admired,
> And valour and heroic virtue called;
> To overcome in battle, and subdue
> Nations, and bring home spoils with infinite
> Manslaughter, shall be held the highest pitch
> Of human glory, and for glory done
> Of triumph, to be styled great conquerors,
> Patrons of mankind, gods, and sons of gods,
> Destroyers rightlier called and plagues of men.
> Thus fame shall be achieved, renown on earth,
> And what most merits fame in silence hid.[34]

To give a voice to 'what most merits fame' is the chief purpose of the poem. Milton himself tells us he is:

> Not sedulous by nature to indite
> Wars, hitherto the only argument
> Heroic deemed, chief mastery to dissect
> With long and tedious havoc fabled knights
> In battles feigned; the better fortitude
> Of patience and heroic martyrdom
> Unsung

It is something other than martial action and military success which 'justly gives heroic name/To person or to poem'. The unexpected positioning of this apology itself introduces us to what that is, what constitutes 'the better fortitude'. Milton declares himself not, where we might expect him to do so, at the beginning of the poem, but here at the opening of its ninth book as he is about to recount the Fall. To announce his true theme as he embarks upon this 'sad task', and to describe that task as 'argument/Not less but more heroic than the wrath/Of stern Achilles', is inescapabably to associate the better fortitude of true heroism with the Fall, with failure and with weakness.[35] We are invited to contemplate Adam and Eve on their knees in tears as a scene more heroic than the traditional one with which the poem began, to prefer submission to mastery, obedience to domination, the trust of the weak to the power of the strong:

> What better can we do, than ...
>   confess
> Humbly our faults, and pardon beg, with tears
> Watering the ground, and with our sighs the air
> Frequenting, sent from hearts contrite, in sign
> Of sorrow unfeigned, and humiliation meek.

The rhetorical question requires no answer. This is the lesson taught by history, mankind's accumulated experience:

> Henceforth I learn, that to obey is best,
> And love with fear the only God, to walk
> As in his presence, ever to observe
> His providence, and on him sole depend,
> Merciful over all his works, with good
> Still overcoming evil, and by small
> Accomplishing great things, by things deemed weak
> Subverting worldy strong, and worldly wise
> By simply meek; that suffering for truth's sake
> Is fortitude to highest victory,
> And to the faithful death the gate of life.[36]

So it is that Milton can describe the action of *Paradise Regained* as a tale 'of deeds/Above heroic' when there is no action – and certainly no martial action – at all. The Son is to be 'proved' by a 'great duel', but 'not of arms'. In his youthful heart 'victorious deeds' and 'heroic acts' had 'flamed', but this is not the way nor the victory subsequently revealed and promised. He is to

> Be tried in humble state, and things adverse,
> By tribulations, injuries, insults,
> Contempts, and scorns, and snares, and violence,
> Suffering, abstaining, quietly expecting
> Without distrust or doubt

Heroism is attained by rejecting the temptation to be heroic:

> he who reigns within himself, and rules
> Passions, desires, and fears, is more a king.[37]

Just so Bunyan wrote:

> Know then true Valour there doth dwell
> Where Men engage for God,
> Against the Devil, Death and Hell,
> And bear the Wickeds rod.
>
> These be the Men that God doth count
> Of high and noble Mind;
> These be the men that do surmount
> What you in Nature find.

If, as Defoe's Roxana was to remark in the early eighteenth century, 'Knight-Errantry is over', the reason is not far to seek.[38]

Bunyan's *Prison Meditations* were written explicitly for persecuted saints. Milton's anticipated readership may not have been so exclusive, but that, in his own mind, he was proposing a nonconformist ideal is no matter for conjecture. When Abdiel returns to Heaven having refused to join Satan's rebellion, he is thus commended by the Father:

> Servant of God, well done, well hast thou fought
> The better fight, who single hast maintained
> Against revolted multitudes the cause
> Of truth, in word mightier than they in arms;
> And for the testimony of truth hast borne
> Universal reproach, far worse to bear
> Than violence: for this was all thy care
> To stand approved in sight of God, though worlds
> Judged thee perverse.

The 'better fight' (I Tim. vi.12) anticipates the 'better fortitude': this is true heroism. Though couched in general terms, the Father's description of its manners and circumstances, his identification of the true servant (Matt. xxv.21) as an individual standing against 'revolted multitudes' and 'Universal reproach' (Ps. lxix.7), has an inescapable contemporary reference. Throughout this study examples have been cited of judgements passed upon the nonconformists as perverse and of reproaches heaped upon them by the majority of their countrymen who had returned to royalism and episcopalianism. When Abdiel later confronts Satan on the field of Heaven, however, the identification of his cause with that of nonconformity becomes all but explicit:

> there be who faith
> Prefer, and piety to God, though then
> To thee not visible, when I alone
> Seemed to thy world erroneous to dissent
> From all: my sect thou seest, now learn too late
> How few sometimes may know, when thousands err.[39]

Only one group of people was known as 'dissenters' and 'sectarians'. Their nonconformity is here identified with the unwavering opposition to Satan of the loyal angels. And Milton counts himself of their number: Abdiel cannot 'change his constant mind'; Milton sings 'unchanged'.[40]

Whereas the old heroism has been typified in rare exempla, this heroism, if it was to be an ideal of practical attainment, had to be compatible with the variety of human nature and experience. And so it was. Nonconformist writing does not reduce human character to conformity. It cannot, wrote Howe with reference to debate over the relative merits of a liturgy and extempore prayer,

> be universally laid, it is a better Judgment, or more Grace, that determines Men the one way or the other; but somewhat in the Temper of their Minds distinct from both, which I know not how better to express than by *mental Tast*, the acts whereof (as the Objects are suitable or unsuitable) are relishing or disrelishing, liking or disliking: And this hath no more of Mystery in it, than that there is such a thing belonging to our Natures, as Complacency and Displicency in reference to the Objects of the Mind. And this, in the kind of it, is as common to Men, as human Nature, but as much diversify'd in Individuals, as Mens other Inclinations are, that are most fixed, and least apt to admit of Change.

'No Man's Judgment (or relish of things, which influences his Judgment, tho he know it not) is at the command of his Will; and much less of another Man's'; 'no man's genius can be forced in these things.' The repressive and punitive attempt to enforce conformity flouts the simple fact of human individuality: those who attempt it, or suppose religious debates are a matter either of whim or of perversity, 'show they understand little of human nature'; 'How comes one man in the matter of literature to savour metaphysics, another mathematics, another history, and the like? ... Why may there not be the like difference in the matters of religion?' Those who find the *Book of Common Prayer* edifying are hence 'no rule to us; but it would less become us, hereupon to suspect their sincerity than our own'.[41]

Nonconformity was hence a defence of human individuality:

> if there was an Act of Parliament, that all men should have faces one like another, and propose one man for a Pattern, it would be as easily brought to pass, as to compel all men to be of one Judgment; for he that hath a hand in forming the face, hath a hand in forming the Judgment.

It was also a defence of the variety of human experience and circumstances. 'All barks that sail to heaven', wrote Manton, 'draw not a like depth of water. And partly because of the remainders of corruption in all. Inordinate self-love is not in all alike broken and mortified, and so their particular interests have an influence upon their opinions. And partly because of the accidental prejudices of education and converse, &c.' 'God sendeth forth his servants with divers dispositions ... [he] fits his servants severally to do good.' 'Very excellent men excel in different ways' asserted Howe, with uncharacteristic brevity. The way of God's dealing with men is 'with great latitude and variety'; 'The grace and Spirit of Christ ought to be reverenced in the various appearances thereof' (II Cor. v.13–14). Baxter similarly concluded from his own experience, and from observation, that God broke not all men's hearts alike.[42] Bunyan was equally sensitive to psychological and experiential diversity. In Part II of *The Pilgrim's Progress* the calls of Christiana and Mercy are distinguished, but Mercy's fear that hers is therefore invalid proves groundless: the Keeper of the Gate, who is later identified as Christ, prays 'for all them that believe on me, by what means soever they come unto me'. This is, indeed, only the first of many episodes in the book which stress the variety of the experience of grace. It is also only the first of many distinctions between the characters and dispositions of the pilgrims. Their fictional reality resides in their individuality. In nonconformity, fidelity to truth compelled fidelity to the variety of natures in the Creator's work, Nature. From its essential conviction that 'Christians should be wary of making themselves standards to one another' there thus emerged a defining feature of literary realism.[43]

Individual and susceptible to a variety of experience, the nonconformist hero had one other distinctive feature. The traditional hero was socially and intrinsically eminent: nonconformity admitted the socially inconspicuous and the personally inadequate. Though by no means all nonconformists were sympathetic towards the democratic tendencies of radical Puritanism, none of them was as excited by the prospect of royalty and nobility as Donne had been, or as royalists and episcopalians continued to be.[44] Their common concern was for those who had no part to play in romance. 'Many times', wrote Manton in an exposition of Isaiah liii.2 drawing out the implications of Christ's own 'meaness', 'God singleth out the meanest. Our Saviour sent fishermen to conquer the world.' Furthermore, we are enjoined to have a special care for the psychologically, emotionally, or spiritually immature, as well as for the socially underprivileged:

> The strong are not to deal rigorously with the weak, nor insult over them, nor pursue them with censures, but wait till God declare the truth unto them, and must promote their conviction with all gentleness and condescension ... [and] not break the bruised reed [Isa.xlii.3; Matt. xii.20] Infants must not be turned out of the family because they cry, and are unquiet and troublesome; though they be peevish and froward, yet we must bear it with gentleness and patience, as we do the frowardness of the sick.

The Quaker Francis Howgill develops the same point from the variety of human nature: conformists

> would have all Shoos made by their Last, though they will not fit every mans feet. Faith is the gift of God, there are divers degrees and measures according to the

mind and good pleasure of the giver; so that he that hath received any measure or degree, must not be excluded as having no faith, though he attain not to that degree that some do enjoy; and the Apostles Doctrine was, *that every one should be perswaded in his own mind, and if any was otherwise minded*, they were to be let alone till God revealed it to them [Rom. xiv.1–14][45]

A comprehensive and catholic sympathy for those generally beneath the notice of Restoration literature is hence the mark of nonconformist writing. 'And now abideth', wrote St Paul, 'faith, hope and charity, these three; but the greatest of these is charity' (I. Cor. xxiii.13). In this respect, nonconformist writing was emphatically Pauline.

What excites nonconformist writers, then, is not the splendours of state (Milton's 'tedious pomp') but the splendour of the least soul shining as brightly in heaven as the greatest star. In *The Greatness of the Soul* (1683), Bunyan encourages those 'small in esteem', 'little accounted of', 'small in the world's eyes', that 'if thou feareth God, thou are sure to be blessed', and those negligible 'in thine own thoughts or in the thoughts of others ... small in grace, small in gifts' that 'The least Star stands as fixed, as the biggest of them all, in Heaven.' Similarly, in his sermons after 1662 Baxter dealt with 'what tendeth most to your strength & Stedfastness' and encouraged 'all poor weak Christians' to 'grow to a greater measure in Grace'. II Corinthians xx.9, 'my strength is made perfect in weakness', on which Baxter preached in 1680, and which serves as an epigraph to this chapter, became a key text.[46]

Sceptics may see in this thrust in nonconformist writing an expedient response to the danger of desertion to the less demanding practices of the parish church, but it is not the language of expediency we hear in Part II of *The Pilgrim's Progress*, still less in its triumphant conclusion. In that book Bunyan deliberately associates with the women Christiana and Mercy the young, the old, the infirm, the despondent, the tiresomely scrupulous, the timid and the fearful. These seem improbable saints. Yet, that they hardly look any different from ordinary people is both the theological point and the source of the fictional verisimilitude. The regenerate are distinguished from the unregenerate not by any exceptional abilities or virtue, and certainly not by their social status: it is, we recall, Mr Worldly-Wiseman who 'looked like a Gentleman'. What distinguishes them is that they keep on going. Such faith, as the stories of Little-faith and Mr Fearing illustrate, is vouchsafed regardless of human weakness. And it is the particular concern of Christian charity, and so of nonconformist writing. Great-heart reassures Mr Feeblemind:

I have it in Commision, to comfort the *feeble minded*, and to support the weak. You must needs go along with us; we will wait for you, we will lend you our help, we will deny our selves of some things, both *Opinionative* and *Practical*, for your sake; we will not enter into doubtful Disputations before you, we will be made all things to you, rather then you shall be left behind.

The margin refers us to Romans xiv, the chapter to which Howgill alluded, and to Matthew xxv.40 when the Shepherds of the Delectable Mountains welcome the pilgrims with the words 'we have for the *Feeble*, as for the *Strong*, our Prince has an eye to what is done to the least of these.'[47]

Bunyan's sure grasp of the psychology of human fallibility and his incisive depiction of the social and domestic world of his characters has led critics to discern in Part II of *The Pilgrim's Progress* the nascent novel,[48] but it is not quite accurate to characterize Part I as, by contrast, 'epic'.[49] Christian is not really cast in the traditional heroic mould. It is only in Part II, when the pilgrims have the benefit of his example to guide them, that he is likened to Hercules. In Part I, Evangelist discerns 'many weaknesses' in both Christian and Faithful. Christian trembles for fear of the lions before the Palace Beautiful; he confesses to Prudence that 'when I would be doing of that which is best, that which is worst is with me'; he remains vulnerable to doubt and despair, and, even at the end, nearly drowns in the river. It is this fallibility which arouses our sympathy and creates tension in the book, but this is no mere fictional device: it is the point Bunyan would impress upon us. Christian can hardly be said to deserve salvation. Left to his own devices, he never would have achieved the quest: yet quite against the odds, he does achieve it. Any person may, through grace, become a Christian hero: 'all the Kings Subjects are not his Champions: nor can they, when tried, do such feats of War as he.'[50]

4 THE COMPANY OF THE SAINTS

In neither part of *The Pilgrim's Progress* do pilgrims travel alone. Bunyan's are stories of mutual encouragement and support: Hopeful prevents Christian from committing suicide in Doubting Castle and Christian prevents Hopeful from sleeping in the Enchanted Ground. This is fiction, but biographies afford many comparable examples. The Quaker Thomas Green, to take only one case, recalled that when imprisoned with John Samm, 'our hearts was knit together, even as Jonathans was to David [I Sam. xviii.1]; and as Iron sharpeneth Iron, so did the Lord by the manifestation of his love and life [to] our hearts, cause us often to refresh each other'. '*Two are better than one*' says Hopeful in the words of Ecclesiastes iv.9. 'Man is a sociable creature' writes Manton, citing the same text from Ecclesiastes: 'The Lord appointed mankind to live in society, that they might be mutually helpful to one another. Surely God never made them to live in deserts.' By having Peter, James and John accompany him to the Transfiguration (Matt. xvii.1) Christ hallowed and commended 'spiritual friendship'. As he consecrated it in his own person, choosing some of his disciples 'for intimacy and special converse', so the disciples themselves exemplified it, for example in the friendship between Peter and John. 'An heavenly, faithful friend is one of the greatest treasures upon earth.'[51]

The name of Bunyan's Faithful, it appears, denotes a relationship to others as well as to God. What he, like any true friend, offers Christian is encouragement both in the performance of external duties and in the inner quest for assurance. The inward and introspective tendency discussed in the previous chapter conduced not to introversion but to sociability. As Faithful acknowledges, it is '*but seldom*' that a believer can confidently conclude '*this is a work of Grace, because his corruptions now, and his abused reason, makes his mind to mis-judge*'. Such uncertainty generated interest in the experiences of other selves. 'Its a precious thriving course', wrote Baxter, 'for Christians to be communicating experiences' since comparisons and contrasts might clarify one's own state and offer encouragement. Gouge recommends 'communicating your experiences, your comforts and supports to one another, exhorting one another, and provoking one another to love and to good works', and the 'treasuring up [of] those Christian experiences you hear' from others as habits of 'spiritual advantage'. Christiana is greatly cheered by the history of Mr Fearing since it shows she is not alone in her spiritual difficulties. Mercy also finds that 'something of him has also dwelt in me'. How efficacious such sharing of experience might be is illustrated in *Grace Abounding*, where Bunyan's conversion begins when he comes across 'three or four poor women' of Bedford 'sitting at a door in the Sun, and talking about the things of God'. It was their talk of 'a new birth, the work of God on their hearts' which brought home to him the inadequacy of his own profession. No wonder that when a '*profitable question*' is proposed for discussion in *The Pilgrim's Progress* it proves to concern the life of a neighbour. It was the way of Quakers' missions, as of their books, to allow their experiences to speak to others, to evangelize by declaring 'what the Lord hath done for my soul' (Ps. lxvi.16).[52]

Hence derive not only autobiographical testimonies but also the obituaries commonly included in funderal sermons, the narratives of incidents in other people's lives which serve as anecdotal illustrations and cautionary tales in sermons (and in *Mr. Badman*), biographies such as Baxter's of his wife (1681) and Matthew Henry's of his father Philip (1698), and biographical collections such as those compiled by Baxter's friend, the Presbyterian Samuel Clarke. The primary aims of such accounts are exemplary and commemorative, and hortative. The former tends to the representation of typical models for imitation, but the latter, if it is to reach the reader, demands a contrary thrust. Protestant hagiography does not, as Baxter insists in his preface to Samuel Clarke's *The Lives of Sundry Eminent Persons* (1683), depict 'Rarities' but what has been attained, and may be attained, by ordinary people. In the preface to his life of Philip Henry, Matthew Henry acknowledged that his father was neither called nor inclined 'to any very publick scene of action. He was none of the forward men of the age … The world scarce knew that there was such a man in it.' This, however, is the recommendation of his biography: it 'is the more adapted to general use' because of the 'low and narrow sphere' of his father's life, and, especially, because it consists 'not in the extacies and raptures of zeal and devotion, – which are looked upon rather as admirable than imitable, – but, in the long series of an even, regular provident, and well-ordered conversation, which he had in the world and in the ordinary business of it'.[53] The consequent attention to commonplace details tends to individualize the subject, and so renders a particular, rather than (or as well as) a typical, experience of grace. Nonconformist historiography similarly interpreted the past through individual experience. Penn's preface can hence present Fox's autobiographical *Journal* not as one man's partial and imperfect recollections of the past, but as a valid historical vindication of Quakerism. The biographical strategy of Calamy's 1702 *Abridgment* of Baxter's *Reliquiae*, and its successors, similarly insists on the primacy of individual testimony. Ordinary lives have become a fit literary subject, challenging by their very ordinariness the escapades of the picaro and the rogue.

Companionship sought merely out of spiritual self-interest would be as cold-hearted as an exclusively exemplary literature of commemoration and as unwelcome as charity performed solely as duty. That is not the note struck by nonconformist writing. Penn ends his preface to Fox's *Journal* thus: 'I have done when I have left this short epitaph to his name. *Many sons have done virtuously in this day, but dear George thou excellest them all.*' Penn's rephrasing of, and addition to, Proverbs xxxi.29 transforms his biblical allusion into the entirely personal testimony of a friend. The fellowship of the Quakers depended upon affection sustained by literally meeting each other, as well as upon the inner enlightenment of silent worship. Though 'the unity and fellowship of the children of light and truth doth not simply consist in their outward nearness, company or presence', yet 'their being together in the outward ... doth greatly conduce and contribute to increase and strengthen their unity, and to make their fellowship and communion of life'. Families which were not bound together by affection could not aspire to the ideal of being 'little churches' (I Cor. xvi.19). Marvell had celebrated Cromwell as a devoted, even a doting, father, and it is the unashamed enjoyment of intimacy and domesticity which plays through Lucy Hutchinson's account of her childhood, of her courtship by and the early years of her marriage to John Hutchinson, through Baxter's *Breviate* of his wife's life, through Heywood's journals, through Matthew Henry's extended description of life in his childhood home, and through Part II of *The Pilgrim's Progress*.[54] It is there too, as has been noticed, in Milton's paradise. Against Satan's experiential hell is set not Eden but the experience of mutual, human love: Adam and Eve are 'Imparadised in one another's arms/The happier Eden'.[55]

In short, nonconformist literature welcomes and celebrates human affection and love, amongst Christians, between friends and within families. Only a delight and trust in human love can explain that paternal, familial and sexual imagery of the heart used to express the intimacy of God's relationship to his creatures of which several examples have occured in the course of this study.[56] For Howe, this is an essential feature of people's nature:

No one, whose nature is not overrun with barbarism, would entertain the discovery of the harmless, innocent love, though it were not profitable to us, even of a creature like ourselves, otherwise than with complacency, – yea, though it were a much inferior (even a brute) creature. Men are pleased to behold love expressing itself towards them in a child, in a poor neighbour, in an impotent servant, – yea, in their horse or dog.

To know God is to enjoy his 'intimate acquaintance' as 'a friend'; it is to be 'an associate of the Most High, a domestic'; 'no more a stranger, a foreigner, but of his own household; to live wholly upon the plentiful provisions, and under the happy order and government of his family'.[57] As towards God, so between individuals; we declare ourselves by the quality of our relationship to others. 'Men are really what they are relatively' wrote Gouge, a saying often heard from Philip Henry, repeated by his son, and used by the Presbyterian George Swinnock, ejected vicar of Great Kimble, Buckinghamshire.[58]

Though there would for some years be a good deal of poetic lust ('There's something Genrous in meer lust' observed Rochester), the Restoration exiled love as a serious literary subject with remarkable swiftness and finality. Love is the chief butt of Restoration comedy, an emotion beneath a lady or a gentleman, a vulgarity, a delusion, a matter merely of sexual desire or a sport. It later creeps back via the novel, but what had been *the* subject for Spenser, Sidney, Shakespeare and Donne is deemed unworthy of poetry for over a century. And even among these earlier poets (save Spenser) and the lesser Elizabethans, love has little to do with enduring relationships, and even less with marriage (except as contracted to the frustration of the lover.). Donne's tense is the present; the brief moment of his love poems is fleetingly suspended between immaturity and senility, deceit and betrayal, hope and despair. 'Love is a growing, or full constant light;/And his first minute, after noon, is night': and, in love as in nature, night will come.[59] Donne cannot bring himself to mention a wife, and no more could Restoration wits and dramatists, save as an object of mockery. In this context of uncertainty, deceit and lust, nonconformists speak with a single, clear and confident voice of the joy of sexuality and the enduring bond of love, from Lucy Hutchinson's tart remark that Edward the Confessor was 'sainted for his ungodly chastitie' to Milton's celebration of sexual and marital love in *Paradise Lost*. Milton's angels enjoy coitus in heaven, while Satan knows only 'fierce desire ... Still unfulfilled'. Since 'In solitude/What happiness', nonconformist protagonists are almost invariably husbands and wives.[60] The relationship is indeed, a chief means of grace. Christiana is drawn to pilgrimage by her love for her husband, self-recrimination at her treatment of him and the encouragement of his example: 'she had lost her Husband, and ... the loving bond of that Relation was utterly broken betwixt them ... This therefore of her Husband did cost her many a Tear.' As Christiana is moved by love for her husband, so Mercy joins her because 'her Bowels yearned over *Christiana*' (where 'bowels' is to be understood in the obsolete sense of the seat of tender feeling and affection). When, at their departure, Mercy grieves for her relations left behind, Christiana replies:

> Bowels becometh Pilgrims. And thou dost for thy Friends, as my good *Christian* did for me when he left me; he mourned for that I would not heed or regard him, but his Lord and ours did gather up his Tears and put them into his Bottle and now both I, and thou, and these my sweet Babes, are reaping the Fruit and Benefit of them.[61]

There are those who find Christian's abandonment of his family selfish and unfeeling.[62] It is not unfeeling. Christian, like Bunyan himself when he resolved to face imprisonment, is a married man with four children. To leave them is no easier for him than for Bunyan himself – 'as the pulling the flesh from my bones'. At the Palace Beautiful, Christian weeps for loss of them: the marginal note reads 'Christian's love to his Wife and Children'.[63] And Christiana's words show that the decision was not a selfish one either. By refusing to put creaturely love before love to God, Christian secures the salvation of his family: they follow him. Taken together, the two departures reveal not a contempt for human love but a recognition of its strength, an emblem of its sanctifying power and a statement of its subordinate status. For it is subordinate: no nonconformist recommended unconditional surrender to it. That is Adam's sin in *Paradise Lost*, and it earns from the Son the uncompromising severity of 'Was she thy God, that her thou didst obey?' This is however, no more a repudiation of the claims of human love than is Christian's flight from the City of Destruction. To our own age, as to Milton's, to propose moderation ('In loving thou dost well, in passion not') appears cold comfort. It is not. Adam's lines as he takes the apple wring from us – and are meant to wring from us – a heartfelt response; they prompt – and are meant to prompt – approval of this self-sacrificing fidelity as the highest form of love. Those critics who, feeling the pull of these lines, infer that because we succumb to the temptation emotionally to endorse Adam's decision, Milton must also have done so, do not, as they suppose, give the lie to the epic: they merely deny Milton a dramatic imagination.[64] He sees clearly enough that such devotion is not selfless but selfish ('How can I live without thee … '). The fidelity in *Paradise Lost* which is in fact ignoble though it appears noble recognizes, like the desertion in *The Pilgrim's Progress* which is noble though it appears ignoble, that absolute devotion to any human being brings not blissful freedom but enslavement. It is satiety which bedevils the century's literature of love. In nonconformist writing, 'all the charities' of family life are released by the welcome it accords affection, love and sexuality as gifts and means, not appetites and ends. It can depict real homes because home is elsewhere.[65]

Chapter 8 'Answerable style'
the linguistic dissent of nonconformity

I have also spoken by the prophets
and I have multiplied visions, and used
similitudes, by the ministry of the
prophets

Hos. xii.10

I   A PLAIN STYLE?

In his *The Arte of Prophecying*, published in Latin in 1592 and Englished in 1607, the Elizabethan Puritan and 'English Calvin' William Perkins wrote that style should be

> both simple and perspicuous, fit both for the peoples understanding, and to expresse the Majestie of the Spirit ... Wherefore neither the words of arts, nor Greeke and Latine phrases and quirkes must be intermingled in the sermon 1. They disturbe the minde of the auditors, that they cannot fit those things which went afore with those that follow. 2. A strange word hindreth the understanding of those things that are spoken. 3. It drawes the minde away from the purpose to some other matter. Here also the telling of tales and all profane and ridiculous speeches must bee omitted.[1]

This passage strikes the authentic note of Puritan stylistics and encapsulates what literary historians have come to recognize as the Puritan contribution to the development of seventeenth-century prose style: it set the virtues of clarity, simplicity and plainness against the rhetorical excess of Euphuism, the luxuriance of 'tropical' romance styles, the syntactical sophistication of Ciceronianism and the erudite ingenuity of the metaphysicals. It did so on the three grounds touched on by Perkins: the need to communicate effectively and intelligibly ('fit for the peoples understanding' (Rom. x.15)); the obligation to avoid arrogant self-display which attracts attention to manner rather than matter ('fit for the Majestie of the Spirit', alluding to I Cor. ii.4–5); and the desirability of treating holy things with due awe and seriousness ('ridiculous speeches must be omitted' (Prov. xiii.16, xv.21)). [2]

This was not, in the main Puritan tradition at least, to recommend either negligence, a complete reliance upon inspiration and the power of an unprepared, extempore discourse, or infelicity and dullness. 'If any man thinke', wrote Perkins, 'that by this means barbarisme should be brought into pulpits, hee must understand that the Minister may, yea and must privately use at his liberty the arts, Philosophy and variety of reading.' '*Sudden conceits of the minde not digested, must needs be rawly deliuered*', warned Richard Bernard in *The Faithfull Shepheard* (1607). 'The best wit readiest to conceiue, the firmest memoirie to retaine, nor the volublest tongue to utter ... may not exempt a man from studying, reading, writing sometime, meditation and continuall praier.' It was, however, to insist that these preparatory studies should be directed to the end of lucidity and directness. John Wilkins wrote in his *Ecclesiastes: or, A Discourse concerning the Gift of Preaching as it fals under the Rules of Art* (1646) that style 'must be plain and naturall, not being darkned with the affectation of Scholasticall harshnesse, or Rhetoricall flourishes. Obscurity in the discourse is an argument of ignorance in the minde. The greatest learning is to be seen in the greater plainnesse.'[3]

The homiletic, and, by extension, stylistic practice based upon such precepts and axioms was regarded by nonconformists as exemplary. In his biographies of earlier Puritans Samuel Clarke invariably singled out for mention their practical inclination towards plainness in their sermons. John Dod, for example, would not leave 'the text untill he had made it plain to the meanest capacity ... He took great care to speak to the meanest capacity, and to feed the Lambs, saying, he must stoop to the lowest capacity.' Robert Harris 'could preach with a learned plainness, and had learned to conceal his Art'. 'He used to say, that a Preacher had three Books to study, 1. The Bible. 2. Himself. 3. The People.' James Ussher, Archbishop of Armagh, rejected 'that frothy way of preaching by strong lines ... wherein he reproved, and decried the *Corinthian* vanity in this kinde'. As Ussher applied himself '*to the capacities of a common Auditory*' so, too, the 'method' of William Gouge's sermons was equally 'clear ... his expressions plain, always delivering the solid points of Divinity in a familiar stile to the capacity of the meanest'.[4]

It is hence not remarkable that we can illustrate a comparable distaste for erudite and artistic ostentation and an equal commitment to plainness from among the nonconformists themselves. Bunyan reproved learned ministers who, instead of preaching directly 'the simplicity of the Gospel', 'do tickle the ears of their hearers with vain Philosophy' and 'nuzzle up your people in ignorance with *Aristotle, Plato*, and the rest of your heathenish Philosophers'. In *Grace Abounding* he neither adopts a high style nor uses rhetorical embellishment since 'God *did not play in convincing of me; the* Devil *did not play in tempting of me ... wherefore I may not play in my relating of them, but be plain and simple, and lay down the thing as it was.*' In *The Pilgrim's Progress* fine words are associated with hypocrisy, and both, often, with elevated social status: By-ends comes from Fair-speech and has married into high society.[5] Baxter argued the practical Puritan case for plainness throughout his career. Thomas Gouge recommended that discourse should be suited to the hearers' capacity and that, while 'Pleasantness of converse' was welcome, 'liberty of wit' should be restrained. Howe scorned 'rhetorical flourishes, a set of fine words, handsome cadences and periods, fanciful representations, little tricks and pieces of wit ... pitiful quibbles and gingles, inversions of sentences, the pedantic rhyming of words, yea, and an affected tone' as 'things that are neither capable of gratifying the Christian nor the man'. William Bates deplored 'The Affectation of Wit and fla[u]nting Eloquence [which] frustrates the End of Preaching'. He praised Manton, as he praised Baxter and Thomas Jacombe, for a style which 'was natural and free, clear and eloquent, quick and purposeful', without 'vain Ornaments' and 'vain Ostentation of Wit'.[6]

Such a preference might, indeed, be advanced as grounds for nonconformity. An anonymous tract from 1700 allows that the conformist clergy are learned but 'That there is generally in our Parish-Churches, more solid, plain, scriptural, and practical Preaching, fitted for the Capacity and Remembrance of the generality of Men and Women that come to hear, than there is in the *Nonconformists Meetings*, will not easily be allowed by any that commonly heareth both.' If, then, Christians 'cannot ordinarily communicate in all Ordinances with their Parish Ministers, and be equally instructed in the Truths of God, or Hear what they understand, or in such Methods as they can remember ... I think *it is* worth their while, and no Sin against God, to go where they may'. [7]

If, however, we turn from the nonconformists' own account of themselves to conformists' comments upon their style it is to find the boot on the other foot. The nonconformists' want of plainness is the very charge preferred time and again. Conformists present themselves as the guardians of lucidity and perspicuity against the extravagant excesses of the nonconformists' metaphorical and figurative indulgence, imprecise and obscurely evocative phraseology, and wild flights of fancy. Nonconformist writing emerges from their accounts as something altogether too heated and luxuriant for plain tastes. The anonymous *Short Examination* cited above was written in reply to George Hascard's *A Discourse about Edification: In Answer to a Question, Whether it is Lawful for any Man to forsake the Communion of the Church of England, and go to the Separate Meetings, because he can better Edifie there?* (1683). In the course of returning a negative answer to his question, Hascard offers a very different characterization of nonconformist conventicles. Their preference is for 'speculative Notions' rather than 'Edifying Truths', and their desire is to have their hearts 'warm'd' and fancies 'gratifi'd' by 'dark and obscure Discourses'. Their 'silly and phantastick' preachers have but to 'Tickle their imaginations with conjectural Discourses' to win applause. They take

> sudden heats and warmth for true Edification, when melting tones, affectionate expressions, solemn looks, and behaviour, passion and vehemency, and other Arts have play'd upon the fancy, and put their constitutions into different motions, some have thought themselves so strangely Edif'd, as though it was the impulse and powerful acting of the Divine Spirit; which many times is no more than a bright or lowering day can do, acting on the Animal Spirits, and a Dose of Physick will do the same.[8]

Similarly when, in 1700, George Keith bade farewell to Quakerism and accepted ordination by Henry Compton, Bishop of London, he emerged, by his own account, not only from fanciful delusion into rational common sense but also from stylistic obfuscation into lucidity and coherence. Far from being plain, Quaker style is, he alleges, a florid fraud (a fraud because florid) designed to prevent clear thinking and so to maintain the absurdities of the Friends' profession:

> I have found, and have now just Reason to acknowledge, that the greatest part of my Religion, when among them, was made up of senseless and absurd Notions, (which I am now ashamed of) they being (as we were wont) set forth in unintelligible fantastical Phrases; by (as 2 Pet. 3.16 saith) wresting Scripture to our own Destruction: tho' I indeed then, (as well as they) accounted it, the heights of Spirituality and Mystery, upon which we valued and boasted our selves, as the only Knowing and Spiritual People: When as Thanks be to God, it is known now to me, and all Discerning Persons that there was, and is nothing in such pretended Heights and Spiritualities, but only vain Imagination and Dreaming; which are dangerous Deceits. For as the light of Reason and Sense dispels the vain Images of Dreams: So these admitted, would and will cure all Phantastical Impostures and Delusions, for which cause they, as well as I, formerly declared against nothing so vehemently as Reason, under the notion of Carnal, and so an Enemy to the Spirit.[9]

This contention that the irrationality of nonconformity was sustained by the subterfuge of a style which preferred 'fantastical Phrases' to lucidity was by 1700 decidedly *déjà vu*. Conformists had since 1660 been claiming that if only nonconformists would think and write clearly the preposterousness of their position would become plain. In an Oxford University sermon of 29 July 1660 Robert South, a former undergraduate at Owen's Christ Church and afterwards the University's Public Orator and a Canon of Christ Church, had sounded very much like an advocate of Puritan style: 'All vain, luxuriant Allegories, rhiming *Cadencies* of similary Words, are such pitiful Embellishments of Speech, as serve for nothing but to embase Divinity.' Sermons should be carefully prepared, suited to their hearers, plain and natural in expression. But when South defines 'wit' it becomes apparent that, to his mind, Puritans fail to attain this ideal quite as lamentably as metaphysical court preachers:

> Wit in Divinity is nothing else, but Sacred Truths suitably expressed. 'Tis not Shreds of *Latin* or *Greek*, nor a *Deus dixit*, and a *Deus benedixit*, nor those little Quirks, or Divisions into ὅτι, the διότι, and the καθότι, or the *Egress, Regress,* and *Progress,* and other such Stuff (much like the Style of a Lease) that can properly be called *Wit* ... Nor, Is the Contrary of it to be at all more endured in those, who cry up their mean, heavy, careless, and insipid Way of handling Things Sacred, as the only Spiritual and Evangelical Way of Preaching, while they charge all their crude Incoherences, sawcy Familiarities with God, and nauseous Tautologies, upon the Spirit prompting such Things to them, and that as the most elevated, and seraphick Heights of Religion. Both these sorts ... are absolutely to be exploded; and it is hard to judge, which of them deserves it most ... the *Deus dixit,* and the *Deus benedixit,* could not be accounted Wit ... so neither can the whimsical cant of *Issues, Products, Tendencies, Breathings, Indwellings, Rollings, Recumbencies,* and Scriptures misapplyed be accounted Divinity.[10]

South's scorn for Puritan diction is surpassed only by his contempt for the radicals' reliance upon inspiration. Extempore sermons 'they call a *saving Way* of Preaching, as it must be confessed to be a Way to save much Labour, and nothing else that I know of!' In a 1668 Christ Church sermon, South again recommends 'Great clearness and Perspicuity', 'An unaffected Plainness and Simplicity' and, noting that apostolic preaching was 'in the plainest and most intelligible Language', 'easy, obvious and familiar; with nothing in it strained or far fetched', he claims 'there is a certain Majesty in Plainness': 'All Dress and Ornament supposes Imperfection ... Gaudery is a pitiful and a mean thing.' Once again, however, he associates nonconformist preaching not with such plainness but with an uncritical reliance upon the Spirit which leads to '*Lies* and *Nonsense*': 'Christ defend his Church from such inspired Impostors.'[11]

Imposture is the burden of the strictures on nonconformist style in the *Continuation* of *A Friendly Debate between a Conformist and a Nonconformist* (1669) by Simon Patrick, afterwards Bishop successively of Chichester and Ely, and of the criticisms of Owen's *A Discourse of Communion with God* (1657) made by William Sherlock, afterwards a prebend of St Paul's. So is it, too, of Anthony à Wood's remarks that in that same book Owen

> doth strangely affect in ambiguous and uncouth words, canting, mystical and unintelligible phrases to obscure sometimes the plainest and most obvious truths: And at other times he endeavours by such a mist and cloud of sensless terms to draw a kind of vail over the most erroneous doctrines.[12]

In his *Essay Concerning Preaching* (1678), Joseph Glanvill, a fellow of the Royal Society and, though an admirer of Baxter, a conformist polemicist against nonconformists in his *The Zealous and Impartial Protestant* (1681), advocated, as South had done, 'Plain, Practical, Methodical and Affectionate' preaching, a 'manly unaffectedness, and simplicity of Speech', since 'plainness is for ever the best Eloquence'. Glanvill, however, can no more discern these qualities in nonconformist sermons than could South. He finds there the 'foolish affectations' of such phrases as 'roll upon *Christ*, close with *Christ*, get into *Christ*' which 'rouse people up, but convey no knowledge to them'. He is distressed, too, by the vulgarity of nonconformist style, 'a certain sordidness, which though Ignorant People may like as plain, and familiar Preaching; yet 'tis such a familiarity as breeds contempt. Such is the use of vulgar Proverbs, and homely Similitudes, and rude clownish Phrases.' The plainness of which Glanvill approves as 'the best Character of Speech' is not the same as 'Bluntness; this degenerates into sordidness, and rusticity'.[13] That Bunyan was thus degenerate was the burden of such comments as were subsequently made on his style. Measured by Augustan canons it appeared to be a 'prophanation', the work of a Grub Street hack quite lacking in 'sublimity', a view which culminated in David Hume's assertion in 1757 that regard for Bunyan was proof merely of bad taste.[14]

It appears, then, that, as Roger Pooley has observed, 'The terms of the argument between Puritans and Laudians in the 1630s (plainness versus ostentation) are almost exactly reversed in the 1660s and 1670s, when it is the new Anglicans who emphasize plainness against what they see as Puritan and nonconformist excess.'[15] This conviction that they were on the side of common sense, clarity and good taste enabled conformists to characterize (and stigmatize) nonconformists as literary and linguistic, as well as religious, dissenters, distinguishable by an abuse of language which was an affront to all who valued plain, rational and civil discourse. Their style was neither civil nor sensible, but vulgar, indulgent and idiosyncratic. This was most glaringly the case in the Quaker habit of addressing all individuals by the familiar 'thou' rather than by the polite (and, in strict grammar, plural) form of the pronoun, 'you'.[16] In 1660 Fox, John Stubbs and Benjamin Furly defended this plain form of address with a wealth of linguistic evidence in *A Battle-Door for Teachers & Professors to Learn Singular and Plural; You to Many, and Thou to One*.[17] Their adherence to this practice in the Restoration world of elaborately formal and self-consciously ostentatious manners marked out Quakers from society and identified them as members of a separate group with an alternative culture. It was, as Penn describes it, a 'piece of our nonconformity to the world that renders us very clownish to the breeding of it'.[18]

This was, however, only the most obvious example of a thorough-going linguistic nonconformity. The Quaker's religion, wrote the conformist Samuel Austin, 'is, *Not to speak like his Neighbours*'. His '*Babylonish Rhetorick*' consists in 'a *Rhapsody* of oft repeated *Non-sense*; and when he has darkned your understanding with a cloud of insignificant *Babble*, he cries, *Ah! friends mind the Light.*' And what was true of Quakers was true of nonconformists generally. In *The Zealous Protestant* Glanvill pointed to the nonconformists' linguistic habits as defining their separate status:

> *all* are zealous for their particular Conceits, *all* call their own imaginations by the most sacred names, *Light, God's Truth, Gospel Ways, Holy Mysteries, Daunings, Illuminations, Refinings*, and a world more of such fondness; by which they are infinitely puff'd up in their own Phancies, as the only *Knowing*, the only *Spiritual* Christians.[19]

L'Estrange, who could be percipient in his polemics, similarly recognized the powerfully cohesive force of the nonconformists' language:

> Mr *Baxters* Works will be as good as a *Non-conformists Dictionary* to us: and assist the World toward the Understanding of the *Holy Dialect*, in a Wonderful manner. For the *Purity of the Gospel*; the *ways of Christ*: the *Ordinances of the Lord*; the *Power of Godlynesse*; the *Foundations of Faith*; *the Holy Discipline*: A *Blessed Reformation*, &c. These are *Words*, and *Expressions*, that signify quite another thing to *Them*, then they do to *Us. Faithful Pastors; Laborious Ministers; Heavenly Guides; Zealous Protestants*; The *Upright in the land*: *Humble Petitioners; Just Priviledges; Higher Powers; Glorious Kings*; Holy *Covenanting unto the Lord*, &c. This is not to be taken now, as the *Language Currant* of the *Nation*, but only as a Privy *Cypher of Intelligence* betwixt Themselves, and the *Cant*, or *Jargon* of the *Party*. Nay, they fly from us in their *Speech*, their *Manners*, their *Meaning*, as well as in their *Profession*. The very *Christ-Crosse* in the *Horn-Book* is as much a Scandal to them, as the *Crosse* in *Baptisme*; and they make it a point of *Honour* to maintain the Freedome of their

Own Tongue; in token, that they are not as yet a *Conquer'd Nation*.[20]

L'Estrange here recognizes what we heard Penn say: that nonconformity to the world involves rejection of its ways and manners, of which speech and literary style are part. The language of nonconformity could not conform to a model which expressed values from which it dissented. The distinction between *'Them'* and *'Us'* hence depended on, and was expressed by, a style which defied that *'Currant* of the *Nation'*.

2   'THE THING AS IT WAS'

And yet, that they were the plain style men was a conviction held by nonconformists quite as tenaciously as by conformists. How can this paradox be resolved? It is the usual way for diverging literary movements to distinguish themselves with distinctive terms and titles: how did it come about that in this dispute both parties laid claim to the same title? Part of the answer lies, of course, in the word 'plain' itself, which, as Glanvill remarked, is a term 'of great latitude'. A great variety of styles may shelter beneath it. And when we deal with a movement as individualistic as nonconformity, that variety will be particularly pronounced. When he commended Bates's 'inimitably polite and fine' style, Howe cautioned against imitation of it since what was 'natural' from Bates would be unnatural, and so unconvincingly forced, from another, 'style being to any man as appropriate, upon the matter, as his visage or voice: and as immediately depending upon the temper of the mind, – in conjunction with fancy, as that is more or less brisk, lively and vigorous, – as the other do on the complexion of the body or the disposition of the organs of speech'.[21] The inclination of nonconformity was to allow such particular tempers freer expression than did the conservative and conformist tendencies of episcopalians. There is consequently no such thing as a 'nonconformist style'. No single epithet could encompass Howe's own inelegancy, Bate's fluency, Penn's poised and often aphoristically pointed lucidity, Baxter's unpretentious and direct urgency, Owen's ponderous comprehensiveness, Fox's visionary fervour and admonitory trenchancy, or the shifting registers of Bunyan's prose, colloquial, biblical, theological, personal, narrative; nor do any of these phrases adequately represent the variety within the writings of any one individual. It would consequently be entirely possible to assemble extracts to prove nonconformist writing was plain, or, equally, that it was not.

Nevertheless, we can still attach some significance to the word 'plain' as used by conformists and nonconformists and understand how both could, quite sincerely and justifiably, appeal to it as a stylistic ideal. The situation came about because they were not actually arguing about style at all, or rather, were arguing about it only as a consequence of a deeper disagreement. The opposing premises upon which that disagreement was founded generated contrary tendencies in the writing of each party, but they also bred differing notions of what constituted plainness. The passages which have been quoted from conformists do not prefer a plain over an ornate style *per se* but as the fit (and inevitable) form of expression for a particular set of intellectual, religious and ethical ideals. Their irritation with nonconformist writing is not exclusively, or even primarily, an aesthetic distaste for its style but a reproof to its way of thinking, a way of thinking which to conformists seems not to deserve the name of 'thought' at all. The style of nonconformists is berated as a glaring example of the culpable consequences of erroneous conceptions. 'Suitable expression', 'nothing strained or far-fetched', 'clearness and perspicuity', 'unaffected plainness', 'manly unaffectedness' are preferred to 'affectionate expression', 'dark and obscure Discourses', 'fantastical Phrases', 'whimsical cant', 'ambiguous and uncouth words', since the former are the natural expression of 'obvious truths' apparent to 'discerning Persons' by the 'light of Reason'; the latter are the product of 'sudden heats', 'passion and vehemency', 'Animal spirits', 'imagination and fancy', 'absurd Notions' and 'Delusions'. The one is a rational demonstration of 'Edifying Truths'; the other an expression of 'only vain Imagination and Dreaming', mere 'lies and nonsense'. Conformists, in short, could not understand what nonconformists were talking about; and if their writing did not make sense, it could not be plain. The debate over plainness thus resolves itself into a debate over what constituted 'sense', what 'senselessness'; what was affected, what genuine. It was, in fact, a debate about the nature of truth.

This fundamental disagreement was recognized by Samuel Parker to be at the heart of the debate over style. When, in his *Discourse of Ecclesiastical Politie* (1670), he writes of stylistic differences he ascribes them to conflicting theological emphases: conformists locate the essence of Christianity in the moral life; nonconformists locate it in the experience of grace. Morality is, in Parker's view, commonsensical and universal, and therefore susceptible of plain and rational demonstration; grace is an individual's illusion, sustainable only by reliance upon vague, and vaguely emotive, language which refuses to define facts:

> And what is it than Men set up against Morality, but a few figurative Expressions of it self, that without it are utterly insignificant? 'Tis not enough (say they) to be completely Vertuous, unless we have Grace too: But when we have set aside all manner of Vertue, let them tell me what remains to be call'd *Grace*, and give me any Notion of it distinct from all Morality, that consists in the right order and government of our Actions in all our Relations, and so comprehends all our Duty: and therefore if Grace be not included in it, 'tis but a Phantasm, and an Imaginary thing. So that if we strip those Definitions that some Men of late have bestowed upon it, of Metaphors and Allegories, it will plainly signifie nothing but a vertuous temper of Mind.

Although he mocks, Parker's derision is based upon an acute perception: that it is their refusal to identify 'true and real Righteousness' with a morally blameless life which gives rise to the 'Metaphors and Allegories' of nonconformist style: they have found out, in lieu of Moral Vertue, a *Spiritual Divinity*, that is made up of nothing else but certain Trains and Schemes of effeminate Follies and illiterate Enthusiasms; and instead of Sober Devotion, a more spiritual and intimate way of Communion with God, that in truth consists in little else but meeting together in private to prate Phrases, make Faces, and rail at Carnal Reason (*i.e.* in their sense all sober and sincere use of our Understandings in Spiritual Matters) whereby they have effectually turn'd all Religion into unaccountable Fansies and Enthusiasms, drest it up with pompous and empty Schemes of Speech, and so embrace a few gaudy Metaphors and Allegories, instead of the substance of true and real Righteousness. And herein lies the most material difference between the sober Christians of the Church of *England*, and our modern Sectaries, That we express the Precepts and Duties of the Gospel in plain and intelligible Terms, whilst they trifle them away by childish Metaphors and Allegories, and will not talk of Religions but in barbarous and uncouth Similitudes.[22]

Parker is quite right: the nonconformists did propose 'a more spiritual and intimate way of Communion with God'. This 'enthusiasm', as he called it, was for Parker imposture all, a fraud fabricated by deceitful and deceiving language. For nonconformists, the fraud was Parker's plainness and moralism. Marvell, referring to Parker as 'his Morality' rather than 'his Grace', replied to him, much as did Howe to the deists, that Parker's view reduced God from a living deity to a mere abstract sanction for certain forms of behaviour: 'if Grace be resolv'd into Morality, I think a man may almost as well make God too to be only a Notional and Moral existence.' The answer to Parker's question 'let them tell me what remains to be call'd Grace' lay in the intimacy of the saving relationship, the personal response of an individual. For Sherlock, the biblical metaphors which describe 'the Relation and Union between Christ and Christians, do primarily refer to the Christian Church, no to every individual Christian': 'the Union of particular Christians to Christ is by means of their Union to the Christian Church.' For Owen, they describe something far more intimate. Where Sherlock argues it is 'unsafe to found Religion upon a pretended acquaintance with Christ's Person', Owen insists that just such an 'acquaintance' is the essence of the Christian Life. I Corinthians vi. 17 was frequently cited by nonconformists as evidence of, in Bates's phrase, the '*Vital Bond*' between Christ and each individual believer.[23]

To be plain was consequently, for nonconformists, to declare not 'Precepts and Duties' but 'what I smartingly do feel'. Precepts and duties of course follow, but as the consequence not the condition of grace. Keach's allegorial figure True Godliness has a 'friend and honest neighbour Morality, one that I love very well', but not one who would 'say his name is True Godliness' as the character Legalist supposes. Just so, in *Truth and Innocence Vindicated* (1671), his reply to Parker, Owen insisted that nonconformists 'Moral duties do esteem, commend, count as necessary in religion as any men', but they do not hold that such works are 'available unto the salvation of the souls of men': 'They say, moreover, that for men to rest upon their performance of these moral duties for their justification before God, is but to set up their own righteousness through an ignorance of the righteousness of God, for we are freely justified by his grace.' Parker, in fact, is Bunyan's Ignorance.[24]

Hence, whereas 'plainness' meant for the conformist the instruction of others by the clear exposition of moral duties, for the nonconformist to be plain was not to appeal dispassionately to universals but to encourage others by being authentic, true to the experience of grace within oneself. Plain style was for the former explicatory and discursive, for the latter confessional and hortatory. It was what Heywood called 'the language of my heart'. We heard Bunyan say that he took up a plain style to recount truthfully *'the thing as it was'*: that 'thing' was not an ethical code but an autobiographical fact; to describe it was to write, in the Quaker terminology of William Britten, not 'by hearsay ... [but] upon experience from Christ within me'. Thus was it possible for 'the conflict between Puritan soteriology and Anglican moralism' to present itself, as Dr Pooley has said, as 'the conflict between two plain styles'.[25]

3 'FINE METAPHORS AND GLITTERING ALLUSIONS'

Parker's reiterated taunting of the nonconformists with their 'Metaphors and Allegories' usefully narrows the area of discussion. Clearly, he felt it was their analogical method which distinguished their style and, from his point of view, invalidated it. He goes on to recommend 'an Act of Parliament to abridge Preachers the use of fulsom and lushious Metaphors' since this 'might perhaps be an effectual Cure of all our present Distempers':

> Let not the Reader smile at the odness of the Proposal: For were Men obliged to speak Sense as well as Truth, all the swelling *Mysteries of Fanaticism* would immediately sink into flat and empty Nonsense; and they would be ashamed of such jejune and ridiculous Stuff as their admired and most profound Notions would appear to be, when they want the Varnish of fine Metaphors and glittering Allusions.[26]

Imagery was under attack throughout the later seventeenth century. Parker's remarks take their place beside the distrust of metaphor felt by such philosophers as Hobbes and by such scientists as Robert Boyle. As is well known, this repudiation of figurative language became the orthodoxy of the Royal Society in its *History* (1667) by Thomas Sprat, Bishop of Rochester.[27]

The scientific conviction that truth is objective, a fact independent of the individual who observes it and incomprehensible only in so far as it has not yet yielded to rational investigation, characterizes the temper of the conformist plain-style men. Since Christianity does not consist in personal conviction and private illumination it is, for Parker and Sherlock, not mysterious either. It is a matter of common (that is, universal and natural) sense; an affair of external and demonstrable duties. In his reply to Parker's *Ecclesiastical Politie*, Owen wondered (rhetorically) 'what if the things condemned as "fulsome metaphors" prove to be scriptural expressions of gospel mysteries?' That is the phrase which Sherlock's *Discourse Concerning the Knowledge of Jesus Christ* (1674, licensed by Parker) repeated derisively from Owen's *Discourse of Communion with God*, and we have heard both Parker and Glanvill pick it up. 'Mystery' is one of the features of nonconformist religion with which Patrick's Conformist has no patience:

> Though you talk of *Gospel-light*, and *Gospel-discoveries*, and *Gospel-manifestations*, yet there is little or nothing all this while to be known or understood. Religion you will have to be such a Mystery, that if a man thinks he understands it, he ought to conclude he is not acquainted with it. It is a certain sign a man hath no skill in it, if he imagine he knows the plain meaning of it. It must be look't upon as a *Great something*. A thing to be star'd at and admired, but no body knows what.[28]

By contrast, for nonconformists the Bible was no lucid handbook of ethics but an inexhaustible storehouse of wonders and revelations. We recall the 'riddles of secrets' of Bunyan's Emanuel. So, too, was a life founded upon it. Keach, the opening pages of whose *Travels of True Godliness* are devoted to denying that godliness is equivalent to a moral life, puts into the mouth of his Dr Self-love (a divine) a parodic exaggeration of the position of Parker and Patrick: 'let me tell you, that natural religion is sufficient, and that what this traveller [True Godliness] saith, is but mysterious nonsense.' It is indeed a 'supernatural' mystery argues Keach (citing I Tim. iii. 16), but to those with a 'saving and experimental knowledge of God and Jesus Christ' far from nonsense. 'The great Mysteries of Godliness ... are of impossible Discovery without Revelation', wrote Bates. 'They only know [Christ]', wrote Penington, 'who are his Sheep, who are quickned and made alive by him. And this Life is a Mystery: none can understand it, but they that partake of it.' 'Truly to know Christ crucified', said his fellow Quaker George Whitehead, 'is a Mystery which none but the Children of the Light know.' It is, significantly, a character called 'Secret' who calls Christiana to pilgrimage. The name suggests divine knowledge of, and concern about, people's innermost longings and anxieties, and underlines the essentially private nature of the saints' experience of grace as they are let into the secret of God's mercy (Ps. xxv. 14; Prov. iii. 32; Matt. xiii. 35; Rom. xvi. 25).[29]

To convey that secret only metaphor would serve. What is uniquely an individual's possession, rather than the common knowledge of all, can be conveyed only be analogy. To quote Roger Pooley again, 'the crucial Reformation doctrine of justification by faith ... needs an analogical imagination to grasp it.'[30] If 'Faith is the substance of things hoped for, the evidence of things not seen' (Heb. xi. 1), it not only realizes the invisible but metamorphoses the visible. It alters the perception, both of the self and the world the self inhabits. It may still be, materially, the old, unregenerate world which is inhabited: but to the regenerate it looks and feels quite different. When Fox came to see 'all the world could do me no good' it became for him 'a briery, thorny wilderness': 'It is the great love of God to make a wilderness of that which is pleasant to the outward eye and fleshly mind.' Penington writes of 'the eye of my spirit' discerning what is invisible to physical eyes. It was not a turn of phrase peculiar to Quakers. Manton wrote on Hebrews xi. 1 that faith 'gives a being, a kind of existence, to things future and afar off, and sets them before the eyes of our mind, and gives us some sight of them, as if they were already come', and directed his readers 'with an eye of faith' to 'look within the veil [Heb. vi. 19–20] ... The great work of faith is to see him that is invisible.'[31]

All these examples resort to images, for only similitudes could convey this changed perspective. Conversion brings metaphor inevitably after it. The New England Puritan John Cotton defined a regenerate person as 'He that hath a new mind, and a new heart, new affections, new Language', for what is, in the experience of the individual, unique and unprecedented, cannot be told in the old language. It was not easy to tell. In his study of *The Holy Spirit in Puritan Faith and Experience*, Geoffrey F. Nuttall pointed out that the inner certitude of the presence of the Holy Spirit in the Puritan tradition was accompanied by a consciousness of the difficulty of describing its experience to others.[32] While yet a Quaker, Keith exclaimed

> how insufficient words, (even the best of words, Scripture words, though there were as many books of Scripture as the whole world could contain) are to reveal or to give the knowledge of God unto man, many, yea the most of things natural, and created cannot be understood by words, words being but figures, emblems or signs and representations of things, come always short of the things themselves ... can the best Orator tell a blind man, what the Sun is.

Yet words were, if not all that was available (for the witness of a reformed life could communicate tellingly), the readiest form of communication. Awareness of their insufficiency ('Humane language is not so copious as the hearts conceivings are' wrote Baxter) led not to a resigned silence but to a redoubled effort to communicate effectively. And, since the experience of conversion and the knowledge of grace it brought were not common or plain but as marvellous and mysterious as the sun to a blind man, only an analogical attempt to convey some sense of the awesome otherness and yet merciful condescension of God could be made. It is, wrote Baxter, an error to suppose 'That God may be *formally* conceived of and comprehended by man, and not only known analogically and as in glass'. 'The Notions we have of God, though *Borrowed* and *Analogical*, are not useless nor fallacious, but imperfect and such as lead to perfect knowledge. And he that will not use them, must use none.'[33]

The readiest source of such analogies was the Bible: 'Where', asked Gale, 'can we find more *proper* and *significant Symbols, Metaphors*, and other such like *Rhetorick shadows*, and *Images*, than in sacred Scripture?' Indeed, so complete was the nonconformists' sympathetic identification with biblical texts that they often ceased to express themselves by likening their situation to a biblical precedent and came instead to speak through, and in the words of, such precedents. They did not so much refer to the Bible as appropriate it. The 'intertextuality' of their writing, as current critical terminology would call it, extended to the frequent omission of quotation marks, parentheses, or italics to distinguish quotations and allusions. Biblical diction and phraseology, particularly its pastoral and apocalyptic imagery, became their diction, as we heard Owen protest to Parker. The following passage, in which William Dundas writes of his own conversion and his experimental justification for addressing his reader, is straightforward and restrained, and yet is, even so, a catena of biblical allusions:

> It is from a deep Sense of a clear and through Experience that I am moved to lay before you, having fresh in my Thoughts your Conditions; for upon that Ground did I set up my Tent for many Years, and was most unwilling to remove it, till the Lord by Fire and Sword did pursue me, and did tumble me out of all my False Rests; and whilst I was settling upon my Lees, he poured me from Vessel to Vessel, where I never had a settled *Peace* nor *Comfort*, till the Lord settled the Ark of my Soul upon the Mountains of *Ararat*; then did I see all the World (I mean those of that spirit) lying as so many Dead Corps, swimming upon the waters; and then my Soul was refreshed with the Sense of God's Love.[34]

The absence of cited texts in this passage is characteristic of Quaker writing (though less so in the 1680s and 1690s), and points to the fact that its biblical allusions are less specific references than general evocations. They conjure states of being. That 'Tent' recalls the nomadic life of Abraham (Gen. xiii. 18), but through him the unsettled condition of those who have not yet fulfilled their destiny. It suggests only temporary settlement, and so passes into the 'False Rests' which contrast with the true rest promised the saints (Heb. iii. 11, 18). 'Tumble' reduces Dundas's unregenerate confidence to the ignominy of a lazy lie-a-bed, but there lurks behind it the far more ominous power of God to 'put out' and to 'put down' the wicked (Ps. ix. 5; Luke i. 52) and to 'put all things under his feet' (Ps. viii. 6). That power comes to the fore in the phrases 'settling upon my lees' and 'from Vessel to Vessel', which set Dundas's particular experience in the larger context of God's Providence, his dealings with nations (Jer. xlviii. 11), and so leads to the allusion to Noah (Gen. viii. 4): Dundas's own world has been destroyed and saved. This movement culminates in the apocalyptic image of judgement to all the world, recalling Ezekiel's lament over Egypt (Ezek. xxxii. 6), the vengeance of the angel of the Lord on the Assyrians (II Kings xix. 35; Isa. xxxvii. 36) and Nahum's oracle of the destruction of the bloody city of Ninevah (iii. 3). The 'Lord of Fire and Sword' (Isa. lxvi. 16) who has been active in all history is yet active, in the life of nations and of such individuals as Dundas, slaying many, but saving many.

Even such a cursory reading illustrates how suggestive a style this is. Its allusiveness sets up trains of thought which reach out beyond the individual to all time and space. In that sense, nonconformist style is expansive: it begins in the experience of the individual and comes to encompass all experience. Whatever particular subject is handled is related, implicitly and allusively, to everything else. The conformist and scientific ideal of a plain style which, denuded of connotative suggestiveness and figurative vagueness, isolates, categorizes and contains phenomena, was for nonconformists reductive and simplistic. It was founded upon an inadequate conception of people as purely rational creatures, of nature as legalistically predictable and of God as a distant moral benevolence. Nonconformist style sought clarity and understanding through the interaction and relationships of phenomena, a realization of the complex nature of human beings, of nature's mystical and revelatory power and of God's immanence. It strove for the encyclopaedic comprehensiveness of a Milton, whose marvellous fecundity of reference is no mere display of erudition, nor a vaguely incantatory and evocative chanting of proper nouns,[35] but a way of setting every moment in time in a context of anticipations and reiterations, antecedents and consequences, parallels and contrasts. It discerns patterns in whatever it touches, and hence by its very manner asserts the never-ending conflict between the serpent's seed and the woman's seed (Gen. iii. 15) which underlies every event and is the driving force of history. It is, as it were, a Providential style: all-encompassing, confident that all things exemplify eternal verities and that, to the God who made all things (Prov. xxvi. 10; Acts xiv. 15) for himself (Prov. xvi. 4; Rev. iv. 11), who is in all things (Deut. iv. 7) and performs all things (Ps. lvii. 2), all things are possible (Matt. xix. 26).

Such a style deals in ultimate realities. The following passage from Keith's *Immediate Revelation* (1668) transports its reader into a realm of terrifying horrors and miraculous wonders. It contrasts in illuminating ways with the passage quoted from him on p. 243, written when he had forsaken Quakerism, and is replete with the 'fantastical Phrases' he there repudiates:

> O house of *Jacob*, O ye lost scattered sheep, who have been driven from the fold of rest, the sweet, pleasant green pasture of your souls, the still running waters, the pure sweet Christaline river of life, that issueth fresh in living streams from the fountain it self, Lo every one that thirsteth come unto the waters and drink without Money and price that your souls may live, for of a truth, the Lord God has opened unto us a fountain, a vein of life, a well-spring of life a well of living water … which who so drinketh off, will never any more drink or thirst to drink of these dead waters, that is the good words, uttered from a dead killing spirit, the waters of the Whore on which she sits, and holds forth the cup of fornications, unto the inhabitants of the earth … And now I say for your sake, ye my kinsfolk according to the flesh, my little Sister who hath no breasts, ye scattered sheep who have no pasture for your souls, but that which feedeth death, and maketh you live in the earthly corrupt principle, which is the Serpents meat, that if by any means I may provoke some of you … [to] return unto the Bishop and Shepherd of your Souls, I am drawn in the tender love of God to write unto you concerning this principle, to wit, Jesus Christ revealed and revealing in man, God, and the things of his Kingdom …[36]

In the passage previously quoted there is only one biblical citation (duly referenced); here, virtually every phrase is biblical, adopted, from Genesis to Revelation, without regard for its original context.[37] Nor is Keith at all dismayed by any incongruity between the world his imagery conjures and that of his readers' experience. This, indeed, is a common trait: Heywood can regret his 'carrying womb and dry breasts' (Hos. ix. 14); Terrill likened Mrs Hazzard to 'a he-goat before the flock' (Jer. 1.8); and the Quaker Richard Crane warned the guilty that they would not escape God's judgement by fleeing the Great Plague 'though they mount upon dromadaries for hast', which, in London, they were not likely to do.[38] The effect of Keith's phrases derives from accumulation and reiteration, but he is not thoughtlessly collecting them like magic charms. This passage does not proceed, like the later one, dialectically, but it does proceed: it first arrests attention with its opening apostrophe, then disorientates and dismays, but also entices and arouses its reader with a series of spiritual oppositions, so 'provoking' him, finally, to enter Christ's kingdom. It does not persuade by force of argument, but it does persuade, by its vivifying of spiritual states and needs and the authenticity of its personal appeal. Above all, it addresses its reader not as a coolly commonsensical individual but as a sentient being for whom water, sweetness, freshness and greenness are alluring and enticing. Spiritual longing is here no idle curiosity but a yearning as irresistible as physical appetite and thirst. When, later, Keith rejected all this as 'the vain Images of Dreams' dispelled by 'the light of Reason and Sense', he was severely restricting his conception of human nature. Flesh and blood have come to count for very little. Furthermore, no longer daunted by what had been the horrors of carnal reason and moralism, Keith has also banished fear and despair: to substitute for ecstasy a life of decent behaviour is to substitute reassuring confidence for dread of defeat in the eternal warfare. The earlier Keith is far more dramatic: the stakes are higher. The Quaker opposes not reason and nonsense but life and death, nourishment and poison, purity and corruption, love and hypocrisy, the Serpent and the Lamb of God, all and nothing, for so they are opposed from the Fall to the Last Things.

The business of Quaker style, that is to say, was to express, as they believed the Bible expressed, transcendental truths. To the confusion of categoric distinctions between the literal and the metaphorical, the real and the imaginary, it handled history and experience, as Quakers believed the Bible handled them, not as mutable circumstances but as revelations of the immutable.[39] Sometimes vehicle and tenor, biblical history and its import, were kept distinct. The behaviour of the Restoration authorities shows a heart

hardned ... far beyond *Pharaoh*, and your cruelty towards the Lords people hath far exceeded his towards *Israel*, he never imprisoned the *Israelites*, neither did he ever shut them up that they might not labour for their livelihood, but you have shut up thousands of the Lords people in *Prisons* and *Dungeons* ... O cruelty far exceeding *Egipts* bondage, and *Pharoah's* sin was, he would not have had *Israel* gone from him out of his Country ... but your sin is this, you have made a Law to force the Lords people out of their Native Country [by transportation] ... therefore as you have exeeded them in cruelty, towards the Lords people, so will the Lord multiply his Plagues upon you as upon *Egipt*, untill you be made to let *Israel* alone to Worship the Lord.[40]

This passage draws firm parallels and contrasts between Israelites/Quakers and Egyptian/Restoration authorities, but past and present, biblical history and current English affairs, remain distinct, separate exemplifications of the trials of the saints and the certainty of judgement (in the Great Plague of London and those of Egypt). Often though, and particularly in the early years of the Restoration, this temporal divide collapses as we lose touch with the specifics of the history of both Israel and England, to confront instead ultimate powers. We do so in a cascade of talismanic phrases, a rhapsody which cannot stay for syntax. This is Willaim Brend in 1662 threatening carnal powers that they

> shall be brought to nought and confounded by the Power, Dominion, and Authority of this most high born Prince of Peace, who is of the Royalty of the Infinite Majesty of the most High God, whose Word abides and endures for ever and ever, which is the seed of everlasting bliss, and in which seed all the Nations of the earth shall be blessed: and this seed shall have the Dominion, whose right alone it is, and to all the Dominions and Kingdoms of the whole World belongs; and therefore there hath been so many overturns, overturns [*sic*], and must be till he be acknowledged whose right it is, and his Royal Scepter bowed down unto, which is the Scepter of Righteousness: And therefore Nations and Kingdoms, and inhabitable parts of the whole earth, look not for peace whilst your whoredomes remain; for you are all gone a whoreing from this Noble and Renowned seed, the Covenant of God, which is his Light ... [41]

But what, Parker would say to this, am I supposed to do? For Brend, being is before doing, and to be is to transcend the natural, to be initiated into the power of the Lord. 'Dear valiant Vessels of the Host of the mighty strength of Heaven' Dewsbury addresses his fellow Quakers, with what is virtually a single compound epithet. Its alliteration holds in intimate proximity power and its recipient, transforming suffering and derided individuals into members of the company of the Most High. The authenticity of Quaker style lay in this determination to render what was seen in terms of the unseen, the only true reality. And for that, only 'fantastical Phrases' would serve. The point had been made by John Webster, who, though not a Quaker, shared many of their radical convictions. Writing of anatomy in *Academarium Examen* (1654), he rejected analytical and scientific accuracy as appropriate to theology and spiritual discourse:

> though it be grown to a mighty height of exactness, in vulgar *Anatomy* and dissection of the dead bodies of men, or the living ones of beasts, birds, and fishes; yet it is defective as to that vive and *Mystical Anatomy* that discovers the true *Schemastism* or signature of that invisible *Archeus* or *spiritus mechanicus*.[42]

4 'GLORY STAMPED ON EVERY CREATURE'

Quaker style was thus of a piece with their mission to bring people off from the 'outward', to rescue them from a merely implicit faith in the efficacy of past events. Biblical events may have happened then, but they also (and more importantly) happen now. If Quaker eschatology was 'realized', so was their style. Its consequent figurative use of the Bible – or 'spiritualizing' as it was called – was regarded with considerable suspicion by other nonconformists, as well as by conformists. Quakers were accused of undercutting the historical foundation of Christianity by neglecting, if not denying, the historicity of Christ and the factuality of the biblical record. 'Ask our *trembling Saint*', wrote Austin, 'if he believe the *Resurrection of the dead*, he shall answer *yea*, but tell you another time, he meant only an *arising from sin*; by *Heaven* and *Hell* he intends no more but several *Scenes* transacted *within us*, and abuses *holy Scripture* into a mystical *Romance*.' 'When he mentions *Christ* he does it Allegorically.' This was the burden of Baxter's and Bunyan's pieces against the Quakers. For Owen in *Of the Divine Originall . . . of the Scriptures* (1659) the Bible was the primary witness to the Spirit; for Fox, the Spirit, which was the inspiration of the Bible, took precedence over it. Quakers might claim, as did Fox, that they recognized the historical Jesus, and that, in Whitehead's words, 'the Appearance of Christ within, and his Manifestation in Spirit, doth neither deny nor oppose his Manifestation or Suffering in the Flesh, but rather answereth and fulfilleth the Intent and End thereof', but their critics remained sceptical.[43]

Their wariness led other nonconformists to be less free with biblical images and phrases. They read Scripture in a more critical and scholarly way, sensitive to the historical facts of Jewish culture and customs and to the textual problems posed by the transmission of the text and by its translation. They were more concerned to understand particular texts in context, and in their exegesis kept a firmer (but not pedantic) hold on the literal. On Matthew vi. 6 ('when thou prayest, enter into thy closet, and when thou hast shut the door, pray to thy Father which is in secret'), Manton wrote:

> These words are not to be taken metaphorically, nor yet pressed too literally. Not metaphorically, as some would carry them. Descend into thy heart, be serious and devout with God in the closet of thy soul, which is the most inward recess and retiring place of man. This were to be wanton with scripture. The literal sense is not to be left without necessity, nor yet pressed too literally, as if prayer should be confined to a chamber and a closet ... The meaning is, private prayer must be performed in a private place.

Gale disapproved of an unrestrained *'Mythologising humor'* and Bunyan, like Owen, insisted that the Bible was a guide to experience and not vice versa. There is often a stubborn literalness about his representations of biblical texts in *The Pilgrim's Progress*. In the *'Man cloathed with Raggs'* (Isa. lxiv. 6), the son of Great- grace who 'tumbled the Hills about with words' (Mark xi. 23–4) and the 'wide field full of dark Mountains' (Jer. xiii. 16), for example, Bunyan is faithful to the particularities of his source texts.[44]

However, when Christian and Pliable, having fallen 'suddenly into the bogg', 'wallowed for a time, being grieviously bedaubed with dirt; And *Christian*, because of the burden that was on his back, began to sink in the Mire', we are no longer witnessing a biblical scene. The 'horrible pit' of Psalm xl.2 and the 'burden' of Psalm xxxviii. 4 have been combined and transformed into an everyday and contemporary incident. Throughout *The Pilgrim's Progress*, Bunyan thus recognizes and realizes the didactic and edificatory – that is, the biblical – force of the least detail in the world around him, and feels no compunction about allegorizing it. Indeed, he writes 'realistic allegory' with little tension and no indecorousness precisely because he finds his biblical matter exemplified in the world around him, in muddy roads, boys stealing apples and tavern suppers. He is habituated to treating the visible as an allegory of the invisible, to discerning in the sublunary translunary truths. In his *Book for Boys and Girls* (1688) he can draw moral profit from eggs, candles, frogs, snails, sheets of paper and their like, for, as he wrote in *Solomon's Temple Spiritualised* (1688) of the cedar which lines the inner temple in I Kings vi. 16,

> since it is the wisdom of God to speak to us ofttimes by trees, gold, silver, stones, beasts, fowls, fishes, spiders, ants, frogs, flies, lice, dust, &c., and here by wood; how should we by them understand his voice, if we count there is no meaning in them?

The emblems in the Interpreter's House, or Prudence's answers to Matthew's emblematic catechism, exemplify just the alchemy of which William Spurstowe wrote in *The Spiritual Chymist* (1666), which consists in taking 'all objects and providences, [and] turning every thing by a Divine Chymistry, *in succum, &* sanguinem, into spirit and nourishment'.[45]

Spurstowe's title was almost certainly a deliberate echo of Robert Boyle's *The Sceptical Chymist* (1661). Boyle's book is an argument for the inductive and experimental investigation of nature as the only proper scientific method and a refutation of the occult and magical suppositions of Hermetic philosophy.[46] In the two chief characters of his dialogue, Carneades (Boyle) and Themistus (an Hermetic philosopher), modern chemistry confronts traditional alchemy. Nonconformists were well aware of contemporary scientific advances – Baxter was a friend of Boyle – but the universe imaged in their writing shares more with the convictions of Themistus than of Carneades. It was not magical, but it was mysterious and numinous. In 1691 Baxter could still write of *The Certainty of the Worlds of Spirits*. These mysteries were not unfathomable, but they would not yield to purely scientific enquiry. Nonconformists inhabited a universe neither mechanistic nor self-containedly comprehensible, but vital, animistic and significant, a revelation of its divine creator and providential sustainer. They continued to conceive of it as a series of correspondences, the great chain of being of which Milton wrote in *Paradise Lost*, in which every part is linked both to every other part and to God, and in which everything is an image of every particular and of the whole. It is a conception in which universals are as real, and distinct from, particulars, but can be known only through them: 'Nature', wrote Howe, 'is nothing else but divine art.'[47]

The nonconformist interest in the created world was consequently less in the natural laws of its operation, in 'secondary causes', than in its emblematic significance, its capacity to reveal truths about the primary cause, God. On the Pauline authority of Romans i. 20 ('for the invisible things of [God] from the creation of the world are clearly seen, being understood by the things that are made'), nonconformists continued, as Puritans had done, to encourage observation of, and meditation on, the creation as a second revelation, and to read this 'book of the creatures' as a series of metaphors, exempla and allegories.[48] Thomas Adams had long ago written that 'A good Christian, that like the Bee workes honey from euery flower, suffers no action, demonstration, euent, to slip by him without a question. All objects to a meditating *Solomon*, are like wings to reare and mount up his thoughts to Heauen'; and the New England Puritan Anne Bradstreet wrote 'There is no object that we see, no action that we do, no evil that we feel, or fear, but we may make some spiritual advantage of all.' Just so, Gouge wrote that

> There is no creature in which there are not manifest foot-steps of the power, wisdom and goodness of God ... As Christians see all things in God, so may they see God in all things, and thereby make some spiritual use and improvement of them. He may with the bee suck sweetness out of every flower, not only for sensual delight, but also for spiritual profit.[49]

So to do would, wrote Baxter, be to find that *'every creature'* may 'become a *Preacher* to us'.[50]

It was its failure to do this which invalidated mere *'Creature-knowledge'*, knowing 'the creatures as *Aristotle*', a purely scientific attention to cause and effect:

> We know little of the creature, till we know it as it standeth in its Order and respects to God: single letters and syllables uncomposed are non-sence. He that over-looketh the *Alpha* and *Omega*, and seeth not the beginning and end, and him in all, who is the *all* of *all*, doth see nothing at all. All creatures ... signifie nothing as separated from God.

If 'Every creature hath the name of God ... upon it; which a considerate believer may as truly discern, as he can read upon a post or hand in a cross way, the name of the Town or City which it points to', then a natural philosophy which confines itself to physics misconstrues its object and method of study:

> This spiritual use of creatures and providence, is Gods great End in bestowing them on man; And he that overlooks this End, must needs rob God of his chiefest praise ... The Relation that our present mercies have to our great Eternal mercies, is the very quintessence and spirits of all these mercies. Therefore they do loose the very spirits of their mercies, and take nothing but the husks and bran, who do overlook this Relation, and draw not forth the sweetness of it in their contemplation.

As Baxter's image of 'husks and bran' suggests, to deny the interpenetration of the natural by the supernatural and to rest content with an analytical and plain scientific account of creation was to reduce the world to sterile forms and appearances. It was, in Howe's view, a kind of atheism:

What a dismal Chaos is this world while we see not God in it. To live destitute of a divine presence, to discern no beam of the heavenly glory ... This is *disconsolate* as well as *sinful* darkness. What can we make of Creatures, what of the daily events of Providence, if we see not in them the glory of God ... diffused everywhere. Our practical Atheism and inobservance of God, makes the World become to us the *region and shadow of death*, states us as among Ghosts and Spectres, makes all things look with a ghastly face, imprints death on every thing we see.[51]

By contrast, 'To spiritualize all outward objects and ordinances' was to restore to the natural world its true vitality and beauty. It was to perceive it imaginatively. To be sure the imagination may, as Bunyan warns, lead us astray, but precisely because 'the *imagination is* such a power, that if it putteth forth it self to dress up and present a thing to the Soul, whether that thing be evil or good, the rest of the faculties cannot withstand it', the imagination alone could present the world in its truly divine nature. Rather in the way of Wordsworth's imagination, which half-perceived and half-created the intimations of immortality celebrated in his poems, nonconformist faith created its perception of 'glory stamped on every creature, sparkling in every providence' by its literary transformations of the perceived world. Howe can write with the kind of Platonic imagery we associate with Vaughan and Traherne ('Beams of his glory do everywhere break forth, through every creature'), and with an ecstatic wonder:

> To eye Him in all his Creatures, and observe the various prints of the Creators glory instampt upon them. With how lively a lustre would it cloath the world, and make every thing look with a pleasant face! What an heaven were it to look upon God, as filling all in all; and how sweetly would it, ere-while, raise our Souls into some such sweet seraphick strains, *holy, holy, – the whole earth is filled with his glory.*[52]

The comprehensiveness of many of these remarks was not casual but deliberate: God's glory was as evident in the '*ordinary*' as in the '*extraordinary*'. Nonconformists were as anxious as Wordsworth would be to rescue the commonplace from the dullness of familiarity: 'let us admire God in the Sun and Stars, in Sea and Land, as if this were the first time that ever we had seen them' wrote Baxter. The wonder of the everyday is a recurrent motif: 'We vainly hunt with a lingering mind after miracles; if we did not more vainly mean by them nothing else but novelties, we are compassed about with such; and the greatest wonder is that we see them not.' Howe described as 'the most vulgar and meanest disease of the mind' a 'disregard for what is common, and an aptness to place more in the strangeness of new, unexpected and surprising events': 'all the works of God, even those that are of every day's observation, do some way or other represent God to us.' But if, as Gouge wrote, 'every flower, or spire of grass, every worm or fly, declares the power of our great Creator', only the observant will perceive the meanest flower that blows.[53] Nonconformist writing is consequently as curious and particular as it is celebratory and enthusiastic. Philip Henry was as attentive to the details of his gardening as he was to improving 'for spiritual purposes' the cultivation and growth of his plants. The many intimations of the divine in the journals of Oliver Heywood are not vaguely asserted but, as in Bunyan, derived from circumstantially accurate and anecdotally familiar accounts of what he has seen and heard.[54]

The conformist and scientific plain style could not answer to a world so vibrantly significant and instinct with the divine. It was analytically descriptive rather than imaginatively interpretative: 'what men commonly call universal nature, if they would be content no longer to lurk in the darkness of an obscure and uninterpreted word, they must confess is nothing else but common Providence; that is, the Universal Power which is everywhere active in the world.' In what interested other plain stylists, nonconformists can seem curiously uninterested: Howe does not 'understand' nor is he 'solicitious to know' how comets are formed neither is he worried lest it prove to be 'as naturally as can be supposed', for 'that hinders not their being signs to us, more than the natural causation of the bow in the cloud'. This divorce between scientific and divine truth, and unequivocal preference for the latter, was not obscurantism. By retaining a sense of the mystery of creation it continued to uphold the legitimacy, indeed the necessity, of a sentient response to it. Reason alone could not encompass it: the senses could. 'The Understanding', wrote Baxter, 'is not the whole soul, and therefore cannot do the whole work': we must 'call in our Sense to its assistance'. Nonconformists welcomed, and delighted in, people's capacity to respond feelingly: 'God would not have given us, either our Senses themselves, or their usual objects, if they might not have been serviceable to his own praise.'[55] And they delighted equally in those 'objects'. Matter is celebrated as good, most sustainedly in Book VII of *Paradise Lost*, where Milton is entranced by God's creative power. We may understand his adoption of the doctrine of *creatio ex deo*, rather than *ex nihilo*, as an expression of this conviction.[56] And to enjoy it is a good: Manton contrasts with John the Baptist the Christ who 'came eating and drinking; that is, using the ordinary diet of men, and eating promiscuously with all company, in a more free use of the creatures, taking the fare as he found it, and conversing with all sorts of men in a familiar course of life'.[57]

A literature founded on such convictions will not be satisfied with the ethical compliance or intellectual assent of its reader: it will seek to move him emotionally. The final failing of the conformist plain style was that it was deliberative and directive, not affective. Its ascetic avoidance of sensory pleasure and effects was reductive, a denial of the true nature of the universe, of man, and of the experience of grace as conceived by nonconformists. Sense impressions are an essential part of nonconformist writing: it aspires to a kind of comprehensive synaesthesia. Keith writes of regeneration thus:

> this seed and Birth of God upon the saints [is] a substantial living principle in which they have all the spiritual and supernatural sensations of spiritual and supernatural objects, really present and manifest, seen, heard, smelled, tasted and

felt, as really as the outward birth is a substantial living principle, in which we have the natural and animal sences and sensations of outward and natural things, ... [according to those who] only conceive regeneration to be but an accidental (though supernatural) change on the mind ... it putteth on no substantial principle ... but we know it to be a substance and feel it to be so, as manifestly as we feel and know this outward birth of flesh and blood to be a substance, for it hath all the properties and characters of a substance, that the outward hath, it giveth us to see, hear, smel, taste and feel the substantial things of the spiritual inward and invisible world.

He adds an extensive list of examples of 'spiritual discerning' being 'held forth' in the Bible 'under the names of all the five senses' which, though they are metaphors, are images of sensation greater, not lesser, than the physical. Bunyan similarly chooses to describe 'the Soul by its *Senses*, its *spiritual Senses*, for so I call them: for the body hath Senses pertaining to it, and as it can see, hear, smell, feel and tast, so can the Soul'. It tastes, 'even as really as doth the palate belonging to the body': 'Nothing is so sensible [ie. sensitive] as the Soul, nor feeleth so quickly the love and mercy, or the anger and wrath of God.'[58]

When, then, in his plain style, Bunyan comes to describe a state of spiritual bliss, he does so like this:

I saw then that they went on their way to a pleasant River, which *David the King* called the *River of God* [Ps.lxv.9]; but, *John*, *The River of the water of life* [Rev. xxii.1]. Now their way lay just upon the bank of the River: here therefore *Christian* and his Companion walked with great delight; they drank also of the water of the River, which was pleasant and enlivening to their weary Spirits: besides, on the banks of this River, on either side, were *green Trees*, that bore all manner of Fruit; and the leaves of the Trees were good for Medecine; with the Fruit of these Trees they were also much delighted; and the leaves they eat to prevent Surfeits, and other Diseases that are incident to those that heat their blood by Travels. On either side of the River was also a Meadow, curiously beautified with Lilies; And it was green all the year long. In this Meadow they lay down and slept, for here they might *lie down safely* [Isa. xiv.30]. When they awoke, they gathered again of the Fruit of the Trees, and drank again of the Water of the River: and then lay down again to sleep. Thus they did several days and nights. Then they sang,

> Behold ye how these Christal streams do glide
> (To comfort Pilgrims) by the High-way side;
> The Meadows green, besides their fragrant smell,
> Yield dainties for them: And he that can tell
> What pleasant Fruit, yea Leaves, these Trees do yield,
> Will soon sell all, that he may buy this Field.[59]

The reader's attention is drawn to the biblical and emblematic nature of this scene by its opening marginal glosses from the Psalms and Revelation. Its details derive predominantly from the descriptions of cultic shrines and the pastoral imagery of the Pentateuch, the Prophets and the Psalms. There is nothing naturalistically English here, nothing accurately and plainly delineated. Bunyan, however, is imprecise about flora and location to specific effect: freeing the scene from exclusive particularities enables him to engage all his reader's senses in an appreciation of it. The insistence on the one place ('here

... here') and on its immutability ('green all the year long') does exclude the world and time and invest the scene with a stasis which the pilgrims' repeated actions ('again ... again') only enforce. Bunyan's paratactic style, the parallel clauses and co-ordinating conjunctions, and his reiterative and repetitive diction work to the same effect. This image of spiritual liberation from sublunary circumstances is not, however, couched in terms of insensate and artificial immobility. Quite the contrary. It establishes a series of oppositions rendered in terms of physical wants and states: thirst/refreshment, hunger/food, weariness/rest, sickness/health, torpor/vitality, anxiety/repose. The scene thus answers to every physical need and desire, but it offers more than the simple satisfaction of appetite: it is a place of 'great delight'. It offers not merely food but '*dainties*'; it refreshes not only with water but with '*fragrant smell*' and the sight of 'a Meadow, curiously beautified with Lilies'; it provides '*pleasant Fruit*' as well as medicinal cures. If it lacks the tactile sensuality of Marvell's 'The Garden', touch is implicitly present in the plucking of the leaves and fruit. And the scene closes with the pilgrims' own song. By thus supplying the missing sense, they themselves become part of the scene, its completion and perfection. Bunyan does not, of course, depict any pantheistic communion with nature. The vehicle of his allegory is, nevertheless, people responding sensitively and gratefully to natural beauty and provision. The joy of the saints is akin to a walk by a river: and that, Samuel Parker would have thought very silly indeed.

Chapter 9 'The world was all before them'

nonconformist story

> *These all died in faith, not having received the promises, but*
> *having seen them afar off, and were persuaded of them, and*
> *embraced them, and confessed that they were strangers and*
> *pilgrims in the earth.*

> Heb. xi. 13

I 'THE TRUE CHILDREN OF ABRAHAM'

'As I walk'd through the wilderness of this world, I lighted on a certain place, where was a Denn.' Even before he enters Bunyan's dreamworld, the reader of *The Pilgrim's Progress* is transported by its opening words into a curious and, apparently, improbable landscape. Bedfordshire, after all, was no wilderness. It is, furthermore, a landscape ordinarily to avoid, to go round or away from, or, at worst, hurry across. Yet Bunyan is walking there, and not merely wandering aimlessly: both verb and preposition are purposeful. To walk *through* a wilderness is to be going somewhere, and to *walk* through it is to be going unhurriedly but steadily. The marginal gloss 'Gaol' upon 'Denn' alerts us (should we need it) to the figurative nature of this language, and Bunyan's address, twelve years earlier, of the preface to *Grace Abounding* 'from the *Lions Dens*', from the prison where 'I stick between the Teeth of the Lions in the Wilderness', points to the source of its imagery.[1] Dens are inhabited by lurking lions in the wildernesses of biblical story (Ps. x.9; Amos iii.4), and by cockatrices (Isa. xi.8) and dragons (Jer. ix.11, x.22) too. They are, indeed, fearful places, their floors strewn with torn carcases (Nahum ii.12), the haunt of robbers (Jer. vii.11) and defeated Israelite refugees (Judg. vi.2). That single monosyllable hence tells a good deal about the plight of nonconformists under the Great Persecution and of Bunyan's relationship to the authorities of the Restoration, but his wilderness is not merely that created by Charles II, Clarendon, Sheldon and the Cavalier Parliament. His words, unobtrusively recalling the geography of a far distant place and the journeys of a far distant time, set his own and his readers' experiences in that larger biblical perspective nonconformist writing habitually adopted. They not only, and incidentally, gloss Bunyan's situation, but also, and more significantly, introduce the imaginative idea which will shape his autobiographical and fictional narratives. The Bible supplied more than Parker's 'glittering Allusions': it in large part determined the form of nonconformist story.

The Old Testament recounts the history of the election of Israel and the course of its covenant relationship with Jehovah in narratives in which religious dedication and desert journeys are so interconnected that by the time of the prophets the landscapes of these nomadic wanderings had become symbols of spiritual states. The prophecies of a return from Babylonian exile are inspired by, and articulated in terms of, the Exodus. The Deuteronomic and post-Exilic redactors of the Pentateuch discerned in the two traditions of Israel's origins in the Abraham legends and the Exodus saga the same pattern of decision to leave, journey under divine guidance, testing in the wilderness and covenant. That pattern underlies nonconformist story, as it had done Puritan narratives. To the Puritan and nonconformist mind both personal history and national English history were comprehensible only in terms of Israel's history, and, since the latter was as vividly present to their imagination as the former, it offered not only an interpretative key but a narrative model. In this complex of Old Testament stories was found a spiritual geography and a structure by means of which to recount both 'what the Lord hath done for my soul' (Ps. lxvi.16) and the 'great and mighty signs and wonders' of God (Dan. iv.3). Biblically inspired 'Storytelling was one strategy of the plain style' of the Puritans which was adopted by nonconformists and was by Bunyan brought to its apogee.[2]

These twin preoccupations – the personal experience of saving grace and the operation of Providence – were never for long kept apart. It is this which gives to these narratives their distinctive resonance. Within the unified structure created by the image of the journey, various levels of significance are constantly in play: many journeys go forward at once. *The Pilgrim's Progress* is 'about' Christian; but it is also about Bunyan himself, is, indeed, a reworking of *Grace Abounding*; it is about the state of England during the Restoration period, to which topical and satirical reference is several times made; it is about the Old Testament experience of similar circumstances; and it is about the New Testament resolution of both Israel's earlier and England's later history. The mode of nonconformist story, that is to say, is at once realistic, allegorical in the old medieval sense, picturing forth theological abstractions, and symbolic in the manner of modern subjectivism, investing particular experiences with figurative significance. Its method was a peculiarly intimate and personal use of the traditional typological exegesis of the Old Testament which survived the Reformation and continued to be promoted in the seventeenth century by such works as the Puritan Thomas Taylor's *Christ Revealed: or the Types and Shadows of Our Saviour in the Old Testament* (1635) and, later, Benjamin Keach's massive *Tropologia: a Key to Open Scripture Metaphors* (1681). The details of Old Testament narratives became something more than 'some outward or sensible thing ordained of God under the Old Testament to represent and hold forth something of Christ in the New'. They were read as symbolic anticipations of the individual's personal experience and as allegorical representations of the general experience of saints, sinners and nations. It had 'happened to *Israel*' as it happens to Christian, and to all Christians.[3]

A good deal happened to, and in, Israel, but it was from only a few biblical episodes and images that the common structure and recurrent motifs of non-conformist narratives were derived. The first of these was the emigration of Abraham. That Abraham was a type of Christ continued to be in Puritan and nonconformist interpretations of Genesis the commonplace it had been in medieval hermeneutics. Edward Taylor, who had in 1668 emigrated to New England and become minister of Westfield, Massachusetts, wrote in a meditation on Galatians iv.24 addressed to Christ:

> Nay, Abram's Shine to thee's an Allegory,
> Or fleeting Sparke in th'Smoake, to typify
> Thee, and thy Glorious Selfe in mystery.

But Abraham was often, more pressingly and immediately, found by the seventeenth-century Puritan to typify himself, or, at least, the self that he would be. There was, for him, a particular relevance in the story of Abraham being called from Haran to 'get thee out of thy country ... unto a land that I will show thee', and of his exodus, in obedient response, from a centre of civilization and from his family, who remained in Mesopotamia, to live as a nomadic tent-dweller in the foreign and hostile land of Canaan (Gen. xii.1–10, xxiv.4,10). Puritans themselves, in biographical fact, undertook such journeys occasioned by religious commitment. Many felt compelled by their 'differences about Religious Matters' with the Royalists to take up what Baxter called 'this moving Life' in the New Model army. Many resolved, like Abraham in the gloss of the Elizabethan homily *Of Faith* on Genesis xii 'to go unto a far country' for the same reason.[4] One such group was John Robinson's separatist church at Scrooby in Nottinghamshire, which, in 1608, decided to emigrate to Amsterdam, 'to go into a country they knew not ... for their desires were set on the ways of God'. In 1620 that same commitment took them, as the colonists known to history as the Pilgrim Fathers, to New England: they were, Cotton Mather later wrote, '*satisfy'd*, they had as plain a command of Heaven to attempt a Removal, as ever their Father *Abraham* had for his leaving the *Caldean* Territories'. William Bradford, Plymouth colony's historian and governor for most of its first 35 years, could with justice claim that, like Paul (II Cor. xi.26–7), the Pilgrims had been 'in journeyings often ... in perils in the wilderness' and reflect, in a poem published in *New England's Memorial* (1669), Nathaniel Morton's history of Plymouth based on Bradford's own journal:

> [God] call'd me from my native place
> For to enjoy the means of grace.
> In wilderness he did me guide,
> And in strange lands for me provide.
> In fears and wants, through weal and woe
> A pilgrim passed I to and fro.[5]

Experience continued thus to chime with the Abraham story for nonconformists. Fox had been but the most remarkable of many seekers after truth who left their home environment to travel 'up and down as a stranger on the earth' 'to look for comfort' from despair, and he was but one of many nonconformists who pursued an itinerant ministry after the Restoration. What Ambrose Rigge wrote in one of several testimonies prefaced to Fox's collected works, *Gospel-Truth Demonstrated* (1706), that 'He travelled thro' many Sufferings, Tryals and Tribulations; in Perils (by Sea and Land)', could have been said not only of other Quakers but of other nonconformists. Oliver Heywood, for example, regularly detailed in his jounals his 'many years travels in my Lords work', setting down 'my journeyings and labours in the gospel since my ejection'. Between 1665 and 1700 he travelled over 1,000 miles in each of 14 years (1,400 miles in 1681 and 1687) and never less than 600 miles, save in 1670 and 1685 (when he was imprisoned in York Castle), until, in 1698 when 68 years old, age began to take its toll. In Derbyshire 'the Apostle of the Peak' William Bagshaw, ejected Presbyterian vicar of Glossop, preached throughout the country, as did the Presbyterian Stephen Hughes, ejected from Meidrim, in Carmarthenshire. And even for those who did not physically travel, to choose nonconformity was effectively to choose exile. Many knew the social ostracism which, in his biblical commentary (1708–10), the Presbyterian Matthew Henry conjectured was Abraham's lot since the Canaanites 'were likely to be but bad neighbours, and worse landlords'.[6]

So to share in the experience of exile and a nomadic life known to Abraham was also, for nonconformists, to share in something else. The circumstances of his life were determined, as were theirs, by an act of deliberate self-denial and obedience. Writing of mortification, Penn adduced the patriarch's example to this effect: 'In several most remarkable instances, his life was made up of self-denial. First, in quitting his own land, where we may well suppose him settled in the midst of plenty, at least sufficiency: and why? Because God called him.' To 'walk in the steps of Abraham' as one of his 'true children' was to walk 'according to the obedience of faith'. If, however, the Abraham story offered encouragement to obedience, in that he was rewarded with the covenant promise (Gen. xv, xvii.1–5), it also exemplified the challenge and the demand of such faith. The observation in the Epistle to the Hebrews (xi.8) that 'by faith' Abraham 'went out, not knowing whither he went' had been picked up in the gloss in the Genevan version of the Bible (1560) on Genesis xii.1: 'In appointing him no certaine place, he [God] proueth so much more his fayth and obedience.' Matthew Henry enlarged the point: Abraham's removal 'was designed to try his faith and obedience, and also to separate him, and set him apart, for God'. He was 'tried whether he loved God better than he loved his native soil and dearest friends' and, as he was told nothing about the promised land, he 'had no particular securities given him that he should be no loser by leaving his country to follow God. Note, those that deal with God must deal on trust.'[7]

Nonconformist story takes its rise from such an act of trust, which is represented time and again in the decision to leave what is known and stable and to venture into the unknown against, as it seems, common sense. This is nowhere more dramatically the case than in the beginning of *The Pilgrim's Progress*, whose seventeenth-century title-pages significantly hold out the discovery of 'The manner of his setting out'. That departure repeatedly affronts the advocates of worldly caution: Faithful's prudent neighbours, for example, stigmatize his pilgrimage as a 'desperate Journey', and Mrs Timorous leaves Mercy 'to go a fooling' with the sharp observation 'while we are out of danger we are out; but when we are in, we are in.' Safety-first is proverbially recommended to a true pilgrim in one of Keach's allegorical dialogues:

> Who would for Things which so uncertain are,
> Such losses suffer, and such Labour bear?
> A Bird i'th' Hand's worth two i' th' Bush, you know,
> This Zeal, poor Lad, will work thy Overthrow.

The determination of their protagonists to resist such appeals had been characteristic of earlier Puritan narratives. In his history of the Massachusetts Bay emigration, *Wonder-Working Providence of Zion's Saviour* (1654), Edward Johnson had, when depicting the farewells at Southampton in 1630, presented all the ties of creaturely affection and worldly interest in the 'expostulations' and pleas of friends and relatives to remain, which 'With bold resolvedness these stout Souldiers of Christ' rejected, preferring 'that far remote, and vast wilderness'. In a similar vein, Thomas Shepherd, when defending the ecclesiastical polity of the Massachusetts Bay colony in 1648, had expressed 'wonder' that 'so many' should 'against so many perswasions of friends' leave 'accommodations and comforts' and 'dearest relations' to 'go to a wilderness'.[8]

To make a decision of such apparent recklessness and to insist on undertaking such a foolhardy journey argues an audacious and intrepid character. 'Hee that at euery steppe, lookes at euery stoppe, and numbers his perils with his paces, either turnes aside faintly, or turns back cowardly' and there would be an end to his story. The nonconformist protagonist is, as Johnson's had been, boldly defiant: 'The boldness of Christians is the honour of Christ' wrote Henry. 'Play the man' echoes like a refrain through *The Pilgrim's Progress*: Christian is not to be deterred from his pilgrimage any more than is Valiant-for-Truth by hearing of the dangers he will encounter. Cowardice is not the least of Harapha's failings as he faces Samson. William Penn's encomium of Fox invokes a similar image: he never knew Fox 'out of his place, or not a match for every service and occasion', 'For in all things he acquitted himself like a man, yea, a strong man.'[9] It was, of course, a theme which found martial imagery particularly serviceable.[10]

With this boldness goes a sense of adventure. A recent study, sub-titled *Spiritual Adventure in Two Worlds*, distinguishes this as the essential quality of the work of the New England divine Thomas Hooker, but it was not peculiar to him.[11] It was, for example, by appealing to their sense of adventurousness that, in his *Young Man's Guide* (1670), the English Presbyterian Thomas Gouge sought to arouse his readers: 'Faith is an adventuring upon the truth of God, an adventuring our lives, and adventuring our souls ... Believers are merchants, Matt. xiii.45. Merchant-adventurers, that will adventure all they have, their whole stock and patrimony, for the riches of that good land.' The initial act of faith was such a leap in the dark: of his early spiritual experience Heywood wrote that 'I did not know indeed whether I was fit to come to cht. ... but ... I knew there was no other course to be taken but venturing my soul on cht.' So, too, was a life of continuing obedience: 'Faith', wrote Manton, citing Hebrews xi.8, 'was ever a venturing all, and a forsaking all, upon the belief of God's veracity'; 'Here was trusting and venturing all upon God's call. [Abraham] forsook his kindred, and father's house, and all, to seek an abode he knew not where.' And so, too, was adherence to nonconformity: 'I must venture' resolves Christian confronted by the lions of persecution before the Palace Beautiful.[12] By daring to venture, to take the risk, the hero embarks upon a journey which perforce involves excitement and unpredictability, the modern sense of 'adventure'.[13] Though this journey will not lie through Logres, Faeryland, or Arcadia, and there will be less of chivalry and romance in it than in the *aventures* of medieval and Renaissance knights errant, it will nevertheless be quite as challenging, and far more momentous.

2   'TO BE A PILGRIM'

A leaving is also a setting out, and there was only one way to set out: 'Enter ye in at the strait gate, for wide is the gate, and broad is the way, that leadeth to destruction, and many there be that go in thereat: Because strait is the gate, and narrow is the way, which leadeth unto life, and few there be that find it' (Matt. vii.13–14). The stress in Matthew upon both the straitness of the gate and the difficulty of finding it, coupled with the exclusivity of the dominical glosses upon the inscrutable Jehovah of Exodus (iii.14), 'I am the door', 'I am the way' (John x.9, xiv.6), made pressing the need first to locate it and then to pass through it. 'Conversion and regeneration are *the gate* by which we enter into this way' wrote Henry; 'This is a *strait gate*, hard to find, and hard to get through, like a passage between two rocks, I Sam. xiv.4'. In Keach's dialogue *War with the Devil* (1673), Truth cautions Youth, who has undergone the kind of formal conversion Bunyan recounts in the early paragraphs of *Grace Abounding*, that

> Conversion's hard: It is a Thing so rare,
> That very few that narrow Passage enter,
> Tho' for that Way there's Thousands do adventure.
> Yet miss their Mark: For all their inward Strife,
> They fall far short of the New Creature, Life.

So Bunyan's Christian, who 'could not tell which way to go' and has his own flirtation with formalism and moralism, experiences considerable difficulty reaching the Wicket-gate, and admits he 'should never have found it' but for Evangelist's help. The Lucan form of the saying emphasizes the point: 'Strive to enter in at the strait gate' (Luke xiii.24). 'The word in the Greek *Agonizesthe*', explained Gouge, 'signifies a striving with our utmost skill, strength, and activity, as wrestlers do for mastery.' The Greekless Bunyan adduced Ephesians vi.12 to the same purpose: 'Wrestle for heaven, or you are like to go without it.'[14]

It is in such terms of prolonged search and physical exertion that in *Grace Abounding* Bunyan depicts his desire to join John Gifford's Bedford church by passing through the 'narow gap, like a little door-way ... very straight and narrow' which he imagined himself finding, after much 'prying', in the wall separating him from its members:

> I made many offers to get in, but all in vain, even untill I was well nigh quite beat out by striving to get in: at last, with great striving, me thought I at first did get in my head, and after that, by a side-ling striving, my shoulders, and my whole body; then was I exceeding glad, and went and sat down in the midst of them.

The additional trope of the 'Sunny side of some high Mountain', where 'these poor people of *Bedford*' were 'refreshing themselves' in contrast to 'the cold ... frost, snow and dark clouds' in which Bunyan is 'shivering and shrinking', enforces his isolation and his desperate need to find his way to them. Such urgent necessity prompts Gouge to admonish his reader that 'A man that hath a work of great consequence to be done, and but one day for the doing it, had need rise early in the morning and with all possible speed fall upon it.' The saying thus supplied one argument against those unregenerate souls who took refuge in the doctrine of predestination: Increase Mather warned his Boston congregation that 'Sinners can do more towards their own Conversion than they do or will do. They should give *diligence* to make sure of their being effectually called. They should strive to enter in at the strait gate.' Perhaps inappropriately recalling Abraham in a maritime image intended to dissuade his readers from delaying until they are old, Gouge wrote: 'Is it not extreme folly, while the ship is sound, the tackle good, the mariners whole and strong, to be playing and sporting at road; and when the ship is crazy, the tackle weak, and rotten, the mariners sick, then to hoist sail for a voyage into a far country?'[15]

A gate, however, leads somewhere: it is the beginning, not the end, of a journey. The saying in Matthew recalls the Old Testament imagery of the two ways: 'There are but two ways, right and wrong, good and evil, the way to heaven and the way to hell, in the one of which we are all of us walking' Henry categorically asserted. In the wisdom literature, particularly, these two paths or ways are opposed, often within the parallel structure of individual proverbs (e.g. Prov. ii.20–2, xi.5, xiv.8, xxi.8): on the one hand, the straight way of the righteous (Ps. v.8), which is 'a shining light' (Prov. iv.18), 'in the pathway thereof there is no death' (Prov. xii.28); on the other, the crooked way of the wicked (Prov. ii.15), in the dark turnings of which sinners stumble and die

(Prov. iv.19; Isa. lix.7–10).It was a figurative antithesis particularly serviceable to Calvinist theologies which adopted the Pauline distinction between the 'children of light' and the darkness of the fallen world (Eph. v.8; I Thess. v.5). It found expression in such starkly diagrammatic schemes of the two ways as Bunyan's *A Mapp Shewing the Order and Causes of Salvation and Damnation*. Both imaginative and theological logic led Bunyan to follow the First Part of *The Pilgrim's Progress* with its sequel *The Life and Death of Mr. Badman* (1680), in which, as he had previously written 'of him that was going to heaven', Bunyan now writes 'of the life and death of the ungodly, and of their travel from this world to hell'. Bunyan's fellow Baptist Benjamin Keach similarly published *The Progress of Sin: or the Travels of Ungodliness* (1684) one year after his 'apt and pleasant Allegory' of *The Travels of True Godliness*.[16]

The metaphorical use of 'way' for Judaism in the Old Testament and for Christianity in the New Testament is associated with the use of 'walk' in a moral sense throughout the Bible, a sense known in English from the early sixteenth century. The combination of verb and noun clearly has metaphorical potential. Its appeal to the Puritan imagination is testified by the number of works of practical divinity which figure 'guide', 'walking', 'pathway', 'progress' and their like in their titles. The admonition most earnestly urged in such works is to alert watchfulness. The Old Testament insistence on the straightness of the way, passing through hazards on either side (e.g. Deut. vi. 14; Pss. xii.8, cxxxviii.7), means, as Paul wrote to the Ephesians, that it requires circumspection to be walked (Eph. v.15). The traveller must, therefore, keep his eyes and ears open and be prepared for every eventuality, as John Robinson advised in his farewell letter to the departing Pilgrim Fathers.[17]

This journey has, in consequence, something of the quality of a detective story. Christian is constantly taxed to distinguish his friends from his foes and is repeatedly in danger of being turned from the way which is 'as straight as a Rule can make it'. He must pass 'right up' Hill Difficulty, straight between the lions, and keep his footing between the 'very deep ditch' of doctrinal error on the one side and the 'very dangerous Quagg' of moral failing on the other. Attempts to go around such obstacles or to take short cuts invariably lead to disaster. It is, significantly, after turning aside into the lands of Giant Despair that he meets the Shepherds Watchful and Experience. 'Do not step over it, nor crosse it, nor walke beside it, nor neere it, but walke *in it*' the Puritan Thomas Adams had written. The same caution was to be heard from nonconformists. Ellwood wrote that, after his convincement by Nayler and Burrough,

> here began to be a Way cast up, before me, for me to walk in: A direct and plain Way; so plain, *that a way-faring Man*, how weak and simple so-ever (though a Fool, to the Wisdom, and in the Judgment of the World) *could not err*, while he continued to walk in it: the Error coming in, by his going out of it.

Narrative accounts of this way have not, therefore, the casually episodic structure of picaresque fiction. Fielding's Parson Adams could be going anywhere, and, indeed, spends most of the book going in the opposite direction to the one he had intended. Nor is progress in any direction under his control: he is the victim of a succession of arbitrary mishaps which delay and mislead him. The nonconformist journey, by contrast, is dominated by the desire to keep going straight on: and its progress is proportionate to the dedication and discernment of the traveller.[18]

This narrative strategy embodies a dynamic conception of the Christian life as a progress in grace through devotion and moral effort. As has been remarked, this Puritan conviction remained characteristic of the teaching of nonconformists.[19] It may be, as Adams wrote on Ephesians v.2, that works do not earn salvation, that 'Loue is not a cause to justifie, but a *Way* for the justified ... Faith is *Causa iustificandi: Loue is Via iustificati*', but works were the single most reliable means of assurance that conversion was genuine, that the gate had been found. Only by travelling the way can you prove that you are in it. For Baxter it was axiomatic that '*Your Conversion is not sound if you are not heartily desirious to encrease*. Grace is not true, if there be not a desire after more':

> I doubt it is the undoing of many to imagine, that if once they are sanctified, they are so sure in the hands of Christ, that they have no more care to take, nor no more danger to be afraid of, and at last think they have no more to do, as of necessity to Salvation; and thus prove that indeed they were never sanctified.

Christ 'never intended to *justifie or sanctifie us perfectly* at the first ... but to carry on both proportionably and by degrees'. Hence, '*Much of the Work of your Salvation is yet to do, when you are Converted*. You have happily begun; but you have not finished.'[20] Baxter's friend Gouge was of the same mind: saints 'content not themselves with any measure or degree of grace, but labour and strive after perfection'; 'prove that your grace is true ... Let your love prove your faith, and your labours of love prove your love, and the fruit of your labours prove that you have not either believed or laboured in vain.' True spirituality, wrote Howe, is 'growing spirituality'. Manton agreed: 'illumination is given by God by degrees.' Although the 'legal perfection' of 'unsinning obedience' is impossible and unattainable (Rom. viii.3), the 'evangelical perfection' of 'sincere obedience' is not only possible but is the essential mark of an imperfect believer's longing to realize the 'immaculate purity' of eternity: 'He that looketh not for a Turkish paradise, but a sinless estate, will endeavour it now, get as much as he can of it. When you cease to grow in holiness you cease to go any farther to salvation.' Evangelical obedience hence admits of 'several degrees of grace, and diversities of growth among Christians'.[21] And even Bunyan, whose Calvinism was a good deal purer than that of this Baxterian tradition, wrote *Christian Behaviour* (1663) to show 'the beauty and excellency' of good works and allowed that there are 'degrees of grace in the world'. The fate of Ignorance should not blind us to Christian's declaration, in dismising Talkative, 'The Soul of Religion is the practick part.' Adams had made the same point: 'The *Apostle* chargeth vs to walke, not to talke of loue: One steppe of our feet, is worth ten words of our tongues.'[22]

This gives to nonconformist story an insistent onward pressure. The word 'progress' impels the saint forward, denying him any antinomian rest just within the gate: 'It may justly be doubted, whether there be any truth of grace where there is not a desire and endeavour after an increase therein' wrote Gouge. In terms of the image with which we are becoming familiar this means 'You have hit of the right way, but you have your Journey yet to go.' And it is a long journey.

> after the work of grace hath been wrought in you, there is a great deal more work to be wrought in you; many lusts to be conquered, much corruption to be subdued, many temptations to be resisted, many graces to be exercised, several duties to be performed ... bitter things to be endured.[23]

This is precisely the matter of *The Pilgrim's Progress*. 'Departing from iniquity', wrote Bunyan, 'is not a work of an hour, or a day, or a week, or a month, or a year: *But it's a work that will last thee thy life-time.*' It is 'a work of continuance ... of time, of all thy time; no wonder if it dogs thee'. Hence, what marks out Bunyan's pilgrims is less any remarkable degree of grace than that they keep on going. This sense of dedicated effort was caught in the Pauline imagery of the race (I Cor. ix.24; Gal. v.7; Phil.ii.16; Heb. xii.1), and it was from *The Heavenly Footman*, a tract on this theme, that *The Pilgrim's Progress* probably developed. In his 1662 farewell sermon Manton had taken up the same image: 'a Christian's life is like a race from earth to heaven ... Now, in this race we must run, and so run that we may obtain the crown ... Running is a motion, and a speedy motion; there is no lying, sitting or standing, but still there must be running.' And, as he then foresaw, there would for nonconformists be small encouagement:

> Because the spectators will be ready to discourage us. We are set forth not only as a spectacle to God and angels [I Cor. iv.9], but to the world; and they will be ready to deride, scorn, and oppose us for our zeal to God, and our forwardness in the ways of God, to discourage us by bitter mockery &c.[24]

Despite this, Christians are not to shrink from the challenge, either by lapsing into formal conformity or by turning papist and shunning the world. Matthew xix.21 does not mean we should all 'turn monks or anchorites' but that we should witness to the world in the world. Just so, 40 years before, in a sermon delivered at Plymouth colony in 1621, Robert Cushman warned the settlers 'you are not in a retired monastical course' to live 'as retired hermits'. 'Hermit' may be an etymological derivative of ερημος, but the Puritans had quite another way with wildernesses. Johnson envisaged the Massachusetts Bay settlers 'marching manfully on (the Lord assisting)' through the 'howling Desert'. In his elegy for Bradford, Josiah Winslow celebrated the governor's service of God: 'If not in one place, he'll go forward still'; no suffering or pain could 'Discourage him, he'll follow God again'. It is the very thought of Bunyan's more famous poem 'Who would true Valour see'.[25]

3 'OUT OF EGYPT'

Just how difficult it was to continue 'manfully on' once one had set out, and how perilous abandoning the attempt might be, nonconformists found represented in Exodus. John v.46 encouraged them to find there 'more types of Christ ... than perhaps in any other book of the Old Testament' and to see in it 'The way of reconciliation to God'. That way was the way of mortification. Israel's exodus was, like Abraham's, a calling out from civilization: 'When Israel was a child, then I loved him, and called my son out of Egypt' (Hos. xi.1). It was also, explicitly, a testing in the wilderness (Exod. xvi.4). The Israelites' want of complete commitment is depicted in Exodus in their repeated longings to return to an Egypt which, in the context of wilderness, came to represent the ready provision of material needs (Exod. xiv.11ff., xvi.3ff., xvii.3ff.; Num. xi.3ff., xiv.1ff.). Indeed, for Abiram and Dathan, when they revolted against Moses' authority, the 'land flowing with milk and honey' was no longer Canaan but Egypt (Num. xvi.13). The physicality of these repinings (Ps. cvi.14) showed, in Henry's firm words, 'the dominion of the carnal mind', and since Canaan was attainable only by those who, like Moses, freely and whole-heartedly preferred 'rather to suffer affliction' than to enjoy 'the felicity of this world' (Heb. xi.25), freely to choose the wilderness became in the Puritan tradition a signal mark of the saint. Lady Arbella Fermore, who gave her name to Winthrop's flagship, 'left an earthly *Paradice* in the Family of an *Earldom*, to encounter the Sorrows of a Wilderness, for the Entertainments of a *pure Worship*'. Johnson depicted the 1630 emigrants as undertaking 'voluntary banishment'; Morton insisted that the Pilgrim Fathers, like Moses and the Israelites, were not 'driven out' but left 'of their own free choice and motion'. Instancing Bradford's self-denial, Cotton Mather made the same point: 'The Leader of a People in a *Wilderness* has need to be a *Moses*.'[26]

Moses had, indeed, been in Bradford's own mind when he recorded the Pilgrims' first view of the 'hideous and desolate wilderness' of America from the *Mayflower*, and Winthrop, in 1629 anticipating the hazards of 'a barbarous place' with 'no learnynge and less civilitie', reflected that as the Israelites had been led 'into the wildernesse and made [to] forgette the fleshpotts of Egipt', so this too would be an exercise in mortification. On board the *Arbella*, he explicitly paralled the Massachusetts venture with Exodus.[27] The term 'wilderness', which throughout the seventeenth century remained the colonists' usual designation for their new environment, itself owed as much to Exodus as to observation. America was perceived in the image of Sinai: Mather's *Magnalia Christi Americana* was the history 'of a *New English Israel*', of the journey to and the resettling of that 'holy-land', as Thomas Tillam, later a republican Baptist, in 1638 hailed America 'Uppon the first sight of New-England'. No wonder a common form of eulogy for first-generation New England ministers was to liken them to Moses, 'Renouncing honour, profit, pleasure, ease', while their successors were hailed as Joshuas 'to lead us in the remaining part of our pilgrimage'.[28]

Colonists who, for religious reasons and to escape persecution, literally crossed a sea to find themselves in a land devoid of civilization and, if not a desert, uncultivated and hostile, might be expected to discern in the Exodus story a compelling precedent. The insistence in their histories that the colonists chose freely to emigrate implies, however, that the real journey was not physical but psychological and spiritual. In this sense, Exodus was as relevant to English nonconformists as to New England settlers. On Bartholomew Day, 1662, Philip Henry 'imitated the self-denial of Moses ... *rather choosing to suffer affliction with the people of God, than to enjoy the good things of this world*'. Before his conversion to Quakerism, William Dundas was 'long in *Egypt*'. Exodus, that is to say, was less the history of a migration than an exemplification of spiritual commitment, of the liberation of those who, in faith, spurned the world. Edward Taylor, in a meditation on Matthew ii.15, treated the Exodus as a type not only of the holy family's return from Egypt but also of the individual's escape from sin:

> But Isra'ls coming out of Egypt thus,
> Is such a Coppy that doth well Descry
> Not onely Christ in person unto us.
> But Spirituall Christ, and Egypt Spiritually.
> Egyptian Bondage whence gates Israel shows
> The Spiritual bondage whence Christs children goe.[29]

This Egypt all may choose to leave. 'Every small content glews us to our Egypt': it is open to every person to esteem 'the reproach of Christ greater riches than the treasures in Egypt' (Heb. xi.26) by forsaking the Egypt of carnality through the Red Sea of conversion and baptism for the wilderness of trial in hope of the Canaan of salvation. 'Out of Egypt', wrote Bunyan, 'thou must go through the Red Sea; thou must run a long and tedious journey, through the vast howling wilderness, before thou come to the land of promise.' Therein lies the real challenge: having resolved upon a mortified life and left Egypt, to stand by that choice throughout 'a long and tedious journey'; to continue to believe that Christ, the eternal manna, will prevent hunger and thirst in this desert (John vi.31–5). To his *War with the Devil* Keach appended a dialogue on the need for perseverance which he organized around, and articulated in terms of, the Exodus migration. It opens with an old man, Apostate, who, having abandoned the journey to Canaan, is making his way back to Egypt:

> How many Straits and Crosses have I met,
> Since I myself to seek for *Canaan* set!
> *Red-Seas* and Wildernesses lie between;
> Why venture I for what I ne'er have seen? ...
> Ah! would to God, in *Egypt* I'd remain'd,
> For there's no *Canaan* likely to be gain'd ...
>   back to *Egypt* I will now retire,
> Where I'll have all Things to my Heart's Desire.

Apostate meets a young man, Professor, who is travelling in the opposite direction. Professor is of another mind:

> What *Moses* chose of old, the same do I,
> All vain Allurements I do quite defy.
> I knew, when first my Journey I did take,
> I must my Father's House learn to forsake;
> In *Abraham's* Steps I am resolv'd to go,
> Whatever I exposed am unto.

This is the tenacity required of the saint: he must be not merely bold in undertaking his pilgrimage and watchful in pursuing it but also resolutely determined to complete it. This is the most demanding quality of all, for 'Man is naturally like a horse that loueth short journeys; and there are few that hold out.'[30]

This spiritualization of Exodus, which interpreted Moses as a type of Christ who 'openeth the way of the Red Sea to believers, giving the grace of baptism through the Red Sea of his blood', was encouraged by the parallel drawn between the historical Exodus and the new exodus of Christ in the Epistle to the Hebrews, the book which Tyndale had thought most 'playnlye declareth the meaninge and significacions of the sacrifices, ceremonies and fygures of the old testament'. However, its 'deep author', as Penn called him, believed by Owen and prevalent opinion to be Paul,[31] stresses that as the Israelites who wavered and rebelled perished in the wilderness, so must Christians 'hold fast', 'steadfast unto the end' (Heb. iii.6, 14). As in I Corinthians x.1–6, sin is held to have denied entry to Canaan to those 'whose carcasses fell in the wilderness' (Heb. iii.17–19). On this reading, the promised land was offered only conditionally: as some of those who enjoyed liberation from Egypt failed to reach Canaan, so the promise of salvation is conditional on constancy (Heb. iii.14, iv.1–11). There were few more sensitive topics of debate amongst Puritan and nonconformist divines than the doctrines of assurance and perseverance, but there was recognition that assurance was a gift, which may be withheld, and that uncritical reliance upon the doctrine of the necessary perseverance of the saints fostered complacency and hypocrisy. It is, after all, when he sleeps in the Arbour on Hill Difficulty that Christian loses the roll which was 'the assurance of his life, and acceptance at the desired Haven'. Christian's experience can encompass Doubting Castle because doubts and misgivings do not deny election: only abandoning the way does that, for 'he that keepes the way, is sure to come to the end'. While it may be true that, as one of Baxter's admired English practical divines, Robert Bolton, wrote, 'Grace once truely rooted in the heart, can never be remooved', the rootedness of one's faith remains open to question.[32]

Nonconformist story is hence without not only the arbitrariness of picaresque fiction but also the structural inevitability of the folktale (despite *The Pilgrim's Progress*'s affinities with the genre). The experiential fact of uncertainty is incontrovertible. When Bunyan's Honest, 'an old Man' who has 'bin a

Traveller in this Rode many a day', has seen pilgrims 'set out as if they would drive all the World afore them. Who yet have in a few days, dyed as they in the Wildnerness, and so never gat sight of the promised Land', it would be a foolhardy wayfarer who supposed that once he was through the gate all was well: 'you have your Journey yet to go.' It was in Exodus, as well (we may suppose) as in personal observation, that Bunyan found reason for Honest's caution: 'Almost all the many thousands of the children of Israel in their generation, fell short of perseverance when they walked from Egypt towards the land of Canaan. Indeed, they went to work at first pretty willingly, but they were very short-winded, they were quickly out of breath.' The saint only gains final assurance of perseverance when he has persevered. As Coleridge annotated *The Pilgrim's Progress*, the argument from predestination is 'a mere identical proposition followed by an assertion of God's prescience. Those who will persevere, will persevere, and God foresees.' Or, as the Shepherd answers Christian's query '*How far is it thither?*', 'Too far for any, but those that *shall* get thither indeed'. The discovery of their identity must await the end of the story. And so tension and suspense are inevitable, as James, to Great-heart's approval, comments on the case of Mr Fearing, who 'was always afraid that he should come short of whither he had desire to go', 'No fears, no Grace'. Truth doubts the sincerity of Youth's conversion in *War with the Devil* precisely because

> Thou seem'st too confident, 'tis a sad Sign:
> For Fears attend where saving-Grace doth shine.[33]

To resolve to leave Egypt was not, then, to ensure a happy ending; but, though it was to exchange the assurance of the familiar for the unknown and the uncertain, it was the only choice which made a happy ending possible. It is with a finely poised and yet positive ambivalence that *Paradise Lost* closes in a recollection of Israel's desert wanderings:

> Some natural tears they dropped, but wiped them soon;
> The world was all before them, where to choose
> Their place of rest, and providence their guide:
> They hand in hand with wandering steps and slow,
> Through Eden took their solitary way.

In this depiction of the direst journey in human history there is certainly sorrow and regret, yet it is tempered. This is less a leaving than a setting out. Milton concludes his epic not with judgement nor with expulsion, not with the 'flaming brand' and 'dreadful faces thronged and fiery arms' of the preceding lines, but with the prospect of people meeting an opportunity offered. In Books XI and XII Adam's contrition has turned to affirmative faith. The grim course of human history as presented by Michael has not denied the capacity of divine mercy to frustrate evil: 'O goodness infinite, goodness immense!/That all this good of evil shall produce,/And evil turns to good'. It is determined to obey, and so to share in this mercy, that, 'hand in hand', an emblem of fellowship, Adam and Eve begin their journey. An uninhabited world, a wilderness, awaits them, but 'The world was all before them' suggests less exile from bliss than limitless opportunities for discovery and joy. What is made of those opportunities depends upon Adam and Eve: they are, we might say, being given their chance. Lonely exile is not God's judgement, but they may, through their own exercise of free will ('where to choose'), so condemn themselves. Only their own disobedience and wrong choices, not their fallibility ('wandering steps'), can deny them Providence as a guide. And we have good cause to be hopeful. The echo of Psalm cvii.4 in the final line recalls not only Israel's wanderings in the wilderness but also that, when Israel 'cried unto the Lord', he 'led them forth by the right way'. The prospect of a wilderness may – indeed, should – prompt 'natural' sorrow, but 'nothing is here for tears': Milton ends by alluding to a psalm of thanksgiving and praise to the Lord whose 'mercy endureth for ever' for having redeemed the faithful 'from the hand of the enemy'.[34]

4 'THE WILDERNESS OF THIS WORLD'

It is not only by uncertainties and misgivings that the nonconformist protagonist is tried. Although the 'Den' of the dungeon of Doubting Castle renders concrete such inner doubts, the external adversity of that first 'Denn' is no less real or testing. Apollyon had good reason to threaten the potential convert Thoughtful in Keach's *Travels of True Godliness* with 'great persecution, it being the portion of all who entertained True Godliness, insomuch that his very life might be in danger'. In these extremities, the prophets of the Exile, addressing a people, like Bunyan in his 'Den', 'robbed and spoiled', 'snared in holes' (or 'dongeons', as Geneva has it) and 'hid in prison-houses' (Isa. xlii.22), offered the assurance that this trial was 'for their good' (Jer. xxiv.5). Unlike the waste land of Arthurian story, this wilderness may be not a curse but a blessing, for, as we noticed in Chapter 6, it is a necessary part of the journey and may assure the traveller that he is in the way.[35] Like Abraham, like the Israelites, whose 40 years of trial were re-enacted in Christ's 40 days in the wilderness (Matt. iv.1–11), Christians must expect to be tried, for those 'whom the Lord loveth he chasteneth' (Heb. xii.6).

Their story thus invites analysis in Aristotelian terms. Its beginning is no random point, no mere accident of the hero's birth or upbringing, but the genuine beginning of the 'new birth', which, since it is the unprompted operation of grace, 'is not itself necessarily after anything else'. It does, however, have 'naturally something else after it', the sustained testing of the validity of that beginning in the middle section, for it is by *firm obedience fully* tried/Through *all* temptation' that paradise is regained.[36] Upon the protagonist's performance during this middle section of trial depends the ending. And that resolution constitutes a final and irrevocable climax. The apparently slippery notion of 'progress', which has much exercised critics of Bunyan, may be understood in these terms. What begins as flight from sin, Egypt, Babylon, becomes for the saint a pilgrimage to Canaan. As his experience grows during the middle of his story, 'progress' shifts from its original sense of 'journey' to its modern sense of 'improvement', 'movement towards'. Christian early learns the importance of proceeding along the way, and the whole of the way, in the direction Evangelist sends him; but for the unregenerate there is no progress in this second sense, only a picaresque wandering: Formalist and Hypocrisy 'tumble over the Wall' midway, Atheist goes in the opposite direction, and Simple, Sloth and Presumption remain stationary, asleep. 'We must', as the Genevan version glossed John xiv.6, 'begin in him, continue in him, and end in him.'[37]

More pointedly, the oracles of the restoration of Israel explicitly invoked the Exodus saga. The location of Canaan midway between two scenes of bondage and exile encouraged the depiction of the way of Israel, no less than that of the individual, as a straight middle way between alternatives, the 'great dragon' of Egypt (Ezek. xxix.3) and the 'great whore' of Babylon (Rev. xvii.1–6). As Jehovah has led his people home through the wilderness from the former, so would he from the latter (e.g. Isa. xi.16, xxxv.8–10, xlviii.20–2, xlix.10–11; Jer. xxxi.2–5; Ezek. xx.5–38, xxxiv.11–15, xxxvi.22–38). These oracles had put sprightliness into the step of earlier Puritan travellers. The vision of Eden in the desert (Isa. li.3; Ezek. xxxvi.35), of a new heaven and a new earth (Isa. lxv.17), encouraged New England settlers in what Samuel Darnforth called their *Errand into the Wilderness* (1670). Jeremiah's castigation of the wickedness of Babylon with the call to 'go out of the midst of her', echoed in the potent context of Revelation (Jer. li.45; Rev. xviii.4; cf. Isa. lii.11), supported both those colonists in their emigration, giving a millenarian expectancy to their founding of the New Jerusalem, and those separatists who rejected an episcopal for a gathered church. John Lilburne entitled a 1639 pamphlet *Come Out of her My People*; John Robinson, citing Revelation, wrote that 'as the people of God in old time, were called out of Babylon civil ... so are the people of God now to go out of Babylon spiritual'; and John Winthrop 'led the van 'gainst Babylon.[38]

A liberation no less exhilarating was offered to nonconformists. The 'Precious promises of a return out of captivity', wrote Henry, may be received as our own whatever our situation, since Cyrus is 'a type of Christ' and the chapters we now distinguish as Deutero-Isaiah are 'for the consolation of all God's faithful worshippers'. Their oracles concerning 'the deliverance of the Jews out of Babylon' are 'applicable to the great salvation Christ hath wrought out for us'. Deutero-Isaiah's promise that God 'will bring the prisoner from the prison' (Isa. xlii.7, xlix.9) underlies many a depiction of conversion. Souls unregenerate are 'in bondage', wallowing 'in the Egyptian sea': Fox had been 'in spiritual Babylon ... Egypt'. Friends are to minister to 'captive' souls which 'must be led out of captivity' 'to walk cheerfully over the world'. To the boldness and resolution of the journey is, therefore, to be added, despite its trials and sufferings, the joy of liberation, a joy most exuberantly caught in 'lightsom' Christian's 'three leaps for joy'.[39]

This was, furthermore, a liberation available to the weak and downhearted. These Old Testament oracles recognized frankly that many who follow the Lord may well find the wilderness way exhausting. Their assurance that Jehovah will 'bind up that which was broken and will strengthen that which was sick', that he will 'give power to the faint' and lead the weary 'by the rivers of water, in a straight way, where they shall not stumble' (Isa. xl.28–31; Jer. xxxi.2, 8–9; Ezek. xxxiv.16), informs the pastoral concern of nonconformist divines for human fallibility and incapacity. The nonconformists' rejection of traditional heroism was neither expedient nor the (however humorous) self-interested casuistry of a Falstaff but a biblically inspired confidence that those willing to undertake an impossible adventure in the full knowledge of personal insufficiency do so with 'providence their guide'. Another of old Honest's experiences was of those 'that have promised nothing at first setting out to be Pilgrims, and that one could a thought could not have lived a day, that have yet proved very good Pilgrims'.[40]

Unlike New England colonists, who, for some years at least, had hopes that they were in the way to settle a 'New English Canaan', English nonconformists had weaned themselves from expectations of any significant change in their earthly condition. For them to apply to themselves, as Henry advised, Old Testament narratives and prophecies of liberating journeys was hence not only to interpret figuratively their geography but also to relocate their destination. 'I haue', wrote Heywood 'a building not made with hands, but eternal in the heauens [II Cor. v. 1] ... woe is me that I am forced to dwel in meshech [Ps. cxx.5], and sojourne in this weary wildernes, when shal my soul be set at liberty out of the mouldy cage.' The wilderness has come to encompass all of human life, as it does in the opening sentence of *The Pilgrim's Progress*: the end of the way lies, as it does for Christian, beyond time and space. The source of this resigned comprehensiveness lies in Hebrews.[41]

In the passage which inspired Baxter's *Saints Everlasting Rest* (1650), the Epistle, noting that in Psalm xcv.11 God is said to deny the erring Israelites not Canaan but 'my rest', argues that survival in the wilderness was a way not merely to a homeland but to an eternal salvation (Heb. iii.7–4, 16). This inclination to read Old Testament peregrinations as journeys not for temporal possession but for an eternal kingdom is more pronounced in the handling of Abraham and patriarchs in chapter xi. Genesis had allowed that, throughout his life, Abraham, like Isaac and Jacob after him, remained a nomadic 'stranger' in Canaan (xii.9, xiii.3, xvii.8). 'My country' is Mesopotamia, even at the end of his life (xxiv.4). He is, in the Septuagint, περάτης, or, in the Authorised Version, 'Abraham the Hebrew' (xiv.13). His last act was to ensure the continuance of his family's alien status by arranging Isaac's marriage not to a native Canaanite but to the granddaughter of his brother Nahor, Rebekah, who, still living in Mesopotamia, responded with the simple words which echo through biblical and nonconformist story alike: 'I will go' (xxiv.58). This preference for exile over return to Mesopotamia led the author of Hebrews to construe Abraham's faith as the hope 'for a better country, that is, an heavenly'. Consequently, not only Abraham but all the faithful become, in the words with which Jehovah himself had described the patriarchs (Exod. vi.4), 'strangers and pilgrims in the earth' (Heb. xi.8–16). As the Elizabethan homily *The Fear of Death* had it, 'life in this world is resembled and likened to a pilgrimage in a strange country far from God; and ... death, delivering us from our bodies, doth send us straight home into our country'. 'Bear yourselves as inhabitants of another country' said Howe.[42]

Although the characterization of the 'strange country' of this world as a wilderness is not directly biblical, biblical deserts of exile, trial and spiritual enlightenment supplied the most frequent metaphor to express the homelessness of saints whose destination was the New Jerusalem (Rev. xxi). Anne Bradstreet could, like many New Englanders, present the journey as a sea voyage, the saint 'sailing through this world unto his heavenly country', but when, in her untitled poem 'As weary pilgrim', she longs 'to be at rest/ And soar on high among the blest', it is a wilderness she creates as the context of her mortal life, beset by 'dangers', 'travails', 'burning sun', 'briars and thorns', 'hungry wolves', 'erring paths' and 'parching thirst'.[43] She might more plausibly have claimed to inhabit a wilderness than English nonconformists, but her poem is metaphorical, not mimetic. It need not have been written in, and is not about, New England. The wilderness which is its subject is not an observable, geographical location but a spiritual conviction unrestricted by time or place, the universal perception of faith. That perception and conviction were shared equally by English nonconformists. In Henry's gloss on Genesis xii.6–9, 'All good people must look upon themselves as strangers and sojourners in this world, and by faith sit loose to it, as "a strange country"', the phrases 'look upon' and 'by faith' are parallel. The nonconformist who, as Keach's Professor protests to Apostate, walked not by 'Sight and Sense' but 'by Faith' (II Cor. v.7), perceived himself a pilgrim providentially led like the Israelites through the desert. As we have heard Fox say, 'It is the great love of God to make a wilderness of that which is pleasant to the outward eye and fleshly mind.'[44]

The wilderness image was hence quite as serviceable in London as in New England, and was deployed by English nonconformists quite as pertinently as by New Englanders. They could not, like Morton, set it in the recent historical context which enabled him to hope that his *New England's Memorial* would, though an historiographical work, be a practical and devotional 'help to thee in thy journey through the wilderness of this world, to that Eternal Rest which is only to be found in the Heavenly Canaan'. It nevertheless lay all around them.

The full title of the work in which Gouge wrote that we are to live 'as a citizen of heaven, and a pilgrim on earth' is *The Young Man's Guide through the Wilderness of this World to the Heavenly Canaan*. It is through 'the wilderness of this world' that Keach's True Godliness, like Bunyan at the start of *The Pilgrim's Progress*, goes 'up and down'. It was with a terse statement of this commonplace that Bunyan concluded the preface to *Grace Abounding*: 'The Milk and Honey is beyond this Wilderness.'[45]

But what, then, of that joy in the created world which was claimed for nonconformists in the previous chapter?[46] Unexpectedly, and perhaps ironically, yet quite understandably, the representation of the general state of mortal life through the image of the wilderness was entirely compatible with delight in the observed features of the physical world. Indeed, the two were mutually reinforcing. No sensualist would undertake a pilgrimage, but neither would a dullard insensitive to worldly joys. Nonconformist writing avoided both extremes. For those who, alive to natural beauty, retained their awareness that it was only natural, the more sensitive their responsiveness to it the greater would be their apprehension of that 'other country'. We should, wrote Baxter, argue 'from sensitive delights as from the less to the greater': 'How delightful are pleasing odors to our smel? how delightful is perfect musick to the ear? how delightful are beauteous sights to the eye? ... O then think every time thou seest or remembrest these, what a fragrant smell hath the pretious ointment which is poured on the head of our glorified Saviour.'[47] The image of the wilderness did not contradict such sensory pleasure but directed it as Baxter recommended. Christian and Hopeful are not persuaded by their delight at the river's side to give over their journey: it encourages them to continue on their way. This is not 'Journeys end' but a foretaste of that end. Just so, in one of the sources of this scene, the Song of Songs, the prospect of natural beauty and fecundity arouses the yearnings of love for fulfilment (ii.4, 10–12). It is in Bunyan's 'sweet and pleasant' country of Beulah (Isa. lxii.4), which draws on these same verses from the Song, that the pilgrims 'with desire fell sick'. Only the capacity at once to perceive the world as a wilderness and to respond to its beauty and joy could both set the pilgrim in the way to the Celestial City and arouse in him those longings which would keep him in it.[48]

Nonconformist story follows a protagonist who, discontented and dimly aware that there may be that which answers to his need, sets out on a quest for fulfilment. This structure shares something with the scope of the novel as it evolved in the work of Defoe and later eighteenth-century writers. Where it differs is in its refusal to complete the quest in this world. It offers not the this-worldly comfort achieved by a Crusoe or a Moll Flanders, only the challenge of continuing trial allayed by the increasingly intense expectation of final rest. Eighteenth-century fictional heroes may travel, but they arrive at their point of departure (with some wealth, a wife and perhaps a little wisdom). The nonconformists' fondness for the journey as an image of spiritual development, an expression of the yearning of the mortal and mutable for the immortal and immutable, will not again be current until the Romantic period, and we do not too absurdly reach for the word 'romantic' to suggest the subjective basis and revelatory force of quest narratives which thus trace in the visible the invisible. We might, indeed, apply the term to the idealism (if not Platonism) of their literary inspiration, the interpretation of the Old Testament by the author of the Epistle to the Hebrews. For nonconformists, as for him, archetypal biblical narratives told of 'a way in the wilderness', 'The way of holiness', in which those who walked should 'find rest for their souls' (Isa. xliii,19, xxxv.8; Jer. vi.16). There was no other story to tell: 'I am', says Keach's Professor, 'a Stranger, and I am going Home.'[49]

Conclusion

the literary temper of nonconformity

The literary culture of nonconformity was not moribund but vital. This study has attempted to show that writing was essential to the survival of nonconformity and that, in meeting the adverse circumstances of the late seventeenth century, nonconformity created a committed Christian literature of distinctive character. It was a literature which in its premises and procedures dissented from evolving literary canons as did nonconformists themselves from the developing values of what came to be called Anglicanism. This literary dissent was misrepresented by contemporary conformists as introvertedly sectarian, retrogressive and obscurantist. It was rather creative, positive and salutary in its demotic realism, its subjective authenticity, its metaphorical richness and its sensitivity to the numinous. In these respects it anticipated a later, and greater, literary movement: its tendency is towards the work not of Pope but of Blake, Wordsworth and Coleridge, men who admired not only the genius of Milton, as the eighteenth century had done, but also that of Bunyan and Baxter, as the eighteenth century had not.[1]

This affinity between nonconformist writing and Romanticism has been noticed before.[2] In 1910 Joseph Ritson published an historical appreciation of the nonconformist tradition in order to inspire his younger contemporaries to continue to work for a free church in a free state. He called it *The Romance of Nonconformity*, meaning by that title 'an imaginative reconstruction of the facts of a wonderful story'. The resulting pious, but partisan, account finds romance in the extraordinary, the heroic, the adventurous and the resilient in nonconformist history. These qualities are real enough, but stretch somewhat even the capacious term 'romantic'. Something more specific is, however, suggested by Ritson's approving quotation of R. A. Scott-James's definition of the romantic response as 'when suddenly a thought, an action, the gleam of a moment makes us leap to our feet as at a vision, as at the promise of some instant fulfilment of life'.[3] Scott-James is recalling the 'visionary gleam' of Wordsworth's 'Immortality Ode', the visionary trance of 'Tintern Abbey' and the 'spots of time' of *The Prelude*, and in this sense nonconformist writing was indeed romantic.[4] While the world moved on to rationalism, scepticism and pragmatism, it retained its commitment to the visionary. It told of a faith which was not, in Keach's entirely representative words, 'a bare living up to the natural principles of morality' but 'a faithful living up to the supernatural principles of grace and the gospel'.[5]

This the seventeenth century knew as enthusiasm, and it was the enthusiastic in older literature which the Romantics valued most highly. Coleridge drew a distinction between fanaticism ('the *fever* of *superstition*') and enthusiasm ('an undue (or when used in a good sense, an unusual) vividness of ideas') and recognized in Bunyan the genius of the latter: 'Bunyan was a man of too much genius to be a fanatic ... Enthusiasm, indeed, ὁ Θεὸς ἐν 'ημῖν, is almost a synonym of genius; the moral life in the intellectual life, the will in the reason.' This degree of self-involvement and commitment does not obliterate but realize individuality. It is fanatical spirits, 'who catch heat by crowding together round the same *Fane*', who lose themselves.[6] The enthusiast becomes himself, dares to dissent by being himself. If the nonconformist's faith in an immanent and supernatural deity was not of a sort to commend him to his age, no more was his evidence for that faith: 'I, by Experience, can confute them all.'[7]

This, as they called it, 'experimental' knowledge of God had little time for literary fashions or poses. It spoke directly to the reader with the urgent immediacy of personal conviction and with the persuasive authenticity of varied, and variously modulated, individual voices. It spoke with an honest awareness, born of personal experience, of people's imperfect natures and of the complexity of worldly affairs, but, though it toyed with no extravagant impossibilities, it spoke also with the sure confidence that the world could be overcome, that in the sufferings of nonconformists lay the promise of final victory. Hence, as its experiential basis preserved nonconformist writing from the escapist flights of romance, so its supernatural faith preserved it from sardonic preoccupation with political machinations and social *mores*. Although this refusal to take refuge in either the ideal or the material was also a refusal to prefer either romance or realism, it denied neither: rather, it admitted both. It married the alternative worlds that literary fashions and genres tended to divorce. Nonconformity's commitment to God and to man resulted in that literary equipoise exemplified in different ways in the 'realistic allegory' of Bunyan; in the metaphorical plainness of Quaker prose; in the psychological accuracy Milton discerned in biblical folktale, or in the subjectivity of his epic voice, or in the revolving of the grandeur of *Paradise Lost* around a story of human inadequacy. It is there in the restrained politeness with which Howe insists on emotional responsiveness, in the equal hostility in Keach of both Riches and Poverty to True Godliness, in the rationalism of Baxter's mysticism, in the inconsequentiality of incidents which manifest the Lord's power in Fox's *Journal*.

Even the apparently clear, and clearly exceptional, case of Marvell's later work affords neither an example conveniently classifiable as unique (witness Alsop), nor a readily categorizable and straightforward assumption of the persona of a Restoration satirist. Although the movement of his literary career from introspective lyric to topical satire runs counter to that sketched in this study as characteristic of nonconformist writing generally, Marvell did not simply exchange a private for a public world. As his earlier poetry had pressed the lyric to meditate upon the personal implications of public events,[8] so his later satires serve not society but the individual in society. Marvell is no disillusioned observer like Rochester nor a Classical satirist like Dryden defending the status quo. The wit which in Rochester mocks all idealistic aspiration, in Marvell affirms that conscientious individuality which in Dryden is ridiculed as enthusiastic chicanery and the subversion of all right order and social decency.[9] Though obviously a Restoration satirist in his methods, Marvell will not fit: he contrives to be at one and the same time an individualistic outsider like Rochester and a party man like Dryden; but his kind of individuality and of partisanship were scorned equally by Rochester and Dryden.

But, then, something would be amiss if a nonconformist did fit in.[10] We may recall again St Paul's words, 'And be not conformed to this world: but be ye transformed by the renewing of your mind' (Rom. xii.2). It was, as St Paul himself demonstrated, a part of such nonconformity to dissent from, and to transform, the world's literary presuppositions, prejudices and traditions. The nonconformist transformed epic into anti-epic, heroes into villains, failures into heroes, stories into homilies, sermons to fables, divinity to allegory, allegory to realism, realism to metaphor, this world to a wilderness and a wilderness into a wonder. Bunyan's 'Apology' entices the would-be reader of *The Pilgrim's Progress* with a string of oxymorons and paradoxes advertising his book's generic elusiveness, its mingling of literary techniques and moods:

> *Art thou for something rare, and profitable?*
> *Wouldest thou see a Truth within a Fable? ...*
> *It seems a Novelty, and yet contains*
> *Nothing but sound and honest Gospel-strains*
> *   Wouldst thou divert thy self from Melancholly?*
> *Would'st thou be pleasant, yet be far from folly? ...*
> *Would'st thou be in a Dream, and yet not sleep?*
> *Or would'st thou in a moment Laugh and Weep?*
> *Wouldest thou loose thy self, and catch no harm?*
> *And find thy self again without a charm?*
> *Would'st read thy self, and read thou know'st not what*
> *And yet know whether thou art blest or not,*
> *By reading the same lines? O then come hither,*
> *And lay my Book, thy Head and Heart together.*

Whatever else it might be, reading this book is going to be a novel and unpredictable experience; we are going to lose our bearings, our common sense challenged by a mystery.[11]

'Behold, I make all things new' (Rev. xxi.5): the nonconformist exercised his own divine gift of creativity to renovate and originate, though not that literature might be reborn. It was the reader he would transform: '*This Book*', hoped Bunyan, '*will make a Travailer of thee.*'[12]

Notes

NOTE Places of publication are given only for works published outside the United Kingdom.

INTRODUCTION

1. Edmund Calamy, *Memoirs of John Howe* (1724), 213.
2. John Ferguson, *Pelagius* (1956), 45, 77–8, 93–5; F. L. Cross (ed.), *Oxford Dictionary of the Christian Church* (1958), s.vv. Germanus, Pelagianism, Semi-Pelagianism. For the controversies with Jerome see also J. N. D. Kelly, *Jerome* (1975), 309–23.
3. Geoffrey of Monmouth, *Historia Regum Britanniae*, XI.xii, as translated by Lewis Thorpe, *The History of the Kings of Britain* (1966), 266.
4. Bede, *Historia Ecclesiastica Gentis Anglorum*, II.ii, V.xxii and xxiii, as translated by Leo Sherley-Price, revised by R. E. Latham, *A History of the English Church and People* (1968), 100–3, 328–9, 331; Thomas Stapleton (trans.), *Ecclesiastical History of the English People*, ed. Philip Hereford (1935), p. xxxiv.
5. Peter A. Fiore, *Milton and Augustine* (1981), 1–11.
6. John Foxe, *Acts and Monuments*, ed. Josiah Pratt, 4th edn rev., 8 vols ([1877]), I.305–8, 337–8; cf. Thomas Fuller, *Church-History of Britain*, ed. James Nichols, 3rd edn, 3 vols (1868), I.106–7 (II.ii.3). For an account convinced Celtic independence 'handed down the torch of truth' to Hussites, Lollards and Reformers, see Thomas M'Crie, *Annals of English Presbytery* (1872), 18–22, from which the Bale reference is taken. For similar parallels between the later Cistercians and Congregationalists see Geoffrey F. Nuttall, *Visible Saints* (1957), 3–4. On the Culdees see William Reeves, *The Culdees* (Dublin, 1864), esp. 27–32, and on the polity of the British church, Nora Chadwick, *The Age of the Saints in the Early Celtic Church* (1961), 63–88, and Nora Chadwick *et al.*, *Studies in the Early British Church* (1958), index, *s.v. clas.*

7. Jonathan F. Post, *Henry Vaughan* (Princeton, NJ, 1982), 123–6; Milton, *CPW*, V.i.192–3; Marvell, *RT*, 115, 16.
8. Geoffrey Chaucer, 'General Prologue', *The Canterbury Tales*, I.477–528. William Haller, *The Rise of Puritanism* (1938; rpt New York, 1957), 3–4 quotes Chaucer's character of the Parson as an exemplification of that spirit of Christian commitment which would later be called 'Puritan'.
9. Chaucer, 'Epilogue to the Man of Law's Tale [The Shipman's Prologue]', *Canterbury Tales*, II.1173. On Chaucer and Lollardy see H. Simon, 'Chaucer a Wyclifite', *Chaucer Society Essays*, III (1876), 227–92; John S. P. Tatlock, 'Chaucer and Wyclif', *MP*, XIV, 5 (1916), 257–68; and Roger S. Loomis, 'Was Chaucer a Laodicean?', in *Essays and Studies in Honor of Carleton Brown* (New York, 1940), 129–48.
10. Possible etymologies are succinctly listed in F. N. Robinson (ed.), *The Works of Geoffrey Chaucer*, 2nd edn (1957), 697, n. to l. 1173, and in H. B. Workman, *John Wyclif*, 2 vols (1926), I.327. A derivation from Old Dutch 'lollen' (to mutter, mumble) would anticipate the similar scornful allusion to habits of worship and devotion in 'Ranter' and 'Quaker'.
11. Milton, *CPW*, I.525–6, II.552–3.
12. Foxe, *Acts and Monuments*, II.790–6; Margaret Aston, 'John Wycliffe's Reformation reputation', *Past and Present*, 30 (1965), 23–51; Anne Hudson (ed.), *Selections from English Wycliffite Writings* (1978), 155, 183. Chaucer and Langland were read and edited to similar purpose: see John N. King, *English Reformation Literature* (Princeton, NJ, 1982), 50–2, 319–39.
13. K. B. McFarlane, *Wycliffe and English Non-Conformity* (1952; rpt 1972), xiii; Watts, *DRR*, 7–14; Claire Cross, *Church and People 1450–1660* (1976; rpt 1979),

14–44, 73–5; A. G. Dickens, *The English Reformation* (1966), 33–7; *id., Lollards and Protestants in the Diocese of York 1509–1558* (1959), *passim*; John Thomson, *The Later Lollards 1414–1520* (1965), esp. 239–53; Margaret Aston, 'Lollardy and the Reformation: survival or revival?', *History*, XLIX (1964), 149–70.

14. Watts, *DRR* 9–10; George H. Williams, *The Radical Reformation* (1962), 401–3, 778–9.

15. Foxe, *Acts and Monuments*, VII.550. On the vogue and influence of Foxe see William Haller, *Foxe's Book of Martyrs and the Elect Nation* (1963), 13–15 and *passim*; J. F. Mozley, *John Foxe and his Book* (1940), 137–9.

16. N. H. Keeble, *Richard Baxter: Puritan Man of Letters* (1982), 38, 115; John Brown, *John Bunyan (1628–88)*, rev. F. M. Harrison (1928), 153–4; Bunyan, *GA*, 122, 153; Bunyan, *PP*, 97, 260, 328; Bunyan, *MW*, II.239, VIII.383–4, 412, IX.309, 345; Bunyan, *CW*, II.700b, 717a.

17. John Crooke, *The Cry of the Innocent* (1662), sig. A2ᵛ; William Sachse (ed.), *The Diary of Roger Lowe* (1938), 99; Fox, *JGF*, 484.

18. See C. H. Garrett, *The Marian Exiles* (1938).

19. W. H. Frere and C. E. Douglas (eds), *Puritan Manifestoes* (1907), 9. The *Admonition* was the work of John Field and Thomas Wilcox: see Patrick Collinson, *The Elizabethan Puritan Movement* (1967), 118–20.

20. Thomas Fuller dated it from 1564 in his *Church-History*, II.540 (IX.i.67); Peter Heylyn from 1565 in *Ecclesia Restaurata* (1661), 172 (both cited in A. F. Scott-Pearson, *Thomas Cartwright* (1925), 18 n. 5) and from 1566 in *Examen Historicum* (1659), 149; John Stow from 'about' 1567 in *The Chronicles of England* in *Three Fifteenth-Century Chronicles*, ed. J. Gardiner, Camden Society, n.s.XXVIII (1880), 143. *OED*'s first citation is from 1572, with 'Puritanism' following in 1573, 'Puritant' in 1604, 'Puritanize' in 1605, 'Puritanic' in 1606 and 'Puritanical' in 1607. The related term 'Precisian' is known from 1571 and 1572. The origin, senses and early currency of the term are documented in M. Van Beek. *An Enquiry*

into *Puritan Vocabulary* (Groningen, 1969), 32–5.

21. Collinson, *Puritan Movement*, 29–35, 92–7; M. M. Knappen, *Tudor Puritanism* (1939; rpt Chicago, 1965), 168–71.

22. Watts, *DRR*, 18–25; Cross, *Church and People*, 136–9; Collinson, *Puritan Movement*, 69–83; Knappen, *Tudor Puritanism*, 187–216. The *Advertisements* are excerpted in Henry Bettenson (ed.), *Documents of the Christian Church*, 2nd edn (1967), 239–40.

23. Bolam, *EP*, 30–2; Collinson, *Puritan Movement*, 109–21, 131–45, 243–72, 314–15; Knappen, *Tudor Puritanism*, 221–5, 265–82.

24. Watts, *DRR*, 56–62; Bolam, *EP*, 33; Collinson, *Puritan Movement*, 273–316; Knappen, *Tudor Puritanism*, 285–8; Haller, *Rise of Puritanism*, 49–82.

25. Fuller, *Church-History*, III.36(IX.v.2); cf. III.112 (IX.vii.21–3). For a description of this pastoral reformation in the late Elizabethan period, see Collinson, *Puritan Movement*, 328–82.

26. *OED*, s.vv. 'Nonconformist, 1a', 'Nonconformity, 1'; John Geree, *The Character of an Old English Puritane, or Non-Conformist* (1646), 1, 4; Watts, *DRR*, 16.

27. *Rel. Bax.*, I.13–14, §§17–19.

28. Bolam, *EP*, 36–8, 46–72; Geoffrey F. Nuttall and Owen Chadwick (eds), *From Uniformity to Unity* (1962), 49–51; J. C. Spalding and M. F. Bras, 'Reduction of episcopacy', *CH*, XXX (1961), 414–32; A. H. Wood, *Church Unity without Uniformity* (1963), 71–9, 81–96, 118. The fullest account of the Westminster Assembly is by Robert S. Paul, *The Assembly of the Lord* (1985).

29. [James Webster], *Lawful Prejudices against an Incorporating Union with England* (1707), 8; *Rel. Bax.*, II.146, §23; II.278, §113; II.284, §128; II.373, §242; III.41, §91; Keeble, *Baxter*, 28, 152–3.

30. *Rel. Bax.*, II.146, §23; Alexander Gordon, *Heads of English Unitarian History* (1895), 64–5.

31. Jones, *CE*, 28; Watts, *DRR*, 66–7, 84–6, 96, 99–100; *DNB*, s.v. Burton; Nuttall, *Visible Saints*, 8 n. 4; *OED*, s.vv. 'Independency, 1', 'Congregationalism'. The *Apologeticall Narration* is included in

William Haller (ed.), *Tracts on Liberty in the Puritan Revolution*, 3 vols (New York, 1934), II.305–39, and was edited by Robert S. Paul in 1963. For the 'Dissenting Brethren', see Paul, *Assembly*, 121–7.

32. H. G. Tibbutt (ed.), *The Minutes of the First Independent Church (now Bunyan Meeting) at Bedford* (1976), 19; Albert Peel (ed.), *The Savoy Declaration of Faith and Order* (1939), 28.

33. Peel (ed.), *Savoy Declaration*, 70, 71, 73, 75; Nuttall, *Visible Saints*, 15–16; Jones, *CE*, 34–8; P. Toon, *God's Statesman: The Life and Work of John Owen* (1971), 103–5.

34. Peel (ed.), *Savoy Declaration*, 29, 31; Milton, 'On the New Forcers of Conscience', ll. 6, 20, in *PJM*, 296, 298; Watts, *DRR*, 103.

35. B. R. White, *The English Separatist Tradition* (1971), 2–19.

36. Watts, *DRR*, 19–40; White, *Separatist Tradition*, 20–90. On the elusive connections between early Independency, Congregationalism and separatism, see Nuttall, *Visible Saints*, 4–13; Watts, *DRR*, 50–6, 94–9, 108–9, 151–60, and references there cited.

37. Watts, *DRR*, 41–9; Underwood, *EB*, 33–8, 40–1, 46–7, Whitley, *BB*, 20–1; B. R. White, *The English Baptists of the Seventeenth Century* (1983), 23–9.

38. Watts, *DRR*, 65–6; Underwood, *EP*, 57; Bunyan, *PP*, 207; White, *English Baptists*, 58–64.

39. [Edward Terrill], *Records of a Church of Christ meeting in Broadmead, Bristol*, ed. E. B. Underhill (1847), 19–20; Henry Newcome, *The Autobiography*, ed. Richard Parkinson (1852), 118–19; Andrew Marvell, 'The first anniversary of the government under O.C.', ll. 299, 313–14, in *P&L*, I.116. On Munster, see Williams, *Radical Reformation*, 362–86, and on Canne, J. Wilson, 'Another look at John Canne', *CH*, XXXIII (1964), 34–47 which, following Champlin Burrage, confirms that the Bristol visit occurred not in 1640 but in 1648 and that Canne was never a Baptist (pp. 36–8). Terrill's remark nevertheless illustrates the contemporary force of the term 'Anabaptist'.

40. For succinct summaries of their opinions and history see Watts, *DRR*, 117–42, 179–208, and for the current historiographical view of them, J. F. McGregor and B. Reay (eds), *Radical Religion in the English Revolution* (1984). For the view that these enthusiasts constituted a third, revolutionary, culture in earlier seventeenth-century England see Christopher Hill, *The World Turned Upside Down* (1972; rpt 1975).

41. Fox, *JGF*, 58; Braithwaite, *BQ*, 57–8; Penney, *ESP*, 1; *OED*, sv. 'Quaker, 2'. For the relationship between Quakers and Interregnum radicals, see Braithwaite, *BQ*, chapters i–iv *passim*.

42. John Milton, *Areopagitica* (1644) and *Doctrine and Discipline of Divorce* (1643), in *CPW*, II.223, 224, 543, 551; W. T. Whitley (ed.), *The Works of John Smyth*, 2 vols (1915), II.564 (and cf. II.752); [Terrill], *Records*, 8–26.

43. Fox, *JGF*, 3, 4, 6, 10, 11; Braithwaite, *BQ*, 30–9; Richard Baxter, *Directions for Weak Christians* (1669), sigs G8–G8ᵛ; *id.*, *The Life of Faith* (1670), 196.

44. Richard Baxter, *The Second Part of the Nonconformists Plea for Peace* (1680), sig. a1ᵛ; Whitley (ed.), *Works of Smyth*, II.748 (and cf. I.cxx); Thomas Helwys, *Mistery of Iniquity*, facsimile rpt (1935), 69; Underwood, *EB*, 42–7; Watts, *DRR*, 48, 49.

45. W. C. Abbott (ed.), *Writings and Speeches of Oliver Cromwell*, 4 vols (Cambridge, Mass., 1937–47), I.360, 377, III.62, 459, IV.276.

46. [Edward Burrough], *A Visitation of Love* (1660), 14; R. S. Bosher, *The Making of the Restoration Settlement* (1957), 265.

47. Hill, *World Turned Upside Down*, 77–8, 153–4; *id.*, *Puritanism and Revolution* (1958), 323–8; Bernard S. Capp, *The Fifth Monarchy Men* (1972), 16–22; William Lamont, *Richard Baxter and the Millennium* (1979), 9–25 and *passim*.

48. Anne Bradstreet, 'Dialogue between Old England and New', ll. 286–93, in *Works*, ed. J. Hensley (Cambridge, Mass., 1967), 187.

49. Abraham Cowley, *The Essays and Other Prose Writings*, ed. Alfred B. Gough (1915), 87; Antonia Fraser, *Cromwell Our Chief of Men* (1973; rpt 1976), 558–68, sees pragmatism as Cromwell's main motive. For a full discussion of the bearing

of millenarianism on the Jewish question, see David S. Katz, *Philo-Semitism and the Re-Admission of the Jews to England 1603–55* (1982), 89–126, and for the 1655 negotiations, *ibid.*, 190–231, which rejects 'economic self-interest' as Cromwell's main motive (pp. 195–6).

50. Abbott (ed.), *Writings … of Cromwell*, I.377, 638, 697; III.53, 64, 591, 592.

51. Andrew Marvell, 'To His Coy Mistress', l. 10; 'Horatian Ode', ll. 9–12; 'First Anniversary', ll. 293–320, 125–30, 144, 109–10, 131–40, in *P&L*, I.27, 91, 116, 111–12.

52. Milton, *CPW*, II.557–8; the allusion to Samson is noted in Edgar F. Daniels, 'Samson in *Areopagitica*', *N&Q*, CCIX (1964), 92–3, and in the annotation in *CPW*, *loc. cit.*

53. *Rel. Bax.*, I.100, §145; Cowley, *Essays*, 46.

54. Sir Giles Isham (ed.) *Correspondence of Bishop Brian Duppa and Sir Justinian Isham*, Northants. Record Soc. Publ. XVII (1956), 180; Christopher Hill, *Milton and the English Revolution* (1973; rpt 1979), 347; Abraham Cowley, 'Upon his Majesty's Restoration and Return', ll. 134–44, and Edmund Waller, 'A Panegyric to my Lord Protector', ll. 169–73, quoted from *Silver Poets of the Seventeenth Century*, ed. G. A. E. Parfitt (1974), 228, 25; John Dryden, 'Heroique Stanzas' and 'Astraea Redux', l. 321, in *Poems and Fables*, ed. James Kinsley (1962), 24; Gilbert Burnet, *The Life and Death of John Earl of Rochester* (1692), 3–4.

55. 'Tom Tell-Troth', *A Letter to the Earl of Shaftesbury* ([1680]), 2.

56. Richard Baxter, *Gildas Salvianus: The Reformed Pastor* (1656), 380.

57. J. P. Kenyon, *Stuart England* (1978; rpt 1982), 182; Bunyan, *PP*, 45–6, 65, 244–5.

58. Raymond Stearns, *The Strenuous Puritan: Hugh Peter* (Urbana, Ill., 1954), 416–20; Milton, *CPW*, VII.463; Thomas Ellwood, *The History of the Life* (1714), 131; Marvell, *RT*, 312; *Rel. Bax.*, II.440, §439 and II.383, §274; N. H. Keeble, 'Richard Baxter's preaching ministry', *JEH*, XXXV (1984), 545–6; Samuel Pepys, *The Diary*,

ed. Robert Latham and William Matthews, 11 vols (1970–83), IV.373–4 (9 Nov. 1663).

59. Hill, *World Turned Upside Down*, 370, 378–9, 256, 332; *id., Some Intellectual Consequences of the English Revolution* (1980) 55; Anthony Fletcher, 'The authority of enthusiam', *TLS*, 4,272 (15 Feb. 1985), 182.

60. J. R. Jones, *Country and Court: England 1658–1714* (1978; rpt 1980), 154–5; Peter Malekin, *Liberty and Love: English Literature and Society 1640–88* (1981), 175; G. B. Harrison, *John Bunyan* (1928), 11.

61. Martin Gray, *A Dictionary of Literary Terms* (1984), 173; James Sutherland, *English Literature in the Later Seventeenth Century* (1969), 25.

62. Sutherland, *English Literature*, 25–31; Kenyon, *Stuart England*, 346.

63. Emile Legouis and Louis Cazamian, *History of English Literature*, rev. edn (1960), 601–2; Hill, *World Turned Upside Down*, 404.

64. Harrison, *Bunyan*, 11; Legouis and Cazamian, *History*, 567.

65. Roberta Florence Brinkley (ed.), *Coleridge on the Seventeenth Century* (New York, 1968), 475; Walter Allen, *The English Novel* (1958), 32; Roger Sharrock (ed.), *The Pilgrim's Progress: A Casebook* (1976), 78.

66. Maurice Ashley, *England in the Seventeenth Century*, 3rd edn (1967), 162, 109.

67. Bruce King, *Seventeenth-Century English Literature* (1982), 256–60, 185–6, 211, 208. For the editing of Fox's *Journal*, see below, n. 55 to ch. 6.

68. Hill, *World turned Upside Down*, 239; Robert Barclay, *Michel Unmasqued* (1672), 2.

69. Macaulay, *The History of England*, ed. C. H. Firth, 6 vols (1913–15), II.867. This is discussed on pp. 61–4.

70. *Rel. Bax.*, I.96–7, §139; Milton, *PR*, III.386–402 and *PL*, XII.585–7, IN *PJM*, 1133–4, 1056.

71. *Rel. Bax.*, II.297, §402. For similar expressions, see pp. 191–3, and with the view that they do constitute something very like capitulation, Hill, *World Turned Upside Down*, 350–1.

72. Nabil I. Matar, 'Peter Sterry, the millennium and Oliver Cromwell',

JURCHS, II (1982), 342; John Howe, *The Blessedness of the Righteous* (1673), 399; Milton, *PR*, II.466–7, in *PJM*, 1115.
73. Hill, *Milton*, 349.
74. Howe, *Blessedness*, 2, 4.

CHAPTER 1

1. Browning, *EHD*, 57–8.
2. *Rel. Bax.*, II.217, §74.
3. For various assessments of Charles's motives, see Watts, *DRR*, 221–2, and below, nn. 16–18.
4. Burnet, *OT*, I.89; Robert S. Bosher, *The Making of the Restoration Settlement* (1957), 146–7; Douglas R. Lacey, *Dissent and Parliamentary Politics in England 1661–1689* (New Brunswick, NJ, 1969), 4–12, 268; David Ogg, *England in the Reign of Charles II*, 2nd edn (1956; rpt 1967), 27–9.
5. Fox, *JGF*, 354; Lacey, *Parliamentary Politics*, 11, 267 n. 32. For Baptist quietism see Underwood, *EB*, 89–91, and for an interpretation of Quaker quietism after the Restoration as a deliberate rejection of their Interregnum activism, see James F. Maclear, 'Quakerism and the end of the Interregnum', *CH*, XIX (1950), 240–70 (and cf. Braithwaite, *BQ*, 460–2, 481).
6. *Rel. Bax.*, II.229, §§87, 88.
7. *Rel. Bax.*, II.230, §90 and II.231, §91.
8. *Rel. Bax.*, II.281–4, §§118–27; Bosher, *Restoration Settlement*, 193–4; I. M. Green, *The Re-Establishment of the Church of England* (1978), 83–8. Only Reynolds accepted.
9. For the debates on this bill, see Bosher, *Restoration Settlement*, 171–9.
10. *Rel. Bax.*, II.259, §105; II.279, §§114, 115. The draft is printed in *Rel. Bax.*, II.259–64, and the final version in Browning, *EHD*, 365–70. The discussions surrounding it are detailed in *Rel. Bax.*, II.265–79, §§106–115, and in Bosher, *Restoration Settlement*, 184–90.
11. *Rel. Bax.*, II.276, §110; II.284–5, §§128–9; II.379–80, §263; II.430, §419; Bosher, *Restoration Settlement*, 187–8, 189–90.
12. John Sudbury, *A Sermon Preached at the Consecration of the Right Reverend Fathers in God ...* (1660), *passim;* Bosher, *Restoration Settlement*, 179–84; Norman Sykes, *From Sheldon to Secker* (1959), 6–8; Green, *Re-Establishment*, 89–98, 255, which argues that the new bishops were less uniformly Laudian than Bosher claimed.
13. Lacey, *Parliamentary Politics*, 12–13; Bosher, *Restoration Settlement*, 195–9; Marvell, *P&L*, II.6; Andrew Marvell (?), 'Third Advice to a Painter', ll. 239–40, in *Complete Poetry*, ed. George de F. Lord (1984), 137.
14. *Rel. Bax.*, II.297, §403; II.281, §121.
15. Bosher, *Restoration Settlement*, 176–7, 180, 190; cf. Watts, *DRR*, 218; J. R. Jones, *Court and Country: England 1658–1714* (1978; rpt 1980), 137.
16. Green, *Re-Establishment, passim;* Anne Whiteman, 'The Restoration of the Church of England', in Geoffrey F. Nuttall and Owen Chadwick (eds), *From Uniformity to Unity* (1962), 71–2.
17. Sir John Reresby, *Memoirs*, ed. Andrew Browning (1936), 112–13.
18. R. A. Beddard, 'The Restoration Church', in J. R. Jones (ed.), *The Restored Monarchy 1660–1688* (1979), 159–61; cf. John Miller, 'The later Stuart monarchy', in *ibid.*, 35.
19. *Rel. Bax.*, II.448, §445; N. H. Keeble, *Richard Baxter* (1982), 152–3.
20. Reresby, *Memoirs*, 36.
21. Champlin Burrage, 'Fifth Monarchy insurrection', *EHR*, XXV (1910), 739–46; P. G. Rogers, *Fifth Monarchy Men* (1966), 110–22 (and for an earlier attempt of this kind by Venner in 1657, pp. 81–7).
22. [George Fox *et al.*], *A Declaration from the Harmles & Innocent People of God called Quakers* (1660[/61]); Fox, *JGF*, 397–404, 410–11; [–], *The Humble apology of some commonly called Anabaptists* (1661); Penney, *ESP*, 117–27; Edward Cardwell, *Documentary Annals of the Reformed Church of England*, 2 vols (1839), II.251–3; Steele, *BRP*, I.3278; Underwood, *EB*, 93–4; Whitley, *BB*, 109; Watts, *DRR*, 222–3; Bosher, *Restoration Settlement*, 205; Braithwaite, *BQ*, 512.
23. Bosher, *Restoration Settlement*, 216; Ogg, *Charles II*, 181–2.
24. Lacey, *Parliamentary Politics*, 30 (and appendix iii, pp. 476–9); if we include Presbyterians who later conformed, the figure is 60 (F. Bate, *Declaration of Indulgence* (1908), 20; Watts, *DRR*, 218).

25. Browning, *EHD*, 63–5, 375–6. For the business of this session, see Lacey, *Parliamentary Politics*, 32–6; Bosher, *Restoration Settlement*, 221–4.

26. Halifax, *A Letter to a Dissenter* (1687), in *Complete Works*, ed. J. P. Kenyon (1969), 116.

27. *Rel. Bax.*, II.336, §192; II.369, §240.

28. *The Bishop of Worcester's Letter to a Friend* (1662), 13; Izaak Walton, *The Lives*, World's Classics (1927; rpt 1966), 403–4; *Rel. Bax.*, II.364–5, §237.

29. Alexander Gordon. *Heads of English Unitarian History* (1895), 72–4; Sykes, *Sheldon*, 4–5. For the proceedings at the Savoy see *Rel. Bax.*, II.303–72, §§170–241; Edward Cardwell, *A History of Conferences . . . connected with the Revision of the Book of Common Prayer* (1840), 257–368; E. C. Ratcliff, 'The Savoy Conference', in Nuttall and Chadwick (eds), *Uniformity to Unity*, 89–146; Bosher, *Restoration Settlement*, 226–30 (which quotes the hostile reactions to Baxter); Horton Davies, *Worship and Theology . . . from Andrewes to Baxter and Fox* (Princeton, NJ, 1975), 365–73.

30. *The Book of Common-Prayer* (1662), Preface, sig. b6; *Rel. Bax.*, II.384, §276; W. H. Hutton, *The English Church from the Accession of Charles I to the Death of Anne* (1903), 188–91; Bosher, *Restoration Settlement*, 244–9. For fuller discussion see James Parker, *An Introduction to the Successive Revisions of the Book of Common Prayer* (1877), pp. xcii–cccclvi; Francis Proctor and W. H. Frere, *History of the Book of Common Prayer* (1902), 196–203; Davies, *Worship and Theology*, 373–89.

31. For its parliamentary history, see Bosher, *Restoration Settlement*, 224–5, 239–44, 249–54; Lacey, *Parliamentary Politics*, 36–7, 48–50; and, more at large, C. A. Swainson, *The Parliamentary History of the Act of Uniformity* (1875) and Parker, *Successive Revisions*, pp. lxxxiii–lxxxvi, cccclvii–cccclxxxvi.

32. Samuel Pepys, *The Diary*, ed. Robert Latham and William Matthews, 11 vols (1970–83), III.97.

33. Browning, *EHD*, 377–82; Henry Bettenson (ed.), *Documents of the Christian Church*, 2nd edn (1967), 235–9. For the established church's earlier views on orders, see Norman Sykes, *Old Priest and New Presbyter* (1957), and for the 'outstanding innovation' of the 1662 'unvarying requirement of episcopal ordination', *ibid.*, 118–41.

34. [A.B.], *A Letter from a Minister . . . showing some Reason for his Non-Conformity* ([1679]), 2. This piece is not by Baxter, as given in Samuel Halkett and John Laing, *Dictionary of Anonymous and Pseudonymous English Literature*, ed. James Kennedy *et al.*, 7 vols (1926–34), VI.382: see N. H. Keeble, 'Some erroneous, doubtful and misleading Baxterian attributions in Wing and Halkett and Laing', *N&Q*, XXXII, 2 (1985), 188.

35. [Daniel Defoe], *A Short View of the Present State of the Protestant Religion* (1707), 14; *CSPD 1663–64*, 63; *Rel. Bax.*, II.385, §279.

36. Matthews, *CR*, p. xiii; *Rel. Bax.*, II.298 [misnumbered 286] –300, §§151–6.

37. John Pinney, *Letters 1679–1699*, ed. Geoffrey F. Nuttall (1939), pp. ix–x; William Addison, *Worthy Dr Fuller* (1951), 98.

38. Matthews, *CR*, pp. xii–xiv; Watts, *DRR*, 219.

39. Watts, *DRR*, 153, 159–64, 219. For Owen, Sterry Jessey and the Mathers, see *DNB* and Matthews, *CR*, *s.vv.* For slightly different Baptist and Independent figures, see Underwood, *EB*, 96–7, and Jones, *CE*, 64.

40. Pepys, *Diary*, III.117, 127, 161, 169, 178, 183, 186, 210; A. G. Matthews, *Mr Pepys and Nonconformity* (1954), 141–3; *CSPD 1661–62*, 418, 428, 488.

41. Bosher, *Restoration Settlement* 250–3, 255–8.

42. Howe, *CW*, V.237; cf. Edmund Calamy, *Memoirs of John Howe* (1724), 141. *Rel. Bax.*, II.387, §285 distinguishes the 'divers sorts' of nonconformists, and summarizes their arguments II.390–429, §§301–416.

43. Gordon, *Heads*, 82; *Rel. Bax.*, II.387, §285(2); Matthews, *CR*, p. lxi; Watts, *DRR*, 219; Manton, *CW*, V.499. For Wilkins, see *DNB*, *s.v.*

44. Manton, *CW*, II.6, 11–13, 68–78; [Andrew Marvell], *Mr. Smirke* (1676), 53, 62, 74, 75.

45. Baxter, *Cure of Church-Divisions* (1670),

296; *id.*, *The True Catholick* (1660), 165; Calamy, *Memoirs*, 36, 30–3. The grounds of Baxter's nonconformity are discussed in Irvonwy Morgan, *The Nonconformity of Richard Baxter* (1946), 90–223; Nuttall and Chadwick (eds), *Uniformity to Unity*, 184–6; Keeble, *Baxter*, 23–8. For the Reconcilers more at large see Roger Thomas, 'The rise of the Reconcilers', in Bolam, *EP*, 46–72, and E. W. Kirby, 'The Reconcilers and the Restoration (1660–62)', in *Essays in ... Honor of Wilbur Cortez Abbott* (Cambridge, Mass., 1941), 49–79.

46. Calamy, *Memoirs*, 39, 12–13; *CSPD 1663–4*, 63.

47. [–], *The Nonconformists Advocate* (1680), 3, 7–8, 33, 39–40 (and cf. [A.B.], *Letter*, 1–2); Burnet, *OT*, I.185; Baxter, *An Answer to Mr. Dodwell and Dr. Sherlock* (1682), 178; [James Owen], *Moderation a Virtue* (1703), 18.

48. [George Trosse], *A Discourse of Schism* (1701), 12–13; [Owen], *Moderation*, 17; Roberta Florence Brinkley (ed.), *Coleridge on the Seventeenth Century* (New York, 1968), 138–9.

49. [Defoe], *Short View*, 11; J[ohn] C[heyney], *The Conforming Non-Conformist* (1680), sig. A2ᵛ; Lacey, *Parliamentary Politics*, 15–16, 24, 27; Edmund Calamy, *Historical Account of my Own Life*, ed. J. T. Rutt, 2 vols (1829), I.473. The Baxter/Bagshaw controversy involved Baxter, *The Cure of Church-divisions* (1670); Bagshaw, *An Antidote against Mr. Baxters Palliated Cure* (1670); Baxter, *A Defence of the Principles of Love* (1671); Bagshaw, *A Defence of the Antidote* (1671); Baxter, *A Second Admonition to Mr. Edward Bagshaw* (1671); Bagshaw, *A Review and Conclusion of the Antidote* (1671); Baxter, *The Church Told of Mr. Ed. Bagshaw's Scandals* (1672). This last appeared when news came of Bagshaw's death. 'While we wrangle here in the dark, we are dying and passing to the World that will decide all our Controversies: And the safest Passage thither is by *peacable Holiness*' (*Rel. Bax.*, III.89, §195).

50. Lacey, *Parliamentary Politics*, 20–1, 23–4; Baxter, *A Christian Directory* (1673), 859; Philip Henry, *Diaries and Letters*, ed. Matthew Henry Lee (1882), 133–5,

177–80; Matthews, *CR, s.vv.* Baldwin, Crofton, Humfrey, Tombes; Underwood, *EB*, 69–70.

51. Burnet, *OT*, I.480; [Daniel Defoe], *Inquiry into the Occasional Conformity of Dissenters* (1701), 23, 11, 13, 10.

52. Howe, *CW*, V.284; Browning, *EHD*, 406–10; [Owen], *Moderation*, 11–12. Owen was answered by [Samuel Grascome], *Occasional Conformity a Most Unjustifiable Practice* (1704), [Charles Leslie], *The Wolf Stript* (1704) and [Daniel Defoe], *The Dissenters Answer* (1704), to which Owen anonymously rejoined in *Moderation Still a Virtue* (1704). Owen has usually been described as a Congregationalist, but in the view of Alan P. Sell, 'Robert Travers', *JURCHS*, III, 7 (1985), 269–70, he 'was more Presbyterian than anything else'. For further defences of occasional conformity by Howe, see his letters printed in Calamy, *Memoirs*, 212–18, and Henry Rogers, *The Life and Character of John Howe* (1836), 424–6. Christopher Hill, in *Reformation, Conformity and Dissent*, ed. R. Buick Knox (1977), 199–220, offers a (largely) sociological account of the practice since Elizabethan times. On the Occasional Conformity and Schism Acts see Sykes, *Sheldon*, 91–104.

53. Calamy, *Memoirs*, 213.

54. [–], *The Case of Mixt-Communion Friendly Discoursed* (1700), 18–22.

55. [Edward Terrill], *The Records of a Church of Christ meeting in Broadmead, Bristol*, ed. E. B. Underhill (1847), 15–18.

56. G[eorge] F[ox], *The Pearle Found in England* (1658), 11; [William Fortescue], *A Short Relation ... of William Simpson* ([1671]), 14.

57. *Rel. Bax.*, III.43, §98; III.196–8, §80; Owen, *CW*, XV.59–185; Joseph Besse, *A Collection of the Sufferings of the People called Quakers*, 2 vols (1753), I.293.

58. *Rel. Bax.*, I.39, §55; *CSPD 1668–9*, 11, 159–60; Lacey, *Parliamentary Politics*, 16–17; Jones, *CE*, 81–2. The most important precedent was the 'semi-separatist' Henry Jacob, for whom see Watts, *DRR*, 50–6, and Geoffrey F. Nuttall, *Visible Saints* (1957), 9, 10–11.

59. *Rel. Bax.*, II.430, §420.

60. Matthews, *CR*, pp. xvi, xvii, lxi, *s.vv.* Baxter, Denton, Howe, Mather, Nuttall,

Owen; Peter Toon, *God's Statesman: The Life and Work of John Owen* (1971), 18–19, 22–4, 26, 27–30, 151; *Rel. Bax.*, I.13, §18; John Brown, *John Bunyan*, rev. F. M. Harrison (1928), 37–51. On the genealogy of nonconformity see Geoffrey F. Nuttall *et al.*, *The Beginnings of Nonconformity* (1964), 11–23.

61. *DNB, s.vv.* Ashurst, Henry; Foley, Thomas and Paul; Hampden, Richard; Holles and Wharton, Philip; Lacey, *Parliamentary Politics*, 375, 395–7, 402–3, 466–9, 473–5; Burnet, *OT*, I.175; Marvell, 'Last Instructions to a Painter', l. 457, in *P&L*, I.159.

62. Sykes, *Sheldon*, 27–9; *The Diary of Ralph Josselin*, ed. Alan MacFarlane (1976), 490–3, 498, 508, 511, 512, 535, 548, 549, 556, 587, 593, 614, 615, 627–8; Alan MacFarlane, *The Family Life of Ralph Josselin* (1970), 27–30; Harold Smith, *The Ecclesiastical History of Essex* ([1932]), 223–4.

63. Howe, *CW*, VI.374; *Rel. Bax.*, III.43, §96.

64. Browning, *EHD*, 382, 373, 388, 387, 84; [Charles Leslie], *A Discourse shewing who they are that are now Qualify'd to Administer Baptism* (1698), sigs A1–A1ᵛ. I am indebted to Mr Norman Arthur for the comment on L'Estrange's usage.

65. [Marvell], *Mr. Smirke*, 3; Gilbert Burnet, *Life of Matthew Hale* (1682), 65–6.

66. [Stephen Lobb], *The True Dissenter* (1685), sig. a7ᵛ (Lobb consequently argues against occasional conformity, *ibid.*, 96–115); Burnet, *Life*, 65–75; Lacey, *Parliamentary Politics*, 57; Celia Fiennes, *The Illustrated Journeys*, ed. Christopher Morris (1984), 13, 132, 135, 138, 139, 161, 179, 182, 200.

67. John King, *Animadversions on a Pamphlet ... To The Churches of the Nonconformists* (1701), 1, 5, 8, 9, *et passim*; Edmund Calamy, *Defence of Moderate Nonconformity*, 3 vols (1703–5), II.87–9; Calamy, *Own Life*, II.31; Roger Thomas in Bolam, *EP*, 127–30; William Lamont, *Richard Baxter and the Millennium* (1979), 274–80. For Mather see Matthews, *CR* amd *DNB, s.v.*

68. Burnet, *Life*, 68; [John Nalson], *The Character of a Rebellion* (1681), 15; [Charles Leslie], *Principles of the Dissenters* (1705), sig. A4. This account differs from Watts,

DRR, 1–2, which sees 'dissenter' as the common term after 1662.

69. [John Tutchin], *A New Test of the Church of England's Loyalty* (1702), 4; John Howe, *Humble Requests both to Conformists and Dissenters, touching their temper and behaviour toward each other, upon the lately passed Indulgence* (1689), in Calamy, *Memoirs*, 166–8.

70. *Rel. Bax.*, II.385, §280.

71. Bettenson, *Documents*, 242–3; Underwood, *EB*, 98; Whitley, *BB*, 114–15; Penney, *FPT*, 360; Braithwaite, *SPQ*, 107.

72. Brown, *Bunyan*, 132, 144–5; Bunyan, *GA*, §333, pp. 118, 120–1; Penney, *FPT*, 156.

73. Underwood, *EB*, 90–2.

74. *The Examination and Trial of Margaret Fell and George Fox* (1664) in *Harl. Misc.*, VI.259 (this is reprinted also in Cobbett, *ST*, VI.630–45); *CSPD 1671–2*, 40; Alfred W. Braithwaite, 'Imprisonment upon a praemunire', *JFHS*, L (1962), 38–40, and 'Early tithe prosecutions', *JFHS*, XLIX (1960), 148–56. For a general survey of this legislation as it related to Quakers, see William Charles Braithwaite's appendix to Penney, *FPT*, 343–63; for vagrancy, unlawful assembly and riot, see Sir William Holdsworth, *A History of English Law*, 17 vols (1903–72; vols I–III, 3rd edn, 1922–3), IV.391–402, VI.350–1, VIII.324–33. A lucid contemporary exposition of the ecclesiastical law in force in the early Restoration period may be found in W[illiam] Shephard, *A Sure Guide for his Majesties Justices of Peace* (1663), 65–201.

75. For this 'code' and its effects on nonconformists in general, see G. R. Cragg, *Puritanism in the Period of the Great Persecution* (1957) and Watts, *DRR*, 221–43; for Baptists see Underwood, *EB*, 89–115 and Whitley, *BB*, 101–20; for Congregationalists, Jones, *CE*, 63–89; for Quakers, Braithwaite, *SPQ*, 21–54, 75–81, 100–15. The 1665 and 1670 Acts are excerpted in Browning, *EHD*, 382–6. For their parliamentary passage, see Lacey, *Parliamentary Politics*, 53–5, 60–1.

76. H. Gee, 'The Derwentdale Plot 1663', *TRHS*, 3rd ser., XI (1917) 124–42; Francis Nicholson, 'The Kaber Rigg Plot, 1663', *Cumberland and Westmorland Antiq. and Arch. Soc. Jnl.*, n.s.XI (1911), 212–33;

James Walker, 'The Yorkshire Plot', *Yorkshire Arch. Soc. Jnl.* XXXI (1934), 348–59.

77. [A. Luders, T. E. Tomlins *et al.* (eds)], *Statutes of the Realm*, 11 vols (1810–28, V.516–20; E[dward] B[illing], *A Faithful Testimony for God* (1664), 9; Penney, *ESP*, 221, 230–1; Braithwaite, *SPQ*, 40–52.

78. Pinney, *Letters*, 127.

79. Penney, *FPT*, 101; Marvell, *P&L*, II.314; Penney, *ESP*, 299–301; Lacey, *Parliamentary Politics*, 61–2.

80. [John Howe], *The Case of the Protestant Dissenters* (1689), 2. Compare [Francis Bampfield], *A Just Appeal from the Lower Courts on Earth to the Highest Court in Heaven* (1683); [Henry Care], *A Perfect Guide for Protestant Dissenters* (1682); [John Owen], *The Case of Present Distresses on Non-Conformists* (1682), in *CW*, XIII.579–82.

81. [Marvell], *Mr. Smirke*, 8.

82. Matthews, *CR.* p. xiii; Watts, *DRR*, 229.

83. Bunyan, *PP*, 101–4, 34–5; [Ralph Wallis], *More News from Rome* (1666), 29; Sykes, *Old Priest*, 123–4; *DNB* and Matthews, *CR, s.v.* Humfrey; Pinney, *Letters*, 125.

84. Matthews, *CR*, p. xiv. *s.vv.* Angier, Ashurst; Milton, *SA*, ll. 692–6, in *PJM*, 369.

85. Penney, *ESP*, 320–1; Watts, *DRR*, 228, 229; *CSPD 1668–9*, 342; [Terrill], *Records*, 105.

86. Watts, *DRR*, 230; Fox, *JGF*, 517–18, 566–7; Jones, *CE*, 78–80; *CSPD 1664–5*, 458–9; Turner, *OREN*, I.3, 10, 53, 107, 113; Penney, *ESP*, 314–15.

87. Bunyan, *GA*, p. 105; [Terrill], *Records*, 76, 80; Billing, *Faithful Testimony*, 3–4; Braithwaite, *SPQ*, 41–2, 49–59; *Rel. Bax.*, II.436, §431; Pepys, *Diary*, V.235 (7 Aug. 1664).

88. Alfred W. Braithwaite, 'Errors in the indictment', *JFHS*, XLIX (1959), 24–30, and *id.*, *Thomas Rudyard*, *JFHS* Supplement (1956); Holdsworth, *English Law*, III.616–20, IV.531, 535–6.

89. Holdsworth, *English Law*, VI.500, 576 (for Hale's character and achievement see VI.574–96); Sir Matthew Hale, *The Works*, 2 vols (1805), I.31; *Rel. Bax.*, III.47, §107.

90. Andrew Marvell, *An Account of the Growth of Popery* ([1678]), 22. On the 'marked deterioration' in the quality of the bench, see Holdsworth, *English Law*, VI.28–9, 213–16, 499, 501–4 (and on Scroggs and Jeffreys, VI.504–7, 527–30).

91. [–], *Another Out-Cry of the Innocent & Oppressed* (1665), 3–4; Billing, *Faithful Testimony*, 8; Alfred W. Braithwaite, 'Early Friends' experience with juries', *JFHS*, L (1964), 217–27.

92. *Rel. Bax.*, III.87, §190. On *Bushel's Case*, see Holdsworth, *English Law*, I.340, 344–7, and Braithwaite, *SPQ*, 71–3. The contemporary account was by Thomas Rudyard in *The Second Part of the Peoples Antient and Just Liberties Asserted* (1670). Vaughan's judgement is given in Cobbett, *ST*, VI.999–1026, and, in brief, in Browning, *EHD*, 86–9.

93. *Trial of Fell and Fox*, in *Harl Misc.*, VI.260, 261, 267, 268. For this trial and the ensuing imprisonment see also Fox, *JGF*, 461–502, and Braithwaite, *SPQ*, 31–9.

94. [William Penn and William Mead], *The Peoples Antient and Just Liberties Asserted* (1670), in John Dunton (ed.), *The Phenix*, 2 vols (1707–8), I.309, 310, 310–12, 319. (This is reprinted also in Cobbett, *ST*, VI.951–1000.)

95. Manton, *CW*, I.5.

96. *A Relation of the Imprisonment of John Bunyan* (1765), in *GA*, pp. 108, 109, 111, 116–117, 118.

97. Bunyan, *GA*, pp. 111, 119, 113.

98. For representative cases see Watts, *DRR*, 244–6. Penney, *FPT*, 370, lists magistrates who became Friends, and Penney, *ESP*, 6–13, 105–15, gives contemporary lists of 'moderate' magistrates.

99. For a discussion of this as the 'central theme' in the history of Charles's reign see Ogg, *Charles II*, 450–72. On these cases and constitutional matters, see Holdsworth, *English Law*, VI.27–8, 48, 52–3, 203–8, 216–25; Browning, *EHD*, 83; Cobbett, *ST*, XI.1166–1316. For the Hampdens, see *DNB*, *s.vv.*, and Lacey, *Parliamentary Politics*, 402–3.

100. Steele, *BRP*, I.3301, 3367; Penney, *ESP*, 132–3, 150; Underwood, *EB*, 98; Braithwaite, *SPQ*, 107–8; Watts, *DRR*, 224; Lacey, *Parliamentary Politics*, 100; Fox, *JGF*, 411–14, 423, 557–8, 576, 683–4, 699–701, 737, 738.

101. Lacey, *Parliamentary Politics*, 48–50;
Bosher, *Restoration Settlement*, 250–3;
Keith Feiling, 'Clarendon and the Act
of Uniformity, 1662–3', *EHR*, XLIV
(1929), 289–91.

102. Lacey, *Parliamentary Politics*, 50–3;
Bosher, *Restoration Settlement*, 258–66
(p. 261 prints the Presbyterian petition);
George Abernathy, 'Clarendon and the
Declaration of Indulgence', *JEH*,
XI (1960), 55–73; Browning, *EHD*,
373; *Rel. Bax.*, II.429–30, §§417–18.

103. *Rel. Bax.*, II.430, §418.

104. J. R. Jones, *Court and Country: England
1658–1714* (1980), 103–5, 170–1; Ogg,
Charles II, 322–56; Browning, *EHD*, 863–
7.

105. Browning, *EHD*, 387–8.

106. Marvell, *RT*, esp. pp. 43–61, 111–13,
278–9 (the editor summarizes Marvell's
case in this respect on pp. xv–xvii);
Browning, *EHD*, 77–81.

107. Sykes, *Sheldon*, 76; Browning, *EHD*, 389–
91. The Second Test Act of 1678
required all MPs to make an extended
declaration repudiating Roman
Catholicism (Browning, *EHD*, 391–4).

108. Gordon, *Heads*, 85 (cf. Watts, *DRR*,
247–8); *Rel. Bax.*, III.99, §214. For Love
see Lacey, *Parliamentary Politics*,
419–20.

109. *CSPD 1671*, 496; *CSPD 1671–2*, 28;
Turner, *OREN*, III.201–2.

110. F. Bastian, *Defoe's Early Life* (1981), 15
(which treats Defoe's Presbyterian
background on pp. 14–17). For
Annesley see *CR*, and *DNB*, *s.v.* The
paternal grandfather and great-
grandfather of Wesley were also ejected
ministers, see Matthews, *CR*, *s.v.*
Westley, Bartholomew and John.

111. This paragraph is chiefly drawn from the
fullest account of these matters, Roger
Thomas, 'Comprehension and
indulgence', in Nuttall and Chadwick
(eds), *Uniformity to Unity*, 190–253, esp.
pp. 196–210; see also Roger Thomas in
Bolam, *EP*, 87–8, 94–101, and Sykes,
Sheldon, 68–73.

112. John Humfrey, *The Authority of the
Magistrate about Religion* (1672), 28
(quoted in Lacey, *Parliamentary Politics*,
65); Baxter's application as a 'mere
Nonconformist' is printed in *The

Autobiography of Richard Baxter*, ed. N. H.
Keeble (1974; rpt 1985), 300, and
Frederick J. Powicke, *The Reverend Richard
Baxter under the Cross* (1927), 71–2.

113. Sykes, *Sheldon*, 77; Fox, *JGF*, 409;
Turner, *OREN*, III.732–6;
Underwood, *EB*, 69, 102–3; Jones,
CE, 92; Matthews, *CR*, p. xv; Watts,
DRR, 248; Bolam, *EP*, 90.

114. Edward Stillingfleet, *The Unreasonableness
of Separation* (1681), p. xxiii; Heywood,
AD, II.20–37, III.139–40 (and cf. III.214),
II.194–7; Gordon, *Heads*, 87–8.

115. R. A. Beddard, in Jones (ed.), *Restored
Monarchy*, 172; J. R. Jones, *The First Whigs*
(1961), 21–2, 155; O. W. Furley, 'The
pope-burning processions of the late
seventeenth century', *History*, XLIV (1959),
16–23; Heywood, *AD*, II.216–20;
Reresby, *Memoirs*, 152. On the Plot see
John Kenyon, *The Popish Plot* (1972) and
John Miller, *Popery and Politics in England
1660–1688* (1973), 154–88.

116. Jones, *Whigs*, 9–19 analyses the
composition of the party; for
nonconformist participation see also
Lacey, *Parliamentary Politics*, 121–49 and
Watts, *DRR*, 251–2.

117. Lacey, *Parliamentary Politics*, 112–16, 119,
135, 144–5, 313–15; Watts, *DRR*, 253; H.
Horwitz, 'Protestant reconciliation in the
Exclusion Crisis', *JEH*, XV (1964), 201–17.

118. Dryden, *Absalom and Achitophel*, ll.
978–80, in *Poems and Fables*, ed. James
Kinsley (1962), 215; Reresby,
Memoirs, 209; James quoted in
Maurice Ashley, *England in the
Seventeenth Century*, 3rd edn (1967),
19.

119. Ogg, *Charles II*, 459; Jones, *Court and
Country*, 204–5, 215–16; Heywood, *AD*,
II.222–5. For the course of events, see
Jones, *Whigs, passim*; Francis S. Ronalds,
The Attempted Whig Revolution (1937); J. P.
Kenyon, 'The Exclusion Crisis 1678–
1681', *History Today*, XIV (1964), 252–9,
344–9; Ogg, *Charles II*, 584–619.

120. Lacey, *Parliamentary Politics*, 157–63;
Doreen M. Milne, 'The results of the
Rye House Plot', *RHST*, 5th ser., I
(1951), 91–108.

121. C. D. Curtis, *Sedgemoor and the Bloody
Assize* (1930), appendix i, 91, 92, 95–6
(and cf. Browning, *EHD*, 119–20); Lacey,

Parliamentary Politics, 168–74; Watts, *DRR*, 256–7; Underwood, *EB*, 108, 109; Burnet, *OT*, I.649; Cobbett, *ST*, XI.410–54. For Ferguson see Matthews, *CR* and *DNB*, *s.vv.*, and for Elizabeth Gaunt, Kenneth W. Wadsworth. 'A tercentenary – Elizabeth Gaunt', *JURCHS*, III (1986, 316–20. On Monmouth's rebellion see, in brief, David Ogg, *England in the reigns of James II and William III* (1984), 144–57 and Jones, *Court and Country*, 227–9; more at large, W. R. Emerson, *Monmouth's Rebellion* (New Haven, Conn., 1951).

122. Seth Ward, *Against Resistabce of Lawful Powers* (1661), 6; Somers, *CT*, VIII.424, IX.262.

123. Steele, *BRP*, I.3828; Lacey, *Parliamentary Politics*, 175–9; John Miller, *James II* (1977), 154–6.

124. Burnet, *OT* I.672; Browning, *EHD*, 395–7; Reresby, *Memoirs*, 450, 452. For an example of nonconformist amazement at their change of fortune, see Heywood, *AD*, III.227.

125. Defoe, *Short View*, 15–16; Philip Nye, *The King's Authority* (1687), sig. A1ᵛ; [Robert Ferguson], *A Representation of the Threatning Dangers, impending over Protestants* ([1687]), 43–9; Lacey *Parliamentary Politics* 180–2; Miller, *James II*, 171–3. For Alsop see *CR* and *DNB*, *s.v.*, and R. A. Beddard, 'Vincent Alsop and the emancipation of Restoration dissent', *JEH*, XXIV (1973), 161–84. This article prompted William Lamont's detailed examination of Baxter's thinking on nonconformity in *Richard Baxter and the Millennium* (1979), 210–84, which concludes that between 1676 and 1684 Baxter himself came very close to believing, like Alsop, that in tolerated dissent lay nonconformity's only possible future. For Penn see *DNB*, *s.v.*, and Vincent Buranelli, *The King and the Quaker* (Philadelphia, Pa, 1962), esp. pp. 67–135.

126. John Dryden, *The Hind and the Panther*, preface and I.1, 35–61, 154–196, 291–2, 311, 314, 328, 409, III.76–9, 672–709, in *Poems and Fables*, 352–3, 355–6,

359–60, 362, 363, 365, 390, 405–6; Godfrey Davies, *Essays on the Later Stuarts* (San Marino, 1958), 72. On the precedents for, and implications of, Dryden's animal symbolism see James Kinsley, 'Dryden's bestiary', *RES*, n.s.IV (1953), 331–6.

127. Sykes, *Sheldon*, 83; Lacey, *Parliamentary Politics*, 185–8, 193–8.

128. [Gilbert Burnet], *An Apology for the Church of England* ([1688]), 2; Burnet, *OT*, I.664; [Ferguson], *Threatning Dangers*, 39.

129. Browning, *EHD*, 83, 399–400, 84; Lacey, *Parliamentary Politics*, 209–11; Roger Thomas, 'The Seven Bishops and their petition', *JEH*, XII (1961), 62–3; G. V. Bennett, 'The Seven Bishops: a reconsideration', in D. Baker (ed.), *Religious Motivation* (1978), 267–87.

130. Browning, *EHD*, 84–5; Cobbett, *ST*, XII.422–6; Reresby, *Memoirs*, 501; Lacey, *Parliamentary Politics*, 211–12; H. C. Foxcroft, *The Character of a Trimmer* (1946), 248 (quoted in Ashley, *England in the Seventeenth Century*, 130); Cardwell, *Documentary Annals*, II.325.

131. Browning, *EHD*, 120–2; Cobbett, *ST*, IX.1054–1126, XI.479–94; Henry Newcome, *The Autobiography*, ed. Richard Parkinson (1852), I.268; [–], *The Address of the Nonconformist Ministers ... to his Highness the Prince of Orange* (1689); Heywood, *AD*, III.234; Fiennes, *Illustrated Journeys*, 226; Lacey, *Parliamentary Politics*, 215, 222–3; Ogg, *James and William*, 201.

132. Browning, *EHD*, 158–9, 122–8; Ogg, *James and William*, 242; Lacey, *Parliamentary Politics*, 226–36; Sykes, *Sheldon*, 85–9; George Every, *The High Church Party* (1956), 19–42; Reresby, *Memoirs*, 541, 567.

133. Sykes, *Sheldon*, 90; Browning, *EHD*, 400–3. For a more general account of the 'Glorious Revolution' see, in brief, Jones, *Court and Country*, 234–55 and Ogg, *James and William*, 195–245; more at large, J. R. Jones, *The Revolution of 1688 in England* (1972).

134. Howe, *CW*, IV.278; Milton, *CPW*, I.585; Calamy, *Memoirs*, 128.

CHAPTER 2

1. Keith Feiling, 'Clarendon and the Act of Uniformity', *EHR*, CLXXIV (1929), 289–91; George R. Abernathy, 'Clarendon and the Declaration of Indulgence', *JEH*, XI (1960), 55–73; George Clark, *The Later Stuarts*, 2nd edn (1955), 21.

2. Turner, *OREN*, III.61, 41–59. Sheldon's was clearly not that 'temperate and homely' Anglicanism Arthur Bryant believed was 're-established by law in 1660' (*The England of Charles II* (1934), 78).

3. Turner, *OREN*, III.61, 71, I.13, 14, 27; Browning, *EHD*, 383, 384; Fox, *JGF*, 563–4. For Durant see Matthews, *CR* and *DNB*, *s.v.*

4. [–] *Reasons why the Church of England as well as Dissenters should make their Address of Thanks to the King* (1687), 5; [William Penn], *A Perswasive to Moderation to Church Dissenters* ([1686]), 1; [William Penn and William Mead], *The Peoples Antient and Just Liberties Asserted* (1670), in John Dunton (ed.), *The Phenix*, 2 vols (1707–8), I.304.

5. Turner, *OREN*, I.181, III.30.

6. [Daniel Defoe], *The Shortest Way with the Dissenters* (1702), 4; [John Tutchin], *A New Test of the Church of England's Loyalty* (1702), 4–5.

7. Richard Baxter, *A Paraphrase on the New Testament*, 2nd edn (1695), sig. 3E3ᵛ; N. H. Keeble, *Richard Baxter* (1982), 21; Geoffrey F. Nuttall, *Richard Baxter* (1965), 109–11. For the trial see Cobbett, *ST*, XI.493–502.

8. [Charles Leslie], *A Case of Present Concern* ([1703?]), 1–3; [*id.*], *The Wolf Stript* (1704), 3; [*id.*], *A Parallel between the Faith and Doctrine of the Present Quakers, and that of the Chief Hereticks* ([1700]), sig. A1.

9. Jones, *CE*, 38–46, 52, 72–3; Peter Toon, *God's Statesman* (1971), 107–20, 130, 151; A. J. Shirren, *The Chronicles of Fleetwood House* (1951; rpt Houston, Texas, n.d.), 74–84. On subversion and plotting among nonconformists see W. C. Abbott, 'English conspiracy and dissent', *American Historical Review*, XIV, 3 and 4 (1908–9),

503–28, 696–722, and Richard L. Greaves's more detailed *Deliver us from Evil: The Radical Underground in Britain 1660–1663* (New York, 1986); for a wide-ranging survey of the ideas, fortunes and actions of defeated Puritans and radicals, see Christopher Hill, *The Experience of Defeat* (1984), which discusses Owen on pp. 170–8.

10. *CSPD 1660–1*, 252, 310, 412; *CSPD 1661–2*, 71, 119, 128, 396, 405, 434, 465, 526, 540.

11. *CSPD 1663–4*, 37, 44, 60, 72, 74, 144, 237, 296, 299; *CSPD 1664–5*, 427, 576, 671; *CSPD 1665–6*, 8, 240.

12. *DNB*, *s.vv.* Ludlow, Lisle. For a detailed account of the circumstances surrounding the composition and publication of Ludlow's *Memoirs*, see A. B. Worden's introduction to his edition of Ludlow, *A Voyce from the Watch Tower* (1978). For other examples of the authorities' conviction and anxiety that old Cromwellians were bent on the overthrow of monarchy see David Ogg, *England in the Reign of Charles II*, 2nd edn (1956; rpt 1967), 209–10.

13. Howe, *CW*, V.252.

14. Turner, *OREN*, I.84–5. For Spencer see Underwood, *EB*, 76, and for Crooke, Fox, *JGF*, 206–7, 226–7, 339; *DNB*, *s.v.*; and H. G. Tibbutt, 'John Crook, 1617–1699', *Publications of the Bedfordshire Historical Record Soc.*, XXV (1947), 110–28.

15. Turner, *OREN*, I.86, 87, 89, 143. Each of these is in Matthews, *CR* and *DNB*, *s.vv.*

16. Howe, *CW*, VI.374.

17. Turner, *OREN*, I.80, 159, 162, 160. For Swift see Matthews, *CR*, *s.v.*

18. Penney, *FPT*, 208, 219, 227, 42, 46, 94–5. For Crossfield and Broughton meeting houses, see David M. Butler, *Quaker Meeting Houses of the Lake Counties* (1978), 39, 47, 52.

19. Marvell, *P&L*, II.343; *CSPD 1670*, 231; TURNER, *OREN*, I.111; *CSPD 1680–1*, 505 (quoted in Matthews, *CR*, *s.v.* Durant). For other cases, see Watts, *DRR*, 244–7. Penney, *FPT*, 370, lists justices who became Friends. For Barrett, see

Matthews, *CR, s.v.*

20. [Stephen Lobb], *The True Dissenter* (1685), 85–6 (the point is developed on pp. 87–96); Albert Peel (ed.), *The Savoy Declaration of Faith and Order 1658* (1939), 73. The phrase 'Society of Friends' did not come into use until 1793 (Braithwaite, *BQ*, 570). Geoffrey F. Nuttall, *Visible Saints* (1957), 75–100, discusses the significance of fellowship in the earlier Congregational tradition, and notes, pp. 70–2, the incidence of 'society', 'company' and analogous terms, and the 'stress on the societary nature of the church'. On the domestic architecture of meeting-houses, see Horton Davies, *Worship and Theology in England ... 1603–1690* (Princeton, NJ, 1975), 60–7.

21. Bunyan, *PP*, 37, 45. Roger Sharrock so interprets the location of the Palace Beautiful in *PP*, p. 821, but see Richard L. Greaves, *John Bunyan* (1969), 125 on the significance of church membership in Bunyan's thought.

22. Bunyan, *PP*, 42–7, 52–3, 55–6. On the admission procedure of Congregational churches see Nuttall, *Visible Saints*, 109–16, and Patricia Caldwell, *The Puritan Conversion Narrative* (1983), esp. pp. 45–80.

23. Matthews, *CR, s.v.* Collins; [–], *Reasons why the Church of England ...* , 8–9; Braithwaite, *SPQ*, 79.

24. For such cases, see Watts, *DRR*, 232–4.

25. *CSPD 1664–5*, 461; Thomas Ellwood, *The History of the Life* (1714), 199, 144; Fox, *JGF*, 442, 446, 514, 687 (temporary liberty), 433, 567 (prison meetings), 440, 457 (prior warning of warrants).

26. Marvell, *P&L*, II.317–18 (my italics); [Edward Terrill], *Records of a Church of Christ meeting in Broadmead, Bristol*, ed. E. B. Underhill (1847), 112–13; Bunyan, *CW*, II.703b. For Pepys see above, p. 50.

27. Bunyan, *GA*, pp. 105–6. For Samsell, see John Brown, *John Bunyan*, tercentenary edn rev. F. M. Harrison (1928), 136. Fox similarly courted arrest (*JGF*, 457, 567, 734).

28. Watts, *DRR*, 229–30; [Terrill], *Records*, 170–1; Roger Sharrock, 'The origins of *A Relation ...* ', *RES*, X, 39 (1959), 253–6; Maria Webb, *The Penns & Peningtons of the Seventeenth Century* (1867), 190–207 (for later letters see pp. 305–15). Nuttall, *Visible Saints*, 95–9, treats Congregational correspondence in the Interregnum period.

29. Ellwood, *History*, 93–7.

30. Peter Fraser, *The Intelligence of the Secretaries of State ... 1660–1688* (1956), 1–2, 9, 20–34, 140–4; Mark A. Thomson, *The Secretaries of State 1681–1782* (1932), 2–3; William Dundas, *A Few Word of Truth from the Spirit of Truth* (1673), 9; Ellwood, *History*, 79–90 (cf. Fox, *JGF*, 398); R. A. Beddard, 'Vincent Alsop and the emancipation of Restoration dissent', *JEH*, XXIV (1973), 170–1.

31. Marvell, *P&L*, II.113, 166, 169. Annabel M. Patterson, *Marvell and the Civic Crown* (Princeton, NJ, 1978), 10–12, discerns in such passages not merely prudence but also that 'Irony and detachment *about himself* generally characteristic of Marvell.

32. Marvell, *P&L*, II.101–2, 314, 104, 316, 327–8 (this point is made in Christopher Hill, *Writing and Revolution in 17th Century England* (1984), 51, 170). For Popple see *DNB* and Caroline Robbins, 'Absolute liberty: the life and thought of William Popple 1638–1708', *William and Mary Quarterly*, 3rd ser., XXIV, 2 (1967), 190–223, which takes its title from the passage quoted.

33. Penney, *ESP*, 143–5. For Tickell and Portinscale meeting houses, see Butler, *Quaker Meeting Houses*, 39, 51, and for the meetings and meeting-houses at Carlisle, Cockermouth and Mosedale, *ibid.*, 1–3, 39, 48, 51.

34. Penney, *ESP*, 127; Penney, *FPT*, 1–4; Braithwaite, *BQ*, 538–40; Braithwaite, *SPQ*, 281–4; Fox, *JGF*, 715–16.

35. Geoffrey F. Nuttall, 'Richard Baxter's correspondence: a preliminary survey', *JEH*, I, 1 (1950), 85–95; *Rel. Bax.*, III.90, §202.

36. John Brown, *John Bunyan*, tercentenary edn rev. F. M. Harrison (1928), 260; Henri Talon, *John Bunyan*, trans. Barbara Wall (1951), 202–3; Macaulay and Charles Firth, in Roger Sharrock (ed.), *The Pilgrim's Progress; A Casebook* (1976), 75, 100; Richard L. Greaves, 'John Bunyan's "Holy War" and London nonconformity', *BQ*, XXVI, 4 (1975), 158–68.

37. Edmund Gosse, *The Life and Letters of John*

Donne, 2 vols (1899), I.303–4.

38. Edith Klotz, 'A subject analysis of English imprints … 1480 to 1640', *Huntingdon Library Quarterly*, I, 4 (1938), 417–18; Andrew Maunsell, *The First Part of the Catalogue* … (1595); William Jaggard, *A Catalogue of … English Bookes* (1618); William London, *A Catalogue of the Most Vendible Books* (1657); [G. K. Fortescue (ed.)], *Catalogue of the Pamphlets … Collected by George Thomason, 1640–1661*, 2 vols (1908), I, pp. xx–xxi; Arber, *TC*, *passim*.

39. Richard Baxter, *True Christianity* (1655), sig. A4^v.

40. *Rel. Bax.*, III.179, §8; Keeble, *Baxter*, 149–55.

41. Bunyan, *GA*, §320.

42. Alastair Fowler summarizes what is known about the composition of *PL* in *PJM*, 419–23. There is no doubt it was completed after the Restoration or that *PR* was written in the late 1660s (*PJM*, 1063). The traditional allocation of the composition of *SA* to the same period, and probably after *PR*, was first challenged by William Riley Parker ('The date of *Samson Agonistes*', *PQ*, XXVIII (1949), 145–66, and its 'Postscript', *N&Q*, V (1958), 201–2), who favoured 1646/7–53, a dating promoted in his biography, *Milton*, 2 vols (1968), II.903–17, and in 'The date of *Samson Agonistes* again', in Joseph A. Wittreich (ed.), *Calm of Mind* (Cleveland, Ohio, 1971), 163–74, and followed by John Carey in *PJM*, 320–2. John T. Shawcross, 'The chronology of Milton's major poems', *PMLA*, LXXVI, 4 (1961), 345–58, came to the same conclusion on the evidence of prosodic analysis. For convincing refutations of the 'early daters', see Christopher Hill, *Milton and the English Revolution* (1977; rpt 1979), 481–6, and Mary Ann Radzinowicz, *Towards Samson Agonistes* (Princeton, NJ, 1978), 387–407.

43. John Dryden, *Discourse concerning … Satire* (1693), in John Dryden, *Selected Criticism*, ed. James Kinsley and George Parfitt (1970), 217; Ellwood, *History*, 233–4.

44. Milton, *PL*, XII.531–3, in *PJM*, 1053.

45. Milton, *PR*, I.36, 410–20, 227–93, 185–6, in *PJM*, 1079, 1085–8.

46. Milton, *PR*, I.91 (cf. II.136, IV.196–9, 389–90, 501, 514–28), IV.561–2, in *PJM*, 1081, 1163. The poem is so interpreted by Elizabeth Marie Pope, *Paradise Regained* (Baltimore, Md, 1947), 22, 24–5, 30–41, 80–4, 93–107; Barbara Lewalski, *Milton's Brief Epic* (Providence, RI, 1966), 133–5, 159–63, 188–92, 315–21; Louis L. Martz, *Poet of Exile* (New Haven, Conn., 1980), 252–4; Douglas Bush (ed.), *Milton: Poetical works* (1966; rpt 1973), 461–2, 509. For the dissenting views that Christ's words cannot mean 'Tempt not me' see Arnold Stein, *Heroic Knowledge* (Minneapolis, Minn., 1957), 128–9, and that Satan's protestations of ignorance about Christ's identity are a mere stratagem, Don Cameron Allen, *The Harmonious Vision* (Baltimore, Md, 1954), 111–14.

47. Milton, *PL*, VII.24, in *PJM*, 776; *Richard Baxter's Farewel Sermon* (1683), 5.

48. Dunton (ed.), *The Phenix*, I.306, 304–5 (this pamphlet is printed also in Cobbett, *ST*, VI.951–99).

49. Dunton (ed.), *The Phenix*, I.304–5, 306, 311–12, 319, 321; Marvell, *P&L*, II.318; *id.*, *RT*, 314.

50. Dunton (ed.), *The Phenix*, I.312, 321; [–], *The Voice of the Innocent uttered forth* (1665), 8. For Fox's arrest see Braithwaite, *BQ*, 475–6, and *JGF*, 378–87.

51. [Benjamin Coale], *To the Bishops* (1671), 3; Robert Barclay, *William Michel Unmasqued* (1672), sig. A2^v; W[illiam] B[rend], *A Short Declaration of the Purpose and Decree of the Everlasting Counsel of Gods Heavenly Host* (1662), 4.

52. Jones, *CE*, 70; Owen, *CW*, XIII.583–6; Matthews, *CR*, *s.v.* Humfrey; Douglas R. Lacey, *Dissent and Parliamentary Politics in England* (New Brunswick, NJ, 1969), 226.

53. Fox, *JGF*, 754–5, 760.

54. Fox, *JGF*, 60, 499, 559–60, 705–6.

55. Bunyan, *GA*, pp. 1–3; Margaret Olofson Thickstun, 'The preface to Bunyan's *Grace Abounding* as Pauline epistle', *N&Q*, CCXXX (1985), 180–2.

56. William Dewsbury, *The Word of the Lord* ([1663]), 2, 3, 5, 7; [–], *The True and Faithful Relation of the People of God (called) Quakers, in Colchester* (1664), 18; John Samm, *A Salutation to the Little Flock* ([1663?]), 1–2, 7.

57. [Ralph Wallis], *More News from Rome* (1666), sig. A4^v.

CHAPTER 3

1. Baxter, *A Christian Directory* (1673), I.ii.60.
2. Milton, *CW*, II.502; Frederick S. Siebert, *Freedom of the Press in England 1476–1776* (Urbana, Ill., 1952), 21–3, 30–51; W. W. Greg, *Some Aspects and Problems of London Publishing between 1550 and 1650* (Oxford, 1956), 1–3; Cyprian Blagden, *The Stationers' Company: A History 1403–1959* (1960), 29–30; Steele, *BRP*, I.114, 122, 176, 253, 271, 295.
3. Printed and translated in Edward Arber (ed.), *A Transcript of the Registers of the Company of Stationers of London; 1554–1640*, 5 vols (1875–94; rpt New York, 1950), I.xxviii–xxxii, and summarized in R. B. McKerrow, 'Booksellers, printers and the stationers' trade', in [C. T. Onions (ed.)], *Shakespeare's England*, 2 vols (Oxford, 1916), II.216–17.
4. Marjorie Plant, *The English Book Trade*, 2nd edn (1965), 126; Blagden, *Stationers' Company*, 31–3, 43–4. On the form and significance of entries in the Company's Register see Greg, *Aspects and Problems*, 41–62, and Leo Kirschbaum, *Shakespeare and the Stationers* (Columbus, Ohio, 1955), 35–9.
5. Blagden, *Stationers' Company*, 41–4; Greg, *Aspects and Problems*, 5–6, 46; Siebert, *Freedom of the Press*, 56–8; Kirschbaum, *Shakespeare and the Stationers*, 32–5, 39–42; Phoebe Sheavyn, *The Literary Profession in the Elizabethan Age*, 2nd edn (1967), 51–3; Arber, *Transcript*, I.xxxviii (which prints the 1559 Injunctions relating to printing).
6. Blagden, *Stationers' Company*, 33; Frank A. Mumby, *Publishing and Bookselling*, 5th edn rev. (1974), 57; Arber, *Transcript*, I.xxviii, xxxii.
7. Blagden, *Stationers' Company*, 65–6, 71–3; Gregg, *Aspects and Problems*, 6, 9, 50–3; Siebert, *Freedom of the Press*, 58–62, 82–7; Plant, *Book Trade*, 144. The Decrees of 1566 and 1586 are printed in Arber, *Transcript*, I.322, 807–12.
8. Blagden, *Stationers' Company*, 117–25.

Arber, *Transcript*, IV.528–36 prints the 1637 Decree.

9. Blagden, *Stationers' Company*, 145–7; Siebert, *Freedom of the Press*, 165–233; William M. Clyde, 'Parliament and the press, 1643–7', *The Library*, 4th ser., XIII, 4 (1933), 399–424. The Ordinances and Acts are printed in C. H. Firth and R. S. Rait (eds), *Acts and Ordinances of the Interregnum 1642–1660*, 3 vols (1911), I.184–6, 1021–3, II.245–54, 696–9. For pleas for liberty of the press, see Don M. Wolfe (ed.), *Leveller Manifestoes of the Puritan Revolution* (New York, 1944), 128, 207, 326–30, 364, and William Haller (ed.), *Tracts on Liberty in the Puritan Revolution*, 3 vols (New York, 1934), III.84, 182–3, 220.
10. Steele, *BRP*, I.3239, and 3258, 3337, 3371, 3516, 3570, 3595, 3624, 3699, 3859, 3888, 3891, 3997, 4016, 4101. On this continuing use of proclamations see Siebert, *Freedom of the Press*, 237–8, 250–1, and Sir William Holdsworth, *A History of English Law*, 17 vols (1903–72; vols I–III, 3rd edn, 1922–3), IV.305–6, VI.303, 311–12, 373 (VI.360–79 offers a legal discussion of press legislation up to 1695). For Goodwin see Matthews, *CR*, and *DNB, s.v.*
11. Blagden, *Stationers' Company*, 130, 148, 153–9, 164. The Act is excerpted in Browning, *EHD*, 67–9; for a full text see [A. Luders, T. E. Tomlins *et al.* (eds)], *Statutes of the Realm*, 11 vols (1810–28), V.428–33.
12. Arthur W. Pollard, 'Some notes on the history of copyright in England, 1662–1774', *The Library*, 4th ser., III, 2 (1922), 103–4; Christopher Hill, *Writing and Revolution in 17th Century England* (1985), 54; Baxter, *The Second Part of the Nonconformists Plea for Peace* (1680), sig. A2^v; N. H. Keeble, *Richard Baxter* (1982), 19–20.
13. J. R. Jones, *Court and Country: England 1658–1714* (1978; rpt 1980), 14, 209–10; *id.*, *The First Whigs* (1961), 159–61; Peter Fraser, *The Intelligence of the Secretaries of State & Their Monopoly of Licensed News 1660–1688* (1956), 14–32; George Kitchin, *Sir Roger L'Estrange* (1913), 264–7, 270–88; M. Dorothy George, 'Elections and electioneering 1679–81', *EHR*, XLV

(1930), 552–78 (esp. pp. 567–8, 572–7); E. Lipson, 'The elections to the Exclusion Parliaments', *EHR*, XXVIII (1913), 78–9; *Statutes of the Realm*, VI.20. The fullest account of the government's campaign of judicial press control is Timothy Crist, 'Government control of the press after the expiration of the Printing Act in 1679', *Publishing History*, V (1979), 49–77.

14. See Raymond Astbury's extremely detailed account 'The renewal of the Licensing Act in 1693 and its lapse in 1695', *The Library*, 5th ser., XXXIII, 4 (1978), 296–322, and cf. Siebert, *Freedom of the Press*, 262–3; Kitchin, *L'Estrange*, 129; Christopher Hill, *The World Turned Upside Down* (1975), 385; *id.*, *Writing and Revolution*, 54.

15. Charles Blount, *Just Vindication of Learning* (1679), in *Harl. Misc.*, VI.72, 75–6, 77; Astbury, 'Renewal of the Licensing Act', 302–9. For Blount's wholesale indebtedness to *Areopagitica*, see George F. Sensabaugh, *That Grand Whig Milton* (Stanford, Calif., 1952), 58–60, 155–62. Locke's 'Memorandum' is printed in Peter King, *Life of John Locke*, new edn (1858), 202–9 (quotation from p. 203).

16. Cobbett, *ST*, VI.564 (cf. p. 548); J. Walker, 'The censorship of the press during the reign of Charles II', *History*, n.s. XXXV (1950), 228 (which quotes Hyde's ruling).

17. Cobbett, *ST*, VII.926–59, 1111–30, XI.493–502; Wing, *STC*, B.5492, 5495–8, 5506–7, 5524, 5536, 5544, 5554, 5555, 5560, 5586, 5590, 5593, 5593B. For the trials of Harris, Smith, Curtis and Carr, see Crist, 'Government control of the press', 56–63.

18. The law in this respect is discussed in Holdsworth, *English Law*, V.208–9, VIII.333–78, and Siebert, *Freedom of the Press*, 116–26, 269–75.

19. Cobbett, *ST*, VII.929, VI.548, 552, 558.

20. Cobbett, *ST*, VII.1114, XI.493–502. Matt.v.19, Mark ix.39, xi.31, xii.38–40, Luke x.2. John xi.57, Acts xv.2 prompted the cited glosses. For Wallop see *DNB*, *s.v.*

21. Cobbett, *ST*, IX.1333–58, 819, 839–40, 854–60, XII.278–9.

22. Cobbett, *ST*, XIV.1128 (quoted in Holdsworth, *English Law*, VIII.

341, and Siebert, *Freedom of the Press*, 271).

23. Cobbett, *ST*, VI.549, IX.902–16; Baxter, *A Paraphrase on the New Testament*, 2nd edn (1695), sig. 3E3ᵛ.

24. Browning, *EHD*, 63–4. The law of treason is discussed in Holdsworth, *English Law*, VIII.314–16; in Siebert, *Freedom of the Press*, 265–9; and by Jennifer Carter in J. R. Jones (ed.), *The Restored Monarchy* (1979), 81–3.

25. Cobbett, *ST*, X.147–308; *CSPD 1684–5*, 171, 184, 187, 221–4, 226, 297. For Rosewell see Matthews, *CR*, *s.v.*

26. Cobbett, *ST*, VI.514–17, 519–34. To Secretary Bennet the author of *Mene Tekel* was later reported to be Roger Jones (*CSPD 1664–5*, 6), whose authorship is accepted as 'probable' in Richard L. Greaves's account of the episode in *Deliver us from Evil: The Radical Underground in Britain 1660–1663* (New York, 1986), pp. 222–3, 224, and under whom it is listed in Wing, *STC*, J988. For Twyn see Henry R. Plomer, *A Dictionary of the Booksellers ... 1641 to 1667* (1907; rpt 1968), *s.v.*

27. Cobbett, *ST*, VII.1128 (quoted in part in Holdsworth, *English Law*, VIII.343–4).

28. Cobbett, *ST*, XII.324–5, VI.707–10; *CSPD 1663–4*, 595. For Keach see Underwood, *EB*, 111–12, 132–3, and for his trial and bearing in the pillory, Thomas Crosby, *The History of the English Baptists*, 4 vols (1738–40), II.185–209.

29. Cobbett, *ST*, VI.708, XI.501–2.

30. Carl S. Meyer, 'Henry VIII burns Luther's books, 12 May 1521', *JEH*, IX (1958), 173–87; Charles R. Gillett, *Burned Books*, 2 vols (New York, 1932), I.19–20. This was not the earliest example of ecclesiastical censorship of printed books in England: John B. Gleason, 'The earliest evidence for ecclesiastical censorship', *The Library*, 6th ser., IV, 2 (1982), 137–41, finds John Colet acting as a prepublication censor in (or about) 1510.

31. Gillett, *Burned Books*, I.53–4, 61–2, 90–1, 150–8, 187–9, 238–47, 248–63, II.419–21, 429–34, 443–6, 449–54; W. H. Hart, *Index Expurgatorius Anglicanus*, 4 vols (1872–7), nos 14, 28–9, 62, 117, 132, 187, 190, 193, 194, 211, 213, 225;

DNB, s.v. Delaune; *Delaune's Plea for the Non-Conformists ... With a Preface by the Author of the Review* (1706), sigs. a1, a1ᵛ.

32. Somers, *CT*, VIII.420–4 (the Decree is printed also in Gillett, *Burned Books*, II.516–20, and, in part, in J. P. Kenyon (ed.), *The Stuart Constitution 1603–1688* (1966), 471–4).

33. Gillett, *Burned Books*, II.511, 513; Owen, *CW*, VIII.127–62. William Lamont, *Richard Baxter and the Millennium* (1979), 102–5, discusses Baxter's political thought in relation to the Decree's charges (concluding that only the charge of allowing resistance to Charles I has any plausibility in a collection of otherwise wrong-headed, imprecise and contrived allegations), and in a long account of *The Holy Commonwealth* (pp. 124–209) challenges the view of Richard B. Schlatter (ed.), *Richard Baxter and Puritan Politics* (New Brunswick, NJ, 1957), 26 and *passim* that Baxter's chief political concern was to defend 'the mixed species of government'.

34. Bunyan, *HW*, 31–2. The identification of Mr Filth suggested in the editors' note on this passage is made almost certain by L'Estrange's reputation for lecherous immorality (see p. 108), though he did not, as Bunyan here alleges, automatically allow bawdy material (see Paul Salzman, *English Prose Fiction 1558–1700* (1985), 221).

35. Kitchin, *L'Estrange*, 43–66, 74–84. For Baxter's disavowal of responsibility for the publication of the *Petition for Peace* see *Rel. Bax.*, II.379, §§261–3, and for further details of the controversy with Bagshaw, N. H. Keeble, 'Richard Baxter's preaching ministry', *JEH*, XXXV (1984), 545–6.

36. L'Estrange, *A Memento* (1682), 6–7; [*id.*], *A Seasonable Memorial* (1680), 12; [*id.*], *An Account of the Growth of Knavery* (1678), 9; *id.*, *A Word Concerning Libels* (1681), 10; *id.*, *Truth and Loyalty Vindicated* (1662), sig. A2ᵛ.

37. *CSPD 1661–2*, 282–3; Kitchin, *L'Estrange*, 105–7; L'Estrange, *Considerations and Proposals* (1663), sigs. A3–A3ᵛ, p. 6.

38. L'Estrange, *Considerations*, sig. A4ᵛ, pp. 1, 24–5; *CSPD 1663–4*, 240 (the warrant is printed also in Plomer, *Dictionary 1641 to 1667*, pp. xxi–xxii); Kitchin, *L'Estrange*, 126–30. In *Economics of the British Book Trade*, ed. Robin Myers and Michael Harris (1985), pp. 32–59, John Hetet analyses 'The Wardens' accounts of the Stationers' Company' for evidence of the Company's enforcement of the Licensing Act, to conclude that, in so far as it acted as an agent of state censorship, it did so out of self-interest.

39. *Rel. Bax*, III.102, §221. On 'the Grotian religion' see Keeble, *Baxter*, 117–18, and Geoffrey F. Nuttall, 'Richard Baxter and *The Grotian Religion*', in *Reform and Reformation*, ed. Derek Baker (1979), 245–50.

40. *CSPD 1663–4*, 446, 586, 616, 621. For Forbes, Nicholson and Warmestry see *DNB, s.vv.*, and for Forbes, also Matthews, *CR, s.v.*, and Geoffrey F. Nuttall, 'George Whitefield's "Curate"', *JEH*, XXVII, 4 (1976), 371–3.

41. [Ralph Wallis], *More News from Rome* (1666), sigs. A3ᵛ–A4.

42. [Wallis], *More News*, sig. A4, pp. 16, 25. Baxter mentions Warmestry's 'vehement tedious Invectives' at Kidderminster in *Rel. Bax.*, II.149, §30 and II.376, §251.

43. *CSPD 1664–5*, 8, 19.

44. *CSPD 1664–5*, 24, 45, 156–7. Browne (for whom see *DNB, s.v.*) may have had little regard for the episcopal clergy, but he was, equally, a noted persecutor of the Quakers (see Braithwaite, *SPQ*, 24, and *Rel. Bax.*, II.436, §431). Wing, *STC*, W616–18, knows only a 1666 edn of *More News*, *Magna Charta* only as an alternative title for it and no edn of *The Honour of a Hangman*.

45. *CSPD 1664–5*, 309–10; *CSPD 1667–8*, 357–8.

46. Sheila Williams, 'The pope-burning processions of 1679, 1680 and 1681', *Journal of the Warburg and Courtauld Institutes*, XXI (1958), 109–10; Mumby, *Publishing and Bookselling*, 122; John Dunton, *The Life and Errors*, 2 vols (1818), I.266; [Wallis], *More News*, sig. A4.

47. Blagden, *Stationers' Company*, 172–3 (on the English Stock, see *ibid.*, 75–7, 92–106). For an example of L'Estrange's

irritation with the Company see *CSPD 1673*, 413.

48. L'Estrange, *Considerations*, 2, 5, 30–1; Kitchin, *L'Estrange*, 142–4. In his reply to the *Account* L'Estrange pointed to Marvell as its author (*Account of the Growth of Knavery*, 6, 27, 34).

49. Mark A. Thomson, *The Secretaries of State 1681–1782* (1932), 150–5; Fraser, *Intelligence of the Secretaries of State*, 9–34, Siebert, *Freedom of the Press*, 252–3.

50. Cobbett, *ST*, VI.526, 560; Siebert, *Freedom of the Press*, 255.

51. *CSPD 1663–4*, 8, 11, 18, 19 (Leach), 179, 180, 213–14, 230, 267, 268 (Lillicrap), 211, 270, 278, 334, 497, 503 (Marsh), 211, 334, 255, 272 (Brudenell), 225 (Cutler). The very varied, often popular, and frequently conformist and royalist, titles listed under these men in Paul G. Morrison, *Index of Printers, Publishers and Booksellers in Donald Wing's Short-Title Catalogue* (Charlottesville, VA, 1955) hardly suggest any particular commitment in them. Leach and Lillicrap were probably after something marketable. Morrison's list, though, does not tell the whole story: stationers would not advertise their names on unlicensed publications (so Brudenell does not appear on the imprint of the *The Kingdome Saved* (Wing, *STC*, L2641)). For further details of these men see Plomer, *Dictionary 1641–67*, *s.vv.*, and Greaves, *Deliver us from Evil*, pp. 218–20.

52. *CSPD 1663–4*, 186, 193, 216, 295, 311, 338, 426, 465, 537, 549. Uncertainty attends the conjectural dating of Elizabeth Calvert documents in *CSPD*. [Althea E. Terry], 'Giles Calvert's publishing career', *JFHS*, XXXV (1938), 46, proves from his will that Giles Calvert died between 11 and 28 August 1663. Elizabeth's 'July 4? 1663' petition, which speaks of her 'late' husband, must therefore have been drawn up some weeks later at the earliest (*CSPD 1663–4*, 193), and her 'April ? 1664' petition pleading her bereavement (her dead husband 'yet unburried') must derive from August or early September 1663 (*ibid.*, 549). Evidently, she was not released from the Gatehouse until after her husband's death.

53. Milton, *CPW*, VI.23–35 (*De Doctrina* was refused a licence in 1676, two years after

Milton's death (*CPW*, VI. 39–40));
Christopher Hill, *Milton and the English Revolution* (1977; rpt 1979), 234–5. Hill's essay 'Censorship and English literature', in *Writing and Revolution*, pp. 32–71, collects a great many examples (drawn chiefly from the earlier seventeenth century) of the effects of censorship and the steps taken to counter it.

54. Hill, *Writing and Revolution*, 52; F. Bastian, *Defoe's Early Life* (1981), 56 (and see pp. 48–65 for Defoe's education at Morton's academy); Marvell, *P&L*, I.225–32, II.357 (and n. on p. 396). For Morton see Matthews, *CR, s.v.*

55. Matthews, *CR, s.v.* Morrice; Philip Henry, *Diaries*, ed. M. H. Lee (1882), 173; Douglas R. Lacey, *Dissent and Parliamentary Politics* (New Brunswick, NJ, 1969), 369; Steele, *BRP*, I.3622, 3623, 3625.

56. Hill, *Writing and Revolution*, 52, 53; *id.*, *Milton and the English Revolution*, 355; Milton, *CPW*, VIII.408. Baxter occasionally had his books vetted before publication by such nonconformist friends as John Corbet (*Rel. Bax.*, III.72, §155).

57. Braithwaite, *SPQ*, 279–81; Russell S. Mortimer, 'The first century of Quaker printers, Part I', *JFHS*, XI (1948), 38–9, 40; Thomas P. O'Malley, 'The press and Quakerism', *JFHS*, LIV (1979), 173–4; Luella Wright, *The Literary Life of the Early Quakers* (Columbia, Miss., 1932), 95–109; Fox, *JGF*, 732–3.

58. E[dward] B[illing], *A Faithful Testimony for God* (1664), 4; Franklin B. Williams, 'The Laudian imprimatur', *The Library*, 5th ser., XV (1960), 96–7; Kirschbaum, *Shakespeare and the Stationers*, 57–74; Arber, *TC*, I.xi, §27.

59. *Rel. Bax.*, II.379, §261; Baxter, *Catholick Communion Doubly Defended* (1681), 29; *id.*, *A Defence of the Principles of Love* (1671), I.40; *Rel. Bax.*, I.123, §211(2); Wing, *STC*, B1263, B1380; Heywood, *AD*, III.224 (and cf. III.335).

60. Wing, *STC, s.v.* Owen, *passim*, B5534, B5541, B5506 (Bunyan), K68, K69, K84 (Keach), F1746, F1750, F1764, F1774, F1922, F1928, etc. (Sowle), F1794, F1795, F1799, F1803A, F1812, etc. (Bringhurst), P1356, P1327 (Penn); *CSPD 1668–9*, 98, 102. Each of these

stationers is in Henry R. Plomer, *A Dictionary of the Printers ... 1668 to 1725* (1922; rpt 1968), *s.vv.*; for Ponder, see also Frank M. Harrison, 'Nathaniel Ponder', *The Library*, 4th ser., XV (1934), 257–94, and for Sowle and Bringhurst see Mortimer, 'First century, Part I', 47–9, and 'Part II', *JFHS*, XLI (1949), 74–6.

61. Helen Darbishire (ed.), *The Early Lives of Milton* (1932), 75–6, 185–6; Arber, *TC*, I.56, 172; J. Milton French, *The Life Records of John Milton*, 5 vols (1949–58; rpt New York, 1966), V.25–6, 72–4, 79–80, 84; William Riley Parker, *Milton*, 2 vols (1968), I.637; Keeble, *Baxter*, 115–21.

62. *Rel. Bax.* I.120, §206; Burnet, *OT*, I.467; Kitchin, *L'Estrange*, 192n., [Robert Ferguson], *A Representation of the Threatening Dangers* [1687]), 9; Wing, *STC*, M878, A2905, A2917. The publishing history of Marvell's *Rehearsal* is detailed see *RT*, pp. xx–xxv, and see Marvell's own remarks, *RT*, 173–4.

63. [Herbert Croft], *The Naked Truth* (1675), sig. A3ᵛ; [Peter Gunning], *Lex Talionis* (1676), 1; [Francis Turner], *Animadversions upon ... The Naked Truth*, 2nd edn (1676), sig. A2; [Andrew Marvell], *Mr. Smirke* (1676), 9–10, 13.

64. Marvell, *RT*, 166, 9. Marvell's title alludes to *The Rehearsal*, I.i.80–92, in *Burlesque Plays of the Eighteenth Century*, ed. Simon Trussler (1969), 9. This, and the satiric strategy of *RT*, are discussed in Warren L. Chernaik, *The Poet's Time* (1983), 182–94, and Annabel M. Patterson, *Marvell and the Civic Crown* (Princeton, NJ, 1978), 175–210.

65. Marvell, *P&L*, II.346, 357, 328 (and see above, n. 48).

66. John N. King, *English Reformation Literature* (Princeton, NJ, 1982), 21, 72, 418; Leona Rostenberg, *The Minority Press* (New York, 1971), 170–86, 190–8; Siebert, *Freedom of the Press*, 96–100; Watts, *DRR*, 68–9; John F. Wilson, 'Another look at John Canne', *CH*, XXXIII (1964), 34–47. For illegal Catholic printing see Rostenberg, *Minority Press*, 111–31, and A. F. Allison and D. M. Rogers, *A Catalogue of Catholic Books Printed Abroad or Secretly in England 1558–*

1640 (1956.).

67. *CSPD 1667–8*, 294, 319, 360, 361, 363, 378; Kitchin, *L'Estrange*, 110n., 176–7; Walker, 'Censorship', 225, 235.

68. Wing, *STC*, L3460 (Ludlow), M860, M861, M878 (Marvell), W616 (Wallis). Under the title *The Second Part of the Growth*, Wing, *STC*, refers to Ferguson where the publication is not, however, listed (in either 1st or 2nd edns of *STC*). It is listed, with the imprint described as 'fictitious', in vol. 258 of the *British Library Catalogue*, under the pseudonym 'Philo-Veritas', with a queried ascription to Ferguson. Ferguson's authorship and the London printing were first alleged in Anthony à Wood, *Athenae Oxonienses*, 4 vols (1813–20), IV.232 (noted in *DNB*, *s.v.* Ferguson). For the case of Ludlow, see *Memoirs*, ed. C. H. Firth, 2 vols (1894), I.xiii, and Ludlow, *A Voyce from the Watch Tower*, ed. A. B. Worden (1978), 18–21.

69. *CSPD 1675–6*, 547; *CSPD 1676–7*, 543, 544, 550, 555, 565; *CSPD 1677–8*, 1, 3, 47, 135, 188. See also Matthews, *CR*, *s.v.* Cary.

70. *Rel. Bax.*, III.61, §140; Marvell, *RT*, 205, 166 (and cf. 196–8).

71. *Rel. Bax*, I.123, §211(2); Wood, *Athenae Oxonienses*, I.534; *CSPD 1689–90*, 30; *CSPD 1691–2*, 438, 450; Edmund Bohun, *The Diary and Autobiography*, ed. S. Wilton Rix (1853), 93–8, 1011–17. For Bohun see *DNB*, *s.v.*, and for both this affair and the vulnerability of licensers generally, Siebert, *Freedom of the Press*, 243–4, and Astbury, 'Renewal of the Licensing Act', 298. Blount had set out deliberately to trap Bohun by tempting him to license a manuscript which appealed to his Tory sympathies: see Sensabaugh, *Grand Whig Milton*, 156–7.

72. *Rel. Bax.*, I.123, §211(2), III.61, §§137, 140 and III.86, §186; Keeble, *Baxter*, 20; Peter Toon, *God's Statesman* (1971), 127; Owen, *Exercitations on the Epistle to the Hebrews* (1668), sig. A2; Kitchin, *L'Estrange*, 200–3; Marvell, *RT*, 22–3.

73. Cobbett, *ST*, VII.959–60; Milton, *CPW*, II.529; *CSPD 1675–6*, 544; *CSPD 1676–7*, 92; Bohun, *Autobiography*, 98; *Harl Misc.*, VI.74; Darbishire, *Early Lives*, 180;

Parker, *Milton*, I.600–1, 613–14; Milton, *PL*, IV.193, V.354–5, VI.146–8, VII.24–8, XII.521–2.

74. Hill, *Writing and Revolution*, 32, 40, 50, 157–8; id., *Milton and the English Revolution*, 64–5, 216–18, 404–10, 471–2; id., *Some Intellectual Consequences of the English Revolution* (1980), 46–9.

75. *Rel. Bax.*, I.123, §211(2); Manton, *CW*, II.11; William Bates, *The Works*, 2nd edn (1723), 343–4; Cobbett, *ST*, XI.499–501.

76. Joan Bennett, 'God, Satan and King Charles', *PMLA*, XCII (1977), 441–57; Bunyan, *PP*, 19, 21; Bunyan, *HW*, 228, 230, 233, 205, 172, 158; *Rel. Bax.*, II.448, §445.

77. Siebert, *Freedom of the Press*, 269n. lists prosecuted printers.

78. Turner, *OREN*, III.482–91; B. R. White, *The English Baptists* (1983), 127; Underwood, *EB*, 93–4 (Wing, *STC*, H3404); [Terry], 'Giles Calvert', 48. These stationers are all noted in Plomer, *Dictionary 1641 to 1667* or *1668–1725*, *s.vv.*

79. *CSPD 1654*, 378, 389; *CSPD 1659–60*, 572, 575; *CSPD 1661–2*, 23, 173; Wing, *STC*, M2101, S4875, D2034, A3247; B. R. White, 'Henry Jessey in the Great Rebellion', in R. Buick Knox (ed.), *Reformation, Conformity and Dissent* (1977), 152. There are accounts of these publishing ventures in Walker, 'Censorship', 226–36 (an unsympathetic appraisal), Leona Rostenberg, *Literary, Politic ... Printing ... in England, 1551–1700*, 2 vols (New York, 1965), I.203–36 (an essay on Livewell Chapman), esp. pp. 230–4, and Greaves, *Deliver us from Evil*, pp. 212–15.

80. L'Estrange, *Truth and Loyalty*, 56; Kitchin, *L'Estrange*, 112–13.

81. CSPD *1661–2*, 23, 106, 156, 166, 572; Penney, *ESP*, 155–7; Wing, *STC*, P1216, F1894. For accounts of Giles Calvert's publishing career see [Terry], 'Giles Calvert', 45–9; Mortimer, 'First Century, Part I', 148–9; O'Malley, 'Press and Quakerism', 175–6; Plomer, *Dictionary 1641–67*, *s.v.* Calvert.

82. *CSPD 1663–4*, 71, 101, 124, 180, 349, 430, 510, 581, 582. Chapman is in Plomer, *Dictionary 1641–67*, *s.v.*

83. Cobbett, *ST*, VI.539–64; *CSPD 1663–4*, 37, 43, 297, 319, 326, 574. Brewster is noticed in Plomer, *Dictionary 1641–67*, *s.v.* Greaves, *Deliver us from Evil*, pp. 219, 223–5, summarizes L'Estrange's campaign against the Confederates.

84. *CSPD 1661–2*, 87. Cobbett, *ST*, VII.937–60 prints extracts from one of Smith's two accounts of his experiences. For them, and a summary, see Plomer, *Dictionary 1668–1725*, *s.v.* Smith. Smith's authors were primarily Baptists, men such as Thomas Collier, whose work Calvert, Brewster and Hills had formerly seen through the press (Wing, *STC*, C5275), Thomas Grantham, for whom Darby worked (G1528), Hanserd Knollys, a former author of Chapman's, as was Vavasor Powell (K705, P3090), and Henry Denne (H1020, 11024). Smith's radicalism did not extend to sympathy for the Quakers (see e.g. B5426A, H2271).

85. *CSPD 1664–5*, 191; *CSPD 1667*, 290, 395; *CSPD 1667–8*, 178, 201, 360, 363, 372–3, 378; [Terry], 'Giles Calvert', 46; Marvell, *RT*, pp. xxi, xxiii; Wing, *STC*, M878–881; Dunton, *Life and Errors*, I.247.

86. Penney, *ESP*, 229–30; Plomer, *Dictionary 1641–1667*, *s.vv.* Dover, Inman. Neither of these women left any imprints to be recorded in Morrison's *Index*.

87. Cobbett, *ST*, VII.959–60; *CSPD 1682*, 68, 564; *CSPD Jan. 1 to June 30 1683*, 37, 38, 278; *CSPD July 1 to Sept. 30 1683*, 432; Plomer, *Dictionary 1668–1725*, *s.v.* Curtis.

88. Mortimer, 'First century, Part I', 40–1, 47–9; Percy H. Muir, 'English imprints after 1640', *The Library*, 4th ser., XIV (1933–4), 160–2; Norman Penney, 'George Fox's writings and the Morning Meeting', *Friends' Quarterly Examiner* (1902), 63–72.

89. Plomer, *Dictionary 1641–67* and *1668–1725*, *s.vv.* the various Simmons. For Nevill see also Giles Hester, *Nevill Simmons: Bookseller and Publisher* (1893).

90. Dunton, *Life and Errors*, I.205, 206; *Rel. Bax.*, III.85, §183. For all these stationers, see Dunton, and Plomer, *Dictionary 1668–1725*, *s.vv.* For the Poultry's earlier history as a publishing centre, see Henry Plomer, 'The Long Shop in the Poultry', *Bibliotheca*, II (1895–7), 61–80. The cited

Aylmer publications are Wing, *STC*, M2117, M2096 (Milton), B933, B925–7 (Barrow), T1185–1272 (Tillotson), K396–421A (Kidder), F1695–1729 (Fowler).

91. Wing, *STC*, P970–73A, P983A–6 (Pearse), B1100, B1128, B1115 (joint publication of Bates), B1101–12, B1118–24, B1126 (Bates), B1101, B1104, B1109, B1111, B1113, B1122–6 (printed by Darby), H3023, H3024, H3030, H3035, H3036, H3038 (Howe), H3028 (funeral sermon for Bates), M536, M522 (Manton), M526 (*195 Sermons*), K137, K150, K156, K160, K161, K163, K196, K204, K206A, K207–9A, K212, K222, K226 (Keith).

92. Alexander Pope, *The Dunciad Variorum*, n. to II.136, in *The Poems*, ed. John Butt (1963), 383; Dunton, *Life and Errors*, I.38–9, 62–3, 64–5, 77–9; Stephen Parks, *John Dunton and the English Book Trade* (New York, 1976), 8–16, 17–21; Bastian, *Defoe's Early Life*, 157–8; Wing, *STC*, D1885, A3225, A3228, A3240, W1374.

93. Dunton, *Life and Errors*, I.79–80, 87–90, 94, 130, 138–9, 147–8; Parks, *Dunton*, 24–37, 66–7, 405 n. 63; Wing, *STC*, M1096, M1120, M1246.

94. Wing, *STC*, B1350, B1370 (Baxter), W2646, W2648, W2649, W2653, W2657 (Williams), H1281A (*Heads*), K161, K166 (Keith), K80, K97 (Keach); Parks, *Dunton*, 46; Dunton, *Life and Errors*, I.205; [Charles Leslie], *A Case of Present Concern* ([1703?]), 2; Arber, *TC*, III.308. A full list of Dunton's publications is appended to Parks, *Dunton*.

95. Wing, *STC*, M526, C3711, P2820–3; Sarah Clapp, 'Subscription publishers prior to Jacob Tonson', *The Library*, 4th ser., XIII (1932), 173–6; Dunton, *Life and Errors*, I.211; Arber, *TC*, I.469, 500, II.22, 79, 121, III.180, 206.

96. John Alden, 'Pills and publishing', *The Library*, 5th ser., VII (1952), 21–37; Parks, *Dunton*, 205–6, 207.

CHAPTER 4

1. Marvell, *RT*, 4–5. Milton had used the dragon's teeth analogy with reference to printing in *Areopagitica* (*CPW*, II.492), but with the intellectual fertility of books rather than the productivity of the press in mind.

2. See pp. 95, 96 above.

3. Marjorie Plant, *The English Book Trade*, 2nd edn (1965), 86–8; L'Estrange, *Considerations and Proposals* (1663), 27; Edward Arber (ed.). *A Transcript of the Registers of the Company of Stationers of London; 1554–1640*, 5 vols (1875–94; rpt New York, 1950), I.14–15; Henry R. Plomer, *A Dictionary of the Booksellers . . . 1641 to 1667* (1907; rpt 1968), *s.v.* Fletcher, and *1668 to 1725* (1922; rpt 1968), *passim*. Plant, *Book Trade*, 64 computes 50 English printers and 27 booksellers and printers in 1700.

4. Plant, *Book trade*, 91 (see pp. 88–92 for an account of output), 92–5. Marjorie Plant does not identify the catalogue she used, but it was presumably the *General Catalogue* advertised by Robert Clavell in Arber, *TC*, I.436.

5. John Dunton, *Life and Errors*, 2 vols (1818), I.175, 177. See above, p. 122.

6. *Rel. Bax.*, I.115, §174; Wing, *STC*, B1196–1204, B1383–95, B5557–75A.

7. Wing, *STC*, B5523–29A, B5539–40, B5550–3 (Bunyan), B1113–16, B1118–21 (Bates), C6255–7, C6265–7 (Corbet), K64–5, K80–2, K87–92A, K96–100, K103–7 (Keach), H1762–4 (Heywood), H3015–17 (Howe), O729–31 (Owen).

8. Wing, *STC*, B720–3, 725–9 (Barclay), P1328–32 (Penn), P1149–1221 (Penington; some dates are conjectural).

9. David Runyan, 'Types of Quaker writing', in H. Barbour and A. Robert (eds), *Early Quaker Writings* (Grand Rapids, Mich., 1973), 567–73. Isaac Sharp, 'Joseph Smith', *JFHS*, XI (1914), 9, quoting the figures of William C. Westlake in *The Friends' Quarterly Examiner* (1868), put the total at 6,092 titles by 1700; Luella Wright, *The Literary Life of Early Friends* (New York, 1932), 8, at 2,678 by 1725.

10. H. S. Bennett, *English Books and Readers 1603 to 1640* (1970), 216–17, 222–4; Plant, *Book Trade*, 247–53.

11. William Penn, *No Cross, No Crown*, ed. Norman Penney (1930; rpt 1981), pp. xxvii–xxx. Wright, *Literary Life of Early Friends*, 58–60, 64–6, discusses, with evidence from Penn, the relationship

between reader and author in Quaker literature.

12. Dunton, *Life and Errors*, I.159, II.491–509; Stephen Parks, *John Dunton and the English Book Trade* (New York, 1976), 133–47; Plomer, *Dictionary 1668–1725, s.v.* Millington; William Riley Parker, *Milton*, 2 vols (1968), I.578, 607–8.

13. Arber, *TC*, II.534; *Rel. Bax.*, III.190, §70.

14. Arber, *TC*, I.159, II.326; Sarah Clapp, 'Subscription publishers prior to Jacob Tonson', *The Library*, 4th ser., XIII, 2 (1932), 158–83, esp. pp. 172–6; Plant, *Book Trade*, 227–32; and for earlier precedents, Phoebe Sheavyn, *The Literary Profession in the Elizabethan Age*, 2nd edn (1967), 85–6.

15. Arber, *TC*, I.389–90; Parks, *Dunton*, 311; Parker, *Milton*, I.651–2, 662–3.

16. *CSPD 1663–4*, 37, 43, 297; J. Walker, 'The censorship of the press during the reign of Charles II', *History*, new ser., XXXV (1950), 227–8; Heywood, *AD*, II.213–15, III.51–7, IV.259–63.

17. L'Estrange, *Considerations and Proposals* (1663), 1; *Rel. Bax.*, I.4, §3; *CSPD 1664–5*, 400. The figure of 10,000 is from *The Trade of England Revived* (1681), quoted in Margaret Spufford, *Small Books and Pleasant Histories* (1981), 115, which, on pp. 111–28, gives a detailed account of the trade of late seventeenth-century pedlars as it contributed to the dissemination of cheap books.

18. William Dundas, *A Few Words of Truth* (1673), 13 (and cf. p.16); Arber, *TC*, III.296; Russell S. Mortimer, 'The first century of Quaker printers, Part I', *JFHS*, XL (1948), 39–40; Penney, *ESP*, 228–9; Penney, *FPT*, 161; Wright, *Literary Life of Early Friends*, 74–86. For Hookes see Braithwaite, *SPQ*, 282–3, 288–9, and Norman Penney, 'Our recording clerks: (i) Ellis Hookes', *JFHS*, I, 1(1903), 12–22.

19. Heywood, *AD*, I.246, II.211–16, III.66–73, 229, IV.259–63.

20. Baxter, *An Apology for the Nonconformists Ministry* (1681), 10, 73 (cf. *Rel. Bax.*, I.89, §137(14)); *Rel. Bax.*, III.190, §69; Baxter, *Two Sheets for Poor Families* (1665), 2nd pag., 10; *id.*, *Poor Man's Family Book* (1674), pref. 'A request to the rich'; *id.*, *A Call to the Unconverted*, 13th edn with additions (1669), 2nd pag., 1.; *id.*, *The Reverend Richard Baxter's Last Treatise*, ed. F. J. Powicke (1926), 42; *id.*, *A Paraphrase on the New Testament* (1685), sig. A4; David Cressey, *Literacy and the Social Order* (1980), 50–1.

21. Baxter, *Five Disputations of Church Government and Worship* (1659), 491; *Rel. Bax.*, appendix vii, 117–18.

22. Gregory King's statistical and economic table is printed in Browning, *EHD*, 515–17, in George Clark, *The Later Stuarts*, 2nd edn (1955), 15–6, and in Peter Laslett, *The World We Have Lost*, 3rd edn (1983), 32–3, with a caution as to its reliability on p. 298, n. 4. The labourers' figure is from Joan Thirsk (ed.), *The Agrarian History of England and Wales 1500–1640* (1967), 435–8, 864. For an account of book production costs and prices in the seventeenth century, see Plant, *Book Trade*, 220–45, and, for the cheaper market, Spufford, *Small Books*, 48, 50, 91–8, 130–1. My generalizations about retailing prices are derived from Arber, *TC, passim.*

23. Spufford, *Small Books*, 130, 134, 135, 197, 198, 200, 211; N. H. Keeble, 'Some erroneous, doubtful and misleading Baxterian attributions in Wing and Halkett and Laing', *N&Q*, XXXII, 2 (1985), 188–9. For a sympathetic appraisal of these chapbooks, see Eamon Duffy, 'The godly and the multitude in Stuart England', *The Seventeenth Century*, I.1 (1986), 31–55.

24. Arber, *TC*, I.65, 71 (Baxter), I.216, 245 (Bunyan), I.449 (Corbet), I.449 (Vincent), I.244 (Keach), II.237 (Doolittle); [William Roberts], 'Bookselling in the Poultry', *The City Press*, XXXIV, 86 (16 Aug. 1890), 7.

25. Arber, *TC*, I.70, 88, 90, 102, 109–10, 115, 146, 328, 402, 449, 492, II.94, 388, 407 (Baxter), I.12, 116, 182 (Bunyan), I.381 (Cheyney), I.449 (Corbet), I.39, II.427–8 (Doolittle), II.25 (Firmin), I.140 (Gale), I.148 (Gouge), I.328 (Humfrey), I.125, 146 (Janeway), I.300, II,317 (Keach), I.8, 288, 502, II.229, 238, 377, 473, 556 (Owen), III.270 (Penn), I.140 (Poole), I.18 (Tombes), I.54, 95 (Vincent).

26. Arber, *TC*, I.299, II.24, I.192; [Roberts], 'Bookselling in the Poultry', 7.
27. Arber, *TC*, I.1, 42, 47, 62, 101, 102, 123, 192.
28. Arber, *TC*, I.29, 34, 108, 280.
29. Arber, *TC*, I.56.
30. Arber, *TC*, I.146, II.11.
31. Milton, *CPW*, I.810 (and cf. 'Ad Joannem Rousium', ll. 73–87, in *PJM*, 302–3); Baxter, *The Life of Faith*, enlarged edn (1670), sig. a2; Milton, *PL*, I.26, in *PJM*, 462. The significance of the reader to *PL* is the subject of Stanley E. Fish, *Surprised by Sin* (1967; rpt Berkeley, Calif., 1971).
32. Milton, *PL*, VII.30–9, in *PJM*, 777.
33. E. A. Wrigley and R. S. Schofield, *The Population History of England, 1541–1871* (1981), 93, 207–10, 212, 528–9, 532–3 (referred to in Laslett, *World We Have Lost*, 106–7).
34. Cressey, *Literacy and Social Order*, 73–4, 118–74 (cited in Laslett, *World We Have Lost*, 229–32); Laslett, *World We Have Lost*, 9; Margaret Spufford, 'First steps in literacy', in Harvey J. Graff (ed.), *Literacy and Social Development in the West* (1981), 126.
35. Cressey, *Literacy and Social Order*, 42, takes it as a reliable guide to full literacy, but see Spufford, *Small Books*, 27.
36. Spufford, *Small Books*, 1–82 *passim* (quotations from pp. xviii, 32, 36); *id.*, 'First steps in literacy', 126–50.
37. Spufford, *Small Books*, 6–8, 23, 25, 30–1, 35, 46; Heywood, *AD*, I.58, 157; Roger Lowe, *The Diary*, ed. William L. Sachse (1938), 19, 29, 43, 62, 69; Joseph Lister, *The Life* (1860), 7.
38. Bunyan, *MW*, VI.194–6; Braithwaite, *SPQ*, 288–9.
39. Algernon Sidney, *Discourses concerning Government* (1763), 101 (quoted in Clark, *Later Stuarts*, 27, and in H. Horwitz, 'Protestant reconciliation in the Exclusion Crisis', *JEH*, XV (1964), 204); [Francis Turner], *Animadversions upon … The Naked Truth*, 2nd edn (1676), 31–2; Marvell, *RT*, 47; Duncan Coomer, *English Dissent under the Early Hanoverians* (1946), 60.
40. Turner, *OREN*, III.28, 58, 59, 60, 69, 70, 72; quotations from *ibid.*, I.5, 33, 88, 140.
41. Turner, *OREN*, III.114–20, 142–3.

42. *CSPD 1693*, 448–50; E. D. Bebb, *Nonconformity and Social and Economic Life 1660–1800* (1935), 33.
43. Bebb, *Social and Economic Life*, 35–40, 45 (Bebb's findings are reported in Clark, *Later Stuarts*, 27, and Coomer, *English Dissent*, 60); Watts, *DRR*, 267–89; Braithwaite, *BQ*, 512, and *SPQ*, 459, estimates a total Quaker population of 30,000–40,000 in 1661, and of 40,000–50,000 ('at most') in 1670–9. Barry Reay, *The Quakers and the English Revolution* (1985), 26–7, believes the total may have been as high as 60,000 in the 1660s.
44. James Sutherland, *English Literature of the Late Seventeenth Century* (1969), 26, 30. On the age structure of the population, see Wrigley and Schofield, *Population History*, 215–17, 528–9.
45. Bunyan, *PP*, 6.
46. *Rel. Bax.*, I.114, §174; Baxter, *A Call to the Unconverted* (1658), sigs A2–A3; N. H. Keeble, *Richard Baxter* (1982), 73–6.
47. Benjamin Keach, *The Child's Instructor* (1679); Bunyan, *MW*, VI.183; Theophilus Gale, *The Court of the Gentiles*, 5 vols (1669–78), I, sigs *4–*4^v; Baxter, *Compassionate Counsel to all Young-Men* (1681); Howe, *CW*, II.1–3.
48. Peter Toon, *God's Stateman* (1971), 17–18; Howe, *CW*, II.vii–viii; Bunyan, *MW*, IX.xxv, xxxiv.
49. On the differences between Owen and Baxter, the Happy Union and its collapse in the midst of doctrinal controversy, see Watts, *DRR*, 289–97, Jones, *CE*, 109–19, and Alexander Gordon (ed.), *Freedom after Ejection* (1917), 26–8, 95–7; more at large, Roger Thomas in Geoffrey F. Nuttall *et al.*, *The Beginnings of Nonconformity* (1964), 33–60, and in Bolam, *EP*, 95–8, 101–25.
50. Manton, *CW*, III.225; Howe, *The Blessedness of the Righteous* (1673), 113–14; Howe, *CW*, III.58.
51. Howe is discussed in this respect on pp. 165–7 above.
52. Baxter, *A Christian Directory* (1673), III, questions 173–4, pp. 917–28; Bunyan, *PP*, 21, 99, 226.
53. Watts, *DRR*, 285–8, 349, 360; the analysis and its interpretation occupy pp. 346–66 (cf. Bebb, *Social and Economic Life*, 46–50).

54. Penney, *ESP*, 194; [Amor Stodard *et al.*], *To the King and both Houses of Parliament* (1666), 11.

55. Turner, *OREN*, I.14, 34, 38, 82, 164 (cf. Braithwaite, *SPQ*, 460–1).

56. Braithwaite, *SPQ*, 461; Penney, *FPT*, 179 (cf. pp. 370–1); Bebb, *Social and Economic Life*, 46–8; Reay, *Quakers and the English Revolution*, 143–4.

57. Turner, *OREN*, I.17, 28, 29, 35, 41, 110, 63; Bunyan, *GA*, §2; Howe, *CW*, I.445. H. G. Tibutt, *Bunyan Meeting Bedford 1650–1950* ([1950]), 20, lists church members in 1670, with their occupations.

58. Turner, *OREN*, I.33, 48–9, 110, 116, 125, 139, 143; Watts, *DRR*, 350–1.

59. [–], *Reasons why the Church of England . . .* (1687), 7; [Charles Leslie], *A Snake in the Grass*, 3rd edn (1698), pp. xxix–xxx; Jones, *CE*, 126–7; Watts, *DRR*, 360–5. Nonconformist divines were alive to the possible consequences; see, e.g., William Bates, *The Danger of Prosperity* (1685), in *Works*, 2nd edn (1723), 275–308.

60. Burnet, *OT*, I.260; Bunyan, *PP*, 169.

61. Cf. Spufford, *Small Books*, 47. Dr Isabel Rivers points out to me that the passage bewailing the youthful reading of romances in Bunyan, *MW*, I.332–3, is put into the mouth of a damned soul and so should not be taken, as it commonly is, as Bunyan's own confession, though that he had read romances is not, of course, in doubt. On their influence on him, see Vincent Newey (ed.), *The Pilgrim's Progress: Critical and Historical Views* (1980), 49–68, 182–250, and the articles by Harold Golder there cited; Roger Sharrock (ed.), *The Pilgrim's Progress: A Casebook* (1976), 88–93; Henri Talon, *John Bunyan*, trans. Barbara Wall (1951), 172–8.

62. Laslett, *World We Have Lost*, 22–52 (and for the paucity of nobility and gentry, esp. pp. 39–40, 42–3); *OED*, s.v. 'Vulgar, sb.3' (and cf. its use in *SA*, l. 1659, to distinguish 'the throng' from 'lords and each degree/ Of sort', ll. 1607–10, in *PJM*, 397, 398).

63. Barbour and Roberts (eds.), *Early Quaker Writings*, 14; [Charles Leslie], *The Wolf Stript* (1704), preface, p. 3; [Daniel Defoe], *The Dissenters Answer* (1704), 7–9

64. F. J. Powicke, 'Richard Baxter and the Countess of Balcarres', *BJRL*, IX, 2 (1925), 585–99; Watts, *DRR*, 250–1.

65. All these men were ejected Presbyterians or Congregationalists. Details are from Matthews, *CR*, s.vv. On Wharton's patronage of nonconformists see A. G. Matthews, *Mr. Pepys and Nonconformity* (1954), 76–94.

66. Though there were particular exceptions, only in the early eighteenth century did the Baptists as a body begin to arrange for the regular maintenance of their pastors, and the Quakers not even then (Underwood, *EB*, 125–6, 129–32; Braithwaite, *SPQ*, 360–5).

67. Turner, *OREN*, I.63; Underwood, *EB*, 60, 61, 110, 111, 114, 126.

68. Braithwaite, *BQ*, 28, 30, 63, 89, 501; Braithwaite, *SPQ*, 333, 334–5, 403–4.

69. Gordon (ed), *Freedom after Ejection*, 177–8.

70. Bennett, *English Books and Readers*, 59–66; Sheavyn, *Literary Profession* 75–9; Leo Kirschbaum, *Shakespeare and the Stationers* (Columbus, Ohio, 1955), 56–148; Frank Mott Harrison, 'Nathaniel Ponder', *The Library*, 4th ser., XV, 3 (1934), 268–74, 284–6.

71. Bunyan, *PP*, 8; Frank J. Warnke, in C. A. Patrides (ed.), *Approaches to Sir Thomas Browne* (Columbia, Miss. 1982), 49–59 (quotation from p. 54).

72. Christopher Hill, *Milton and the English Revolution* (1977; rpt 1979), 413; Wordsworth, Prospectus to *The Excursion*, ll. 51–2, 55, in *Poetical Works*, ed. Thomas Hutchinson, rev. Ernest de Selincourt, Oxford Standard Authors (1936; rpt 1964), 590; Milton, *PL*, XII.561–87, in *PJM*, 1055–6.

73. Bunyan, *PP*, pp. xlvi, xciv–xcv, ci–cii, cxvi.

74. Bunyan, *PP*, 4, 164; Bunyan, *HW*, 5; Rosemary Freeman, *English Emblem Books* (1948), 207.

75. Bunyan, *PP*, 171; Bunyan, *HW*, 116.

76. Bunyan, *MW*, VI.4, 191–2; Freeman, *Emblem Books*, 213.

77. Bunyan, *HW*, 31, 8, 9, 22, 206; Bunyan, *PP*, 7, 188, 28, 301, 262, 214.

78. Bunyan, *HW*, 204 (cf. pp. 150, 189); Bunyan, *PP*, 245.

79. Bunyan, *HW*, 78–9, 161; Bunyan, *PP*, 137, 177, 195, 196, 203, 229; Bunyan,

CW, III.590a, 599b, 607b, 608b, 611b, 622a, 637a.

80. Bunyan, *PP*, 7, 136.

81. Howe, *CW*, I.384.

82. Bunyan, *PP*, 7, 171, 173.

83. Bunyan, *PP*, 34, 171, 200–1, 263.

84. Bunyan, *CW*, III.626a; Bunyan, *PP*, 84, 107, 127, 251.

85. Bunyan, *HW*, 33, 39, 167–70, 209; Bunyan, *PP*, 77, 183, 271.

86. This point is made in Dayton Haskin, 'The burden of interpretation in *The Pilgrim's Progress*', *SP*, LXXIX, 3 (1982), 273–5.

87. Thomas Ellwood, *The History of the Life* (1714), 14, 15 (cf. p. 26); Howe, *CW*, III.19; [Daniel Defoe], *The True-Born Englishman* (1701), 6; Bunyan, *MW*, IX.282, 306–7, 308; Penn, *No Cross, No Crown*, 3–4 (I.iii–iv), 106 (VII.xvi).

88. John Corbet, *Self Imployment in Secret* ([1700?]), 36, 37; Bates, *Works*, 345–6; Howe, *CW*, I.384, 403–4; Penn, *No Cross, No Crown*, 54, 59 (V.ii, vi); [James Owen], *Church-Pageantry Display'd* (1700), 17, 18; Howe, *Blessedness of the Righteous*, 218; [Andrew Marvell], *An Account of the Growth of Popery* ([1678]), 12.

89. Manton, *CW*, II.93–4, 98; Milton, *PL*, IV.748–9, in *PJM*, 658; Keeble, *Baxter*, 25–6; Howe, *CW*, II.215; Bunyan, *PP*, 52, 258–71.

90. Bunyan, *MW*, IX.254.

91. Milton, *SA*, 'Of that Sort of Dramatic Poem ... ', in '*PJM*, 343–5; Thomas Gouge, *The Works* (1798), 430; Marvell, *RT*, 9, 11, 12, 13; Gale, *Court*, I.296.

92. Bunyan, *PP*, 2–7 (quotations from p. 7); Bunyan, *MW*, VI.44; Bunyan, *HW*, 1; Samuel Butler, *Hudibras*, ed. John Wilders (1967), 29, 100 (I.ii.5–6; II.i.1.). For Penn's remarks, and further discussion of this topic, see pp. 228–9.

93. Milton, *PL*, IX.30–8, in *PJM*, 855–6; Parker, *Milton*, I.190; Lucy Hutchinson, *Memoirs ... of Colonel Hutchinson*, ed. James Sutherland (1973), 3–4, 28–30, 32.

94. For Keach see Underwood, *EB*, 132–3, and for him and the general nonconformist contribution to early hymnody see Horton Davies, *Worship and Theology in England from Andrewes to Baxter and Fox* (Princeton, NJ, 1975), 281–5.

95. Corbet, *Self-Imployment*, 43; Howe, *CW*, VI.297. For Baxter's similar rejection of 'sourness' and his ready admission of poetry and music, see Keeble, *Baxter*, 103–8.

CHAPTER 5

1. Baxter, *A Christian Directory* (1673), I.ii.60; Bunyan, *PP*, 7; Bunyan, *GA*, §§117, 3. Under Gifford the Bedford church was in 1650 founded on Congregational principles, and though in the 1660s many of its members (including Bunyan) supported believers' baptism this was never a condition of membership. See Bunyan, *CW*, II.605–15, 617–57; H. G. Tibbutt, *Bunyan Meeting Bedford 1650–1950* ([1950]), 12, 13, 25, 33, 35.

2. Bunyan, *GA*, §§15, 129. On Bunyan's reading see Richard L. Greaves, *John Bunyan* (1969), esp. pp. 153–60, and Greaves's introduction to Bunyan, *MW*, II, pp. xvi–xxi.

3. Bunyan, *MW*, VIII.51, I.12, 243, II.16; *PP*, 229; *GA*, §276. For Gibbs, see Matthews, *CR*, *s.v.*

4. Bunyan, *GA*, §119; *Rel. Bax.*, I.1–5, §§1–5; cf. *Richard Baxter's Penitent Confession* (1691), 9; Baxter, *Cain and Abel Malignity* (1689), 134–5; *id.*, *Against the Revolt to a Foreign Jurisdiction* (1691), 540; N. H. Keeble, *Richard Baxter* (1982), 34.

5. Keeble, *Baxter*, 35–6; Geoffrey F. Nuttall, 'A transcript of Richard Baxter's library catalogue', *JEH*, II, 2, and III, 1 (1951–2), 207–21, 74–100.

6. *Rel. Bax.*, I.3, §2; I.5, §5(4); I.6, §5; Baxter, *The Saints Rest* (1650), 807 (cf. *Rel. Bax.*, I.134, §213(31)).

7. Baxter, *Poetical Fragments* (1971), 16–17; *id.*, *Christian Directory*, I.ii.60. For the Dutch scholar Heinsius, Scaliger's successor at Leiden, editor of Classical, biblical and Patristic texts, see John Edwin Sandys, *History of Classical Scholarship*, 3 vols (1908), II.313–15.

8. Bunyan, *GA*, §§74, 263, 73, 62, 67, 111, 195, 140, 61, 101, 98.

9. Bunyan, *GA*, §§193, 201, 204, 93, 181, 176, 107, 114, 233, 63. On this quality in Bunyan's writing see Brainerd P. Stranahan, 'Bunyan's special talent:

biblical texts as "events" in *Grace
Abounding* and *The Pilgrim's Progress'*, *ELR*,
XI, 3 (1981), 329–43, and Peter J. Carlton,
'Bunyan: language, convention, authority',
ELH, LI, 1 (1984), 17–32

10. *Rel. Bax.*, I.6–7, §6; I.5, §5; I.3, §3 (cf.
Potential Fragments, 13–15); Keeble,
Baxter, 32, 134. Baxter argues that a
distinct awareness of '*the very time and
manner of your Conversion*' is not an
essential sign of election in *The Right
Method for a Settled Peace of Conscience*
(1653), 136–44, 406–11. This advice
consoled Heywood when he feared his
faith was 'onely the fruit of education, and
common workings of the spirit' (*AD*,
I.155).

11. *Richard Baxter's Dying Thoughts* (1683), 9;
Baxter, *The Cure of Church-divisions*
(1670), 5–6; *id.*, *The Catechizing of Families*
(1683), 4–5; *id.*, *Christian Directory*,
II.xxi.580.

12. Baxter, *Christian Directory*, III, question
158, p. 907, and III, question 166, pp.
912–13; *id.*, *The Life of Faith*, 2nd enlarged
edn (1670), 248–9, 509–11; *id.*, *Saints
Rest*, 176; *id.*, *Dying Thoughts*, 80; Keeble,
Baxter, 30–2, 33.

13. *Rel. Bax.*, I.128, §213(5); Baxter, *Right
Method*, 119–68, 189–226; Bunyan, *PP*, 1,
27. Francis John [Jayne] (ed.), *An Excerpt
from Reliquiae Baxterianae* (1910), 16,
noted that the Hooker reference should be
not to *Ecclesiastical Polity* but to Hooker's
first sermon on Habakkuk i.4 and his
'Answer to the Supplication that Mr
Travers made' (in *The Works*, ed. John
Keble, 3 vols, 2nd edn (1841), III.469–81,
577–8).

14. Samuel How, *The Sufficiency of the Spirit's
Teaching, without Human Learning* (1826),
12, 13, 19, 24–6; Watts, *DRR*, 69–70.

15. Christopher Hill, *The World Turned Upside
Down* (1975), *passim*, esp. pp. 296–305,
which quotes William Dell, *Several
Sermons* (1709), 398, 403, 144, on pp. 94,
303; William Penn, *No Cross, No Crown*,
ed. Norman Penney (1930; rpt 1981),
20–1 (II.vi); Leo. F. Solt, 'Anti-
Intellectualism in the Puritan Revolution',
CH, XXIV (1956). 306–16.

16. William Erbery, *Testimony of William
Erbery* (1658), 86, 193; Isaac Penington,
The Way of Life (1658), 7; James Nayler,
All Vain Jangler ([1654?]), 5; *id.*, *A
Discovery of the First Wisdom* (1653), 6. For
Erbery, Penington and Nayler, see
Christopher Hill, *The Experience of Defeat*
(1984), 83–97, 118–28, 138–42, which
refers to these passages. For Penington
and Nayler see also Maria Webb, *The
Penns and Peningtons of the Seventeenth
Century* (1867); Geoffrey F. Nuttall, *James
Nayler*, Supplement 26 to *JFHS* (1954);
DNB and Braithwaite, *BQ* and *SPQ*,
indexes, *s.vv.* Penington and Nayler.

17. Isaac Penington, *Many Deep Considerations
have been upon my Heart concerning the State
of Israel* ([1664?]), 3–4; Fox, *JGF*, 7, 11;
Dryden, 'Religio Laici', ll. 406–8, in
Poems and Fables, ed. J. Kinsley (1962),
292.

18. Samuel Butler, *Hudibras*, ed. John Wilders
(1967), 2–7, 14, 15, 16 (I.i.51–186, 189,
460, 473–8, 505); Watts, *DRR*, 146–50;
Peter Toon, *God's Statesman: The Life and
Work of John Owen* (1971), 61 n. 3, and, for
Owen's Oxford career at large, pp. 50–79.
For Cole, see Matthews, *CR, s.v.*, and for
the debate on tithes, Geoffrey F. Nuttall,
Visible Saints (1957), 138–41.

19. Toon, *God's Statesman*, 79; J. Hallett (ed.),
The Life of Geo. Trosse (1714), 81; Matthew
Henry, *An Account of the Life and Death of
Philip Henry* (1698), 10 (both quoted by
Toon, *loc. cit.*). For Owen's conservatism
at Oxford, see Hugh Kearney, *Scholars and
Gentlemen: Universities and Society . . .
1500–1700* (1970), 120–1. For Henry see
Matthews, *CR*, and *DNB, s.v.*

20. Edmund Calamy, *Memoirs of the Life of . . .
Mr. John Howe* (1724), 10–11, 21–3
(Calamy prints fragmentary notes of the
sermon on pp. 262–8); W. Major Scott,
Life of John Howe ([1911]), 18–19; Robert
F. Horton, *John Howe* (1895), 52–3. For
Goodwin see Matthews, *CR* and *DNB, s.v.*

21. Howe, *CW*, I.401–2.

22. Howe, *CW*, II.22, 69, 74–5, 76–80.

23. Howe, *The Blessedness of the Righteous*
(1673), 114.

24. Calamy, *Memoirs*, 7; Scott, *Howe*, 6;
Howe, *CW*, III.30, 37, 294, 296, IV.200.

25. Howe, *Blessedness*, 106, 198–200; Howe,
CW, I.397–9, 430–9.

26. Theophilus Gale, *The Court of the Gentiles*,
5 vols (1669–78), I, sigs *2-*4.

27. E.g. Gale, *Court*, I.13, 61, 63–4, II.83, 84,

227; B. Jowett (trans.) *The Dialogues of Plato* (1871), 682.

28. Gale, *Court*, I.19–59, II.21–42, 84, 107, 128–9, 239 (quotations from *seriatim* I.26, II.38, 28–9, 30, 39–40).

29. Donald Harden, *The Phoenicians*, rev. edn (1980), 18–20, 44, 46; W. F. Albright, 'The role of the Canaanites in the history of civilisation', in G. Ernest Wright (ed.), *The Bible and the Ancient Near East* (1961), 328; John Bright, *A History of Israel* (1960), 107.

30. Bright, *Israel*, 326–7, 397–9; Harden, *Phoenicians*, 18, 47–8, 107–9, 149–51; D. Diringer, *The Alphabet*, 2nd edn (1949), 210–17, 235–43, 450–1; I. J. Gelb, *A Study of Writing* (1952), 132ff., 176–8; W. K. C. Guthrie, *A History of Greek Philosophy*, 6 vols to date (1962–), I.29–37, 52–3.

31. Gale, *Court*, I. 60–102, 104–274, 275–393, II.21–448. For Canaanite influence on the Israelites, see Albright, 'Role of the Canaanites', 328, 339, 343–51; John Drane, *The Old Testament Story* (1983), 66–8.

32. Gale, *Court*, I.104, 163, 168, 112–14, 282, 335, 336, 350, 352, II.138–56. On the general acceptance of the primacy of Hebrew, see David S. Katz. *Philo-Semitism and the Re-Admission of the Jews to England 1603–1655* (1982), 52–71, which treats Gale on pp. 63–4.

33. Gale, *Court*, II.5, I.12, 392–8, II, sig.a2ᵛ

34. Milton, *CPW*, IV.i, 612; Ben Jonson, *Timber or Discoveries* (1640), in *The Complete Poems*, ed. G. Parfitt (1975), 448–9; Webb, *Penns & Peningtons*, 244.

35. Milton, *PR*, IV.287–90, 291–2, 295, 338, in *PJM*, 1150–6.

36. Milton, *PL*, V.224–45 (the allusion to Exodus is noted by the editor, Alastair Fowler), 541–62 VII.61–2, 118–30, VIII.8, in *PJM*, 688, 708–9, 778, 781–2, 813.

37. Noted by Fowler in *PJM*, 782; see *OED*, *s.v.* Invention. If so, the Milton who gave Galileo honourable mention in *PL*, I.288–91, is almost certainly not opposing scientific investigation *per se* (as argued in Grant McColley, 'Milton's dialogue on astronomy', *PMLA*, LII (1937), 759–60, but rather, unduly speculative investigation pursued for its own sake (as

argued in Kester Svendsen, *Milton and Science* (Cambridge, Mass., 1956), 77–8, 240–3, and Howard Schultz, *Milton and Forbidden Knowledge* (New York, 1955), *passim*.

38. Milton *PL*, VIII.528–59, 560, 588–94, in *PJM*, 843–6.

39. Milton, *PL*, VIII.13–38, 66, 71, 75–158, 167–78, VII.115–18, in *PJM*, 813–24, 781.

40. Milton, *PL*, VIII.437–51, 66–9, 188–94, in *PJM*, 837–8, 817, 825.

41. Milton, *PL*, IX.602, 680, 908, in *PJM*, 892, 896, 909. My exposition follows that of Fowler in *PJM*, see e.g. nn. on pp. 814, 820, 824, 825. Cf. Douglas Bush (ed.), *Milton: Poetical Works* (1966), nn. on pp. 359, 360, 367. On the Augustinian distinction between *scientia* and *sapientia* and its relevance to Milton, see Barbara Lewalski, *Milton's Brief Epic* (Providence, RI, 1966), 291–5.

42. Milton, *PR*, II.410–12 (cf. III.351–6), IV.221–2, in *PJM*, 1113, 1145; Milton, *CPW*, II.282–3.

43. Milton, *PR*, IV.288–90, III.96–9, in *PJM*, 1150, 1120; Thomas Ellwood, *The History of the Life* (1714), 131–6. That the repudiation is relative, not absolute, is the argument of Irene Samuel, 'Milton on learning and wisdom', *PMLA*, LXIV (1949), 708–23, and Arnold Stein, *Heroic Knowledge* (Minneapolis, Minn., 1957), 97. For a contrary view, see G. F. Sensabaugh, 'Milton on learning', *SP*, XLIII (1946), 258–72; Louis L. Martz, *Poet of Exile* (New Haven, Conn., 1980), 265–8; Alan Sinfield, *Literature in Protestant England 1560–1660* (1983), 26–7.

44. Richard L. Greaves, *The Puritan Revolution and Educational Thought* (New Brunswick, NJ, 1969), *passim*; Norman Wood, *The Reformation and English Education* (1931), 304–41; Kearney, *Scholars and Gentlemen*, 117–20; Christopher Hill, 'Puritans and "The Dark Corners of the Land"', *RHST*, 5th ser., XIII (1963), 77–102.

45. E. C. Walker, *William Dell: Master Puritan* (1970), 98–118, 137–78; Christopher Hill, *Some Intellectual Consequences of the English Revolution* (1980), 55; Olive M. Griffiths, *Religion and Learning* (1935), 35.

On the academies, see Irene Parker, *Dissenting Academies in England* (1914) and H. McLachlan, *English Education under the Test Acts* (1931).

46. Matthews, *CR* and *DNB, s.v.* Gale; Whitley, *BB*, 182–4; [Edward Terrill], *Records of a Church of Christ meeting at Broadmead, Bristol*, ed. E. B. Underhill (1847), pp. xci–xciii; Bunyan, *GA*, §3; Bunyan, *HW*, 51–2; Bunyan, *MW*, VI.193–6.

47. Ellwood, *History*, 5, 131, 202–3; G[eorge] F[ox], *The Pearle* (1658), 13; George Keith, *The Woman-Preacher of Samaria* (1674), 2, 9; *id.*, *Universal Free Grace* (1671), sig. A2; Braithwaite, *SPQ*, 333–4. After controversies with the main Quaker body and organizing his own 'Christian Quakers' Keith in 1700 conformed: see his *Farewell-Sermon* (1700); Braithwaite, *SPQ*, 482–7; and Ethyn W. Kirby, *George Keith* (1942).

48. Robert Barclay and George Keith, *Quakerism Confirmed* (1676), 4, 9–10.

49. Keith, *Universal Free Grace*, 10; *id.*, *Immediate Revelation* (1668), 24–7, 42–4; F[rancis] H[owgill], *The Great Case of Tythes* (1665), 55–6. For Howgill see *DNB, s.v.*, and Braithwaite, *BQ*, index, *s.v.*

50. Baxter, *Gildas Salvianus ... The Reformed Pastor* (1656), 390; *id.*, *The Life of Faith* (1670), 146, 172; *id.*, *Directions for Weak Christians* (1669), 106–7; *Rel. Bax.*, I.126, §213(3) and I.129, §213(11) (Keeble, *Baxter*, 39–41); Gale, *Court*, III, sig. b1; Christopher Hill, *Milton and the English Revolution* (1977; rpt 1979), 103.

51. Howe, *CW*, II.24, III.51, 61, V.18, II.80–4.

52. For Baxter's sympathy for the Cambridge Platonists see *Rel. Bax.*, II.386–7, §284(2) and for his rationalism Roger Thomas in Geoffrey F. Nuttall *et al.*, *The Beginnings of Nonconformity* (1964), 51–60, and in Bolam, *EP*, 103–12; Frederick J. Powicke, *The Reverend Richard Baxter under the Cross* (1927), 53–6, 238–51. The balance in Baxter and Howe was not maintained by many of their successors: for the transformation of Presbyterianism into the Unitarianism of the 'Rational Dissenters' (as they called themselves), see Bolam, *EP*, 113ff., and Olive M. Griffiths, *Religion and Learning: A Study in English Presbyterian Thought to the ... Unitarian Movement* (1935), esp. pp. 54–89.

53. Howe, *CW*, III.177, 179, 186, 189, 180, 182. Henry Rogers, *The Life ... of John Howe* (1836), 509–28 discusses this text as one of the earliest contributions to the deistic controversy.

54. Milton, *CPW*, VIII.420–1; Baxter, *Directions and Persuasions to a Sound Conversion* (1658), 34–5; Manton, *CW*, II.145.

55. Milton, *CPW*, VIII.423 (*Of True Religion*), VI.459, 471–6, 128–9 (*De Doctrina*); *PL*, IX.644, 659, V.900, VI.113, in *PJM*, 894, 895, 729, 735; Baxter, *A Treatise of Knowledge and Love Compared* (1689), 211; *id.*, *The Scripture Gospel Defended* (1690), sig. A2.

56. William Blake, 'There is no Natural Religion (Second Series)', in *The Complete Writings*, ed. Geoffrey Keynes, Oxford Standard Authors (1957; corrected rpt 1966), 97.

57. Charles Leslie, *The Snake in the Grass*, 3rd edn (1698), 314; Edward Phillips, *New World of Words* (1658), *s.v.* enthusiasts; Robert Burton, *The Anatomy of Melancholy*, Everyman's Library, 3 vols (1932; rpt 1948–9), III.326, 344, 364, 368, 370; Benjamin Whichcote quoted from C. A. Patrides (ed.), *The Cambridge Platonists* (1969), 330; Thomas Hobbes, *Leviathan*, Everyman's Library (1914; rpt 1965), 37 (I.viii). Susie I. Tucker, *Enthusiasm: A Study in Semantic Change* (1972), cites seventeenth-century definitions on pp. 15–17, and illustrates the derogatory connotations of the word on pp. 26–32, 52–3.

58. John Locke, *An Essay Concerning Human Understanding*, ed. Peter H. Nidditch (1975; rpt 1979), 697–703 (IV.xix.1–11); Butler, *Hudibras*, 16 (I.i.477–8).

59. Leslie, *Snake in the Grass*, sig. A2, p. xxxi. Nor will it do, of course, to lump together everyone else as 'Augustan' or all early nineteenth-century writers as 'Romantic'. These vague and time-worn terms obscure the variety within the literature of both periods and cannot be applied to individuals without extensive qualification and explanation. They are used in this study merely as a brief way of suggesting the general emphases of these periods in

the hope that the reader will allow them to stand for their prevailing temper, the Zeitgeist.

60. Penington, *Many Deep Considerations*, 1–2; *Letters of John Keats*, ed. Frederick Page, World's Classics (1954; rpt 1965), 49.

61. Coleridge, *Biographia Literaria*, ed. George Watson, Everyman's Library (1956; rpt 1971), 167; *Shelley's Literary and Philosophical Criticism*, ed. John Shawcross (1909; rpt 1969), 120; Wordsworth, *The Prelude* (1850), XII.207–18 and 'Resolution and Independence', ll. 50–5, in *Poetical Works*, ed. Thomas Hutchinson, rev. Ernest de Selincourt, Oxford Standard Authors (1936; rpt 1964), 577, 156; *Letters of Keats*, 84; [Charles Leslie], *The Wolf Stript* (1704), 82–3; Sir William Davenant, *Gondibert*, ed. David F. Gladish (1971), 7, 22, 49; H. James Jensen, *A Glossary of John Dryden's Critical Terms* (Minneapolis, Minn., 1969), *s.vv.* Fancy, Imagination, Judgment, Reason; Hobbes, *Leviathan*, 33 (I.viii); Jonson, *Complete Poems*, 448–9.

62. Bunyan, *PP*, 1–2; Milton, *PL*, IX.21–4 (cf. VII.28–31, III.29–32), in *PJM*, 854; Helen Darbishire (ed.), *The Early Lives of Milton* (1932), 291; Ellwood, *History*, 77–8; William Bates, *Funeral Sermon for ... Baxter* (1692), in *Works*, 2nd edn (1723), 729.

63. Howard was a Dover shoemaker and Crane a London distiller (Braithwaite, *BQ*, 186, 456). Philly's mission is described in Braithwaite, *SPQ*, 216n.

64. Wordsworth, 'Expostulation and Reply', ll. 21–2, 'The Tables Turned', ll. 26–32, 'Tintern Abbey', ll. 35–49, in *Poetical Works*, 377, 164; Milton, *PL*, III.32–55, in *PJM*, 562–4 (and cf. *CPW*, V.i, 589–92). For such royalist charges, see William Riley Parker, *Milton*, 2 vols (1968), I.571.

65. Milton, *PJM*, 457; Gale, *Court*, I.283–4.

66. Ellwood, *History*, 175–97, 291; John Crooke, *A True ... Testimony concerning John Samm* (1664), 6–11; Heywood, *AD*, I.39–40, 130–1; Baxter, *Poetical Fragments*, sig. A3ᵛ.

67. Gale, *Court*, I.286–8.

68. Gale, *Court*, I.288–9; Benjamin Keach, *War with the Devil*, 22nd edn (1776), p. iv.

69. Milton, *PL*, I.7–8, and 'At a Vacation

Exercise', ll. 19–20, in *PJM*, 459–60, 76–7; Milton, *CPW*, II.403, 516. Alastair Fowler in *PJM*, 459, notes Davenant's remark. The 1633 edition of Donne's poems was addressed to 'The Understanders' (*The Poems*, ed. Herbert J. Grierson, 2 vols (1912; rpt 1966), I.1). For Dryden's request to 'tag' *PL* see Darbishire, *Early Lives*, 7, 296.

CHAPTER 6

1. Christopher Hill, *Milton and the English Revolution* (1977; rpt 1979), 344. See Godfrey Davies, *The Restoration* (San Marino, 1955) and Ronald Hutton, *The Restoration* (1985) for accounts of these events.

2. Braithwaite, *SPQ*, 115.

3. Braithwaite, *SPQ*, 115, Bunyan, *PP*, 8, 87; Edmund Calamy, *Memoirs of the Life of ... John Howe* (1724), 115; Howe, *CW*, IV.102; *id.*, *The Blessedness of the Righteous* (1673), 514; John Corbet, *Self Imployment in Secret* ([1700?]), 36.

4. Milton, *SA*, ll. 7–9, 633–45, 667–704, in *PJM*, 347, 367–70. For a sustained reading of *SA* in such contemporary terms, see Hill, *Milton*, 428–48.

5. John Crooke, *The Cry of the Innocent* (1662), sig. A2.

6. Crooke, *Cry of the Innocent*, sig. A2; G[eorge] F[ox] and E[llis] H[ookes], *A Primmer and Catechism* (1670), 35 [misnumbered 45]–8; William Penn, *No Cross, No Crown*, ed. Norman Penney (1930; rpt 1981), 105; Bunyan, *CW*, II.692a, 700b, 701b, 702, 715b, 716–17, 722a–23b, 727b, 737b–38a.

7. *The New Testament translated by William Tyndale*, ed. N. Hardy Wallis (1938), 517–18; Milton, *CPW*, II.515; *id.*, *Comus*, ll. 328–9, in *PJM*, 192. This aspect of *Comus* is explored in Maryann Cale McGuire, *Milton's Puritan Masque* (Athens, Georgia, 1983), 60–96.

8. [Thomas Goodwin], *Patience and its Perfect Work* (1666), 1, 3, 12–13, 14; Penn, *No Cross, No Crown*, 7; Bunyan, *CW*, II.713a, 736b; Howe, *CW*, II.238; Milton, *PL*, XII.515–18, 532–3, in *PJM*, 1053. William Bates treats this theme in *The Great Duty of*

Resignation (1684), in *Works*, 2nd edn (1723), 235–74, esp. pp. 243–6.

9. Manton, *CW*, II.113–21, I.262, 266, 333, 336; Penn, *No Cross, No Crown*, 87, 34; Crooke, *Cry of the Innocent*, sig. A2; Bunyan, *CW*, II.693a.

10. *Rel. Bax.*, I.132–3, §213(28).

11. Fox, *JGF*, 380, 419–20.

12. Fox, *JGF*, 362, 398–404; Manton, *CW*, II.14–25; Bunyan, *PP*, 86.

13. Howe, *The Blessedness of the Righteous*, 4; Howe, *CW*, I.436; Bunyan, *CW*, II.692a, 706b, 707a, 711a, 736b, 738a.

14. George Fox, *The Summ of Such Particulars as are Charged against George Fox* (1660), 3; Fox, *JGF*, 354, 357, 398–404, 420; [Amor Stoddard *et al.*], *To the King and Both Houses of Parliament* (1666), 3–4.

15. On Quaker pacifism and the currency of this phrase, see Geoffrey F. Nuttall, *Christianity and Violence* (1972), 10–15. For their earlier active political involvement and the process by which Fox's quietism became Quaker orthodoxy, see James F. MacLear, 'Quakerism and the end of the Interregnum: a chapter in the domestication of radical Puritanism', *CH*, XIX (1950), 240–70; Alan Cole, 'The Quakers and the English Revolution', *Past and Present*, 10 (1956), 39–54; Hugh Barbour, *The Quakers in Puritan England* (New Haven, Conn., 1964), 181–246; Barry Reay, *The Quakers and the English Revolution* (1985), 37–45, 103–22. For the extent to which they did continue to press for legislative changes after the Restoration, see Ethyn Williams Kirby, 'The Quakers' efforts to secure civil and religious liberty 1660–96', *Journal of Modern History*, VII, 4 (1935), 401–21.

16. Thomas Ellwood, *Davideis*, ed. Walter Fischer (Heidelberg, 1936), 23 (I.252); Milton, *PR*, II.410–11, III.194–6, 354–6, 386–402, in *PJM*, 1113, 1124, 1132, 1133–4. For a sustained exposition of *PR* along these lines see Michael Fixler, *Milton and the Kingdoms of God* (1964), 221–71.

17. Milton, *SA*, ll. 1663, 1709–12, 1726, 1728, in *PJM*, 399, 400, 401.

18. Milton, *PJM*, 335, with reference to the argument that this bloodthirstiness denies *SA* a Christian theme in Kenneth Burke,

'The imagery of killing', *Hudson Review*, I (1948), 151–67, and K. Fell, 'From myth to martyrdom', *English Studies*, XXXIV (1953), 145–55. *SA*'s vengefulness similarly leads Irene Samuel, '*Samson Agonistes* as tragedy', in Joseph Wittreich, Jr (ed.), *Calm of Mind* (Cleveland, Ohio, 1971), 235–57, to argue that its subject 'cannot be Samson restored to divine favor'. R. W. Condee, *Structure in Milton's Poetry* (Philadelphia, PA, 1974), 143–52, uses this aspect of the poem as an argument for its early composition: the 'violent, vengeful and bloody' heroism of *SA* is so much at odds with *PL*, XII.561–70, as to suggest composition in the 1640s before Milton had modified his ideas of heroism.

19. Andrew Milner, *John Milton and the English Revolution* (1981), 167–8, 174–5, 182–91.

20. Milton, *SA*, ll. 1381–9, in *PJM*, 390–1. Milner, *John Milton*, 186–7, instances Pepys' comment in this context, but as illustrating a disquiet with meek submissiveness such as Milner believes Milton to have had in *SA*. Pepys' remark is quoted above, p. 50.

21. Milton, *SA*, ll. 102, 120, 460–1, 595–8, in *PJM*, 350, 362, 366.

22. Samuel Johnson, 'Milton', *Lives of the Poets*, 2 vols, World's Classics (1906; rpt 1967–8), I.131; Milner, *John Milton*, 184; Hill, *Milton*, 433.

23. Milner, *John Milton*, 191–2; Hill, *Milton*, 428–48 (esp. pp. 446–7).

24. Milton, *SA*, ll. 1715–16, 1452–84 (cf. ll. 481–6), 1490–4, 1721, in *PJM*, 400, 392–3.

25. Milton, *SA*, ll. 1605–6, in *PJM*, 397.

26. Hence, though I agree with E. L. Marilla, '*Samson Agonistes*: an interpretation', *Studia Neophilologica*, XXIX (1957), 67–76, and John Dale Ebbs, 'Milton's treatment of poetic justice in *Samson Agonistes*', *Modern Language Quarterly*, XXII (1961), 377–89, that the point of the drama lies in the primacy of Samson's own restored faith, I disagree with them that it encourages the faithful to suicidal action or to anticipate any such bloody climax to their witness (cf. the similar view of Mary Ann Radzinowicz, *Towards Samson*

Agonistes (Princeton, NJ, 1978), 264–5).

27. W[illiam] B[ayly], *The Travels of the Bowels of Sion*, appended to *The Life of Enoch again Revived* (1662), 12–14; John [Philly], *The Arraignment of Christendom* (1664), 85, 91, 108.

28. Goodwin, *Patience*, 4, 7–8, 31–2; Manton, *CW*, II.413, I.73–8. Just so, the radical Ludlow, writing almost certainly with an eventual nonconformist readership in mind, encourages to patience with no expectation of an imminent apocalyptic deliverance: see Ludlow, *A Voyce from the Watch Tower*, ed. A. B. Worden (1978), 10–12.

29. Goodwin, *Patience*, 98–102; Howe, *CW*, IV.98–9, 106–7; Manton, *CW*, IV.27–34, V.490 (cf. Bates, *Works*, 238–9); Milton, *PL*, IX.31–2, *PR*, I.14–15, III.90–2, *SA*, ll. 1287–91, in *PJM*, 855, 1078, 1119, 388 (and on Milton see Gerald J. G. Schiffhorst, 'Satan's false heroism in *Paradise Lost* as a perversion of patience', *Christianity and Literature*, XXXIII, 2 (1984), 13–20). Texts commonly cited to encourage to a heavenly-minded disdain for the world included Matt. vi.19–21; Rom. ii.1–8; II Cor. iv.8–18; Phil. iii.7–21; Col. iii.1–5; Heb. x.31–9, xi.1, 13–16.

30. P[atrick] Livingstone, *Plain and Downright Dealing* ([1667]), 10.

31. Goodwin, *Patience*, 16–18, 21; Howe, *CW*, VI.13, 14–16.

32. Penn, *No Cross, No Crown*, 2, 3, 21–2, 30, 36, 40–1, 92 (I.ii, II.vi, III.i, IV.ii, x, VI.xviii); Manton, *CW*, IV.30; Howe, *CW*, IV.248–9.

33. Bunyan, *MW*, VI.45; Milton, *PL*, IV.294, XII.561, in *PJM*, 631, 1055.

34. Theophilus Gale, *The Court of the Gentiles*, 5 vols (1669–78), IV.95; Howe, *CW*, II.65, I.454; *id.*, *Blessedness of the Righteous*, 168; Fox, *JGF*, 493.

35. Bunyan, *CW*, II.701a; Edmund Calamy, *An Abridgment of Mr. Baxter's History*, 2 vols, 2nd edn (1713), II.232; Roger Lowe, *The Diary*, ed. William L. Sachse (1938), 18–19; John Pinney, *Letters*, ed. Geoffrey F. Nuttall (1939), 1–2; Matthews, *CR*, *s.v.* Clifford.

36. Richard Lovelace, *The Poems*, ed. C. H. Wilkinson, corrected reissue (1953), 78–9.

37. Bunyan, *MW*, VI,42–51, 320n. (quotations from stanzas 43, 15, 24, 40, 41, 24, 5, 61).

38. Manton, *CW*, I.202, IV.30; Heywood, *AD*, III.218, 221; J[ohn] Swintoun, *Some Late Epistles to the Body* (1663), 3; cf. Bates, *Works*, 347.

39. C. A. Patrides, *Milton and the Christian Tradition* (1966), 145; Milton, *SA*, l. 1719, in *PJM*, 400. See above, pp. 84–5.

40. Howe, *CW*, I.443–6; *id.*, *Blessedness*, 399; Robert Barclay and George Keith, *Quakerism Confirmed* (1676), 70; Milton, *PL*, I.18. XII.587, in *PJM*, 461, 1056; Penn, *No Cross, No Crown*, 58; Fox, *JGF*, 261, 500.

41. Fox, *JGF*, 34–5; Penn, *No Cross, No Crown*, 121. See Maurice A. Creasey, *'Inward' and 'Outward': A Study in Early Quaker Language*, Supplement no. 30 to *JFHS* (1962).

42. Robert Barclay, *Truth Cleared of Calumnies* (1670), 25 [misprinted 52]. See Lief Eeg-Olofsson, *The Conception of the Inner Light in Robert Barclay's Theology* (Lund, 1954).

43. Geoffrey F. Nuttall, *The Holy Spirit in Puritan Faith and Experience*, 2nd edn (1947), 6–8 and *passim*; M. Van Beek, *An Enquiry into Puritan Vocabulary* (Groningen, 1969), 68–9, 117–20.

44. The literary consequences of the introspective bias of Puritanism are discussed in: Patricia Caldwell, *The Puritan Conversion Narrative* (1983), *passim*; William Haller, *The Rise of Puritanism* (1938; rpt New York, 1957), 95–101; U. Milo Kaufmann, *The Pilgrim's Progress and Traditions in Puritan Meditation* (New Haven, Conn., 1966), 196–216; N. H. Keeble, *Richard Baxter* (1982), 132–55; Kenneth B. Murdock, *Literature and Theology in Colonial New England* (1949; rpt New York, 1963), 99–116; Roger Sharrock, *John Bunyan* (1954; rpt 1968), 55–61; G. A. Starr, *Defoe & Spiritual Autobiography* (Princeton, NJ, 1965), 3–50; W. Y. Tindall, *John Bunyan: Mechanic Preacher* (New York, 1934), 22–31; Owen C. Watkins, *The Puritan Experience* (1972), 9–36 and *passim*.

45. Bunyan, *GA*, pp. 110–11, 117–18. The 'experimental' in the religious sense is associated with Baconian experimentation

in Sargent Bush, Jr, *The Writings of Thomas Hooker* (Madison, Wis., 1980), 231–41.

46. Bunyan, *HW*, 186–7; Goodwin, *Patience*, 53–4; Penney, *ESP*, 122–3.

47. Penn. *No Cross, No Crown*, 25, 31, 120–1.

48. Howe, *Blessedness*, 323–8.

49. For discussion of Baxter's teaching on this topic see Keeble, *Baxter*, 133–9.

50. Bunyan, *PP*, 123–4, 147–9, 163. For discussion of Ignorance, whose treatment by Bunyan has disturbed some readers, see Maurice Hussey, 'Bunyan's Mr. Ignorance', in Rogert Sharrock (ed.), *The Pilgrim's Progress: A Casebook* (1976), 128–38; James F. Forrest, 'Bunyan's Ignorance and the Flatterer', *SP*, LX (1963), 12–22; Kaufmann, *Traditions in Puritan Meditation*, 113–14; Vincent Newey (ed.), *The Pilgrim's Progress: Critical and Historical Views* (1980), 40–4, 145–6, 149–50.

51. Baxter, *The Mischiefs of Self-Ignorance* (1662), 304; Isaac Ambrose, *Media: The Middle Things*, 3rd edn (1657), esp. pp. 43, 61, 73, 84–6. The suggestion of Ambrose's influence in the north is made by William L. Sachse in his edition of Roger Lowe's *Diary* (1938), 2.

52. Heywood, *AD*, I.134, 151, II.226.

53. John Corbet, *Self-Imployment in Secret* ([1700?]), 9.

54. See the bibliography in Watkins, *Puritan Experience*, 241–59. A. N. Wilson, *The Life of John Milton* (1983), noting (pp. 99, 103) Milton's 'unwavering interest in himself', considers it 'simply impossible' to read *SA* save as 'a thinly veiled spiritual autobiography' (p. 232).

55. Edmund Calamy's *Abridgment of Mr Baxter's History of his Life and Times* (1702) rearranged and rewrote as a third-person history of nonconformity Baxter's original *Reliquiae* (1696), itself already somewhat restrained by Matthew Sylvester's editing (see Geoffrey F. Nuttall, 'The MS. of *Reliquiae Baxterianae* (1696)', *JEH*, VI, I (1955), 73–9, and William Lamont, *Richard Baxter and the Millennium* (1979), 79–88). Thomas Ellwood's edition of Fox's *Journal*, prepared for the Morning Meeting and published in 1694, with a preface by Penn, ordered and polished the style of Fox's original dictated to Thomas Lower in 1674/5 (and preserved in the Spence MSS). The *Ellwood Journal* was reprinted until 1902, and is the basis of the revised edition by Norman Penney included in Everyman's Library in 1924 (and often reprinted), which may be compared with Norman Penney's *verbatim* transcript of the Spence MSS in the *Cambridge Journal*, namely *The Journal of George Fox*, ed. Norman Penney, introd. T. Edmund Harvey, 2 vols (1911). On these matters (and for the nature of the 1952 text used in his study), see Fox, *JGF*, pp. vii–xvi, 754–5; Braithwaite, *BQ*, 531–7; *Cambridge Journal*, I.x–xl; Norman Penney, 'George Fox's writings and the Morning Meeting', *Friends' Quarterly Examiner* (1902), 63–9.

56. Alexander Pope, 'An Essay on Man', epistle ii, l. 2, in *The Poems*, ed. John Butt (1963; rpt 1965), 516. The trends here alluded to are summarized in James Sutherland, *A Preface to Eighteenth Century Poetry* (1948; rpt 1963), 1–43.

57. Alexander Pope, 'An Essay on Criticism', l. 71, 'Epitaph ... for Sir Isaac Newton', l. 2, 'An Essay on Man', epistle iv, ll. 35–6, in *Poems*, 146, 537, 808, 522; Charles Leslie, *The Wolf Stript* (1704), 82–3.

58. Bunyan, *CW*, III.590; Bunyan, *MW*, VI.105, 119–20; Bunyan, *GA*, §285.

59. Milton, 'At a Vacation Exercise', l. 21, in *PJM*, 77; Keeble, *Baxter*, 83–6, 97, 150.

60. *The Book of Common Prayer* (1662), sig. b5; John Dryden, 'The Hind and the Panther', I.62–3, in *Poems and Fables*, ed. James Kinsley (1962), 356.

61. Milton, *PL*, I.253–4, IV.17–23, 73–8, in *PJM*, 477, 609, 612; Bunyan, *PP*, 113–18; Matthew Henry, *The Life of Philip Henry*, ed. J. B. Williams, in *The Lives of Philip and Matthew Henry* (1974), 159. For discussion of this internalization of hell, see C. A. Patrides, *Premises and Motifs in Renaissance Thought and Literature* (Princeton, NJ, 1982), 182–99; Christopher Hill, *The World Turned Upside Down* (1972; rpt 1975), 151–83; *id., Milton*, 306–16.

62. Milton, *PR*, I.15, IV,638–9, in *PJM*, 1078, 1167 (and cf. *SA*, l. 1733, in *PJM*, 401).

63. Joseph Addison, *The Spectator*, ed. D. Bond, 5 vols (1965), IV.252 (cited by Caldwell, *Puritan Conversion Narrative*,

163); Bunyan, *PP*, 72, 83; Bunyan, *MW*, VI.47; Benjamin Keach, *The Travels of True Godliness* (1799), 30, 84.

64. Works against hypocrisy include Baxter's *Vain Religion of the Formal Hypocrite* (1660) and the second part of his *Directions for Weak Distempered Christians* (1669); [Giles Firmin], *The Real Christian Discovered* (1670); and Matthew Mead, *The Almost Christian Discovered* (1662). For a discussion of this topic see Richard L. Greaves's introduction to Bunyan, *MW*, IX, pp. xxxii–xxxiv.

65. Howe, *Blessedness*, 379–81; Howe, *CW*, II.36; Matthew Henry, *Life of Philip Henry*, 77–8; Isaac Penington, *Many Deep Considerations have been upon My Heart* ([1664?]), 4.

66. Manton, *CW*, III.236; Howe, *CW*, II.235, 240–1.

67. Thomas Gouge, *The Works* (1798), 392, 399–400; Howe, *CW*, II.244; Heywood, *AD*, I.142, 300, 302.

68. James Sutherland, *English Literature of the Late Seventeenth Century* (1969), 14.

CHAPTER 7

1. *The Letters of Dorothy Osborne to William Temple*, ed. G. C. Moore Smith (1928; rpt 1959), 21, 24, 31, 81–2, 85. For Madame de Scudéry and the romance vogue in Restoration England see Paul Salzman, *English Prose Fiction 1558–1700* (1985), 177–201, and the works cited *ibid.*, p. 177 n.2.

2. John Dryden, *Selected Criticism*, ed. James Kinsley and George Parfitt (1970), 109. 110. 112; Buckingham, *The Rehearsal*, I.i.32–2, in *Burlesque Plays of the Eighteenth Century*, ed. Simon Trussler (1969), 8.

3. William Congreve, *Incognita*, preface, in *Shorter Novels: Seventeenth Century*, ed. Philip Henderson, Everyman's Library (1930; rpt 1962), 241.

4. The action of *The English Rogue* is summarized and discussed in Salzman, *Prose Fiction*, 223–38.

5. William Congreve, *The Way of the World*, ed. Brian Gibbons, 3rd impression (1979), II.i.228–9; Sir George Etherege, *She*

Would if She Could, II.ii.224–5, in *Plays*, ed. Michael Cordner (1982), 142, and editor's note p. 110 (cf. *OED*, s.v. 'Honest, 1a, c); William Wycherley, *The Country-Wife*, I.i.357–8, in *Plays*, ed. Arthur Friedman (1979), 261.

6. Rochester, '[On King Charles]', l. 2, in *The Poems of John Wilmot, earl of Rochester*, ed. Keith Walker (1984), 122. For characterizations of Charles and his court along these lines by historians see: J. R. Jones, *Court and Country: England 1658–1714*(1978; rpt 1980), 2–3, 141–2; J. R. Jones (ed.), *The Restored Monarchy* (1979), 10–12, 37–9; Sir George Clark, *The Later Stuarts*, 2nd edn (1955), 2; Thomas Babington Macaulay, *The History of England*, ed. C. H. Firth, 6 vols (1913–15), I. 146–7, 358–60.

7. For representative contemporary comments on Charles's political insincerity and elusiveness see Sir John Reresby, *Memoirs*, ed. Andrew Browning (1936), 174, 210: Burnet, *OT*, I.93–4; [Sir William Temple], *Memoirs 1672–9*, 2nd edn (1692), 25, 30–4, 84, 273–4; Samuel Pepys, *The Diary*, ed. Robert Latham and William Matthews, 11 vols (1970–83), VIII.342 (17 July 1667), 355–6 (27 July 1667); John Evelyn, *Diary*, ed. E. S. de Beer, 6 vols (1955), IV.410–11 (6 Feb. 1685); Halifax, *A Character of King Charles the Second*, in *Complete Works*, ed. J. P. Kenyon (1969), 251–2.

8. Rochester, 'Tunbridge Wells. A Satyr', ll. 180–1, in *Poems*, 73; Halifax, *The Character of a Trimmer*, in *Complete Works*, 45–102; Pope, *The Rape of the Lock*, V.9–34, in *The Poems*, ed. John Butt (1965), 237–8.

9. Fox, *JGF*, 36. William Penn, *No Cross, No Crown*, ed. Norman Penney (1930; rpt 1981), 117–51 (IX.iii–xl), gives a full account of the reasons why Quakers decline 'as vain and foolish, several worldly customs and fashions of respect, much in request at this time of day'.

10. Howe, *CW*, II.443–4; Thomas Gouge, *The Works* (1798), 447; Matthew Henry, *The Life of Philip Henry*, in J. B. Williams (ed), *The Lives of Philip and Matthew Henry* (1974), 5; Bunyan, *PP*, 19; Defoe, *Roxana*, ed. David Blewett (1982), 290.

11. Manton, *CW*, II.15.

12. Manton, *CW*, II.13–20.

13. Penn, *No Cross, No Crown*, 212, 213, 228, 229–30, 236, 238, 239 (XIV.i, XV.ii, vii, viii).

14. Milton, *CPW*, II.515; Penn, *No Cross, No Crown*, 62, 64 (V.xi, xiii).

15. Notably by J. Sears McGee, *The Godly Man in Stuart England* (New Haven, Conn., 1976), esp. pp. 71–94, which argues that Puritans may in this way be distinguished from 'Anglicans', who promoted the Second Table.

16. Manton, *CW*, II.7–8; Penn, *No Cross, No Crown*, 62 (V.xi); Baxter, *The Divine Life* (1664), 342.

17. Gouge, *Works*, 401, 402, 403; Bunyan, *MW*, IX.43, 251–2, 326; Bunyan, *PP*, 148.

18. Baxter, *A Christian Directory* (1673), sigs A2–A3ᵛ; id., *The Right Method for a Settled Peace of Conscience* (1653), 4–5. On the practical bias in Baxter see N. H. Keeble, *Richard Baxter* (1982), 29–30, 39–41, 72–86.

19. Etherege, *She Would if She Could*, I.i.52–5, 92–3, and *The Man of Mode*, I.i.204–11, V.ii.154–73, in *Plays*, 113, 114, 226–7, 322–3; Wycherley, *The Country-Wife*, I.i.106–9, 201–2, II.i.25–7, 400–1, in *Plays*, 252, 255, 266, 277; Congreve, *Way of the World*, IV.i.100–1; Rochester, 'An Allusion to Horace', ll. 120–4, in *Poems*, 102; Buckingham, *The Rehearsal*, I.ii.74, in *Burlesque Plays*, 12.

20. William Bates, *The Works*, 2nd edn (1723), 499; Milton, *PL*, V.354–5, in *PJM*, 696; Penn, *No Cross, No Crown*, 168–74 (XI.ii–viii).

21. Penn, *No Cross, No Crown*, 223–4 (XV.v).

22. Bunyan, *PP*, 17–20, 46–7, 77–9, 103–6, 109, 128–30; *OED*, s.v. 'Discretion, 3'.

23. Celia Fiennes, *The Illustrated Journeys*, ed. Christopher Morris (1984), 27, 167, 101–2, 113, 204.

24. Fiennes, *Journeys*, 95, 98, 103, 104, 107–8, 120.

25. Fiennes, *Journeys*, 102, 174.

26. Fiennes, *Journeys*, 158–9, 94, 42, 186.

27. [–], *A True and Faithful Relation From the People of God (called) Quakers, in Colchester* (1664), 5, 6, 7, 8, 9.

28. [–], *True and Faithful Relation*, 7, 11.

29. [Edward Burrough], *A Visitation of Love unto the King* (1660), 4, 7, 8, 10.

30. Penn, *No Cross, No Crown*, 252–3 (XVII.i).

31. Samuel Johnson, *Rasselas*, cap. x, in *Shorter Novels: Eighteenth Century*, ed. Philip Henderson, Everyman's Library (1930; rpt 1967), 22.

32. See on this subject T. J. B. Spencer, '*Paradise Lost*: the Anti-Epic', in C. A. Patrides (ed.), *Approaches to Paradise Lost* (1968), 81–98; Davis P. Harding, *The Club of Hercules* (Urbana , Ill., 1962), 24–66; John M. Steadman, *Milton and the Renaissance Hero* (1967); Alan Sinfield, *Literature in Protestant England 1560–1660* (1983), 37–44; James A. Freeman, *Milton and the Martial Muse* (Princeton, NJ, 1980).

33. Milton, *PL*, I.286–7, 539, 550, 551–4, 561–2, in *PJM*, 478–9, 493–5.

34. Milton, *PL*, I.157, 263, 529, IV.749, IX.129, 825, XI.689–99, in *PJM*, 471, 477, 493, 658, 863, 904, 1017.

35. Milton, *PL*, IX.13–15, 27–33, 40–1, in *PJM*, 854–6.

36. Milton, *PL*, X.1086–92, XII.561–71, in *PJM*, 980, 1055.

37. Milton, *PR*, I.11, 14–15, 174, 215–16, II.466–8, III.189–93, in *PJM*, 1078, 1084, 1086, 1115, 1123.

38. Bunyan, *MW*, VI.50; Defoe, *Roxana*, ed. David Blewett (1982), 262.

39. Milton, *PL*, VI.29–37, 143–8, in *PJM*, 731, 736.

40. Milton, *PL*, V. 902, VII.24, in *PJM*, 729, 776.

41. Edmund Calamy, *Memoirs of the Life of . . . John Howe* (1724), 172, 174; Howe, *CW*, IV.279–81.

42. [Ralph Wallis], *More News from Rome* (1666), 9; Manton, *CW*, II.69, 93–4; Howe, *CW*, II.89–90, VI.302; *Rel. Bax.*, I.7, §6(3) (quoted above, p. 161).

43. Bunyan, *PP*, 190, 209; Howe, *CW*, II.95.

44. For Donne's responsiveness in this regard, see John Carey, *John Donne* (1981; rpt 1983), 94–6, 112–15.

45. Manton, *CW*, III.219–47 (quotation from pp. 224–5), II.72; Francis Howgill, *The True Rule* (1665), 9.

46. Bunyan, *MW*, IX.86–7; *Richard Baxter's Farewell Sermon* (1683), 5; id., in *A Collection of Farewell Sermons* (1662), 156;

id., *A Sermon at the Funeral of John Corbet* (1680); N. H. Keeble, 'Richard Baxter's preaching ministry', *JEH*, XXXV, 4 (1985), 554–5.

47. Bunyan, *PP*, 21, 125–9, 249–53, 270–1, 284.

48. E.g. Charles Firth and F. R. Leavis in Roger Sharrock (ed.), *The Pilgrim's Progress: A Casebook* (1976), 102. 216–19.

49. E.g. E. M. W. Tillyard, *The English Epic and its Background* (1954), 393, and, in slightly different terms, Henri Talon, *John Bunyan*, trans. Barbara Wall (1951), 219; Roger Sharrock, *John Bunyan*, corrected reissue (1968), 138.

50. Bunyan, *PP*, 46, 50, 86, 130, 157–8, 240.

51. Bunyan, *PP*, 115–16, 136; Manton, *CW*, I.340–1; John Crooke, *A True and Faithful Testimony concerning John Samm* (1664), 13.

52. Baxter, *A Treatise of Self-Denyall* (1660), 124; Gouge, *Works*, 447, 473; Bunyan, *PP*, 83, 151, 254; Bunyan, *GA*, §37.

53. Samuel Clarke, *The Lives of Sundry Eminent Persons* (1683), sig. a3 (cf. Baxter's preface to James Janeway, *Invisibles, Realities, Demonstrated in the Holy Life ... of Mr. John Janeway* (1673), sigs A6ᵛ–A7); Matthew Henry, *Life of Philip Henry*, pp. xxxvii–xxxviii.

54. Fox, *JGF*, p. xlviii; George Keith, *The Benefit, Advantage and Glory of Silent Meetings* (1670), 12; Marvell, 'A Poem upon the Death of O.C.', ll. 201–12, in *P&L*, I.134; Lucy Hutchinson, *Memoirs of the Life of Colonel Hutchinson*, ed. James Sutherland (1973), 28–34, 282–9; Matthew Henry, *Life of Philip Henry*, 64–86. For some account of Baxter's *Breviate*, see Keeble, *Baxter*, 127–31.

55. Milton, *PL*, IV.506–7, in *PJM*, 642. See above, pp. 211–12.

56. See above, pp. 177, 205, 213.

57. Howe, *CW*, II.12, 38–9, 84.

58. Gouge, *Works*, 486; Matthew Henry, *Life of Philip Henry*, 69; George Swinnock, *Heaven and Hell Epitomized* (1663), pref. (taken from J. B. Williams's note in Henry's biography, *loc. cit.*).

59. Rochester, 'A Ramble in St James's Parke', l. 98, in *Poems*, 66; John Donne, 'A Lecture upon the Shadow', ll. 25–6, in

The Complete English Poems, ed. A. J. Smith (1971), 63.

60. Lucy Hutchinson, *Memoirs*, 280; Milton, *PL*, IV. 509–11, 741–75, VIII.364–5, 618–29, in *PJM*, 642, 657–9, 834, 848–9. For a summary of nonconformist teaching on the family, see Richard B. Schlatter, *The Social Ideas of Religious Leaders 1660–1688* (1940), 1–83, which stresses companionship and love on pp. 11–17, 21–2, and for the development of the affectionate nuclear family in the Puritan and nonconformist traditions, Lawrence Stone, *The Family, Sex and Marriage 1500–1800*, abridged edn (1979; rpt 1984), 101–3, 156–8, 176–7, 234–5. Edmund S. Morgan, *The Puritan Family*, rev. edn (New York, 1966), draws its evidence from New England, but the emphases of its chapters on marital and parental relations would hold for England. For a stimulating psychological (largely Freudian) analysis of Puritan family relationships, which draws evidence from such nonconformists as Heywood, see David Leverenz, *The Language of Puritan Feeling* (New Brunswick, NJ, 1980).

61. Bunyan, *PP*, 177–8, 183, 186; *OED*, *s.v* 'Bowel, 3'.

62. Notably Robert Bridges in Sharrock (ed.), *Casebook*, 107–8, 112.

63. Bunyan, *PP*, 50, 51; Bunyan, *GA*, §327; John Brown, *John Bunyan*, tercentenary edn rev. F. M. Harrison (1982), 388–9.

64. Milton, *PL*, X.145, VIII.588, in *PJM*, 932, 846. For examples of the view that the force of *PL*, IX.904–16, frustrates and ruptures the poem, see A. J. Waldock, *Paradise Lost and its Critics* (1947), 42–64; Hill, *Milton*, 129, 337, 354–5, 411 (and cf. William Empson, *Milton's God*, rev. edn (1965), 182–210).

65. Milton, *PL*, IX.908, IV.756, in *PJM*, 909, 658. Some phrases in this paragraph are taken from N. H. Keeble, 'Christiana's key', in Vincent Newey (ed.), *The Pilgrim's Progress: Critical and Historical Views* (1980), 13, which discusses this matter more at large, pp. 9–13.

CHAPTER 8

1. William Perkins, *The Workes*, 3 vols

(Cambridge, 1616–18), II.670b–617a.

2. For accounts of Puritan thinking on style, see: Perry Miller, *The New England Mind: The Seventeenth Century* (1939; rpt Boston Mass., 1961), 331–62; Kenneth B. Murdock, *Literature and Theology in Colonial New England* (1949; rpt New York, 1963), 34–50, 57–65; Harold Fisch, 'The Puritans and the reform of prose style', *ELH*, XIX, 4 (1952), 229–47; Laurence A. Sasek, *The Literary Temper of the English Puritans* (Baton Rouge, La, 1961), 39–56; and for a summary of the received view, James D. Boulger, *The Calvinist Temper in English Poetry* (The Hague, 1980), 123–9.

3. Perkins, *Workes*, II.670b; Richard Bernard, *The Faithfull Shepheard* (1607), 11, 12; John Wilkins, *Ecclesiastes* (1646), 72. W. F. Mitchell, *English Pulpit Oratory from Andrewes to Tillotson* (1932) places such remarks in the larger context of seventeenth-century homiletics.

4. Samuel Clarke, *A Generall Martyrologie* (1660), 208; *id.*, *A Collection of the Lives of Ten Eminent Divines* (1662), 106, 216, 311, 312.

5. Bunyan, *MW*, I.345; Bunyan, *GA*, pp. 3–4; Bunyan, *PP*, 98–9.

6. N. H. Keeble, *Richard Baxter* (1982), 48–54; Thomas Gouge, *The Works* (1798), 447, 449; Howe, *CW*, II.128; William Bates, *The Works*, 2nd edn (1723), 651, 707, 724.

7. [–] *A Short Examination of a Discourse concerning Edification* (1700), 8, 9, 10.

8. [George Hascard], *A Discourse about Edification* (1683), 14–15, 18.

9. George Keith, *Mr George Keith's Farewel Sermon* (1700), 11. For an account of Keith's increasing disillusion with Quakerism and the stages by which he became 'the most formidable' of all its opponents, see Braithwaite, *SPQ*, 482–93.

10. Robert South, *Sermons*, 6 vols (1715–17), IV.10–14, 21–34, 46, 47–9, 51.

11. South, *Sermons*, V.488–95, 504–5 (and cf. V.108–73).

12. [Simon Patrick], *A Continuation of the Friendly Debate* (1669), 81–91, 110 [misnumbered 112], 154–5; [William Sherlock], *A Discourse Concerning the Knowledge of Christ* (1674), 79–80;

Anthony à Wood, *Athenae Oxonienses*, ed. Philip Bliss, 4 vols, 3rd edn (1813–20), IV.105. For Owen's *Discourse*, see *CW*, II.1–274.

13. Joseph Glanvill, *An Essay Concerning Preaching*, 2nd edn (1703), 11, 25, 27, 77.

14. Edward Smith, *A Poem on the Death of Mr John Philips* ([1708]), 8; Joseph Addison, *The Spectator*, ed. Donald F. Bond, 5 vols (1965), IV.365; John Dennis, *The Critical Works*, ed. E. N. Hooker, 2 vols (Baltimore, Md, 1939–43), II.29–30; John Arbuthnot, *The History of John Bull*, ed. A. W. Bower and R. A. Erickson (1976), 63, 92; David Hume, *The Philosophical Works*, ed. T. H. Green and T. H. Grose, 4 vols (1882; rpt 1964), III.268–9.

15. Roger Pooley, 'Language and loyalty: plain style at the Restoration', *Literature & History*, VI, 1 (1980), 4. To this article, which is the most penetrating and suggestive discussion of the religious debates over style in the late seventeenth century, my own account is much indebted.

16. Fox, *JGF*, 36 (quoted above, p. 218); cf. Thomas Ellwood, *The History of the Life* (1714), 27; William Penn, *No Cross, No Crown*, ed. Norman Penney (1930; rpt 1981), 152–66.

17. On the *Battle-Door*, see Braithwaite, *BQ*, 496–9. For discussions of pronominal usage, the shift from 'thou' to 'you' and Quaker practice in relation to seventeenth-century forms of address, see Kathleen M. Wales, '*Thou* and *You* in Early Modern English', *Studia Linguistica*, XXXVII, 2 (1983), 107–25, esp. pp. 119–20, and the studies listed in this article's appended bibliography.

18. Penn, *No Cross, No Crown*, 152. Modern philologists incline to the view that it was the Quaker insistence on using 'thou' which sealed the fate of the pronoun: see Wales, '*Thou* and *You*', 119, and opinion there cited.

19. [Samuel Austin], *Plus Ultra or the Second Part of the Character of a Quaker* (1672), 2, 3, 8; [Joseph Glanvill], *The Zealous and Impartial Protestant* (1674), 25.

20. L'Estrange, *The Casuist Uncas'd*, 2nd edn (1680), sigs A2ᵛ–A3.

21. Glanvill, *Essay*, 12; Howe, *CW*, VI.300.

22. [Samuel Parker], *A Discourse of Ecclesiastical Politie* (1670), 71–2, 74–5.
23. Marvell, *RT*, 62, 53 (cf. pp. 263–9); [Sherlock], *Discourse*, 142–3, 143–4; Bates, *Works*, 380–8. Owen replied to Sherlock in *A Vindication of . . . A Discourse Concerning Communion with God* (1674), in *CW*, II.274–364 (see esp. pp. 286–92, and cf. II.46–59, 117–32).
24. Benjamin Keach, *The Travels of True Godliness* (1799), 114; Owen, *CW*, XIII.361.
25. Heywood, *AD*, I.205; Bunyan, *GA*, pp. 3–4 (quoted above, p. 241); [William Britten], *Silent Meeting a Wonder to the World* (1671), 5; Pooley, 'Language and loyalty', 10–11. For Britten, successively beneficed minister, Baptist and Quaker, see Braithwaite, *BQ*, 509–11.
26. [Parker], *Ecclesiastical Politie*, 76.
27. The scientific inclination towards plainness was the subject of 1930s articles by R. F. Jones, reprinted in Stanley Fish (ed.), *Seventeenth-Century Prose* (New York, 1971), 53–89, 94–111, which discuss the cases of Hobbes, Sprat and Boyle on pp. 54–5, 57–8, 59, 99–100, quoting the relevant Sprat passage in full on pp. 61–3.
28. Owen, *CW*, XIII.350; [Sherlock], *Discourse*, 40–1; [Patrick], *Continuation*, 110–11 [misnumbered 112–13].
29. Bunyan, *HW*, 116 (quoted above, p. 147); Keach, *True Godliness*, 7–12, 38; Bates, *Works*, 642; Isaac Penington, *Naked Truth* (1674), 78; George Whitehead, *The Nature of Christianity in the True Light Asserted* (1671), 13; Bunyan, *PP*, 179; cf. Owen, *CW*, V.44–55. For Whitehead see Braithwaite, *SPQ*, index *s.v.*
30. Pooley, 'Language and loyalty', 5.
31. Fox, *JGF*, 12, 13, 33; Isaac Penington, *Many Deep Considerations* ([1664?]), 3–4; Manton, *CW*, I.64, III.16.
32. John Cotton, *Christ the Foundation of Life* (1651), 98–9, quoted in Patricia Caldwell, *The Puritan Conversion Narrative* (1983), 92, which discusses subjectivity and authenticity in Puritan style on pp. 91–108; Geoffrey F. Nuttall, *The Holy Spirit in Puritan Faith and Experience*, 2nd edn (1947), 138.
33. George Keith, *Immediate Revelation* (1668), 38 (cf. pp. 92–7); Baxter, *The*

Saints Rest (1650), 89; *id.*, *The True and Only Way of Concord* (1680), 1st pag., 292; *id.*, *The Second Part of the Nonconformists Plea for Peace* (1680), 1st pag., 9; Nuttall, *Holy Spirit*, 141.
34. Theophilus Gale, *The Court of the Gentiles*, 5 vols (1669–78), I.392; William Dundas, *A Few Words of Truth from the Spirit of Truth* (1673), 3.
35. As F. R. Leavis, *Revaluation* (1936; rpt 1964), 45, said it was in a now notorious essay. The standard refutation is Christopher Ricks, *Milton's Grand Style* (1963).
36. Keith, *Immediate Revelation*, 31–2.
37. A single search discloses the following (there are certainly others): Gen. iii.1–6; Ps. xxiii.2; Prov. xvi.22, xviii.14; Song of Sol., iv.15, viii.8; Isa. xxxii.12, lv.1, lxv.25, lxvi.12; Jer. ii.13, xvii.13, l.17; Mic. ii.12; Matt. v.6, x.6, xv.24; John iv.14; Acts ii.30; Heb. iii.11, 18; Rev. ii.21, xii.9, xiv.8, xvii.1, 2, 4, 15, xviii.3, xix.2, xxi.6, xxii.1.
38. Heywood, *AD*, I.139; [Edward Terrill], *Records of a Church of Christ*, ed. E. B. Underhill (1847), 10; R[ichard] C[rane], *A Lamentation Over Thee, O London* (1665), 4.
39. For a fine account of early Quaker style, see Jackson I. Cope, 'Seventeenth-century Quaker style', in Fish (ed.), *Seventeenth-Century Prose*, 200–35, which makes this point on pp. 201–4; see also Luella M. Wright, *The Literary Life of Early Friends* (New York, 1932), 68–72.
40. [–], *Another Out-Cry of the Innocent & Oppressed* (1665), 7.
41. W[illiam] B[rend], *A Short Declaration of the Purpose and Decree of . . . Gods Heavenly Host* (1662), 3.
42. W[illiam] D[ewsbury], *To All the Faithful Brethren* (1661), 1; John Webster, *Academarium Examen* (1654), 74 (facsimile reprint in Allen G. Debus, *Science and Education in the Seventeenth Century: The Webster-Ward Debate* (1970)). Webster's terminology here derives from the Swiss Hermetic and Cabbalistic philosopher and physician Paracelsus, for whom see Walter Pagel, *Paracelsus: An Introduction* (Basle and New York, 1958), which explains 'Archeus' on pp. 104–13. For Webster see Charles Webster, *The Great Instauration*

(1975), 198–202, 331–5, and Debus, *Science and Education, passim.*

43. [Austin], *Plus Ultra*, 5, 10; Owen, *CW,* XVI.295–343 (esp. pp. 318–29); Fox, *JGF*, 63, 159, 332, 360, 445; Whitehead, *Nature of Christianity*, 33. See on this subject Geoffrey F. Nuttall, '"Nothing else would do": early Friends and the Bible', *The Friends Quarterly*, XXVII, 10 (1982), 651–9.

44. Manton, *CW*, I.8; Gale, *Court*, I.393–4; Bunyan, *MW*, IX.xxviii–xxx; Bunyan, *PP*, 8, 42, 285. John R. Knott, Jr, *The Sword of the Spirit* (Chicago, 1980) discusses the various exegetical and imaginative responses to the Bible in the Puritan tradition (including those of Baxter, Bunyan and Milton).

45. Bunyan, *PP*, 14; Bunyan, *CW*, III.500 (quoted in Roger Sharrock, *John Bunyan* (1968), 100); William Spurstowe, *The Spiritual Chymist* (1666), sig.A3ᵛ.

46. For Hermetic philosophy see Francis Yates, *Giordano Bruno and the Hermetic Tradition* (1964), 1–83 and *passim.*

47. Milton, *PL*, II.1004–6, 1051–2, III.501–15, V.469–90, in *PJM*, 555, 557–8, 590–1, 704–5; Howe, *CW*, III.56. The idea is discussed in C. A. Patrides, *Premises and Motifs in Renaissance Thought and Literature* (Princeton, NJ, 1982), 31–51; *id., Milton and the Christian Tradition* (1966), 54–90; and more at large in Arthur O. Lovejoy, *The Great Chain of Being* (New York, 1960).

48. On this tradition see U. Milo Daufmann, *The Pilgrim's Progress and Traditions in Puritan Meditation* (New Haven, Conn., 1966), esp. pp. 175–95, and Miller, *New England Mind*, 207–35.

49. Thomas Adams, *The Workes* (1630), 252–3; Anne Bradstreet, *The Works*, ed. Jeannine Hensley (Cambridge, Mass., 1967), 272; Gouge, *Works*, 404.

50. Baxter, *The Divine Life* (1664), 170. For Baxter's meditative advice and responsiveness to the created world, see Knott, *Sword of the Spirit*, 67–84, and Keeble, *Baxter*, 100–13 (which is drawn on in what follows) and references cited *ibid.,* 200 n. 13.

51. Baxter, *Gildas Salvianus: The Reformed Pastor* (1656), 265; *id., A Treatise of Knowledge and Love Compared* (1689), 158;

52. Gouge, *Works*, 404; Bunyan, *MW*, IX.195; Howe, *CW*, II.247, III.169; *id., Blessedness*, 394 (alluding to Isa. vi.2–3).

53. Baxter, *The Life of Faith*, enlarged edn (1670), 183; Howe, *CW*, III.61, 71–2, IV.147; Gouge, *Works*, 404.

54. Matthew Henry, *The Life of Philip Henry*, in *The Lives of Philip and Matthew Henry*, ed. J. B. Williams (1974), 118–19; Heywood, *AD*, I.344ff., II.237ff., III.103ff., IV.17ff.

55. Howe, *CW*, III.55, 140–1; Baxter, *Saints Rest*, 691, 756–7.

56. Milton, *CPW*, VI.300–8. Milton's doctrine of the Creation is discussed in Denis Saurat, *Milton, Man and Thinker*, rev. edn (1944), 102–4, 236–8; A. S. P. Woodhouse, 'Notes on Milton's views on Creation', *PQ*, XXVIII (1949), 211–36; Harry F. Robins, *If This Be Heresy* (Urbana, Ill., 1963), 45–55; Patrides, *Milton and the Christian Tradition*, 29–45; Gordon Campbell, 'Milton's theological and literary treatments of the Creation', *Journal of Theological Studies*, n.s. XXX, 1 (1979), 128–37. Milton's 'pleasure in the fecundity of the universe' is noted in Christopher Hill, *Milton and the English Revolution* (1977; rpt 1979), 259–62, and contrasted with Donne in John Carey, *John Donne* (1981; rpt 1983), 123.

57. Manton, *CW*, II.93–4.

58. Keith, *Immediate Revelation*, 6–7, 9, 10; Bunyan, *MW*, IX.148, 149–50. For earlier Puritan examples, see Nuttall, *Holy Spirit*, 38–42.

59. Bunyan, *PP*, 110–11.

CHAPTER 9

1. Bunyan, *PP*, 8; Bunyan, *GA*, p. 1 (with a reference to Song of Sol. iv.8).

2. Phyllis M. Jones, '"Puritan's progress": the story of the soul's salvation in early New England sermons', *Early American Literature*, XV (1980), 16. For some account of this aspect of Puritan writing, see this article, pp. 14–28; Sargent Bush, Jr, *The Writings of Thomas Hooker* (Madison, Wis.,

1980), 163–85, 216–20, 312–13; Sacvan Bercovitch, 'The American Puritan imagination', in *The American Puritan Imagination*, ed. Sacvan Bercovitch (1971), 1–16.

3. Bunyan, *PP*, 44; Samuel Mather, *The Figures or Types of the Old Testament*, 2nd edn (1705), 52, quoted in Mason I. Lowance, 'Images or shadows of divine things', *Early American Literature*, V, 1 (1970), 141. For discussion of the literary consequences of typology see Sacvan Bercovitch (ed.), *Typology and Early American Literature* (Amherst, Mass., 1972); Paul J. Korshin, *Typologies in England 1650–1820* (Princeton, NJ, 1982); Mason I. Lowance, Jr, *The Language of Canaan* (Cambridge, Mass., 1980).

4. Edward Taylor, *The Poems*, ed. Donald E. Stanford (New Haven, Conn., 1960), 87; *Rel. Bax.*, I.31, §49, and I.58, §85; [John Griffiths (ed.)], *Certain Sermons or Homilies* (1908), 37–8.

5. William Bradford, *Of Plymouth Plantation*, ed. Samuel Eliot Morrison (New York, 1952), 11, 329; Cotton Mather, *Magnalia Christi Americana: or, The Ecclesiastical History of New England* (1702), I.6, §3; Nathaniel Morton, *New England's Memorial*, in *Chronicles of the Pilgrim Fathers*, [ed. Alexander Young], Everyman's Library (1910), 173.

6. Fox, *JGF*, 3–4, 5, 6, 10; George Fox, *Gospel-Truth Demonstrated* (1706), sig. A2; Heywood, *AD*, II.225, 227–8 (cf. III. 247, 254, 262, 264, 267, 274, 278); Watts, *DRR*, 280–1; Matthew Henry, *An Exposition of All the Books of the Old and New Testament*, 3 vols (1867), I.42. Isabel Rivers, '"Strangers and pilgrims": sources and patterns of Methodist narrative', in *Augustan Worlds*, ed. J. C. Hilson *et al.* (1978), 189–203, argues that the reflection of Methodist itinerancy in its writings constitutes a distinct development of the Puritan literature of pilgrimage.

7. William Penn, *No Cross, No Crown*, ed. Norman Penney (1930; rpt

1981), 42, 92; Henry, *Exposition*, I.40–1.

8. Bunyan, *PP*, 67, 183–4; Benjamin Keach, *War with the Devil*, 22nd edn (1776), 107; *Johnson's Wonder-Working Providence*, ed. J. Franklin Jameson (New York, 1959), 50–2; Thomas Shepherd, *A Defence of the Answer* (1648), in *The Puritans: A Sourcebook of their Writings*, ed. Perry Miller and Thomas H. Johnson, 2 vols (1938; rpt New York, 1963), I.121.

9. Henry, *Exposition*, III.863; Thomas Adams, *The Workes* (1630), 652; Bunyan, *PP*, 293, 18; Milton, *SA*, 11. 1074–1243, in *PJM*, 381–6; Fox, *JGF*, p. xlvii.

10. Discussed in William Haller, *The Rise of Puritanism* (1938; rpt New York, 1957), 150–9.

11. Bush, *Thomas Hooker*, *passim*.

12. Thomas Gouge, *The Works* (1798), 383–4; Heywood, *AD*, I.136; Manton, *CW*, II.147–8; Bunyan, *PP*, 43.

13. *OED*, s.v. 'Adventure, 5,6' (noted by S. J. Newman in Vincent Newey (ed.), *The Pilgrim's Progress: Critical and Historical Views* (1980), 239).

14. Henry, *Exposition*, III.45; Keach, *War with the Devil*, 42; Bunyan, *PP*, 9, 48; Gouge, *Works*, 354; Bunyan, *CW*, I.368b–9a.

15. Bunyan, *GA*, §§53–4; Gouge, *Works*, 353, 361; Miller and Johnson (eds), *The Puritans*, I.337.

16. Henry, *Exposition*, III.44; Bunyan, *CW*, III.559, 590. See Gordon Campbell, 'The source of Bunyan's *Mapp*', *Journal of the Warburg and Courtauld Institutes*, XLIV (1981), 240–1, for earlier examples of this caste of mind.

17. *OED*, s.v. 'Walk v., 6'; Haller, *Rise of Puritanism*, 142, 146–50; Bradford, *Plymouth Plantation*, 368–71.

18. Bunyan, *PP*, 27, 41, 45–6, 62, 120; Adams, *Workes*, 802; Thomas Ellwood, *The History of the Life* (1714), 25. Roger Pooley, 'The structure of *The Pilgrim's Progress*', *Essays in Poetics*, IV (1979), 63–4, stresses the straightness of the way,

and, p. 61, contrasts picaresque fiction.

19. See above, pp. 12–14.
20. Adams, *Workes*, 800; Baxter, *Directions for Weak Christians* (1669), pt i, 17–18, sigs G8–G8ᵛ. For further examples of Baxter's views on justification and the significance of works, see N. H. Keeble, *Richard Baxter* (1982), 69–72
21. Gouge, *Works*, 396, 450; Howe, *CW*, II.216; Manton, *CW*, II.57–61, 75; cf. William Bates, *The Works*, 2nd edn (1723), 506–9, 561–73.
22. Bunyan, *CW*, II.549; Bunyan, *MW*, IX.252, 295; Bunyan, *PP*, 79; Adams, *Workes*, 802.
23. Gouge, *Works*, 396, 397; Baxter, *Directions*, pt i, 19.
24. Bunyan, *MW*, IX.276, 277; Bunyan, *PP*, pp. xxxii–xxxiiii; Manton, *CW*, II.419–21
25. Manton, *CW*, II.59–60; [Young (ed.)], *Chronicles*, 174, 236; Johnson, *Wonder-Working Providence*, 115; Bunyan, *PP*, 295. For nonconformist attitudes to monasticism, see above, pp. 220–1.
26. Henry, *Exposition*, I.118, 255; [Griffiths (ed.)], *Homilies*, 38; Mather, *Magnalia*, I.6, §1, I.21, §4, II.5, §8; Johnson, *Wonder-Working Providence*, 50; [Young (ed.)], *Chronicles*, 10.
27. Bradford, *Plymouth Plantation*, 62–3; Peter N. Carroll, *Puritanism and the Wilderness* (New York, 1969), 16; Miller and Johnson (eds), *The Puritans*, I.199.
28. Harrison T. Meserole (ed.), *Seventeenth-Century American Poetry* (New York, 1968), 397; [Young (ed.)], *Chronicles*, 167, 174, 178. For Tillam, see Underwood, *EB*, 92. On the term 'wilderness' see Carroll, *Puritanism and the Wilderness*, *passim*; Alan Heimert, 'Puritanism, the wilderness and the frontier', *New England Quarterly*, XXVI (1953), 361–82; George H. Williams, 'The idea of the wilderness', in Cotton Mather, *Magnalia Christi Americana*, ed. Kenneth B. Murdock (Cambridge,

Mass., 1977), 49–58; and, with particular reference to Bunyan, Roger Pooley, 'The wilderness of this world', *BQ*, XXVII (1978), 290–9.
29. Matthew Henry, *The Life of Philip Henry*, in *The Lives of Philip and Matthew Henry*, ed. J. B. Williams (1974), p. xxxv; William Dundas, *A Few Words of Truth from the Spirit of Truth* (1673), 18; Taylor, *Poems*, 182.
30. Thomas Taylor, *Christ Revealed* (1816), 227; Bunyan, *CW*, III. 382; Keach, *War with the Devil*, 99–100, 115; Adams, *Workes* 652.
31. Taylor, *Christ Revealed*, 213; *The New Testament Translated by William Tyndale 1534*, ed. N. Hardy Wallis (1938), 502; Penn, *No Cross, No Crown*, 89; John Owen, *Exercitations on the Epistle to the Hebrews* (1668), 24–39.
32. Bunyan, *PP*, 42, 44; Adams, *Workes*, 807; Robert Bolton, *Some General Directions for a Confortable Walking with God*, 3rd edn (1630), 22.
33. Bunyan, *PP*, 119, 249, 254, 257; Bunyan, *CW*, III.287; *Coleridge on the Seventeenth Century*, ed. Roberta Florence Brinkley (1955; rpt New York, 1968), 483–4; Keach, *War with the Devil*, 48.
34. Milton, *PL*, XII.469–71, 645–9, in *PJM*, 1050, 1060. The allusion to Ps. cvii.4 is noted by the editor, Alastair Fowler.
35. Benjamin Keach, *The Travels of True Godliness* (1799), 186–7. For discussion of the importance of trial, see above, pp. 187–91.
36. Milton, *PR*, I.4–5 (my italics), in *PJM*, 1077; Aristotle, *Poetics*, 1450b3, in *Aristotle: Poetics*, trans. John Warrington, Everyman's Library (1963), 15.
37. Bunyan, *PP*, pp. 39, 135; *OED*, *s.v.* 'Progress *sb.*, 1, 2, 4b'; Philip Edwards, 'The journey in *The Pilgrim's Progress*', in Newey (ed.), *Pilgrim's Progress*, 112–13.
38. cf. the title essay in Perry Miller, *Errand into the Wilderness* (New York, 1964), 1–15; Robinson cited

from Jesper Rosenmeier, 'William
Bradford's *Of Plymouth Plantation*',
in Bercovitch (ed.), *Puritan
Imagination*, 82; Johnson, *Wonder-
Working Providence*, 76, 268–75.

39. Henry, *Exposition*, II.746, 603, 590,
621; Fox, *JGF*, 13, 15, 21, 263;
Bunyan, *PP*, 38.

40. Bunyan, *PP*, 258. See above, pp. 232–5.

41. Heywood, *AD*, I.150.

42. [Griffiths (ed.)], *Homilies*, 99; Howe, *CW*,
II.217. Brainerd P. Stranahan, 'Bunyan
and the Epistle to the Hebrews', *SP*, LXXIX
(1982), 279–96, examines in detail the
indebtedness of *The Pilgrim's Progress* to
Hebrews.

43. Anne Bradstreet, *The Works*, ed. Jeannine
Hensley (Cambridge, Mass., 1967), 283,
294–5. On the significance of the Atlantic
crossing for New Englanders see Carroll,
Puritanism and the Wilderness, 27–44, and
Cecelia Tichi, 'Spiritual biography', in
Bercovitch (ed.), *Puritan Imagination*, 65–
7; and for its unsettling, even
disillusioning, effect upon the expectations
of emigrants to the New English Canaan
crossing their Red Sea, Patricia Caldwell,
The Puritan Conversion Narrative (1983),
119–34.

44. Henry, *Exposition*, I.42; Keach, *War with
the Devil*, 107; Fox, *JGF*, 13 (quoted
above, pp. 250–1).

45. [Young (ed.)], *Chronicles*, 6; Gouge, *Works*,
403; Keach, *True Godliness*, 56; Bunyan,
GA, p. 4.

46. See above, pp. 257–62.

47. Baxter, *The Saints Everlasting Rest* (1650),
761, 762–3.

48. Bunyan, *PP*, 111, 154–5 (the scene is
discussed above, pp. 261–2). On the
significance of the Song of Solomon for
the Puritan mind and imagination, see
Lowance, *Language of Canaan*, 41–54.

49. Keach, *War with the Devil*, 105.

CONCLUSION

1. Although in *A Gathered Church* (1978)
Donald Davie argues that later
dissenting literature is as Classical as
the work of Pope, he does distinguish
from it the culture of seventeenth-
century nonconformity. His
characterization of the earlier period

as unenlightened, uncivilized and
unattractive (pp. 9–13) may be taken
as an attempt to redress the balance in
favour of the eighteenth century, but
his consequent difficulty in
accommodating the figure of Blake,
to whom he has perforce to deny any
sustaining relationship with the
dissenting tradition (pp. 49–54),
raises a larger question about the
adequacy of his description of the
taste and sentiment of eighteenth-
century dissent.

2. Notably in Vincent Newey,
'Wordsworth, Bunyan and the
Puritan mind', *ELH*, XLI (1974), 212–
32, and *id.*, 'The steadfast self', in R.
T. Davies and B. G. Beatty (eds),
Literature of the Romantic Period
(1976), 43–7. See also R. Parker,
Coleridge's Meditative Art (Ithaca, NY,
1975), 28–45; Dayton Haskin,
'Baxter's quest for origins', *The
Eighteenth Century*, XXI, 2 (1980),
145–61; N. H. Keeble, *Richard Baxter*
(1982), 112–13; James D. Boulger,
Coleridge as a Religious Thinker (New
Haven, Conn., 1961), 37–64 and
passim.

3. Joseph Ritson, *The Romance of
Nonconformity* (1910), pp.iii, 3–4; R. A.
Scott-James, *Modernism and Romance*
(1908), 4.

4. Wordsworth, 'Immortality Ode', l.
56, 'Tintern Abbey', ll. 37–49, *The
Prelude* (1850), XII.207–18, in
Poetical Works, ed. Thomas
Hutchinson, rev. Ernest de
Selincourt (1904; rpt 1964), 163,
460, 577.

5. Benjamin Keach, *The Travels of True
Godliness* (1799), 12.

6. *Coleridge on the Seventeenth Century*,
ed. Roberta Florence Brinkley (1955;
rpt New York, 1968), 329, 477. This
passage from Coleridge is discussed
in Susie I. Tucker, *Enthusiasm: A
Study in Semantic Change* (1972),
47–8.

7. Benjamin Keach, *War with the Devil*,
22nd edn (1776), 80.

8. As is drawn out in Christopher Hill's
essay on Marvell in *Puritanism and
Revolution* (1965; rpt 1968), 324–50.

9. It is the theme of Warren L. Chernaik, *The Poet's Time* (1983) that in Marvell 'the commands of conscience take precedence over the commands of the state' (p. 10). His chapter on 'Christian liberty' (pp. 102–50) is the best exposition we have of Marvell's religious and ecclesiastical position. See also Annabel M. Patterson, *Marvell and the Civic Crown* (Princeton, NJ, 1978), 200–10.

10. As far as is known, Marvell was not a member of any nonconformist church, and he would have had to be at least an occasional conformist to be an M.P. In *RT*, 186, he denies that he is a nonconformist. This may have been rhetorical prudence, securing an appeal to the largest possible readership, though it seems unlikely Marvell would have conceded so much truth to the demands of satire. Even if literally true, there is no doubt where his sympathies lie: it is the nonconformist case he argues, and Milton, Owen, Baxter and Howe whom he defends. See on this matter Chernaik, *Poet's Time*, 121–4, and Caroline Robbins, 'Marvell's religion', *Journal of the History of Ideas*, XXIII, 2 (1962), 268–72, which argues that, theologically at least, Marvell subscribed, like Baxter, to the 'hypothetical universalism' of Moses Amyraut and might be numbered amongst the 'Reconcilers'.

11. Bunyan, *PP*, 7.

12. Bunyan, *PP*, 6.

Bibliography

This bibliography does not attempt to list all the works referred to in this study. It includes the chief primary sources and those secondary studies which bear most directly on nonconformity and its literature. The place of publication is not given if it is London.

A. PRIMARY

I DOCUMENTARY SOURCES

Arber, Edward (ed.) *The Term Catalogues, 1668–1709 A.D.*, 3 vols (1903–6; rpt New York, 1965)
— *A Transcript of the Registers of the Company of Stationers of London; 1554–1640 A.D.*, 5 vols (1875–94; rpt New York, 1950)
Besse, Joseph (ed.) *A Collection of the Sufferings of the People called Quakers*, 2 vols (1753)
Bettenson, Henry (ed.) *Documents of the Christian Church*, 2nd edn (Oxford, 1963)
Browning, Andrew (ed.) *English Historical Documents 1660–1714* (1966)
Calendar of State Papers, Domestic Series, 41 vols (1860–1947)
Cardwell, Edward (ed.) *Documentary Annals of the Reformed Church of England ... 1546–1716*, 2 vols (Oxford, 1839)
— (ed.) *A History of Conferences and other Proceedings connected with the Revision of the Book of Common Prayer 1558–1690* (Oxford, 1840)
Cobbett, William (ed.) *A Complete Collection of State Trials and Proceedings for High Treason and Other Crimes and Misdemeanours*, cont. T. B. and T. J. Howell, 33 vols (1809–26)
[Eyre, G. (ed.)] *A Transcript of the Registers of the Worshipful Company of Stationers: From 1640–1708 A.D.*, 3 vols (1913–14; rpt New York, 1950)
Firth, C. H. and Rait, R. S. (eds) *Acts and Ordinances of the Interregnum 1642–1660*, 3 vols (1911)
French, J. Milton (ed.) *The Life Records of John Milton*, 5 vols (1949–58; rpt New York, 1966)
Gordon, Alexander (ed.) *Freedom after Ejection: A Review (1690–1692) of Presbyterian and Congregational Nonconformity in England and Wales* (Manchester, 1917)
[Luders, A., Tomlins, T. E., *et al.* (eds)] *The Statutes of the Realm*, 11 vols (1810–28)
Peel, Albert (ed.) *The Savoy Declaration of Faith and Order 1658* (1939)
Penney, Norman (ed.) *Extracts from State Papers Relating to Friends 1654 to 1672* (1913)
— (ed.) *'The First Publishers of Truth'* (1907)
[Thomas, Roger (ed.)] *'An Essay of Accommodation': being a scheme for uniting Presbyterians and Congregationals drawn up c. 1680* (1957)
Tibbutt, H. G. (ed.) *The Minutes of the First Independent Church (now Bunyan Meeting) at Bedford 1656–1766* (Bedford, 1976)
Turner, G. Lyon (ed.) *Original Records of Early Nonconformity under Persecution and Indulgence*, 3 vols (1911–14)

2 NONCONFORMIST TEXTS

The Address of the Nonconformist Ministers (in and about the City of London) to his Highness the Prince of Orange (1689)

Alleine, Joseph *An Alarme to Unconverted Sinners* (1672)

[Alleine, Theodosia, *et al.*] *The Life and Death of Mr. Joseph Alleine* (1672)

[Alsop, Vincent] *Anti-Sozzo, sive Sherlocismus Enervatus: in Vindication of some Great Truths Opposed . . . by Mr. William Sherlock* (1675)

[—] *The Mischief of Impositions: Or, An Antidote against a Late Discourse . . . Called the Mischief of Separation* (1680)

Another Out-Cry of the Innocent & Oppressed. Being a True Account of the unjust and illegal proceedings . . . against . . . Quakers . . . in Northampton (1665)

Armitage, Evelyn Noble (ed.) *The Quaker Poets of Great Britain and Ireland* (1896)

B., A. *A Letter from a Minister to a Person of Quality, shewing some Reasons for his Non-conformity* ([1679])

Bagshaw, Edward *An Antidote against Mr. Baxter's Palliated Cure of Church-divisions* (1670)

— *A Defence of the Antidote* (1671)

— *A Review and Conclusion of the Antidote* (1671)

Barbour, Hugh, and Roberts, Arthur (eds) *Early Quaker Writings 1650–1700* (Grand Rapids, 1973)

Barclay, Robert *An Apology for the True Christian Divinity, as the same is held forth, and preached by the People Called, in Scorn, Quakers* (1678)

— *Truth Cleared of Calumnies* (1670)

— *Truth Triumphant Through the Spiritual Warfare, Christian Labours and Writings of . . . Robert Barclay* (1692)

— *William Michel Unmasqued* (1672)

Barclay, Robert, and Keith, George *Quakerism Confirmed, Or A Vindication of the Chief Doctrines and Principles of the people called Quakers* (1676)

[Barrington, John Shute] *An Essay upon the Interest of England; in respect to Protestants Dissenting from the Establish'd Church* (1701)

Bates, William *The Works*, 2nd edn (1723)

Baxter, Richard *Against the Revolt to a Foreign Jurisdiction* (1691)

— *An Apology for the Nonconformists Ministry* (1681)

— *The Autobiography*, abridged J. M. Lloyd Thomas, ed. N.H. Keeble (1974; rpt 1985)

— *Cain and Abel Malignity* (1689)

— *A Call to the Unconverted*, 13th edn with additions (1669)

— *The Catechizing of Families* (1683)

— *Catholick Communion Doubly Defended* (1681)

— *A Christian Directory* (1673)

— *The Church Told of Mr. Ed. Bagshaw's Scandals* (1672)

— *Compassionate Counsel to all Young-men* (1681)

— *The Cure of Church-Divisions* (1670)

— *A Defence of the Principles of Love* (1671)

— *Directions and Perswasions to a Sound Conversion* (1658)

— *Directions for Weak Distempered Christians* (1669)

— *The Divine Life* (1664)

[—] *Fair-warning: or XXV Reasons against Toleration and Indulgence of Popery* (1663)

— *Gildas Salvianus: The Reformed Pastor* (1656)

— *The Life of Faith*, 2nd enlarged edn (1670)

— *The Nonconformists Plea for Peace* (1679)

— *A Paraphrase on the New Testament* (1684)

— *A Paraphrase on the New Testament . . . to which is added . . . Mr. Baxter's Account of his Notes on some particular Texts, for which he was Imprisoned*, 2nd edn (1695)

[—] *A Petition for Peace* (1661)

— *Poetical Fragments*, introd. V. de Sola Pinto (Farnborough, 1971)

— 'The Poor Husbandman's Advocate', *The Reverend Richard Baxter's Last Treatise*, ed.
   F. J. Powicke (Manchester, 1926)
— *The Poor Man's Family Book* (1674)
— *Reliquiae Baxterianae* (1696)
— *Richard Baxter's Dying Thoughts* (1683)
— *Richard Baxter's Penitent Confession* (1691)
— *Richard Baxter and Puritan Politics*, ed. Richard B. Schlatter (New Brunswick, NJ,
   1957)
— *The Right Method for a Settled Peace of Conscience* (1653)
[—] *Sacrilegious Desertion of the Holy Ministry Rebuked* (1672)
— *The Saints Everlasting Rest* (1650)
— *A Second Admonition to Mr. Edward Bagshaw* (1671)
— *The Second Part of the Nonconformists Plea for Peace* (1680)
— *The Scripture Gospel Defended* (1690)
— *A Treatise of Knowledge and Love Compared* (1689)
— *A Treatise of Self-Denyall* (1660)
— *The True and Only Way of Concord* (1680)
— *The True Catholick and Catholick Church Described* (1660)
— *Two Sheets for Poor Families* (1665)
Bayley, Charles *The Causes of God's Wrath Against England ... Fore-told by, and delivered
   in, A Letter to the King* (1665)
B[ayly], W[illiam] *The Life of Enoch again Revived, in which Abels Offering is Accepted and
   Cains Mark Known, and He Rejected* (1662)
B[illing], E[dward] *A Faithful Testimony for God and my Country: Or, Retro-spective Glass
   for the Legislators And the rest of the Sons of the Church of England, (So called) Who are
   Persecuting the Innocent* (1664)
B[rend], W[illiam] *A Short Declaration of the Purpose and Decree of the Everlasting Counsel of
   Gods Heavenly Host* (1662)
A Brief Account of many memorable Passages of the Life and Death of the Earl of Shaftsbury
   ([1683])
[Britten, William] *Silent Meeting A Wonder To the World* (1671)
Bunyan, John *Grace Abounding to the Chief of Sinners*, ed. Roger Sharrock (Oxford, 1962)
— *The Holy War*, ed. Roger Sharrock and James Forrest (Oxford, 1980)
— *Miscellaneous Works*, gen. ed. Roger Sharrock, 12 vols in progress (Oxford, 1976–)
— *The Pilgrim's Progress*, ed. James Blanton Wharey, rev. Roger Sharrock, 2nd edn
   (Oxford, 1960)
— *The Pilgrim's Progress*, ed. N. H. Keeble, World's Classics (1984)
— *The Works of John Bunyan*, ed. George Offor, 3 vols (London, Glasgow and
   Edinburgh, 1860–2)
[Burgess, Cornelius] *Reasons Shewing the Necessity of Reformation of the Publick Doctrine,
   Worship, Rites and Ceremonies, Church-Government and Discipline reputed to be (but
   indeed not) Established by Law* (1660)
Burrough, Edward *The Memorable Works of a Son of Thunder and Consolation* (1672)
[—] *A Visitation of Love unto the King, and Those call'd Royalists* (1660)
Calamy, Edmund *An Abridgment of Mr. Baxter's History of his Life and Times. With an
   Account of many others of those ... who where ejected after the Restauration ... And a
   Continuation of their History, till the Year 1691* (1702)
— *An Abridgment of Mr. Baxter's History ... And the Continuation of their History to ...
   1711*, 2 vols, 2nd edn (1713)
— *Calamy Revised: Being a Revision of Edmund Calamy's Account*, ed. A. G. Matthews
   (Oxford, 1934)
— *A Continuation of the Account of the Ministers ... who were Ejected and Silenced ... by or
   before the Act of Uniformity*, 2 vols (1727)
— *A Defence of Moderate Nonconformity*, 3 vols (1703–5)

— *An Historical Account of my Own Life*, ed. J. T. Rutt, 2 vols (1829)

— *Memoirs of the Life of the Late Revd. Mr. John Howe* (1724)

C[aryl], J[oseph] *Peter's Pattern: Or, The perfect Path to Worldly Happiness* (1659)

The Case of Mixt-Communion Friendly Discoursed, betwixt a Minister and a Nonconforming Parishioner (1700)

The Case of People called Quakers, Relating to Oathes and Swearing (1673)

C[heyney], J[ohn] *The Conforming Non-Conformist and the Non-Conforming Conformist* (1680)

Clarke, Samuel *A Collection of the Lives of Ten Eminent Divines*(1662)

— *A Generall Martyrologie* (1660)

— *The Lives of Sundry Eminent Persons* (1683)

Coad, John *A Memorandum of the Wonderful Providences of God to a poor unworthy Creature, during the time of the Duke of Monmouth's Rebellion* (1849)

[Coale, Benjamin] *To the Bishops and their Ministers* (1671)

Corbert [i.e. Corbet], John *Self-Imployment in Secret* (Edinburgh, [1700?])

[Cowie, John] *Some Queries touching Excommunication Published by the People of God, (termed in derision Quakers)* ([1682])

C[rane], R[ichard] *A Lamentation Over Thee O London* (1665)

Crooke, John *The Cry of the Innocent for Justice: Being a Relation of the Tryal of John Crook* (1662)

— *An Epistle of Love To all that are in present Sufferings, whether Inwardly or Outwardly* (1660)

— *An Epistle for Vnity* (1661)

— *A True and Faithful Testimony concerning John Samm* (1664)

— *Truth's Progress; Or, A Short Relation of Its First Appearance and Publication After the Apostacy* (1667)

[Defoe, Daniel] *The Case of the Protestant Dissenters in Carolina* (1706)

[—] *The Dissenters Answer to the High-Church Challenge* (1704)

[—] *The Dissenters in England Vindicated* ([1707])

[—] *An Enquiry into the Occasional Conformity of Dissenters in Cases of Preferment. With a preface to Mr. How* (1701)

[—] *The Experiment: or, The Shortest Way with the Dissenters Exemplified* (1705)

[—] *A Letter to Mr. How, by way of a reply to his Considerations of the Preface to an Enquiry into the Occasional Conformity of Dissenters* (1701)

[—] *Royal Religion; being some Enquiry after the Piety of Princes* (1704)

[—] *A Short View of the Present State of the Protestant Religion* (Edinburgh, 1707)

[—] *The Shortest-Way with the Dissenters* (1702)

[—] *The True-Born Englishman. A Satyr* (1701)

De Laune, Thomas *A Plea for the Non-Conformists* (1684)

— *De Laune's Plea for the Non-Conformists ... With a Preface by the Author of the Review* (1706)

D[ewsbury], W[illiam] *The Word of the Lord, To his beloved Citty New-Ierusalem* ([1663])

— *To All the Faithful Brethren Born of the Immortal Seed* (1661)

Dundas, William *A Few Words of Truth from the Spirit of Truth* (1673)

Dunton, John *The Life and Errors*, 2 vols (1818)

— (ed.) *The Phenix: or, a Revival of Scarce and Valuable Pieces*, 2 vols (1707–8)

Ellwood, Thomas *Davideis: a reprint of the first edition of 1712*, ed. Walter Fischer (Heidelberg, 1936)

— *The History of the Life* (1714)

[Fell, Margaret, and Fox, George] *The Examination and Trial of Margaret Fell and George Fox at the several Assizes held at Lancaster ... 1663–4* (1664)

[Ferguson, Robert] *A Representation of the Threatning Dangers, impending over Protestants* ([Edinburgh, 1687])

Fiennes, Celia *The Illustrated Journeys ... c. 1682–c.1712*, ed. Christopher Morris (1984)

[Fortescue, William] *A Short Relation Concerning the Life and Death of That man of God . . . William Simpson* (1671)

Fox, George *A Collection of Many Select and Christian Epistles* (1698)

— *A Distinction between the Phanatick Spirit, and the Spirit of God* (1660)

— *An Epistle to be Read in all the Assemblies of the Righteous* (1666)

— *A General Epistle to be read in all the Christian Meetings in the World* (1662)

— *Gospel-Truth Demonstrated, in a Collection of Doctrinal Books* (1706)

— *Journal*, ed. Norman Penney, 2 vols (Cambridge, 1911)

— *Journal*, ed. Thomas Ellwood, rev. Norman Penney, Everyman's Library (1924)

— *Journal*, ed. John L. Nickalls (1952; rpt 1975)

— *The Law of God, The Rule for Law-makers, The Ground of all just Laws, and the corruption of English Laws and Lawyers Discovered* (1658)

— *The Pearle Found in England* (1658)

— *The Summ of Such Particulars as are Charged against George Fox* (1660)

— *Truths Triumph In the Eternal Power Over the Darke Inventions of Fallen Man* (1661)

F[ox], G[eorge], and H[ookes], E[llis] *A Primmer and Catechism for Children* (1670)

Fox, George, Stubs, John, and Furley, Benjamin *A Battle-Door for Teachers and Professors to Learn Singular & Plural; You to Many, and Thou to One* (1660)

[Fox, George, et al.] *A Declaration from the Harmles & Innocent People of God called Quakers against all Plotters and Fighters in the World (*1660[/1])

[Franklin, John] *A Resolution of this Case, Viz. Whether it be Lawful to separate from the Publick Worship of God in the Parochial Assemblies of England* (1683)

Fullertoune, John *A Short Testimony concerning Catherine Allardes, Late Wife to Iohn Fullertoune* (1671)

Gale, Theophilus *The Court of the Gentiles: Or, A Discourse touching the Original of Human Literature, both Philologie and Philosophie, from the Scriptures and Jewish Church*, 5 vols (Oxford and London, 1669–78)

[Goodwin, Thomas] *Patience and its Perfect Work, under Sudden & Sore Tryals* (1666)

Gouge, Thomas *The Works* (1798)

Hamilton, William *Some Necessity of Reformation of the Publick Doctrine of the Church of England* (1660)

Henry, Matthew *An Exposition of All the Books of the Old and New Testament*, 3 vols (London, Glasgow and Edinburgh, 1867)

— *The Life of the Rev. Philip Henry*, in J. B. Williams (ed.), *The Lives of Philip and Matthew Henry* (1825; rpt 1974)

Heywood, Oliver *His Autobiography, Diaries, Anecdote and Event Books*, ed. J. Horsfall Turner, 4 vols (Brighouse and Bingley, 1882–5)

[Holles, Denzil] *The Long Parliament Dissolved* (1676)

Howard, Luke *A Few Plain Words of Instruction* (1658)

Howe, John *The Blessedness of the Righteous* (1673)

— *The Case of the Protestant Dissenters Represented and Argued* (1689)

— *The Works*, ed. Henry Rogers, 6 vols (1862–3)

H[owgill], F[rancis] *The Great Case of Tythes and forced Maintenance Once more Revived* (1665)

— *The True Rule, Judge, and Guide of the True Church of God Discovered* (1665)

[Humphrey, John] *Advice before it be too Late: Or, A Breviate for the Convention* ([1689])

— *The Authority of the Magistrate About Religion* (1672)

[—] *The Healing Attempt . . . in Order to a Comprehension* (1689)

Hutchinson, John *A Narrative of the Imprisonment and Usage of Col. John Hutchinson* (1664)

Hutchinson, Lucy *Memoirs of the Life of Colonel John Hutchinson*, ed. James Sutherland (1973)

Janeway, James *Invisibles, Realities, Demonstrated in the Holy Life . . . of Mr. John Janeway (*1673)

Keach, Benjamin *The Progress of Sin: Or, The Travels of Ungodliness* (Edinburgh, 1799)
— *The Travels of True Godliness* (Edinburgh, 1799)
— *Tropologia: A Key to Open Scripture Metaphors* (1681)
— *War with the Devil: or The Young Man's Conflict with the Powers of Darkness*, 22nd edn (1776)
Keith, George *The Benefit, Advantage and Glory of Silent Meetings* (1670)
— *Immediate Revelation ... Or, The Holy Ghost ... poured forth, and inspiring man, and induing him with power from on high Not Ceased* (1668)
— *Mr. George Keith's Farewel Sermon* (1700)
— *The Universal Free Grace of the Gospell Asserted* (1671)
— *The Woman-Preacher of Samaria, A Better Preacher, and more Sufficiently Qualified to Preach, than any of the Men-Preachers of the Man-made-Ministry* (1674)
A Lamentation over the House of Israel ([1664?])
Lister, Joseph *The Life ... 1627–1709* (Bradford, 1860)
Livingstone, P[atrick] *Plain and Downright Dealing with them that were with us, and are gone out from us* ([1667])
[Lobb, Stephen] *The True Dissenter, Or, The Cause of those that are for Gathered Churches* (1685)
Lowe, Roger *The Diary ... 1663–74*, ed. William L. Sachse (1938)
Ludlow, Edmund *The Memoirs*, ed. C. H. Firth, 2 vols (Oxford, 1894)
— *A Voyce from the Watch Tower: Part Five: 1660–1662*, ed. A.B. Warden, Camden Society, 4th ser., 21 (1978)
Manton, Thomas *The Complete Works*, 5 vols (1870–1)
[Marvell, Andrew] *An Account of the Growth of Popery, and Arbitrary Government in England* (Amsterdam, [1678])
— *Complete Poetry*, ed. George deF. Lord, Everyman's Library (1968; rpt 1984)
[—] *Mr. Smirke: Or, The Divine in Mode* (1676)
— *The Poems and Letters*, ed. H. M. Margoliouth, rev. Pierre Legouis and E. E. Duncan-Jones, 2 vols, 3rd edn (Oxford, 1971)
— *The Rehearsal Transpros'd*, ed. D. I. B. Smith (Oxford, 1971)
Memoirs of Queen Mary's Days ([1679])
Milton, John *Complete Prose Works*, gen. ed. Don M. Wolfe, 8 vols (New Haven, Conn., 1953–82)
— *The Poems*, ed. John Carey and Alastair Fowler, 2nd corrected impression (1980)
Newcome, Henry *The Autobiography*, ed. Richard Parkinson (Manchester, 1852)
The Nonconformists Advocate (1680)
Nye, Philip *The King's Authority in Dispensing with Ecclesiastical Laws, Asserted and Vindicated* (1687)
Nye, Philip, and Robinson, John *The Lawfulness of Hearing the Publick Ministers of the Church of England Proved* (1683)
[Owen, James] *Church-Pageantry Display'd, or, Organ-Worship Arraign'd and Condemn'd* (1700)
[—] *Moderation a Virtue: or, The Occasional Conformist Justify'd from the Imputation of Hyprocrisy* (1703)
[—] *Moderation Still a Virtue* (1704)
Owen, John *The Correspondence*, ed. Peter Toon (Cambridge, 1970)
— *Exercitations on the Epistle to the Hebrews* (1668)
— *The Golden Book of John Owen*, ed. James Moffatt (1904)
— *The Works*, ed. William H. Goold, 16 vols (1850–3; rpt Edinburgh, 1965–8)
Penington, Isaac *Many deep Considerations have been upon my heart concerning the State of Israel* ([1664?])
— *Naked Truth* (1674)
[Penn, William] *Good Advice to the Church of England, Roman Catholick and Protestant Dissenter* (1687)

— *No Cross, No Crown*, ed. Norman Penney (1930; rpt York, 1981)

[—] *A Persuasive to Moderation to Church Dissenters* ([1686])

[Penn, William, and Mead, William] *The Peoples Antient and Just Liberties Asserted* (1670)

[Philly], John *The Arraignment of Christendom, Containing A Revelation of the Rys, Growth & fulness of the Great Whor* (1664)

Picton, Ja[mes] *A Just Plea against Swearing, and against the National Worship of England* (1663)

Pinney, John *Letters*, ed. Geoffrey F. Nuttall (1939)

Prynne, William *The Unbishoping of Timothy and Titus* (1660)

A Renunciation and Declaration of the Ministers of Congregational Churches ... against the Late Horrid Insurrection and Rebellion (1661)

Samm, John *A Salutation to the little flock, Who doe choose Christ to be their Rock* ([1663?])

A Short Examination of a Discourse concerning Edification (1700)

Smith, William *Liberty of Conscience Pleaded* (1663)

— *Joyful Tidings to the Begotten of God* (1664)

Spurstowe, William Σατανα Νοήματα *or, the Wiles of Satan* (1666)

— *The Spiritual Chymist* (1666)

[Stodard, Amor, Whitehead, George, et al.] *To the King and both Houses of Parliament ... Being a Representation of the Cause and Sufferings of the People, called Quakers* (1666)

Stout, William *Autobiography*, ed. J. Harland (Manchester, 1851)

Swintoun, John *Heaven and Earth, Sea and Dry Land, hear the Word of the Lord* (1664)

— *Some Late Epistles to the Body* (1663)

— *To the Inhabitants of the Whole Earth* (1665)

[Terrill, Edward] *The Records of a Church of Christ, meeting in Broadmead, Bristol 1640–1687*, ed. Edward Bean Underhill (1847)

[Trosse, George] *A Discourse of Schism: Design'd For the Satisfaction of Conscientious and Peaceable Dissenters* (1701)

A True and Faithful Relation From the People of God (called) Quakers, in Colchester (1664)

[Tyso, John, et al.] *Another Cry of the Innocent and Oppressed for Justice* (1665)

The Voice of the Innocent uttered forth: Or, The Call of the Harmless and Oppressed for Iustice and Equity (1665)

[Wallis, Ralph] *More News from Rome or Magna Charta, Discoursed of between a Poor Man and his Wife* (1666)

Whitehead, George *The Quakers Plainness Detecting Fallacy* (1674)

— *The Nature of Christianity in the True Light Asserted* (1671)

B. SECONDARY

I STUDIES CHIEFLY HISTORICAL AND ECCLESIASTICAL

Abbott, W. C. 'English conspiracy and dissent', *American Historical Review*, XIV, 3 and 4 (1908–9), 503–28, 696–722

Abernathy, George 'Clarendon and the Declaration of Indulgence', *JEH*, XI (1960), 55–73

Barbour, Hugh *The Quakers in Puritan England* (New Haven, Conn., 1964)

Bebb, Evelyn D. *Nonconformity and Social and Economic Life 1660–1800* (1935)

Beddard, R. A. 'Vincent Alsop and the emancipation of Restoration dissent', *JEH*, XXIV (1973), 161–84

Bolam, C. Gordon 'The ejection of 1662 and its consequences for the Presbyterians in England', *The Hibbert Journal*, LX (1961–2), 184–95

Bolam, C. Gordon, et al. *The English Presbyterians* (1968)

Bosher, Robert, S. *The Making of the Restoration Settlement* (1957)

Braithwaite, Alfred W. 'Early Friends' experience with juries', *JFHS*, I, 4 (1964), 217–27

— 'Early tithe prosecutions: Friends as outlaws', *JFHS*, XLIX, 3 (1960), 148–56

— '"Errors in the Indictment" and pardons: the case of Theophilus Green', *JFHS*, XLIX, 1 (1959), 24–30

— 'Imprisonment upon a praemunire: George Fox's last trial', *JFHS*, I, 1 (1962), 37–43

— *Thomas Rudyard: Early Friends' "Oracle of Law"*, *JFHS* Supplement 27 (1956)

Braithwaite, William C. *The Beginnings of Quakerism*, rev. Henry J. Cadbury, 2nd edn (1955; rpt York, 1981)

— *The Second Period of Quakerism*, rev. Henry J. Cadbury, 2nd edn (1961; rpt York, 1979)

Brown, John *John Bunyan (1628–1688): His Life, Times, and Work*, rev. Frank Mott Harrison, tercentenary edn (1928)

Buranelli, Vincent *The King and the Quaker: a Study of William Penn and James II* (Philadelphia, Pa, 1962)

Butler, David M. *Quaker Meeting Houses of the Lake District* (1978)

Cadbury, Henry J. 'Early use of the word 'Quaker'; *JFHS*, XLIX, 1 (1959), 3–5

Coomer, Duncan *English Dissent under the Early Hanoverians* (1946)

Cragg, G. R. *Puritanism in the Period of the Great Persecution 1660–1688* (Cambridge, 1957)

Cuming, G. J. 'The Grand Debate', *The Church Quarterly Review*, CLXIII (1962), 29–39

— 'The Prayer Book in Convocation, November 1661', *JEH*, VIII, 2 (1957), 182–92

Curtis, C. D. *Sedgemoor and the Bloody Assize* (1930)

Davies, Horton *The English Free Churches* (1952)

— *Worship and Theology in England from Andrewes to Baxter and Fox, 1603–1690* (Princeton, NJ, 1975)

Dobree, Bonamy *William Penn: Quaker and Pioneer* (1932)

Eeg-Olofsson, Leif *The Conception of the Inner Light in Robert Barclay's Theology* (Lund, 1954)

Feiling, Keith 'Clarendon and the Act of Uniformity, 1662–3', *EHR*, CLXXIV (1929), 289–91

Furley, O. W. 'The pope-burning processions of the late seventeenth century', *History*, XLIV (1959), 16–23

Gee, Henry 'The Derwentdale Plot, 1663', *RHST*, 3rd ser., XI (1917), 125–42

George, M. Dorothy 'Elections and electioneering, 1679–81', *EHR*, XLV, 180 (1930), 552–78

Gordon, Alexander *Heads of English Unitarian History with appended lectures on Baxter and Priestley* (1895)

Greaves, Richard L. *Deliver us from Evil: The Radical Underground in Britain 1660–1663* (New York, 1986)

— *John Bunyan* (Abingdon, 1969)

— 'The tangled careers of two Stuart radicals: Henry and Robert Danvers', *BQ*, XXIX, 1 (1981), 32–43

Greaves, Richard L., and Zaller, R. (eds) *A Biographical Dictionary of British Radicals in the Seventeenth Century*, 3 vols (Brighton, 1982–4)

Green, I. M. *The Re-Establishment of the Church of England, 1660–1663* (Oxford, 1978)

Griffiths, Olive M. *Religion and Learning: A Study in English Presbyterian Thought from the*

Bartholomew Ejection (1662) to the Foundation of the Unitarian Movement (Cambridge, 1935)

Hill, Christopher *The Experience of Defeat* (1984)

— *Milton and the English Revolution* (1977; rpt 1979)

— *Puritanism and Revolution* (1965; rpt 1968)

— *Some Intellectual Consequences of the English Revolution* (1980)

— *The World Turned Upside Down* (1972; rpt Harmondsworth, 1975)

Holdsworth, Sir William *A History of English Law*, 17 vols (1903–72; vols I–III, 3rd edn, 1922–3)

Horton, Robert *John Howe* (1895)

Horwitz, H. 'Protestant reconciliation in the Exclusion Crisis', *JEH*, XV (1964), 201–17

Hutton, William *The English Church from the Accession of Charles I to the Death of Anne* (1903)

Jones, J. R. *The First Whigs: The Politics of the Exclusion Crisis 1678–1683* (1961)

— *The Revolution of 1688 in England* (1972)

— (ed.) *The Restored Monarchy* (1979)

Jones, R. Tudur *Congregationalism in England 1662–1962* (1962)

Kenyon, J. P. *The Popish Plot* (1972)

— 'The Exclusion crisis', *History Today*, XIV, 4 and 5 (1964), 252–9, 344–9

Kirby, Ethyn Williams 'The Quakers' efforts to secure civil and religious liberty 1660–96', *Journal of Modern History*, VII, 4 (1935), 401–21

— 'The Reconcilers and the Restoration (1660–1662)', in *Essays in Modern English History in Honor of Wilbur Cortez Abbott* (Cambridge, Mass., 1941)

Knox, R. Buick (ed.) *Reformation, Conformity and Dissent: Essays in honour of Geoffrey F. Nuttall* (1977)

— 'The bishops and the nonconformists in the seventeenth century', *JURCHS*, III, 3 (1984), 78–94

Lacey, Douglas R. *Dissent and Parliamentary Policitics in England 1661–1689* (New Brunswick, NJ, 1969)

Lamont, William *Richard Baxter and the Millennium* (1979)

Laslett, Peter *The World We have Lost Further Explored*, 3rd edn (1983)

Lipson, E. 'The elections to the Exclusion Parliaments 1679–81', *EHR*, XXVIII (1913), 59–85

M'Crie, Thomas *Annals of English Presbytery* (1872)

McGee, J. Sears *The Godly Man in Stuart England: Anglicans, Puritans, and the Two Tables, 1620–1670* (New Haven, Conn., 1976)

MacLear, James F. 'Quakerism and the end of the Interregnum', *CH*, XIX (1950), 240–70

Matar, Nabil I. 'Peter Sterry, the Millennium and Oliver Cromwell', *JURCHS*, II, 10 (1982), 334–42

Matthews, A. G. *Mr. Pepys and Nonconformity* (1954)

Miller, John *Popery and Politics in England 1660–1688* (Cambridge, 1973)

Miller, Perry *The New England Mind: The Seventeenth Century* (1939; rpt Boston, Mass., 1963)

Milne, Doreen J. 'The results of the Rye House Plot', *RHST*, 5th ser., I (1951), 91–108

Morgan, Edmund S. *The Puritan Family*, rev. edn (New York, 1966)

Morgan, Irvonwy *The Nonconformity of Richard Baxter* (1946)

Nicholson, Francis 'The Kaber Rigg Plot, 1663', *Cumberland and Westmoreland Antiq. and Arch. Soc. Journal*, new ser., XI (1911), 212–33

Nuttall, Geoffrey F. *Christianity and Violence* (Royston, 1972)

— *The Holy Spirit in Puritan Faith and Experience*, 2nd edn (Oxford, 1947)

— *Richard Baxter* (1965)

— *Visible Saints: The Congregational Way 1640–1660* (Oxford, 1957)

— 'George Whitefield's "Curate": Gloucestershire dissent and the Revival', *JEH*, XXVII, 4 (1976), 369–86
— 'Lyon Turner's "Original Records": notes and identifications', *Trans. of the Congregational Hist. Soc.*, XIV (1940–4), 14–24, 112–20, 181–7; XV (1945–8), 41–7
— 'Methodism and the older dissent: some perspectives', *JURCHS*, II, 8 (1981), 259–74
— '"Nothing else would do": early Friends and the Bible', *The Friends' Quarterly*, XXII, 10 (1982), 651–9
Nuttall, Geoffrey F., and Chadwick, Owen (eds) *From Uniformity to Unity 1662–1962* (1962)
Nuttall, Geoffrey F., *et al. The Beginnings of Nonconformity* (1964)
Parker, James *An Introduction to the History of the Successive Revisions of the Book of Common Prayer* (Oxford, 1877)
Powicke, Frederick J. *A Life of the Reverend Richard Baxter 1615–1691* (1924)
— *The Reverend Richard Baxter under the Cross (1662–1691)* (1927)
Proctor, Francis, and Frere, Walter *A New History of the Book of Common Prayer* (1902)
Reay, Barry *The Quakers and the English Revolution* (1985)
Ritson, Joseph *The Romance of Nonconformity* (1910)
Robbins, Caroline '"Absolute liberty": the life and thought of William Popple, 1638–1708', *William and Mary Quarterly*, 3rd ser., XXIV, 2 (1967), 190–223
— 'Marvell's religion: was he a New Methodist?', *Journal of the History of Ideas*, XXIII, 2 (1962), 268–72
Rogers, Henry *The Life and Character of John Howe* (1836)
Rogers, P. G. *The Fifth Monarchy Men* (1966))
Schlatter, Richard B. *The Social Ideas of Religious Leaders 1660–1688* (1940)
Scott, W. Major *The Life of John Howe* ([1911])
Sell, Alan P. 'Robert Travers and the Lichfield-Longdon Church Book', *JURCHS*, III, 7 (1985), 268–78
Stearns, Raymond P. *The Strenuous Puritan: Hugh Peter 1598–1660* (Urbana, Ill, 1954)
Swainson, C. A. *The Parliamentary History of the Act of Uniformity* (1875)
Sykes, Norman *Old Priest and New Presbyter* (Cambridge, 1957)
— *From Sheldon to Secker* (Cambridge, 1959)
Thomas, Roger 'The Seven Bishops and their petition, 18 May 1688', *JEH*, XII (1961), 56–70
Tibbutt, H. G. *Bunyan Meeting Bedford 1650–1950* (Bedford, [1950])
— 'John Crook, 1617–1699: a Bedfordshire Quaker', *Publ. of the Bedfordshire Hist. Record Soc.*, XXV (1947), 110–28
Toon, Peter *God's Statesman: The Life and Work of John Owen* (Exeter, 1971)
Underwood, A. C. *A History of the English Baptists*, 2nd edn (1956)
Walker, Eric C. *William Dell: Master Puritan* (Cambridge, 1970)
Walker, James 'The Yorkshire Plot', *Yorkshire Arch. Soc. Journal*, XXXI (1934), 348–59
Watts, Michael R. *The Dissenters: From the Reformation to the French Revolution* (Oxford, 1978)
Webb, Maria *The Penns and Peningtons of the Seventeenth Century* (1867)
White, B. R. *The English Baptists of the Seventeenth Century* (1983)
Whitley, W. T. *A History of British Baptists*, 2nd edn (1932)
— 'The great raid of 1670 on certain London churches under the new Conventicle Act', *BQ*, new ser., IX (1938–9), 247–51
Williams, Sheila 'The pope-burning processions of 1679, 1680 and 1681', *Journal of the Warburg and Courtauld Institutes*, XXI (1958), 104–18
Wood, A. H. *Church Unity without Uniformity* (1963)

2   STUDIES CHIEFLY LITERARY AND BIBLIOGRAPHICAL

Allen, Don Cameron *The Harmonious Vision: Studies in Milton's Poetry*
   (Baltimore, Md, 1954)
Astbury, Raymond 'The renewal of the Licensing Act in 1693 and its lapse in
   1695', *The Library*, 5th ser., XXXIII, 4 (1978), 296–322
Bastian, F. *Defoe's Early Life* (1981)
Beek, M. Van *An Enquiry into Puritan vocabulary* (Groningen, 1969)
Bennett, Joan 'God, Satan, and King Charles: Milton's royal portraits', *PMLA*,
   XCII, 3 (1977), 441–57
Bercovitch, Sacvan (ed.) *The American Puritan Imagination* (Cambridge, 1971)
—   *Typology and Early American Literature* (Amherst, Mass., 1972)
Blagden, Cyprian *The Stationers' Company: A History 1403–1959* (1960)
Boulger, James D. *The Calvinist Temper in English Poetry* (The Hague, 1980)
Brinkley, Roberta Florence (ed.) *Coleridge on the Seventeenth Century* (1955; rpt
   New York, 1968)
Burke, Kenneth 'The imagery of killing', *Hudson Review*, I (1948), 151–67
Bush, Sargent, Jr *The Writings of Thomas Hooker: Spiritual Adventure in Two
   Worlds* (Madison, Wis., 1980)
Caldwell, Patricia *The Puritan Conversion Narrative* (Cambridge, 1983)
Campbell, Gordon 'Milton's theological and literary treatments of the
   Creation', *Journal of Theological Studies*, new ser., XXX, 1 (1979),
   128–37
—   'The source of Bunyan's *Mapp*', *Journal of the Warburg and Courtauld
   Institutes*, XLIV (1981), 240–1
Carlton, Peter J. 'Bunyan: language, convention, authority', *ELH*, LI, 1 (1984),
   17–32
Chernaik, Warren L. *The Poet's Time: Politics and Religion in the Work of Andrew
   Marvell* (Cambridge, 1983)
Clapp, Sarah L.C. 'Subscription publishers prior to Jacob Tonson', *The
   Library*, 4th ser., XIII, 2 (1932), 158–83
Clyde, William M. 'Parliament and the press, 1643–7' *The Library*, 4th ser.,
   XIII, 4 (1933), 399–424
Condee, Ralph W. *Structure in Milton's Poetry* (1974)
Cope, Jackson I. 'Seventeenth-century Quaker style', in Stanley Fish (ed.),
   Seventeenth-Century Prose (New York, 1971)
Creasey, Maurice A. *"Inward" and "Outward": A Study in Early Quaker Language*,
   JFHS Supplement 30 (1962)
Crist, Timothy 'Government control of the press after the expiration of the
   Printing Act in 1679', *Publishing History*, V (1979), 49–77
Davie, Donald *A Gathered Church: The Literature of the English Dissenting Interest,
   1700–1930* (1978)
Dexter, H.M. 'Collections towards a bibliography of Congregationalism', *The
   Congregationalism of the Last Three Hundred Years* (New York, 1880)
Ebbs, John Dale 'Milton's treatment of poetic justice in *Samson Agonistes*',
   Modern Language Quarterly, XXII (1961), 377–89
Empson, William *Milton's God*, rev. edn (1965)
Fiore, Peter A. *Milton and Augustine* (University Park, PA, 1981)
Fisch, Harold 'The Puritans and the reform of prose style', *ELH*, XIX, 4 (1952),
   229–47
Fish, Stanley E. *Surprised by Sin: The Reader in Paradise Lost* (1967; rpt
   Berkeley, Calif., and Los Angeles, 1971)
Fixler, Michael *Milton and the Kingdoms of God* (1964)

Forrest, James F. 'Bunyan's Ignorance and the Flatterer', *SP*, IX (1963), 12–22

Forrest, James F., and Greaves, Richard *John Bunyan: A Reference Guide* (Boston, Mass., 1982)

Freeman, James A. *Milton and the Martial Muse* (Princeton, NJ, 1980)

Gillett, Charles R. *Burned Books: Neglected Chapters in British History and Literature*, 2 vols (New York, 1932)

Greaves, Richard L. 'John Bunyan's 'Holy War' and London nonconformity', *BQ*, XXVI, 4 (1975), 158–68

Greg, W. W. *Some Aspects and Problems of London Publishing between 1550 and 1650* (Oxford, 1956)

Halkett, Samuel, and Laing, John *Dictionary of Anonymous and Pseudonymous English Literature*, ed. James Kennedy, W. A. Smith and A. F. Johnson, 7 vols (1926–34)

Haller, William *The Rise of Puritanism* (1938; rpt New York, 1957)

Hanson, Laurence *Government and the Press, 1695–1763* (1936; rpt Oxford, 1967)

Harding, Davis P. *The Club of Hercules: Studies in the Classical Background of Paradise Lost* (Urbana, Ill., 1962)

Harrison, Frank Mott 'Nathaniel Ponder: the publisher of *The Pilgrim's Progress*', *The Library*, 4th ser., XV, 3 (1934), 257–94

Harrison, G. B. *John Bunyan: A Study in Personality* (1928)

Hart, W. H. *Index Expurgatorius Anglicanus*, 4 vols (1872–7)

Harvey, T. Edmund *Quaker Language*, *JFHS* Supplement 15 (1928)

Haskin, Dayton 'Baxter's quest for origins', *The Eighteenth Century*, XXI, 2 (1980), 145–61

— 'The burden of interpretation in *The Pilgrim's Progress*', *SP*, LXXIX, 3 (1982), 256–78

Hetet, John 'The Wardens' accounts of The Stationers' Company, 1663–79', in Robin Myers and Michael Harris (eds), *Economics of the British Book Trade* (1985), 32–59.

Hill, Christopher *Writing and Revolution in 17th Century England* (Brighton, 1985)

Jones, Phyllis M. 'Biblical rhetoric and the pulpit literature of New England', *Early American Literature*, XI, 3 (1976–7), 245–58

— '"Puritan's Progress": the story of the soul's salvation in early New England sermons', *Early American Literature*, XV, 1 (1980), 14–28

Kaufmann, U. Milo *The Pilgrim's Progress and Traditions in Puritan Meditation* (New Haven, Conn., 1966)

Keeble, N. H. *Richard Baxter: Puritan Man of Letters* (Oxford, 1982)

— '*The Pilgrim's Progress*: a Puritan fiction', *BQ*, XXVIII, 7 (1980), 321–36

— 'Richard Baxter's preaching ministry: its history and texts', *JEH*, XXXV, 4 (1984), 539–59

— 'Some erroneous, doubtful and misleading Baxterian attributions in Wing and Halkett and Laing', *N&Q*, CCXXX (1985), 187–91

— 'The way and the ways of Puritan story', *English*, XXXIII, 147 (1984), 209–32

Kirschbaum, Leo *Shakespeare and the Stationers* (Columbus, Ohio, 1955)

Kitchin, George *Sir Roger L'Estrange* (1913)

Knott, John R., Jr *The Sword of the Spirit: Puritan Responses to the Bible* (Chicago, 1980)

— 'Bunyan and the holy community', *SP*, LXXX, 2 (1983), 200–25

Korshin, Paul J. *Typologies in England 1650–1820* (Princeton, NJ, 1982)

Leverenz, David *The Language of Puritan Feeling* (New Brunswick, NJ, 1980)

Lewalski, Barbara *Milton's Brief Epic* (Providence, RI, 1966)

Lowance, Mason I., Jr *The Language of Canaan: Metaphor and Symbol in New England* (Cambridge, Mass., 1980)

McColley, Grant 'Milton's dialogue on astronomy', *PMLA*, LII (1937), 728–62

McLachlan, Herbert *English Education under the Test Acts* (1931)

Marilla, E. L. '*Samson Agonistes*: an interpretation', *Studia Neophilogica*, XXIX (1957), 67–76

Martz, Louis L. *Poet of Exile: A Study of Milton's Poetry* (New Haven, Conn., 1980)

Matthews, A. G. *The Works of Richard Baxter: An Annotated List* (1932)

Milner, Andrew *John Milton and the English Revolution* (1981)

Mitchell, W.F. *English Pulpit Oratory from Andrewes to Tillotson* (1932)

Morrison, Paul G. *Index of Printers, Publishers and Booksellers in Donald Wing's Short-Title Catalogue* (Charlottesville, VA, 1955)

Mortimer, Russell S. 'The first century of Quaker printers', *JFHS*, XL (1948), 37–49; XLI (1949), 74–84

Mumby, Frank, and Norrie, Ian *Publishing and Bookselling*, 5th edn rev. (1974)

Murdock, Kenneth B. *Literature and Theology in Colonial New England* (1949; rpt New York, 1963)

Newey, Vincent (ed.) *The Pilgrim's Progress: Critical and Historical Views* (Liverpool, 1980)

Nuttall, Geoffrey F. 'The *MS.* of *Reliquiae Baxterianae* (1696)', *JEH*, VI, 1 (1955), 73–9

— 'Richard Baxter's correspondence: a preliminary survey', *JEH*, I, 1 (1950), 85–95

— 'A transcript of Richard Baxter's library catalogue', *JEH*, II 2 (1951), 207–21; III, 1 (1952), 74–100

O'Malley, Thomas P. 'The press and Quakerism 1653–1659, *JFHS*, LIV, 4 (1979), 169–84

Parker, Irene *The Dissenting Academies* (1914)

Parker, William Riley *Milton: A Biography*, 2 vols (Oxford, 1968)

— 'The date of *Samson Agonistes*', *PQ*, XXVIII (1949), 145–66

— 'The date of *Samson Agonistes*: a postscript', *N&Q* new ser., V (1958), 201–2

Parks, Stephen *John Dunton and the English Book Trade* (New York, 1976)

Patrides, C. A. *Milton and the Christian Tradition* (Oxford, 1966)

— (ed.) *Approaches to Paradise Lost* (1968)

Patterson, Annabel *Marvell and the Civic Crown* (Princeton, NJ, 1978)

Penney, Norman 'George Fox's writings and the Morning Meeting', *Friends' Quarterly Examiner* (1902), 63–72

— 'Our recording clerks: (i) Ellis Hookes', *JFHS*, I, 1 (1903), 12–22

Plant, Marjorie *The English Book Trade*, 2nd edn (1965)

Plomer, Henry R. *A Dictionary of the Booksellers and Printers who were at work ... from 1641 to 1667* (1907; rpt Oxford, 1968)

— *A Dictionary of the Printers and Booksellers ... 1668 to 1725* (1922; rpt Oxford, 1968)

— 'A lawsuit as to an early edition of the 'Pilgrim's Progress', *The Library*, 3rd ser., V, 17 (1914), 60–9

— 'The Long Shop in the Poultry', *Bibliotheca*, II (1895–7), 61–80

Pollard, Alfred W. 'Some notes on the history of copyright in England, 1662–1774', *The Library*, 4th ser., III, 2 (1922), 97–114

Pooley, Roger 'Language and loyalty: plain style at the Restoration', *Literature & History*, VI, 1 (1980), 2–18

— 'The structure of *The Pilgrim's Progress*', *Essays in Poetics*, II (1979), 59–69

— 'The wilderness of this world – Bunyan's *Pilgrim's Progress*', *BQ*, XXVII, 7 (1978), 290–9

Pope, Elizabeth M. *Paradise Regained: The Tradition and the Poem* (Baltimore, Md, 1947)

Radzinowicz, Mary Ann *Towards Samson Agonistes: The Growth of Milton's Mind* (Princeton, NJ, 1978)

Ricks, Christopher *Milton's Grand Style* (Oxford, 1963)

[Roberts, William] 'Bookselling in the Poultry', *The City Press*, XXXIV, 86 (16 August 1890), 7

Robins, Harry F. *If This Be Heresy: A Study of Milton and Origen* (Urbana, Ill., 1963)

Rostenberg, Leona *Literary, Politic, Scientific, Religious & Legal Publishing, Printing & Bookselling 1551–1700*, 2 vols (New York, 1965)

— *The Minority Press and the English Crown: A Study in Repression 1558–1625* (New York, 1971)

Sasek, Lawrence A. *The Literary Temper of the English Puritans* (Baton Rouge, 1961)

Samuel, Irene 'Milton on learning and wisdom', *PMLA*, LXIV (1949), 708–23

Saurat, Denis *Milton: Man and Thinker*, rev. edn (1944)

Schiffhorst, Gerald 'Satan's false heroism in *Paradise Lost* as a perversion of patience', *Christianity and Literature*, XXXIII, 2 (1984), 13–20

Schultz, Howard *Milton and Forbidden Knowledge* (New York, 1955)

Sensabaugh, George F. *That Grand Whig Milton* (Stanford, Calif., 1952)

— 'Milton on learning', *SP*, XLIII (1946), 248–72

Sharrock, Roger *John Bunyan*, corrected reissue (1968)

— 'The origins of *A Relation of the Imprisonment of Mr. John Bunyan*', *RES*, new ser., X, 39 (1959), 250–6

— 'Spiritual autobiography in *The Pilgrim's Progress*', *RES*, XXIV (1948), 102–20

— (ed.) *The Pilgrim's Progress: A Casebook* (1976)

Shawcross, John T. 'The chronology of Milton's major poems', *PMLA*, LXXVI, 4 (1961), 345–58

Siebert, Frederick *Freedom of the Press in England 1476–1776* (Urbana, Ill., 1952)

Sinfield, Alan *Literature in Protestant England 1560–1660* (1983)

Smith, Joseph *Bibliotheca Anti-Quakeriana* (1873)

— *A Descriptive Catalogue of Friends' Books*, 2 vols (1867)

— *Supplement to a Descriptive Catalogue* (1893)

Spufford, Margaret *Small Books and Pleasant Histories: Popular Fiction and its Readership in Seventeenth-Century England* (1981)

— 'First steps in literacy', in Harvey J. Graff (ed.), *Literacy and Social Development in the West* (Cambridge, 1981)

Starr, G. A. *Defoe & Spiritual Autobiography* (Princeton, NJ, 1965)

Steadman, John M. *Milton and the Renaissance Hero* (Oxford, 1967)

Stein, Arnold *Heroic Knowledge: An Interpretation of Paradise Regained and Samson Agonistes* (Minneapolis, Minn., 1957)

Stranahan, Brainerd 'Bunyan's special talent: biblical texts as 'Events' in *Grace Abounding* and *The Pilgrim's Progress*', *ELR*, XI, 3 (1981), 329–43

— 'Bunyan and the Epistle to the Hebrews', *SP*, LXXIX, 3 (1982), 279–96

Talon, Henri *John Bunyan*, trans. Barbara Wall (1951)

Tanner, Tony 'Licence and licensing: To the presse or to the spunge', *Journal of the History of Ideas*, XXXVIII, 1 (1977), 3–18

[Terry, Althea E]. 'Giles Calvert's publishing career', *JFHS*, XXXV (1938), 45–9

Thickstun, Margaret 'The preface to Bunyan's *Grace Abounding* as Pauline epistle', *N&Q*, CCXXX (1985), 180–2

Tindall, William Y. *John Bunyan: Mechanick Preacher* (New York, 1934)

Waldock, A. J. A. *Paradise Lost and its Critics* (Cambridge, 1947)

Wales, Kathleen M. '*Thou* and *You* in early modern English', *Studia Linguistica*, XXXVII, 2 (1983), 107–25

Walker, J. 'The censorship of the press during the reign of Charles II', *History*, new ser., XXXV (1950), 218–38

Watkins, Owen *The Puritan Experience* (1972)

Whitley, W. T. *A Baptist Bibliography*, 2 vols (1916–22)

Wilson, A. N. *The Life of John Milton* (Oxford, 1983)

Wing, Donald *Short-Title Catalogue of Books ... 1641–1700*, 3 vols (New York, 1945–51; vols I–II, 2nd edn, 1972–82)

Wittreich, Joseph, Jr (ed.) *Calm of Mind: Tercentenary Essays on Paradise Regained and Samson Agonistes* (Cleveland, Ohio, 1971)

Wright, Luella M. *The Literary Life of the Early Friends 1650–1725* (New York, 1932)

Index

NOTES

1. The churchmanship of later seventeenth-century English nonconformists is parenthetically indicated by the following abbreviations: P = Presbyterian; C = Congregational; B = Baptist; Q = Quaker.
2. There are three listings under 'Nonconformists': the first is of historical matters; the second of bibliographical topics and the circumstances of book production; the third of literary and thematic aspects of nonconformist writings.
3. Published works are indexed under their authors, where known; anonymous works of uncertain authorship and composite works are indexed under their titles.
4. Parliamentary Acts and Ordinances are indexed under 'Parliament, Acts of'.